P9-CEL-570

Fodor's 2016
LONDON

WELCOME TO LONDON

History and tradition greet you at every turn in London; it's also one of the coolest, most modern cities in the world. If London contained only landmarks such as Westminster Abbey and Buckingham Palace, it would still rank as one of the world's great destinations, but Britain's capital is much more. People come to glimpse the royals and stop by hot galleries; to take in theater and trendy shops; to sample tea and scones or cutting-edge cuisine. When you need a break from the action, pop into a pub, relax in a park—or take a walk and make London your own.

TOP REASONS TO GO

★ **Architectural Icons:** The Tower of London and Big Ben are quintessential London.

★ **Art Museums:** From the National Gallery to the Tate Modern, a visual feast awaits.

★ **Top Theater:** Whether it's Shakespeare or avant-garde drama, the play's the thing.

★ **City of Villages:** Unique neighborhoods from Mayfair to the East End invite discovery.

★ **Shopping:** Fun markets, famous flagship department stores, chic boutiques.

★ **Parks and Squares:** Distinctive green spaces large and small are civilized retreats.

Fodor's LONDON 2016

Publisher: Amanda D'Acierno, *Senior Vice President*

Editorial: Arabella Bowen, *Editor in Chief*; Linda Cabasin, *Editorial Director*

Design: Tina Malaney, *Associate Art Director*; Chie Ushio, *Senior Designer*

Photography: Jennifer Arnow, *Senior Photo Editor*; Mary Robnett, *Photo Researcher*

Production: Linda Schmidt, *Managing Editor*; Evangelos Vasilakis, *Associate Managing Editor*; Angela L. McLean, *Senior Production Manager*

Maps: Rebecca Baer, *Senior Map Editor*; David Lindroth, Mark Stroud (Moon Street Cartography), *Cartographers*

Sales: Jacqueline Lebow, *Sales Director*

Marketing & Publicity: Heather Dalton, *Marketing Director*; Katherine Punia, *Publicity Director*

Business & Operations: Susan Livingston, *Vice President, Strategic Business Planning*; Sue Daulton, *Vice President, Operations*

Fodors.com: Megan Bell, *Executive Director, Revenue & Business Development*; Yasmin Marinaro, *Senior Director, Marketing & Partnerships*

Writers: Jo Caird, Kate Hughes, Jack Jewers, James O'Neill, Ellin Stein, Alex Wijeratna

Lead Editor: Kristan Schiller

Editors: Stephen Brewer, Robert I. C. Fisher, Jess Moss

Production Editor: Elyse Rozelle

ISBN 978–1–101–87828–6

ISSN 0149–631X

SPECIAL SALES

This book is available at special discounts for bulk purchases for sales promotions or premiums. For more information, e-mail specialmarkets@penguinrandomhouse.com.

PRINTED IN THE UNITED STATES OF AMERICA

10 9 8 7 6 5 4 3 2 1

CONTENTS

CONTENTS

ABOUT THIS GUIDE

Fodor's Ratings

Everything in this guide is worth doing—we don't cover what isn't—but exceptional sights, hotels, and restaurants are recognized with additional accolades. **Fodor's Choice ★** indicates our top recommendations, and **Best Bets** call attention to notable hotels and restaurants in various categories. Care to nominate a new place? Visit Fodors.com/contact-us.

Trip Costs

We list prices wherever possible to help you budget well. Hotel and restaurant price categories from $ to $$$$ are noted alongside each recommendation. For hotels, we include the lowest cost of a standard double room in high season. For restaurants, we cite the average price of a main course at dinner or, if dinner isn't served, at lunch. For attractions, we always list adult admission fees; discounts are usually available for children, students, and senior citizens.

Hotels

Our local writers vet every hotel to recommend the best overnights in each price category, from budget to expensive. Unless otherwise specified, you can expect private bath, phone, and TV in your room. For expanded hotel reviews, facilities, and deals visit Fodors.com.

Top Picks	Hotels &
★ Fodor'sChoice	**Restaurants**
	🖼 Hotel
Listings	⬟ Number of
✉ Address	rooms
✉ Branch address	⦿ Meal plans
☎ Telephone	✕ Restaurant
🖷 Fax	✍ Reservations
⊕ Website	🏛 Dress code
✎ E-mail	▭ No credit cards
🎫 Admission fee	$ Price
⊙ Open/closed	
times	**Other**
Ⓜ Subway	⇨ See also
⊹ Directions or	☞ Take note
Map coordinates	🏌 Golf facilities

Restaurants

Unless we state otherwise, restaurants are open for lunch and dinner daily. We mention dress code only when there's a specific requirement and reservations only when they're essential or not accepted. To make restaurant reservations, visit Fodors.com.

Credit Cards

The hotels and restaurants in this guide typically accept credit cards. If not, we'll say so.

EUGENE FODOR

Hungarian-born Eugene Fodor (1905–91) began his travel career as an interpreter on a French cruise ship. The experience inspired him to write *On the Continent* (1936), the first guidebook to receive annual updates and discuss a country's way of life as well as its sights. Fodor later joined the U.S. Army and worked for the OSS in World War II. After the war, he kept up his intelligence work while expanding his guidebook series. During the Cold War, many guides were written by fellow agents who understood the value of insider information. Today's guides continue Fodor's legacy by providing travelers with timely coverage, insider tips, and cultural context.

EXPERIENCE LONDON

LONDON TODAY

Welcome to London—variously described by great poets and statesmen as "modern Babylon," "Unreal City," "enormous Babel," and "...the City of the free." Indeed, majestic London's always been a city in flux and these days it's hard to turn a corner without stumbling into some work-in-progress crater so vast you can only imagine what was there before. This latest wave of development was turbo-charged as the city became a safe haven during the global economic crisis. New neighborhoods continually rise up and burst to the fore—a visit to Shoreditch at the eastern edge of the city should provide you with your quotient of London hipness. The creative fervor that swirls through London like a pea souper fog shows up in DIY galleries, mini-boutiques, pop-up restaurants, and ace hipster hotels.

Although many images are seared on your consciousness before you arrive—the guards at Buckingham Palace, big red double-decker buses, Big Ben, and the River Thames—time does not stand still in this ancient and yet gloriously modern city. Instead, "London, the buskin'd stage...The heart, the centre of the living world!" is in permanent revolution, and evolves, organically, mysteriously, historically through time. Ask any time-pressed, phlegmatic but savvy local and they'll tell you that London is...

Soaring into the Stratosphere
London has loosened its collar and showcases some spectacular new architecture, with the Shard providing a pyramid-shape iconic beacon for the city. With the exceptions of Canary Wharf, the former Swiss Re HQ ("the Gherkin"), the Lloyd's of London building and the London Eye, London's skyline has traditionally been low-key, with little of the sky-scraping swagger of, say, Shanghai or Manhattan. But a spectacular crop of soaring new office towers with wonderful monikers—the Quill, the Shard, the Pinnacle, the Cheese Grater, and the Walkie-Talkie—is revitalizing the city skyline. With an astonishing 230 new towers being built or planned, opinions are heavily divided. Not everyone loves Renzo Piano's jagged pointy Shard and its 95-floor cloud-piercing "Vertical City" at London Bridge, which has a stunning viewing gallery on the 72nd floor. However, once you whizz up and visit it, your understanding of the wonderful immensity of London is transformed forever.

Reflecting the Global Community
The nationalities *keep* coming, and London now swipes the crown as one of *the* most cosmopolitan cities on Earth. White Britons are in the minority for the first time (according to the latest census), representing 45% of London's population of 8.2 million, while Asians make up 18%, black Londoners 13%, European "White Others" 13%, and mixed-race residents at 5%. But London's always been a city of immigrants—from the 10th century, the city had Cymric Brythons, Belgae and Gauls, East Saxons, and Mercians, Danes, Swedes, and Norwegians, plus Jutes, Franks, and Angles. Today, Londoners simply shrug, *harrumph*, and are "Begone with their business."

Teeming with Arts and Culture
Have you picked up one of those free daily London *Evening Standard* newspapers at a Tube stop lately? They're stuffed with a smorgasbord of world-class shows, plays, performances, readings, recitals, concerts, fashion follies,

lectures, talks, cabaret auctions, and blockbuster art exhibitions. Whether it's contemporary art *and* old masters paintings at the sold-out Frieze London art fair or a monthlong Michelin-star chef pop-up "non-restaurant" restaurant in Spitalfields, London is one of the most happening places on the planet.

Getting Around Town

Finally, you'll notice that the public transport's gotten more frequent and more reliable. While London's traffic often seems more chaotic than New York City's, the Congestion Charge, the £11.50-per-day fee imposed on vehicles entering central London during the day, has reduced both traffic and pollution. Although the Underground now runs 24 hours a day on weekends on six key "night Tube" lines, massive tunneling continues apace on London's flagship, high-speed, Cross Rail Underground railway line, which includes spanking new interchanges at Paddington, Tottenham Court Road, and Farringdon stations, slated to open in 2018. Meanwhile, don't miss London's distinctive sky-blue hire bikes, Barclay's Cycle Hire bike-sharing scheme, known locally as "Boris Bikes," after flamboyant former London Mayor Boris Johnson. With 10,445 bikes available at 722 docking stations, you'll find (after laying down £2 for a 24-hour pass) that the first half hour's free, an hour's a quid, and two hours is only £6.

WHAT'S NEW

We really shouldn't begrudge it, but some of London's top cultural attractions seem to be caught in a Cold War upgrade arms race and are investing heavily in new galleries, exhibits, refurbs, rehangs, expansions, and assorted shiny new bells and whistles. Look, then, for the £40-million major upgrade of the Imperial War Museum, which includes a giant atrium filled with a dramatically suspended Spitfire, V-1 Rocket, and Harrier Jump jet, or admire Rubens, Titian, and Velázquez masterpieces in a new light at the £5-million revamped capsule Wallace Collection in Marylebone. Similarly, Shakespeare's Globe has re-created an atmospheric and intimate 16th-century replica oak-panel candlelit 350-seat Jacobean *indoor* theater—the Sam Wanamaker Playhouse—where you'll catch intimate bawdy and bloody Jacobean plays, historical music recitals and vocalists, and groundbreaking collaborations with groups like the Royal Opera House.

WHAT'S WHERE

The following numbers refer to chapters.

2 Westminster, St. James's, and Royal London. This is the place to embrace the "Gran turismo" label. Snap pictures of the mounted Horse Guards, watch kids clambering onto the monumental bronze lions in Trafalgar Square, and visit stacks of world-class art in the fantastic national galleries. Do brave the crowds to peruse historic Westminster Abbey and its ancient narrative in stone.

3 Mayfair and Marylebone. You might not have the wallet for London's most prestigious shops, but remember window-shopping in Mayfair is free. Meanwhile, chic boutique shops in Marylebone are a refreshing change from gaudy Oxford Street a few blocks south.

4 Soho and Covent Garden. More sophisticated than seedy these days, the heart of London puts Theatreland, strip joints, Chinatown, burger boîtes, and the trendiest of film studios side by side. And hold tight among the hectic hordes in Leicester Square. Covent Garden's historic piazza is one of the most raffishly enjoyable parts of the city.

5 Bloomsbury and Holborn. Once the bluestocking and intellectual center of London, elegant 17th- and 18th-century Bloomsbury is now also a mixed business district. The British Museum has enough amazing *objets* and artifacts to keep you busy for a month; the Law Courts, University of London, and quaint Lamb's Conduit Street are worth a gander. Clerkenwell, meanwhile, is a hotbed of culinary invention.

6 The City. London's Wall Street might be the oldest part of the capital, but thanks to new skyscrapers and a sleek Millennium Bridge, it looks like the newest. History fans won't be short-changed, however: head for St. Paul's Cathedral, Tower Bridge, and the Tower of London.

7 East London. Once famed for the noxious 19th-century slums immortalized by Charles Dickens and Jack the Ripper, today the area has become a fulcrum of London's contemporary art scene and a trendy new media, youth-quake party zone. For spit-and-sawdust sensations of market London on the weekend, dive headfirst into the eclectic wares at Spitalfields, Brick Lane (popular for Bangladeshi curry houses and 24-hour Jewish bagel bakeries), and Columbia Road's much-loved early-morning flower street market.

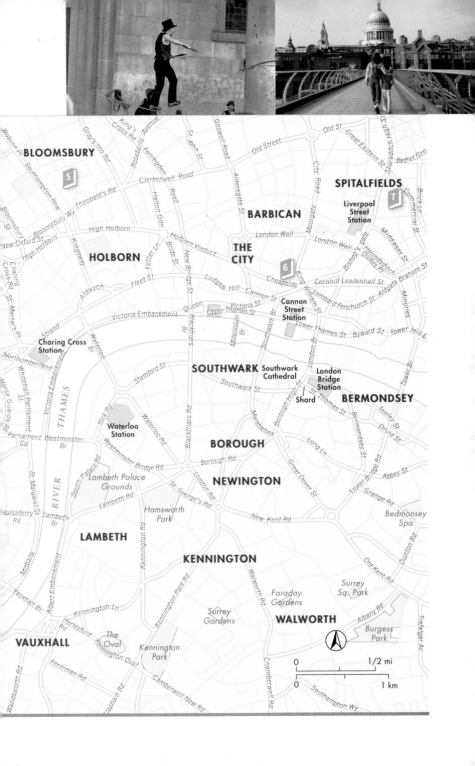

WHAT'S WHERE

8 South of the Thames. The Southbank Centre—including the National Theatre and Royal Festival Hall, the Haywood Gallery, Purcell Room and Queen Elizabeth Hall, plus the nearby Shakespeare's Globe and Tate Modern—showcases the capital's crowning artistic glories. Or put it all in aerial perspective from the 72nd floor of the mesmerizing pyramid-shape Shard.

9 Kensington, Chelsea, Knightsbridge, and Belgravia. Although the many boutiques of King's Road have lost much of their heady '60s swagger, the free museums are as awe-inspiring as ever. Kensington High Street (or "Ken High" to locals) is slightly more affordable than the King's Road; otherwise, flash your cash at London's snazziest department stores, Harrods and Harvey Nichols.

10 Notting Hill and Bayswater. North of Kensington, around Portobello Road, Notting Hill Gate is a trendsetting square mile of multiethnic finds, photographers galleries, bookshops, and see-and-be-seen-in restaurants. Nearby, Bayswater mixes eclectic ethnic fashions, organic fresh-food shops, and spangly Chinese restaurants.

11 Regent's Park and Hampstead. Surrounded by elegant "terraces"—in truth, mansions as big as palaces—designed by 19th-century architect John Nash, Regent's Park is a Regency extravaganza. The nearby hilltop villages of Hampstead and Primrose Hill attract residents like Kate Moss and Jude Law.

12 Greenwich. The Royal Observatory, Sir Christopher Wren architecture, the Old Royal Naval College, *Cutty Sark*, and Greenwich and the Prime Meridian all add up to one of the best Thames-side excursions beyond the cut-and-thrust of central London.

13 The Thames Upstream. As an idyllic retreat from the city, stroll around London's historic gardens and enjoy the stately homes of Kew, Richmond, and Putney. Better yet, take a gentle river cruise and end up at the famous Hampton Court Maze.

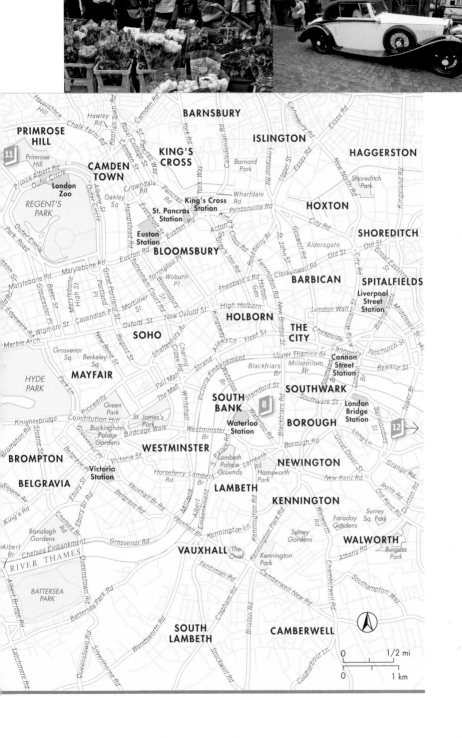

LONDON PLANNER

When to Go

The heaviest tourist season runs April through September, with another peak around Christmas. Late spring is the time to see the Royal Parks and gardens at their freshest; fall brings autumnal beauty and fewer people. Summer gives the best chance of good weather, although the crowds are intense. Winter can be dismal—it's dark by 5—but all the theaters, concerts, and exhibitions go full-speed ahead, and Christmas lights bring a touch of festive magic. Weather-wise, winter is cold and wet with occasional light snow and spring is colorful and fair. June to August can range from a total washout to a long hot summer and anything in between. Autumn, finally, ranges from warm to cool to mild. In short, layers and a brolly are your best friends. It's impossible to forecast London weather but you can be certain that it will *not* be what you expect.

When Not to Go

The October "half-term," when schools in the capital take a break for a week or two, results in most attractions being overrun by children. The start of August can be a very busy time, and hot weather makes Tube travel a sweltering and sweaty nightmare. Air-conditioning is far from the norm in London, even in hotels; so although it rarely tops 90°F, it can feel much hotter. And festive shopping in central London just before Christmas borders on the insane.

Addresses

Central London and its surrounding districts are divided into 32 boroughs—33, counting The City of London. More useful for navigating, however, are the subdivisions of London into postal districts. Throughout the guide we've given the abbreviated postal code for most listings. The first one or two letters give the location: N means north, NW means northwest, and so on. Don't expect the numbering to be logical, however. (You won't, for example, find W2 next to W3.) The general rule is that the lower numbers, such as W1 or SW1, are closest to the city center.

Getting Around

London is, above all, a walker's city, and will repay every moment you spend exploring on foot. But if you're in a rush, there are other options. By far the easiest and most practical way to get around is on the Underground, known as the Tube. Trains run daily from early morning to beyond midnight during the week and 24 hours on weekends on six key lines. Frequent all-cash-free buses crisscross London and often have their own lanes, which only buses and black taxis can use. They are a great way to see London, but routes are more complicated than the Tube's; scan the route posted at the bus stop and check the number and destination on the front of the bus. Ask the bus conductor if in doubt.

Put a deposit on an Oyster card for £5, which will allow you to use London's transport—including bus, Tube, tram, DLR, London Overground, and most National Rail services in London—at a lower cost than using paper tickets. The plastic card can be topped up as often as you want, and your £5 deposit will be reimbursed when you hand the card back.

Alternatively, buy a Travelcard pass (from £9 per day in the central Zones 1 and 2), which offers unlimited use of the Tube, buses, and the commuter rail. Check ⊕ *www.tfl.gov.uk* for details on ongoing Tube renovations.

1

WHAT IT COSTS		
	IN LONDON	**IN NEW YORK**
Pair of theater tickets	£40–£100	$70–$240
Museum admission	Usually free; sometimes £4–£16	Usually $8–$30; rarely free
Fast-food value meal	£7	$8
Tall latte	£3.90	$4
Pint of beer in a pub	£3.70 and up	$6 and up
1-mile taxi ride before tip	£7.50	$7
Subway ride within city center	Up to £8.40 without Oyster or Travelcard	$2.75

⇨ *For further details on transport around London, see the Travel Smart section at the end of this book.*

London Hours

The usual shop hours are Monday–Saturday 9–6 and Sunday 11–5. Around Oxford Street, Kensington High Street, and Knightsbridge, hours are 9:30–6, with late-night hours (until 7:30 or 8) on Wednesday or Thursday.

Many businesses are closed on Sunday and national (bank) holidays, except in the center, where most open 10–4. Banks are open weekdays 9:30–4:30; offices are generally open 9–6.

The major national museums and galleries are open daily, mainly 10–6, and often they're open late one night a week.

Deal or No Deal?

There's no getting around it: London can be as expensive as—or even *more* expensive than—New York, Paris, or any other large global city. So it's much better to accept this fact in advance and factor it into your vacation planning, tailoring outings and trips that will reflect your interests—and your budget.

Often, booking in advance, harnessing cut-price and low-season deals, and taking advantage of Internet specials for flights and hotel rooms can cut down on costs. London is also great at offering things for free (particularly the museums), and the quality of the culture, entertainment, parks, relaxation, and general fun to be had in the city means that if you target your spending wisely, you'll go home penny-pinched but deeply satisfied.

LONDON
TOP ATTRACTIONS

Westminster Abbey

(A) The front towers of this soaring early–English Gothic edifice stand around the tombs of British monarchs and the great men and women who built Britain. The Abbey plays a preeminent role in the spiritual life of the nation, from the coronation of 38 sovereigns to royal weddings and state funerals.

Buckingham Palace

(B) Not the largest or prettiest royal residence, the palace at the heart of London is nonetheless a must-see. The opulence of the 19 State Rooms open to the public are jaw-dropping, and don't overlook the collection of old master paintings and gilded state carriages at the Queen's Gallery.

Tower of London

(C) The 900-year-old Tower is London at its historic, gory best. Every brick tells a grisly story, and the axe blows and fortunes that have risen and fallen within this 20-towered mini-city provide an inexhaustible supply of intrigue.

St. Paul's Cathedral

(D) Sir Christopher Wren's neoclassical masterpiece never fails to take the breath away. Climb the enormous 360-foot dome, one of the world's finest and largest, to experience the acoustics of the Whispering Gallery, and higher still to the Golden Gallery for far-reaching views across London.

British Museum

(E) The oldest public museum in the world has been wowing visitors to London since 1753. Its unrivaled 8-million-strong collection spans all recorded history, including the 4th-century BC Egyptian mummies, the Elgin Marbles, the Rosetta Stone, and the Anglo-Saxon warrior treasures of Sutton Hoo.

Shakespeare's Globe

(F) You can catch a Shakespeare play any evening in London. But standing in the open-air "pit" or yard with the "groundlings" on a floor of sawdust watching King Lear in a *scrupulously* re-created oak version of the original Tudor theater for which Shakespeare wrote is a genuine thrill.

Tate Modern

(G) The world's most visited modern art gallery, Tate Modern is a hip and massively successful feature of London's artistic landscape. Passing wry judgment on the latest exhibit inside the giant Turbine Hall at this former Bankside Power Station is a civic duty among art-loving Londoners.

London's Central Parks

(H) A whopping 25% of London is parkland, so it is mighty hard to choose between St. James's Park (those fairy-tale views), Kensington Gardens (the beloved *Peter Pan* statue), Hyde Park (pedalos on the Serpentine Lido), and Regent's Park's fragrant rose gardens.

Hampton Court Palace

(I) Henry VIII's palace has a majestic Tudor-turreted charm, augmented by Sir Christopher Wren's touch, and a picturesque Thames-side location, all of which make for a great day out. Not even dour Lord Protector of the Realm Oliver Cromwell, who moved here in 1653, could resist its charms.

National Gallery

(J) There are enough world-class paintings—from da Vinci to Valázquez—at this collection of 2,300 works to have the most indifferent art enthusiast drool with delight. Note the raised front entrance and its great photo op: Big Ben and Nelson's Column framed by Trafalgar Square.

LONDON ROYAL LEGACY

The Rocky Monarchy

From medieval castles and keeps, to Royal Parks, palaces, pageants, ceremonies and processions, London has had a tumultuous and sometimes bloody royal history, which can still be glimpsed or encountered at practically every second turn. London has been the royal capital of England since 1066, when William the Conquerer began the tradition of royal coronations at Westminster Abbey. Every reigning monarch since then—including Richard I (the *Coeur de Lion*) in 1189, to the current Queen Elizabeth II in 1953—has been crowned at the Abbey, and many of England's illustrous—and sometimes *notorious* —kings and queens have left a legacy or their majestic mark on the city. Many of the finest places in this book have royal associations: William I subjugated London with the imposing Tower of London; Henry VIII hunted deer at Hampton Court; Elizabeth I enjoyed bear baiting in Southwark; and Charles I was executed on Whitehall. Tyranical but weak monarchs like King John (1199–1216) granted the City of London more powers under Magna Carta, while the first "Parliament" sat at the royal Palace of Westminster in 1240 under Henry III. The Tudors rarely brooked dissent; Elizabeth I's half-sister, "Bloody" Mary I (1553–58), burned heretic Protestant bishops at the stake, and traitors were hung, drawn, and quartered, with their heads stuck on pikes on London Bridge.

A Cultural Renaissance

Peace under Elizabeth I "The Virgin Queen" saw a cultural renaissance and the great flowering of English theater, poetry, and drama, centered on Shakespeare's Globe and the open-air playhouses of Southwark. Charles I was captured by the formidable Puritan Oliver Cromwell during the English Civil War, and beheaded on a freezing day outside Banqueting House in 1649. Although the Interregnum lasted only 16 years (outlawing simple pleasures, such as dancing and theater), the Restoration of Charles II in 1660 and subsequent monarchs including the Protestant William III and Mary II—who moved into Kensington Palace, now the current home of the Duke and Duchess of Cambridge—and the House of Hanover's four Georgian kings and later Queen Victoria saw London grow into a teeming metropolis.

The Down-to-Earth Duke and Duchess

These days you might spot the heartthrob Duke and Duchess of Cambridge walking with their kids in Kensington Gardens, or elegantly stepping out onto the red carpet at a royal gala performance in the West End. Besides the color, pageantry, and marching bands of the Changing the Guard ceremony at Buckingham Palace, there's a rich calendar of royal ceremonies. The Ceremony of the Keys to lock up the Tower of London has taken place at 9:53 pm each night for more than 700 years, and you can see the Queen take the Royal Salute from the Household Division at the annual Trooping the Colour march from Horse Guards Parade to St. James's Park. The Queen is also drawn by four horses in the dazzling Irish State Coach from Buckingham Palace to the Palace of Westminster in a huge royal procession for the State Opening of Parliament each autumn, and you can see her pay homage to the war dead at the Cenotaph on Remembrance Sunday.

GIVE THE SPORTS SCENE A GO

Sport in the capital is best watched, rather than participated in. If you're lucky enough to score a ticket for a Premier League football match, you'll experience a seething mass of mockery and chanting. Tennis, horse racing, and cricket impinge on Londoners' horizons at crucial times of the year, too, but you're unlikely to see grown men crying at the outcome of the Wimbledon Men's Final.

Boating

The Boat Race. Join more than a quarter of a million devotees along the banks of the River Thames between Putney and Mortlake for a glimpse of the annual Oxford and Cambridge University Boat Race, held on the last Saturday of March or first Saturday of April. Sink a few pints and soak up the tweed cap and Barbour–clad Oxbridge-y Thames-side atmosphere as these heavyweight eight-man university crews clash oars and tussle head-to-head for supremacy. First raced in 1829, the 4-mile route is a picturesque stretch between Putney and Chiswick Bridges. ⊠ *Putney Bridge, Putney* ⊕ *www.theboatrace.org.*

Cricket

At its best, Test cricket can be a slow build of smoldering tension and unexpected high-wire excitement. At its worst, it can be too slow and uneventful for the casual observer, as five-day games crawl toward a draw, or as rain stops play. But try to visit Lord's—the home of cricket—for just one day of a Test match to hear the *thwack* of leather on willow and to see the English aristocracy and upper middle classes on full display.

Lord's. Lord's Cricket Ground—home of the venerable 1787 Marylebone Cricket Club (MCC)—has been hallowed cricketing turf since 1814 and MCC rules codified the game. Tickets for major Test matches are hard to come by: obtain an application form online and enter the ballot (lottery) to purchase them. ⊠ *Marylebone Cricket Club, Lord's Cricket Ground, St. John's Wood Rd., St. John's Wood* ☎ *020/7432–1000* ⊕ *www.lords.org* Ⓜ *St. John's Wood.*

Football

London's top teams—Chelsea, Tottenham Hotspur, Arsenal, West Ham, and Queens Park Rangers—are top-class and the first three often progress in the European-based Champions League. It's unlikely you'll get tickets for anything except the least popular Premier League games during the August–May season, despite the high ticket prices—£43 for a walk-up match day seat at Chelsea, and £122 for the most expensive tickets at Arsenal. QPR has a raucous match-day atmosphere and is a good bet with General Sale tickets from £25.

Tennis

Wimbledon Lawn Tennis Championships. The All England Club's Wimbledon Lawn Tennis Championships are famous for Centre Court, rain, strawberries and cream, and an old-school insistence on players wearing white. Thankfully, the rain has been banished on Centre Court by the retractable roof, but whether you can get tickets for Centre Court all comes down to the luck of the draw—there's a ballot system for advance purchase. See *www.wimbledon.com* for details. ⊠ *The All England Lawn Tennis Club, Church Rd.* ☎ *020/8944–1066 for general inquiries* ⊕ *www.wimbledon.com.*

FREE AND CHEAP

The exchange rate may vary a bit, but there is one conversion that will never change: £0 = $0. Here are our picks for the top free things to do in London.

Concerts

St. Martin-in-the-Fields, St. Stephen Walbrook, St. Olaves in the City, and St. James's Church Piccadilly have free lunchtime concerts and recitals, as does St. Giles-in-the-Fields on Friday and St. George, Bloomsbury on Sunday afternoon. There are also regular organ recitals at Westminster Abbey.

Of the music colleges, the Royal Academy of Music, the Royal College of Music, the Guildhall, Trinity College, and the Royal Opera House have free recitals. For contemporary ears, there's free jazz and classical music on an exquisite 1897 Bechstein on the first Sunday of the month at the Dysart Petersham restaurant (*0208/940–8005*) in Richmond and live jazz at the Lamb & Flag (*33 Rose St., 0207/497–9504*) in Covent Garden, from 8 pm one Sunday a month. For free blues on Sunday to Thursday or before 8:30 pm on Friday and Saturday, head to the Ain't Nothin But . . . honky-tonk blues bar in Soho (*20 Kingly St., 020/7287–0514*).

Film, Theater and Opera

If all seats have been sold, the National Theatre sells unobstructed-view £5 standing tickets on the day of performances at their Olivier and Lyttleton theaters. Standing-only tickets are between £10 and £15 at the Royal Opera House, and 67 tickets are available in person from the box office from 10 am on the day of most performances. Under 30 or a full-time student? Becoming an Access all Arias member of the English National Opera is free, and allows you to buy £10 to £30 tickets. There are 700 £5 standing-only tickets available for every performance at the historical replica and half-covered Shakespeare's Globe theater, as well as £10 standing tickets for evocative candle-lit plays and concerts at the adjacent indoor Sam Wanamaker Playhouse. At Sloane Square, the Royal Court Theatre has four standing-only tickets for *10 pence* each at the Jerwood Theatre Downstairs, available an hour before performances; otherwise *all* tickets at both theaters there are £10 on Monday.

Sightseeing on the Cheap

Prop yourself on the top deck of a red double-decker bus for a ride through the most scenic parts of the city. Routes 9 and 15 also operate Heritage routes on the traditional Routemaster buses. With all buses now cashless, instead you can use your Oyster card or buy tickets from machines at the bus stops for the following routes:

Bus 11: King's Road, Sloane Square, Victoria Station, Westminster Abbey, Houses of Parliament and Big Ben, Whitehall, Trafalgar Square, the Strand, the Royal Courts of Justice, Fleet Street, and St. Paul's Cathedral.

Bus 19: Sloane Square, Knightsbridge, Hyde Park Corner, Green Park, Piccadilly Circus, Shaftsbury Avenue, Bloomsbury, Sadler's Wells Theatre and The Angel, Islington.

Bus 88: Oxford Circus, Conduit Street, Piccadilly Circus, Haymarket, Trafalgar Square, Whitehall, Horse Guards Parade, Westminster Station, Westminster Abbey, Horseferry Road, and Tate Britain.

THE ARTS FOR FREE

Classical Music and Jazz

The Barbican, the Royal National Theatre, and the Royal Opera House often have free music in their foyers or in dedicated spaces. On the South Bank, free festivals and take place alongside the river.

Many of London's music colleges give free concerts several times a week. The Royal Academy of Music and the Royal College of Music have free recitals. St. Martin-in-the-Fields has free lunchtime concerts, as does St. James's Piccadilly. Westminster Abbey and St. Paul's in Covent Garden also have frequent free music. For the BBC Proms, hundreds of standing tickets are available at £5: not quite free, but almost.

Contemporary Music

Brixton's Dogstar pub has a great selection of DJs, often playing for free on weekday evenings. Ain't Nothing But Blues Bar in Soho has live music most nights, often without a cover charge, and pubs such as the Monarch and the Hawley Arms near Camden Market offer the chance to see tomorrow's indie stars. East London establishment Stories hosts free acoustic acts, while Cecil Sharp House in Camden, the home of folk, has tickets for as little as £3. There's no cover charge at Piano Kensington, where talented pianists delight often raucous crowds.

Drama and Performance Arts

Look out for occasional festivals where innovative performances take place on the South Bank. Check the newspapers and *Time Out* for upcoming performances.

Museums and Galleries

Few if any other cities in the world offer the number of free art venues available in London. Most of the city's museums and galleries do not charge entrance fees. The monthly *Galleries* magazine, available from galleries themselves or online at ⊕ *www.galleries.co.uk*, has listings for all private galleries in the capital.

Park Life

London's parks come to life in summer with a wide-ranging program (⊕ *www.royalparks.org.uk* for details, or 020/7298–2000). There are several summer festivals in London parks, some with lots of pop stars, like British Summer Time in Hyde Park (⊕ *www.bst-hydepark.com*; day tickets around £80) and the more indie Field Day in Victoria Park (⊕ *www.fielddayfestivals.com*; day tickets around £40, weekend tickets around £80). Notable contemporary art fairs are October's Frieze in Regent's Park (⊕ *www.friezelondon.com*; around £35) and the Affordable Art Fair in Battersea Park and Hampstead Heath in spring (⊕ *www.affordableartfair.com*; weekdays £12, weekends £15).

Radio and Television

With so much broadcast material recorded in front of live London audiences, there are often opportunities to watch a free quiz show, current-affairs debate, comedy, or even drama. (⊕ *www.bbc.co.uk/showsandtours/tickets*).

LONDON MUSEUMS, AN OVERVIEW

London's museums are one of the capital's crown jewels, and many have free entry. *This list includes museums listed elsewhere in our content (check index for full listings), plus extras.*

Major Galleries

Giddy art lovers will target the big four—the **National Gallery**, the **National Portrait Gallery**, **Tate Britain**, and **Tate Modern**. The National Gallery has more than 2,300 masterpieces from 1250 to 1900, while the world's largest collection of portraits is next door at the National Portrait Gallery. Tate Britain takes you on a chronological walk through 500 years of British art and Tate Modern showcases contemporary art and installations.

Academies and Galleries

Must-visits include the 1768 **Royal Academy of Arts** for its sell-out exhibitions on artists like Monet and the diminutive **Courtauld Gallery** at Somerset House, which has an exceptionally classy capsule collection from the early medieval period to the Postimpressionists. The **Queen's Gallery** at Buckingham Palace showcases the Royal Collection and hosts blockbusters on world-class greats like Leonardo da Vinci. The historic and underrated **Dulwich Picture Gallery** exhibits exquisite European old masters from 1600 to the 1700s and the **Guildhall Art Gallery** has awesome Pre-Raphaelites.

House Museums

London's historic house museums are treats within treats: the art and the house itself. One of the finest is the private **Wallace Collection** at the majestic 1788 Hertford House on Manchester Square in Marylebone, which hosts European old masters and fine French decorative arts. Other historic humdingers with old masters include **Apsley House, Kenwood House,** and **Leighton House** in Holland Park.

Contemporary Art

With London now a top-two global art hub, you'll find excellent contemporary art galleries splattered around. The **Serpentine Gallery** in Hyde Park may be small but packs a mean modern art punch. The **Hayward Gallery** at the Southbank Centre concentrates on bleeding-edge exhibitions while the **Whitechapel Gallery** kindles the smoldering East London art scene. Private galleries like the **Saatchi Gallery,** Hauser & Wirth, and **Maureen Paley** push up-and-comers and unknowns.

Major Museums

The **British Museum** was the world's first national public museum in 1753 and still captivates with its vast collection of artifacts from the Rosetta Stone to Ramesses the Great. A 105-foot Diplodocus greets you at the **Natural History Museum** with its trove of 70 million artifacts spanning 4.5 billion years while the **Science Museum** has a collection of 300,000 items showcased in 12 galleries. The **Victoria & Albert Museum** is stuffed with amazing jewelry and design exhibits. At St. Pancras, the permanent exhibition at the **British Library** has manuscripts like Magna Carta, a Gutenberg Bible, and Shakespeare's First Folio from 1623.

British History

The **Museum of London** explores London since way before Roman times while the **Museum of London Docklands** tells the 2,000-year story of the port of London. The **Royal Observatory, Greenwich,** tells of Britain's role in the story of navigation and astronomy, and is the home of the Prime Meridian while the **National Maritime Museum** charts British naval ascendancy. The **National Army Museum,**

Imperial War Museum, and **Household Cavalry Museum** venerate Britain's military history, while the **Royal Air Force Museum** houses Spitfires and a Lancaster bomber. You'll find all the clocks have stopped at 4:58 pm at the **Churchill War Rooms,** which preserves the bunkered World War II Cabinet War Rooms, and you can operate a "dead man's handle" on a 1930s Underground train at the **London Transport Museum. Shakespeare's Globe** and adjacent indoor candlelit **Sam Wanamaker Playhouse** theaters are enthralling replicas of the originals.

Royal Palaces

London's a royal wonderland, with royal palaces doubling down as de facto royal museums. You can get into **Buckingham Palace** from August 1 to late September and tour 19 impossibly grand State Rooms, including the Queen's Throne Room. **Kensington Palace** is home to the Duke and Duchess of Cambridge and you can glide through former King William III and Queen Mary II's closet. The Tudor turrets, tapestries, and historic kitchens fascinate all-comers at **Hampton Court Palace,** as do the sparkling Crown Jewels regalia at the Royal Palace and Fortress at the **Tower of London.** Pocket-size **Kew Palace** and **Eltham Palace** are two other prize royal retreats.

Best for Kids

Kids adore the gory Black Death scenes and gruesome Jack the Ripper scenes at the **London Dungeon** and are always intrigued by the waxwork models of celebs at **Madame Tussauds.** The eclectic **Horniman Museum** in Forest Hill has 350,000 quirky objects amassed by a Victorian tea trader and there are scientific, medical, and surgical specimens galore at the **Wellcome Collection, The Royal Institution,** and **Hunterian Museum.** The **London Fire Brigade Museum,** tiny **Pollock's Toy Museum Trust,** and **The Guards Museum** on Birdcage Walk all cater brilliantly to the whims of kids of all ages.

One-Man Shows

London is fab at preserving the homes of illustrious native sons and daughters, with the best including the **Charles Dickens Museum, Florence Nightingale Museum, Freud Museum, Handel House Museum,** plus artist William **Hogarth's House** and essayist Thomas **Carlyle's House** on Cheyne Row. Candlelit tours at **Dennis Severs' House** in Spitalfields chart the tale of a 17th-century French Huguenot silk merchants' family, and the **Sir John Soane's Museum** is crammed with a magpie collection of antiquities from the namesake neoclassical architect and collector.

A LONDON HISTORIC PUB CRAWL

A brilliant, beery, and *traditional* way to see London and its medieval backstreets is on a pub crawl. This walk takes you through some of the city's most historically textured and resonant neighborhoods. Settle back with a pint of English ale and drink in all the history.

Bankside

Like Geoffrey Chaucer's *Canterbury Tales* pilgrims, we start in Southwark near London Bridge. Head down Borough High Street to the **George Inn**, a long black-and-white affair with wonky galleries, warped beams, open fires, and oak wooden stairs. First chronicled in 1542, the pub's mentioned in Charles Dickens's *Little Dorrit*. Cross Borough High Street and take the Bedale Street entrance to **Borough Market**; walk along until it turns into Cathedral Street, with the striking 12th-century **Southwark Cathedral** on your right. At the fork head left to Sir Francis Drake's **Golden Hinde II** replica galleon and walk past **The Clink Prison Museum** to reach the **Anchor Bankside**. This old tavern was built in 1615 and was frequented by William Shakespeare and other players and actors from the nearby Globe, Swan, and Rose theaters. Head up to the roof terrace for sweeping views of the River Thames, **London Bridge,** and **St. Paul's Cathedral.**

Across the Thames

Cross Southwark Bridge to The City. Turn left along Cannon Street and on the corner of Bow Lane, **Ye Olde Watling** was built before the Great Fire, and promptly torched. Rebuilt around 1668, again in 1901, and then again after the Blitz, it's named after Watling Street, the original Roman road on which it sits.

Head west along Watling Street to St. Paul's Cathedral and take a left down Creed Lane from Ludgate Hill. Turn right onto Carter Lane and wind left into Blackfriars Lane. At the bottom, turn right to **The Blackfriar** at No. 174 Queen Victoria Street. The Grade II–listed spectacular interior is all marble and brass bas-reliefs of Dominican friars interspersed with aphorisms and quotes. Head north up New Bridge Street and turn left onto Fleet Street to the 1667 **Ye Olde Cheshire Cheese** at No. 145. Dr. Samuel Johnson, author of the first dictionary, used to drink here, as did Samuel Pepys, Charles Dickens, Voltaire, Mark Twain, Oscar Wilde, and Teddy Roosevelt.

Bloomsbury

Wander west along Fleet Street, then walk north up Fetter Lane, cross Holborn Viaduct into Hatton Garden, head down a brick alley to **Ye Olde Mitre** at 1 Ely Court, which has served brews since 1546. Look for the maypole cherry tree trunk that Elizabeth I once danced around. For the final stretch, walk north via Hatton Garden and Leather Lane, left into Baldwin Gardens, amble up Gray's Inn Road, then left onto Theobald's Road before turning right onto quaint Lamb's Conduit Street, to find **The Lamb**, notable for its 1720s horseshoe bar with etched-glass "snob screens" to shield the well-to-do from women of dubious distinction. Head west along Great Ormond Street to Queen Square to find **The Queens Larder,** where Queen Charlotte reputedly rented out a cellar to store foods for her sickly husband, George III.

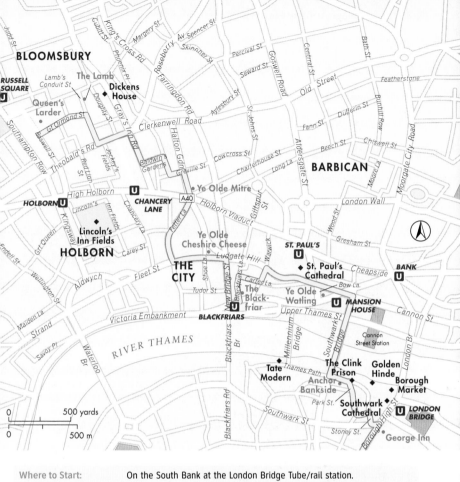

Where to Start:	On the South Bank at the London Bridge Tube/rail station.
Length:	4 miles (about 1½ hours without stopping). Just part of this walk will give you a taste of the oldest bits of London.
Where to Stop:	Russell Square Tube station or Tottenham Court Road.
Best Time to Go:	Weekday afternoons (most pubs open late in the morning).
Worst Time to Go:	Busy summer weekends may be too crowded.
Eating and Drinking:	All the pubs will serve food at lunchtime. Stop when you're hungry or pick up some tasty grub in Borough Market and stop in either Gray's Inn Fields or Lincoln's Inn Fields for a picnic.
Diversions:	From the Anchor Bankside, consider continuing along the riverside to Tate Modern, before crossing over the River Thames to ferret out Ye Olde Watling or The Blackfriar.
Pub Highlights:	George Inn, The Anchor Bankside, Ye Olde Watling, The Blackfriar, Ye Olde Cheshire Cheese, Ye Olde Watling, Ye Olde Mitre, The Lamb.

IN PURSUIT OF THE EAST END ART SCENE

From the atmospheric period Georgian streets of Whitechapel and Spitalfields to the grittier warehouses-turned-galleries of Hackney, a tour of the burgeoning East End's art spaces presents the area in all its rich variety.

Whitechapel and Bethnal Green

To start your tour, Tube it to Aldgate East Station, then walk east along Whitechapel High Street to the **Whitechapel Gallery,** a center for exciting exhibitions since its founding in 1901. Head back toward the Tube, then turn right into Commercial Street, go north past Spitalfields Market, then right, at The Ten Bells pub into Fournier Street, with its handsome, 18th-century former Protestant French Huguenot silk weavers' townhouse workshops. Turn left into Brick Lane, then right past the railway lines into Cheshire Street, known for quirky shops like the Duke of Uke (for all your ukulele needs). The shops give way to a railway line as Cheshire Street turns into Dunbridge Street, and then Three Colts Lane, as you walk directly east, until you come to industrial Herald Street, where you'll turn left. At No. 21 is the **Maureen Paley** gallery, founded by an American expat who's now a doyenne of the East End artster scene.

Hackney

Turn right onto Witan Street and then left onto Cambridge Heath Road. The **V&A Museum of Childhood** is just past Bethnal Green Tube station. Continue heading north (take Bus 106 or 254 if you're flagging) to just past Hackney Road. A few yards on the right is **Vyner Street,** not quite as sizzling as it used to be, but still a gallery hot spot (try **Wilkinson Gallery**). Cross back over Cambridge Heath Road and head west along Andrews Road, paralleling Regent's Canal with its residential houseboats. Here you can either turn right to visit **Broadway Market** or left, going straight until you reach Hackney Road. Turn right and then take your first left at the Ion Square Gardens. Bear right onto **Columbia Road** (helpfully signed for Shoreditch), site of London's best flower street market on Sunday morning.

Shoreditch

A short way past where the indie shops of Columbia Road end, you'll see another sign for Shoreditch on the left at Virginia Road. Turn left here, bear right, and then turn left again at Hocker Street. This brings you to **Arnold Circus**, an early Arts and Crafts housing development. From the southern end of the Circus, take the first right off Club Row into Old Nichol Street. Here you'll find the **Kate MacGarry** gallery, known for its cutting-edge conceptual and video art. Turn left into Boundary Street at the end of the road and stop for a restorative coffee or egg-and-bacon bap at hipster-vogue **Albion** English "caff" at the end of Boundary Street. At this point you can either turn left around the corner to explore more indie boutiques on **Redchurch Street,** or right, which will bring you almost immediately to Shoreditch High Street and the huge Tea Building to the left. Turn left onto Bethnal Green Road, where you'll find the Shoreditch High Street Overground station just above the spunky **Boxpark** metal shipping container pop-up mall.

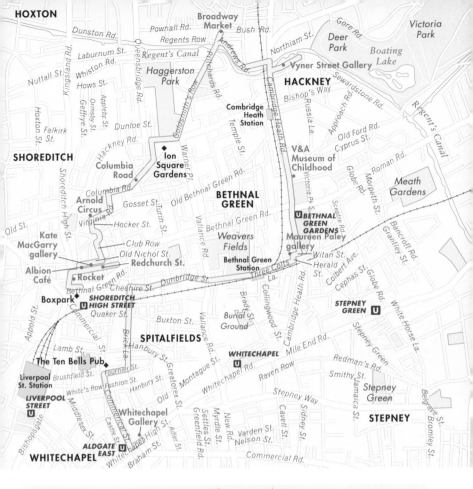

Where to Start:	At Aldgate East Tube station in Whitechapel.
Length:	3½ miles (about 2 hours without stopping).
Where to Stop:	Shoreditch High Street Overground station.
Best Time to Go:	Weekdays for galleries, weekends for markets.
Worst Time to Go:	Busy summer weekends may be crowded.
Eating and Drinking:	Wine and small plates of charcuterie at Brawn on Columbia Road; excellent modern British food at Upstairs at the Ten Bells on Commercial Street; coffee and light bites at Sir Terence Conran's Albion café on Boundary Street.
Diversions:	Consider crossing to the west side of Shoreditch High Street to explore London's new media hub near the Old Street (aka Silicon) roundabout. The digerati gather at The Book Club on Leonard Street for coffee by day and drinks by night.
Gallery Highlights:	Maureen Paley gallery, Whitechapel Gallery, V&A Museum of Childhood, Kate MacGarry gallery, and Wilkinson Gallery.

DID YOU KNOW?

Trafalgar Square is home to
gatherings from New Year's
Eve celebrations to rowdy
political demonstrations.
Statues, monuments, bronze
lions, and fountains fill this
intersection of Whitehall and
The Mall.

AFTERNOON TEA

An Age-Old Tradition

So what is Afternoon Tea, exactly? Well, it is real loose-leaf tea—Earl Grey, English Breakfast, Ceylon, Darjeeling, or Assam—brewed in a fine bone china or porcelain pot and served with cups and saucers, milk or lemon, and silver spoons, taken between noon and 6 pm. For the full monty there should be elegant finger foods on a three-tiered silver cake stand: crustless finger cucumber sandwiches on the bottom; scones with Devonshire clotted cream and strawberry jam in the middle; and rich English fruit cake, shortbread, patisseries, macaroons, and dainty fancies on top.

Teagoers dress smartly, and conversation by tradition should naturally avoid politics and religion. Here are some top places in town to head:

Classic Choices

Hands down, **The Savoy** on the Strand offers one of the most beautiful settings for tea. The Thames Foyer, a symphony of grays and golds centered on a winter garden wrought-iron gazebo, is just the place for the house pianist to accompany you as you enjoy 76 house teas along with finger sandwiches, homemade scones, and pastries.

Setting the standard in its English Tea Room for some of London's best-known traditional teas, **Brown's Hotel**, at 33 Albermarle Street offers afternoon tea for £41.50 or, if you wish to splash out, Champagne Tea for £110 for two people.

If you seek timeless chic, the 1920s dining room at the **Wolseley** Viennese grand café on Piccadilly remains a fashionable hangout. The silver service teas here—light Cream Tea is £10.75 and Champagne Tea £33.50—are among the best in town.

Something Different

Add spice to your afternoon tea by trying a popular Moroccan-style Afternoon Tea (£22) at the souk-chic tearoom at **Momo** off Regent Street, where you'll enjoy sweet mint tea plus scones with fig jam, Maghrebian pastries, Moroccan chicken wraps, and honey-and-nut-rich Berber-style crepes.

Alternatively, you can sit looking out onto immaculate lawns amid mini-potted orange trees at **The Orangery** in Prince William and Kate's London pad, Kensington Palace, inside resplendent Kensington Gardens. Afternoon Tea is £24 and a suitably Royal Afternoon Tea (with a glass of Laurent-Perrier NV) is £34.

Bea's of Bloomsbury is one of the best afternoon tea stops around. Bea's churns out freshly baked delights like blackberry cupcakes or heavenly chocolate fudge cupcake with fudge icing. Cheery afternoon tea services (noon–7 pm daily) with loose-leaf Jing tea, cupcakes, scones with jam and clotted cream, mini-meringues, marshmallows, and Valrhona brownies is £19, or £26 with Champagne.

An Edwardian Escape

For frilly trompe l'oeil grandeur, few can compete with afternoon tea at **The Ritz** on Piccadilly. It's served in the impressive Palm Court, replete with marble tables, Louis XVI chaises, resplendent bouquets, and musical accompaniment: a true taste of Edwardian London in the 21st century. Afternoon Tea is £50 and Champagne Tea £77. Reserve months ahead and remember to wear a jacket and tie.

For more information on the above places, see our Where to Eat, Where to Stay, and Shopping chapters.

LONDON WITH KIDS

Education Without Yawns

Kew Gardens. Kew Gardens is great for kids, with activities, the "climbers and creepers" play zone, treetops Sky Walk, zip wires, scramble slides, and children's trails; it's free for kids.

London Dungeon. Gore galore (did you ever see a medieval disembowelment?) plunges you into the depths of London history, with gruesome Jack the Ripper rides and special effects scary enough to frighten the coolest of kids.

London Zoo. Disappear into the animal kingdom among the enclosures, complete with sessions for kids about all kinds of bugs and spiders in this popular animal retreat in Regent's Park.

Natural History Museum. It doesn't get more awe-inspiring than bloodsucking bats, a cabinet of hummingbirds, simulated Kobe earthquakes, and a life-size blue whale. Just make sure you know your dodo from your diplodocus.

Science Museum. Special effects, virtual space voyages, 800 interactive exhibits, puzzles, and mysteries from the world of science can keep kids effortlessly amused all day.

Tower of London. Perfect for playing prince and princess in front of the Crown Jewels, but not so perfect for imagining what becomes of the fairy tale—watch your royal necks.

Performances

Covent Garden street performers. You can't beat the open-air gaggle of jugglers, fire-eaters, unicyclists, mime artists, and the human statues tantalizing crowds at Covent Garden piazza.

Regent's Park Open-Air Theatre. Welcome to the land of fairy dust and magic. Don't miss an evening performance under the stars of *A Midsummer Night's Dream* in high summer.

Activities

Ride the London Eye. Europe's biggest observation wheel looks like a giant fairground ride, and you can see across what seems like half of London from the top.

Pose with a Queen's Horse Guard. There's always an erect soldier in uniform standing watch by the entrance to Horse Guards on the Trafalgar Square end of Whitehall. They don't mind posing for pictures, but they're not allowed to smile (which some kids see as a challenge).

Ice-skating at the Natural History Museum. Send your kids whizzing, arms whirling, across ice from mid-November to January at this spotlighted ice rink right outside the museum.

Night at the Natural History Museum. Find out what the dinosaurs really do when the lights go out at the monthly Dino Snores sleepover (minimum of one adult and five kids per group).

Pedalo on the Serpentine. Pack a picnic and take a blue pedalo out into the middle of Hyde Park's famed Serpentine lake; settle back and tuck in to lunch.

Lose the kids at Hampton Court Maze. The topiary might be more than 300 years old, but the quest to reach the middle of Hampton Court's world-famous trapezoid-shape yew hedge maze remains as challenging as ever.

West End musicals. Foot-stompingly good West End musicals and shows like *Les Misérables, Billy Elliot, Matilda, Mamma Mia!, War Horse, Oliver!, Grease,* and *The Phantom of the Opera* will mesmerize the over-seven-years-old crowd.

Millennium Bridge and St. Paul's Cathedral.

THE BUILDING OF LONDON

The past is knit into the very fabric of the lives of Londoners: they live in Regency townhouses, worship in Baroque churches, and chill out in Edwardian-era parks. Unfolding like a gigantic historical pop-up book, London reveals—building by building—the pageant of a nation's history. To make sense of it all, here's a quick architectural tour through time.

Despite invading tribes, an epic fire, and 20th-century bombing, London has always survived, and a surprising amount of yesterday remains visible in its streets today. Starting with remnants of Londinium, the early Roman city contained by a defensive wall some 2,000 years ago, you can trace the city's beginnings. Only pieces of the wall remain, but the name of each entrance to the city has been preserved: Aldgate, Newgate, Bishopsgate, Cripplegate, Aldersgate, and Ludgate.

As commerce grew the city over the centuries, London expanded between two centers of power, Westminster in the west and the Tower of London in the east. Following both the Great Fire and World War II destruction, the need to rebuild outweighed the desire for sensible street layouts, and often any aesthetic considerations. In fact, London as a whole has rarely been planned, and the financial center is still roughly in the shape of that original Roman wall. London's haphazard streets and alleys are filled with diverse architectural styles side-by-side, each representing a piece of the city's history.

TIMELINE

55, 54 BC Julius Caesar arrives on Britain's shores	43 AD–410 AD Roman rule	61 AD Boudica attacks and destroys Londinium		600s Anglo-Saxon Lundenwic settlement in Covent Garden area
	0	250	500	750

(top left) Statue of the Roman Emperor Trajan (r. AD 98-117) outside the largest remaining section of the Roman wall at Tower Hill. (right) Tower of London; (left) Carausius coin struck circa 288-290 AD at the Londinium mint.

Pre–410 — Roman Londinium

As the Roman Empire expanded, Britain was conquered and the first city where London now stands began to develop along the Thames. Among many building projects, the Romans enclosed Londinium with a ragstone wall to protect against invading tribes after the Celtic warrior queen Boudica razed the city. Today chunks of the ancient barrier remain in the City, and at the Guildhall Art Gallery you can see a partial Roman amphitheatre from this time.

■ Visit: Guildhall (Ch. 6), London Wall at Tower Hill Tube station (Ch. 6), Museum of London (Ch. 5)

410–1485 — Saxon and Medieval London

Little is known of the 250 years after the Romans left London. Following these "Dark Ages," most medieval houses and bridges were built of timber or wattle and daub and the perishable materials didn't last in the changing city.

England's royalty began building heavily in the capital as a sign of strength and power, focusing on defensive structures. In 1042, the Saxon King Edward the Confessor moved his court and began a church on the site of the current Westminster Abbey, where almost all the monarchs of England have been crowned since. From

across the English Channel, William the Conqueror brought Norman architectural styles with him. William built the White Tower; later expanded, the solid castle became the heart of the Tower of London complex. His son and heir William II saw the construction of Westminster Hall, the oldest part of the Palace of Westminster (today's Houses of Parliament). St. Bartholomew's Hospital, founded in 1123, and the Guildhall, a center of commerce from the early 15th century, are among the few buildings that survived the later Great Fire in 1666.

■ Visit: Guildhall (Ch. 6), St. Bartholomew's Hospital (Ch. 6), Tower of London (Ch. 6)

1000	1250	1500	1750
1066 William the Conqueror becomes King of England	1240 Parliament sits at Westminster for the first time · 1348 The Black Death	1605 Guy Fawkes's Gunpowder Plot uncovered · 1536 Dissolution of the Monasteries	1642–51 Civil War · 1666 Great Fire

1

IN FOCUS THE BUILDING OF LONDON

(top left) Painted ceiling of Banqueting House by Sir Peter Paul Rubens; (top right) *The Great Fire of London, with Ludgate and old St Paul's;* (bottom right) St. Paul's Cathedral, built 1675–1708, designed by Sir Christopher Wren

1485–1714

Tudor and Stuart London

As London grew, the Tudor royals influenced the architecture of London not only by creating, but also by destroying. Henry VII continued the expansion of Westminster Abbey and his successor, Henry VIII, resided at Hampton Court. The arts flourished under Elizabeth I, and the original Globe Theatre was built in 1599. Yet many fine medieval churches were torn down as England. separated from the Roman Catholic Church.

Architects brought continental ideas to London, notably the influential Italian Palladian style introduced by Inigo Jones. You can see this neo-classical style with it's mathematical proportions and balanced lines at the Queen's House in Greenwich and at Banqueting House, where Charles I was executed following the English Civil War. Eleven years later, Charles II was restored to the throne, returning from exile in France.

The Great Fire of 1666 destroyed five-sixths of London, but it also wiped out the plague that had ravaged the impoverished and overcrowded population the year before. Sir Christopher Wren was given the Herculean task of rebuilding London. He wanted to map out a more organized grid for the city, but it was rebuilt on the old haphazard lines. It took Wren 35 years to build his baroque masterpiece, St. Paul's Cathedral. Wren also designed 52 other churches (only 23 still stand, including St. Bride's and St. Stephen Walbrook) and Monument to commemorate the fire. Nicholas Hawksmoor assisted Wren and designed his own highly original churches including the splendid Christ Church in Spitalfields.

■ Visit: Banqueting House (Ch. 2), Christ Church, Spitalfields (Ch. 7), Shakespeare's Globe theater (Ch. 8), Queen's House, Greenwich (Ch. 12), St. Bride's (Ch. 6), St. Paul's Cathedral (Ch. 6), St. Stephen Walbrook (Ch. 6), Hampton Court (Ch. 13)

| 1721–42 Robert Walpole, serves as first Prime Minister | 1776 Declaration of American Independence | 1803–1815 Napoleonic Wars | 1837 Queen Victoria comes to the throne |

| 1750 | 1780 | 1810 | 1840 |

(top left) Courtyard of neo-classical Somerset House, built for George III. (right) The Rotunda of the Victoria and Albert (V&A) Museum with modern Chihuly sculpture; (bottom left) St Martin-in-the-Fields on Trafalgar Square.

1714–1830 Georgian Era

By the beginning of the 18th century, London was the biggest city in Europe and a center of world trade. This growth led to changes in politics, as power moved to a parliamentary system. Increased wealth led to an explosion of art and architecture.

Many different styles flourished—Rococo, neo-classical, Regency, and Gothic Revival. The predominant neo-classical, based on the styles of ancient Greece, can be seen in many stately homes. You can admire the elegant Regency terraces around John Nash's Regent's Park.

■ Visit: Regent's Park (Ch. 11), Somerset House (Ch. 4), St. Martin-in-the-Fields (Ch. 2)

1837–1901 Victorian Age

Queen Victoria ruled the British Empire for 63 years. London experienced the growth of wealth, industrialization, and philanthropy; this was also a period of desperate poverty, as depicted in Charles Dickens's novels. At the start of the 19th century the population of the city was over a million; by the end of Victoria's reign it was over six million.

This rapid growth required many building programs, from worker housing to even bigger projects such as the bridges, government buildings, and the first subway system in the world. Businessmen, artists, and architects helped create many institutions that still exist today, from the Tate Britain to the Ragged Schools and Foundling hospitals.

The clean, classical lines of the previous era gave way to more elaborate styles—which were considered more "English"—such as the Gothic Revival Houses of Parliament. Other Victorian projects included covered markets, canal locks, arcades, palaces, memorials, museums, theaters, and parks. So much building took place during this period that it's hard to miss the style: look for elaborate, highly decorated architecture.

■ Visit: Burlington Arcade (Ch. 3), Houses of Parliament (Ch. 2), Leadenhall Market in The City (Ch. 6), V&A and Natural History Museum (Ch. 9)

1851 Great Exhibition held in Hyde Park	1901 Death of Queen Victoria	1939–1945 WWII	1951 Festival of Britain
1863 Underground opens	1914–1918 WWI		
1870	1900	1930	1960

1

IN FOCUS: THE BUILDING OF LONDON

(left) Theatergoers at The National Theatre on the South Bank of the River Thames; (right) Tower block at Barbican Centre, a 1970s complex of art venues and apartments.

20th-century building

1901–1979

The turn of the 20th century saw wealthy Westminster widening its streets to accommodate the arrival of motor cars and department stores. Even after the First World War, a "live for today" attitude continued among the upper classes, while the poorest Londoners suffered increasing prices and low wages. While Modernism—a cultural movement embracing the future and rejecting anything associated with the past—was gathering pace in 1920s Europe, conservative British architecture continued to hark back to traditional influences of ancient Greece and the middle ages.

The WWII devastation of the Blitz bombings changed this and an enormous amount of post-war building was needed quickly. Émigrés such as Hungarian Ernö Goldfinger and Russian-born Berthold Lubetkin brought the modernist architectural movement to London with their high-rise buildings—a solution to the desperate housing shortage. One of the most exciting post-war projects was the 1951 Festival of Britain, celebrating the great inventions of the century. Out of a host of new architecture at the South Bank for this event, only the Royal Festival Hall remains.

Mass-produced concrete, steel, and glass ushered in the Brutalist style in the '60s. This outgrowth of

modernism can be seen in the Hayward Gallery and National Theatre. It was not a popular style, partly because the use of raw concrete—pioneered in the sunny south of France— looked gray, ugly, and even sinister against the backdrop of wet and windy London.

London's powers-that-be haven't always embraced modernist architecture, and many examples have been torn down. Today some iconic buildings are protected and the massive concrete Barbican Centre finally brought modernism right into the conservative City.

■ Visit: The Barbican Centre (Ch. 6), Hayward Gallery (Ch. 8), National Theatre (Ch. 8), Royal Festival Hall (Ch. 8)

1979–1990 Margaret Thatcher
Prime Minister

1991 Canary
Wharf is opened

2012 Summer
Olympics

1960　　　　　　1980　　　　　　2000　　　　　　2020

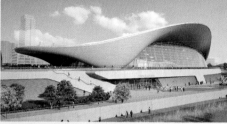

(left) The Shard; (top right) The London Aquatics Centre by Zaha Hadid. (bottom right) The 2000 Great Court at the British Museum by Sir Norman Foster.

1980–Present

Modern and Millennium London

While the sun may have set on the British empire, London remains a global city, perhaps more now than ever before. The '80s saw changes in economic policy and ambitious building projects, including the Jubilee Line extension to the Underground system. Great business and banking centers reached higher into the sky as London's importance in financial markets increased. London's disused Docklands area got a revitalizing boost with the Canary Wharf development and the DLR (Docklands Light Railway).

Internationally-known architects began to make their mark on the city with creative projects. Known as Tower 42, the NatWest Tower opened in 1981 as the tallest skyscraper in the city—for a great view, head to its cocktail bar on the 42nd floor. The Richard Rogers Partnership designed the fabulous 1986 Lloyd's building. Sir Norman Foster and his associates have designed the Sackler Galleries at the Royal Academy of Arts, the British Museum's Great Court, City Hall, and the former Swiss Re Building (known as "The Gherkin").

Building projects to celebrate the Millennium are now so beloved it's hard to imagine London without the pedestrian-only Millennium Bridge and the London Eye.

The current crop of stunning skyscrapers is the largest transformation in London's skyline… *ever*. Big-name starchitects have been given *carte blanche* to reach for the clouds in the higgledy-piggledy medieval heart of town. While not everyone is enamored by Renzo Piano's 95-story pyramid-shaped "Shard," the tallest building in Western Europe, near the London Bridge, you can't help marveling at its magnificence. Other stunners like the "Helter Skelter" or "Cheese Grater" add Manhattan-esque *Oooomph!* to the skyline.

■ Visit: Canary Wharf (Ch. 12), Lloyd's Building (Ch. 6), Shard (Ch. 8), Swiss Re (Ch. 6)

WESTMINSTER, ST. JAMES'S, AND ROYAL LONDON

GETTING ORIENTED

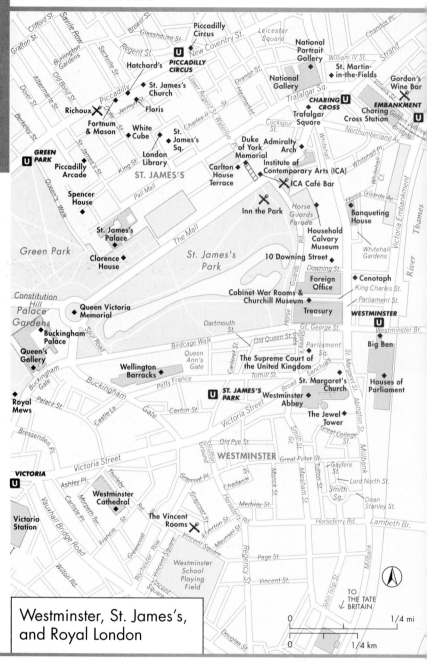

Westminster, St. James's,
and Royal London

TOP REASONS TO GO

Glorious Westminster Abbey: This Gothic church was not only the site of William and Kate's marriage but has also seen 38 coronations, starting with William the Conqueror's in 1066.

Calling on Buckingham Palace: Even if you miss the palace's summer opening, keep pace with the marching soldiers as they enact the time-honored "Changing the Guard."

Masterpieces Theater: Leonardo, Raphael, Van Eyck, Rembrandt, and many other artistic greats are shown off in the gorgeous rooms at the National Gallery.

Discover the unspoiled Churchill War Rooms: Listen to Churchill's radio addresses to the British people as you explore this cavernous underground wartime hideout.

Hear Big Ben's chimes: As the Eiffel Tower is to Paris, so is Big Ben to London—just follow your ears from Trafalgar Square to catch sight of the 320-foot-high Clock Tower.

FEELING PECKISH?

Gordon's Wine Bar. Gordon's is the oldest wine bar in the city (est. 1890). The Thames used to lap almost at its doors and Rudyard Kipling was a tenant in the rooms upstairs. Faded art still fills almost every inch of wall and there's World War II blackout paint on the windows. Head to the back room, windowless and still lit entirely by candles, it's been used as a wine cellar for 800 years. The excellence of the wine list only makes it easier for time to disappear here. ✉ *47 Villiers St., Trafalgar Sq.* ☎ *020/7930–1408* ⊕ *www.gordonswinebar. com* Ⓜ *Embankment, Charing Cross.*

GETTING THERE

Trafalgar Square is in the center of the action. Take the Tube to Embankment (Northern, Bakerloo, District, and Circle lines) and walk north until you cross the Strand, or get off at the Charing Cross (Bakerloo and Northern lines) Northumberland Avenue exit. Buses are another great option, as almost all roads lead to Trafalgar Square.

Two Tube stations are right in the heart of St. James's: Piccadilly Circus (Piccadilly or Bakerloo lines), and Green Park (Piccadilly, Victoria, or Jubilee lines).

MAKING THE MOST OF YOUR TIME

For royal pageantry begin with Buckingham Palace, Westminster Abbey, and the Guards Museum, followed by the Houses of Parliament and Big Ben. For art, the National Gallery, Tate Britain, and the Queen's Gallery head anyone's list.

NEAREST PUBLIC RESTROOMS

Paid loos (£1.50) are across the street from Westminster Abbey at the bottom of Victoria Street. Banqueting House and the Queen's Gallery have elegant restrooms.

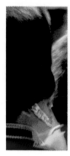

Sightseeing
★★★★★
Nightlife
★★
Dining
★★★
Lodging
★
Shopping
★★

This is postcard London at its best. Crammed with historic churches, grand state buildings, and some of the world's best art collections, Royal London and Westminster unite politics and high culture. (Oh, and the Queen lives here, too.) The places you'll want to explore are grouped into four distinct areas—Trafalgar Square, Whitehall, St. James's, and Buckingham Palace—each nudging a corner of triangular St. James's Park. There is as much history in these few acres as in many whole cities, so pace yourself—this is concentrated sightseeing.

WESTMINSTER

Updated By
James O'Neill

Home to London's most photogenic pigeons, **Trafalgar Square** is not only the official center of the district known as **Westminster,** nominally a separate city but in fact the official center of London. What will bring you here are the two magnificent museums on the northern edge of the square, the **National Gallery** and the **National Portrait Gallery.** From the square, two boulevards lead to the seats of different eras of governance. The avenue called **Whitehall** drops south to the neo-Gothic **Houses of Parliament,** where members of both Houses (Commons and Lords) hold debates and vote on pending legislation. Just opposite, **Westminster Abbey** is a monument to the nation's history and for centuries the scene of daily worship, coronations, and royal weddings. Poets, political leaders, and 17 monarchs are buried in this world-famous, 13th-century Gothic building. Sandwiched between the two is the **Jewel Tower,** the only surviving part of the medieval Palace of Westminster (a name still given to Parliament and its environs). Halfway down Whitehall, **No. 10 Downing Street** is both the residence and the office of the prime minister. One of the most celebrated occupants, Winston Churchill, is commemorated in the **Churchill War Rooms,** his underground wartime headquarters off Whitehall. Just down the road is the **Cenotaph,** built for the dead of World War I and since then a focal point for the annual remembrance of others lost in war.

The Mall, a wide, elegant avenue beyond the stone curtain of **Admiralty Arch,** heads southwest from Trafalgar Square toward the **Queen Victoria Memorial** and **Buckingham Palace,** the sovereign's official residence. The building is open to the public only in summer, but you can see much of the royal art collection in the **Queen's Gallery** and spectacular ceremonial coaches in the **Royal Mews,** both open all year. Farther south toward Pimlico, **Tate Britain** focuses on prominent British artists from 1500 to today.

This area can be considered "Royal London" partly because it is neatly bounded by the triangle of streets that make up the route that Queen Elizabeth II usually takes when processing from Buckingham Palace to Westminster Abbey or to the Houses of Parliament on state occasions, and also because it contains so much of British history going back a thousand years.

The main drawback to sightseeing here is that half the world is doing it at the same time. So, for a large part of the year a lot of Royal London is floodlit at night (when there's more elbow room), adding to the theatricality of the experience.

TOP ATTRACTIONS

FAMILY
Fodor's Choice
★
Churchill War Rooms. It was from this small warren of underground rooms—beneath the vast government buildings of the Treasury— that Winston Churchill and his team directed troops in World War II. Designed to be bombproof, the whole complex has been preserved almost exactly as it was when the last light was turned off at the end of the war. Every clock shows almost 5 pm, and the furniture, fittings, and paraphernalia of a busy, round-the-clock war office are in situ, down to the colored map pins.

During air raids, the leading government ministers met here, and the Cabinet Room is still arranged as if a meeting were about to convene. In the Map Room, the Allied campaign is charted on wall-to-wall maps with a rash of pinholes showing the movements of convoys. In the hub of the room, a bank of differently colored phones known as the "Beauty Chorus" linked the War Rooms to control rooms around the nation. The Prime Minister's Room holds the desk from which Churchill made his morale-boosting broadcasts; the Telephone Room (a converted broom cupboard) has his hotline to FDR. You can also see the restored rooms that the PM used for dining and sleeping. Telephonists (switchboard operators) and clerks who worked 16-hour shifts slept in lesser quarters in unenviable conditions.

A great addition to the War Rooms is the Churchill Museum, a tribute to the great wartime leader himself. ⊠ *Clive Steps, King Charles St., Westminster* ☎ *020/7930–6961* ⊕ *www.iwm.org.uk* 🎫 *£18* ☯ *Daily 9:30–6; last admission 5* Ⓜ *Westminster.*

Downing Street. Looking like an unassuming alley but for the iron gates (and armed guards) that block the entrance, this is the location of the

A BRIEF HISTORY OF WESTMINSTER

The Romans may have shaped The City, but England's royals created Westminster. Indeed, technically it's still a separate city—notice it says "City of Westminster" on the street signs, not "City of London"—although any formal divide between the two vanished centuries ago, along with the open countryside that once lay between them. Edward the Confessor started the first Palace of Westminster in the 11th century; he also founded Westminster Abbey in 1050, where every British monarch since then has been crowned.

The district became the focus of political power in England after the construction of Whitehall Palace in the 16th century; a vast and opulent building, it was the official residence of the monarch until it burned down in 1698. It survives both as the name of Westminster's most important road, and a term still used in Britain to refer to the seat of government in general. The first Parliament building was part of the same complex; it, too, was nearly destroyed by the Gunpowder Plot of 1605 (still commemorated annually on November 5, Guy Fawkes Day) and eventually succumbed to fire in 1834. The Westminster we see today took shape during the Georgian and Victorian periods, as Britain reached the zenith of its imperial power. Grand architecture sprang up, and Buckingham Palace became the principal royal residence in 1837, when Victoria acceded to the throne. Trafalgar Square and Nelson's Column were built in 1843, to commemorate Britain's most famous naval victory, and the Houses of Parliament were rebuilt in 1858 in the trendy neo-Gothic style of the time. The illustrious Clarence House, built in 1825 for the Duke of Clarence (later William IV), is now the home of Prince Charles and Camilla, Duchess of Cornwall.

famous **No. 10,** London's modest equivalent of the White House. The Georgian entrance to the mid-17th century mansion is deceptive; it's actually a huge complex of discreetly linked buildings. Since 1732 it has been the official home and office of the Prime Minister—the last private resident was the magnificently named Mr. Chicken—although the current Prime Minister actually lives in the private apartments above No. 11, because those in No. 10 are too small to house a family. (No. 11 is traditionally the residence of the Chancellor of the Exchequer, the head of the treasury.) There are no public tours, and you can't get past the wrought-iron gates into Downing Street itself, but the famous black front door to No. 10 is clearly visible from Whitehall. Just south of Downing Street, in the middle of Whitehall, is the **Cenotaph,** a stark white monolith built to commemorate the 1918 armistice. On Remembrance Day (the Sunday nearest November 11) it's strewn with red poppy wreaths to honor the dead of both world wars and all British and Commonwealth soldiers killed in action since; the first wreath is traditionally laid by the Queen. ⊠ *Whitehall* ⊕ *www.number10.gov.uk* Ⓜ *Westminster.*

QUICK BITES

Notes Music and Coffee. Next door to the London Coliseum (home of the English National Opera), this hip café serves some of the best sandwiches, salads, and coffee in the neighborhood. Keep an eye out for their popular jazz nights. ✉ *31 St. Martin's La., Westminster* ☎ *020/7240–0424* ⊕ *notes-uk.co.uk* Ⓜ *Charing Cross.*

FAMILY **Horse Guards Parade.** Once the tiltyard for jousting tournaments, Horse Guards Parade is best known for the annual Trooping the Colour ceremony, in which the Queen takes the salute on her official birthday tribute, on the second Saturday in June. (Though it's called a birthday it's actually the anniversary of her coronation—the current Queen's real birthday is April 21.) It's a must-see if you're around, with marching bands and throngs of onlookers. Throughout the rest of the year the changing of two mounted sentries known as the **Queen's Life Guard** at the Whitehall facade of Horse Guards provides what may be London's most popular photo opportunity. The ceremony lasts about half an hour. At 4 pm daily is the dismounting ceremony, aka the 4 O'Clock Parade, during which sentries are posted and horses returned to their stables. ✉ *Whitehall* ☎ *020/7930–4832* ⊗ *Changing of the guard 11 am Mon.– Sat., 10 am Sun.; dismounting ceremony daily at 4 pm* Ⓜ *Westminster.*

Houses of Parliament.

See the highlighted listing in this chapter.

The Jewel Tower. Overshadowed by the big-ticket attractions of Parliament to one side and Westminster Abbey to the other, this is the only portion of the Palace of Westminster complex to have survived intact from medieval times. Built in the 1360s to contain treasures belonging to Edward III, it once formed part of the palace's defensive walls—hence the fortresslike appearance. Check out the original ribbed stone ceiling on the ground floor; look up to see the carved stone images of men and beasts. The Jewel Tower was later used as a records office for the House of Lords, but hasn't served in any official function since the rest of the old palace was destroyed by fire in 1834 and the ancient documents were moved to the greater safety of the Tower of London. Today it contains an exhibition on the history of Parliament. ✉ *Abingdon St., Westminster* ☎ *020/7222–2219* ⊕ *www.english-heritage.org.uk* 🎫 *£4* ⊗ *Mar.–Oct., daily 10–5; Nov.–Feb., weekends 10–4; last admission 30 mins before closing* Ⓜ *Westminster.*

FAMILY **National Gallery.**
Fodor's Choice *See the highlighted listing in this chapter.*
★

FAMILY **National Portrait Gallery.** The National Portrait Gallery was founded in
Fodor's Choice 1856 with a single aim: to gather together portraits of famous (and infa-
★ mous) Britons throughout history. More than 150 years and 160,000 portraits later, it is an essential stop for all history and literature buffs. If you visit with kids, ask at the desk about the excellent Family Trails, which make exploring the galleries with children much more fun. On the top floor, the Portrait Restaurant has one of the best views in London—a panoramic vista of Nelson's Column and the backdrop along Whitehall to the Houses of Parliament.

Galleries are arranged clearly and chronologically, from Tudor times to contemporary Britain. A Holbein miniature of Henry VIII is among the most famous image in the Tudor Gallery, although the enormous portrait of Elizabeth I—bejeweled and literally astride the world in

HOUSES OF PARLIAMENT

✉ *St. Stephen's Entrance, St. Margaret St., Westminster* ☎ *020/7219–4272 information and tours, 0161/425–8677 public tours (from overseas), 0207/219–4114 public tours* ⊕ *www.parliament.uk/visiting* 🎟 *Free; tours £16.50 (booking ahead)* ⊘ *Tour times and hrs for Visitor's Gallery vary wk to wk.* Ⓜ *Westminster.*

TIPS

■ Public tours of Parliament cost £25 and must be booked in advance online or by phone.

■ Other tours, including afternoon tea on the Pavillion Terrace, overlooking the Thames, are also available for £52.50.

■ The easiest time to get into the Commons is during an evening session—Parliament is still sitting if the top of the Clock Tower is illuminated.

■ The best view is from the opposite (south) bank, across Lambeth Bridge. It is most dramatic at night when lit green and gold.

The Palace of Westminster, as the complex is called, was first established on this site by Edward the Confessor in the 11th century. William II started building a new palace in 1087, and this became the seat of English power. Fire destroyed most of the palace in 1834, and the current complex dates largely from the mid-19th century.

Highlights

The **Visitors' Galleries** of the House of Commons provide a view of democracy in action when the benches are filled by opposing MPs (members of Parliament). Debates are formal but raucous, especially during the **Prime Minister's Questions** (PMQs), when any MP can put a question to the nation's leader. Tickets to PMQs are free but highly sought after, so the only way for non-U.K. citizens to gain access is by lining up on the day and hoping for returns or no-shows. The action starts at 1 pm every Wednesday when Parliament is sitting, and the whole shebang is broadcast live on television.

There are also Visitors Galleries for The House of Lords.

Westminster Hall, with its remarkable hammer-beam roof, was the work of William the Conqueror's son William Rufus. It's one of the largest remaining Norman halls in Europe, and its dramatic interior was the scene of the trial of Charles I.

After the 1834 fire, the Clock Tower—renamed **Elizabeth Tower** in 2012, in honor of the Queen's Diamond Jubilee—was completed in 1858, and contains the 13-ton bell known as **Big Ben.** At the southwest end of the main Parliament building is the 323-foot-high Victoria Tower.

a powerful display of Imperial intent—may be the most impressive. The huge permanent collections include portraits of Shakespeare, the Brontë sisters, and Jane Austen. Look for the four Andy Warhol *Queen Elizabeth II* silkscreens from 1985 and Maggi Hambling's surreal self-portrait. Contemporary portraits range from the iconic (*Julian with T-shirt*—an LCD screen on a continuous loop—by Julian Opie) to the extreme (Marc Quinn's *Self*, a realization of the artist's head done in frozen blood). Temporary exhibitions can be explored on the first three floors, particularly in the Wolfson and Porter galleries, on the ground floor. ⊠ *St. Martin's Pl., Westminster* ☎ *020/7306–0055, 020/7312–2463 information line* ⊕ *www.npg.org.uk* ✉ *Free; charge for special exhibitions; audiovisual guide £3; family audio guides £6 for 5 people, £4 for 2 people* ☉ *Mon.–Wed. and weekends 10–6, Thurs. and Fri. 10–9; last admission 10 mins before closing* Ⓜ *Charing Cross, Leicester Sq.*

FAMILY **St. Martin-in-the-Fields.** One of London's best-loved and most welcoming of churches is more than just a place of worship. Named after St. Martin of Tours, known for the help he gave to beggars, this parish has long been a welcome sight for the homeless, who have been given soup and shelter at the church since 1914. The church is also a haven for music lovers; the internationally known Academy of St. Martin-in-the-Fields was founded here, and a popular program of concerts continues today. (Although the interior is a wonderful setting for a recital, beware the hard wooden benches!) The crypt is a hive of activity, with a popular café and shop. Here you can also make your own life-size souvenir knight, lady, or monarch from replica tomb brasses, with metallic waxes, paper, and instructions (about £5). ⊠ *Trafalgar Sq., Westminster* ☎ *020/7766–1100* ⊕ *www.smitf.org* ✉ *Free; concerts £7–£30* ☉ *Open all day for worship; sightseeing: Mon., Tues., and Fri. 8:30–1 and 2–6; Wed. 8:30–1:15 and 2–5; Thurs. 8:30–1 and 2–6; Sat. 9:30–6; Sun. 3:30–5* Ⓜ *Charing Cross, Leicester Sq.*

QUICK BITES

The atmospheric **St. Martin's Café in the Crypt**, with its magnificent high-arched brick vault and gravestone floor, has a superb setting at the heart of London. It serves full English and continental breakfasts, sandwiches, salads, snacks, afternoon tea, and wine. Lunch and dinner options include vegetarian meals.

FAMILY
Fodor'sChoice
★

Tate Britain. First opened in 1897, and funded by the sugar magnate Sir Henry Tate, this stately neoclassical institution may not be as ambitious as its sibling Tate Modern on the South Bank, but its bright galleries lure only a fraction of the Modern's overwhelming crowds and are a great place to explore British art from 1500 to the present. The museum includes the Linbury Galleries on the lower floors, which stage temporary exhibitions, and a permanent collection on the upper floors. And what a collection it is—classic works by John Constable, Thomas Gainsborough, David Wilkie, Francis Bacon, Duncan Grant, Barbara Hepworth, and Ben Nicholson, and an outstanding display from J. M. W. Turner in the Clore Gallery, including many later vaporous and light-infused works such as *Sunrise with Sea Monsters*. Sumptuous

NAL GALLERY

r Sq., Westminster
☎ 020/7747-2885 ⊕ www.
nationalgallery.org.uk ✉ Free;
charge for special exhibitions;
audio guide £4 ⊗ Sun.–Thurs.
10–6, Fri. 10–9 Ⓜ Char-
ing Cross, Embankment,
Leicester Sq.

TIPS

■ Color coding throughout the galleries helps you keep track of the period in which you're immersed.

■ Begin at an "Art Start" terminal in the Sainsbury Wing or East Wing Espresso Bar. The interactive screens give you access to information on all of the museum's holdings; you can choose your favorites, and print out a free personal tour map.

■ Try a free weekday lunch-time lecture, or Ten Minute Talk, which illuminates the story behind a key work of art. One-hour free, guided tours start at the Sainsbury Wing every weekday at 11:30 and 2:30 (also Friday at 7 pm), and on weekends at 11:30, 2:30, and 4.

■ If you are eager for even more insight into the art, pick up a themed audio guide. Special audio tours include "sounds of the gallery," which are soundscapes to accompany the paintings.

■ If you visit with children, don't miss special programs for young visitors, including free Family Sundays (every Sunday). Check the website for other events.

Standing proudly on the north side of Trafalgar Square, this is truly one of the world's supreme art museums, with more than 2,300 masterpieces on show. Michelangelo, Leonardo, Turner, Monet, van Gogh, Picasso, and more—all for free. Watch out for outstanding temporary exhibitions, too.

Highlights

This brief selection is your jumping-off point, but there are hundreds of other paintings to see, enough to fill a full day. In chronological order: (1) **Van Eyck** (c. 1395–1441), *The Arnolfini Portrait*—a solemn couple holds hands, the fish-eye mirror behind them mysteriously illuminating what can't be seen from the front view. (2) **Holbein** (1497–1543), *The Ambassadors*—two wealthy visitors from France stand surrounded by what were considered luxury goods at the time. Note the elongated skull at the bottom of the painting, which takes shape only when viewed from an angle. (3) **Da Vinci** (1452–1519), *The Virgin and Child*—this exquisite black-chalk "Burlington Cartoon" depicts the master's most haunting Mary. (4) **Velázquez** (1599–1660), *Christ in the House of Martha and Mary*—in this enigmatic masterpiece the Spaniard plays with perspective and the role of the viewer. (5) **Turner** (1775–1851), *Rain, Steam and Speed: The Great Western Railway*, the whirl of rain, mist, steam, and locomotion is nothing short of astonishing (spot the hare). (6) **Caravaggio** (1573–1610), *The Supper at Emmaus*—a freshly resurrected Christ blesses bread in an astonishingly domestic vision from the master of chiaroscuro. (7) **Van Gogh** (1853–90), *Sunflowers*—painted during his sojourn with Gauguin in Arles, this is quintessential Van Gogh. (8) **Seurat** (1859–91), *Bathers at Asnières*—this summer day's idyll is one of the master pointillist's extraordinaire's best-known works.

The Tate Britain showcases British art from the last 500 years, including contemporary works.

Pre-Raphaelite pieces are a major draw, while the Contemporary British Art galleries bring you face to face with Damien Hirst's *Away from the Flock* and other recent conceptions. The Tate Britain also hosts the annual Turner Prize exhibition, with its accompanying furor over the state of contemporary art, from about October to January each year. There's a good little café, and the excellent Rex Whistler Restaurant has been something of an institution since it first opened in 1927. It's open daily for lunch, and for dinner on semiregular **Late at Tate** Friday evening events, when the gallery is open late for talks or performances—check the website for details.

Craving more art? Head down the river on the Tate to Tate boat (£6.80 one-way) to the Tate Modern, running between the two museums every 40 minutes. A River Roamer ticket (£16.50) permits a day's travel, with stops including the London Eye and the Tower of London. You get a discount of roughly a third if you have a Travelcard. ⊠ *Millbank, Westminster* ☎ *020/7887–8888* ⊕ *www.tate.org.uk/britain* 🖾 *Free, special exhibitions extra* ⏲ *Daily 10–6; last ticket sold and special exhibitions close 5:15* Ⓜ *Pimlico.*

Fodor's Choice ★ **Trafalgar Square.** This is officially the center of London: a plaque on the corner of the Strand and Charing Cross Road marks the spot from which distances on U. K. signposts are measured. (London's *actual* geographic center, as measured in 2014, is a rather dull bench on the Victoria Embankment). Medieval kings once kept their aviaries of hawks and falcons here; today the humbler grey pigeons flock en masse to the open spaces around the ornate fountains (feeding them is banned). The square was designed in 1830 by John Nash, who envisaged a new public space with striking views of the Thames, the Houses of Parliament, and Buckingham Palace. Of those, only Parliament is still clearly visible from the square, but it remains a magnet for open-air concerts, political demonstrations, and national celebrations, such as New Year's Eve. Dominating the square is the 170-foot **Nelson's Column**, erected as a monument to the great admiral in 1848. Note that the lampposts on the south side, heading down Whitehall, are topped with ships—they all face Portsmouth, home of the British

ST. MARTIN'S CONCERTS
Classical concerts (some by candlelight) are held every Thursday to Saturday (and some Tuesdays) at 7:30 pm with evening jazz concerts in the crypt every Wednesday at 8 pm. Tickets are available from the box office in the crypt. Free (£3.50 donation suggested) lunchtime concerts take place Monday, Tuesday, and Friday 1–2 pm.

navy. The column is flanked on either side by enormous bronze lions. Climbing them is a very popular photo op, but be extremely careful, as there are no guardrails and it's a long fall onto concrete if you slip. Four plinths border the square; three contain militaristic statues, but one was left empty—it's now used for contemporary art installations, often with a wry and controversial edge. Surprisingly enough, given that this was a square built to honor British military victories, the lawn at the north side, by the National Gallery, contains a statue of George Washington—a gift from the state of Virginia in 1921. At the southern point of the square is the **equestrian statue of Charles I**. After the Civil War and the king's execution, Oliver Cromwell, the antiroyalist leader, commissioned a brazier, John Rivett, to melt the statue down. The story goes that Rivett instead merely buried it in his garden. He made a fortune peddling knickknacks wrought, he claimed, from its metal, only to produce the statue miraculously unscathed after the restoration of the monarchy—and then made another fortune reselling it. In 1667 Charles II had it placed where it stands today, near the spot where his father was executed in 1649. Each year, on January 30, the day of the king's death, the Royal Stuart Society lays a wreath at the foot of the statue. ⊠ *Westminster* Ⓜ *Charing Cross.*

Fodor'sChoice **Westminster Abbey.**
  ★ *See the highlighted listing in this chapter.*

WORTH NOTING

Admiralty Arch. This stately gateway is an impressive counterpoint to Buckingham Palace, at the opposite end of the Mall (rhymes with "shall"). On the southwest corner of Trafalgar Square, the arch, named after the adjacent Royal Navy headquarters, was designed by Sir Aston Webb and completed in 1912 as a memorial to Queen Victoria. Actually comprised of five arches—two for pedestrians, two for traffic, and the central arch which is only opened for state occasions—it was a government building until 2012, and even served as an alternative residence for the Prime Minister when Downing Street was under renovation. It

Continued on page 58

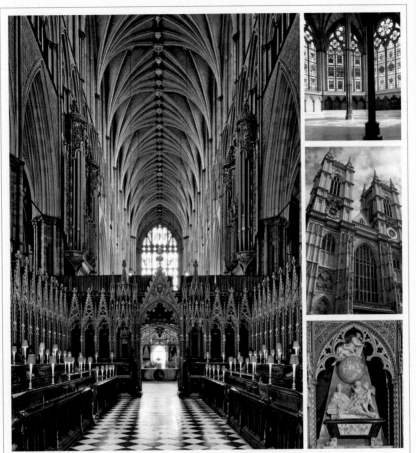

WESTMINSTER ABBEY

A monument to the rich—and often bloody and scandalous—history of Great Britain, Westminster Abbey rises on the Thames skyline as one of the most iconic sites in London.

The mysterious gloom of the lofty medieval interior is home to more than 600 monuments and memorial statues. About 3,300 people, from kings to composers to wordsmiths, are buried in the abbey. It has been the scene of 14 royal weddings and no less than 38 coronations—the first in 1066, when William the Conqueror was made king here.

TOURING THE ABBEY

There's only one way around the abbey, and as there will almost certainly be a long stream of shuffling tourists at your heels, you'll need to be alert to catch the highlights. Enter by the north door.

When you enter the church, turn around and look up to see the ❶ **painted-glass rose window**, the largest of its kind.

The ❷ **Coronation Chair**, at the foot of the Henry VII Chapel, has been briefly graced by nearly every regal posterior since Edward I ordered it in 1301. Look for the graffiti on the back of the Coronation chair. It's the work of 18th- and 19th-century visitors and Westminster schoolboys who carved their names there.

The ❸ **Henry VII's Lady Chapel** contains the tombs of Henry VII and his queen, Elizabeth of York. Close by are monuments to the young daughters of James I, and an urn purported to hold the remains of the so-called Princes in the Tower—Edward V and Richard. Interestingly, arch enemies Elizabeth I and her half-sister Mary Tudor share a tomb here. Begun in 1503, the chapel is famed for its ceiling—a dazzling fan-vaulted roof with carved pendants—and the heraldic banners of living knights that hang above its oak stalls.

In front of the ❹ **High Altar**, which was used for the funerals of Princess Diana and the Queen Mother, is a black-and-white marble pavement laid in 1268. The intricate Italian Cosmati work contains three Latin inscriptions, one of which states that the world will last for 19,683 years.

The ❺ **Shrine of St. Edward the Confessor** contains the shrine to the pre-Norman king. Because of its great age, you must join a tour with the verger to be admitted to the chapel. (Details are available at the admission desk; there is a small extra charge.)

Geoffrey Chaucer was the first poet to be buried in ❻ **Poets' Corner** in 1400. Other memorials include: William Shakespeare, William Blake, John Milton, Jane Austen, Samuel Taylor Coleridge, William Wordsworth, and Charles Dickens.

A door from the south transept and south choir aisle leads to the calm of the ❼ **Great Cloisters.**

West Entrance

College Hall

Dean's Court

Deanery

Choir

Site of Refectory

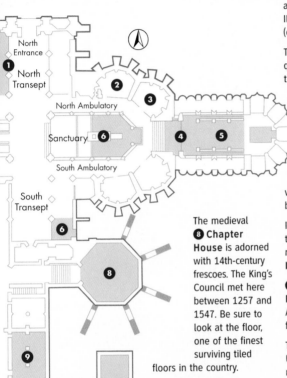

North Entrance

1 North Transept

North Ambulatory

Sanctuary **6**

South Ambulatory

South Transept

6

8

9

11

2

3

4   **5**

8

10

and actual clothing of Charles II and Admiral Lord Nelson (complete with eye patch).

The **10** **Little Cloister** is a quiet haven, and just beyond, the **11** **College Garden** is a delightful diversion. Filled with medicinal herbs, it has been tended by monks for more than 900 years.

The **12** **Dean's Yard** is the best spot for a fine view of the massive flying buttresses above.

The medieval **8** **Chapter House** is adorned with 14th-century frescoes. The King's Council met here between 1257 and 1547. Be sure to look at the floor, one of the finest surviving tiled floors in the country.

The **9** **Abbey Museum** includes a collection of deliciously macabre effigies made from the death masks

In the choir screen, north of the entrance to the choir, is a marble **13** **monument to Sir Isaac Newton.**

14 **A plaque to Franklin D. Roosevelt** is one of the Abbey's very few tributes to a foreigner.

The **15** **Grave of the Unknown Warrior,** in memory of the soldiers who lost their lives in both world wars, is near the exit of the abbey.

QUIRKY LONDON

Near the Henry VII chapel, keep an eye open for St. Wilgefortis, who was so concerned to protect her chastity that she prayed to God for help and woke up one morning with a full growth of beard.

A BRIEF HISTORY

960 AD Benedictine monastery founded on the site by King Edward and King Dunstan.

1045–65 King Edward the Confessor enlarges the original monastery, erecting a stone church in honor of St. Paul the Apostle. Named "west minster" to distinguish from "east minster" (St. Paul's Cathedral).

1065 The church is consecrated on December 28. Edward doesn't live to see the ceremony.

1161 Following Edward's canonization, his body is moved by Henry III to a more elaborate resting place behind the High Altar. Other medieval kings are later buried around his tomb.

1245–54 Henry III pulls down the abbey and starts again with a new Gothic style influenced by his travels in France. Master mason Henry de Reyns ("of Rheims") constructs the transepts, north front, and rose windows, as well as part of the cloisters and Chapter House.

1269 The new abbey is consecrated and the choir is completed.

1350s Richard II resumes Henry III's plan to rebuild the monastery. Henry V and Henry VII continue as benefactors.

1503 The Lady Chapel is demolished and the foundation stone of Henry VII's Chapel is laid on the site.

1540 The abbey ceases to be used as a monastery.

1560 Elizabeth I refounds the abbey as a Collegiate Church. From this point on it is a "Royal Peculiar," exempt from the jurisdiction of bishops.

1745 The western towers, left unfinished from medieval times, are finally completed, based on a design by Sir Christopher Wren.

1995 Following a 25-year restoration program, saints and allegorical figures are added to the niches on the western towers and around the Great West Door.

PLANNING YOUR DAY

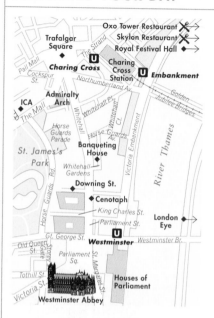

GETTING HERE: The closest Tube stop is Westminster. When you exit the station, walk west along Great George Street, away from the river. Turn left on St. Margaret Street.

CONTACT INFO: ✉ Broad Sanctuary, Westminster SW1 P3PA ☎ 020/7222-5152 ⊕ www.westminster-abbey.org.

ADMISSION: Adults: Abbey and museum £20. **Family tickets:** 2 adults and 2 children, £45. **Children under 11:** free.

HOURS: The abbey is a house of worship. Services may cause changes to the visiting hours on any given day, so be sure to call ahead.
Abbey: Weekdays 9:30–6; Sat. Apr.–Sept. 9:30–3:30, Oct.–Mar. 9:30–1:30 (last admission 1 hour before closing); Sun, worship only.
Museum: Mon.–Sat. 10:30–4.
Cloisters: Daily 8–6
College Garden: Apr.–Sept.: Tues.–Thurs. 10–6; Oct.–Mar.: Tues.–Thurs. 10–4.
Chapter House: Mon.–Sat. 10–4

WHAT'S NEARBY: To make the most of your day, arrive at the abbey early (doors open at 9:30), then make an afternoon visit to the Parliament buildings and finish with a sunset ride on the **London Eye.** Post-flight, take a walk along the fairy-lit South Bank and have dinner (or a drink in the bar) with a view, at the **Oxo Tower Restaurant** (☎ 020/7803–3888) or the Royal Festival Hall's **Skylon Restaurant** (☎ 020/7654–7800).

Please note that overseas visitors can no longer visit the **Houses of Parliament** during session. However, tours of the buildings are available in August and September. For more information and booking call ☎ 0844/847–1672. Also, it's advisable to prebook tickets for the London Eye. Do this online at www.londoneye.com, or call 0871/781–3000.

IN A HURRY?

If you're pressed for time, concentrate on the following four highlights: the Coronation Chair; Chapter House; Poets' Corner; and Grave of the Unknown Warrior.

THINGS TO KNOW

■ Photography and filming are not permitted anywhere in the abbey.

■ In winter the interior of the abbey can get quite cold; dress accordingly.

■ For an animated history of the Abbey, join one of the verger-led tours (90 minutes) that depart from the North Door: Apr.–Sept.: Mon.–Fri. 10, 10:30, 11, 2, 2:30, Sat. 10, 10:30, 11; Oct.–Mar.: Mon.–Fri. 10:30, 11, 2, 2:30, Sat. 10:30, 11. Ask at information desk, £3 per person (in addition to entrance charge).

■ Touring the abbey can take half a day, especially in summer, when lines are long.

■ To avoid the crowds, make sure you arrive early. If you're first in line you can enjoy parts of the abbey in relative calm before the mad rush descends.

■ If you want to study up before you go, visit www.westminster-abbey.org, which includes an in-depth history and self-guided tour of the abbey. Otherwise pick up a free leaflet from the information desk.

■ On Sundays the abbey is not open to visitors. Join a service instead. Check the Web site for service times, as well as details of concerts, organ recitals, and special events.

is now being turned into a luxury hotel. Look out for the bronze nose grafted onto the inside wall of the right- hand traffic arch (when facing the Mall); it was placed there in secret by a mischievous artist in 1997 and has been allowed to stay ever since. ⊠ *The Mall, Cockspur St., and Trafalgar Sq., Westminster* Ⓜ *Charing Cross.*

Banqueting House. James I commissioned Inigo Jones, one of England's great architects, to undertake a grand building on the site of the original Tudor Palace of Whitehall, which was (according to one foreign visitor) "ill-built, and nothing but a heap of houses." Jones's Banqueting House, finished in 1622 and the first building in England to be completed in the neoclassical style, bears all the hallmarks of the Palladian sophistication and purity which so influenced Jones during his time in Italy. James's son, Charles I, enhanced the interior by employing the Flemish painter Peter Paul Rubens to glorify his father and himself (naturally) in a series of vibrant painted ceiling panels called "The Apotheosis of James I." As it turned out, these allegorical paintings, depicting a wise monarch being received into heaven, were the last thing Charles saw before stepped through the open first-floor window onto the scaffold, which had been erected directly outside for his execution by Cromwell's Parliamentarians in 1649. Twenty years later his son, Charles II, would celebrate the restoration of the monarchy in the exact same place. ⊠ *Whitehall, Westminster* ☎ *084/4482–7777* ⊕ *www.hrp.org.uk* ☒ *£6.60* ☉ *Daily 10–5; last admission 45 mins before closing. May close at short notice for events; call ahead.* Ⓜ *Charing Cross, Embankment, Westminster.*

Carlton House Terrace. Architect John Nash designed Carlton House, a glorious example of the Regency style, under the patronage of George IV (the Prince Regent, who ruled in place of George III while the "mad king"was considered too unstable to rule). Carlton House was considered a most extravagant building for its time; it was demolished after the prince's accession to the throne in 1820. In its place Nash built Carlton House Terrace—no less imposing, with white-stucco facades and massive Corinthian columns. Carlton Terrace was a smart address, home to several of the 19th century's greatest luminaries—including two prime ministers, William Gladstone (1856) and Lord Palmerston (1857–75). Today Carlton House Terrace houses the Royal Society (No. 6–9), Britain's most prestigious society of scientific minds; still active today, its previous members have included Isaac Newton and Charles Darwin. ⊠ *The Mall, St. James's* Ⓜ *Charing Cross.*

FAMILY **Household Cavalry Museum.** Hang around Horse Guards for even a short time and you'll see a member of the Household Cavalry on guard, or trotting past on horseback, resplendent in a bright crimson uniform with polished brass armor. Made up of soldiers from the British Army's most senior regiments, the Life Guards and the Blues and Royals, membership is considered a great honor; they act as the Queen's official bodyguards and play a key role in state occasions. (It is they who perform the Changing of the Guard ceremony every day at 11 am [10 am on Sundays].) Located in the cavalry's original 17th-century stables, the museum has displays of uniforms and weapons going back to 1661 as well as interactive exhibits on the regiments' current operational roles. In the tack room you can handle saddles and bridles, and try on a trooper's uniform, including a distinctive brass helmet with horsehair plume. You can also observe the working horses being tended to in their stable block behind a glass wall. ⊠ *Horse Guards, Whitehall* ☏ *020/7930–3070* ⊕ *www.householdcavalrymuseum.co.uk* ▭ *£7* ⊙ *Mar.–Sept., daily 10–6; Oct.–Feb., daily 10–5; last admission 45 mins before closing* Ⓜ *Charing Cross, Westminster.*

St. Margaret's Church. Dwarfed by its neighbor, Westminster Abbey, St. Margaret's was founded in the 11th century and rebuilt between 1488 and 1523. It's the unofficial parish church of the House of Commons—Winston Churchill tied the knot here in 1908. Samuel Pepys, Geoffrey Chaucer, and John Milton worshipped here, and since 1681, a pew off the south aisle has been set aside for the Speaker of the House (look for the carved portcullis). The stained glass in the north windows is classically Victorian, facing abstract glass from John Piper in the south. These were to replace the originals, which were ruined in World War II. ⊠ *St. Margaret's St., Parliament Sq., Westminster* ☏ *020/7654–4840* ⊕ *www.westminster-abbey.org/st-margarets* ⊙ *Weekdays 9:30–3:30, Sat. 9:30–1:30, Sun. 2–4:30 (entry via east door). Church may close on short notice for services, so call ahead.* Ⓜ *Westminster.*

The Supreme Court. The highest court of appeal in the United Kingdom is housed in the carefully restored Middlesex Guildhall. Visitors are welcome to drop by and look at the three courtrooms, including the impressive Court Room 1 on the second floor, with its magnificent carved wood ceiling. The Court's art collection, on permanent display, includes portraits by Thomas Gainsborough and Joshua Reynolds. Guided tours are available on Friday (book ahead). There is a café downstairs. ⊠ *Parliament Sq., Westminster* ☏ *020/7960–1500* ⊕ *supremecourt.uk* ▭ *Free; guided tour £5; audio guide £1* ⊙ *Weekdays 9:30–4:30; guided tours Fri. 11 am, 2 and 3 pm* Ⓜ *Westminster (take Exit 6 for Whitehall west).*

FAMILY **Wellington Barracks and the Guards Museum.** These are the headquarters of the Guards Division, the Queen's five regiments of elite foot guards (Grenadier, Coldstream, Scots, Irish, and Welsh), who protect the sovereign and, dressed in tunics of gold-purled scarlet and tall bearskin caps, patrol her palaces. Guardsmen alternate these ceremonial postings with serving in current conflicts, for which they wear more practical uniforms. If you want to learn more about the guards, visit the **Guards Museum,** which has displays on all aspects of a guardsman's life in conflicts dating back to 1642; the entrance is next to the Guards Chapel. Next door is the **Guards Toy Soldier Centre,** a great place for a souvenir. ⊠ *Birdcage Walk, Westminster* ☏ *020/7414–3428* ⊕ *www.theguardsmuseum.com* ▭ *£5* ⊙ *Daily 10–4; last admission 3:30* Ⓜ *St. James's Park, Green Park.*

Westminster Cathedral. Tucked away on traffic-clogged Victoria Street lies this remarkable neo-Byzantine gem, seat of the Archbishop of Westminster, head of the Roman Catholic Church in England and Wales. Faced with building a church with Westminster Abbey as a neighbor, architect John Francis Bentley looked to the east for inspiration, to the basilicas of St. Mark's in Venice and the Hagia Sofia in Istanbul.

The asymmetrical redbrick edifice, dating from 1903, is banded with stripes of Portland stone and abutted by a 273-foot-high bell tower (the bell is nicknamed "Big Edward") at the northwest corner, ascendable by elevator for sterling views. The interior remains incomplete, but the unfinished overhead brickwork of the ceiling lends the church a dark, brooding intensity. Several side chapels, such as the Chapel of the Blessed Sacrament and the Holy Souls Chapel, are beautifully finished in glittering mosaics. The Lady Chapel—dedicated to the Virgin Mary—is also sumptuously decorated. Look out for the Stations of the Cross, done here by Eric Gill, and the striking baldachin—the enormous stone canopy standing over the altar with a giant cross suspended in front of it. The nave, the widest in the country, is constructed in green marble, which also has a Byzantine connection—it was cut from the same place as the marble used in the Hagia Sofia, and was almost confiscated by warring Turks as it traveled west. All told, more than 200 different types of marble can be found within the cathedral's interior. Just inside the main entrance is the tomb of Cardinal Basil Hume, head of the Catholic Church in England and Wales for more than 25 years. There's a café in the crypt. ⊠ *Ashley Pl., off Victoria St., Westminster* ☎ *020/7798–9055* ⊕ *www.westminstercathedral.org.uk* ✉ *Bell Tower and viewing gallery £5; Treasures of the Cathedral exhibition £5; joint ticket for Bell Tower and exhibition £8* ☯ *Cathedral weekdays 7–6, weekends 8–7; Bell Tower and Treasures of the Cathedral exhibition weekdays 9:30–5, weekends 9:30–6* Ⓜ *Victoria.*

ST. JAMES'S

As a fitting coda to all of Westminster's pomp and circumstance, St. James's—packed with old-money galleries, restaurants, and gentlemen's clubs that embody the history and privilege of traditional London—is found to the south of Piccadilly and north of the Mall.

When Whitehall Palace burned down in 1698, all of London turned its attention to St. James's Palace, the new royal residence. In the 18th and 19th centuries, the area around the palace became the place to live, and many of the estates surrounding the palace disappeared in a building frenzy, as mansions were built and streets laid out. Most of the homes here are privately owned and therefore closed to visitors, but there are some treasure houses that you can explore (such as Spencer House), as well as many fancy shops that have catered to the great and good for centuries.

Today, St. James's remains a rather masculine enclave, containing most of the capital's celebrated gentlemen's clubs (especially the classic Atheneum), long-established men's outfitters and clothiers, and some interesting art galleries and antiques shops. In one corner is St. James's Park, framed on its western side by the biggest monument in the area: Buckingham Palace, official residence of the Queen. The smaller St. James's Palace is where much of the office work for the House of Windsor gets done; nearby is Clarence House, London home of Prince Charles and his wife, Camilla.

2

ROYALTY WATCHING

You've seen Big Ben, the Tower, and Westminster Abbey. But somehow you feel something is missing: a close encounter with Britain's most famous attraction—Her actual Maj, Elizabeth II. The Queen and the Royal Family attend hundreds of functions a year, and if you want to know what they are doing on any given date, turn to the Court Circular, printed in the major London dailies, or check out the Royal Family website, ⊕ www.royal.gov.uk, for the latest events on the Royal Diary. Trooping the Colour is usually held on the second Saturday in June, to celebrate the Queen's official birthday. This spectacular parade begins when she leaves Buckingham Palace in her carriage and rides down the Mall to arrive at Horse Guards Parade at 11 exactly. To watch, just line up along the Mall with your binoculars.

Another time you can catch the Queen in all her regalia is when she and the Duke of Edinburgh ride in state to open the Houses of Parliament. The famous black and gilt-trimmed Irish State Coach travels from Buckingham Palace—on a clear day, it's to be hoped, for this ceremony takes place in late October or early November. The Gold State Coach, an icon of fairy-tale glamour, is used for coronations and jubilees only.

But perhaps the most relaxed, least formal time to see the Queen is during Royal Ascot, held at the racetrack near Windsor Castle—a short train ride out of London— usually during the third week of June (Tuesday–Friday). The Queen and members of the Royal Family are driven down the track to the Royal Box in an open carriage, giving spectators a chance to see them. After several races, the famously horse-loving Queen invariably walks down to the paddock, greeting race goers as she proceeds. If you meet her, the official etiquette is to first make a short bow or curtsy, and then to address her first as "Your Majesty," and then "Ma'am" (to rhyme with "ham," not "farm") thereafter.

TOP ATTRACTIONS

Fodor's Choice **Buckingham Palace.**
★ *See the highlighted listing in this chapter.*

The Mall. This stately, 115-foot-wide processional route sweeping from Admiralty Arch to the Queen Victoria Memorial at Buckingham Palace is an updated 1904 version of a promenade laid out around 1660 for the game of *paille-maille* (a type of croquet crossed with golf), which also gave the parallel road Pall Mall its name. (That's why Mall is pronounced to rhyme with "pal," not "ball.") The tarmac is colored red, to represent a ceremonial red carpet. The **Duke of York Memorial** up the steps toward Carlton House Terrace is a towering column dedicated to George III's second son, further immortalized in the English nursery rhyme "The Grand Old Duke of York." Sadly, the internal spiral steps are inaccessible. Be sure to stroll along The Mall on Sunday when the road is closed to traffic, or catch the bands and troops of the Household

A classic photo op: cavalry from the Queen's Life Guard at Buckingham Palace

Division on their way from St. James's Palace to Buckingham Palace for the Changing of the Guard. ⊠ *St. James's* Ⓜ *Charing Cross, Green Park.*

Piccadilly Circus. The origins of the name "Piccadilly" relate to a humble 17th-century tailor from the Strand named Robert Baker who sold picadils—a stiff ruffled collar all the rage in courtly circles—and built a house with the proceeds. Snobs dubbed his new-money mansion Piccadilly Hall, and the name stuck.

Pride of place in the circus—a circular junction until the construction of Shaftesbury Avenue in 1886— belongs to the statue of **Eros,** dating from 1893 (although even most Londoners don't know that it is, in reality, a representation of Eros's brother Anteros, the Greek God of requited love). The other instantly recognizable feature of Piccadilly Circus is the enormous bank of lit-up billboards on the north side; if you're passing at night, frame them behind the Tube entrance sign on the corner of Regent Street for an unforgettable photo. ⊠ *St. James's* Ⓜ *Piccadilly Circus.*

The Queen's Gallery. Technically speaking, the sovereign doesn't "own" the rare and exquisite works of art in the Royal Collection, she merely holds them in trust for the nation—and what a collection it is! Only a selection is on view at any one time, presented in themed exhibitions. Let the excellent (free) audio guide take you through the elegant galleries filled with some of the world's greatest artworks.

A rough time line of the major royal collectors starts with Charles I (who also commissioned Rubens to paint the Banqueting House ceiling). An avid art enthusiast, Charles established the basis of the Royal Collection, purchasing works by Raphael, Titian, Caravaggio, and

Dürer. During the Civil War and in the aftermath of Charles's execution, many masterpieces were sold abroad and subsequently repatriated by Charles II. George III, who bought Buckingham House, scooped up a notable collection of Venetian (including Canaletto), Renaissance (Bellini and Raphael), and Dutch (Vermeer) art, and a large number of baroque drawings, in addition to patronizing English contemporary artists such as Gainsborough and Beechey. The Prince Regent, later George IV, had a particularly good eye for Rembrandt, equestrian works by Stubbs, and lavish portraits by Lawrence. Queen Victoria had a penchant for Landseer animals and landscapes, and Frith's contemporary scenes.

> ### THE GUARDMEN'S BEARSKINS
>
> While on duty, guardsmen take their job very, very seriously. They don't speak, don't acknowledge anyone (even those tourists trying in vain to make them laugh), don't even swat away troublesome flies from their noses. And they're certainly not allowed to keel over under the weight of their enormous hats. Called "bearskins" (and still made from the pelts of Canadian black bears), the headdresses were first worn by the French Imperial Guard defeated in the Battle of Waterloo in 1815.

Later, Edward VII indulged Queen Alexandra's love of Fabergé, and many royal tours around the empire produced gifts of gorgeous caliber, such as the Cullinan diamond from South Africa and an emerald-studded belt from India. ⊠ *Buckingham Palace, Buckingham Palace Rd., St. James's* ☎ *020/7766–7301* ⊕ *www.royalcollection.org.uk* ⊠ *£9.75; joint ticket with Royal Mews £16.75; joint ticket with Mews and Buckingham Palace £35.60* ☉ *Daily 10–5:30; last admission 1 hr before closing. Closed for 2 wks in Oct./early Nov.* Ⓜ *Victoria, St. James's Park, Green Park.*

FAMILY **Royal Mews.** Fairy-tale gold-and-glass coaches and sleek Rolls-Royce state cars emanate from the Royal Mews, next door to the Queen's Gallery. Designed by John Nash, the Mews serves as the headquarters for Her Majesty's travel department (so beware of closures for state visits), complete with the Queen's own special breed of horses, ridden by wigged postilions decked in red-and-gold regalia. Between the stables and riding school arena are exhibits of polished saddlery and riding tack. The highlight of the Mews is the splendid Gold State Coach, a piece of art on wheels, with its sculpted tritons and sea gods. There are activities for children, and free guided tours are available April to October; daily at 10:15, then hourly from 11 am to 4 pm. ⊠ *Buckingham Palace Rd., St. James's* ☎ *020/7766–7302* ⊕ *www.royalcollection. org.uk* ⊠ *£9; joint ticket with Queen's Gallery £16.75; joint ticket with Queen's Gallery and Buckingham Palace £35.60* ☉ *Apr.–Oct., daily 10–5; Nov., Feb., and Mar., Mon.–Sat. 10–4; last admission 45 mins before closing. Closed Dec. and Jan.* Ⓜ *Victoria, St. James's Park.*

St. James's Palace. Commissioned by Henry VIII, this Tudor brick palace was the residence of kings and queens for more than 300 years; indeed, while all monarchs have actually lived at Buckingham Palace since Queen Victoria's day, it is still the official residence of the Sovereign.

BUCKINGHAM PALACE

✉ *Buckingham Palace Rd., St. James's* ☎ *020/7766–7300* ⊕ *www.royalcollection.org. uk/visit* ✑ *£20.50; joint ticket with Queen's Gallery and Royal Mews £35.60* ☉ *Aug., daily 9:30–7:30 (last admission 5:15); Sept., daily 9:30–6:30 (last admission 4:15). Times subject to change; check website* Ⓜ *Victoria, St. James's Park, Green Park.*

TIPS

■ If bought directly from the palace ticket office, tickets are valid for a repeat visit over the course of 12 months from the first visit.

■ Admission is by timed ticket with entry every 15 minutes throughout the day. Allow up to two hours.

■ A Royal Day Out ticket, available only in August and September, gives you the regal triple whammy of the Royal Mews, the Queen's Gallery, and the State Rooms, and is valid throughout the day. Tickets cost £33.25. Allow four hours.

■ Get there by 10:30 to grab a spot in the best viewing section for the Changing the Guard (www.changing-the-guard.com), daily at 11:30 from May until the end of July (varies according to troop deployment requirements) and on alternate days for the rest of the year, weather permitting.

The doors of the monarch's official residence are only open to the public in August and September, when the Queen heads off to Scotland on her annual summer holiday. (Want to know if the Queen's at home? If she's in residence the Royal Standard flies above the palace; if not, it's the more famous red, white, and blue Union Flag.) The standard tour covers the palace's 19 State Rooms. With fabulous gilt moldings and walls adorned with old masters.

Highlights

The **Grand Hall,** followed by the **Grand Staircase** and **Guard Room,** are visions in marble and gold leaf, filled with massive, twinkling chandeliers. Don't miss the theatrical **Throne Room,** with the original 1953 coronation throne, or the sword in **the Ballroom,** used by the Queen to bestow knighthoods and other honors with a touch on the recipient's shoulders. Royal portraits line the **State Dining Room,** and the **Blue Drawing Room** is dazzling in its splendor. The bow-shape **Music Room** features lapis lazuli columns between arched floor-to-ceiling windows, and the alabaster-and-gold plasterwork of the **White Drawing Room** is a dramatic statement of wealth and power.

Changing the Guard remains one of London's best free shows and culminates in front of the palace. Marching to live military bands, the old guard proceeds up the Mall from St. James's Palace to Buckingham Palace. Shortly afterward, the new guard approaches from Wellington Barracks. Then within the forecourt, the captains of the old and new guards symbolically transfer the keys to the palace.

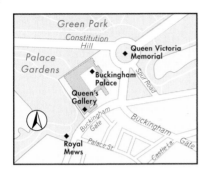

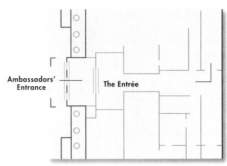

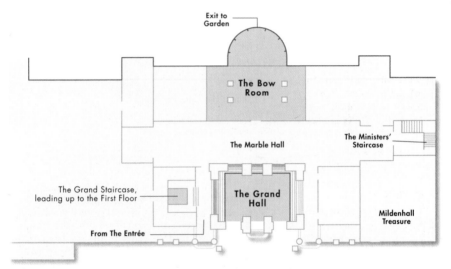

BUCKINGHAM PALACE: GROUND FLOOR

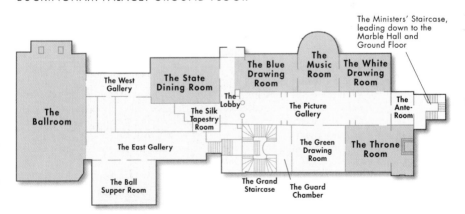

BUCKINGHAM PALACE: FIRST FLOOR

Gentlemen's shops in St. James's specialize in high-quality, handmade goods.

(Foreign ambassadors, for instance, are received by the "Court of St. James.") Today it contains various royal apartments and offices, including the working office of Prince Charles. The palace is not open to the public but the surprisingly low-key Tudor exterior is well worth the short detour from the Mall to see. Friary Court out front is a splendid setting for Trooping the Colour, part of the Queen's official birthday celebrations. Everyone loves to take a snapshot of the scarlet-coated guardsman standing sentry outside the imposing Tudor gateway. Note that the Changing the Guard ceremony at St. James's Palace occurs only on days when the guard at Buckingham Palace is changed. If you're approaching from St. James Street, take a quick peek at the delightfully old-looking **Berry Bros. & Rudd** wine store at No. 3, near the back entrance to the palace; it's been trading here continuously since 1698. ⊠ *Friary Ct., St. James's* ⊕ *www.royal.gov.uk* Ⓜ *Green Park.*

FAMILY
Fodor's Choice
★

St. James's Park. In a city of royal parks, this one—bordered by three palaces (the Palace of Westminster, St. James's Palace, and Buckingham Palace)—is the most regal of them all. It's not only London's oldest park, but also its smallest and most ornate. Once marshy meadows, the land was acquired by Henry VIII in 1532 as royal deer-hunting grounds (with dueling and sword fights strictly forbidden). Later, James I drained the land and installed an aviary and zoo (complete with crocodiles, camels, and an elephant). When Charles II returned from exile in France, where he had been hugely impressed by the splendor of the gardens at the Palace of Versailles, he transformed the park into formal gardens, with avenues, fruit orchards, and a canal. Lawns were grazed by goats, sheep, and deer, and in the 18th century the park became a

2

different kind of hunting ground, for wealthy lotharios looking to pick up nighttime escorts. A century later, John Nash redesigned the landscape in a more naturalistic, romantic style, and if you gaze down the lake toward Buckingham Palace, you could easily believe yourself to be on a country estate.

A large population of waterfowl—including pelicans, geese, ducks, and swans (which belong to the Queen)—breed on and around Duck Island at the east end of the lake. From April to September, the deck chairs (charge levied) come out, crammed with office workers at midday, eating lunch while being serenaded by music from the bandstands. One of the best times to stroll the leafy walkways is after dark, with Westminster Abbey and the Houses of Parliament rising above the floodlit lake. The popular Inn the Park restaurant is a wood-and-glass pavilion with a turf roof that blends in beautifully with the surrounding landscape; it's an excellent stopping place for a meal or a snack on a nice day. ✉ *The Mall or Horse Guards approach or Birdcage Walk, St. James's* ⊕ *www.royalparks.org.uk* ⊙ *Daily 5 am–midnight* Ⓜ *St. James's Park, Westminster.*

WORTH NOTING

Clarence House. The London home of the Queen Mother for nearly 50 years until her death in 2002, Clarence House is now the residence of Prince Charles, the Prince of Wales; his wife, Camilla, the Duchess of Cornwall; and Prince Harry. The Regency mansion was built by John Nash for the Duke of Clarence (later to become William IV) who considered next-door St. James's Palace to be too cramped for his liking, although postwar renovation work means that little remains of Nash's original. Since then it has remained a royal home for princesses, dukes, and duchesses, including the present monarch, Queen Elizabeth, as a newlywed before her coronation. The rooms have been sensitively preserved to reflect the Queen Mother's taste, with the addition of many works of art from the Royal Collection, including works by Winterhalter, Augustus John, and Sickert. Clarence House is usually open only for the month of August and tickets must be booked in advance. ✉ *St. James's Palace, The Mall, St. James's* ☎ *020/7766–7300* ⊕ *www. royalcollection.org.uk* 🎟 *£9.50; exclusive guided tour £35* ⊙ *Aug. weekdays 10–4:30; weekend 10–5:30; last admission 1 hr before closing* Ⓜ *Green Park.*

Institute of Contemporary Arts (ICA). You would never suspect that behind the stately white-stucco facade in the heart of Establishment London is to be found that champion of the avant-garde, the ICA. Since 1947, the ICA has been pushing boundaries in visual arts, performance, theater, dance, and music. There are two movie theaters, a performance theater, three galleries, a highbrow bookstore, a reading room, a café, and a bar. ✉ *The Mall, St. James's* ☎ *020/7930–3647* ⊕ *www.ica.org.uk* 🎟 *Free; films £8–£11; performances and exhibitions vary (most are free)* ⊙ *Galleries Tues.–Sun. 11–11; exhibitions Tues., Wed., and Fri.–Sun. 11–6, Thurs. 11–9.* Ⓜ *Charing Cross, Piccadilly Circus.*

ICA Café Bar. Overlooking The Mall, this café and bar offers a tasty, reasonably priced lunch and dinner menu, with coffees and snacks available throughout the day. Like the venue itself, it's open Tuesday–Sunday 11–11. ⊠ *The Mall, St. James's* 🕾 *020/7930–8619* ⊕ *www.ica.org.uk* ⊙ *Closed Mon.*

Spencer House. Ancestral abode of the Spencers—Princess Diana's family—this is perhaps the finest example of an elegant 18th-century town house extant in London. Reflecting his passion for the Grand Tour and classical antiquities, the first Earl Spencer commissioned architect John Vardy to adapt designs from ancient Rome for a magnificent private palace. Vardy was responsible for the exteriors, including the gorgeous west-facing Palladian facade, its pediment adorned with classical statues, and the ground-floor interiors, notably the lavish Palm Room, with its spectacular screen of columns covered in gilded carvings that resemble gold palm trees. The lavish style was meant not only to attest to Spencer's power and wealth but also to celebrate his marriage, a love match then rare in aristocratic circles (the palms are a symbol of marital fertility). Midway through construction—the house was built between 1756 and 1766—Spencer changed architects and hired James "Athenian" Stuart, whose designs were based on a classical Greek aesthetic, to decorate the gilded State Rooms on the first floor. These include the Painted Room, the first completely neoclassical room in Europe. Since the 1940s the house has been leased by the Spencers to a succession of wealthy residents. ⊠ *27 St. James's Pl., St. James's* 🕾 *020/7499–8620 recorded information, 020/7514–1958 tour reservations* ⊕ *www.spencerhouse.co.uk* 🎟 *£12* ⊙ *Sept.–Dec. and Feb.–July, Sun. 10:30–5:45; last tour 1 hr before closing. No children under 10 admitted.* Ⓜ *Green Park.*

St. James's Church. Bombed by the German Luftwaffe in 1940 and not restored until 1954, this was one of the last of Sir Christopher Wren's London churches—and his favorite. Completed in 1684, it contains one of the finest works by the master carver Grinling Gibbons (1648–1721)—an ornate limewood reredos (the screen behind the altar). The church is a lively place, with all manner of lectures and concerts (some are free). A café occupies a fine location right alongside the church, while a small, sedate garden is tucked away at the rear. The market out front is full of surprises; come on Tuesday for antiques, Wednesday to Saturday for arts and crafts. ⊠ *197 Piccadilly, St. James's* 🕾 *020/7734–4511, 020/7381–0441 concert program and tickets* ⊕ *www.sjp.org.uk* 🎟 *Free* ⊙ *Daily, generally about 9–6 (exact times vary; call to check)* Ⓜ *Piccadilly Circus, Green Park.*

MAYFAIR AND
MARYLEBONE

GETTING ORIENTED

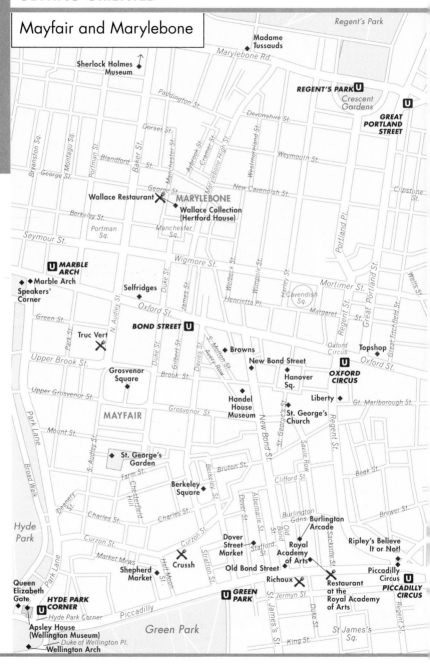

Mayfair and Marylebone

TOP REASONS TO GO

At home with the Duke of Wellington: His Apsley House is filled with splendid salons lined with grand old master paintings.

Get a passion for fashion: Bond and Mount streets are filled with great shopping. McQueen and McCartney will keep your credit card occupied, but don't forget stylish, gigantic Selfridges.

London's most charming shopping arcade: Built for Lord Cavendish in 1819, the beautiful Burlington Arcade is right out of a Victorian daguerreotype.

The Wallace Collection: Savor room after room of magnificent furniture, porcelain, silver, and top old master paintings, in the former residence of the marquesses of Hertford.

Dress to impress at Claridge's: Afternoon tea at this sumptuous art deco gem is the perfect end to a shopping spree in Mayfair.

FEELING PECKISH?

Crussh. This successful chain serves up delicious juices and smoothies, as well as sandwiches, soups, and wraps. Decamp to nearby Green Park, where—if you're lucky—you can grab one of the deck chairs. Not open on weekends. ⊠ *1 Curzon St., Mayfair* ☎ *020/7629-2554* ⊕ *www.crussh. com* Ⓜ *Green Park.*

Richoux. Since 1909, Richoux has been an affordable refuge from busy Piccadilly. Simple but well-executed French bistro food is served all day, as well as scrumptious afternoon tea. ⊠ *172 Piccadilly, Mayfair* ☎ *020/7493-2204* ⊕ *www.richoux. co.uk* Ⓜ *Green Park, Piccadilly Circus.*

Truc Vert. Before crossing Oxford Street, fortify yourself in this rustic French café. Open for breakfast, lunch, and dinner, Truc Vert has a menu that changes daily. ⊠ *42 N. Audley St., Mayfair* ☎ *020/7491-9988* ⊕ *www.trucvert.co.uk.*

GETTING THERE

Three Tube stations on the Central line are handy for reaching these neighborhoods: Marble Arch, Bond Street (also on the Jubilee line), and Oxford Circus (also on the Victoria and Bakerloo lines).

You can also take the Piccadilly or Bakerloo line to the Piccadilly Circus Tube station, the Piccadilly line to the Hyde Park Corner station, or the Piccadilly, Victoria, or Jubilee line to the Green Park station.

The best buses are the 8, which takes in Green Park, Berkeley Square, and New Bond Street, and the 9—London's oldest existing bus route—which runs along Piccadilly.

MAKING THE MOST OF YOUR TIME

Set aside at least a day to experience Mayfair and Marylebone. Leave enough time for shopping and also to wander casually through the streets and squares.

The only areas to avoid are the Tube stations at rush hour, and Oxford Street if you don't like crowds. At all costs, stay away from Oxford Circus around 5 pm, when the commuter rush can, at times, resemble an East African wildebeest migration—but without the charm.

The area becomes quiet at night—so plan to party elsewhere.

3

Sightseeing
★★★★
Nightlife
★
Dining
★★★★
Lodging
★★★★
Shopping
★★★★

Mayfair forms the core of London's West End, the city's most stylish central area. This neighborhood oozes class and old-school style. The sense of being in one of the world's most wealthy and powerful cities is palpable as you wander along its grand and graceful streets. Scoot across the district's one exception to all this elegance—Oxford Street—and you'll discover the pleasant streets of Marylebone, the most central of London's many "villages."

MAYFAIR

Updated By
James O'Neill

Ultraritzy Mayfair, lined with beautiful 18th-century mansions (along with Edwardian apartment buildings made of deep-red brick), is the address of choice for many of London's wealthiest residents. Once you note the sheer number of Rolls-Royces, Bentleys, and Jaguars, you may become acutely aware of how poor you are. Even the delivery vans hereabouts all seem to bear some royal coat of arms, advertising that they've been purveyors of fine goodies for as long as anyone can remember.

The district can't claim to be stuffed with must-sees—but that is part of its appeal. There is no shortage of history and gorgeous architecture; the streets here are custom-built for window-shopping, expansive strolling, and getting a peek into the lifestyles of London's rich and famous, past and present. Mayfair is primarily residential, so its homes are off-limits except for one satisfyingly grand example: Apsley House, the Duke of Wellington's home, built by Robert Adam in 1771, and once known as No. 1, London.

Despite being bordered by four of the busiest streets in London—the busy budget-shopping mecca Oxford Street (to the north), the major traffic artery Park Lane with Hyde Park beyond (to the west), and the bustling Regent Street and Piccadilly (to the east and south, respectively)—Mayfair itself is remarkably traffic-free and a delight to explore. Starting at **Selfridges,** on Oxford Street, a southward stroll will take you through quiet streets lined with Georgian town houses (the area was largely developed in the 17th and 18th centuries). From there, with a bit of artful navigating, you can reach four pleasant patches of green: **Grosvenor Square, Berkeley Square, Hanover Square,** with its splendid **St. George's Church** where Handel worshipped, and the quiet **St. George's Gardens,** bounded

A BRIEF HISTORY

The name Mayfair derives from the 15-day May fair that was once held in the charming warren of narrow streets known as Shepherd Market. But in the 18th century, the residents of this now-fashionable neighborhood felt the fair was lowering the tone and so put a stop to it.

by a maze of streets and mews. Some of London's most exclusive shopping destinations are here, among them **Mount Street, Bruton Street, Savile Row,** and the **Burlington Arcade.** At the western end of Mayfair at Hyde Park corner are two memorials to England's great hero, the Duke of Wellington: **Wellington Arch** and the duke's restored London residence, **Apsley House.**

The **Royal Academy of Arts** is at the southern fringe of Mayfair on Piccadilly, and just across the road begins more sedate St. James's, with its old-money galleries, restaurants, and gentlemen's clubs that echo the privilege of traditional London. You'll get the best sense of the neighborhood just to the south on **St. James's Square** and **Pall Mall,** with its private clubs tucked away in 18th- and 19th-century patrician buildings.

TOP ATTRACTIONS

Fodor'sChoice ★ **Apsley House (Wellington Museum).** Apsley House was built by Robert Adam and presented to the Duke of Wellington as thanks for his victory over Napoléon at the Battle of Waterloo, in 1815. Long known simply as No. 1, London, on account of its being the first mansion at the old tollgate from Knightsbridge village, the building reopened in early 2015 after a major refurbishment. Victory over the French made Wellington—born in Ireland as Arthur Wellesley—the greatest soldier and statesman in the land. The so-called Iron Duke lived here from 1817 until his death in 1852. Opposite the house, and now marooned in a roundabout in the middle of the constant Hyde Park traffic, is the **Wellington Arch,** designed by Decimus Burton and unveiled in 1828, although Burton's original plan to have a sculpture of the Angel of Peace descending upon a chariot of war at the arch's pinnacle wasn't realized until 1912. As you'd expect, the mansion has many uniforms and weapons on display, but it also houses a celebrated art collection, the bulk of which was once owned by Joseph Bonaparte, onetime King of Spain and younger brother of Napoléon. With works by Brueghel, Van Dyck, and Rubens, as well as the Spanish masters Velázquez and Murillo (note the former's famous portrait of Pope Innocent X), the collection also includes a Goya portrait of the duke himself on horseback. An 11-foot-tall statue of a nude (fig-leafed) Napoléon looms over you as you approach the grand central staircase. The statue was taken from the Louvre and given as a gift to Wellington from the grateful British government in 1816. ⊠ *149 Piccadilly, Hyde Park Corner, Mayfair* ☎ *0870/333–1181* ⊕ *www.english-heritage.org.uk* ☎ *£6.90; joint ticket with Wellington Arch £8.90* ☉ *Apr.–Oct., Wed.–Sun. and bank holiday Mon. 11–5; Nov.–Feb., weekends 10–4* Ⓜ *Hyde Park Corner.*

WORD OF MOUTH

"I think Mayfair is a great location…you have access to three major tube lines…[and] if you need to hop on a cab, Mayfair is about as central as you can be, so fares won't break the bank."

—hsv

Bond Street. This world-class shopping haunt is divided into northern "New" (1710) and southern "Old" (1690) halves. You can spot the juncture by a bronzed bench on which Franklin D. Roosevelt sits companionably next to Winston Churchill. At No. 35, on New Bond Street, you'll find **Sotheby's,** the world-famous auction house, as well as upscale retailers like Asprey's, Burberry, Louis Vuitton, Georg Jensen, and Church's. You'll find even more opportunities to flirt with financial ruin on Old Bond Street, with flagship boutiques of top-end designers like Chanel, Gucci, and Yves St. Laurent; an array of fine jewelers including Tiffany; and art dealers Colnaghi, Spink Leger, and Agnew's. **Cork Street,** which parallels the top half of Old Bond Street, is where many top dealers in contemporary art have their galleries. ⊠ *Mayfair* Ⓜ *Bond St., Green Park.*

Fodor'sChoice ★ **Burlington Arcade.** With ceilings and lights now restored to how they would have looked when it was built in 1819, Burlington Arcade is the finest of Mayfair's enchanting covered shopping alleys. Originally built for Lord Cavendish, it was meant to stop the hoi polloi from flinging rubbish into his garden at next-door Burlington House. Top-hatted watchmen called beadles—the world's smallest private police force—still patrol, preserving decorum by preventing you from singing, running, or carrying an open umbrella. The arcade is also the main link between the Royal Academy of Arts and its extended galleries at 6 Burlington Gardens. ⊠ *Piccadilly, Mayfair* ☎ *020/7493–1764* ⊕ *www.burlington-arcade.co.uk* ☉ *Mon.–Sat. 9–8, Sun. 11–6* Ⓜ *Green Park, Piccadilly Circus.*

QUICK BITES Several of London's most storied and stylish hotels are in Mayfair. Even if you're not staying at one, sample the high life by popping into their glamorous bars for a cocktail or some afternoon tea. **Claridge's Bar** takes its cue from art deco, as do the intimate **Rivoli Bar** (at the Ritz) and **The Connaught's** bar; the bar at **Brown's Hotel** is modernist.

Marble Arch. John Nash's 1827 arch, moved here from Buckingham Palace in 1851, stands amid the traffic whirlpool where Bayswater Road segues into Oxford Street, at the top of Park Lane. The arch actually contains three small chambers, which served as a police station until the mid-20th century. Search the sidewalk on the traffic island opposite the movie theater for the stone plaque recalling the Tyburn Tree, an elaborately designed gallows that stood here for 400 years, until 1783.

Each June for the past 240 years, the iconic Royal Academy of Arts has put on its Summer Exhibition, a huge draw for art-loving visitors and Londoners alike.

The condemned would be conveyed here in their finest clothes from Newgate Prison in The City, and were expected to affect a casual indifference or face a merciless heckling from the crowds. Towering across the grass from the arch toward Tyburn Way is *Horse at Water,* a vast patina-green statue of a horse's head by sculptor Nic Fiddian. Cross over (or under) to the northeastern corner of Hyde Park for Speakers' Corner, a parcel of land long-dedicated to the principle of free speech. On Sunday people of all views—or none at all—come to pontificate, listen, and debate about everything under the sun. ⊠ *Park La., Mayfair* Ⓜ *Marble Arch.*

Fodor'sChoice ★ **Royal Academy of Arts.** Burlington House was built in 1664, with later Palladian additions for the 3rd Earl of Burlington in 1720. The piazza in front dates from 1873, when the Renaissance-style buildings around the courtyard were designed by Banks and Barry to house a gaggle of noble scientific societies, including the Royal Society of Chemistry and the Royal Astronomical Society.

The house itself is home to the Royal Academy of Arts. In a city with many major public galleries, the Royal Academy more than holds its own. The statue of the academy's first president, Sir Joshua Reynolds, palette in hand, is prominent in the piazza, while within the house are statues of the major painters J. W. M. Turner and Thomas Gainsborough. Free tours show off part of the collection and the excellent temporary exhibitions. Every June, the RA puts on its Summer Exhibition, a huge and eclectic collection of art by living Royal Academicians and many other contemporary artists. ⊠ *Burlington House, Piccadilly, Mayfair* ☎ *020/7300–8000, 020/7300–5839 lectures and family programs* ⊕ *www.royalacademy. org.uk* ✉ *Prices vary with exhibition, £8–£16* ⊙ *Sat.–Thurs. 10–6, Fri. 10–10; tours Tues. and Wed. 1, Thurs. and Fri. 3, Sat. 11:30* Ⓜ *Piccadilly Circus, Green Park.*

QUICK BITES

The RA Grand Café. With its walls covered in Gilbert Spencer murals, the Royal Academy's café is almost as beautiful as the art hanging in the galleries. The accent is on variety, with hearty dishes like fish pie, cold cuts, and upscale salads and sandwiches. It's open daily from 10 to 6, except Friday, when it closes at 11 pm. ✉ *Burlington House, Piccadilly, Mayfair* ☎ *020/7300–5608* ⊕ *www. royalacademy.org.uk* Ⓜ *Piccadilly Circus, Green Park.*

ROYALTY IN AISLE 9

Shoppers and historians alike will enjoy **Fortnum & Mason** at 181 Piccadilly. This old-fashioned fine-foods store, built in 1788, seems stuck in another century, with ornate murals decorating the walls, glass cabinets, and brass fixtures casting a dazzling glow all around. The store is especially famous for its loose-leaf tea and luxury picnic hampers (a tempting purchase, given that St. James's Square is just a stone's throw away). Fortnum & Mason sent hams to the Duke of Wellington's army and baskets of treats to Florence Nightingale in the Crimea. (It also happens to be the Queen's grocery store.)

Wellington Arch. Opposite the Duke of Wellington's mansion, Apsley House, this majestic stone arch surveys the traffic rushing around Hyde Park Corner. Designed by Decimus Burton and completed in 1828, it was created as a grand entrance to the west side of London and echoes the design of that other landmark gate, Marble Arch. Both were triumphal arches commemorating Britain's victory against France in the Napoleonic Wars. Atop the building, the Angel of Peace descends on the quadriga, or four-horse chariot of war. This replaced the Duke of Wellington on his horse, which was considered too large and moved to an army barracks in Aldershot. Inside the arch, three floors of permanent and temporary exhibits reveal the monument's history. ✉ *Hyde Park Corner, Mayfair* ☎ *020/7930–2726* ⊕ *www.english-heritage.org.uk* ✉ *£4.20* ⊙ *Daily 10–4, but platform sometimes closed for exhibition installations* Ⓜ *Hyde Park Corner.*

WORTH NOTING

Grosvenor Square. Pronounced *Grove* -na, this leafy square was laid out in 1725–31 and is as desirable an address today as it was then. Americans have certainly always thought so—from John Adams, the second president, who as ambassador lived at No. 38, to Dwight D. Eisenhower, whose wartime headquarters was at No. 20. Now the massive 1960s block of the U.S. Embassy occupies the entire west side, and a British memorial to Franklin D. Roosevelt stands in the center. There is also a classically styled memorial to those who died in New York on September 11, 2001. Grosvenor Chapel, completed in 1730 and used by Eisenhower's men during World War II, stands a couple of blocks

Marble Arch was originally a gateway to Buckingham Palace before it was moved to the corner of Hyde Park.

south of the square on South Audley Street, with the entrance to pretty **St. George's Gardens** to its left. ✉ *Mayfair* Ⓜ *Bond St.*

Handel House Museum. The former home of the composer, where he lived for more than 30 years until his death in 1759, is a celebration of his genius. It was the first museum in London solely dedicated to one composer. In rooms decorated in fine Georgian style you can linger over original manuscripts and gaze at portraits—accompanied by live music if the adjoining music rooms are being used by musicians in rehearsal. Some of the composer's most famous pieces were created here, including the *Messiah* and *Music for the Royal Fireworks*. To hear a live concert here is to imagine the atmosphere of rehearsals and "salon" music in its day. The museum occupies both No. 25 and the adjoining house, No. 23, where another musical star, Jimi Hendrix, lived for a brief time in the 1960s, as a blue plaque outside the house indicates. ✉ *25 Brook St., entrance in Lancashire Court, Mayfair* ☏ *020/7495–1685* ⊕ *www. handelhouse.org* 🎟 *£6.50* 🕐 *Tues., Wed., Fri., and Sat. 10–6; Thurs. 10–8; Sun. noon–6 (last admission ½ hr before closing)* Ⓜ *Bond St.*

MARYLEBONE

A favorite of newspaper style sections everywhere, Marylebone High Street forms the heart of Marylebone (pronounced "Marr-le-bone") Village, a vibrant, upscale neighborhood that encompasses the squares and streets around High Street and nearby Marylebone Lane. The district took its name from a church dedicated to St. Mary and the bourne (another word for "stream") that ran through the original village. Its

Regent Street, home to Liberty department store and Hamleys toy shop, decorated for the holidays

development, by various members of the aristocracy, began in the early 18th century. Today, it's hard to believe that you're just a few blocks north of gaudy Oxford Street as you wander in and out of Marylebone's small shops and boutiques, the best of which include La Fromagerie (2–6 Moxon Street), an excellent cheese shop; Daunt Books (Nos. 83–84), a travel bookshop; "Cabbages and Frocks" market on the grounds of the St. Marylebone Parish Church, held Saturday 11–5, which purveys specialty foods and vintage clothing; and on Sunday 10–2, a large farmers' and artisanal-food market in a parking lot on Cramer Street, just behind High Street. But some memorable sights await, too, including that best remnant of ancien régime France in London, the fabled Wallace Collection. The best metro stop for the area is Bond Street.

TOP ATTRACTIONS

Sherlock Holmes Museum. Outside Baker Street station, by the Marylebone Road exit, is a 9-foot-high bronze statue of Arthur Conan Doyle's celebrated detective, who "lived" around the corner at number 221B Baker Street—now a museum to all things Sherlock. Inside, Mrs. Hudson, Holmes's housekeeper, guides you into a series of Victorian rooms where the great man lived, worked, and played the violin. It's all carried off with such genuine enthusiasm and attention to detail that you could be forgiven for thinking that Mr. Holmes actually *did* exist. ⊠ *221B Baker St., Regent's Park* ☎ *020/7224–3688* ⊕ *www.sherlock-holmes. co.uk* ☜ *£10* ⊙ *Daily 9:30–6* Ⓜ *Baker St.*

FAMILY **Wallace Collection.** With its Great Gallery stunningly refurbished in 2014,
Fodor'sChoice there's even more reason to visit this exquisite gem of an art gallery—
★ although housing one of the world's finest collections of old master
paintings is reason enough. This glorious collection and the 18th-cen-
tury mansion in which it's located were bequeathed to the nation by
the widow of Sir Richard Wallace (1818–90). Wallace's father, the 4th
Marquess of Hertford, took a house in Paris after the French Revolution
and set about snapping up paintings by what were then dangerously
unpopular artists, for a song. Frans Hals's *Laughing Cavalier* is probably the most famous painting here, or perhaps Jean-Honoré Fragonard's
The Swing. The full list of painters in the collection reads like a who's-
who of classical European art: from Rubens, Rembrandt, and Van Dyck
to Canaletto, Titian, and Velázquez. English works include paintings
by Gainsborough and Turner. There are also fine collections of furniture, porcelain, Renaissance gold, and majolica (15th- and 16th-century
Italian tin-glazed pottery). The conditions of the bequest mean that no
part of the collection can leave the building; this is the only place in the
world you'll ever be able to see these works. ⊠ *Hertford House, Manchester Sq., Marylebone* ☎ *020/7563–9500* ⊕ *www.wallacecollection.
org* ⊠ *Free* ☉ *Daily 10–5 (except Dec. 24–26)* Ⓜ *Bond St.*

▮ QUICK
BITES

Wallace Restaurant. Bringing the outside in, this café and restaurant is in
the Wallace Collection's glass-roofed courtyard. It's open daily for breakfast, lunch, and afternoon tea (from 10 to 4:30), and for dinner on Friday
and Saturday evenings (last seating is at 9:30 pm). The menu includes
Scottish pheasant, Dover sole, and other upscale offerings. If you don't
want to strain your budget too much, you can just linger over coffee in
the gorgeous surroundings. ⊠ *The Wallace Collection, Hertford House,
Manchester Sq., Marylebone* ☎ *020/7563–9505.*

WORTH NOTING

FAMILY **Madame Tussauds.** One of London's busiest tourist attractions, this is
nothing less—but also nothing more—than the world's most famous
exhibition of lifelike waxwork models of celebrities. Madame T. learned
her craft while making death masks of French Revolution victims, and
in 1835 she set up her first show of the famous ones near this spot. Top
billing still goes to the murderers in the Chamber of Horrors, who stare
glassy-eyed at visitors—one from an electric chair, one sitting next to
the tin bath where he dissolved several wives in quicklime. ▮TIP➔ Beat
the crowds by booking timed entry tickets in advance. You can also
buy nondated, "priority access" tickets via the website (at a premium).
⊠ *Marylebone Rd., Regent's Park* ☎ *0870/400–3000 for timed entry
tickets* ⊕ *www.madametussauds.com* ⊠ *£19–£65 according to time;
call or check website. Combination ticket with London Eye, London
Dungeons, and London Aquarium £40–£58.* ☉ *Early Apr. and mid-
July–Aug., daily 9–7; Sept.–Mar. and mid-Apr.–mid-July, weekdays
9–5:30, weekends 9:30–6* Ⓜ *Baker St.*

221B Baker Street and "Holmes" himself

FAMILY **Ripley's Believe It Or Not!** Inspired by the legendary American traveler/cartoonist/curator Robert Ripley, this museum has six floors of the weird, the wacky, and the downright bizarre (life-size knitted Ferrari, anyone?)—to delight even the most tired and jaded among us. Nothing is too unusual or outlandish to take its place among the 700-plus authentic artifacts. From dinosaur eggs to a sculpture of the Beatles made from chewing gum (yes, chewing gum!), there is so much to see, with interactive exhibits aplenty. ⊠ *The London Pavilion, 1 Piccadilly Circus, Mayfair* ☎ *020/3238–0022* ⊕ *www.ripleyslondon.com* 🖃 *£26.95* ⊘ *Daily 10 am–midnight (last admission 10:30 pm)* Ⓜ *Piccadilly Circus (use exit 4 to Coventry St.).*

SOHO AND
COVENT GARDEN

GETTING ORIENTED

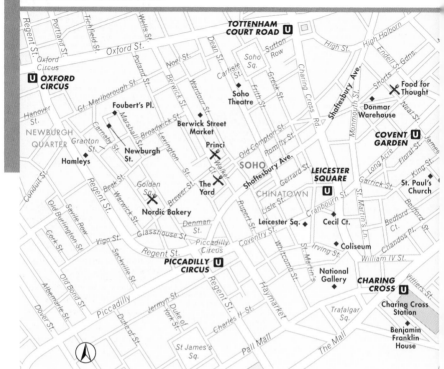

GETTING THERE	TOP REASONS TO GO

Almost all Tube lines cross the Covent Garden and Soho areas, so it's easy to hop off for a dinner or show in one of the hippest parts of London. For Soho, take any train to Piccadilly Circus, or Leicester Square, Oxford Circus, or Tottenham Court Road. For Covent Garden, get off at Covent Garden station on the Piccadilly line. It might be easier to exit the Tube at Leicester Square or Holborn and walk. Thirty buses connect to the Covent Garden area from all over London; check out the area's website, ⊕ *www.coventgarden. uk.com.*

Find tomorrow's look in the Newburgh Quarter: Head to this adorable warren of cobblestone streets for stylish boutiques, edgy stores, and young indie upstarts.

Indulge yourself in Gourmet Country: London has fallen in love with its chefs, and Soho is home to many of the most talked-about restaurants in town.

Covent Garden Piazza: Eliza Doolittle's former backyard has been taken over by fun boutiques and street performers (who play to the crowds at night).

Royal Opera House: Even if you're not going to the opera or ballet, take in the beautiful architecture and sense of history.

See a West End hit in Theatreland: Shaftesbury Avenue is the heart of London's theater district, where more than 40 West End theaters pull in the crowds with a mix of extravagant musicals, Shakespeare, and new plays.

Soho and Covent Garden

4

MAKING THE MOST OF YOUR TIME

You can comfortably tour all the sights around Soho and Covent Garden in a day. Visit the small but perfect Courtauld Gallery on Monday, when entry costs just £3. That leaves plenty of time to watch street entertainment or shop at the stalls around Covent Garden Piazza or in the fashion boutiques of Soho. Save some energy for a night on the town in Soho.

FEELING PECKISH?

The coffee shops on Covent Garden Piazza can be overpriced and mediocre. Head north for Neal Street or west for Soho when the munchies strike.

Food for Thought. This place is always crowded, with hungry customers lining up outside for a delicious range of vegetarian dishes. ⊠ *31 Neal St., Covent Garden* ☎ *020/7836–0239* ⊕ *foodforthought-london.co.uk* Ⓜ *Covent Garden, Leicester Sq.*

Nordic Bakery. On quiet Golden Square, this is an immaculately designed Scandinavian café that serves dark breads and the city's best cinnamon rolls. ⊠ *14A Golden Sq., Soho* ☎ *020/3230–1077* ⊕ *www.nordicbakery.com* Ⓜ *Piccadilly Circus.*

Princi. This chic Italian bakery and café fills up around lunchtime with office workers who come for the colorful salads, oozingly fresh lasagna, and warm-from-the-oven cakes and pastries. ⊠ *135 Wardour St., Soho* ☎ *020/7478–8888* ⊕ *princi.com* Ⓜ *Tottenham Court Rd., Piccadilly Circus.*

GAY LONDON

Old Compton Street in Soho is the epicenter of London's affluent, stylish gay scene. There are some fun nightclubs in the area, with crowds forming in Soho Square, south of Oxford Street. Some of the more well-known clubs and bars in the area include Friendly Society, Ku Bar, and the Yard and the Shadow Lounge.

Sightseeing
★★★

Nightlife
★★★★

Dining
★★★★

Lodging
★★

Shopping
★★★

A red-light district no more, today's Soho is more stylish than seedy and offers some of London's best bars, live music venues, restaurants, and theaters. By day, this hotbed of media production reverts to the business side of its late-night scene. If Soho is all about showbiz, neighboring Covent Garden is devoted to culture. Both districts offer an abundance of narrow streets packed with one-of-a-kind shops and lots of antique character.

SOHO

Updated By
Jo Caird

Soho, which, along with Covent Garden, is loosely known as "the West End," has long been known as the entertainment and arts quarter of London's center. Bordered to the north by Oxford Street, Regent Street to the west, and Chinatown and Leicester Square to the south, the narrow, winding streets of Soho are unabashedly devoted to pleasure. Wardour Street bisects the neighborhood, with lots of interesting boutiques and some of London's best-value restaurants to the west (especially around Foubert's Place and on Brewer and Lexington streets). Most nightlife lies to the east—including the gay clubs of Old Compton Street—and beyond that is the city's densest collection of theaters, on Shaftesbury Avenue. London's compact Chinatown is wedged between Soho and **Leicester Square.** A bit of erudition surfaces to the east of the square on Charing Cross Road, famous for its secondhand bookshops, and on tiny **Cecil Court,** a pedestrianized passage lined with small antiquarian booksellers.

TOP ATTRACTIONS

Fodor's Choice
★

Newburgh Quarter. Want to see the hip style of today's London? Find it one block east of Carnaby Street—where the look of the '60s "Swinging London" was born—in an adorable warren of cobblestone streets now

A BRIEF HISTORY

Almost as soon as a 17th-century housing development covered what had been a royal park and hunting ground, Soho earned a reputation for entertainment, bohemianism, and cosmopolitan tolerance. When the authorities introduced zero tolerance of soliciting in 1991 (the most recent of several attempts to end Soho's sex trade), they cracked down on an old neighborhood tradition that still resurfaces from time to time.

Successive waves of refugees—French Huguenots in the 1680s, followed by Germans, Russians, Poles, Greeks, Italians, and Chinese—settled and brought their ethnic cuisines with them. So when dining out became fashionable after World War I, Soho was the natural place for restaurants to flourish (as they continue to do today).

Among the luminaries who have made their home here are landscape painter John Constable; Casanova; Canaletto, the great painter of Venice; the poet William Blake; and Karl Marx. In the 1950s and '60s, Soho was London's artists' quarter and the place to find the top jazz clubs and art galleries.

The outlines of present-day Covent Garden took shape in the 1630s, when Inigo Jones turned what had been agricultural land into Britain's first planned public square. After the Great Fire of 1666, it became the site of England's largest fruit-and-vegetable market (the flower market arrived in the 19th century). This, along with the district's many theaters and taverns, gave the area a somewhat dubious reputation, and after the produce market relocated in 1973, the surviving buildings were scheduled for demolition. A local campaign saved them, and the restored market opened in 1980.

lined with specialty boutiques, edgy stores, and young indie upstarts. Here, not far from roaring Regent Street, the future of England's fashion is being incubated in stores like Lucy in Disguise and Flying Horse Jeans. A check of the ingredients reveals one part '60s London, one part Futuristic Fetishism, one part Dickensian charm, and one part British street swagger. The Nouveau Boho look best flourishes in shops like Peckham Rye, a tiny boutique crowded with rockers and fashion plates who adore its grunge–meets– *Brideshead Revisited* vibe. Quality independent coffee shops abound—take a break at Speakeasy Espresso & Brew Bar, where you can also browse for home coffee-making equipment. ⊠ *Newburgh St., Foubert's Pl., Ganton St., and Carnaby St., Soho* ⊕ *carnaby.co.uk.*

COVENT GARDEN

To the east of Charing Cross Road lies Covent Garden, the famous marketplace turned shopping mall. Although boutiques and haute fashion shops line the surrounding streets, many Londoners come to Covent Garden for its two outposts of culture: the **Royal Opera House** and the **Donmar Warehouse,** one of London's best and most innovative theaters. The area becomes more sedate just to the north, at the end

You can't miss the buskers performing in the streets of Soho and Covent Garden.

of Wellington Street, where semicircular Aldwych is lined with grand buildings, and from there the Strand leads to the huge, stately piazza of **Somerset House**, a vibrant center of contemporary arts and home to the many masterpieces on view at the **Courtauld Gallery**. You'll get a sense of old-fashioned London just behind the Strand, where small lanes are little changed since the 18th century. On the way to the verdant **Embankment Gardens** bordering the Thames, you may pass the **Adam Houses**, the remnants of a grand 18th-century riverside housing development, and the **Benjamin Franklin House**, where the noted statesman lived in the years leading up to the American Revolution.

Covent Garden joins Soho as an arts-and-entertainment center in the city, popularly referred to as "the West End." The neighborhood centers on the Piazza, site of the original Covent Garden market. High Holborn to the north, Kingsway to the east, and the Strand to the south form its other boundaries.

TOP ATTRACTIONS

Fodor's Choice
★
The Courtauld Gallery. One of London's most beloved art collections, the Courtauld is to your right as you pass through the archway into the grounds of the beautifully restored, grand 18th-century neoclassical **Somerset House**. Founded in 1931 by the textile magnate Samuel Courtauld to house his remarkable private collection, this is one of the world's finest Impressionist and post-Impressionist galleries, with artists ranging from Bonnard to van Gogh. A déjà-vu moment with Cézanne, Degas, Seurat, or Monet awaits on every wall (Manet's *Bar at the Folies-Bergère* and *Le Déjeuner sur L'Herbe* are two of the

stars). Botticelli, Bruegel, Tiepolo, and Rubens are also represented, thanks to the exquisite bequest of Count Antoine Seilern's Princes Gate collection. German Renaissance paintings, bequeathed in 1947, include the colorful and sensual *Adam and Eve* by Lucas Cranach the Elder. The second floor has a more provocative, experimental feel, with masterpieces such as Modigliani's iconic *Female Nude*. Don't miss the little café downstairs—a perfect place for a spot of tea. ⊠ *Somerset House, Strand, Covent Garden* ☎ *020/7848–2526* ⊕ *www.courtauld.ac.uk* 🎟 *£6* ☉ *Daily 10–6; last admission 5:30* Ⓜ *Temple, Covent Garden.*

> ### ICE-SKATING
>
> It's hard to beat the skating experience at Somerset House, where from November through January a rink is set up in the grand courtyard of this central London palace. Check the website for current prices; its popularity is enormous, and if you can't get a ticket, other venues such as Hampton Court, the Tower of London, the London Eye, and the Natural History Museum are following Somerset House's lead in having temporary winter rinks. ☎ *0844/847–1520* ⊕ *www.somersethouse.org.uk/ice-rink.*

Covent Garden Piazza. Once home to London's main flower market, where *My Fair Lady's* Eliza Doolittle peddled her blooms, the square around which Covent Garden pivots is known as the Piazza. In the center, the fine old market building now houses stalls and shops selling expensive clothing, plus several restaurants and cafés, and knickknack stores that are good for gifts. One particular gem is Benjamin Pollock's Toyshop at No. 44 in the market. Established in the 1880s, it sells delightful toy theaters. The superior **Apple Market** has good crafts stalls on most days, too. On the south side of the Piazza, the indoor **Jubilee Market,** with its stalls of clothing, army-surplus gear, and more crafts and knickknacks, feels a bit like a flea market. In summer it may seem that everyone in the huge crowds around you in the Piazza is a fellow tourist, but there's still plenty of office life in the area. Londoners who shop here tend to head for Neal Street and the area to the north of Covent Garden Tube station rather than the market itself. In the Piazza, street performers—from global musicians to jugglers and mimes—play to the crowds, as they have done since the first English Punch and Judy Show, staged here in the 17th century. ⊠ *Covent Garden* ⊕ *www.coventgardenlondonuk.com* Ⓜ *Covent Garden.*

FAMILY **London Transport Museum.** Housed in the old flower market at the southeast corner of Covent Garden, this stimulating museum is filled with impressive vehicle, poster, and photograph collections. As you watch the crowds drive a Tube-train simulation and gawk at the horse-drawn trams (and the piles of detritus that remained behind) and steam locomotives, it's unclear who's enjoying it more, children or adults. Best of all, the kid-friendly museum (under 17 admitted free) has a multilevel approach to education, including information for the youngest visitor to the most advanced transit aficionado. Food and drink are available at the Upper Deck café and the shop has lots of good options for gift-buying. Tickets are valid for unlimited entry for 12 months.

DID YOU KNOW?

Somerset House was lapped by the River Thames before the Victoria Embankment was built in the 19th century. The neoclassical building's grand courtyard is home to ice-skating in winter and dancing fountains in summer.

⊠ Covent Garden Piazza, Covent Garden ☎ *020/7379–6344* ⊕ *www. ltmuseum.co.uk* ✉ *£15* ⏱ *Sat.– Thurs. 10–6 (last admission 5:15), Fri. 11–6 (last admission 5:15)* Ⓜ *Covent Garden, Leicester Sq.*

FAMILY

Fodor's Choice

★

Somerset House. In recent years this huge complex—the work of Sir William Chambers (1723–96), and built during the reign of George III to house offices of the Navy—has been transformed from dusty government offices to one of the capital's most buzzing centers of culture and the arts, often hosting several interesting exhibitions at one time. The cobblestone Italianate courtyard, where Admiral Nelson used to walk, makes a great setting for 55 playful fountains and is transformed into a romantic ice rink in winter; the grand space is the venue for music and outdoor movie screenings in summer. The **Courtauld Gallery** occupies most of the north building, facing the busy Strand. Across the courtyard are the Embankment Galleries, with a vibrant calendar of design, fashion, architecture, and photography exhibitions. Creative activities for children are a regular feature (the website has details). The East Wing has another fine exhibition space and events are sometimes also held in the atmospherically gloomy cellars below the Fountain Court. Tom's Kitchen offers fine dining and the Deli has mouthwatering cakes and pastries. In summer eating and drinking spills out onto the large terrace next to the Thames. *⊠ Strand, Covent Garden* ☎ *020/7845–4600* ⊕ *www.somersethouse.org.uk* ✉ *Embankment Galleries price varies, Courtauld Gallery £7, other areas free* ⏱ *Daily 10–6; last admission 5:15* Ⓜ *Charing Cross, Waterloo, Blackfriars.*

CHEAP TICKETS

One landmark certainly worth a visit by theatergoers is the **Society of London Theatre ticket kiosk (TKTS)**, on the southwest corner of Leicester Square, which sells half-price tickets for many of that evening's performances. It's open Monday to Saturday from 9 to 7, and Sunday from 11 to 4:30. The kiosk also sells advance tickets for many shows. Watch out for illegal ticket touts (scalpers), who target tourists around the square.

WORTH NOTING

The Adam Houses. Only a few structures remain of what was once a regal riverfront row of houses on a 3-acre site, but such is their quality that they are worth a detour off the Strand. The work of 18th-century Scottish architects and interior designers (John, Robert, James, and William Adam, known collectively as the Adam brothers), the original development was damaged in the 19th century during the building of the Embankment, and mostly demolished in 1936 to be replaced by an art deco tower. The original houses still standing are protected, and give a glimpse of their former grandeur. Nos. 1–4 Robert Street and Nos. 7 and 10 Adam Street are the best. *⊠ Robert St. and Adam St., off The Strand, Covent Garden* Ⓜ *Charing Cross, Embankment.*

Royal Society of Arts. At the Royal Society of Arts, you can sometimes see a suite of Adam rooms; ring ahead to check. *⊠ 8 John Adam St.*

Leicester Square is home to many cinemas and a half-price theater ticket booth.

☎ *020/7930–5115* ⊕ *www.thersa.org* ✉ *Free* ◷ *Weekdays 8–8* Ⓜ *Charing Cross, Embankment.*

Benjamin Franklin House. This architecturally significant 1730 house is the only surviving residence of American statesman, scientist, writer, and inventor Benjamin Franklin, who lived and worked here for 16 years preceding the American Revolution. The restored Georgian town house has been left unfurnished, the better to show off the original features—18th-century paneling, stoves, beams, bricks, and windows. Visitors are led around the house by the costumed character of Polly Hewson, the daughter of Franklin's landlady, who interacts with engaging video projections and recorded voices. On Monday you can take a guided tour focusing on the architectural details of the building. ✉ *36 Craven St., Covent Garden* ☎ *020/7839–2006, 020/7925–1405 booking line* ⊕ *www.benjaminfranklinhouse.org* ✉ *Historical Experience £7; architectural tour £3.50* ◷ *Historical Experience Wed.–Sun. noon, 1, 2, 3:15, and 4:15; architectural tour Mon. noon, 1, 2, 3:15, and 4:15.*

Leicester Square. Looking at the neon of the major movie houses, the fast-food outlets, and the disco entrances, you'd never guess that this square (pronounced *Lester*) was a model of formality and refinement when it was first laid out around 1630. By the 19th century the square was already bustling and disreputable, and although it's not a threatening place, you should still be on your guard, especially at night—any space so full of people is bound to attract pickpockets, and Leicester Square certainly does. Although there's a bit of residual glamour (red-carpet film premieres) Londoners generally tend to avoid the place, though it's worth a visit for its hustle and bustle, its mime artists, and the pleasant modern fountain at its center. Also in the middle is a statue of a sulking Shakespeare, perhaps remembering the days when the movie houses were live theaters—burlesque houses, but live all the same. On the northeast corner, in Leicester Place, stands the church of **Notre Dame de France,** with a wonderful mural by Jean Cocteau in one of its side chapels. For more in the way of atmosphere, head north and west from here, through Chinatown and the narrow streets of Soho. ⊠ *Covent Garden* Ⓜ *Leicester Sq.*

St. Paul's Church. If you want to commune with the spirits of Vivien Leigh, Noël Coward, Edith Evans, or Charlie Chaplin, this might be just the place. Memorials to them and many other theater greats are found in this 1633 work of the renowned Inigo Jones, who, as the King's Surveyor of Works, designed the whole of Covent Garden Piazza. St. Paul's Church has been known as "the actors' church" since the Restoration, thanks to the neighboring theater district and St. Paul's prominent parishioners. (Well-known actors often read the lessons at services, and the church still hosts concerts and small-scale productions.) Fittingly, the opening scene of Shaw's *Pygmalion* takes place under its Tuscan portico (you might know it better from the musical *My Fair Lady,* starring Audrey Hepburn). The western end of the Piazza is a prime pitch for street entertainers, but if they're not to your liking, you can repair to the serenity of the garden entered from King or Bedford streets. Charming open-air theater performances of Shakespeare plays and other works are staged there in the summertime. ⊠ *Bedford St., Covent Garden* ☏ *020/7836–5221* ⊕ *www.actorschurch.org* Ⓜ *Covent Garden.*

Theatre Royal, Drury Lane. This is London's best-known auditorium and almost its largest. Since World War II, Drury Lane's forte has been musicals (from *My Fair Lady* and *South Pacific* to *Miss Saigon* and *Shrek*)—though David Garrick, who managed the theater from 1747 to 1776, made its name by reviving the works of the by-then-obscure William Shakespeare. Drury Lane enjoys all the romantic accessories of a London theater—a history of fires (it burned down three times), riots (in 1737, when a posse of footmen demanded free admission), attempted regicides (George II in 1716 and his grandson George III in 1800), and even sightings of the most famous phantom of theaterland, the Man in Grey (in the Circle during matinees). Seventy-five-minute dramatized tours, led by actors, are available. ⊠ *Catherine St., Covent Garden* ☏ *0844/412–4660, 0871/297–0777 Tour bookings* ⊕ *www. reallyuseful.com* ☐ *Tours £10.50* ☉ *Tours daily; times vary* Ⓜ *Covent Garden.*

BLOOMSBURY
AND HOLBORN

GETTING ORIENTED

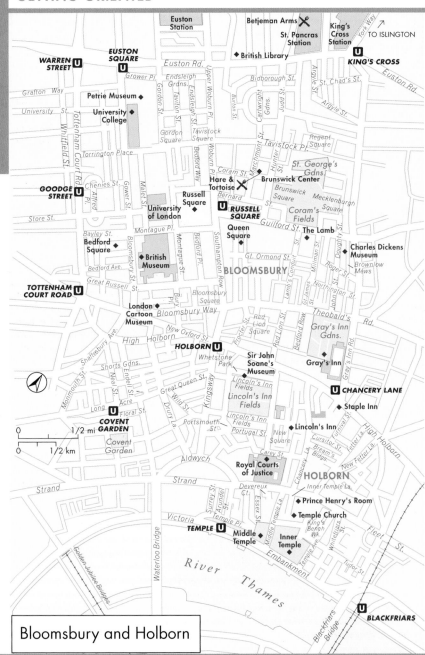

Bloomsbury and Holborn

TOP REASONS TO GO

Take a tour of "Mankind's Attic": From the Rosetta Stone to the Elgin Marbles, the British Museum is the golden hoard of booty amassed over centuries by the British Empire.

Stroll through the Inns of Court: The quiet courts, leafy gardens, and magnificent halls that comprise the heart of Holborn are the closest thing to the spirit of Oxford in London.

Time travel at Sir John Soane's Museum: Quirky and fascinating, the former home of the celebrated 19th-century architect is a treasure trove of antiquities and oddities.

View rare treasures at the British Library: In keeping with Bloomsbury's literary traditions, this repository holds the Magna Carta, a Gutenberg Bible, and Shakespeare's First Folio.

Pay your respects to Charles Dickens: The former residence of the *Oliver Twist* author is now a fascinating museum.

FEELING PECKISH?

The Betjeman Arms. Inside St. Pancras International's renovated Victorian station, this pub is the perfect place to grab a pint and some pub fare. ✉ *Unit 53, St. Pancras International Station, Pancras Rd., King's Cross* ☎ *020/7923–5440* Ⓜ *King's Cross St. Pancras.*

The Hare and Tortoise Dumpling & Noodle Bar. This café serves scrumptious Asian fast food from noon to 11 pm: ingredients are all natural, the portions are huge, and the price is reasonable. ✉ *15–17 Brunswick Shopping Centre, Brunswick Sq., opposite Renoir Cinema, Bloomsbury* ☎ *020/7278–9799* ⊕ *www.hareandtortoise.co.uk/bloomsbury* Ⓜ *Russell Sq.*

Truckles of Pied Bull Yard. The main attraction of this wine bar and café is the Georgian courtyard, where you can relax within a stone's throw of the museum. The London Review Bookshop is here, too. ✉ *Off Bury Pl.,* ☎ *020/7404–5338* ⊕ *www.davy.co.uk/truckles.*

GETTING THERE

The Russell Square Tube stop on the Piccadilly line leaves you right at the corner of Russell Square.

The best Tube stops for the Inns of Court are Holborn on the Central and Piccadilly lines or Chancery Lane on the Central line.

Tottenham Court Road on the Northern and Central lines is best for the British Museum.

Once you're in Bloomsbury, you can easily get around on foot.

MAKING THE MOST OF YOUR TIME

If you plan to visit the Inns of Court as well as the British Museum, and you'd like to get a feel for the neighborhood, then devote an entire day to this literary and legal enclave.

An alternative scenario is to set aside a separate day for a visit to the British Museum, which can easily consume as many hours as you have to spare.

It's a pleasure to wander through the leafy squares at your leisure, examining historic Blue Plaques or relaxing at a street-side café. The students in the neighborhood add a bit of street life.

5

With the British Library, the British Museum, and countless colleges of the University of London among its residents, Bloomsbury might appear all bookish and cerebral—but fear not, it's much more than that. There's a youthfulness about its buzzing thoroughfares, and this vitality extends from down-by-the-Thames Holborn—once Dickens territory, now the heartbeat of legal London—way up to revamped King's Cross and classy Islington to the north, and cool Clerkenwell out east

BLOOMSBURY

Updated By
James O'Neill

Fundamental to the region's spirit of open expression and scholarly debate is the legacy of the Bloomsbury Group, an elite corps of artists and writers who lived in this neighborhood during the first part of the 20th century. **Gordon Square** was at one point home to Virginia Woolf, John Maynard Keynes (both at No. 46), and Lytton Strachey (at No. 51). But perhaps the best-known square in Bloomsbury is the large, centrally located **Russell Square**, with its handsome gardens. Scattered around the **University of London** campus are Woburn Square, Torrington Square, and Tavistock Square. The **British Library,** with its vast treasures, is a few blocks north, across busy Euston Road.

Bloomsbury is bordered by Tottenham Court Road on the west, Euston Road on the north, Woburn Place (which becomes Southampton Row) on the east, and New Oxford Street on the south.

The area from Somerset House on the Strand, all the way up to Kingsway to the Euston Road, is known as London's **Museum Mile** for the myriad historic houses and museums that dot the area. **Charles Dickens Museum,** where the author wrote *Oliver Twist,* pays homage to the master, and artists' studios and design shops share space near the majestic **British Museum.** And guaranteed to raise a smile from the most blasé and footsore tourist is **Sir John Soane's Museum,** where the colorful collection reflects the eclectic interests of the namesake founder.

Bloomsbury's liveliness extends north to the exciting redevelopment of King's Cross—once the ugly sister of *all* ugly sisters, now fast becoming a cultural and foodie destination in its own right. Newly polished King's Cross merges seamlessly into upmarket Islington, with its bustling streets and elegant squares. Due south of Islington, and east of Bloomsbury, don't miss out on the charms of easygoing, fashionable Clerkenwell.

TOP ATTRACTIONS

FAMILY **British Library.** Once a part of the British Museum, the 18-million-volume collection of the British Library has had its own state-of-the-art home since 1997. The library's greatest treasures are on view to the general public: the Magna Carta, the Codex Sinaiticus (an ancient bible containing the oldest complete copy of the New Testament), Jane Austen's writings, and Shakespeare's First Folio. Musical manuscripts by G.F. Handel as well as Sir Paul McCartney are on display in the Sir John Ritblat Gallery. ⊠ *96 Euston Rd., Bloomsbury* ☎ *0330/333–1144* ⊕ *www.bl.uk* ✉ *Free, donations appreciated; charge for special exhibitions* ⊙ *Mon.–Thurs. 9:30–8, Fri. 9:30–6, Sat. 9:30–5, Sun. and public holidays 11–5* Ⓜ *Euston, Euston Sq., King's Cross St. Pancras.*

Fodor's Choice **British Museum.**
★ *See the highlighted listing in this chapter.*

Charles Dickens Museum. This is one of the few London houses Charles Dickens (1812–70) inhabited that is still standing, and it's the place where the master wrote *Oliver Twist* and *Nicholas Nickleby* and finished *Pickwick Papers.* The house looks exactly as it would have in Dickens's day, complete with first editions, letters, and a tall clerk's desk (Dickens wrote standing up). The museum also houses a shop and café. ⊠ *48 Doughty St., Bloomsbury* ☎ *020/7405–2127* ⊕ *www.dickensmuseum.com* ✉ *£8* ⊙ *Daily 10–5 (last admission 4)* Ⓜ *Chancery La., Russell Sq.*

Lamb's Conduit Street. If you think Bloomsbury is about all things intellectual, then think again. Lamb's Conduit Street, a pedestrianized street of gorgeous Georgian town houses nestled to the east of Russell Square, is building a reputation as one of the capital's most charming—and fashionable—shopping thoroughfares. Avail yourself to what the boutique shops have to offer, from fashion to ceramics, bookstores to jewelry, fine art to flowers; there's even an excellent run-by-locals food cooperative called The People's Supermarket. Alternatively, you could just window-shop your way down to **The Lamb—** a Victorian-era pub whose patrons have included Ted Hughes, Sylvia Plath, and Mr. Dickens himself. ⊠ *Lamb's Conduit St., Bloomsbury* Ⓜ *Russell Sq.*

The Lamb. Originally established in 1729 but largely rebuilt during the early 1900s, this is a beautifully preserved Victorian pub with an impressive roll call of past clients, including Charles Dickens who lived nearby. Note the frosted "snob screens" above the bar; these

Continued on page 106

THE BRITISH MUSEUM

Anybody writing about the British Museum had better have a large stack of superlatives close at hand: most, biggest, earliest, finest. This is the golden hoard of nearly three centuries of the Empire, the booty brought from Britain's far-flung colonies.

The first major pieces, among them the Rosetta Stone and the Parthenon Sculptures (Elgin Marbles), were "acquired" from the French, who "found" them in Egypt and Greece. The museum has since collected countless goodies of worldwide historical significance: the Black Obelisk, some of the Dead Sea Scrolls, the Lindow Man. And that only begins the list.

The British Museum is a vast space split into 94 galleries, generally divided by continent or period of history, with some areas spanning more than one level. There are marvels wherever you go, and—while we don't like to be pessimistic—it is, yes, impossible to fully appreciate everything in a day. So make the most of the tours, activity trails, and visitors guides that are available.

The following is a highly edited overview of the museum's greatest hits, organized by area. Pick one or two that

whet your appetite, then branch out from there, or spend two straight hours indulging in the company of a single favorite sculpture. There's no wrong way to experience the British Museum, just make sure you do!

✉ Great Russell St., Bloomsbury WC1

☎ 020/7323–8299

⊕ www.britishmuseum.org

🎟 Free; donations encouraged. Tickets for special exhibits vary in price.

🕙 Galleries (and Reading Room exhibition space): Sat.–Thurs. 10–5:30, Fri. 10–8:30. Great Court: Sat.–Thurs. 9–6, Fri. 9–8:30.

Ⓤ Russell Square, Holborn, Tottenham Court Rd.

(left) The Great Court
(top) *Cradle to Grave* by Pharmacopoeia

MUSEUM HIGHLIGHTS

Ancient Civilizations

The Rosetta Stone. Found in 1799 and carved in 196 BC by decree of Ptolemy V in Egyptian hieroglyphics, demotic, and Greek, it was this multilingual inscription that provided French Egyptologist Jean-François Champollion with the key to deciphering hieroglyphics. *Room 4.*

Colossal statue of Ramesses II. A member of the 19th dynasty (ca. 1270 BC), Ramesses II commissioned innumerable statues of himself—more than any other preceding or succeeding king. This one, a 7-ton likeness of his perfectly posed upper half, comes from his mortuary temple, the Ramesseum, in western Thebes. *Room 4.*

(top) Portland vase
(bottom) Colossal statue of Ramesses II

The Parthenon Sculptures. Perhaps these marvelous treasures of Greece shouldn't be here—but while the debate rages on, you can steal your own moment with the Elgin Marbles. Carved in about 440 BC, these graceful decorations are displayed along with an in-depth, high-tech exhibit of the Acropolis; the **handless, footless Dionysus** who used to recline along its east pediment is especially well known. *Room 18.*

Mausoleum of Halikarnassos. All that remains of this, one of the Seven Wonders of the Ancient World, is a fragmented form of the original "mausoleum," the 4th-century tomb of Maussollos, King of Karia. The highlight of this gallery is the marble forepart of the **colossal chariot horse from the** *quadriga. Room 21.*

The Egyptian mummies. Another short flight of stairs takes you to the museum's most popular galleries, especially beloved by children: the Roxie Walker Galleries of Egyptian Funerary Archaeology have a fascinating collection of relics from the Egyptian realm of the dead. In addition to real corpses, wrapped mummies, and mummy cases, there's a menagerie of animal companions and curious items that were buried alongside them. *Rooms 62–63.*

Portland Vase. Made in Italy from cameo glass at the turn of the first century, it is named after the Dukes of Portland, who owned it from 1785 to 1945. It is considered a technical masterpiece—opaque white mythological figures cut by a gem-cutter are set on cobalt-blue background. *Room 70.*

The **Enlightenment Gallery** should be visited purely for the fact that its antiquarian cases hold the contents of the British Museum's first collections—Sir Hans Sloane's natural-history loot, as well as that of Sir Joseph Banks, who acquired specimens of everything from giant shells to fossils to rare plants to exotic beasts during his voyage to the Pacific aboard Captain Cook's *Endeavour.* *Room 1.*

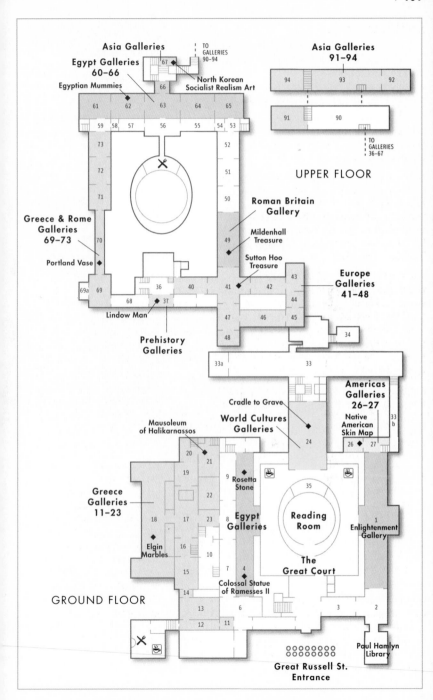

Asia Galleries

Egypt Galleries
60–66

Egyptian Mummies

TO GALLERIES 90–94

North Korean
Socialist Realism Art

Asia Galleries
91–94

UPPER FLOOR

Roman Britain
Gallery

Mildenhall
Treasure

Sutton Hoo
Treasure

Europe
Galleries
41–48

Greece & Rome
Galleries
69–73

Portland Vase

Lindow Man

Prehistory
Galleries

TO GALLERIES 36–67

Americas
Galleries
26–27

Native American
Skin Map

Cradle to Grave

World Cultures
Galleries

Mausoleum
of Halikarnassos

Greece
Galleries
11–23

Elgin
Marbles

Rosetta
Stone

Egypt
Galleries

Reading
Room

Enlightenment
Gallery

The
Great Court

Colossal Statue
of Ramesses II

GROUND FLOOR

Paul Hamlyn
Library

Great Russell St.
Entrance

Asia

The Korea Foundation Gallery. Delve into striking examples of **North Korean Socialist Realism art** from the 1950s to the present and a reconstruction of a **sarangbang,** a traditional scholar's study, complete with hanji paper walls and tea-making equipment. *Room 67.*

The Percival David Collection. More than 1400 pieces of Chinese ceramics (the most comprehensive collection outside China) are on display. *Room 95.*

World Cultures

The JP Morgan Chase North American Gallery. This is one of the largest collections of native culture outside North America, going back to the earliest hunters 10,000 years ago. Here a 1775 **native American skin map** serves as an example of the importance of such documents in the exploration and cartography of North America. Look for the beautifully displayed **native American costumes.** *Room 26.*

The Mexican Gallery. The most alluring pieces sit in this collection side by side: a 15th-century **turquoise mask of Xiuhtecuhtli,** the Mexican Fire God and Turquoise Lord, and a **double-headed serpent** from the same period. *Room 27.*

Britain and Europe

The Mildenhall Treasure. This glittering haul of 4th-century Roman silver tableware was found beneath the sod of a Suffolk field in 1942. *Room 49.*

The Sutton Hoo Treasure. Next door to the loot from Mildenhall—and equally splendid, including brooches, swords, and jewel-encrusted helmets—the treasure was buried at sea with (it is thought) Redwald, one of the first English kings, in the 7th century, and excavated from a Suffolk field in 1938–39. *Room 41.*

Lindow Man. "Pete Marsh"—so named by the archaeologists who unearthed the body from a Cheshire peat marsh—was ritually slain, probably as a human sacrifice, in the 1st century and lay perfectly pickled in his bog until 1984. *Room 50.*

Theme Galleries

Living & Dying. The "Cradle to Grave" installation pays homage to the British nation's wellbeing—or ill-being, as it were. More than 14,000 drugs (the number estimated to be prescribed to every person in the U.K. in his lifetime) are displayed in a colorful tapestry of pills and tablets. *Room 24.*

Colossal chariot horse from the *quadriga* of the Mausoleum at Halikarnassos

LOWER GALLERY

The three rooms that comprise the **Sainsbury African Galleries** are of the main interest here: together they present a staggering 200,000 objects, featuring intricate pieces of old ivory, gold, and wooden masks and carvings—highlighting such ancient kingdoms as the Benin and Asante. The displays include a collection of **55 throwing knives**; ceremonial garments including a dazzling pink and green **woman's coif** (*qufiya*) from Tunisia made of silk, metal, and cotton; and the *Oxford Man, a* 1992 woodcarving by Owen Ndou, depicting a man of ambiguous race clutching his Book of Knowledge.

DID YOU KNOW?

Galleries help divide this sprawling space into manageable sizes for visitors. The Sainsbury African Galleries are just some of the 94 galleries; the British Museum's collection totals more than 7 million objects.

THE NATION'S ATTIC: A HISTORY OF THE MUSEUM

The collection began when Sir Hans Sloane, physician to Queen Anne and George II, bequeathed his personal collection of curiosities and antiquities to the nation. The collection quickly grew, thanks to enthusiastic kleptomaniacs after the Napoleonic Wars—most notoriously the seventh Earl of Elgin, who obtained the marbles from the Parthenon and Erechtheion on the Acropolis in Athens during his term as British ambassador in Constantinople.

Soon thereafter, it seemed everyone had something to donate—George II gave the old Royal Library, Sir William Hamilton gave antique vases, Charles Townley gave sculptures, the Bank of England gave coins. When the first exhibition galleries opened to visitors in 1759, the trustees agreed to admit only small groups guided by curators. The British Museum quickly became one of the most fashionable places to be seen in the capital, and tickets, which had to be booked in advance, were treated like gold dust.

The museum's holdings quickly outgrew their original space in Montague House. After the addition of such major pieces as the Rosetta Stone and other Egyptian antiquities (spoils of the Napoleonic War) and the Parthenon sculptures, Robert Smirke was commissioned to build an appropriately large and monumental building on the same site. It's still a hot ticket: the British Museum now receives more than 5 million visitors every year.

THE GREAT COURT & THE READING ROOM

The museum's classical Greek-style facade features figures representing the progress of civilization, and the focal point is the awesome Great Court, a massive glass-roofed space. Here is the museum's inner courtyard (now the largest covered square in Europe) that, for more than 150 years, had been used for storage.

The 19th-century Reading Room, an impressive 106-foot-high blue-and-gold-domed library, forms the centerpiece of the Great Court. H.G. Wells, Thomas Hardy, Lord Tennyson, Oscar Wilde, George Orwell, T.S. Elliot, and Beatrix Potter are just a few writers who have used this space as a literary and academic sanctuary over the past 150 years or so. Temporary exhibitions here now include "Vikings: life and legend" and "Ming: 50 years that changed China."

(above) Reading Room

PLANNING YOUR VISIT

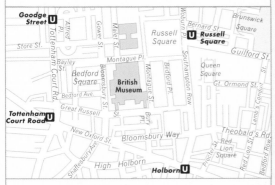

Tours

The **30–40 minute eyeOpener tour (free)** by Museum Guides does just what it says; ask for details at the information desk. After this tour, you can then dip back into the collections that most captured your imagination at your leisure.

An excellent **multimedia guide (£5)** is a good way to explore the galleries at your own pace, via a series of differently-themed tours.

Alternatively, the **Visitor's Guide (£3.50)** gives a brief but informative overview of the museum's history and is, again, divided into self-guided themed tours.

Before you go, take a look at the online **COMPASS tour** using the museum's navigation tool (www.thebritishmuseum.org/compass), which allows users to browse past and present exhibits as well as search for specific objects. A children's version can also be found here. Computer stations in the Reading Room offer onsite access to COMPASS.

■ TIP→ **The closest underground station to the British Museum is Russell Square on the Piccadilly line. However, since you will be entering via the back entrance on Montague Place, you will not experience the full impact of the museum's grand facade. To do so, alight at Holborn on the Central and Piccadilly lines or Tottenham Court Road on the Central and Northern lines. The walk from these stations is about 10 minutes.**

WITH KIDS

■ Take a look at the "Family Visits" page online for the top 12 objects to see with children.

■ The Families Desk in the Great Court has trails for kids ages 3 to 5 and 6 to 11. The Ford Centre for Young Visitors has free activity backpacks.

■ Art materials are available for free from information points, where you can also find out about workshops, performances, storytelling sessions, and other free events.

■ Around the museum, there are Hands On desks open daily 11–4, which let visitors handle objects from the collections.

WHERE TO REFUEL

The British Museum's self-service **Gallery Café** gets very crowded but serves an acceptable menu beneath a plaster cast of a part of the Parthenon frieze that Lord Elgin didn't remove. It's open daily, but isn't particularly family friendly.

The **café in the Great Court** keeps longer hours and is a great place to people-watch and admire the spectacular glass roof while you eat your salad and sandwich.

If the weather is nice, exit the museum via the back entrance on Montague Place and amble over to **Russell Square,** which has grassy lawns, water fountains, and a glass-fronted café for post-sandwich coffee and ice cream.

hinged panes of glass enabled the publican to serve up drinks without disturbing his customers' privacy. The kitchen serves tasty food. ✉ *94 Lamb's Conduit St., Bloomsbury* ☎ *020/7405–0713* ⊕ *www.youngs. co.uk/pubs/lamb* Ⓜ *Russell Sq.*

Fodor's Choice ★ **Sir John Soane's Museum.** Sir John (1753–1837), architect of the Bank of England, bequeathed his eccentric house to the nation on one condition: nothing be changed. It's a house full of surprises. In the Picture Room, two of Hogarth's famous *Rake's Progress* paintings swing away to reveal secret gallery recesses where you can find works by Canaletto and Turner. Everywhere, mirrors play tricks with light and space, and split-level floors worthy of a fairground funhouse disorient you. Ongoing restoration work, due to be completed by 2016, will see Soane's private apartments finally opened up to the public, as well as the catacombs in the basement. ✉ *13 Lincoln's Inn Fields, Bloomsbury* ☎ *020/7405–2107* ⊕ *www.soane.org* ✉ *Free; tours £10* ⊙ *Tues.–Sat. 10–5; also 6–9 on 1st Tues. of month* Ⓜ *Holborn.*

> ### KING'S CROSS STATION
>
> Sick of living in the shadow of its sumptuously renovated next-door neighbor, St. Pancras station, King's Cross—and the area behind it—has undergone a major makeover of its own, with bars, restaurants, shops, cultural venues, and a stunning fountain display for all to enjoy. It's also a place dear to Harry Potter fans everywhere, because it was from the imaginary platform 9¾ that our hero boarded *Hogwarts Express* (the station has helpfully put up a sign for platform 9¾ if you want to take a picture there).

WORTH NOTING

Lincoln's Inn. There's plenty to see at one of the oldest, best preserved, and most attractive of the Inns of Court—from the Chancery Lane Tudor brick gatehouse to the wide-open, tree-lined, atmospheric Lincoln's Inn Fields and the 15th-century chapel remodeled by Inigo Jones in 1620. The chapel and the gardens are open to the public, but to see more you must prebook a place on one of the official tours. But be warned: they tend to prefer group bookings of 15 or more, so it's best to check the website or call for details and note that there are no tours at weekends or in August. ✉ *Chancery La., Bloomsbury* ☎ *020/7405–1393* ⊕ *www. lincolnsinn.org.uk* ✉ *Free* ⊙ *Gardens weekdays 7–7; chapel weekdays 9–5* Ⓜ *Chancery La.*

Royal Courts of Justice. Here is the vast Victorian Gothic pile of 35 million bricks containing the nation's principal law courts, with 1,000-odd rooms running off 3½ miles of corridors. This is where the most important civil law cases—that's everything from divorce to fraud, with libel in between—are heard. You can sit in the viewing gallery to watch any trial you like, for a live version of Court TV. The more dramatic criminal cases are heard at the Old Bailey. Other sights are the 238-foot-long main hall and the compact exhibition of judges' robes. Guided tours must be booked in advance. ✉ *The Strand, Bloomsbury* ☎ *020/7947– 6000, 07789/751–248 tour reservations* ⊕ *www.hmcourts-service.gov.*

uk (search for Royal Courts of Justice in A–Z option) ✉ *Free; tours £12* ⊙ *Weekdays 9–4:30* Ⓜ *Temple, Holborn, Chancery La.*

Temple Church. As featured in *The Da Vinci Code* , this church was built by the Knights Templar in the late 12th century. The Red Knights held their secret initiation rites in the crypt here. Having started poor, holy, and dedicated to the protection of pilgrims, they grew rich from showers of royal gifts until, in the 14th century, they were stripped of their wealth, charged with blasphemy and sodomy, and thrown into the Tower. So it goes. ✉ *King's Bench Walk, The Temple, Bloomsbury* ☎ *020/7353–3470* ⊕ *www.templechurch.com* ✉ *£4* ⊙ *Generally weekdays 10–2 but check website beforehand* Ⓜ *Temple.*

University College London. Founded in 1826 the college is set in a classical edifice designed by the architect of the National Gallery, William Wilkins. Committed to providing higher education without religious exclusion, in 1878 it also became the first British University to accept women on an equal footing with men. The college has within its portals the **Slade School of Fine Art,** which did for many of Britain's artists what the nearby Royal Academy of Dramatic Art (on Gower Street) did for actors. The South Cloisters contain one of London's weirder treasures: the skeleton of one of the university's founders, Jeremy Bentham, who bequeathed himself to the college. ✉ *Malet Pl., Bloomsbury* Ⓜ *Euston Sq., Goodge St.*

Petrie Museum. If you didn't get your fill of Egyptian artifacts at the British Museum, you can see more in the neighboring Petrie Museum, located on the first floor of the DMS Watson library. The museum houses an outstanding collection of Egyptian and Sudanese archaeological objects—jewelry, toys, and some of the world's oldest garments. ✉ *Malet Pl.* ☎ *020/7679–2884* ⊕ *www.ucl.ac.uk/museums/ petrie* ✉ *Free, donations appreciated* ⊙ *Tues.–Sat. 1–5; closed over Christmas and Easter holidays.*

**OFF THE
BEATEN
PATH**

London Canal Museum. This quirky little museum, dedicated to the rise and fall of London's once-extensive canal network, is based in the former warehouse of ice-cream maker Carlo Gatti (hence it also partly features the ice-cream trade as well as London's canals). Children enjoy the activity zone and learning about Henrietta, the museum's horse. Outside, on the Battlebridge Basin, float in the painted narrowboats of modern canal dwellers—a stone's throw from the hustle and bustle of the King's Cross redevelopment. You can walk to the museum along the towpath from Camden Lock—download a free audio tour from the museum's website to accompany the route. ✉ *12–13 New Wharf Rd., King's Cross* ☎ *020/7713–0836* ⊕ *www.canalmuseum.org.uk* ✉ *£4* ⊙ *Tues.–Sun. and bank holiday Mon. 10–4:30; last admission 30 mins before closing. First Thurs. in month open until 7:30.* ⊙ *Closed Dec. 23–Jan. 1* Ⓜ *King's Cross.*

HOLBORN

Southeast of Bloomsbury and west of The City, Holborn may appear to be little more than a buffer zone between the two—but although it may lack the panache of its neighbors, don't underestimate this varied slice of the capital. Home to legal London and the impressive Inns of Court, this is also Charles Dickens territory, with the Old Curiosity Shop snug within its borders and the Dickens museum close by (*see listing above*). Add to that its fair share of churches and quirky places of interest, and you'll soon discover that Holborn can be a rewarding place to while away an hour or three. Holborn's massive Gothic-style **Royal Courts of Justice** ramble all the way to the Strand, and the **Inns of Court — Gray's Inn, Lincoln's Inn, Middle Temple,** and **Inner Temple** —are where most British trial lawyers have offices to this day. Geographically, Holborn is probably best defined as: west, Kingsway; north, Theobald's Road; east, Gray's Inn Road; south, where the Strand becomes Fleet Street.

WORTH NOTING

Gray's Inn. Although the least architecturally interesting of the four Inns of Court and the one most damaged by German bombs in the 1940s, Gray's still has romantic associations. In 1594 Shakespeare's *Comedy of Errors* was performed for the first time in the hall—which was restored after World War II and has a fine Elizabethan screen of carved oak. You must make advance arrangements to view the hall, but the secluded and spacious gardens, first planted by Francis Bacon in 1597, are open to the public. The four Inn's of the Court—Gray's Inn, Lincoln's Inn, Middle Temple, and Inner Temple—are where most British trial lawyers have office to this day. In the 14th century, the inns were lodging houses where the barristers lived so that people would know how to easily find them (hence, the label "inn"). ✉ *Gray's Inn Rd., Holborn* ☎ *020/7458–7800* ⊕ *www.graysinn.org.uk* ✆ *Free* ☉ *Weekdays noon–2:30* Ⓜ *Holborn, Chancery La.*

ISLINGTON

Islington is one of the most fashionable of London's village-like neighborhoods. Upper Street, with its high-street stores, independent boutiques, and myriad restaurants and bars, is where most of the action takes place. But wander off the main drag and you'll discover elegant residential streets and squares, as well as bustling charming markets. You'll also find a handful of topflight Off West End theaters and music venues in the area, including the Almeida, the hugely atmospheric Union Chapel, and—down on Islington's border with Clerkenwell—the renowned contemporary dance venue, Sadler's Wells.

Camden Passage. A pretty pedestrian thoroughfare just off Upper Street, Camden Passage is famous for its many antiques shops selling everything from vintage furniture to period jewelry to timeless timepieces. In recent years, a sprinkling of independent boutiques, delis, and cafés has given the passage an eclectic, vibrant feel. Check out the antiques market held on Wednesday and Saturday mornings. ⊠ *Camden Passage, Islington* Ⓜ *The Angel.*

Chapel Market. Chapel Market is what Islington used to be: an unpretentious, working-class enclave. There's a lively food market that runs for half the length of the street every day except Monday—just listening to the stallholders advertising their wares can be entertainment enough. Although trendy eateries are beginning to pop up here and there, it is still home to London's oldest eel, pie, and mash shop, Manze's, with its marble tables and tiled interior largely untouched since its establishment in 1902. ⊠ *Chapel Market, Islington* Ⓜ *The Angel.*

KING'S CROSS

What a difference a decade makes! Until recently King's Cross was a byword for sleaze and street crime, but after a multibillion-pound redevelopment—actually, make that transformation—it's become a lively new urban quarter. On what was once postindustrial wasteland and railway yards, the 67-acre site is now home to bars, restaurants, street-food vendors, and shops. What's more, with the capital's premier art college—the University of the Arts in London—having relocated to Granary Square, alongside a raft of cultural venues, this former urban black-spot now has a certain artistic credibility about it, too. If all that weren't enough, by courtesy of the Regent's Canal, this bustling quarter even has the occasional splendid oasis of calm as well.

Camley Street Natural Park. These 2 acres of splendid calm are slap-bang in the middle of the King's Cross hustle and bustle. This urban nature reserve, just across the road from the concrete and glass of the Eurostar terminal, provides a habitat for birds, butterflies, bats, and a wide variety of plant and pond life. It's a delightful gem that's popular with schoolchildren and office workers on lunch break, but chances are you could have the whole place pretty much to yourself! ⊠ *12 Camley St., King's Cross* ☎ *020/7833–2311* ⊕ *www.wildlondon.org.uk/reserves/camley-street-natural-park* ☉ *Summer, daily 10–5; winter, daily 10–4* Ⓜ *King's Cross-St. Pancras.*

Granary Square. The heart of the new King's Cross, Granary Square is London's liveliest open space. Pride of place is the ever-changing 1,000-strong fountain display, which is even more spectacular by night when lights accompany the choreography. The immense, six-story granary building—designed in 1852 to store wheat for London's bakers—has been renovated to house the University of the Arts in London (parts of which are open to the public), as well as a selection of excellent eateries. The square's south-facing steps double as an amphitheater for site-specific arts events; at times, the steps themselves *become* the installation—such as when they're lined with pumpkins at Halloween or green grass in summer. ⊠ *Granary Sq., King's Cross* Ⓜ *King's Cross-St. Pancras.*

CLERKENWELL

Once home to medieval religious orders such as the Knights of the Hospitallers of St. John of Jerusalem, Clerkenwell later became an epicenter of the industrial revolution in the capital and, subsequently, of political radicalism (a young Joseph Stalin is said to have met a young Vladimir Lenin at the Crown Tavern pub in Clerkenwell Green). The monks are long gone, so, too, the communists, and the neighborhood's warehouses and factory floors are now home to cutting-edge design agencies, new media start-ups, and übertrendy apartments. With its fashionable boutiques, bars, and restaurants, Clerkenwell can be a pleasant place to spend an hour, or three. Like its neighbor immediately to its east—the City of London—the area can be quite deserted on weekends.

Exmouth Market. A pedestrianized thoroughfare of trendy independent stores and eateries, all with one thing in common: understated quality. Music stores, bookshops, and gift shops jostle for space with Exmouth Market's highly regarded cafés and restaurants, many of which offer outdoor seating. At its southern end is the 19th-century Church of Our Most Holy Redeemer, the only Italian basilica-style church in London. There's an excellent food market on weekdays serving gourmet street food. ⊠ *Exmouth St., Clerkenwell* Ⓜ *Farringdon, The Angel.*

Museum of the Order of St. John. This fascinating museum tells the story of the Knights Hospitallers of St. John, from the Order's 11th-century Crusader origins in Jerusalem to its present-day incarnation as the St. John Ambulance service. The museum is spread across two adjacent sites: the arched St. John's Gatehouse, which dates back to 1504, and the Priory Church with its atmospheric Norman crypt. An excellent interactive display explores the Order's past as both as military force and a religious institution, which cared for sick pilgrims, and the eclectic variety of objects on display reflects that colorful history: from antique medicinal jars and medical equipment to pieces of armor worn by the Knights when they defended Malta from the Ottomans in the 16th century, as well as a bronze cannon given by Henry VIII before he dissolved the Order altogether a few years later. ⊠ *St. John's Gate, St. John's La., Clerkenwell* ☎ *020/7324–4005* ⊕ *www.museumstjohn.org. uk* 🖃 *Free; for guided tours, a suggested donation of £5* ⊙ *Mon.–Sat. 10–5; guided tours on Tues., Fri., and Sat. 11 am and 2:30 pm (see website for details)* Ⓜ *Farringdon.*

6

THE CITY

GETTING ORIENTED

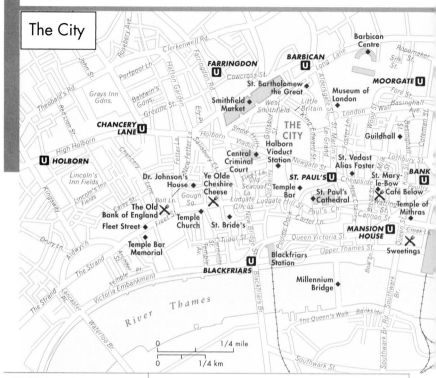

The City

The City area is well served by a concentrated selection of Tube stations—St. Paul's and Bank are on the Central line, and Mansion House, Cannon Street, and Monument are on the District and Circle lines. Liverpool Street and Aldgate border The City's eastern edge, while Chancery Lane and Farringdon lie to the west. Barbican and Moorgate provide easy access to the theaters and galleries of the Barbican, and Blackfriars, to the south, leads to Ludgate Circus and Fleet Street.

St. Paul's Cathedral, the "Symbolic Heart of London": Now increasingly crowded by skyscrapers, St. Paul's still manages to dominate the skyline. Once inside, you'll see the beauty of this 17th-century masterpiece of Sir Christopher Wren.

Linger on the Millennium Bridge: Hurtle across centuries with this promenade between Tate Modern and St. Paul's—and get a great river view, too.

Treachery and treasures at the Tower: This mini-city of melodramatic towers is stuffed to bursting with history, pageantry, and the stunning Crown Jewels (bring sunglasses).

Channel history at the Museum of London: A Roman leather bikini and Queen Victoria's crinoline gowns; Selfridges's art deco elevators and a diorama of the Great Fire (sound effects! flickering flames!)—this gem of a museum's got it all.

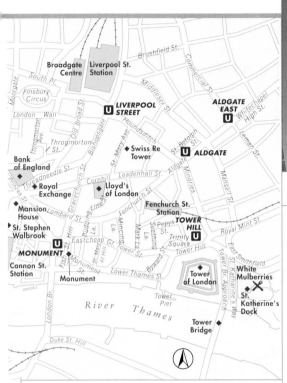

MAKING THE MOST OF YOUR TIME

The "Square Mile" is as compact as the nickname suggests, with little distance between points of interest, making an afternoon stroll a rewarding experience. For full immersion in the Tower of London, however, set aside half a day, especially if seeing the Crown Jewels is a priority. Allow an hour minimum each for the Museum of London, St. Paul's Cathedral, and Tower Bridge. On weekends, without the scurrying suits, The City is nearly deserted, making it hard to find lunch—and yet this is when the major attractions are at their busiest.

A GOOD WALK

Crossing the Millennium Bridge from Tate Modern to St. Paul's is one of the finest walks in London—with the river to either side and Christopher Wren's iconic dome towering at one end. Dubbed the "blade of light," the shiny aluminum-and-steel bridge was the result of a collaboration between architect Norman Foster and sculptor Anthony Caro.

FEELING PECKISH?

The Old Bank of England. It's fun for locals to give directions to this grand pub next to the Royal Courts of Justice on Fleet Street—you just tell people to look for the place with the flaming torches next to the statue of a dragon. They serve hearty pub food—try one of the tasty pies. ✉ *194 Fleet St., The City* ☎ *020/7430–2255* ⊕ *www.oldbankofengland. co.uk* Ⓜ *Temple.*

White Mulberries. This friendly coffee shop at St. Katharine Docks serves an outstanding cup of joe, and tasty cakes, and light bites. ✉ *D3 Ivory House, St. Katharine Docks, The City* ☎ *07507/572600* ⊕ *www.whitemulberries.com* ⊗ *Weekdays 7:30–5, Sat. 8–5, Sun. 9–5* Ⓜ *Tower Hill; Tower Gateway (DLR).*

Ye Olde Cheshire Cheese. This wonderfully higgledy-piggledy, multilevel inn on Fleet Street was built in 1667, but the basement bar is centuries older, making this possibly London's oldest pub. It's closed on Sunday. ✉ *145 Fleet St., The City* ☎ *020/7353–6170* Ⓜ *St. Paul's.*

Sightseeing
★★★★★
Nightlife
★
Dining
★★★
Lodging
★
Shopping
★★★

The City is the capital's fast-beating financial heart, with a powerful architectural triumvirate at its epicenter: the Bank of England, the Royal Exchange, and Mansion House. The "Square Mile" also has historic currency, as the place where London began. St. Paul's Cathedral has been looking after Londoners' souls for hundreds of years, and the Tower of London—a royal fortress, prison, and jewel house surrounded by a moat—has occasionally taken care of their heads.

Updated By
Jack Jewers

The City is a dizzying juxtaposition of the old and the new. You'll find yourself immersed in historic London if you begin your explorations on **Fleet Street,** the site of England's first printing press and the undisputed seat of British journalism until the 1980s. Nestled behind Fleet Street is **Dr. Johnson's House,** former home of the author of *A Dictionary of the English Language,* who claimed that "when a man is tired of London, he is tired of life." The nearby church of **St. Bride's,** recognizable by its tiered-wedding-cake steeple, is a Sir Christopher Wren gem and still the church for journalists, while eastward rises the iconic **St. Paul's Cathedral,** also designed by Wren and largely considered the architect's masterpiece. You'll encounter more of traditional London at the **Central Criminal Court** (nicknamed **The Old Bailey,** and home to London's most sensational criminal trials) and the 800-year-old **Smithfield Market,** whose Victorian halls are the site of a daily early-morning meat market. Nearby are the ancient church of **St. Bartholomew the Great** and **St. Bartholomew Hospital,** both begun in 1123; the **Guildhall,** the site of the only Roman amphitheater in London; the church of **St. Mary-le-Bow;** and the maze of charmingly old-fashioned, narrow streets around **Bow Lane.**

You can put all this history into context at the **Museum of London,** where archaeological displays include a portion of the original **Roman Wall** that ringed The City.

Just beyond rises the modern **Barbican Centre,** a concrete complex of arts venues and apartments that was controversial at the time it was built, but now has become an indispensable part of the London landscape. The sight of several new structures rising above The City—most famously the **Lloyd's of London Building** and the **Swiss Re Tower,** popularly known as "the Gherkin"—may or may not be more reassuring.

The **Monument,** near the banks of the Thames, was built to commemorate the Great Fire of London of 1666. From here, the river leads to one of London's most absorbing and bloody attractions, the **Tower of London. Tower Bridge** is a suitably giddying finale to an exploration of this fascinating part of London.

There is another reason that makes The City such an intriguing place to visit at the moment: with the constant building of new skyscrapers in the financial district, the ancient skyline is changing at a rapid pace. Cross the Thames anywhere from Waterloo to Tower Bridge and half the people you'll see taking in the view are probably Londoners, paused to wonder in astonishment as yet another glass-and-steel monolith seems to have popped up since last week. You could leave years between your visits, or merely months; either way The City will never be the same as when you saw it last.

TOP ATTRACTIONS

FAMILY **Monument.** Commemorating the "dreadful visitation" of the Great Fire of London, in 1666, this huge stone column stands both 202 feet tall and exactly 202 feet from Farrier's baking house in Pudding Lane, where the fire started. (Note the gilded orb of fire at the column's pinnacle.) It was designed by Sir Christopher Wren and Dr. Robert Hooke, who were asked to erect it "on or as neere unto the place where the said Fire soe unhappily began as conveniently may be." The view of The City from the viewing platform at the top is spectacular, but if climbing the 311 steps seems too arduous, you can watch a live view relayed on a screen at the entrance. ⊠ *Monument St., The City* ☎ *020/7626–2717* ⊕ *www.themonument.info* 🎫*£4; combined ticket with Tower Bridge £10.50* ⊙ *Apr.–Sept., daily 9:30–6; Oct.–Mar., daily 9:30–5:30; last admission 30 mins before closing* Ⓜ *Monument.*

FAMILY **Museum of London.** If there's one place to absorb the history of London,
Fodor'sChoice from 450,000 BC to the present day, it's here. There are 7,000 objects
★ to wonder at in all, including Oliver Cromwell's death mask, Queen Victoria's crinoline gowns, Selfridges's art deco elevators, and an original door from the infamous Newgate Prison. The collection devoted to Roman London contains some extraordinary gems, including an astonishingly well-preserved floor mosaic uncovered just a few streets away. (Appropriately enough the museum itself shelters a section of the 2nd- to 4th-century London wall, which you can view through a window.) Permanent displays highlight prehistoric, medieval, and Tudor London. The Galleries of Modern London are equally enthralling: experience the "Expanding City," "People's City," and "World City," each gallery dealing with a section of London's history from 1666 until the 21st century. Innovative interactive displays abound, and there's also a

A BRIEF HISTORY

Although there is evidence of Celtic habitation on the north bank of the Thames, in many ways London begins with the Romans, who established the settlement of Londinium in AD 47 as an outpost of the Empire (before those pesky Celts, led by Queen Boudicca, returned and burned it to the ground 17 years later). The Saxons came and stayed for a while, as did the Vikings, and by the time the Normans turned up in the 11th century and declared it the capital of England, London was already established as the most important city in the realm. William the Conqueror began building the palace that was to become the Tower of London, which by Tudor times was known as the world's most forbidding prison, and where two of Henry VIII's six wives were executed. During the Middle Ages, powerful guilds that nurtured commerce took root in the capital, followed by the foundation of great trading companies, such as the Honourable East India Company, which started up in 1600.

London's history has often been one of disaster and renewal. The Great Fire of 1666 spared only a few of the cramped, labyrinthine streets where the Great Plague had delivered such devastation the previous year. Yet the gutted wastelands ushered in an era of architectural renaissance, led by Sir Christopher Wren. Further punishment would come during the Blitz of World War II, when German bombers destroyed many buildings—but yet again London rebounded. As it likely always will.

fine schedule of temporary exhibitions. Meanwhile, locals are waiting with bated breath for the display of an extraordinary hoard of artifacts, including some from the Bronze Age and Roman periods, which were uncovered during the building of the Crossrail Underground railway. Check the website for details about the fantastic **Street Museum** app, which allows you to hold up your phone in many London streets and be shown pictures of how things looked in the past. ⊠ *London Wall, The City* ☎ *020/7001–9844* ⊕ *www.museumoflondon.org.uk* 🎟 *Free* ⊙ *Daily 10–6; last admission 5:30; galleries start to close 5:40* Ⓜ *Barbican, St. Paul's.*

Fodor's Choice
★

St. Paul's Cathedral.
See the highlighted listing in this chapter.

FAMILY
Fodor's Choice
★

Tower Bridge. Despite its medieval, fairy-tale appearance, Britain's most iconic bridge was actually built at the tail end of the Victorian age, first opening to traffic in 1894. Constructed of steel, then clothed in Portland stone, the Horace Jones masterpiece was built in the Gothic style that was highly popular at the time (and it nicely complements the Tower of London, next door). The bridge is famous for its enormous bascules—the 1,200-ton "arms" that open to allow large ships to glide beneath. This still happens a few times per month (the website lists upcoming times), but when river traffic was dense, the bascules were raised about five times a day.

The **Tower Bridge Exhibition** is a family-friendly tour where you can discover how the bridge actually works before heading out onto the

Continued on page 124

ST. PAUL'S CATHEDRAL

Sir Christopher Wren's maxim "I build for eternity" proves no empty boast.

Sublime, awesome, majestic, and inspirational are just some of the words to describe Wren's masterpiece, St. Paul's Cathedral—and thanks to a painstaking, recently-completed 15-year restoration project, it's now looking better than ever.

This is the spiritual heart of the nation, where people and events are celebrated, mourned, and honored. As you approach the cathedral your eyes are inevitably drawn skyward to the great dome, one of the largest in the world and an amazing piece of engineering. Visit in the late afternoon for evensong, and let the choir's voices transport you to a world of absolute peace in a place of perfect beauty, as pristine as the day it was completed.

TOURING ST. PAUL'S

Enter the cathedral via the main west entrance, and walk straight down the length of the nave to the central Dome Altar. Nobody can resist making a beeline for the dome, so start your tour beneath it, standing dead center on the beautiful sunburst floor, Wren's focal mirror of the magnificent design above. A simple quotation marks the floor "Lector si momentum requiris, circumspice" (Reader if you seek his monument, look around). The dome crowns the center of the cathedral and rises to 364 feet—but save your strength for the "great climb" to get some fantastic views.

THE CATHEDRAL FLOOR

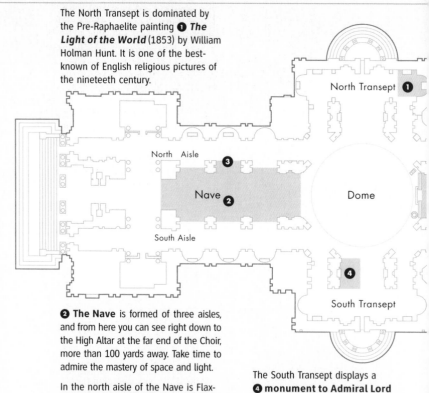

The North Transept is dominated by the Pre-Raphaelite painting ❶ *The Light of the World* (1853) by William Holman Hunt. It is one of the best-known of English religious pictures of the nineteeth century.

North Transept ❶

North Aisle

❸

Nave ❷

Dome

South Aisle

❹

South Transept

❷ **The Nave** is formed of three aisles, and from here you can see right down to the High Altar at the far end of the Choir, more than 100 yards away. Take time to admire the mastery of space and light.

In the north aisle of the Nave is Flaxman's grandiose ❸ **monument to the Duke of Wellington,** who sits astride his faithful charger, Copenhagen, the horse that carried him through the Battle of Waterloo.

The South Transept displays a ❹ **monument to Admiral Lord Nelson,** Britain's favorite naval hero, with an anchor. Other memorials commemorate the explorer Captain Robert Scott and the darling of British landscape painting J.M.W. Turner.

CELEBRITY STATUS

St. Paul's has witnessed many momentous processions along its checkered nave. The somber state funerals of heroes Admiral Lord Nelson and the Duke of Wellington, and of Sir Winston Churchill, drew huge crowds. It was here, also, that the fairy-tale wedding of Prince Charles and Lady Diana Spencer took place, and the jubilees of Queen Victoria, George V, and the present Queen were celebrated.

The North Choir Aisle features the beautiful ❺ **gilded gates** by Jean Tijou, perhaps the most accomplished artist in wrought iron of all time, as well as Henry Moore's sculpture ❻ *Mother and Child,* its simple lines complementing the ornate surroundings.

The Choir contains the ❽ **Bishop's Throne** or cathedra, hence the name cathedral. Look aloft to the fabulous mosaics. Don't miss the exquisite, delicate carvings by Grinling Gibbons, in particular on the case of the ❾ **grand organ,** one of the Cathedral's greatest artifacts. It was designed by Wren and played by such illustrious figures as Handel and Mendelssohn.

❿ **The High Altar,** with its glorious canopy, is a profusion of marble and carved and gilded oak.

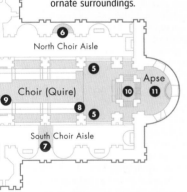

North Choir Aisle

Choir (Quire)

Apse

South Choir Aisle

The Apse is home to the ⓫ **American Memorial Chapel,** which honors the more than 28,000 U.S. soldiers who died while stationed in the U.K. during World War II. The lime-wood paneling incorporates a rocket as a tribute to the United States' achievements in space.

The South Choir Aisle contains a ❼ **marble effigy of poet John Donne,** who was Dean of old St. Paul's for his final 10 years (he died in 1631). This is the only statue to have survived the Great Fire of London intact. You can see the scorch marks at the base of the statue.

MUSICAL FRICTION

The organ, with its cherubs and angels, was not installed without controversy. The mighty instrument proved a tight fit, and the maker, known as Father Schmidt, and Wren nearly came to blows. Wren was reputed to have said he would not adapt his cathedral for a mere "box of whistles."

THE DOME

The dome is the crowning glory of the cathedral, a must for visitors.

At 99 feet, the **❶ Whispering Gallery** is reached by 259 spiral steps. This is the part of the cathedral with which you bribe children—they will be fascinated by the acoustic phenomenon: whisper something to the wall on one side, and a second later it transmits clearly to the other side, 107 feet away. The only problem is identifying your whisper from the cacophony of everyone else's. Look down onto the nave from here and up to the monochrome frescoes of St. Paul by Sir James Thornhill.

More stamina is required to reach the **❷ Stone Gallery,** at 173 feet and 378 steps from ground level. It is on the exterior of the cathedral and offers a vista of the city and the River Thames.

For the best views of all—at 280 feet and 530 steps from ground level—make the trek to the small **❸ Golden Gallery,** the highest point of the outer dome. A hole in the floor gives a vertiginous view down. You can see the lantern above through a circular opening called the oculus. If you have a head for heights you can walk outside for a spectacular panorama of London.

The top of the dome is crowned with a **❹ ball and cross.** At 23 feet high and weighing approximately 7 tons, it is the pinnacle of St. Paul's.

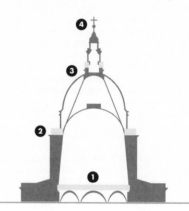

A BRIEF HISTORY

The cathedral is the masterpiece of Sir Christopher Wren (1632–1723), completed in 1710 after 35 years of building and much argument with the Royal Commission. Wren had originally been commissioned to restore Old St. Paul's, the Norman cathedral that had replaced, in its turn, three earlier versions, but the Great Fire left so little of it standing that a new cathedral was deemed necessary.

Wren's first plan, known as the New Model, did not make it past the drawing board; the second, known as the Great Model, got as far as the 20-foot oak rendering you can see here today before it, too, was rejected, whereupon Wren is said to have burst into tears. The third, however, known as the Warrant Design (because it received the royal warrant), was accepted, with the fortunate coda that the architect

be allowed to make changes as he saw fit. Without that, there would be no dome, because the approved design had featured a steeple. Parliament felt that building was proceeding too slowly (in fact, 35 years is lightning speed, as cathedrals go) and withheld half of Wren's pay for the last 13 years of work. He was pushing 80 when Queen Anne finally coughed up the arrears.

■TIP→ **To see Wren's Great Model, you must join a Triforium Tour, held Monday, Tuesday, and Friday. These one-hour tours include a visit to the library and a glimpse of the famous Geometric staircase. The visit ends in the Trophy Room, where Wren's Great Model is on display. The tour costs £8 (in addition to admission to the Cathedral). It's best to book in advance by calling ☎ 020/7246–8357 or sending an e-mail to admissions@stpaulscathedral.org.uk.**

THE CRYPT

A visit to the vast crypt is a time for re-flection and contemplation, with some 200 memorials to see. If it all becomes too somber, take solace in the café or shop near the crypt entrance.

Here lies ❶ **Admiral Nelson,** killed at the Battle of Trafalgar in 1805. His body was preserved in alcohol for the journey home, and his pickled remains were buried here beneath Cardinal Wolsey's unused 16th-century sarcophagus.

The ❷ **tomb of the Duke of Wellington** comprises a simple casket made from Cornish granite. He is remembered as a hero of battle, but his name lives on in the form of boots, cigars, beef Wellington, and the capital of New Zealand.

Surrounded by his family and close to a plethora of iconic artists, musicians, and scientists, the ❸ **tomb of Sir Christopher Wren** is a modest simple slab.

The beautiful ❹ **O.B.E. Chapel** (dedicated 1960) is a symbol of the Order of the British Empire, an order of chivalry established in 1917 by George V. The theme of sovereign and Commonwealth is represented in the glass panels.

The vast ❺ **treasury** houses the cathedral's plate, although a good deal has been lost or stolen over the centuries—in particular in a daring robbery of 1810—and much of the display comes from other London churches.

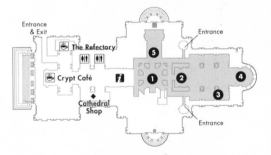

PLANNING YOUR DAY

WHAT'S NEARBY: Stroll over the Millennium Bridge (look back for a great view of St. Paul's) and have lunch at Tate Modern. The restaurant at the top of the gallery has spectacular views of London. ■ TIP➜ To avoid lines visit early in the morning. For a different experience return for Evensong at 5 pm.

CONTACT INFO: ✉ *St. Paul's Churchyard, Ludgate Hill EC4 8AD* ☎ *020/7246–8350* ⊕ *www.stpauls.co.uk* Ⓤ *St. Paul's.*

ADMISSION: Adults: cathedral, crypt, ambulatory, and gallery £18 (includes multimedia guides and guided tours). **Family ticket** (2

adults, 2 children): £44. **Children:** £8.

TOURS: A guided tour of the cathedral, choir, Geometric staircase, and crypt lasts 1½–2 hours and is included in the price of admission (as are the multimedia guides). Tours start at 10, 11, 1, and 2.

HOURS: The cathedral is a house of worship. Services may cause changes to the visiting hours on any given day, so be sure to call ahead.

Cathedral: Mon.–Sat. 8:30–4.
Shop: Mon., Tues., Thurs.–Sat. 8:30–5, Wed. 9–5, Sun. 10–4:30.
Crypt café: Mon.–Sat. 9–5, Sun. 10–4.

walkways for wonderful city views. First, take in the romance of the panoramas from the east and west walkways between those grand turrets. On the east are the modern superstructures of the Docklands, and on the west is the Tower of London, St. Paul's, the Monument, and the misshapen steel-and-glass egg that is Greater London Assembly's City Hall (memorably described as "a glass testicle" by former mayor Ken Livingstone).

> ### A VIEW TO REMEMBER
>
> At the top of the Monument's 311-step spiral staircase (think of it as the trip to the gym you didn't make that day) is a gallery providing fantastic views from the heart of The City. It is helpfully caged to prevent suicide attempts, which were a trend for a while in the 19th century.

Then it's back down to explore the Victorian engine rooms and discover the inner workings, which you learn about through hands-on displays and films. ⊠ *Tower Bridge Rd., The City* ☎ *020/7403–3761* ⊕ *www. towerbridge.org.uk* ▣ *£9* ⊙ *Apr.–Sept., daily 10–5:30; Oct.–Mar., daily 9:30; last admission 30 mins before closing* Ⓜ *Tower Hill.*

Fodor's Choice   **Tower of London.**
★   *See the highlighted listing in this chapter.*

WORTH NOTING

Bank of England. The United Kingdom's main bank has been central to the British economy since 1694. Known for the past couple of centuries as "the Old Lady of Threadneedle Street," after the name appeared in a caption to a political cartoon (which can be seen in the museum), the bank manages the national debt and the foreign exchange reserves, issues banknotes, sets interest rates, looks after England's gold, and regulates the country's banking system. Sir John Soane designed the neoclassical hulk in 1788, wrapping it in windowless walls, which are all that survives of his original building. The bank's history is traced in the surprisingly varied Bank of England Museum (the entrance is around the corner on Bartholomew Lane). In addition to the bank's original Royal Charter, there's a lively program of special exhibitions, plus interactive displays (try your hand at controlling inflation!). Still, most visitors make a beeline for the solid-gold bar that can be stroked and held in the central trading hall—before you get any ideas, there's security everywhere. ⊠ *Threadneedle St., The City* ☎ *020/7601–4878* ⊕ *www.bankofengland.co.uk* ▣ *Free* ⊙ *Weekdays 10–5; last admission 4:45* Ⓜ *Bank, Monument.*

Dr. Johnson's House. Built in 1700, this elegant Georgian residence, with its paneled rooms and period furniture, is where Samuel Johnson lived between 1748 and 1759. The Great Bear (as he was affectionately known) compiled *A Dictionary of the English Language* in the attic as his health deteriorated. Two early editions are on view, among other mementos of Johnson and his friend, diarist, and later, his biographer, James Boswell. After soaking up the atmosphere, repair around the corner in Wine Office Court to the famed **Ye Olde Cheshire Cheese** pub, once Johnson and Boswell's favorite watering hole. ⊠ *17 Gough Sq.,*

Interior of the "Inside-Out" Lloyd's of London building, designed by Richard Rogers Partnership

The City ☎ *020/7353–3745* ⊕ *www.drjohnsonshouse.org* ✉ *£4.75* ⏰ *May–Sept., Mon.–Sat. 11–5:30; Oct.–Apr., Mon.–Sat. 11–5* Ⓜ *Holborn, Chancery La., Temple.*

Guildhall. The Corporation of London, which oversees The City, has ceremonially elected and installed its Lord Mayor here for the last 800 years. The Guildhall was built in 1411, and though it failed to avoid the conflagrations of either 1666 or 1940, its core survived. The Great Hall is a psychedelic patchwork of coats of arms and banners of the City Livery Companies, which inherited the mantle of the medieval trade guilds. Tradesmen couldn't even run a shop without kowtowing to these prototypical unions, and their grand banqueting halls, the plushest private dining venues in The City, are testimony to the wealth they amassed. Inside the hall, Gog and Magog, the pair of mythical giants who founded ancient Albion and the city of New Troy, which London was said to have been built on, glower down from their west-gallery grandstand in 9-foot-high painted lime wood. The hall was also the site of famous trials, including that of Lady Jane Grey in 1553, before her execution at the Tower of London. To the right of Guildhall Yard is the **Guildhall Art Gallery,** which includes portraits of the great and the good, cityscapes, famous battles, and a slightly cloying pre-Raphaelite section. The construction of the gallery in the 1980s led to the exciting discovery of London's only **Roman amphitheater,** which had lain underneath Guildhall Yard undisturbed for more than 1,800 years. It was excavated and now visitors can walk among the remains, although most of the relics are now at the Museum of London. ✉ *Aldermanbury, The City* ☎ *020/7606–3030, 020/7332–3700 gallery* ⊕ *www.cityoflondon.gov.*

uk 🖼 *Free (fee for some gallery exhibitions)* ⊙ *Hall Mon.–Sat. 10–4:30 (also Sun. 10–4:30 1st weekend in May to last weekend in Sept.). Last admission 30 mins before closing. Sometimes closed for events; call to check* Ⓜ *St. Paul's, Moorgate, Bank, Mansion House.*

The Old Bailey. England and Wales don't allow cameras in courtrooms, so the only way to see a trial in action is to show up. The most high-profile ones usually happen here, at any of the 16 public courtrooms of the **Central Criminal Court** (universally known as "The Old Bailey"—a reference to the fact that it sits atop a section of the old London wall, or "bailey" in Medieval English). Oscar Wilde stood trial here for "gross indecency" (homosexuality) in 1895, but far darker souls than his have passed through these doors, including the nation's most notorious murderers, fraudsters, gangsters, and traitors. The day's proceedings are posted outside; there are security restrictions and children under 14 are not allowed. The Old Bailey was originally part of Newgate Prison, England's most feared *gaol* (jail) after the Tower, in use from the 12th century all the way to 1902. The present building dates from 1907. Note the 12-foot gilded statue of Justice perched on top; she's not, as she usually is, wearing a blindfold—her female form was thought by the Edwardians to imply virtue and impartiality enough. ✉ *Newgate St., The City* ☎ *020/7248–3277 information* ⊕ *www.cityoflondon.gov.uk* 🖼 *Free* ⊙ *Public Galleries weekdays 9:55–12:40, 1:55–3:40 (approx.). Line forms at Newgate St. entrance or in Warwick St. Passage; closed Mon. holidays and day after* Ⓜ *St. Paul's.*

St. Bartholomew the Great. This is one of London's oldest churches. Construction on the church and the hospital nearby was begun in 1123 by Henry I's favorite courtier, Rahere, who, surviving malaria, dedicated his life to serving the saint who had visited him in his fevered dreams. With the dissolution of the monasteries, Henry VIII had most of the place torn down; the Romanesque choir loft is all that survives from the 12th century. In recent times, this ancient church has become a bit of a movie star, having appeared in *The Other Boleyn Girl*, *Four Weddings and a Funeral*, and *Shakespeare in Love*, to name but a few. ✉ *Cloth Fair, West Smithfield, The City* ☎ *020/7606–5171* ⊕ *www. greatstbarts.com* 🖼 *Church £4 (free for prayer); photography £1* ⊙ *Church mid-Feb.–mid-Nov., weekdays 8:30–4, Sat. 10:30–4, Sun. 8:30–8; mid-Nov.–mid-Feb., weekdays 8:30–5, Sat. 10:30–4, Sun. 8:30–8* Ⓜ *Barbican, Farringdon.*

St. Bride's. According to legend, the distinctively tiered steeple of this Christopher Wren–designed church gave rise to the shape of the traditional wedding cake. One early couple inspired to marry here were the parents of Virginia Dare, the first European child born in colonial America in 1587. As St. Paul's (in Covent Garden) is the actors' church, so St. Bride's belongs to journalists, many of whom have been buried or memorialized here. By 1664 the crypts were so crowded that diarist Samuel Pepys, who was baptized here, had to bribe the gravedigger to "justle together" some bodies to make room for his deceased brother. Now the crypts house a museum of the church's rich history, and a bit of Roman sidewalk. Ninety-minute guided tours are held on some Tuesday afternoons (call or check website for dates). ✉ *Fleet St., The*

Continued on page 134

THE TOWER OF LONDON

The Tower is a microcosm of the city itself—a sprawling, organic hodgepodge of buildings that inspires reverence and terror in equal measure. See the block on which Anne Boleyn was beheaded, marvel at the Crown Jewels, and pay homage to the ravens who keep the monarchy safe.

An architectural patchwork of time, the oldest building of the complex is the fairytale White Tower, conceived by William the Conqueror in 1078 as both a royal residence and a show of power to the troublesome Anglo-Saxons he had subdued at the Battle of Hastings. Today's Tower has seen everything, as a palace, barracks, a mint for producing coins, an armoury, and the Royal menagerie (home of the country's first elephant). The big draw is the stunning opulence of the Crown Jewels, kept on-site in the heavily fortified Jewel House. Most of all, though, the Tower is known for death: it's been a place of imprisonment, torture, and execution for the realm's most notorious traitors as well as its martyrs. These days, unless you count the killer admission fees, there are far less morbid activities taking place in the Tower, but it still breathes London's history and pageantry from its every brick and offers hours of exploration.

TOURING THE TOWER

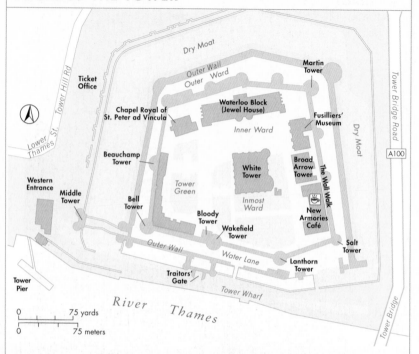

Entry to the Tower is via the **Western Entrance** and the **Middle Tower,** which feed into the outermost ring of the Tower's defenses.

Water Lane leads past the dread-inducing **Traitors' Gate,** the final point of entry for many Tower prisoners.

Toward the end of Water Lane, the **Lanthorn Tower** houses by night the ravens rumored to keep the kingdom safe, and by day a timely high-tech reconstruction of the Catholic Guy Fawkes's plot to blow up the Houses of Parliament in 1605.

The **Bloody Tower** earned its name as the apocryphal site

of the murder of two young princes, Edward and Richard, who disappeared from the Tower after being put there in 1483 by their uncle, Richard III. Two little skeletons (now in Westminster Abbey) were found buried close to the White Tower in 1674 and are thought to be theirs.

The **Beauchamp Tower** housed upper-class miscreants: Latin graffiti about Lady Jane Grey can be glimpsed today on its walls.

Like a prize gem set at the head of a royal crown, the **White Tower** is the centerpiece of the complex. Its four towers dominate the Inner

GOLD DIGGER?

Keep your eyes peeled as you tour the Tower: according to one story, Sir John Barkstead, goldsmith and Lieutenant of the Tower under Cromwell, hid £20,000 in gold coins here before his arrest and execution at the Restoration of Charles II.

Ward, a fitting and forbidding reminder of Norman strength at the time of the conquest of England.

Once inside the White Tower, head upstairs for the **Armouries,** where the biggest attraction, quite literally,

Jewel House, Waterloo Barracks

ROYAL BLING

The Crown of Queen Elizabeth, the Queen Mother, from 1937, contains the exotic 105-carat Koh-i-Noor (mountain of light) diamond.

TIME KILLERS

Some prisoners managed to keep themselves plenty amused: Sir Walter Raleigh grew tobacco on Tower Green, and in 1561 suspected sorcerer Hugh Draper carved an intricate astronomical clock on the walls of his Salt Tower cell.

is the suit of armor worn by a well-endowed Henry VIII. There is a matching outfit for his horse.

Other fascinating exhibits include the set of Samurai armor presented to James I in 1613 by the emperor of Japan, and the tiny set of armor worn by Henry VIII's young son Edward.

The **Jewel House** in Waterloo Block is the Tower's biggest draw, perfect for playing pick-your-favorite-crown from the wrong side of bul-

letproof glass. Not only are these crowns, staffs, and orbs encrusted with heavy-duty gems, they are invested with the authority of monarchical power in England, dating back to the 1300s.

Outside, pause at **Tower Green,** permanent departure point for those of noble birth. The hoi polloi were dispatched at nearby Tower Hill. The Tower's most famous female victims—Anne Boleyn, Margaret Countess of Salisbury, Catherine Howard, and Lady Jane Grey—all went this "priviledged" way.

Behind a well-kept square of grass stands the **Chapel Royal of St. Peter ad Vincula,** a delightful Tudor church and final resting place of six beheaded Tudor bodies. ■TIP→ **Visitors are welcome for services and can also enter after 4:30 pm daily.**

The **Salt Tower,** reputedly the most haunted corner of the complex, marks the start of the **Wall Walk,** a bracing promenade along the stone spiral steps and battlements of the Tower that looks down on the trucks, taxis, and shimmering high-rises of modern London.

The Wall Walk ends at the **Martin Tower,** former home of the Crown Jewels and now host to the crowns and diamonds exhibition that explains the art of fashioning royal headwear and tells the story of some of the most famous stones.

On leaving the Tower, browse the **gift shop,** and wander the wharf that overlooks the Thames, leading to a picture-postcard view of Tower Bridge.

6

IN FOCUS THE TOWER OF LONDON

WHO ARE THE BEEFEATERS?

First of all, they're Yeoman Warders, but probably got the nickname "beefeater" from their position as Royal Bodyguards which entitled them to eat as much beef as they liked. Part of the "Yeoman of the Guard," started in the reign of Edmund IV, the warders have formed the Royal Bodyguard as far back as 1509 when Henry VIII left a dozen of the Yeoman of the Guard at the Tower to protect it.

Originally, the Yeoman Warders also served as jailers of the Tower, doubling as torturers when necessary. (So it would have been a Beefeater tightening the thumb screws, or ratcheting the rack another notch on some unfortunate prisoner. Smile nicely.) Today 36 Yeoman Warders (men and women since 2007), along with the Chief Yeoman Warder and the Yeoman Gaoler, live within the walls of the Tower with their families, in accommodations in the Outer Ward. They stand guard over the Tower, conduct tours, and lock up at 9:53 pm every night with the Ceremony of the Keys.

■TIP➔ Free tickets to the Ceremony of the Keys are available by writing several months in advance; check the Tower Web site for details.

HARK THE RAVENS!

Legend has it that should the hulking black ravens ever leave, the White Tower will crumble and the kingdom fall. Charles II, no doubt jumpy after his father's execution and the monarchy's short-term fall from grace, made a royal decree in 1662 that there should be at least six of the carrion-eating nasties present at all times. There have been some close calls. During World War II, numbers dropped to one, echoing the precarious fate of the war-wracked country. In 2005, two (of eight) died over Christmas when Thor—the most intelligent but also the largest bully of the bunch—killed new recruit Gundolf, named after the Tower's 1070 designer. Pneumonia put an end to Bran, leaving lifelong partner Branwen without her mate.

■ DID YOU KNOW? In 1981 a raven named Grog, perhaps seduced by his alcoholic moniker, escaped after 21 years at the Tower. Others have been banished for "conduct unbecoming."

The six that remain, each one identified by a colored band around a claw, are much loved for their fidelity (they mate for life) and their cheek (capable of 440 noises, they are witty and scolding mimics). It's not only the diet

of blood-soaked biscuits, rabbit, and scraps from the mess kitchen that keeps them coming back. Their lifting feathers on one wing are trimmed, meaning they can manage the equivalent of a lop-sided air-bound hobble but not much more. For the first half of 2006 the ravens were moved indoors full-time as a preventive measure against avian flu but have since been allowed out and about again. In situ they are a territorial lot, sticking to Tower Green and the White Tower, and lodging nightly by Wakefield Tower. They've had free front-row seats at all the most grisly moments in Tower history—Anne Boleyn's execution included.

■TIP➔ Don't get too close to the ravens: they are prone to pecking and not particularly fond of humans, unless you are the Tower's Raven Master.

And *WHAT* are they wearing?

A **pike** (or halberd), also known as a partisan, is the Yeoman Warder's weapon of choice. The Chief Warder carries a staff topped with a miniature silver model of the White Tower.

Anyone who refers to this as a costume will be lucky to leave the Tower with head still attached to body: this is the ceremonial uniform of the Yeoman Warders, and it comes at a cool £13,000 a throw.

The black Tudor **bonnet** is made of velvet; the blue undress consists of a felt top hat, with a single Tudor rose in the middle.

This **Tudor-style ruff** helps date the ceremonial uniform, which was first worn in 1552.

Insignia on a Yeoman Warder's upper right arm denote the rank he carried in the military.

The **medals** on a Yeoman Warder's chest are more than mere show: all of the men and women have served for at least 22 years in the armed forces.

This version of the **royal livery** bears the insignia of the current Queen ("E" for Elizabeth) but originally dates from Tudor times. The first letter changes according to the reigning monarch's Christian name; the second letter is always an "R" for *rex* (king) or *regina* (queen).

Slits in the **tunic** date from the times when Beefeaters were expected to ride a horse.

Red socks and **black patent shoes** are worn on special occasions. Visitors are more likely to see the regular blue undress, introduced in 1858 as the regular working dress of the Yeoman Warders.

The **red lines down the trousers** are a sign of the blood from the swords of the Yeoman Warders in their defense of the realm.

(IN)FAMOUS PRISONERS OF THE TOWER

Anne Boleyn   Lady Jane Grey   Sir Walter Raleigh

Sir Thomas More. A Catholic and Henry VIII's friend and chancellor, Sir Thomas refused to attend the coronation of Anne Boleyn (Henry VIII's second wife) or to recognize the multi-marrying king as head of the Church. Sent to the Tower for treason, in 1535 More was beheaded.

Anne Boleyn. The first of Henry VIII's wives to be beheaded, Anne, who failed to provide the king with a son, was accused of sleeping with five men, including her own brother. All six got the chop in 1536. Her severed head was held up to the crowd, and her lips were said to be mouthing prayer.

Margaret, Countess of Salisbury. Not the best-known prisoner in her lifetime, she has a reputation today for haunting the Tower. And no wonder: the elderly 70-year-old was condemned by Henry VIII in 1541 for a potentially treacherous bloodline (she was the last Plantagenet princess) and hacked to death by the executioner after she refused to put her head on the block like a common traitor and attempted to run away.

Queen Catherine Howard. Henry VIII's fifth wife was locked up for high treason and infidelity and beheaded in 1542 at age 20. Ever eager to please, she spent her final night practicing how to lay her head on the block.

Lady Jane Grey. The nine-days-queen lost her head in 1554 at age 16. Her death was the result of sibling rivalry gone seriously wrong, when Protestant Edward VI slighted his Catholic sister Mary in favor of Lady Jane as heir, and Mary decided to have none of it.

Guy Fawkes. The Roman Catholic soldier who tried to blow up the Houses of Parliament and kill the king in the 1605 Gunpowder plot was first incarcerated in the chambers of the Tower, where King James I requested he be tortured in ever-worsening ways. Perhaps unsurprisingly, he confessed. He met his seriously grisly end in the Old Palace Yard at Westminster, where he was hung, drawn, and quartered in 1607.

Sir Walter Raleigh. Once a favorite of Elizabeth I, he offended her by secretly marrying her Maid of Honor and was chucked in the Tower. Later, as a conspirator against James I, he paid with his life. A frequent visitor to the Tower (he spent 13 years there in three stints), he managed to get the Bloody Tower enlarged on account of his wife and growing family. He was finally executed in 1618 in Old Palace Yard, Westminster.

Josef Jakobs. The last man to be executed in the Tower was caught as a spy when parachuting in from Germany and executed by firing squad in 1941. The chair he sat in when he was shot is preserved in the Royal Armouries' artifacts store.

FOR FURTHER EVIDENCE . . .

A trio of buildings in the Inner Ward, the **Bloody Tower, Beauchamp Tower,** and **Queen's House,** all with excellent views of the execution scaffold in Tower Green, are the heart of the Tower's prison accommodations and home to a permanent exhibition about notable inmates.

TACKLING THE TOWER (without losing your head)

✉ H.M. Tower of London, Tower Hill
☎ 0844/482-7777 ⊕ www.hrp.org.uk
🎟 Adult: £24.50, children under 16: £11, Family tickets (2 adults, 3 children): £60,70 children under 5, free. ⊙ Mar.–Oct., Tues.–Sat. 9–5:30, Sun. and Mon. 10–5:30; last admission at 5. Nov.–Feb., Tues.–Sat. 9–4:30, Sun. and Mon. 10–4:30; last admission at 4 Ⓤ Tower Hill

■TIP➡ You can buy tickets from automatic kiosks on arrival, or up to seven days in advance at any Tube station. Avoid lines completely by booking by telephone (☎ 0844/482-7777/7799 weekdays 9–5), or online.

MAKING THE MOST OF YOUR TIME: Without doubt, the Tower is worth two to three hours. A full hour of that would be well spent by joining one of the Yeoman Warders' tours (included in admission). It's hard to better their insight, vitality, and humor—they are knights of the realm living their very own fairytale castle existence.

The Crown Jewels are worth the wait, the White Tower is essential, and the Medieval Palace and Bloody Tower should at least be breezed through.

■TIP➡ It's best to visit on weekdays, when the crowds are smaller.

WITH KIDS: The Tower's centuries-old cobblestones are not exactly stroller-friendly, but strollers are permitted inside most of the buildings. If you do bring one, be prepared to leave it temporarily unsupervised (the stroller, that is—not your child) outside the White Tower, which has no access. There are baby-changing facilities in the Brick Tower restrooms behind the Jewel House. Look for regular free children's events such as the Knight's school where children can have a go at jousting, sword-fighting, and archery.

■TIP➡ Tell your child to find one of the Yeoman Warders if he or she should get lost; they will in turn lead him or her to the Byward Tower, which is where you should meet.

IN A HURRY? If you have less than an hour, head down Wall Walk, through a succession of towers, which eventually spit you out at the Martin Tower. The view over modern London is quite a contrast.

TOURS: Tours given by a Yeoman Warder leave from the main entrance near Middle Tower every half-hour from 10–4, and last about an hour. Beefeaters give occasional 30-minute talks in the Lanthorn Tower about their daily lives. Both tours are free. Check website for talks and workshops

City ☎ 020/7427–0133 ⊕ www. stbrides.com ⌨ Free; guided tours £6 ⊗ Weekdays 9–6, Sat. hrs vary (call to confirm), Sun. 10–6:30; tours Tues. at 3 Ⓜ St. Paul's, Blackfriars.

St. Mary-le-Bow. Various versions of this church have stood on the site since the 11th century. In 1284 a local goldsmith took refuge here after committing a murder, only to be killed inside by enraged relatives of his victim. The church was abandoned for a time afterward, but was rebuilt as its current form by Sir Christopher Wren after the Great Fire. This 1673 incarnation has a tall steeple (in The City, only St. Bride's is taller) and one of the most famous sets of bells in England—technically, a Londoner must be born within the sound of the "Bow Bells" to be a true Cockney. The origin of that idea may have been the curfew rung on the bells during the 14th century. The Bow takes its name from the bow-shaped arches in the Norman crypt. The church was rebuilt again after severe bomb damage in World War II. The garden contains a statue of local boy Captain John Smith, who founded Virginia in 1606 and was later captured by Native Americans. (His wife, Pocahontas, is buried 25 miles away in Gravesend, Kent.) ✉ Cheapside, The City ☎ 020/7248–5139 ⊕ www.stmarylebow.co.uk ⊗ Mon.–Wed. 7:30–6, Thurs. 7:30–6:30, Fri. 7:30–4 Ⓜ Mansion House, St. Paul's.

QUICK BITES

Café Below. In St. Mary-le-Bow's Norman crypt, this café is packed with City workers weekdays from 7:30 am until 2:30 pm for a menu covering breakfasts, scrumptious light lunches, and delicious cakes. It's also open for dinner Wednesday, Thursday, and Friday. ✉ Cheapside, The City ☎ 020/7329–0789 ⊕ www.cafebelow.co.uk Ⓜ Mansion House, St Paul's.

7

EAST LONDON

GETTING ORIENTED

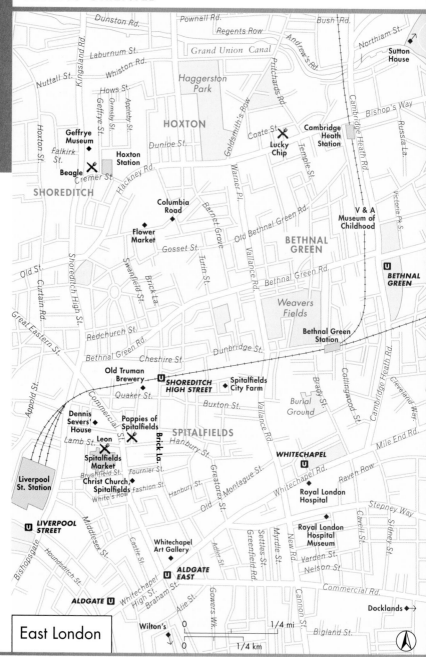

East London

TOP REASONS TO GO

Dennis Severs's House by candlelight: The atmospheric set-pieces in this Georgian town house use visuals, sounds, and aromas to evoke the lives of its fictional previous inhabitants.

Eat artisanal at Broadway Market: Check out the more than 100 food stalls that are here on Saturday, with everything from cheeses to oysters.

Immerse yourself in London's hottest art scene: Edgy galleries mix with large collections.

Trace the footsteps of Jack the Ripper: Track Britain's most infamous serial killer through the streets that were part of major slum in Victorian times.

Peek into the lives of Londoners at the Geffrye Museum of the Home: This former almshouse showcases middle-class domestic interiors over the centuries.

FEELING PECKISH?

Beagle. A great spot (with terrace) for weekend brunch after a morning's shopping. Beagle also serves lunch and dinner, including venison, oysters, and house-smoked salmon. ⊠ *397–400 Geffrye St.* ☎ *020/7613–2967* ⊕ *www.beaglelondon.co.uk* Ⓜ *Overground: Hoxton.*

Poppies of Spitalfields. Poppies of Spitalfields strikes a balance between trendy and traditional with retro-diner decor and efficient service. The specialty is fish-and-chips, but if fish isn't your thing, free-range grilled chicken is also available. ⊠ *6–8 Hanbury St., Spitalfields* ☎ *0207/247–0892* ⊕ *www.poppiesfishandchips.co.uk.*

SAFETY

Around Shoreditch, Spitalfields, and Brick Lane, streets are largely safe during daylight hours. Be cautious on the rougher streets of Whitechapel, Bethnal Green, and Hackney at night.

GETTING THERE

The London Overground, with stops at Shoreditch High Street, Hoxton, Whitechapel, Dalston Kingsland, and Hackney Central, is the easiest way to reach East London. Alternatively, the best Tube stations to use are Old Street on the Northern line, Bethnal Green on the Central line, and Liverpool Street on the Metropolitan and Circle lines.

MAKING THE MOST OF YOUR TIME

To experience East London at its most lively, visit on the weekend. Spitalfields Market bustles all weekend, while Brick Lane and Columbia Road are best on a Sunday morning and Broadway Market on Saturday. If you're planning to explore East London's art galleries, pick up a free map at the Whitechapel Art Gallery. As for the area's booming nightlife scene, there's no time limit.

GUIDED TOURS

The 2½-hour **Jack the Ripper Secret London Tour** (⊕ *london premierwalkingtours.co.uk*), departs from Aldwych Tube station on Tuesday, Wednesday, and Friday at 6:30, Saturday at 6, and Sunday at 1:30. **Street Art London** (⊕ *streetart london.co.uk*) offers two- and four-hour walking tours of East London's street art on Tuesday and Thursday at 10 am and weekends at 11 am.

7

Sightseeing
★★★
Nightlife
★★★★★
Dining
★★★★
Lodging
★
Shopping
★★★★

Made famous by Dickens and infamous by Jack the Ripper, East London is one of London's most enduringly evocative neighborhoods, rich in popular history, architectural gems, and artists' studios. Since the early 1990s, hip gallerists, designers, and new-media entrepreneurs have colonized its handsome Georgian buildings and converted industrial lofts. Today, this collection of neighborhoods lays claim to being the city's most trendsetting area.

Updated By
Ellin Stein

The British equivalent of parts of Brooklyn, East London is a patchwork of districts encompassing struggling artists, ethnic enclaves, upscale professionals, and the digerati, occasionally teetering, like its New York equivalent, on the edge of self-parody. The vast area ranges from gentrified districts like Spitalfields—where bankers and successful artists live in desirable renovated town houses—to parts of Hackney where seemingly derelict, graffiti-covered industrial buildings are hives of exciting creative activity. It remains a little rough around the edges, so stick to busier streets at night.

At the start of the new millennium, Hoxton, an enclave of Shoreditch, became the glossy hub of London's buzzing contemporary art scene, which accelerated the gentrification process. Some artists, such as Tracey Emin and Gilbert & George, long-term residents of Spitalfields' handsome Georgian terraces (and successful enough to still afford the area), have remained.

One such residence, **Dennis Severs's House,** was transformed two decades ago by American artist into a unique "living house museum" that evokes how past generations of a fictional Huguenot family might have lived there. Not far away, Spitalfields Market offers an ever-changing selection of crafts and funky clothes stalls under a glass roof in what was once a Victorian produce market. Across from the market, **Christ Church, Spitalfields,** Nicholas Hawkmoor's masterpiece, soars above Fournier Street.

EAST END STREET SMARTS

Brick Lane and the narrow streets running off it offer a paradigm of East London's development. Its population has moved in waves: communities seeking refuge, others moving out in an upwardly mobile direction.

Brick Lane has seen the manufacture of bricks (during the 16th century), beer, and bagels, but nowadays it's primarily known as the heart of Banglatown—Bangladeshis make up one-third of the population in this London borough, and you'll see that the names of the surrounding streets are written in Bengali—where you find many kebab and curry houses along with shops selling DVDs, colorful saris, and stacks of sticky sweets. On Sunday morning, cars aren't allowed on the upper section of the street. Shops and cafés are open, and several stalls are set up, creating a companion market to the one on nearby **Petticoat Lane.**

Fournier Street contains fine examples of the neighborhood's characteristic Georgian terraced houses, many of them built by the richest of the early-18th-century Huguenot silk weavers (note the enlarged windows on the upper floors to maximize light for the intricate work). Most of those along the north side of Fournier Street have been restored, but some still contain textile sweatshops—only now the workers are Bengali.

Wilkes Street, with more 1720s Huguenot houses, is north of the Christ Church, Spitalfields, and neighboring **Princelet Street** was once important to East London's Jewish community. Where No. 6 stands now, the first of several thriving Yiddish theaters opened in 1886. **Elder Street,** just off Folgate, is another gem of original 18th-century houses. On the south and east side of Spitalfields Market are yet more time-warp streets that are worth a wander, such as **Gun Street,** where artist Mark Gertler (1891–1939) was born, at No. 16.

In the last decade, the streets around the Old Street roundabout (as well as converted warehouses in Hackney and Dalston) have flourished with start-ups, with attendant stylish boutiques (especially on Redchurch Street), destination restaurants, and hipster bars as part of a government initiative to attract IT-oriented businesses to the neighborhood. Old and new Shoreditch meet on **Brick Lane,** the heart of the Bangladeshi community, lined with innumerable curry houses and glittering sari shops, plus vintage-clothing emporia. Here you'll also find the **Old Truman Brewery,** an East London landmark converted into a warren of street fashion and pop-up galleries. On Sunday, the Columbia Road Flower Market to the north of Brick Lane becomes a colorful, fragrant oasis of greenery.

As property prices have climbed, up-and-coming artists have sought more affordable studio spaces in former industrial buildings eastward toward Whitechapel and Bethnal Green, where there are also some notable galleries. Here you'll find the **V&A Museum of Childhood,** a delight for children of all ages, and, a design connoisseur's favorite, the **Geffrye Museum,** a collection of domestic interiors that occupies a row of early-18th-century almshouses.

Probably the best start to an East London tour is via the London Overground, getting off at the Shoreditch High Street station. Immediately northwest of the station, on the west side of Shoreditch High Street, is the heart of the neighborhood that aspires to be the U.K. equivalent to Silicon Valley. To the northeast is Shoreditch's boutique, gallery, and restaurant zone. The subneighborhood of Hoxton is located just above Shoreditch, north of the Old Street roundabout. To the southeast of the station are the handsome Georgian streets of Spitalfields. Bethnal Green is due east, past busy Brick Lane. Whitechapel, formerly Jack the Ripper's patch, is to the south of Spitalfields. All of these neighborhoods are within what is traditionally referred to as the "East End," although East London extends farther to the north and east.

TOP ATTRACTIONS

Fodor's Choice
★
Broadway Market. This parade of shops in hipster-centric Hackney (located north of Regent's Canal) is worth visiting for the specialty bookshops, independent boutiques, organic cafés, neighborhood restaurants, and even a traditional (but now rare) pie-and-mash shop. But wait for Saturday, between 9 and 5, when it really comes into its own with a farmers' market and more than 100 food stalls rivaling those of south London's famed Borough Market. Artisanal breads, cheeses, chocolates, organic meats, produce, oysters, smoked salmon, and ethnic offerings: this is foodie heaven. There are also stalls selling vintage clothes, handmade instruments, and more, which also spill over into the schoolyard at the top of the street. ⊠ *Broadway Market, Hackney* ☎ *0787/246–3409* ⊕ *www.broadwaymarket.co.uk* Ⓜ *Bethnal Green.*

FAMILY
Fodor's Choice
★
Columbia Road Flower Market. On Sunday morning this largely built-up area is transformed into a riot of color and scent as the Columbia Road Flower Market. There's everything from bedding plants to banana trees, including herbs, cut flowers, and bouquets at very reasonable prices. The vendors' patter is part of the fun. Columbia Road itself is lined with some 60 independent shops, so you can pick up some art, antiques, handcrafted jewelry, or, of course, garden accessories to go with your greenery. To avoid the crowds, get here the earlier the better. ⊠ *Columbia Rd., Hackney* ☎ *020/7613–0876* ⊕ *www.columbiaroad. info* ⊙ *Sun. 8–3* Ⓜ *Old St., Northern Line.*

Fodor's Choice
★
Dennis Severs' House. The remarkable interiors of this extraordinary time machine of a house are the creation of Dennis Severs (1948–99), a performer-designer-scholar from Escondido, California, who dedicated his life to restoring this Georgian terraced house. More than that, he created "still-life dramas" using sight, sound, and smell to evoke the world of a fictitious family of Huguenot silk weavers, the Jervises, who might have inhabited the house between 1728 and 1914. Each of the 10 rooms has a distinctive, compelling atmosphere that encourages visitors to become lost in another time, deploying evocative design details like rose-laden Victorian wallpaper, Jacobean paneling, Georgian wing chairs, Baroque carved ornaments, rich "Catholic" wall colors downstairs, and more sedate "Protestant" shades upstairs. The "Silent Night" candlelight tour offered each Monday and Wednesday evening, a silent

Banksy and The East End Art Scene

Banksy, the Bristol-based artist and provocateur who has maintained his anonymity despite works that now commands six figures, is widely credited with making Londoners see street art as more than vandalism. His work can be seen in various locations around the city, from Ladbroke Grove to Fitzrovia to Bemondsey, but he is primarily associated with the East End, where he first came to public attention in the late '80s, and which continues to be an important open-air exhibition space for new talent from around the world. Unfortunately, much of Banksy's early work has been lost, either from being covered over by local councils and building owners, defaced by other graffiti artists, or removed by profiteers. As of this writing, murals remain at Polland Street near Bethnal Green, Rivington Street near Old Street (in the garden of Cargo bar and nightclub), and Stoke Newington Church Street. Shoreditch Street Art Tours (⊕ www. shoreditchstreetarttours.co.uk/) offers a knowledgeable view, guiding not only to the remaining Banksy works but also highlighting the best of his successors.

Today, East London is a global hotbed of contemporary art, but its avant-garde roots go way back. **Shoreditch's** cheap industrial units and Georgian–Victorian terraced streets have attracted artists since the 1960s, when op-art pioneer Bridget Riley established a service to find affordable studio space for her contemporaries. In the early '90s it gained new notoriety when Young British Artists Sarah Lucas and Tracey Emin began selling their own and their friends' work in The Shop, joining Maureen Paley's influential Bethnal Green gallery, and the long-established Whitechapel Art Gallery, where many leading abstract expressionists and pop artists had their first U.K. shows. **Hoxton** truly became a destination for well-heeled collectors when Jay Jopling, the most important modern-art dealer in town, set up his White Cube gallery in 2000 (it's now in Bermondsey), followed by Kate MacGarry's gallery in 2002.

Priced out by the area's fashionability, the emerging artists themselves have relocated farther off the beaten track to edgier neighborhoods such as **Hackney**, with several trendsetting galleries found clustered around **Cambridge Heath Road** and **Vyner Street.**

stroll concluding with Champagne by the fire, is the most theatrical and memorable way to experience the house. Private individual Silent Night tours are available one night per month, and private group visits can also be arranged. ✉ *18 Folgate St., Spitalfields* ☎ *020/7247–4013* ⊕ *www.dennissevershouse.co.uk* ✑ *£10 Sun. and Mon., £15 Mon. and Wed. evenings* ⊙ *Sun. noon–4 (last admission 3:15), Mon. noon–2 (last admission 1:15), Mon. and Wed. 6–9 (last admission 8; reservations essential)* Ⓜ *Overground: Shoreditch High St.*

Fodor'sChoice ★ **Geffrye Museum of the Home.** In contrast to the West End's grand aristocratic town houses, this charming museum is devoted to the life of the city's middle class over the years. Originally a row of almshouses built in 1714 by Sir Robert Geffrye, a former Lord Mayor of London,

020 7843 3788

DID YOU KNOW?

The Columbia Road Flower Market opens at 8 am on Sunday. Arrive early to see the photogenic market at its best and to find the freshest selection. The road is lined with funky shops selling antiques, vintage clothing, horticultural accessories, and more.

it contains a series of 11 period rooms that re-create everyday domestic interiors from the Elizabethan period through the 1950s to the present day. One of the almshouses has been restored to its original condition to offer a glimpse into how the poor and the dependent elderly lived in previous centuries (to visit the almshouse you must go as part of a tour, which is offered at 11, noon, 2, and 3 on specific days each month; check website). Outside, a series of period gardens charts the evolution of the town garden over the past 400 years, and next to them is a walled herb garden. The museum's extension wing houses the 20th-century galleries, a lovely café overlooking the gardens, and a shop. ⊠ *136 Kingsland Rd., Hoxton* ☎ *020/7739–9893* ⊕ *www.geffrye-museum.org.uk* 🖃 *Free (charge for special exhibitions); almshouse £3* ⊙ *Tues.–Sun. 10–5; gardens: Apr. 1–Nov. 2* ⊙ *Closed Mon. (except holidays)* Ⓜ *Old St., then Bus 243; Liverpool St., then Bus 149 or 242. Overground: Hoxton.*

FAMILY **Old Spitalfields Market.** An impressive piece of architecture in itself, this large restored Victorian market hall (covered by a glass canopy) is part bazaar and part food court. The main market days are Thursday through Sunday, with a notable antiques markets on Thursday and a fashion and art market on Friday (plus, on every first and third Friday and second Saturday, a record fair; and a vintage fair every first and third Saturday of the month), as well as markets on other days selling goods that include handmade clothes, toys, hats, and jewelry. While some of the quality is pedestrian, you can also find interesting clothes, accessories, and leather goods by new designers. ⊠ *16 Horner Sq., Spitalfields* ☎ *020/7375–2963* ⊕ *www.oldspitalfieldsmarket.com* 🖃 *Free* ⊙ *Shops daily 10–7; market stalls weekdays 10–5, Sat. 11–5, Sun. 10–5* Ⓜ *Liverpool St.*

FAMILY **V&A Museum of Childhood.** A treat for children of all ages, this East
Fodor'sChoice London outpost of the Victoria & Albert Museum—in an iron, glass,
★ and brown-brick building transported here from South Kensington in 1868—houses one of the world's biggest toy collections. One highlight (among many) is the large Dolls' Houses collection—a bit like a miniature Geffrye Museum with interiors from 1673 up to the present represented. Other favorites range from board games and puzzles to teddy bears and train sets. The collection is organized into galleries: Moving Toys, which includes everything from rocking horses to Xboxes; Creativity, which encompasses dolls, puppets, chemistry sets, play kitchens, construction toys, and musical instruments; and Childhood, with areas devoted to babies, an exhibit of children's clothes from the mid-1600s to the present, and toys inspired by adult pursuits, such as toy soldiers, toy guns, and toy hospitals. Don't miss the magnificent 18th-century commedia dell'arte puppet theater, thought to have been made in Venice. There are special activities for the under-fives. The shop has replica toys that make great presents. ⊠ *Cambridge Heath Rd., Bethnal Green* ☎ *020/8983–5200* ⊕ *www.museumofchildhood.org.uk* 🖃 *Free* ⊙ *Daily 10–5:45* Ⓜ *Bethnal Green.*

Fodor'sChoice **Whitechapel Art Gallery.** Founded in 1901, this internationally renowned
★ gallery mounts shows that rediscover overlooked masters and exhibits tomorrow's legends. Painter and leading exponent of abstract

Jack the Ripper

The spirit of one of the world's most infamous serial killers haunts the "Jack the Ripper Walk" that takes you to the deserted squares and warehouse alleys where he claimed his unfortunate victims, many of them prostitutes.

No. 90 Whitechapel High Street was once the site of the George Yard Buildings, where the body of the Ripper's first victim was discovered in August 1888. His third mutilated victim, Annie Chapman, was left on Hanbury Street, behind what was then a seedy lodging house at No. 29. A double homicide followed, and then, after a month's lull, came the death on the same street of the Ripper's last victim. He had been able to work indoors this time—in a ground-floor apartment today occupied by an Indian restaurant—and left the remains of Mary Kelly, a young widow, strewn around the room. Jack the Ripper's identity has never been established, although theoretical candidates (of varying likelihood) abound, including the grandson of Queen Victoria; the artist Walter Sickert; and Francis Tumblety, an American quack doctor.

Today, many entrepreneurs offer walking tours of the Victorian slums that Jack once stalked. One of the most popular is run by Original London Walks (⊕ www.walks.com); it leaves every night from Tower Hill at 7:30 pm. If you want a walk led by author and Ripper expert Donald Rumbelow, turn up on Sunday nights or alternate Friday nights

---

expressionism, Jackson Pollock was exhibited here in the 1950s as was pop artist Robert Rauschenberg in the 1960s; the 1970s saw a young David Hockney's first solo show. The exhibitions continue to be on the cutting edge of contemporary art. The gallery also hosts talks, film screenings, workshops, and other events. Pick up a free East London art map to help you plan your visit to the area. ⊠ 77–82 Whitechapel High St., Whitechapel ☎ 020/7522–7888 ⊕ www.whitechapelgallery. org ⊡ Free, charge for some special exhibits ☉ Tues., Wed., and Fri.–Sun. 11–6; Thurs. 11–9 Ⓜ Aldgate East.

WORTH NOTING

Fodor's Choice ★   **Christ Church, Spitalfields.** This is the 1729 masterpiece of Sir Christopher Wren's associate Nicholas Hawksmoor, one of his six London churches and an example of English baroque at its finest. It was commissioned as part of Parliament's 1711 "Fifty New Churches" Act, passed in response to the influx of immigrants with the idea of providing for the religious needs of the "godless thousands"—and to help ensure they joined the Church of England as opposed to such nonconformist denominations as the Protestant Huguenots. (It must have worked; you can still see gravestones with epitaphs in French in the crypt.) As the local silk industry declined, the church fell into disrepair, and by 1958 the structure was crumbling, with the looming prospect of demolition. But after 25 years—longer than it took to build the church—and a huge

On Sunday, additional clothing and crafts stalls surround Spitalfields covered market.

local fund-raising effort, the structure was meticulously restored and is a joy to behold, from the colonnaded Doric portico and tall spire to its soaring, heavily ornamented plaster ceiling. Its excellent acoustics make is a superb concert venue. Tours that take you "backstage" to the many hidden rooms and passages, from the tower to the vaults, are offered by appointment. ⊠ *Commercial St., Spitalfields* ☎ *020/7377–6793* ⊕ *www. ccspitalfields.org* ✉ *Free, tours £6* ⊙ *Weekdays 10–4 (may be closed for event; call for info), Sun. 1–4* Ⓜ *Overground: Shoreditch High St.*

Maureen Paley Gallery. Inspired by the DIY punk aesthetic and the funky galleries of New York's Lower East Side, Maureen Paley started putting on exhibitions in her East End home back in 1984, when it was virtually the only gallery in the area. Since then this American artist and gallerist has shown such respected contemporary artists as Gillian Wearing, Helen Chadwick, Jenny Holzer, Peter Fischli, and Wolfgang Tillmans and, today, is considered the doyenne of East End gallerists. The gallery has been in its current home, a converted warehouse in Bethnal Green, since 1999. ⊠ *21 Herald St., Bethnal Green* ☎ *020/7729–4112* ⊕ *www. maureenpaley.com* ⊙ *Daily 11–6* Ⓜ *Bethnal Green.*

FAMILY **Old Truman Brewery.** The last East End brewery still standing—a handsome example of Georgian and 19th-century industrial architecture, and in late Victorian times the largest brewery in the world—has been transformed into a cavernous hipster mall housing galleries, record shops, fashion-forward boutiques, bars, clubs, and restaurants, along with an array of international street-food vendors. The retailers are at street level with offices and studios on the upper floors. Events include fashion shows for both new and established designers, excellent sample sales, art installations, and, on weekends, a food hall and a vintage clothes fair. Truman's Brewery itself, shut down in 1989 but has risen from the ashes in recent years. Its new location out in Hackney Wick is open for brewery tours (6:30 pm Thursday and 2 pm on Saturday). ✉ *91 Brick La., Spitalfields* ☎ *0207/770–6000* ⊕ *www.trumanbrewery. com* Ⓜ *Overground: Shoreditch High St.*

Royal London Hospital Museum. Located in the crypt of a Victorian church, the Royal London Hospital Museum uses exhibits of historic medical equipment, surgical instruments, and archives to document the history of this East London institution from its foundation in 1740 to the present day. Highlights include a forensic medicine section with original materials and documentation connected to the Jack the Ripper murders and the RLH surgeon who helped investigate them. There are also artifacts and documents relating to Joseph Merrick—aka "The Elephant Man"—who spent his final years in the hospital, and a set of dentures worn by George Washington. Opening hours are subject to change on short notice, so call before you go. ✉ *St. Augustine with St. Philip's Church, Newark St., Whitechapel* ☎ *020/7377–7608* ⊕ *www. bartshealth.nhs.uk* ✉ *Free* ⊘ *Tues.–Fri. 10–4:30.*

FAMILY **Spitalfields City Farm.** An oasis of rural calm in an urban landscape, this little community farm raises a variety of animals, including some rare breeds, to help educate city kids about life in the country. A tiny farm shop sells freshly laid eggs, along with organic seasonal produce. Gardening sessions take place on Tuesday (10–2) and Wednesday (11–2). ✉ *Buxton St., Spitalfields* ☎ *020/7247–8762* ⊕ *www. spitalfieldscityfarm.org* ✉ *Free* ⊘ *Tues.–Sun. 10–4* Ⓜ *Overground: Shoreditch High St.*

FAMILY **Sutton House.** Built by a courtier to King Henry VIII, this Tudor mansion has since been home to merchants, Huguenot silk weavers, and, in the 1980s, a group of arty squatters. The house dates back to 1535, when Hackney was a village surrounded by fields and on the outskirts of London. Later, in 1751, it was split into two self-contained houses. Its oak-paneled rooms, tranquil courtyard, and adorable café are an unexpected treat in an area that's yet to entirely shake off its grit. Visit at the weekend for guided tours of the house, or on the first Thursday of the month for an evening tour by candlelight. ✉ *2-4 Homerton High St., Hackney* ☎ *020/8986–2264* ⊕ *www.nationaltrust.org. uk/sutton-house* ✉ *£3.50* ⊘ *Wed.–Sun. noon–5 pm (closed in Jan.)* Ⓜ *Overground: Hackney Central.*

The Ten Bells. Although the number of bells in its name has varied between 8 and 12 (depending on how many bells were used by neighboring Christ Church Spitalfields), this pub retains its authentic mid-Victorian interior and original tiles, including a frieze depicting the area's weaving tradition on the north wall and particularly fine floral tiling on two others. Legend has it the Ripper's third victim, Annie Chapman, had a drink here before meeting her gory end—the pub is depicted in Alan Moore's acclaimed graphic novel *From Hell.* ✉ *84 Commercial St., Spitalfields* ☎ *07530/492986* ⊕ *tenbells.com* Ⓜ *Overground: Shoreditch High St.*

SOUTH OF
THE THAMES

GETTING ORIENTED

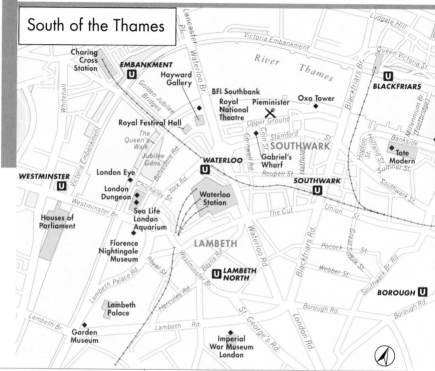

South of the Thames

GETTING THERE

For the South Bank, use Embankment on the District, Circle, Northern, and Bakerloo lines and walk across the Golden Jubilee Bridges; or Waterloo on the Northern, Jubilee, and Bakerloo lines, from where it's a 10-minute walk.

London Bridge on the Northern and Jubilee lines is five minutes from Borough Market and Southwark Cathedral. The station also serves Bermondsey Street, though, confusingly, the next stop on the Jubilee line is called Bermondsey. Brixton has its own stop on the Victoria line.

TOP REASONS TO GO

Join the "groundlings" at Shakespeare's Globe: See one of Shakespeare's plays in this historically accurate replica of the Elizabethan theater where they were first performed.

View a new master at **Tate Modern:** One of the world's great collections of post-1900 modern art, the centerpiece of this Tate branch is the huge renovated electric turbine hall, now an exhibition space used for large installations.

Get bloodthirsty **at the London Dungeon:** Did you ever wonder what a disembowelment looks like? That's just one of the gory tableaux on view in this lively, somewhat jokey history-themed Grand Guignol. You'll be amazed how many children adore this place.

Take in a Waterloo sunset on Waterloo Bridge: This is one of London's most romantic views, with St. Paul's to the east and the Houses of Parliament to the west.

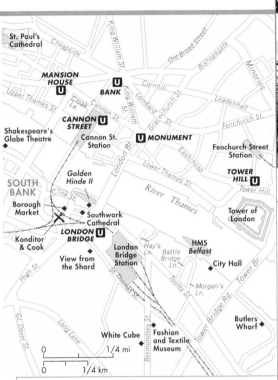

MAKING THE MOST OF YOUR TIME

Don't attempt to visit the area south of the Thames in one go. Tate Modern alone deserves a whole afternoon, especially if you want to do justice to both the temporary exhibitions and the permanent collection. The Globe requires about two hours for the exhibition theater tour and two to three hours for a performance. Finish with drinks at the Oxo Tower or one of the Shard's restaurants, with their spectacular views. You can return across the river to central London via Southwark on the Jubilee line from Tate Modern, although it's a good walk to the station. Crossing the Millennium Bridge for St. Paul's on the Central line or the Golden Jubilee Bridge to Embankment station offer longer but more scenic alternatives.

FEELING PECKISH?

Konditor & Cook. Konditor & Cook. Known for its exquisite cakes and pastries, this chain of patisseries offers daily specials such as paella or vegetarian moussaka. This branch has a Brownie Bar and a Cake School. ✉ *10 Stoney St., Borough* ☎ *020/7633–3300* ⊕ *www.konditorandcook.com* ☽ *Closed Sun.* Ⓜ *London Bridge.*

Pieminister. In the shopping enclave of Gabriel's Wharf, you'll find this branch of Pieminister, which began life in Borough Market. Have a meat pie made with ethically farmed ingredients like chicken and tarragon. ✉ *Gabriel's Wharf, 56 Upper Ground, South Bank* ☎ *020/7928–5755* ⊕ *www.pieminister.co.uk* Ⓜ *Waterloo.*

SAFETY

At night, stick to the Butler's Wharf and Bermondsey Street restaurants, the Southbank Centre, and the Cut near the Old Vic.

8

Sightseeing
★★★★★

Nightlife
★★★★

Dining
★★★

Lodging
★

Shopping
★★

For decades, south London felt down-at-heel, with a considerable criminal element. Tourists rarely ventured across the river to south London except to go to Waterloo station or the Old Vic. But now the area is one of London's leading destinations, with attractions including the IWM London, the Southbank Centre (Europe's largest arts center), and the heavenly Borough Market. Most are clustered around the Southbank and in Bankside and Southwark, but the surrounding neighborhoods of Bermondsey and Lambeth are rising rapidly, with galleries, shops, and restaurants proliferating. And the formerly drab Nine Elms area (near Vauxhall) is in the process of being totally transformed, with luxury high-rises and shops proliferating in anticipation of the huge new U.S. embassy that will open there in 2017.

Updated By
Ellin Stein

A borough of the City of London since 1327, Southwark first became well known for its inns (the pilgrims in Chaucer's *A Canterbury Tale* set off from one), theaters, prisons, tanneries, and brothels, as well as entertainments such as cockfighting. For four centuries, this was a sort of border town outside the city walls (and jurisdiction) where Londoners went to let their hair down and behave badly. Originally, you were just as likely to see a few bouts of bearbaiting at the Globe as you were Shakespeare's most recent work.

But now that south London encompasses high-caliber art, music, film, and theater venues as well as an aquarium, a historic warship, two popular food markets, and greatly improved transportation links, this region has become one of the leading destinations in England.

The restaurant at Tate Modern has some of the best views in London. Here you can see St. Paul's Cathedral in the distance.

Today, you can walk the **Thames Path** along the river from the London Eye all the way to Greenwich. The segment beside the South Bank is alive with skateboarders, secondhand-book stalls, and street entertainers. At one end the **London Eye**, a 21st-century landmark that became an instant favorite with both Londoners and out-of-towners, rises next to the **London Aquarium** and the **Southbank Centre**, home to the **Royal Festival Hall**, the **Hayward Gallery**, the **BFI Southbank**, and the **National Theatre**. Farther east you'll come to a reconstruction of Sir Francis Drake's ship the *Golden Hinde*; **Butler's Wharf**, where some notable restaurants occupy what were once shadowy Dickensian docklands; **The Shard**, at more than 1,000 feet the tallest building in the EU, which offers spectacular views over the city; and, next to **Tower Bridge**, the massive headlight-shape **City Hall**. Nearby Bermondsey Street (the name derives from "Beormund's Eye," as it was known in Saxon times) is home to the bright yellow Fashion Museum, the White Cube Gallery, and lots of trendy shops, restaurants, and cafés. Meanwhile, younger visitors will enjoy the **London Dungeon** and **HMS** *Belfast,* a decommissioned Royal Navy cruiser, while food lovers should make a straight line to London's oldest food market, **Borough Market**, where the independent stallholders sell farm-fresh produce, artisanal bread and cheese, and specialty fish and meat.

Even from the Shard's lofty viewing platform 1,016 feet up, the area south of the Thames still isn't one of London's most beautiful, but you'll be able to see how this patchwork of neighborhoods fits together. The heart is the South Bank, which extends east from the London Eye to Blackfriars Bridge, with the river to the north and Waterloo station to the south. From Blackfriars Bridge east to London Bridge is Bankside, where you'll find the Globe and Tate Modern. Moving east from London Bridge is Borough, with its cobbled streets and former factories now turned into expensive lofts. Next, southeast of Borough, is buzzy, urban Bermondsey, while leafy Dulwich, with its renowned gallery and charming period streets, is quite a distance to the south. Returning up the river to the west of the South Bank is Lambeth and then Vauxhall, with the imposing IWM London (formerly the Imperial War Museum), a thriving gay scene, and scary through-traffic routes. It's a rapidly changing district, thanks to a regeneration spearheaded by the construction of the new U.S. Embassy in adjacent Nine Elms and a slew of upscale riverside residential developments. South of here is Brixton, long the heartland of London's Afro-Caribbean community—with a lively club scene—and now attracting young families priced out of nearby Clapham.

TOP ATTRACTIONS

FAMILY

Fodor'sChoice

★

Dulwich Picture Gallery. Famed for its regal old master painting collection, the Dulwich (pronounced "Dull-ich") Picture Gallery, designed by Sir John Soane, was Britain's first purpose-built art museum when it opened in 1811 (the recent extension was designed by Rick Mather). The permanent collection includes landmark works by Rembrandt, Van Dyck, Rubens, Poussin, and Gainsborough, and the museum also hosts three or so major exhibitions each year. Check the website for its schedule of family activities; there's a lovely café here, too. While you're in the area, take a short wander and you'll find a handful of cute clothing and crafts stores and the well-manicured Dulwich Park, which has lakeside walks and a fine display of rhododendrons in late May. Development in Dulwich Village is tightly controlled, so it feels a bit like a time capsule, with old-fashioned street signs and handsome 18th-century houses on the main street. ⊠ *Gallery Rd., Dulwich* ☎ *020/8693–5254* ⊕ *www. dulwichpicturegallery.org.uk* ⊡ *£6; free guided tours weekends at 3* ☉ *Tues.–Fri. and bank holiday Mon. 10–5, weekends 11–5* ☉ *Closed Mon.* Ⓜ *National Rail: West Dulwich from Victoria or North Dulwich from London Bridge.*

Fashion and Textile Museum. The bright yellow and pink museum (it's hard to miss) designed by Mexican architect Ricardo Legorreta features changing exhibitions devoted to developments in fashion design, textiles, and jewelry from the end of World War II to the present. Founded by designer Zandra Rhodes, and now owned by Newham College, the FTM is a favorite with fashionistas. There are weekday lectures on aspects of fashion history and fashion-based workshops; the excellent gift shop sells books on fashion and one-of-a-kind pieces by local designers. After your visit, check out the many trendy restaurants, cafés, and boutiques that have bloomed on Bermondsey Street. ⊠ *83 Bermondsey St., Bermondsey* ☎ *020/7407–8664* ⊕ *www.ftmlondon.org* ⊡ *£8.80* ☉ *Tues., Wed., Fri., and Sat. 11–6; Thurs. 11–8; Sun. 11–5. Last admission 45 mins before closing* Ⓜ *London Bridge.*

FAMILY **The Globe Theatre.**
Fodor'sChoice *See the highlighted feature in this chapter.*
★ **Gabriel's Wharf.** This is a cluster of small shops specializing in jewelry, art, clothing, and ceramics by designer-manufacturers with an adjoining cluster of informal restaurants and cafés, most with outdoor seating. A project of the Coin Street Community Builders, a social enterprise group, it bustles with activity. The same group converted the nearby **Oxo Tower Wharf,** an art deco warehouse with three levels of designer studios that also serve as retail outlets. The Oxo Tower Restaurant, Bar and Brasserie, a pricey restaurant operated by the swish department store Harvey Nichols, occupies the top floor, and you can see the same spectacular views from an adjacent free public viewing area (open daily). ⊠ *56 Upper Ground, South Bank* ☎ *020/7021–1600* ⊕ *www. coinstreet.org* ✉ *Free* ☉ *Shops and studios Tues.–Sun. 11–6* Ⓜ *Black-friars, Waterloo.*

FAMILY **Golden Hinde II.** This is a full-size reconstruction of the little galleon in which the famed Elizabethan explorer Sir Francis Drake circumnavigated the globe. Launched in 1973, the exact replica made one full and one partial round-the-world voyage, calling in at ports—many along the Pacific and Atlantic coasts of the United States—to do duty as a maritime museum. Now berthed at the St. Mary Overie Dock, the ship continues its educational purpose, complete with a "crew" in period costumes and three decks of artifacts. Call for information on guided tours. ⊠ *1 Pickfords Wharf, Clink St., Bankside* ☎ *020/7403–0123* ⊕ *www.goldenhinde.com* ✉ *£6; 1-hr. guided tour £7* ☉ *Daily 10–5:30* Ⓜ *London Bridge.*

FAMILY **London Dungeon.** Saved by a keen sense of its own borderline ridiculousness, this gory attraction is more funny than frightening, with tableaux depicting the bloody demise of famous figures alongside the torture, murder, and ritual slaughter of lesser-known victims, all to a sound track of screaming, wailing, and agonized moaning. There are lively dramatizations about the Great Plague, Henry VIII, (the fictional) Sweeney Todd, and Jack the Ripper, to name a few, with costumed characters leaping out of the gloom to bring the information to life and add to the fear and fun. Perhaps most shocking are the crowds of children trying to get in—most kids absolutely love this place, although those with more a sensitive disposition may find it too frightening (that goes for adults as well). If you've ever wondered what a disembowelment looks like, this is your chance to find out. Be sure to get the souvenir booklet to impress all your friends back home. Expect long lines on weekends and during school holidays. Savings are available for online booking. ⊠ *Riverside Building, County Hall, Westminster Bridge Rd., South Bank* ☎ *0870/423–2240* ⊕ *www.thedungeons.com* ✉ *From £17.50* ☉ *Mon., Tues., Wed., and Fri. 10–6:30; Thurs. 11–6:30; weekends 10–7:30. Last entry 90 mins before closing. Hrs may vary—phone or check website to confirm.* Ⓜ *Waterloo.*

FAMILY **London Eye.** To mark the start of the new millennium, architects David
Fodor'sChoice Marks and Julia Barfield devised an instant icon that allows Londoners
★ and visitors alike to see the city from a completely new perspective. The

8

giant Ferris wheel was the largest cantilevered observation wheel ever built at the time, and it's one of the city's tallest structures. The 25-minute slow-motion ride inside one of the enclosed passenger capsules is so smooth you'd hardly know you were suspended over the Thames. On a clear day you can see up to 25 miles, with a bird's-eye view of London's most famous landmarks as you circle 360 degrees. If you're looking for a special place to celebrate, Champagne and canapés can be arranged ahead of time. Buy your ticket online to avoid the long lines and get a 10% discount. For an extra £8.55, you can save even more time with a Fast Track flight (check in 15 minutes before your "departure"). You can buy a combination ticket for the Eye and other London attractions—check online for details—and board the London Eye River Cruise here for a 40-minute sightseeing voyage on the Thames. In December, there's a scenic ice rink just below the wheel. ✉ *Jubilee Gardens, South Bank* ☎ *0871/781–3000* ⊕ *www.londoneye.com* ✉ *£20.95; cruise £13 (£11.70 online)* ◷ *Varies; see website.* ◷ *Closed Jan. 7–14* Ⓜ *Waterloo.*

Fodor'sChoice ★ **Southbank Centre.** The public has never really warmed to the Southbank Centre's hulking concrete buildings, products of the Brutalist style popular when the Centre was built in the 1950s and '60s, but they flock to the concerts, recitals, festivals, and exhibitions held here all the same. The **Royal Festival Hall** is truly a People's Palace, with seats for 2,900 and a schedule that ranges from major symphony orchestras to pop stars (catch the annual summer Meltdown Festival, where artists like David Bowie, Patti Smith, or Jarvis Cocker put together a personal selection of concerts by favorite performers). The smaller **Queen Elizabeth Hall** is more strictly classically oriented. It contains the smaller **Purcell Room**, which hosts lectures and chamber performances. For art, head to the **Hayward Gallery,** which hosts shows on top contemporary artists such as Anthony Gormley and Cy Twombly. (The terrace here has some restaurants worth a visit.) Not officially part of the Southbank Centre but moments away on the east side of Waterloo Bridge, the **National Theatre** is home to some of the best productions in London (several, such as *War Horse* and *The History Boys*, have become movies) at prices well below those in the West End. You can hear leading actors, directors, and writers discuss their work at the National Theatre's Platforms, a series of inexpensive early evening and afternoon talks. Meanwhile, film buffs will appreciate the **BFI Southbank** (formerly the National Film Theatre), which has a schedule that true cinema connoisseurs will relish. The Centre's riverside street level has a terrific assortment of restaurants and bars. The BFI's Benugo bar and the Wahaca restaurant at Queen Elizabeth Hall are particularly attractive. Note that renovations of the Hayward Gallery, Purcell Room, and Queen Elizabeth Hall will start in 2015, and the venues will be closed for at least three years while that happens. ✉ *Belvedere Rd., South Bank* ☎ *020/7960–4200* ⊕ *www.southbankcentre.co.uk* ✉ *Varies; check website* ◷ *Varies according to venue; check website* Ⓜ *Waterloo, Embankment.*

Continued on page 160

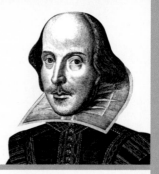

"Within this wooden O..."

—William Shakespeare, Henry V

SHAKESPEARE AND
THE GLOBE THEATRE

At Shakespeare's Globe Theatre, they say the Bard does not belong to the British; he belongs to the world. Not a day has gone by since the Restoration when one of his plays isn't being performed or reinterpreted somewhere. But here, at the site of the original Globe, in a painstaking reconstruction of an open-air theater, is where seeing one of his plays can take on an ethereal quality.

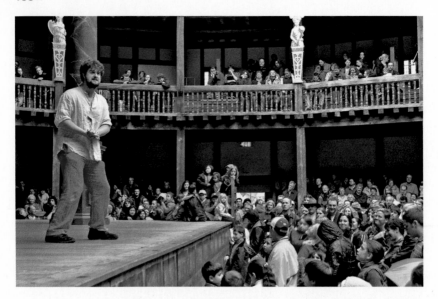

If you are a lover of either British theater or literature, then chances are a pilgrimage to his Globe Theatre is already on your list. But if Shakespeare's works leave you wondering why exactly the play's the thing, then a trip to the Globe—to learn more about his life or to see his words come alive—will reveal all.

The Globe Theatre in Shakespeare's Day

In the 16th and 17th centuries, a handful of theaters—the Rose, the Swan, the Globe, and others whose names are lost—rose above the higgledy-piggledy jumble of rooftops in London's rowdy Southwark neighborhood. They were round or octagonal open-air playhouses, with galleries for the upper classes, and large, open pits for the more lively plebs. People from all social strata, from royalty down, shared the communal experience of drama in these theaters, of which The Globe was one.

A fire in 1613 destroyed the first Globe, which was quickly rebuilt; however, Oliver Cromwell and waves of other puritanical reformers put an end to all the Southwark playhouses in the 1640s. By the time American actor and director Sam Wanamaker visited in 1949, the only indication that the works of the world's greatest dramatist had premiered here was a plaque on a brewery wall. Wanamaker was shocked to find that all evidence of the playwright's legendary playhouse had vanished into air.

And thereby hangs a tale.

Wanamaker's Dream

Over the next several decades, Wanamaker devoted himself to the Bard. He was director of the New Shakespeare Theatre in Liverpool and, in 1959, joined the Shakespeare Memorial Theatre Company (now the Royal Shakespeare Company) at Stratford-upon-Avon. Finally, in the 1970s, he began the project

SHAKESPEARE'S ALL-TIME TOP 10

1. *Romeo and Juliet*. Young love, teenage rebellion, and tragedy are the ingredients of the greatest tearjerker of all time.

2. *Hamlet* (*right*). The very model of a modern antihero and origin of the most quoted line of any play: "To be or not to be…"

3. *A Midsummer Night's Dream*. Spells and potions abound as the gods use humans for playthings; lovers' tiffs are followed by happy endings for all.

4. *Othello*. Jealousy poisons love and destroys a proud man.

5. *The Taming of the Shrew*. The eternal battle of the sexes.

6. *Macbeth*. Ambition, murder, and revenge. Evil gets its just reward.

7. *The Merry Wives of Windsor*. A two-timing rascal gets his comeuppance from a pack of hysterically funny gossips.

8. *Richard III*. One of literature's juiciest villains. The whole audience wants to hiss.

9. *The Tempest*. On a desert island, the concerns of men amaze and amuse the innocent Miranda: "Oh brave new world, that has such people in't."

10. *King Lear*. A tragedy of old age, filial love, and grasping, ungrateful children.

that would dominate the rest of his life: reconstructing Shakespeare's theater, as close to the original site as possible.

Today's Globe was re-created using authentic Elizabethan materials and craft techniques—green oak timbers joined only with wooden pegs and mortise-and-tenon joints; plaster made of lime, sand, and goat's hair; and the first thatched roof in London since the Great Fire of 1666. The complex,

200 yards from the site of the original Globe, includes an exhibition center, cafés, and restaurants, as well as a 17th-century-style theater, modeled on one built adjacent to the Globe to a design by Inigo Jones.

FUN FACT: Plays are presented in the open air (and sometimes the rain) to an audience of 1,000 on wooden benches in the bays, and 500 "groundlings," who stand on a carpet of hazelnut shells and cinder, just as they did nearly four centuries ago.

The eventual realization of Wanamaker's dream, a full-scale, accurate replica of the Globe, was the keystone that supported the revitalization of the entire district. The new Globe celebrates Shakespeare, his work, and his times, and as an educational trust it is dedicated to making the playwright continually fresh and accessible for new audiences. Sadly, Wanamaker died before construction was completed in 1997. A memorial to him stands beside the statue memorializing Shakespeare himself, in Southwark Cathedral, a few hundred yards west of the Globe.

IN FOCUS

8

SHAKESPEARE AND THE GLOBE THEATRE

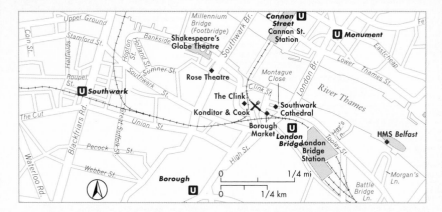

The season of plays is limited to the warmer months, from April 23 (Will's birthday) to the first week in October, with the schedule announced in late January on the theater's website. From November through March, the Sam Wanamaker Playhouse, a re-creation of a Jacobean theater, offers an indoor alternative, with performances by candlelight. Tickets go on sale in mid-February. The box office takes phone and mail orders as well as in-person sales, but the most convenient way to buy tickets is online. Book as early as possible.

FUN FACT: "Groundlings"—those with £5 standing-only tickets—are not allowed to sit during the performance. Reserve an actual seat, though, on any one of the theater's three levels, and you can join the "Elizabethan" crowd.

If you do have a seat, you can rent cushions for £1 (or bring your own) to soften the backless wooden benches. A limited number of backrests are also available for rent for £4. The show must go on, rain or shine, warm or chilly—so come prepared for whatever the weather throws at you. Umbrellas are banned, but you can bring a raincoat or buy a cheap Globe rain poncho, which doubles as a great souvenir.

MAKING THE MOST OF YOUR TIME

Give yourself plenty of time: there are several cafés and restaurants, as well as fascinating interactive exhibitions, and theater tours with occasional live demonstrations. Performances can last up to three hours.

WITH CHILDREN

Childsplay, a program for 8- to 11-year-olds, is held every Saturday during the theatre season. While Mom and Dad enjoy the play, children—helped by actors, musicians, and teachers—learn the background and story and become accustomed to Shakespearean language. By the time they are admitted to the theater for the last 20 minutes of the play, the children have become Shakespeare enthusiasts for life. There is also a children's playground with games and activities. Workshops start at 1:30 pm and tickets are £15; book in advance.

Year-Round at Shakespeare's Globe

Shakespeare's Globe Exhibition is a comprehensive display built under the theater (the entry is adjacent) that provides background material about the Elizabethan theater and about the surrounding neighborhood, Bankside. The exhibition describes the process of building the modern Globe and the serious research that went into it.

FUN FACT: In Shakespeare's day, this was a rough part of town. The Bear Gardens, around the corner from the Globe, was where bear baiting, a cruel animal sport, took place. Farther along, the local *gaol* (jail) stood on the site of what is now the Clink Prison Museum.

Daily live demonstrations include Elizabethan dressing, stage fighting, and swordplay, performed by drama students and stage-fighting instructors from the Royal Academy of Dramatic Art (RADA) and the London Academy of Music and Dramatic Art (LAMDA).

FUN FACT: Many performances are done in Elizabethan dress. Costumes for "original practices" productions, which aim to re-create the production techniques of Shakespeare's day, are handmade from period materials—wool, silk, cotton, animal skins, and natural dyes.

Admission also includes a tour of the theater. On matinee days, the tour visits the archaeological site of the nearby (and older) Rose Theatre.

FUN FACT: Shakespeare's casts were all male, with young men and boys playing the female roles. The live demonstration of Elizabethan dressing that forms part of the "Elizabethan Experience" shows how this was done—and how convincing it can be.

Visiting the Globe

- ✉ 21 New Globe Walk, Bankside, Bankside SE1 9DT

- ☎ 020/7902–1400 box office, 7401–9919 Globe Exhibition & Tour

- 🌐 www.shakespearesglobe.com

- 🎫 Exhibition & tour: £13.50, family ticket (2 adults, 3 children) £36; ticket prices for plays vary (Globe £5–£43, Wanamaker £10–£60).

- 🕐 Exhibition: daily 9–5:30 Globe tours. Plays: Globe, Apr. 23–Oct.; Wanamaker, Nov.–Apr. 23. Call or check website for performance times.

- Ⓤ London Bridge; Mansion House, then cross Southwark Bridge; St. Paul's, then cross the Millennium Bridge.

Borough Market brings hungry shoppers to the London Bridge area every Friday and Saturday.

FAMILY **Tate Modern.**

Fodor'sChoice *See the highlighted listing in this chapter.*

★

WORTH NOTING

Florence Nightingale Museum. Compact, highly visual, and engaging, this museum on the grounds of St. Thomas's hospital is dedicated to Florence Nightingale, who founded the first school of nursing and played a major role in establishing modern standards of health care. Exhibits are divided into three areas: one is devoted to Nightingale's Victorian childhood, the others to her work tending soldiers during the Crimean War (1854–56) and her subsequent health-care reforms. The museum incorporates Nightingale's own books and famous lamp as well as interactive displays of medical instruments and medicinal herbs. ⊠ *2 Lambeth Palace Rd., Lambeth* ☏ *020/7620–0374* ⊕ *www.florence-nightingale. co.uk* ✉ *£7.80* ⊙ *Daily 10–5; last admission 4:30* Ⓜ *Waterloo.*

The Garden Museum. This rather unassuming museum was created in the mid-1970s after two gardening enthusiasts came upon a medieval church, which, they were horrified to discover, was about to be bulldozed. The churchyard contained the tombs of two adventurous 17th-century plant collectors, a father and son both called John Tradescant, who introduced many new species to England. Inspired to action, the gardeners rescued the church and opened this museum. It has subsequently acquired one of the largest collections of historic garden tools, artifacts, and curiosities in Britain, in addition to creating beautiful walled gardens that are maintained year-round by dedicated volunteers. It's also worth visiting the church itself, which contains the tombs of William

TATE MODERN

✉ *Bankside* ☎ *020/7887–8888* ⊕ *www.tate.org.uk/modern* 🎟 *Free, charge for special exhibitions* ◷ *Sun.–Thurs. 10–6, Fri. and Sat. 10–10 (last admission to exhibitions 45 mins before closing)* Ⓜ *Southwark, Mansion House, St. Paul's.*

This spectacular renovation of a mid-20th-century power station is one of the most-visited museums of modern art in the world. Its great permanent collection, which starts in 1900 and ranges from Modern masters like Matisse to the most cutting-edge contemporary artists, is arranged thematically—Landscape, Still Life, and the Nude. Its blockbuster temporary exhibitions showcase the work of individual artists like Gaugin, Roy Lichtenstein, and Gerhard Richter.

TIPS

■ Join a free, 45-minute guided tours. Each covers a different gallery: Poetry and Dream at 11, Structure and Clarity at noon, and Energy and Process at 2. There's also a daily modern art talk at 3.

■ Levels 2 and 3 include temporary exhibitions, for which there's a charge. The main collection is free. Look for the ever-changing video installations scattered throughout the building.

■ Take advantage of the Tate to Tate Boat, which takes visitors back and forth between Tate Britain and Tate Modern every 40 minutes.

■ Private "Tate Tours for Two" can be booked online from £120 to £140, with afternoon tea for an additional £25 or a Champagne dinner or lunch for an additional £100.

Highlights

The vast **Turbine Hall** is a dramatic entrance point used to showcase big, audacious installations that tend to generate a lot of publicity. Past highlights include Olafur Eliasson's massive glowing sun and Carsten Holler's huge metal slides.

The museum is in the process of rearranging its galleries prior to the opening of an ambitious new extension in 2016, so check the website ahead of time. Not to be missed is the new collection of Rothko murals, originally created for the Seagram building in New York, and displays devoted to Cy Twombley and the video pioneer Nam June Paik (both on Level 4.)

Head to the Restaurant on Level 6 or the Espresso Bar on Level 3 for stunning vistas of the Thames. The view of St. Paul's from the Espresso Bar's balcony is one of the best in London.

8

Bligh, captain of the *Bounty*, several members of the Boleyn family, and quite a few Archbishops of Canterbury. As well, there's a green-thumb gift shop and **Garden Café**, serving vegetarian lunches and home-baked cakes—the toffee-apple variety is a standout. ✉ *5 Lambeth Palace Rd., Lambeth* ☎ *020/7401–8865*

⊕ *www.gardenmuseum.org.uk* ✉ *£7.50 (includes garden and all exhibitions)* ◷ *Sun.–Fri. 10:30–5, Sat. 10:30–4. Closed 1st Mon. of month and for occasional events—check website* Ⓜ *Lambeth North, Vauxhall.*

FAMILY **HMS Belfast.** At 613.5 feet, this is one of the last remaining big-gun armored warships from World War II, in which it played an important role in protecting the Arctic convoys and supporting the D-Day landings in Normandy; the ship later saw action during the Korean War. The *Belfast* has been moored in the Thames as a maritime branch of the **IWM London** since 1971. A tour of all nine decks—which include the admiral's quarters, mess decks, bakery, punishment cells, operations room, engine room, and more—gives a vivid picture of life on board the ship, while the riveting interactive gun-turret experience puts you in the middle of a World War II naval battle. ✉ *The Queen's Walk, Borough* ☎ *020/7940–6300* ⊕ *www.iwm.org.uk* ✉ *£15.50* ◷ *Mar.–Oct., daily 10–6; Nov.–Feb., daily 10–5; last admission 1 hr before closing* Ⓜ *London Bridge.*

OFF THE BEATEN PATH

Horniman Museum. Set in 16 acres of gardens, this eclectic museum is considered something of a well-kept secret by the residents of south London—perhaps because of its out-of-the-way location. You can explore world cultures, natural history, and a fine collection of musical instruments (including a giant tuba) here. The emphasis is on fun and a wide range of activities, including London's oldest nature trail. Recent additions include an African Worlds section, an Animal Walk that lets you get up close and personal with domesticated creatures such as sheep, chickens, and alpacas, and an aquarium stocked with endangered species. There's also a café and shop. It's a 15-minute bus ride from here to the Dulwich Picture Gallery. Bus P4, heading toward Brixton, takes you from door to door. ✉ *100 London Rd., Forest Hill* ☎ *020/8699–1872* ⊕ *www.horniman.ac.uk* ✉ *Free; small charge for temporary exhibitions and aquarium* ◷ *Museum daily 10:30–5:30; gardens Mon.–Sat. 7:30 am–dusk, Sun. 8 am–dusk; Animal Walk, daily 12:30–4; Nature Trail, daily 9–4 (may be closed in bad weather; call ahead)* Ⓜ *National Rail: Forest Hill from London Bridge or Victoria.*

FAMILY Fodor'sChoice ★

IWM London. Despite its name, the cultural venue formerly known as the Imperial War Museum (one of five IWM branches around the country) does not glorify either Empire or bloodshed but emphasizes understanding through conveying the impact of 20th- and 21st-century warfare on citizens and soldiers alike. After a major renovation, a dramatic six-story atrium at the main entrance encloses an impressive amount of hardware—including a Battle of Britain Spitfire, a German V2 rocket, tanks, guns, and submarines—along with accompanying interactive

Designed by renowned architect Renzo Piano, The Shard punctures the London skyline with its record-breaking height and spectacular modernity.

material and a café. The "Trench Experiences" in the World War I Galleries uses sights, sounds, and smells to re-create the grimness of life in No Man's Land, while an equally effective "Blitz Experience" in the revamped World War II galleries provides a 10-minute glimpse of an air raid, putting you on a "street" filled with acrid smoke as sirens wail and searchlights glare. Also in the World War II galleries is an extensive and haunting Holocaust Exhibition, while "Conflict Since 1945" documents the fact that there has been fighting somewhere in the world almost continuously since the end of World War II. Other galleries are devoted to works relating to conflicts from World War I to the present day by painters, poets, documentary filmmakers, and photographers (a new exhibition about pioneering female war correspondent Lee Miller opens in late 2015). James Bond fans won't want to miss the intriguing Secret War Gallery, which charts the work of secret agents. ⊠ *Lambeth Rd., South Bank* ☎ *020/7416–5000* ⊕ *www. iwm.org.uk* 🖅 *Free (charge for special exhibitions)* ⊘ *Daily 10–6; last admission 5:30* Ⓜ *Lambeth North.*

FAMILY **Sea Life London Aquarium.** The curved, colonnaded, neoclassic former County Hall that once housed London's local government administration is now home to a superb three-level aquarium full of sharks and stingrays, along with more than 500 other aquatic species, both common and rare. There are also feeding and hands-on displays, including a tank full of shellfish that you can touch. It's not the biggest aquarium you've ever seen, but the educational exhibits are particularly well arranged, with areas for different oceans, water environments, and climate zones, ranging from a stunning coral reef to a rain forest. Regular feeding times and free talks are offered throughout the day. There are also special "experiences" that include behind-the-scenes tours, snorkeling with sharks, or turtle feeding at an extra charge. Admission is by timed slot, but you can purchase flexible priority-entry tickets that also avoid the long lines. ⊠ *County Hall, Westminster Bridge Rd., South Bank* ☎ *0871/663–1678* ⊕ *www.visitsealife.com* 🖃 *£24.95 (up to 17% discount for online booking)* ⊗ *Daily 10–7; last admission 1 hr before closing* Ⓜ *Westminster, Waterloo.*

Southwark Cathedral. Pronounced "Suth-uck," this is the oldest Gothic church in London, with parts dating back to the 12th century. It remains off the beaten track, despite being the site of some remarkable memorials and a concert program that offers regular organ recitals at lunchtime on Monday (except in August and December) and classical music at 3:15 on Tuesday (except in December). Originally the priory church of St. Mary Overie (as in "over the water"—on the South Bank), it became a palace church under Henry VIII and was only promoted to cathedral status in 1905. Look for the gaudily renovated 1408 tomb of John Gower, a poet who was a friend of Chaucer's, and for the Harvard Chapel, where John Harvard, a local butcher's son who went on to found the American university, was baptized. Another notable buried here is Edmund Shakespeare, brother of William. The Refectory serves full English breakfasts, light lunches, and teas 9–6 weekdays, 10–6 weekends. ⊠ *London Bridge, Bankside* ☎ *020/7367–6700* ⊕ *cathedral. southwark.anglican.org* 🖃 *Free, suggested donation £4* ⊗ *Daily 8–6* Ⓜ *London Bridge.*

The View from the Shard. At 800 feet, this 2013 addition to the London skyline currently offers the highest vantage point in Western Europe. Designed by the noted architect Renzo Piano, it has attracted both admiration and disdain. While the building itself is generally highly regarded, many felt it would have been better sited in Canary Wharf (or perhaps Dubai), as it spoils views of St. Paul's Cathedral from traditional vantage points such as Hampstead's Parliament Hill. No matter how you feel about the building, there's no denying that it offers spectacular 360-degree views over London (extending to 40 miles on a clear day) from viewing platforms on floors 68, 69, and 72—almost twice as high as any other viewpoint in the city. Digital telescopes provide information about 200 points of interest. If you find the price as eye-wateringly high as the viewing platforms, there's a less dramatic but still very impressive—and free—view from the lobby of the Shangri-La hotel on floor 35, or, in the evenings, the hotel's chic Gong bar on floor 52 (over-18s only). ⊠ *32 London Bridge St., Borough* ☎ *0344/499–7222* ⊕ *www.theviewfromtheshard.com* 🖃 *From £24.95* ⊗ *Apr.–Oct., daily 10–10; Nov.–Mar., Sun.–Wed. 10–7, Thurs.–Sat. 10–10; admission by timed ticket only. Last admission 90 mins before closing. May be closed for special events, check website.* Ⓜ *London Bridge.*

KENSINGTON, CHELSEA, KNIGHTSBRIDGE, AND BELGRAVIA

GETTING ORIENTED

Kensington, Chelsea, Knightsbridge, and Belgravia

GETTING THERE	TOP REASONS TO GO
Several Tube stations are nearby: Sloane Square and High Street Kensington on the District and Circle lines; Knightsbridge and Hyde Park Corner on the Piccadilly line; Earl's Court, South Kensington, and Gloucester Road on the District, Circle, and Piccadilly lines; Holland Park on the Central line; Ladbroke Grove on the Hammersmith and City line; and Victoria on the District, Circle, and Victoria lines.	**Treasure hunt at the V&A Museum:** The Victoria & Albert is the world's best decorative arts museum. Artists have been sketching in the Sculpture Court since Victorian times.
	Attract a dinosaur's attention at the Natural History Museum: Watch children catch on that the museum's animatronic *T. rex* has noticed *them*—and is licking its rather large chops.
	Glimpse royal domestic life at Kensington Palace: Visit the public areas and gardens of this royal family commune that has housed Queen Victoria, Princess Diana, and (currently) the Duke and Duchess of Cambridge (William and Kate).
SAFETY	**Enter an Orientalist fantasy at Leighton House:** This small museum and "private palace of art" is right out of the Arabian Nights, with peacock-blue tiles and intricate mosaic murals.
This is one of London's safest districts, but beware of pickpockets in shopping areas.	

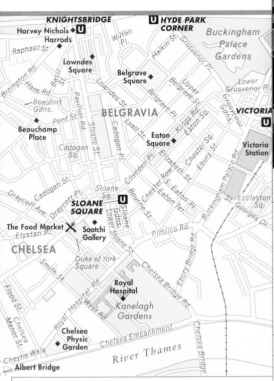

MAKING THE MOST OF YOUR TIME

You could fill three or four days in this borough: A shopping stroll along the length of King's Road is easily half a day. Give yourself a half day, at least, for the Victoria & Albert Museum and a half day for either the Science or Natural History Museum.

A GRAZER'S PARADISE

Duke of York Square Farmers' Market. West London's answer to Borough Market, this Saturday open-air market is in a pedestrianized plaza off Duke of York Square, a chic shopping precinct. It hosts 40 stalls purveying artisanal and locally produced meat, game, fish, breads, cakes, cupcakes, honey, pasta, cheese, fresh oysters, and chocolate from more than 150 small producers. Like Borough Market, this is a grazer's paradise, giving you the chance to sample fresh oysters and cooked sausages as well as yummy hot snacks. ⊠ *Duke of York Sq., Chelsea* ☎ *020/7823-5577* ⊕ *www.dukeofyorksquare. com* ⊙ *Sat. 10–4* Ⓜ *Sloane Sq.*

9

FEELING PECKISH?

The Café at the V&A. Breakfast, light snacks, tea, and full meals are served throughout the day (10–5:15), all in a grand room at modest prices. You can eat in the courtyard if the weather's good, or have a buffet supper on Friday late nights (until 9:30 pm). Stop by just to see the original Arts and Crafts part of the café, one of William Morris's earliest commissions, with stained-glass panels by Edward Burne-Jones. ⊠ *Victoria & Albert Museum, Cromwell Rd., South Kensington* ☎ *020/7942-2000* Ⓜ *South Kensington.*

NEAREST PUBLIC RESTROOMS

Most public restrooms have been replaced by futuristic "autoloos"—booths on street corners that cost £1. If you're not brave enough to try them, head to the restrooms at department stores Peter Jones or Harvey Nichols. Or ask for the "loo" in a pub, but be prepared for "sorry" if you're not a customer.

Sightseeing
★★★★
Nightlife
★★
Dining
★★★★
Lodging
★★★★
Shopping
★★★★★

The Royal Borough of Kensington & Chelsea (or "K&C" as the locals call it) is where you'll find London at its richest, and not just in the moneyed sense. South Kensington offers a concentration of great museums near Cromwell Road, with historic Kensington Palace located nearby in Kensington Gardens. Once-raffish Chelsea, where the Pre-Raphaelites painted and Mick Jagger partied, is now a thoroughly respectable home for the discreetly wealthy, while flashier Knightsbridge has become a haven for international plutocrats, with shopping to match their tastes.

KENSINGTON

Updated By
Ellin Stein

Kensington incorporates the area along the southern edge of Hyde Park from Exhibition Road (where the big museum complex is) and the area to the west of the park bordered by leafy Holland Park Avenue on the north and traffic-heavy Cromwell Road on the south. This more westerly zone includes the satellite neighborhood of Holland Park, with its serenely grand villas and charming park, as well as local shopping mecca Kensington High Street and the antiques shops on Kensington Church Street.

Kensington's first royal connection was created when King William III, fed up with the dampness arising from the Thames, bought a country place there in 1689 and converted it into **Kensington Palace.** Queen Victoria's consort, Prince Albert, added the jewel in the borough's crown when he turned the profits of the Great Exhibition of 1851 into South Kensington's metropolis of museums: The **Victoria & Albert Museum (V&A)**, the **Science Museum,** and the **Natural History Museum.** His namesakes in the area include the **Royal Albert Hall,** with bas-reliefs that make it resemble a giant, redbrick Wedgwood teapot, and the lavish **Albert Memorial.**

Turn into Derry Street or Young Street and enter **Kensington Square,** one of the most complete 17th-century residential squares in London. Holland Park is about ¾ mile farther west; both **Leighton House** and **18 Stafford Terrace,** two of London's most gorgeously decorated Victorian-era houses (the lavish use of Islamic tiles, inlaid mosaics, gilded ceilings, and marble columns make the former into an Arabian Nights fantasy), are nearby as well.

TOP ATTRACTIONS

18 Stafford Terrace. The home of *Punch* cartoonist Edward Linley Sambourne in the 1870s is filled with delightful Victorian and Edwardian antiques, fabrics, and paintings (as well as several samples of Linley Sambourne's work for *Punch*) and is one of the most charming 19th-century London houses extant . The Italianate house was the scene for society parties when Anne Messel was in residence in the 1940s. This being Kensington, there's inevitably a royal connection: Messel's son, Antony Armstrong-Jones, was married to the late Princess Margaret, and their son has preserved the connection by taking the title Viscount Linley. Admission is by guided tour only, and the afternoon tours on weekends are given by costumed actors. ✉ *18 Stafford Terr., Kensington* 🖷 *0207/602–3316* 🌐 *www.rbkc.gov.uk (under Leisure and Libraries)* 🎫 *£8* ☺ *Guided tours Wed. 11:15 and 2:15; weekends 11:15, 1, 2:15, and 3:30. Closed mid-June–mid-Sept.* Ⓜ *High Street Kensington.*

Kensington Palace.
See the highlighted listing in this chapter.

Fodor'sChoice **Leighton House Museum.** Leading Victorian artist Frederic (Lord) Leighton
★ lived and worked in this building on the edge of Holland Park, spending 30 years (and quite a bit of money) transforming it into an opulent "private palace of art" infused with an orientalist aesthetic sensibility. The interior is a sumptuous Arabian Nights fantasy, with walls lined in peacock blue tiles designed by Leighton's friend, the ceramic artist William de Morgan, and beautiful mosaic wall panels and floors, marble pillars, and gilded ceilings. The centerpiece is the Arab Hall, its marble walls adorned with even more intricate murals made from 16th- and 17th-century ceramic tiles imported from Syria, Turkey, and Iran, surmounted by a domed ceiling covered in gold leaf with a gold mosaic frieze running underneath. You can also visit Leighton's studio, with its huge north window and dome, and the house is filled with several of his paintings along with works by other Pre-Raphaelites. ✉ *12 Holland Park Rd., Holland Park* 🖷 *020/7332–3316* 🌐 *www.rbkc.gov.uk (under Leisure and Libraries)* 🎫 *£7* ☺ *Wed.–Mon. 10–5:30* Ⓜ *Holland Park, South Kensington.*

FAMILY **Natural History Museum.**
Fodor'sChoice *See the highlighted listing in this chapter.*
★

FAMILY **Victoria & Albert Museum.**
Fodor'sChoice *See the highlighted listing in this chapter.*
★

9

KENSINGTON PALACE

✉ *The Broad Walk, Kensington Gardens, Kensington* ☎ *0844/482–7799 advance booking, 0844/482–7777 information, 0203/166–6000 from outside U.K.* ⊕ *www.hrp.org.uk* 🎫 *£16.50* ⊙ *Mar.–Sept., daily 10–6; Oct.–Feb., daily 10–5; last admission 1 hr before closing* Ⓜ *Queensway, High Street Kensington.*

TIPS

■ The palace has a wheelchair-accessible elevator, and Kensington Gardens has electric buggies for mobility-impaired visitors.

■ If you also plan to visit the Tower of London, Hampton Court Palace, Banqueting House, or Kew Palace, become a member of Historic Royal Palaces. It costs £46 per person, or £88 for a family, and gives you free entry to all five sites for a year.

■ Picnicking is allowed on the benches in the palace grounds. (You can also picnic anywhere in the adjoining Kensington Gardens.)

■ There's a delightful café in the Orangery, near the Sunken Garden. Built for Queen Anne, it's a great place for formal afternoon tea, although it gets busy during peak hours.

Neither as imposing as Buckingham Palace nor as charming as Hampton Court, Kensington Palace is something of a Royal Family commune, with various close relatives of the Queen occupying large apartments in the private part of the palace. Bought in 1689 by Queen Mary and King William III, it was converted into a palace by Sir Christopher Wren and Nicholas Hawksmoor, and royals have been in residence ever since. Princess Diana lived here with her sons after her divorce, and this is where Prince William now lives with his wife, Catherine, Duchess of Cambridge and their young son, George, and baby daughter, Charlotte.

The State Apartments are open to the public. One permanent exhibition, "Victoria Revealed," is devoted to the private life of Queen Victoria, who was born and grew up at KP. The Queen's State Apartments are given over to William and Mary and the Glorious Revolution. The lavish King's State Apartments, originally build for George I, have a semipermanent exhibit that explores the world of the Georgian Court through the story of George II and his politically active queen, Caroline. There is also a changing temporary exhibition. Through late 2015, this will be "Fashion Rules," a collection of gowns worn by Princess Margaret, Princess Diana, and Queen Elizabeth.

Highlights

Look for the King's Staircase, with its panoramic trompe l'oeil painting, and the King's Gallery, with royal artworks surrounded by rich red damask walls, intricate gilding, and a beautiful painted ceiling. Outside, the grounds are almost as lovely as the palace itself.

Ice-skaters outside the Natural History Museum in South Kensington

WORTH NOTING

FAMILY **Holland Park.** Formerly the grounds of an aristocrat's house and open to the public only since 1952, Holland Park is an often-overlooked gem and possibly London's most romantic park. The northern "Wilderness" end offers woodland walks among native and exotic trees first planted in the early 18th century. Foxes, rabbits, and hedgehogs are among the residents The central part of the park is given over to the manicured lawns—still stalked by raucous peacocks—one would expect at a stately home, although Holland House itself, originally built by James I's chancellor and later the site of a 19th-century salon frequented by Byron, Dickens, and Disraeli, was largely destroyed by German incendiary bombs in 1940. The east wing was reconstructed and has been incorporated into a youth hostel, while the remains of the front terrace provide an atmospheric backdrop for the open-air performances of the April–September **Holland Park Opera Festival** (*0300/999–1000 box office, www.operahollandpark.com*). The glass-walled Garden Ballroom (every home should have one) is now the **Orangery**, which hosts art exhibitions and other public events, as does the **Ice House,** while an adjoining former granary has become the upscale Belvedere restaurant. In spring and summer the air is fragrant with aromas from a rose garden, great banks of rhododendrons, and an azalea walk. Garden enthusiasts will also not want to miss the tranquil, traditional **Kyoto Garden,** a legacy of London's 1991 Japan Festival. The southern part of the park is given over to sport and play: cricket and football (soccer) pitches; a golf practice area; tennis courts; a well-supervised children's Adventure Playground; and a giant outdoor chess set. ⊠ *Ilchester Pl., Holland Park*

NATURAL HISTORY MUSEUM

✉ *Cromwell Rd., South Kensington* ☎ *0207/942–5000* ⊕ *www.nhm.ac.uk* ⊠ *Free (some fees for special exhibitions)* ⊙ *Daily 10–5:50, last admission at 5:30* Ⓜ *South Kensington.*

TIPS

■ "Nature Live" is a program of free, informal talks given by scientists, covering a wildly eclectic range of subjects, usually at 2:30 (and at 12:30 on weekends) in the David Attenborough Studio in the Darwin Centre.

■ The museum has an outdoor ice-skating rink from October to January, and a popular Christmas fair.

■ There are 50-minute Spirit Collection tours at 1:30 daily and 30-minute tours at 10:40, 11:40, and 12:40.

■ Got kids under seven with you? Check out the museum's free "Explorer Backpacks." They contain a range of activity materials to keep the little ones amused.

The ornate terra-cotta facade of this enormous Victorian museum is embellished with relief panels depicting living creatures to the left of the entrance and extinct ones to the right (although some species have subsequently changed categories). Most are represented inside the museum, which contains more than 70 million different specimens. Only a small percentage is on public display, but you could still spend a day here and not come close to seeing everything.

Highlights

A giant diplodocus skeleton dominates the vaulted, cathedral-like entrance hall, affording you perhaps the most irresistible photo opportunity in the building. It's just a cast, but the **Dinosaur Gallery** (Gallery 21) contains plenty of real-life dino bones, fossils, and some extremely long teeth.

You'll also come face-to-face with velociraptors and a giant animatronic *Tyrannosaurus rex* that's programmed to sense when human prey is near and "respond" in character. When he does, you can hear the shrieks of fear and delight all the way across the room.

An escalator takes you into a giant globe in the **Earth Galleries,** where there's a choice of levels to explore. Don't leave without checking out the earthquake simulation in the **Volcanoes and Earthquake Gallery.**

The **Darwin Centre** houses some of the millions of items the museum itself doesn't have room to display, including "Archie," a 28-foot giant squid. If you want to see Archie and some of the other thousands of specimens on the shelves, you'll need to book one of the free behind-the-scenes Spirit Collection tours. These can be booked on the day, but space is limited, so come early. The Centre's **Cocoon Experience** is a 45-minute tour during which you can see specimens from plant and insect collections previously in storage.

VICTORIA & ALBERT MUSEUM

✉ *Cromwell Rd., South Kensington* ☎ *020/7942-2000* ⊕ *www.vam.ac.uk* ⊜ *Free; charge for some special exhibitions (from £5)* ⊘ *Sat.– Thurs. 10–5:45, Fri. 10–10* Ⓜ *South Kensington.*

TIPS

■ The V&A is a tricky building to navigate, so be sure to use the free map.

■ As a whirlwind introduction, you could take a free one-hour tour (10:30, 11:30, 12:30, 1:30, 2:30, or 3:30). There are also tours devoted just to the British Galleries at 2:30. Occasional public lectures during the week are delivered by visiting bigwigs from the art and fashion worlds. There are free lectures throughout the week given by museum staff, who also give an Introductory tour of the collection on Friday nights at 7.

■ Whatever time you visit, the spectacular sculpture hall will be filled with artists, both amateur and professional, sketching the myriad of artworks on display there. Don't be shy; bring a pad and join in.

■ Although the permanent collection is free, the V&A also hosts high-profile special exhibitions that run for several months.

Known to all as the V&A, this huge museum is devoted to the applied arts of all disciplines, all periods, and all nationalities. First opened as the South Kensington Museum in 1857, it was renamed in 1899 in honor of Queen Victoria's late husband and has since grown to become one of the country's best-loved cultural institutions.

Many collections at the V&A are presented not by period but by category—textiles, sculpture, jewelry, and so on. Nowhere is the benefit of this more apparent than in the **Fashion Gallery** (Room 40), where formal 18th-century court dresses are displayed alongside the haute couture styles of contemporary designers. The Fashion Gallery has become known for high-profile temporary exhibitions devoted to icons such as David Bowie and Alexander McQueen.

The **British Galleries** (rooms 52–58 and 118–125), devoted to art and design from 1500 to 1900, are full of beautiful diversions—among them the Great Bed of Ware (immortalized in Shakespeare's *Twelfth Night*). Here, a series of actual rooms have been painstakingly reconstructed piece by piece. These include an ornate music room and the Henrietta St. Room, a breathtakingly serene parlor dating from 1722.

The **Asian Galleries** (rooms 44–47) are full of treasures, but among the most striking items on display is a remarkable collection of ornate samurai armor in the **Japanese Gallery** (room 44). There are also galleries devoted to China, Korea, and the Islamic Middle East. More recently installed areas include the Ceramics gallery and the Medieval and Renaissance galleries, which have the largest collection of works from the period outside of Italy. The Europe Gallery (rooms 1–7), opened after an extensive refurbishment, brings together more than 1,100 objects from 1600 to 1800.

9

Historic Plaque Hunt

As you wander around London, you'll see lots of small blue, circular plaques on the sides and facades of buildings, describing which famous, infamous, or obscure but brilliant person once lived there. The first was placed outside Lord Byron's birthplace (now demolished) by the Royal Society of Arts. There are about 700 blue plaques, erected by different bodies—some green ones originate from Westminster City Council—but English Heritage now maintains the responsibility. If you want to find out the latest, check the website ⊕ www.english-heritage. org.uk. Below are some of the highlights:

James Barrie (100 Bayswater Rd., Bayswater W2); **Frederic Chopin** (4 St. James's Pl., St. James's W1); **Sir Winston Churchill** (28 Hyde Park Gate, Kensington Gore SW7); **Captain James Cook** (88 Mile End Rd., Tower Hamlets E1); **T.S. Eliot** (3 Kensington Court Gardens, Kensington W8); **Benjamin Franklin** (36 Craven St., Westminster WC2); **Mahatma Gandhi** (20 Baron's Court Rd., West Kensington W14); **George Frederic Handel** and **Jimi Hendrix** (23 Brook St., Mayfair W1); **Alfred Hitchcock** (153 Cromwell Rd., Earl's Court SW5); **Karl Marx** (28 Dean St., Soho W1); **Wolfgang Amadeus Mozart** (180 Ebury St., Pimlico SW1); **Horatio Nelson** (103 New Bond St., Mayfair W1); **Sir Isaac Newton** (87 Jermyn St., St. James's SW1); **Florence Nightingale** (10 South St., Mayfair W1); **George Bernard Shaw** (29 Fitzroy Sq., Fitzrovia W1); **Percy Bysshe Shelley** (15 Poland St., Soho W1); **Mark Twain** (23 Tedworth Sq., Chelsea SW3); **H.G. Wells** (13 Hanover Terr., Regent's Park NW1); **Oscar Wilde** (34 Tite St., Chelsea SW3); **William Butler Yeats** (23 Fitzroy Rd., Primrose Hill NW1).

⊕ *www.rbkc.gov.uk (under Leisure and Libraries)* ⊘ *Daily 7:30–30 mins before dusk* Ⓜ *Holland Park, High Street Kensington.*

FAMILY
Fodor's Choice
★

Science Museum. This, one of the three great South Kensington museums, stands next to the Natural History Museum in a far plainer building. It has lots of hands-on painlessly educational exhibits, but don't dismiss the Science Museum as just for kids. Highlights include the Launch Pad gallery, which demonstrates basic laws of physics; *Puffing Billy*, the oldest steam locomotive in the world; and the actual *Apollo 10* capsule. The six floors are devoted to subjects as diverse as the history of flight, space exploration, the large Hadron collider, 3-D printing, and a sublime exhibition on science in the 18th century. The Information Age gallery, devoted to communication networks, including telegraph, television, mobile phones, and Internet, was opened in 2014 by Queen Elizabeth, who marked the occasion by sending her first tweet. The architecturally imaginative Mathematics gallery opens in 2016. Overshadowed by a three-story blue-glass wall, the Wellcome Wing is an annex to the rear of the museum, devoted to contemporary science and technology. It contains a 450-seat IMAX theater and the Legend of Apollo—an advanced motion simulator that combines seat vibration with other technical gizmos to re-create the experience of a moon landing. If you're a family of at least five, you might be able to get a place on one of the popular Science Night sleepovers by booking well in advance. Aimed at kids 7 years old, these nighttime science workshops offer the chance to camp out in one of the galleries, and include a free IMAX show the next morning. Check the website for details. ⊠ *Exhibition Rd., South Kensington* ☎ *0870/870–4868* ⊕ *www. sciencemuseum.org.uk* ✉ *Free; charge for special exhibitions, IMAX, and simulator rides* ⊗ *Daily 10–6; last admission 5:15* Ⓜ *South Kensington.*

Serpentine Gallery. Overlooking the large stream that winds its way through Hyde Park and from which the gallery takes its name, this small brick building set in Kensington Gardens is one of London's foremost showcases for contemporary art, and has featured exhibitions by luminaries such as Louise Bourgeois, John Currin, Gabriel Orozco, and Gerhard Richter. A permanent work on the gallery's grounds, consisting of eight benches and a carved stone circle, commemorates its former patron, Princess Diana. The Serpentine Sackler Gallery, a second exhibition space that's in a small Georgian gunpowder storeroom nearly, has a dramatic extension designed by Zaha Hadid as well as a stylish restaurant. If you're in town between May and September, check out the annual Serpentine pavilion, which each year is commissioned from a leading architect who is given free rein to interpret the brief—leading to imaginative results. Past designers have included Frank Gehry, Daniel Liebeskind, and Jean Nouvel. ⊠ *Kensington Gardens, Kensington* ☎ *0207/402–6075* ⊕ *www.serpentinegallery.org* ✉ *Free* ⊗ *Daily 10–6* Ⓜ *Lancaster Gate, Knightsbridge, South Kensington.*

ARTISTIC CHELSEA

Artists and writers flocked to the area in the 19th century, establishing a creative colony in Cheyne Walk; at one time Turner, Whistler, John Singer Sargent, Dante Gabriel Rossetti, and Oscar Wilde were residents. In the 1960s it was the turn of Mick Jagger and Keith Richards; in the 1970s Bob Marley wrote "I Shot the Sheriff" in a flat off Cheyne Walk. It's now one of London's most expensive streets, completely unaffordable for latter-day Bob Marleys.

CHELSEA

Chelsea was settled before the Domesday Book was compiled and already fashionable when two of Henry VIII's wives lived there. On the banks of the Thames are the vast grounds of the **Royal Hospital,** designed by Christopher Wren. A walk along the riverside embankment will take you to **Cheyne Walk,** a lovely street dating back to the 18th century. Several of its more notable residents—who range from J. M. W. Turner and Henry James to Laurence Olivier and Keith Richards—are commemorated by blue plaques on their former houses.

The **Albert Bridge,** a sherbet-color Victorian confection of a suspension bridge, provides one of London's great romantic views, especially at night. Leave time to explore the tiny Georgian lanes of pastel-color houses that veer off King's Road to the north—especially **Jubilee Place** and **Burnsall Street,** leading to the hidden "village square" of **Chelsea**

Green. On Saturday there's an excellent farmers' market up from the Saatchi Gallery selling artisanal cheese and chocolates, local oysters, and organic meats, plus stalls serving international food.

Residential Chelsea extends along the river from the Chelsea Bridge west to the Battersea Bridge and north as far as the Old Brompton Road.

TOP ATTRACTIONS

Royal Hospital Chelsea. Charles II founded this hospice for elderly and infirm soldiers in 1682 to reward the troops who had fought for him in the civil wars of 1642–46 and 1648. A creation of three of England's greatest architects—Wren, Vanbrugh, and Hawksmoor—this small village of brick and Portland stone set in manicured gardens (which you can visit) surrounds the Figure Court (the figure being a 1682 gilded bronze statue of Charles II dressed as a Roman general), the Great Hall (dining room), and a chapel. The chapel and the Great Hall, where you can see Antonio Verrio's vast oil painting of Charles on horseback, are open to the public at certain times during the day. There is a small museum devoted to the history of the resident "Chelsea Pensioners," but the real attraction, along with the building, is the pensioners themselves. Recognizable by their traditional scarlet frock coats with gold buttons, medals, and tricorne hats, they are all actual veterans, who wear the uniform, and the history it represents, with a great deal of pride. Individuals can visit the grounds, chapel, courts, and museum for free, or for £10 you can go on a guided tour for groups of four or more led by one of the pensioners. ⊠ *Royal Hospital Rd., Chelsea* ☎ *020/7881–5298* ⊕ *www.chelsea-pensioners.co.uk* 🎟 *Free; guided tour (for groups of 4 or more) £10* ⊙ *Grounds, chapel, courts, and Great Hall Mon.–Sat. 10–4:30. Museum weekdays 10–4:30. Closed holidays and for special events* ⊙ *Closed Sun.* Ⓜ *Sloane Sq.*

RHS Chelsea Flower Show. Run by the Royal Horticultural Society, the Chelsea Flower Show, the year's highlight for thousands of garden-obsessed Brits, is held every May (usually the third week) at the Royal Hospital. The mammoth event takes up vast acreage, and the surrounding streets throng with visitors. ⊠ *Chelsea* ☎ *0844/338–7502 in U.K., 121/767–4063 from outside U.K.* ⊕ *www.rhs.org.uk* 🎟 *From £46* ⊙ *Tues.–Fri.,8–8, Sat. 8–5:30.*

Saatchi Gallery. Charles Saatchi, who made his fortune in advertising, is one of Britain's canniest collectors of contemporary art, credited with popularizing the Young British Artists movement through his championing of early works by the likes of Damien Hirst and Tracey Emin. The museum's home—its third in 10 years—is at the former Duke of York's HQ, just off King's Road. Built in 1803, its grand period exterior belies its imaginatively restored modern interior, which was transformed into 15 gallery exhibition spaces of varying size and shape. Unlike Tate Modern, there is no permanent collection beyond an ongoing site-specific installation; instead, at any one time the galleries are given over to between one and three exhibitions that normally run for up to six months. There's also an excellent café, which is open late. ⊠ *Duke*

World-famous Harrods has been luring shoppers with its classic wares since 1834.

of York's HQ Bldg., King's Rd., Chelsea ☎ *020/7811–3085* ⊕ *www.saatchigallery.com* ⊠ *Free* ⊙ *Daily 10–6* Ⓜ *Sloane Sq.*

KNIGHTSBRIDGE

There's no getting away from it. With two world-famous department stores—**Harrods** and **Harvey Nichols,** a few hundred yards apart and surrounded by numerous boutiques selling the biggest names in international luxury and expensive jewelry—London's wealthiest enclave (not many other neighborhoods are plagued with street racers in Maseratis) will appeal most to those who enjoy conspicuous consumption.

Nearby Sloane Street is lined with top-end designer boutiques such as Prada, Dior, and Tods. If it all starts to become a bit generic (although expensive generic), **Beauchamp Place** (pronounced "Beecham") is lined with equally luxe boutiques, but they tend to be one-offs and more distinctive and less global.

Posh Knightsbridge is located to the east of Kensington, bordered by Hyde Park on the north and Pont Street just past Harrods on the south.

BELGRAVIA

Steps away from the roaring traffic of Hyde Park Corner is quiet, fashionable Belgravia, one of the most impressive set pieces of 19th-century urban planning, which lies just to the east of Kensington and Chelsea. Street after street is lined with grand cream stucco terraces, once aristocrats' town houses and most still part of the Grosvenor estate owned by the Duke of Westminster. Many buildings are leased to embassies or organizations, but a remarkable number around **Lowndes Square**, **Eaton Place**, and **Eaton Square** remain in the hands of private owners, whether old money or the oligarchy who put their security guards in the attached mews houses. Some people consider the area near **Elizabeth Street** to be southern Belgravia, others call it Pimlico–Victoria. Either way, you'll find small, unique stores here specializing in baked goods, wine, gifts, and stationery.

> **WORD OF MOUTH**
>
> "We went to the Chelsea Flower Show last year—it was one of the greatest memories from our trip. There was no problem ordering the tickets online and having them delivered. It was just a wonderful day with my Mom! I can't recommend it enough if you love gardening." —willowjane

TOP ATTRACTIONS

Belgrave Square. This is the heart of Belgravia, once the preferred address for the gentry's London town houses, though now mostly occupied by organizations, embassies, and the international rich. The Square and the streets leading off it share a remarkably consistent elegant architectural style thanks to all being part of a Regency redevelopment scheme commissioned by the Duke of Westminster and designed by Thomas Cubitt with George Basevi. The grand, cream-colored stucco terraced houses were snapped up by aristocrats and politicians due to their proximity to Buckingham Palace just around the corner, and still command record prices on the rare occasion when they come onto the market. The private garden in the center is open to the public once a year (*www.opensquares.org*). Walk down Belgrave Place toward Eaton Place and you pass two of Belgravia's most beautiful mews: Eaton Mews North and Eccleston Mews, both fronted by grand rusticated entrances right out of a 19th-century engraving. Traffic can really whip around Belgrave Square, so be careful. ⊠ *Belgrave Sq., Belgravia* Ⓜ *Hyde Park Corner.*

NOTTING HILL
AND BAYSWATER

GETTING ORIENTED

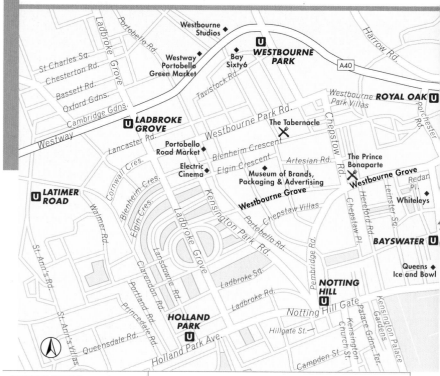

For Portobello Market and environs, the best Tube stops are Ladbroke Grove and Westbourne Park (Hammersmith and City lines); ask for directions when you emerge. The Notting Hill Gate stop on the District, Circle, and Central lines enables you to walk the length of Portobello Road while going slightly downhill.

To find Notting Hill's grandest houses, stroll over to Lansdowne Road, Lansdowne Crescent, and Lansdowne Square—two blocks west of Kensington Park Road.

Unearth a bargain on Portobello Road: The early bird catches the worm; go before 10 am on Saturday to find the good stuff at London's best and most famous antiques market, or come during the week for a leisurely browse.

Refresh in Hyde Park: Explore one of London's largest green spaces by walking, cycling ("Boris bikes" are available at several sites), skating with the Friday Night Skate, or rowing down the Serpentine, the twisty lake that winds through the park.

Take in contemporary art at the Serpentine Gallery: Expand your cultural horizons here at one of London's foremost showcases for modern art, or just have a bite at the café in the extension, designed by the famed architect Zaha Hadid and a piece of artwork in itself.

Notting Hill and Bayswater

MAKING THE MOST OF YOUR TIME

Saturday is the most exciting day for shopping, eating, and drinking here.

The market gets crowded by noon in summer, so come early if you are serious about shopping.

Head south from the north end of Portobello Road, using the parks to take a break on the way.

On Sunday, the Hyde Park and Kensington Gardens railings along Bayswater Road are lined with artists displaying their work, which may slow your progress.

Well-heeled locals are often out on Sunday with friends in the pubs or with kids in the parks.

SAFETY

At night, avoid straying from the main streets north of Westbourne Park Road toward Ladbroke Grove's high-rise estates (projects) and the surrounding areas.

FEELING PECKISH?

The Prince Bonaparte. It recently underwent an art deco makeover, but one thing hasn't changed: the high standard of its modern British food and a fine selection of artisanal ales and carefully chosen wines. This high-ceilinged gastropub is the perfect place for a drink or a bite to eat. ⊠ *80 Chepstow Rd., Bayswater* ☎ *020/7313–9491* ⊕ *theprincebonapartew2. co.uk* ⊗ *Mon.–Sat. noon–11, Sun. noon–10:30* Ⓜ *Notting Hill Gate, Royal Oak.*

The Tabernacle. The Victorian Gothic interior of this combination bar, café, and arts center hosts music gigs (some by big names like Adele), literary events like an evening with Tales of The City's Armistead Maupin, and 15-minute talks with speakers such as Niall Ferguson. The food is Caribbean-influenced, and the atmosphere, especially in the large outdoor courtyard, is relaxed. ⊠ *34–35 Powis Sq., Notting Hill* ☎ *020/7221–9700* ⊕ *www.tabernaclew11.com* ⊗ *Closed Sun.* Ⓜ *Notting Hill Gate.*

10

Sightseeing
★★
Nightlife
★★★
Dining
★★★
Lodging
★★★
Shopping
★★★★

The center of London's West Indian community from the 1950s through the '70s, Notting Hill these days is the address of choice for the well-heeled, be they bankers, rock stars, media and advertising types, or rich hippies. Teeming with trendy restaurants, cool bars, and buzzing street markets, the area is also studded with some of London's most handsome historic residences, crescents, and terraces. Every weekend, the hordes descend on Portobello Road to go bargain-hunting at one of the world's great antiques markets. Holland Park, to the west, has even grander villas, while Bayswater (to the east) has excellent ethnic restaurants.

NOTTING HILL

Updated By
James O'Neill

Notting Hill as we know it emerged in the 1840s when the wealthy Ladbroke family developed a small suburb to the west of London. Before then, the area had the far less glamorous name of "the Potteries and the Piggeries," after the two industries it was best known for: ceramics and pig farming.

During the 1980s, Notting Hill transformed from a lively but down-at-heel and sometimes dangerous West Indian enclave to a supertrendy fashionable neighborhood. However, in London the past is never far behind, and the area's Caribbean legacy persists, not least in the form of the annual Notting Hill Carnival in late August. The new millennium saw the neighborhood's fame go global thanks to the hit romcom of the same name, though the movie itself was criticized by locals for downplaying the area's ethnic diversity. For the Notting Hill of the silver screen, head for fashionable **Westbourne Grove** and **Ledbury Road,** lined with eclectic independent boutiques offering highly desirable designer goods, children's clothing, furniture and home accessories, upscale cookware, shoes, and contemporary art. Prices and taste levels are high.

For less rarefied shopping, try **Portobello Road,** with the beautifully restored early-20th-century **Electric Cinema** at No. 191. The famous Saturday antiques market and shops are at the southern end. The central part of the road is home to a weekday produce market interspersed with vintage clothing shops and hot food stalls. On weekends, the more northerly part of the road sells discounted household goods, secondhand goods, and bric-a-brac, while **the Portobello Green Market** under the Westway overpass has clothing stalls selling everything from supercool baby clothes to jewelry to vintage threads and club wear from youthful new designers. Meanwhile, the boutiques of the **Portobello Green Arcade** carry clothes from more established designers.

To the west of Labroke Grove, before Shepherd's Bush Green, lies the handsome Holland Park neighborhood. On the south side of Holland Park Road (the westerly continuation of Notting Hill Gate) you'll find quiet streets filled with gorgeous stucco villas.

WORD OF MOUTH

"Early in the am on Saturday is great for the Portobello Road Market—by mid-morning it is a zoo." —janisj

"But if you're not that interested in the market, the area of Westbourne Grove/Ledbury Road has some very nice shops and restaurants. Not busy, even on a Saturday." —tulips

"One decade's uninhabitable slum inevitably becomes a global mecca a couple of decades later, often with very little real change in the buildings or street patterns (Notting Hill is possibly the extreme example of this)." —flanneruk

TOP ATTRACTIONS

Graffik. Not everyone thinks graffiti can be a bonus to the urban landscape, but those who do should head for this leading gallery of contemporary street art. The big name here is Banksy, but there are works for sale by several other artists in the same vein such as Trust.iCON and CODE FC, who are more concerned with social commentary than tagging. This is one gallery experience that really appeals to young people, especially if the visit coincides with one of Graffik's two-hour weekend workshops. ✉ *284 Portobello Rd., Notting Hill* ☎ *020/8354–3592* ⊕ *graffikgallery.com* ☉ *Daily 11–6:30* Ⓜ *Notting Hill Gate, Ladbroke Grove.*

FAMILY **Hyde Park and Kensington Gardens.**
See the highlighted listing in this chapter.

Portobello Road. Looking for a 19th-century snuff spoon? Perhaps a Georgian salt cellar ? What about a 1960s-era minidress? Then head to Portobello Road's famous Saturday market. Arrive at about 9 am to avoid the giant crowds. Stretching almost 2 miles from Notting Hill, the market is made up of four sections, each with a different emphasis: antiques, fresh produce, household goods, and a flea market. The antiques stalls are packed in between Chepstow Villas and

10

Continued on page 190

HYDE PARK AND KENSINGTON GARDENS

Two verdant oases in the center of London, the royal parks of Hyde Park and Kensington Gardens, which sit side by side and roll out over 590 acres of grassy expanses, provide a welcome respite from London's frenetic pace. The two parks incorporate formal gardens, fountains, sports fields, an art gallery, a palace, great picnic spots, shady clusters of ancient trees, and even outdoor swimming in a small lake.

Originally the extended backyard of royals, including King William III, Queen Victoria, and today Prince William, the parks remain the property of the Crown, which is why they weren't devoured by the city's late-18th-century growth spurt.

Londoners flock here when the sun is out to sit in a rented deck chair, walk through the formal gardens, engage in a session of tai chi, or even enjoy a mass in-line skate.

KENSINGTON GARDENS

At the end of the 17th century, William III moved his court to what had been Henry VIII's hunting grounds and began the transformation into **Kensington Gardens.** He was attracted to the location for its clean air and tranquillity and subsequently commissioned Sir Christopher Wren to overhaul the original redbrick building, resulting in the splendid **Kensington Palace.**

To the east of the palace complex is the early-20th-century **Sunken Garden,** complete with a living tunnel of lime trees (i.e., linden trees) and golden laburnum.

On western side of the **Long Water** is George Frampton's 1912 *Peter Pan,* a bronze statue of the boy who lived on Bird's island in the Serpentine and never grew up and whose creator, J.M. Barrie, lived at 100 Bayswater Road, not 500 yards from here.

Back toward Kensington Palace is George Frederick Watts's 1904 bronze horse and rider, a commemoration of diamond king Cecil Rhodes, entitled *Physical Energy.* The **Round Pond** is a magnet for model-boat enthusiasts and duck feeders.

Near the Broad Walk, toward Black Lion Gate, is the

- - - - Diana Memorial Walk

LANCASTER U **GATE**

QUEENSWAY U *LANCASTER GATE*

BLACK LION GATE Bayswater Rd. **Italian Gardens** ♦

NOTTING HILL GATE

Kensington Gardens

Diana Princess of Wales ♦ Memorial Playground ✕

The Fountains

Elfin Oak

Peter Pan ♦

Lancaster Walk

The Long Water

Orangery ✕

(RESTRICTED AREA)

Kensington Palace Gardens

Physical Energy ♦

Sunken Garden

The Round Pond

Broad Walk

Kensington Palace

Serpentine Gallery ♦

The Ring

Afternoon tea taken at the Orangery, a short walk from the Sunken Garden on the palace grounds, is a quintessentially English experience.

Flower Walk

Kensington Rd. **QUEEN'S GATE**

Albert Memorial *Kensington*

ALEXANDRA GATE

Diana Princess of Wales Memorial Playground, an enclosed space specially designed to evoke Barrie's Neverland. Hook's ship, crocodiles, and "jungles" of foliage provide a fantasy land for kids—more than 70,000 visit every year. Nearby is Ivor Innes's *Elfin Oak,* the remains of a 900-year-old oak with carvings depicting tiny woodland creatures.

One of the park's most striking monuments is the **Albert Memorial.** This high-Victorian Gothic monument to Prince Albert, is adorned with elaborate ornamentation representing his interests and amusements.

The small **Serpentine Gallery,** now joined by the nearby **Serpentine Sackler Gallery,** is known for its exhibitions of challenging contemporary works.

Hyde Park was once a hunting ground of King Henry VIII, who appropriated it from the monks of Westminster Abbey in 1536. The public wasn't granted access to Hyde Park's delights until George II came to the throne.

It was Charles I, in the early 17th century, however, who

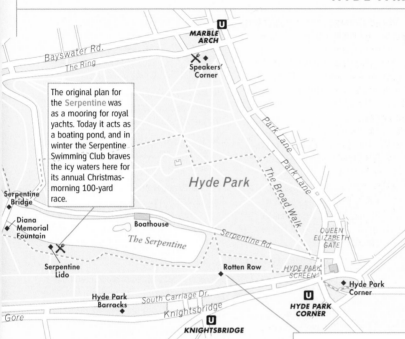

The original plan for the Serpentine was as a mooring for royal yachts. Today it acts as a boating pond, and in winter the Serpentine Swimming Club braves the icy waters here for its annual Christmas-morning 100-yard race.

shaped the Hyde Park that visitors see today, creating **the Ring** (North Carriage Drive), which forms a curve north of the **Serpentine** and boathouses. Charles opened the park to the general public in 1637. During the Great Plague of 1665, people from crowded neighborhoods east of the city camped in the park, seeking refuge from the deadly disease.

The **Serpentine Bridge**, built in 1826 by George Rennie, marks the boundary between Hyde Park and Kensington Gardens. **Rotten Row**, a corruption of the French *route de roi* ("the king's road"), runs

along the southeastern edge of Hyde Park and is still used by the Household Cavalry, who live at the **Hyde Park Barracks**—a high-rise and a long, low, red block—to the left. This is where the regiment that mounts the guard at Buckingham Palace resides; you can see them at about 10:30 am, as they leave in full regalia to perform their ceremonial duties.

On the south side of the 1930s **Serpentine Lido** (open to swimmers from June to September) is the £3.6 million oval **Diana Memorial Fountain.**

Rotten Row was the first artificially lit highway in Britain. In the late 17th century, William III was concerned that his walk from Kensington Palace to St. James's was too dangerous, so he ordered 300 oil lamps to be placed along the route.

Ever since the 1827 legislation of public assembly, **Speakers' Corner** near Marble Arch has provided an outlet for political debate. On Sundays, it's a live version of an Internet chat room, with speakers ranging from calm and sensible to vehement and eccentric.

ENJOYING THE PARKS

Ride. **Hyde Park Riding Stables** keeps horses for hacking the sand tracks. Group lessons (usually just a few people) are £79 per person per hour. Private lessons are £115 weekdays, £125 on weekends. ✉ 63 Bathurst Mews, Bayswater W2 ☎ 020/7723–2813 ⊕ www. hydeparkstables.com Ⓤ Lancaster Gate.

Row. **The Serpentine** has paddleboats and rowboats for £12 per person per hour, kids £5, April through October from 10 am to dusk, later in good weather in summer. ☎ 020/7262–1330.

Run. You can run a **4-mile route** around the perimeter of Hyde Park and Kensington Gardens or a **2½-mile route** in Hyde Park alone if you start at Hyde Park Corner or Marble Arch and encircle the Serpentine.

Skate. On Friday, skaters of intermediate ability and upward meet at 8 pm at the Duke of Wellington Arch, Hyde Park Corner, for the **Friday Night Skate,** a two-hour mass skating session, complete with music and whistles. If you're a bit unsure on your wheels, arrive at 6:30 pm for a free lesson. The **Sunday Rollerstroll,** a more laid-back version of the same thing, runs on Sunday afternoons; meet at 2 pm on the east side of Serpentine Road ⊕ www.thefns.com Ⓤ Hyde Park Corner.

Swim. **Serpentine Lido** is technically a beach on a lake, but a hot day in Hyde Park is surreally reminiscent of the seaside. There are changing facilities, and the swimming section is chlorinated. There is also a paddling pool, sandpit, and kids' entertainer in the afternoons. It's open daily from June through September (and weekends in May), 10–6; admission £4.60, ☎ 020/7706–3422 ⊕ www.royalparks.org.uk Ⓤ Knightsbridge.

WHERE TO REFUEL

✗ The **Lido Café,** near the Diana Memorial Fountain, has plenty of seating with views across the Serpentine Lake.

✗ **Serpentine Bar and Kitchen** on the eastern side of the lake, is a good pit stop for tasty snacks, salads, and sandwiches.

✗ The **Broadwalk Café & Playcafe** next to the Diana Memorial Playground has a children's menu.

✗ The **Orangery** beside Kensington Palace is a distinctly more grown-up affair for tea and cakes.

SPEAKERS' CORNER

Once the site of public executions and the Tyburn hanging trees, the corner of Hyde Park at Cumberland Gate and Park Lane now harbors one of London's most public spectacles: Speakers' Corner. This has been a place of assembly and vitriolic outpourings and debates since the mid-19th century. The pageant of free speech takes place every Sunday afternoon.

Anyone is welcome to mount a soapbox and declaim upon any topic, which makes for an irresistible showcase of eccentricity—one such being the (now-deceased) Protein Man. Wearing his publicity board, the Protein Man proclaimed that the eating of meat, cheese, and peanuts led to uncontrollable acts of passion that would destroy Western civilization. The pamphlets he sold for four decades are now collector's items. Other more strait-laced campaigns have been launched here by the Chartists, the Reform League, the May Day demonstrators, and the Suffragettes.

PRACTICAL INFO

ADMISSION: Free for both parks

HOURS: Kensington Gardens 6 am–dusk; Hyde Park 5 am–midnight

CONTACT INFO: ☎ 030/0061–2000, ⊕ www.royalparks.org.uk

GETTING HERE: Ⓤ **Kensington Gardens:** Kensington High Street, Queensway, Lancaster Gate, South Kensington. **Hyde Park:** Hyde Park Corner, Knightsbridge, Lancaster Gate, Marble Arch

EVENTS: Major events, such as rock concerts and festivals, road races, and talks, are regular features of the parks' calendar; check online for what's on during your visit.

Each summer, a different contemporary architect designs an outdoor pavilion for the Serpentine Gallery. Outdoor film screenings, readings, and other cultural events are held there.

Every June or July, Hyde Park hosts Wireless, one of the U.K.'s biggest music festivals. It's held over a weekend, on several stages, and attracts some of the biggest global names in pop, indie, and rock.

(left) Horseback riding, Hyde Park

(top) The Fountains, Kensington Gardens

(bottom) Both parks are lovely year-round, but spring blooms are spectacular.

TOURS: There are **themed guided walks** about once a month, usually on Thursday or Friday afternoons. They are free but must be booked in advance. Check online or call the park offices for dates and details.

A 45-minute tour (£6) of the **Albert Memorial** is available. It's held at 2 and 3 pm on the first Sunday of the month from March to December. For information call ☎ 0207/936–2568.

Kensington Palace is open daily from 10 am to 6 pm, March to September, and 10 am to 5 pm from October to February. Tickets are £16.50; kids with an adult go free. For information call ☎ 0844/482–7777 or visit ⊕ www.hrp.org.uk.

Westbourne Grove, where you'll also find almost 100 antiques shops plus indoor markets, which are open on weekdays, when shopping is much less hectic. Where the road levels off, around Elgin Crescent, youth culture and a vibrant neighborhood life kicks in, with a variety of interesting small stores and food stalls interspersed with a fruit-and-vegetable market. On Friday and Saturday the section between Talbot Road and the Westway elevated highway becomes one of London's best flea markets, specializing in discounted new household goods, while north of the Westway you'll find secondhand household goods and bric-a-brac. Scattered throughout, but especially under the Westway, are vendors selling a mishmash of designer, vintage, and used clothing, together with jewelry, custom T-shirts, and assorted junk. There's a Trinidad-style Carnival centered on Portobello Road on the August bank-holiday weekend, a tribute to the area's past as a center of the West Indian community. ⊠ *Portobello Rd., Notting Hill* ⊕ *www.portobelloroad.co.uk* Ⓜ *Notting Hill Gate, Ladbroke Grove.*

> ### NOTTING HILL CARNIVAL
>
> Loud, colorful, and very crowded, the annual Carnival (⊕ *www.nottinghillcarnival.biz*) was started by Afro-Caribbean immigrants in the 1960s. Held the last weekend in August, it attracts hundreds of thousands of visitors, mostly the young and raucous. Keep your eyes open for pickpockets—even on "family day."

BAYSWATER

East of Notting Hill Gate Tube station, Notting Hill turns into Bayswater, characterized by wide streets lined with imposing white stucco terraced houses. Traditionally given over to cheap B&Bs, many are being converted back to private homes as the area continues to gentrify. The eastern end of Westbourne Grove and the streets around it are known for their excellent ethnic restaurants, particularly Chinese, Lebanese, and Greek. On **Queensway**, Bayswater's main street, **Whiteleys**, originally a huge department store built in 1912, has been converted into a shopping center containing a luxury movie theater, restaurants (try Le Café Anglais for a swanky evening out), a bowling alley, and, of course, shops.

Nearby **Paddington station** is as well known for its association with the world's most famous marmalade fan, Paddington Bear, as for being one of London's most handsome rail terminals.

REGENT'S PARK
AND HAMPSTEAD

GETTING ORIENTED

Regent's Park and
Hampstead

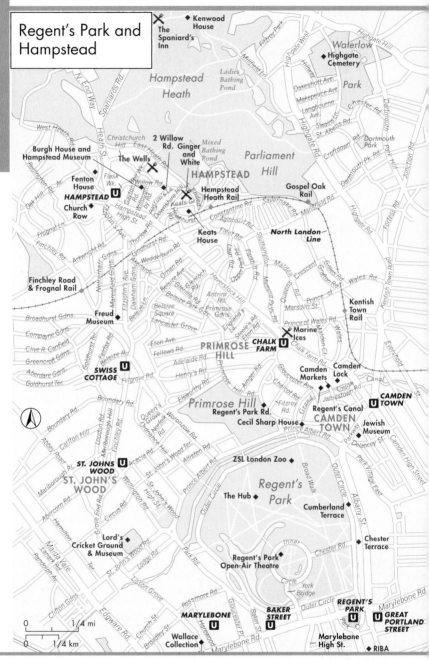

TOP REASONS TO GO

Ramble across Hampstead Heath: Londoners adore the Heath for bringing a bit of countryside to the city.

Go Romantic at Keats House: Visit the rooms where one of England's greatest poets wrote some of his greatest works, inspired by his love for the girl-next-door, Fanny Brawne.

Get sporty in Regent's Park: Cycle past Nash's grand neoclassical stucco terraces or walk up Primrose Hill for a great view over the city.

Gracious living at Kenwood: See one of Britain's best art collections at this 18th-century gentleman's estate largely designed by Robert Adam.

Meet the penguins at the London Zoo: A VIP ticket will let you get up close and personal with the penguins.

FEELING PECKISH?

Ginger and White. Family-friendly and thoroughly modern, Ginger and White is a delightful fusion of continental-style café and traditional British coffee shop—all bound up with a sophisticated Hampstead vibe. ⊠ *4A–5A Perrins Ct., Hampstead* ☎ *020/7431–9098* ⊕ *www.gingerandwhite.com* Ⓜ *Hampstead.*

Marine Ices. Near the Camden Lock market, this place has some of London's best ice cream. ⊠ *Old Dairy Mews, 61 Chalk Farm Rd., Camden Town* ☎ *020/7428–9990* ⊕ *www. marineices.co.uk* ⊙ *Daily 11 am–10 pm* Ⓜ *Chalk Farm.*

SAFETY

Avoid Hampstead Heath, Primrose Hill, and Regent's Park at night unless there's an event; all are perfectly safe during the day. Also to be avoided after dark: the canal towpath in Primrose Hill and Camden.

GETTING THERE

To get to Hampstead by Tube, take the Northern line (the Edgware branch) to Hampstead station, or take the London Overground to Hampstead Heath station. The south side of Hampstead Heath can also be reached by the London Overground Gospel Oak station. To get to Regent's Park, take the Bakerloo line to Regent's Park Tube station or, for Primrose Hill, the Chalk Farm stop on the Northern line. Little Venice is reachable by the Warwick Avenue stop on the Bakerloo line and St. John's Wood has its own stop on the Jubilee Line.

MAKING THE MOST OF YOUR TIME

Regent's Park, Primrose Hill, and Hampstead can be covered in a day. Spend the morning in Hampstead, with a brief foray onto the Heath, then head south to Regent's Park in the afternoon so that you're closer to central London come nightfall, if that is where your hotel is located. (You'll also be heading downhill instead of up.) You can always return to Hampstead another day for a long walk across the Heath or head west to Little Venice's canals.

A GOOD WALK

A walk from Hampstead Village down through Belsize Park, Primrose Hill, and Regent's Park will take you through some of London's leafiest, prettiest scenery.

Sightseeing
★★★★
Nightlife
★★★
Dining
★★
Lodging
★★
Shopping
★★★

Regent's Park, Primrose Hill, Belsize Park, and Hampstead are four of London's prettiest and most civilized neighborhoods. The city becomes noticeably calmer and greener as you head uphill from Marylebone Road through Regent's Park to the refreshing greenery of Primrose Hill and the handsome Georgian houses and Regency villas of Hampstead. To the west, the less bucolic but equally elegant St. John's Wood and Little Venice also provide a taste of moneyed London.

Updated By
Ellin Stein

Leaving the park at the London Zoo, walk up adjoining **Primrose Hill** for one of the most picturesque views of London. Long a magnet for the creative (though these days within reach of only the most well-heeled creatives), this is the kind of neighborhood where the local library's screening of *The Madness of King George* is introduced by its writer, longtime resident Alan Bennett. Peel off from the Hill to explore Regent's Park Road and its attractive independent shops and cafés, as well as the surrounding streets with their pastel Victorian villas.

Alternatively, continue hugging the Hill heading north along Primrose Hill Road. This will take you to Belsize Park, itself a celebrity hot spot (Tim Burton and Hugh Laurie have houses here) with a mixture of Victorian, Arts and Crafts, and art deco buildings. Turn right onto England's Lane, another street full of independent shops and nice cafés, then left onto Haverstock Hill and head farther uphill. At the corner of Pond Street you will see two enormous Victorian Gothic buildings: one, St. Stephen's Church, is now a community arts center. The other, AIR Studios, founded by the Beatles' producer, Sir George Martin, is where scores from movies, including *Iron Man 3*, *Les Misérables*, and *Brave*, have been recorded.

Turn right onto Pond Street and go downhill past the unlovely Royal Free hospital to South End Green and the entrance to **Hampstead Heath**. Or go straight to stay on Rosslyn Hill and then Hampstead High Street, the neighborhood's main drag. Turn left onto Church Row, with its unspoiled early Georgian terraced houses leading to the **St. John's-at-Hampstead**, where the painter John Constable is buried. To the north of Hampstead Heath is Highgate, another upscale north London "village" with a large concentration of Georgian and early Victorian buildings, particularly around The Grove (home to Kate Moss, George Michael, and Sting).

To reach **Little Venice,** go to the west entrance of Regent's Park by the gold-domed London Central Mosque and then north past **Lord's Cricket Ground** to the St. John's Wood Tube stop. Turn left onto Grove End Road, which will bring you to the famous Abbey Road crossroads featured on the Beatles' album of the same name. Head southwest for Little Venice, known as the Belgravia of north London due to its stucco terraces (found on streets such as Randolph Avenue, Clifton Avenue, and Randolph Road) that are very similar to the other neighborhood's. The "Venice" comes from its proximity to a picturesque stretch of the Grand Union Canal along Blomfield Road, where highly decorative houseboats are moored. If you happen to be here on the second Sunday in May, you'll be able to see houseboats from all over London's canals gather here in Paddington Basin for the Blessing of the Boats.

REGENT'S PARK

Commissioned by his patron the Prince Regent (later George IV) to create a master plan for this part of London, formerly a royal hunting ground, London's great urban planner and architect John Nash laid out the plans for the 410-acre Regent's Park in 1812. Bordered by grand neoclassical terraces, the park holds many attractions, including the London Zoo and the summer display of more than 400 varieties of roses in Queen Mary's Gardens.

TOP ATTRACTIONS

FAMILY
Fodor'sChoice
★

Primrose Hill. More conventionally parklike than Hampstead Heath, the rolling lawns of Primrose Hill, the northerly extension of Regent's Park which rises to 256 feet, provide outstanding views over the city to the southeast, encompassing Canary Wharf and the London Eye. Filled with families and picnickers in nice weather, it has featured in books—it was here that Pongo engaged in "twilight barking" in *The Hundred and One Dalmatians*, and the Martians set up an encampment in H.G. Wells's *The War of The Worlds*). It's also been mentioned in songs by Blur, Madness, and Paul McCartney, among others, and served as a location for films, including *Bridget Jones: The Edge of Reason* and *Paddington Bear*. ⊠ *Regent's Park Rd., Regent's Park* ☎ *0300/061–2300* ⊕ *www.royalparks.org.uk* ✉ *Free* Ⓜ *Chalk Farm.*

FAMILY
Regent's Park.
See the highlighted listing in this chapter.

FAMILY
Regent's Park Boating Lake. You can enjoy a pleasant aquatic interlude touring the boating lake in Regent's Park by rowboat or pedalo. Adult rentals cost £9 (£7 before noon) per hour per person, or £7/£5.50 per

A BRIEF HISTORY

Nash's original plan for Regent's Park included a summer palace for his patron the Prince Regent as well as villas for 56 friends, so the concept was to re-create the grounds of a great country estate. The palace was never built (and only eight of the villas were) but Nash's designs for magnificent white-stucco terraces along the park's Outer Circle were, with Cumberland Terrace on the east particularly notable for its neoclassical Ionic columns surmounted by a Wedgewood-blue pediment and statuary personifying Britannia and her empire, an architecturally interesting example of Palladian villa features being incorporated into a residential city terrace. On the opposite side of the park is Winfield House, a neo-Georgian mansion built in the 1930s by the heiress Barbara Hutton. It's now the American Ambassador's (heavily guarded) official residence, with the largest private garden in central London (not counting Buckingham Palace).

In the early 18th century, the commercial development of the mineral springs in Hampstead led to its success as a spa; people traveled from miles around to drink the pure waters from Hampstead Wells, and small cottages were hastily built to accommodate the influx. Though the spa phenomenon was short-lived, the peace and serenity of Hampstead drew many significant artists and writers (from John Keats to George Orwell and Ian Fleming), along with distinguished refugees from Nazi Germany, whose legacy can be found in notable examples of Modernist architecture scattered among the 18th- and 19th-century period houses.

half hour. On weekends and school holidays, children under 12 can take to the waters on a smaller lake, where pedalo rentals are £4. The lake is open daily April through September, 10–6. ✉ ☎ *020/7724–4069.*

FAMILY

Fodor's Choice
★

ZSL London Zoo. Operated by the nonprofit Zoological Society of London, the zoo was begun with the royal animals collection, moved here from the Tower of London in 1828. The zoo itself did not open to the public until 1847. A recent modernization program has seen the introduction of several big attractions, with a focus on education, wildlife conservation, and the breeding of endangered species. The huge **B.U.G.S.** pavilion (Biodiversity Underpinning Global Survival) is a self-sustaining, contained ecosystem for 140 less-cuddly species, including invertebrates such as spiders and millipedes, plus some reptiles and fish. At **Gorilla Kingdom**, a walk-through re-creation of the habitat of the Western Lowland Gorilla, you can watch the four residents at close range. **Rainforest Life** is an indoor tropical rain forest (complete with humidity) inhabited by the likes of armadillos, monkeys, and sloths. A special nighttime section offers glimpses of nocturnal creatures like slow lorises and bats. The **Animal Adventures** Children's Zoo allows kids to get up close to animals including mongooses and llamas, as well as feeding and grooming sheep and goats. Two of the most popular attractions are **Penguin Beach**, especially at feeding time (1:30) and **Meerkat Manor**, where you can see the sociable animals keeping watch over their own sandy territory. If you're feeling flush, try to nab one of the six daily

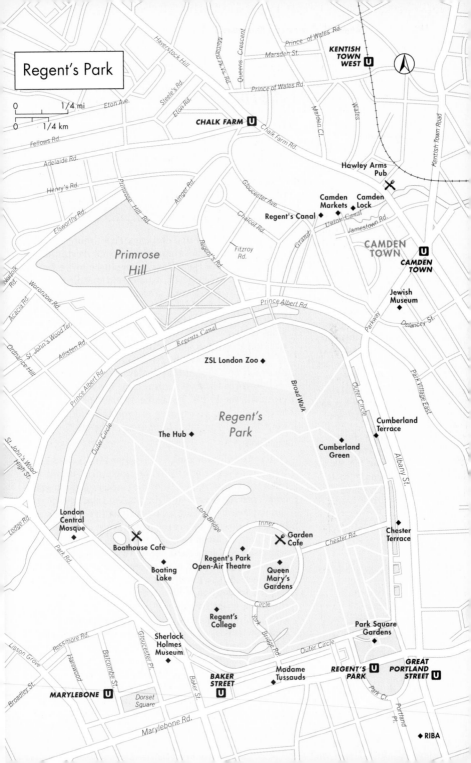

Regent's Park

0   1/4 mi
0   1/4 km

Haverstock Hill
Prince of Wales Rd.
Marsden St.
KENTISH TOWN WEST ⓤ
Queens Crescent
Malden Rd.
Mansfield Rd.
Prince of Wales Rd.
Fellows Rd.
Eton Ave.
Steele's Rd.
Eton Rd.
CHALK FARM ⓤ
Chalk Farm Rd.
Wales
Kentish Town Road
Adelaide Rd.
Henry's Rd.
Elsworthy Rd.
Primrose Hill Rd.
Amyer Rd.
Gloucester Ave.
Chalcot Rd.
Hawley Arms Pub ✕
Camden Markets ♦ Camden Lock ♦
Regent's Canal ♦
Union Canal
Jamestown Rd.
CAMDEN TOWN
CAMDEN TOWN ⓤ
Fellows Rd.
Norfolk Rd.
Acacia Rd.
Woronzow Rd.
St. John's Wood Ter.
Allitsen Rd.
Ordnance Hill
Primrose Hill
Fitzroy Rd.
Regent's Rd.
Grand
Primrose Hill
Prince Albert Rd.
Jewish Museum ♦
Parkway
Delancey St.
Park Village East
Regents Canal
Prince Albert Rd.
ZSL London Zoo ♦
Broad Walk
Outer Circle
Cumberland Terrace ♦
St. John's Wood High St.
Prince Albert Rd.
Outer Circle
The Hub ♦
Regent's Park
Cumberland Green ♦
Albany St.
Lodge Rd.
Park Rd.
London Central Mosque ♦
Boathouse Cafe ✕
Boating Lake
Long Bridge
Inner
Garden Cafe ✕
Chester Rd.
Chester Terrace ♦
Regent's Park Open-Air Theatre ♦
Queen Mary's Gardens
Circle
Lisson Grove
Harewood
Rossmore Rd.
Gloucester Pl.
Balcombe St.
Sherlock Holmes Museum ♦
Regent's College ♦
York Bridge Rd.
Park Square Gardens ♦
Outer Circle
REGENT'S PARK ⓤ
GREAT PORTLAND STREET ⓤ
Broadley St.
Baker St.
Dorset Square
BAKER STREET ⓤ
Madame Tussauds ♦
MARYLEBONE ⓤ
Marylebone Rd.
Park Cr.
Portland Pl.
♦ RIBA

REGENT'S PARK

✉ *Chester Rd., Regent's Park*
☎ *0300/061–2300* ⊕ *www. royalparks.org.uk* ✉ *Free*
Ⓜ *Baker St., Regent's Park, Great Portland St.*

TIPS

■ If watching all this activity works up an appetite, in addition to the Hub's own café there's the Garden Cafe outside the rose garden that serves breakfast, lunch, and supper on a patio, the Smokehouse near the zoo that specializes in BBQ and burgers, the Boatyard Cafe by the boating lake, the Tennis Centre Cafe by the courts, an espresso bar with wraps and cakes, and a kiosk by the children's playground that serves sandwiches and snacks.

■ Regent's Park also hosts two annual events: the prestigious Frieze Art Fair, and the Taste of London, a foodie-oriented extravaganza.

The formal, cultivated Regent's Park, more country house grounds than municipal amenity, began life in 1812, when John Nash was commissioned by the Prince Regent (later George IV) to create a master plan for the former royal hunting ground. Nash's original plan included a summer palace for the prince and 56 villas for friends, none of which were realized except for eight villas (only two survive). However, the grand neoclassical terraced houses on the south, east, and west edges of the park were built by Nash and reflect the scope of his ambitions. Queen Mary's Gardens, which has some 30,000 roses and is a favorite spot for weddings, was created in the 1930s. Today the 395-acre park, with the largest outdoor sports area in central London, draws the athletically inclined from around the city.

Highlights

At the center of the park is the **Queen Mary's Gardens**, a fragrant 17-acre circle containing more than 400 varieties of roses. Just to the east of the Gardens is the **Regent's Park Open-Air Theatre** and the **Boating Lake**, which you can explore by renting a pedalo (paddleboat) or rowboat. Heading east from the rose gardens along Chester Road past the **Broad Walk** will bring you to Nash's iconic white-stucco **Cumberland Terrace,** with its central Ionic columns surmounted by a triangular Wedgwood-blue pediment. At the north end of the Broad Walk you'll find the **London Zoo**, while to the northwest of the central circle is **The Hub** (0300/061–2323), a state-of-the-art community sports center that has changing rooms, exercise classes, and a café with 360-degree views of the surrounding sports fields, used for soccer, rugby, cricket, field hockey, and softball contests. There are also tennis courts toward the park's southeast (Baker Street) entrance, and the park is a favorite north–south route for cyclists.

11

"Meet the Penguins" VIP tickets (2 pm) that offer a 20-minute guided close encounter with the locals (£45 weekdays, £60 weekends.) There are similar VIP encounters with giraffes, lions, owls, meerkats, kangaroos, and aardvarks. Other zoo highlights include **Butterfly Paradise**; the **Blackburn Pavilion,** with its hundreds of tropical bird species; the **Big Cats** enclosure, home to a pride of Asian lions; and **Tiger Territory,** an enclosure for five beautiful endangered Sumatran tigers (including three cubs born at the zoo). For a more grown-up experience, check out Zoo Lates, where comedy, cabaret, and a wine bar are offered to over-18s (in addition to all the usual zoo attractions). These are held on Friday evenings (6–10 pm) in summer. Check the website or the information board out front for free events, including creature close encounters and "ask the keeper" sessions. ✉ *Outer Circle, Regent's Park* ☎ *0844/225–1826* ⊕ *www.zsl. org* 🎫 *£19–£22* ⊙ *Mid-Nov.–Feb., daily 10–4; Mar.–early Sept., daily 10–6; early-Sept.–Oct., daily 10–5:30; early–mid-Nov., daily 10–4:30; last admission 1 hr before closing* Ⓜ *Camden Town, then Bus 274.*

> **HERE'S WHERE**
>
> London Zoo's reptile house is a special draw for Harry Potter fans—it's where Harry first talks to snakes, to alarming effect on his horrible cousin, Dudley.

WORTH NOTING

Cecil Sharp House. The home of the English Folk Dance and Song Society, this soaring building from 1930 hosts concerts by artists ranging from Mumford & Sons and Laura Marling to the Ukulele Orchestra of Great Britain, as well as family barn dances and *céilidhs* (Irish barn dances). Meet the locals at drop-in classes to learn a variety of dance styles, such as morris, baroque, Riverdance-type Irish, zydeco, and the tango. There are also exhibitions on the British folk arts, a café and bar, and a small museum devoted to the composer Ralph Vaughan Williams. ✉ *2 Regent's Park Rd., Primrose Hill* ☎ *020/7485–2206* ⊕ *www. cecilsharphouse.org* 🎫 *Free; classes from £4* ⊙ *Tues.–Fri. 9:30–5:30; 1st and 3rd Sat. of each month (except Aug.) 10–4; call or check website for evening events* Ⓜ *Chalk Farm, Camden Town.*

QUICK BITES

Regent's Park Road in Primrose Hill has several excellent cafés, notably the organic-minded and child-friendly Greenberry and the local favorite Lemonia, which serves Greek food. On Gloucester Avenue at the top of Regent's Park Road, you'll find the landmark gastropubs The Lansdowne and The Engineer, plus the outstanding artisanal deli Melrose & Morgan.

Jewish Museum. This fascinating museum tells the story of the Jewish people in Britain from 1066 to today, including the period between the 13th and 17th century when Judaism was outlawed in England. Using a combination of art, religious artifacts, photographs, manuscripts, and interactive displays, its exhibits include a re-creation of a Jewish East End street from the Victorian era and another documenting the 10,000 Jewish refugee children who came to Britain, although without their parents, as part of the Kindertransport that took place immediately before World War II. There are also temporary themed exhibitions, such as Jews in Football (soccer) or the life of Amy Winehouse. There's a free overview of the collection on the ground floor, including a medieval *mikveh* (ritual bath), excavated a few miles from here in 2001. ⊠ *Raymond Burton House, 129–131 Albert St., Camden Town* ☎ *020/7284-7384* ⊕ *www.jewishmuseum.org.uk* £7.50 ⊙ *Sun.–Thurs. 10–5, Fri. 10–2; last admission 30 mins before closing. Closed on major Jewish holidays.* Ⓜ *Camden Town.*

Lord's Cricket Ground & Museum. During a 100-minute tour, the spiritual home of this most English of games and the headquarters of the MCC (Marylebone Cricket Club), opens its "behind the scenes" areas to visitors. Highlights include the Long Room, a VIP viewing area where portraits of cricketing greats are on display; the players' dressing rooms; and the world's oldest sporting museum, where cricket's 400-year progress from gentlemanly village-green game to worldwide sport is charted via memorabilia, equipment, trophies, and footage of memorable performances. Don't miss the prize exhibit: the urn known as the Ashes—allegedly the remains of a cricket bail (part of the wicket assembly) presented to the English captain in 1883 by a group of Australian women, a jokey allusion to a newspaper's satirical obituary for the death of English cricket published after a resounding defeat. It's been a symbol of the two nations' long-running rivalry ever since. They still play for possession of the Ashes every two years though it's only been an official (as opposed to joke) trophy since 1998. A Waterford crystal version changes hands these days, though the winners still hold a replica of the original urn aloft. Tours are not available during major matches (they're offered during smaller "county" matches), but the museum remains open to match ticket holders. ⊠ *St. John's Wood Rd., St. John's Wood* ☎ *020/7616-8595* ⊕ *www.lords.org* *Tour £18. Museum only £7.50 nonmatch days; £3 with match ticket* ⊙ *Museum weekdays 10–5 (hrs vary on match days, call to confirm). Tours Apr., daily 10–2; May–Oct., daily 10–3 on the hr, except during major matches; Jan.–Mar., weekdays 11– 2 on the hr, weekends 10–2.* Ⓜ *St. John's Wood.*

Regent's Park Open-Air Theatre. There have been works by Shakespeare performed here every summer since 1932, with casts including luminaries such as Vivien Leigh, Dame Judi Dench, and Damien Lewis. Today it also mounts productions of classic plays, musicals, and shows for family audiences among its four annual productions. *A Midsummer Night's Dream* is the one to catch, if it's on—never has that enchanted Greek wood been better evoked, especially if enhanced by genuine birdsong and a rising moon. There's a covered restaurant for pretheater dining, as well as a grill, a buffet, and, of course, a bar. You can also order picnic hampers (meals) in advance. The park can get chilly, so bring a blanket. Performances are rain or shine (umbrellas aren't allowed) with refunds only in case of very heavy downpours. ⊠ *Inner Circle, Regent's Park* ☎ *0844/826-4242 tickets, 0844/375-3460 inquiries* ⊕ *www.openairtheatre.org* *£25–£65* ⊙ *May–mid-Sept., evening performances at 7:45, matinees at 2:15* Ⓜ *Baker St., Regent's Park.*

HAMPSTEAD

Even an impoverished Romantic poet like John Keats could afford **Hampstead.** In 1818 he moved to what is now **Keats House,** a pretty Regency residence where he spent two years and wrote several of his most famous works. Hampstead's bohemian days are long gone, although a few distinguished artists and musicians, plus television stars, still live here. Artisanal food shops and boutiques for the skinny of frame and fat of wallet cluster along Rosslyn Hill, while high-street chains start to proliferate the closer you get to Hampstead Tube station. Be sure to leave the beaten path to explore the numerous narrow charming roads, like Flask Walk, Well Walk, and New End Road. Also hidden among Hampstead's winding streets are **Fenton House,** a Georgian town house with a lovely walled garden, and Burgh House, the oldest (1704) house in the village and a repository of local history. On the way to Highgate you'll find **Kenwood House,** an 18th-century mansion that was designed by Robert Adam and is noted for its remarkable art collection and grounds.

Hampstead's crowning glory, however, is **Hampstead Heath** (known locally as "The Heath"), 791 acres that contain parkland, swimming ponds, and some of Europe's oldest oaks. It's also home to one of London's highest (321 feet) vantage points, Parliament Hill.

TOP ATTRACTIONS

FAMILY **Hampstead Heath.**

Fodor's Choice *See the highlighted listing in this chapter.*
★

Highgate Cemetery. Highgate is not the oldest cemetery in London, but it is probably the best known. After it was consecrated in 1839, Victorians came from miles around to appreciate the ornate headstones, the impressive tombs, and the view. Such was its popularity that 19 acres on the other side of the road were acquired in 1850, and this additional East Cemetery contains what may be the most visited grave—that of Karl Marx (1818–83), only one of several notables interred here. At the summit is the **Circle of Lebanon,** a ring of vaults built around an ancient cypress tree—a legacy of the 17th-century gardens that formerly occupied the site. Leading from the circle is the **Egyptian Avenue ,** a subterranean stone tunnel lined with catacombs, itself approached by a dramatic colonnade that screens the main cemetery from the road. Both sides are impressive, with a grand (locked) iron gate leading to a sweeping courtyard built for the approach of horses and carriages. By the 1970s the cemetery had become unkempt and neglected until a group of volunteers, the Friends of Highgate Cemetery, undertook the huge upkeep. Tours are conducted by the Friends, who will show you the most interesting graves among the numerous statues and memorials once hidden by overgrowth. The West side is can only be seen during a one-hour tour, which you must prebook for weekdays but not weekends. Tours of the East side on Saturday are first come, first serves. You're expected to dress respectfully, so skip the shorts and the baseball cap. Children under eight are not admitted and neither are dogs, tripods, or video

HAMPSTEAD HEATH

✉ *Hampstead* ☏ *020/7332–3322 Heath Education Centre* ⊕ *www.cityoflondon.gov.uk/hampstead* ⬚ *Free* Ⓜ *Overground: Hampstead Heath for south of Heath or Gospel Oak for Lido; Hampstead for east of Heath; Golders Green, then Bus 210, 268 to Whitestone Pond for north and west of Heath.*

TIPS

■ At 321 feet above sea level, Parliament Hill is one of the highest points in London. On clear days you can see all the way to the South Downs, the hills beyond southern London.

■ Perfect for cooling off on a hot day, the Hampstead ponds have been refreshing Londoners for generations. You'll find the "Mens" and "Ladies" ponds to the northeast of Parliament Hill, with a "Mixed" pond closer to South End Green. A £2 donation is requested.

■ Golders Hill Park offers a good café, tennis courts, a duck pond, croquet lawn, and walled flower garden, plus a Butterfly House (open May–September) and a small zoo with inhabitants including lemurs, coatis, and rare birds.

For generations, Londoners have headed to Hampstead Heath to escape the dirt and noise of the city. A unique expanse of *rus in urbe* ("country in the city"), its 791 acres encompass a variety of wildlife as well as habitats: grassy meadows, woodland, scrub, wetlands, and some of Europe's most venerable oak forests. Be aware that, aside from the southern slope of Parliament Hill and Golders Hill Park, it is more like countryside than a park, with signs and facilities in short supply. Pick up a map at Kenwood House, or the **Education Centre** near the Lido off Gordon House Road, where you can also get details about the history of the Heath and the flora and fauna growing there. An excellent alfresco café near the Athletics Field serves Italian food.

Today the Heath is popular with walkers, dog walkers, and swimmers. It has inspired artists from John Constable, who painted views several times, to contemporary author Zadie Smith, to C.S. Lewis, whose *The Lion, The Witch and The Wardrobe* was supposedly inspired by a walk through the Heath's winter landscape.

Highlights

Coming onto the Heath from the South End Green entrance, walk east past a well-equipped children's adventure **Playground** and **Paddling Pool,** turn left, and head to the top of **Parliament Hill.** At 321 feet above sea level, it's one of the highest points in London. You'll find a stunning panorama over the city. On clear days you can see all the way to the South Downs, the hills beyond southern London.

If you keep heading east from the playground instead, you'll come to the **Lido,** an Olympic-size outdoor unheated swimming pool that gets packed on all-too-rare hot summer days.

cameras. ✉ *Swains La., Highgate* ☎ *020/8340–1834* ⊕ *highgatecemetery.org* ✉ *East Cemetery £4, tours £8; West Cemetery tours £12. No credit cards* ⊙ *East: Mar.–Oct., daily 10–5; Nov.–Feb., weekdays 10–4, weekends 11–4. Tours, Sat. at 2. Last admission 30 mins before closing. Hrs may vary—call ahead. West: Tours Mar.–Nov., weekdays at 1:45, weekends half-hourly 11–3* Ⓜ *Archway, then Bus 210, 271, or 143 to Waterlow Park; Belsize Park, then Bus C11 to Brookfield Park.*

Keats House. It was while living in this house between 1818 and 1820 that the major Romantic poet John Keats (1795–1821) fell in love with girl-next-door Fanny Brawne and wrote some of his best-loved poems. (Soon after, ill health forced him to move to Rome, where he died the following year.) After a major refurbishment to make the rooms more consistent with their original Regency decor, the house now displays all sorts of Keats-related material, including portraits, letters, many of the poet's original manuscripts and books, the engagement ring he gave to Fanny, and items of her clothing. A pretty garden contains the plum tree under which Keats supposedly composed *Ode to a Nightingale*. There are frequent guided tours and special events featuring local literary luminaries. The ticket gives you entry for a full year, so you can come back as often as you like. Picnics can be taken into the grounds during the summer. ✉ *10 Keats Grove, Hampstead* ☎ *020/7332–3868* ⊕ *www.keatshouse.cityoflondon.gov.uk* ✉ *£5* ⊙ *Mar.–Oct., Tues.–Sun. 1–5; Nov.–Feb., Fri.–Sun. 1–5 (last admission 4:30)* Ⓜ *Overground: Hampstead Heath.*

Fodor's Choice ★

Kenwood House. This largely Palladian villa was first built in 1616 and later extended, first by Robert Adam starting in 1767 and later by George Saunders in 1795. Adam refaced most of the exterior and added the splendid library, which, with its vaulted ceiling and Corinthian columns, is the highlight of the house's design. A major renovation restored four rooms to reflect Adam's intentions as closely as possible, incorporating the furniture he designed for them and his original color schemes. Kenwood is also home to the **Iveagh Bequest,** a superb collection of 63 paintings that includes masterworks like Rembrandt's *Portrait of the Artist* and Vermeer's *The Guitar Player*, along with major works by Reynolds, Van Dyck, Hals, Gainsborough, and Turner. The grounds, designed by Humphrey Repton and bordered by Hampstead Heath, are equally elegant and serene, with lawns sloping down to a little lake crossed by a trompe-l'oeil bridge. All in all, the perfect home for an 18th-century gentleman. In summer the grounds host a series of popular and classical concerts, culminating in fireworks on the last night. The Brew House café, occupying part of the old coach house, has outdoor tables in the courtyard and a terraced garden. The 2014 movie *Belle*, the story of Kenwood House's 18th-century resident Lord Mansfield and his family, was shot here. ✉ *Hampstead La., Highgate* ☎ *0870/333–1181* ⊕ *www.english-heritage.org.uk* ✉ *Free* ⊙ *House daily 10–5; gardens daily 8–dusk* Ⓜ *Golders Green or Archway, then Bus 210. London Overground: Gospel Oak.*

The fabled cover of the Beatles *Abbey Road* album, with the world's most famous traffic crossing

WORTH NOTING

2 Willow Road. Among the many artists and intellectuals fleeing Nazi persecution who settled in the area was noted architect Erno Goldfinger, who built this outstanding modernist home opposite Hampstead Heath in 1939 as his family residence (his plans drew the ire of several local residents, including novelist Ian Fleming, who supposedly borrowed his neighbor's name for a Bond villain as a result). As well as design touches and pioneering building techniques that were groundbreaking at the time, the unique house, a place of pilgrimage for 20th-century architecture enthusiasts, also contains Goldfinger's impressive collection of modern art and self-designed innovative furniture. Before 2 pm admission is by first come, first served hourly tour only, but you can visit independently after 3. ✉ *2 Willow Rd., Hampstead* ☎ *020/7435–6166* ⊕ *www.nationaltrust.org.uk/2-willow-road* 📧 *£6* ⊙ *Wed.–Sun. 11–2 (guided tour only), 3–5 (last admission 4:30) Closed Nov.–Feb.* Ⓜ *Overground: Hampstead Heath.*

Burgh House and Hampstead Museum. One of Hampstead's oldest buildings, Burgh House was built in 1704 to take advantage of the natural spa waters of the then-fashionable Hampstead Wells. A private house until World War II, it was saved from dereliction in the 1970s by local residents, who have been restoring and maintaining it ever since. The building is a fine example of the genteel elegance common to the Queen Anne period, with redbrick box frontage, oak paneled rooms, and a terraced garden that was originally designed by Gertrude Jekyll. Today the house contains a small but diverting museum on the history of the area, and also hosts regular talks, concerts, and recitals. The secluded

A TRIP TO ABBEY ROAD

The black-and-white crossroads (known as a "zebra crossing") near the Abbey Road Studios at No. 3 is a place of pilgrimage for Beatles' fans from around the world, many of them teenagers born long after the band split up. They converge here to re-create the cover of the Beatles' 1969 *Abbey Road* album, posing on the crossing despite the onrushing traffic. ■TIP→ Be careful if you're going to attempt this. Abbey Road is a dangerous intersection. The studio is where the Beatles recorded their entire output, from "Love Me Do" onward. One of the best—and safer—ways to explore landmarks in the Beatles' story is to take one of the excellent walking tours offered by **Original London Walks** (*020/7624-3978* ⊕ *www.walks. com*). Try **The Beatles In-My-Life Walk** (11:20 am outside Marylebone Underground on Saturday and Tuesday) or **The Beatles Magical Mystery Tour** (Wednesday at 2 pm, February to November, and Thursday and Sunday at 11 am, year-round, at Underground Exit 3, Tottenham Court Road).

garden courtyard of the café is a lovely spot for lunch, tea, or glass of wine on a summer's afternoon. Call ahead if you're visiting on a weekend, however, as the house is often rented out as a wedding venue on Saturday. ⊠ *New End Sq., Hampstead* ☎ *020/7431–0144* ⊕ *www. burghhouse.org.uk* ☒ *Free* ☉ *House, Wed.–Fri. and Sun. noon–5; café, Wed.–Fri. 11–5, weekends 9:30–5:30* Ⓜ *Hampstead.*

Fenton House. This handsome 16th-century merchant's home, Hampstead's oldest surviving house, has fine displays of porcelain, Georgian furniture, and 17th-century needlework. The 2-acre walled garden, with its rose plantings and apple orchard, has been virtually unchanged for 300 years. International musicians give recitals on the important collection of early keyboard instruments throughout the week. Check the website for details. ⊠ *Hampstead Grove, Hampstead* ☎ *020/7435–3471* ⊕ *www.nationaltrust.org.uk* ☒ *£6.50, garden only £2* ☉ *Mar.–Oct., Wed.–Sun. 11–5; Dec. weekends 11–4* Ⓜ *Hampstead.*

Freud Museum London. The father of psychoanalysis lived here with his family for a year, between his escape from Nazi persecution in his native Vienna in 1938 and his death in 1939. His daughter Anna (herself a pioneer of child psychoanalysis), remained in the house until her own death in 1982, bequeathing it as a museum to honor her father. The centerpiece is Freud's unchanged study, containing his remarkable collection of antiquities and his library. Also on display is the family's Biedermeier furniture and, of course, *the* couch. As well, there are lectures, study groups, and themed exhibitions, in addition to a psychoanalysis-related archive and research library. Looking for a unique souvenir for the person who has everything? The gift shop here sells "Freudian Slippers." ⊠ *20 Maresfield Gardens, Swiss Cottage* ☎ *020/7435–2002* ⊕ *www. freud.org.uk* ☒ *£7* ☉ *Wed.–Sun. noon–5* Ⓜ *Swiss Cottage, Finchley Rd.*

St. John's-at-Hampstead. There has been a church here since 1312, but the current building was consecrated in 1747 and later extended in 1877. The Georgian nave's neoclassical serenity is enhanced by Ionic columns and vaulting arches. The church stands at the end of Church Row, a narrow street lined with flat-fronted brick Georgian houses that gives you a sense of what Hampstead was like when it truly was a rural village as opposed to a traffic-clogged North London neighborhood. Many local notables are buried in the picturesque churchyard, including painter John Constable (some of whose most famous works depict the Heath), John Harrison (the inventor of the marine chronometer discussed in the book *Longitude*), members of the artistic du Maurier family, Jane Austen's aunt, and comedy god Peter Cook. ⊠ *Church Row, Hampstead* ☎ *020/7794–5808* ⊕ *www.hampsteadparishchurch.org.uk* 🎟 *Free* Ⓜ *Hampstead.*

GREENWICH

GETTING ORIENTED

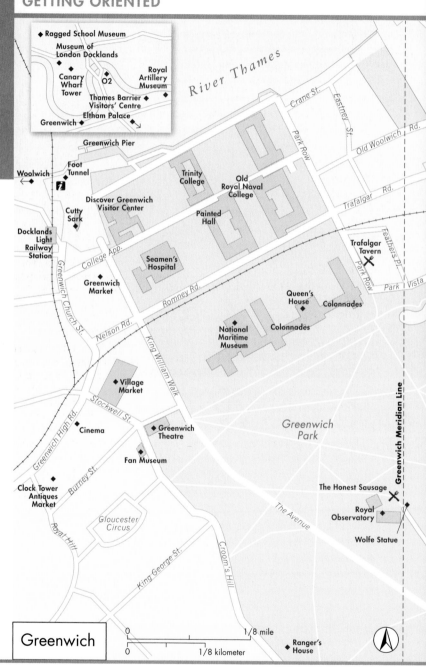

◆ Ragged School Museum

Museum of
London Docklands

◆ Canary Wharf Tower

O2

◆ Royal Artillery Museum

Thames Barrier Visitors' Centre

◆ Eltham Palace

Greenwich ◆

River Thames

Crane St.

Eastney St.

Old Woolwich Rd.

Greenwich Pier

Woolwich

Foot Tunnel

Cutty Sark

Docklands Light Railway Station

Greenwich Church St.

College App.

Greenwich Market

Nelson Rd.

Discover Greenwich Visitor Center

Trinity College

Old Royal Naval College

Painted Hall

Seamen's Hospital

Romney Rd.

Park Row

Trafalgar Rd.

Feathers Pl.

Trafalgar Tavern

Park Row

Park Vista

Queen's House

Colonnades

National Maritime Museum

Colonnades

King William Walk

◆ Village Market

Stockwell St.

Cinema

◆ Greenwich Theatre

Greenwich Park

Greenwich High Rd.

Burney St.

Fan Museum

Clock Tower Antiques Market

Royal Hill

Gloucester Circus

Greenwich Meridian Line

The Honest Sausage

Royal Observatory

Wolfe Statue

The Avenue

King George St.

Croom's Hill

Greenwich

0   1/8 mile

0   1/8 kilometer

Ranger's House

TOP REASONS TO GO

Stand astride the Greenwich Meridian Line: At the Royal Observatory—where the world's time is set—you can be in the eastern and western hemispheres simultaneously.

See the Queen's House, an architectural masterwork: Sir Inigo Jones's 17th-century building was the first in England to embrace the styles of the Italian Renaissance. See what all the fuss was about.

Discover Britain's seafaring past at the **National Maritime Museum:** See how Britannia ruled the waves and helped shape the modern world.

Step aboard the *Cutty Sark*: Take a stroll along the deck of the last surviving 19th-century tea clipper, now shipshape after years of renovation.

FEELING PECKISH?

The Honest Sausage. Inside the park near the Royal Observatory, this delightful little café is a great pit stop for a traditional lunchtime snack. It specializes in straight-down-the-line, traditional sausage or bacon sandwiches, all sourced from an organic, free-range farm in Gloucestershire. And if a porcine snack doesn't curl your tail, you can opt for cake or coffee instead. ⊠ *Pavillion Tea House, Blackheath Ave., Greenwich Park, Greenwich* ☎ *020/8858–9695* ⊕ *www.companyofcooks.com.*

Trafalgar Tavern. With its excellent vista of the Thames, there is no more handsomely situated pub in Greenwich than the Trafalgar Tavern. Featured in Charles Dickens's *Our Mutual Friend*, it's still as grand a place to have a pint and some (upscale) pub grub as it ever was. ⊠ *Park Row, Greenwich* ☎ *020/8858–2909* ⊕ *www.trafalgartavern.co.uk.*

GETTING THERE

Docklands Light Railway (DLR) is a zippy way to get to Cutty Sark station from Canary Wharf and Bank Tube stations in The City. Or take the DLR to Island Gardens and walk the old Victorian Foot Tunnel under the river. (Sitting at the front of a train can be disconcerting, as you watch the controls in the fully automated driver's cab move about, as if a ghost were at the helm.) The best way to arrive, however—time and weather permitting—is like a sea captain of old: by water (though this way takes an hour from central London; ⇨ *for more on cruising the Thames, see Chapter 13*).

MAKING THE MOST OF YOUR TIME

Set apart from the rest of London, Greenwich is worth a day to itself—those who love maritime history will want to spend two—to make the most of walks in the rolling parklands and to immerse yourself in the richness of Greenwich's history, science, and architecture. The boat trip takes about an hour from Westminster Pier (next to Big Ben), or 25 minutes from the Tower of London, so factor in enough time for the round-trip.

NEAREST PUBLIC RESTROOMS

Duck into Discover Greenwich, where loos are free.

12

Sightseeing
★★★★
Nightlife
★
Dining
★★
Lodging
★
Shopping
★★★

About 8 miles downstream—which means seaward, to the east—from central London, Greenwich is a small borough that looms large across the world. Once the seat of British naval power, it is not only home to the Old Royal Observatory, which measures time for our entire planet, but also the Greenwich Meridian, which divides the world into two—you can stand astride it with one foot in either hemisphere.

Updated By
Jack Jewers

Bear in mind that the journey to Greenwich is an event in itself. In a rush, you can take the driverless DLR train—but many opt for arriving by boat along the Thames. This way, you glide past famous sights on the London skyline (there's a guaranteed spine chill on passing the Tower) and ever-changing docklands, and there's usually a chirpy Cock-er-ney navigator enlivening the journey with his fun commentary.

A visit to Greenwich feels like a trip to a rather elegant seaside town—albeit one with more than its fair share of historic sites. The grandiose **Old Royal Naval Hospital,** designed by Christopher Wren, was originally a home for veteran sailors. Today it's a popular visitor attraction, with a more glamorous second life as one of the most widely used movie locations in Britain.

Greenwich was originally home to one of England's finest Tudor palaces, and the birthplace of Henry VIII, Elizabeth I, and Mary I. Inigo Jones built what is considered the first "classical" building in England in 1616—the **Queen's House,** which now houses a collection of fine art. Britain was the world's preeminent naval power for more than 500 years, and the excellent **National Maritime Museum** details that history in an engaging way. Its prize exhibits include the coat worn by Admiral Lord Nelson (1758–1805) in his final battle—bullet hole and all. The 19th-century tea clipper *Cutty Sark* was nearly destroyed by fire in 2007, but reopened in 2012 after a painstaking restoration. Now it's more pristine than ever, and has an impressive new visitor center.

Greenwich Park, London's oldest royal park, is still home to fallow red deer, just as it has been since they were first introduced here for hunting by Henry VIII. The **Ranger's House** now houses a private art collection, next door to a beautifully manicured rose garden. Above it all is the **Royal Observatory**, where you can be in two hemispheres at once by standing along the **Greenwich Meridian Line**, before seeing a high-tech planetarium show.

> **FUN FACT**
>
> Hang out beneath the lightning-cracked Elizabeth Oak in Greenwich Park and you'll be following in illustrious footsteps—Elizabeth I is supposed to have played in its branches as a girl.

Toward north Greenwich, the hopelessly ambitious Millennium Dome has been successfully reborn as the O2 and now hosts major concerts and stand-up comedy gigs. More adventurous visitors can also go **Up the O2** on a climbing expedition across the massive domed surface. Meanwhile, those who prefer excursions of a gentler kind may prefer to journey a couple of miles south of the borough, farther out into London's southern suburbs, to the shamefully underappreciated **Eltham Palace**, once a favorite of Henry VIII. Parts of the mansion were transformed into an art deco masterpiece in the 1930s.

TOP ATTRACTIONS

Fodor'sChoice ★ **Cutty Sark.** This sleek, romantic clipper was built in 1869, one among a vast fleet of tall-masted wooden ships that plied the oceanic highways of the 19th century, trading in exotic commodities—in this case, tea. *Cutty Sark* (named after a racy witch in a Robert Burns poem) was the fastest, sailing the London–China route in 1871 in only 107 days. The clipper has been preserved in dry docks as a museum ship since the 1950s, but was severely damaged in a devastating fire in 2007. But up from the ashes, as the song goes, grow the roses of success—after a major restoration project the visitor facilities are now better than ever. Not only can you tour the ship in its entirety, but the glittering visitor center (which the ship now rests directly above, in an enormous gold mount) allows you to view the hull from below. (And as luck would have it, roughly half the ship had been dismantled and taken away for cleaning at the time of the fire, so the full extent of the damage was much less than it might have been.) There's plenty to see here, and the cramped quarters form a fantastic time capsule to walk around in—this boat was never too comfortable for the 28-strong crew (as you'll see). And don't forget to take in the amusing collection of figureheads. ⊠ *King William Walk, Greenwich* ☏ *020/8858–4422* ⊕ *www.rmg.co.uk* 🎫 *£13.50 (£18.50 with Royal Observatory attractions)* ☉ *Daily 10–5; last admission 4* Ⓜ *DLR: Cutty Sark.*

Discover Greenwich. Intended as a kind of anchor point for Greenwich's big three attractions—the Old Royal Naval College, *Cutty Sark,* and National Maritime Museum—this excellent, state-of-the-art visitor center includes interactive exhibitions on the history of Greenwich, plus an assortment of local treasures and artifacts. Most intriguing among them is a 17th-century "witch bottle," once used to ward off evil spirits. High-tech scans have revealed it to contain a mixture of human

ROYAL OBSERVATORY

⊠ *Romney Rd.,* ☏ *020/8858-*
4422 ⊕ *www.rmg.co.uk/royal-*
observatory 🖾 *Astronomy*
Centre free; Flamsteed House
and Meridian Line courtyard
£8.50; planetarium shows
£6.50; combined ticket £12.50;
combined ticket with Cutty
Sark £18.50 ⊘ *Daily 10–5*
(May–Aug., Meridian courtyard
until 6); last entry 30 mins
before closing; last planetar-
ium show 4:15. Planetarium
closed 1st Tues. of every
month except Aug. and during
Easter. ⊘ *Closed first Tues.*
of every month except Aug.
Ⓜ *DLR: Greenwich.*

TIPS

■ A brass line laid among the cobblestones here marks the meridian. As darkness falls, a green laser shoots out, following exactly the path of the meridian line.

■ The Time Ball atop Flamsteed House is one of the world's earliest public time signals. Each day at 12:55, it rises halfway up its mast. At 12:58 it rises all the way to the top, and at 1 exactly, the ball falls.

■ The hill that is home to the observatory gives fantastic views across London, topped off with £1-a-slot telescopes to scour the skyline. Generally the Planetarium has three themed shows per day.

Greenwich is on the prime meridian at 0° longitude, and the ultimate standard for time around the world has been set here since 1884, when Britain was the world's maritime superpower.

Highlights

The observatory is actually split into two sites, a short walk apart—one devoted to astronomy, the other to the study of time. The enchanting **Peter Harrison Planetarium** is London's only planetarium, its bronze-clad turret glinting in the sun. Shows on black holes and how to interpret the night sky are enthralling and enlightening. Even better for kids are the high-technology rooms of the **Astronomy Centre,** where space exploration is brought to life through cutting-edge interactive programs and fascinating exhibits—including the chance to touch a 4.5-billion-year-old meteorite.

Across the way is **Flamsteed House,** designed by Christopher Wren in 1675 for John Flamsteed, the first Royal Astronomer. A climb to the top of the house reveals a **28-inch telescope,** built in 1893 and now housed inside an onion-shape fiberglass dome. It doesn't compare with the range of modern optical telescopes, but it's still the largest in the United Kingdom. Regular viewing evenings reveal startlingly detailed views of the lunar surface. In the **Time Galleries,** linger over the superb workmanship of John Harrison (1693–1776), whose famous **Maritime Clocks** won him the Longitude Prize for solving the problem of accurate timekeeping at sea, which paved the way for modern navigation.

DID YOU KNOW?

Once sailors could determine their distance from the Greenwich meridian (longitude), maritime navigation was greatly improved. Look for the brass line marking the two hemispheres throughout the cobblestone streets.

THE DOCKLANDS RENAISSANCE

For centuries the Thames was a fevered hub of activity. Great palaces were built along the river, most long gone (such as Whitehall, which dwarfed even Versailles in splendor). Dock warehouses sprang up to the east of London in the 18th century to cater to the burgeoning trade in luxury goods, from tea, coffee, and spices to silks and exotic pets. By the 1950s, however, this trade had all but disappeared—partly due to the devastation of World War II, but also because trading vessels had simply gotten too big to fit along the river. The area all but died away until a massive regeneration scheme known as Docklands was completed in the 1980s. It brought renewal in the form of cutting-edge architecture, galleries, restaurants, and bars. Many of the old warehouses were restored and are now used as museums or shopping malls, such as Hay's and Butler's wharves. The best way to explore is on the **Docklands Light Railway (DLR)**, an elevated track that appears to skim over the water past the swanky glass buildings. (Sit at the very front for a roller-coaster-like driver's-eye view). If you explore on foot, the Thames Path has helpful plaques along the way, with nuggets of historical information.

Firepower Royal Artillery Museum. Adjacent to the old Royal Dockyard at Woolwich is a brilliant exhibition, the Firepower Royal Artillery Museum. Housed in the old Royal Arsenal leading down to the river shore, the museum's setting provides an evocative sense of the Thames and its lingering effect on the capital's history. Inside, the **Field of Fire** experience is a powerful re-creation of what it was actually like to be in the thick of the London Blitz or the D-Day Landings, complete with giant projections of archive film on all sides, live smoke effects, and a floor that quakes in time to the roar of exploding bombs. The **Modern Gunner** exhibition explores the conflicts in which the Royal Artillery Regiment has taken part, from the discovery of gunpowder to the present day. Also on show are tanks and guns—some complete with battle scars. During school holiday periods there are plenty of activities for kids, such as learning the basic skills of a field medic, or even "battle wound" face painting. ⊠ *Royal Arsenal, Woolwich* ☎ *020/8855–7755* ⊕ *www.firepower. org.uk* 🖼 *£5.30* ⊙ *Tues.–Sat. 10–5; last admission 4* Ⓜ *DLR: Woolwich Arsenal.*

12

hair, fingernails, and urine. ⊠ *Pepys Bldg., King William Walk, Greenwich* ☎ *020/8269–4799* ⊕ *www.ornc.org/visit/attractions/discover-greenwich-visitor-centre* 🖼 *Free* ⊙ *Daily 10–5* Ⓜ *DLR: Greenwich.*

Fodor's Choice ★ **Eltham Palace.** Once a favorite getaway for Henry VIII (who liked to spend Christmas here), Eltham Palace has been drastically remodeled twice in its lifetime; once during the 15th and 16th centuries, and again during the 1930s, when a grand mansion was annexed onto the Tudor great hall by the superwealthy Coulthard family. Today it's an extraordinary combination of late medieval grandeur and art deco masterpiece, laced with an eccentric whimsy—the Coulthards even built an entire room to be the personal quarters of their beloved pet lemur. The house and its extensive gardens were fully restored when the palace finally entered public ownership in the late 1990s. At this writing yet another renovation was underway. This will add a new visitor center and reveal new rooms previously closed to the public—including, most enticingly, a "luxury bomb shelter." ✉ *Court Rd., Eltham* 🕾 *020/8294–2548* ⊕ *www.english-heritage.org.uk* 💷 *£10.20* ⏱ *Apr.–Oct. and late Feb., Sun.–Wed. 10–5; Nov.–Mar., Sun. 10–4* Ⓜ *Eltham.*

Greenwich Market. Established as a fruit-and-vegetable market in 1700, the covered market now offers around 120 mixed stalls of art and crafts on Wednesday, Saturday, and Sunday; antiques and collectibles on Tuesday, Thursday, and Friday. You can get food to go on each market day, although the offerings are usually best on weekends. Shopping for handicrafts is a pleasure here, as in most cases you're buying directly from the artist. ✉ *College Approach, Greenwich* 🕾 *020/8269–5096* ⊕ *www.greenwichmarketlondon.com* ⏱ *Tues.–Sun. 10–5:30* Ⓜ *DLR: Cutty Sark.*

Museum of London Docklands. This wonderful old warehouse building, on a quaint cobbled quayside beside the tower of Canary Wharf, is worth a visit in its own right. With uneven wood floors, beams, and pillars, the museum used to be a storehouse for coffee, tea, sugar, and rum from the West Indies—hence the name West India Quay. The fascinating story of the old port and the river is told using films, together with interactive displays and reconstructions. Excellent permanent exhibitions include City and River, which chronicles the explosion of trade and industry that, by the mid-19th century, had transformed this district into the world's most important port. Sailortown is an effective reconstruction of the Wapping district in Victorian times, complete with period shops, a pub, spooky alleys, and costumed guides. Special events happen year-round; check the museum's website for details. ✉ *No. 1 Warehouse, West India Quay, Canary Wharf* 🕾 *020/7001–9844* ⊕ *www. museumoflondon.org.uk/docklands* 💷 *Free* ⏱ *Daily 10–6; last admission 20 mins before closing* Ⓜ *Canary Wharf; DLR: West India Quay.*

Fodor's Choice ★ **National Maritime Museum.** From the time of Henry VIII until the 1940s Britain was the world's preeminent naval power, and the collections here trace half a millennia of that seafaring history. The story is as much about trade as it is warfare; the "Atlantic: Slavery, Trade and Empire" gallery explores how trade in goods—and people—irrevocably changed the world, while "Voyagers: Britons and the Sea" focuses on stories of the ordinary people who took to the waves over the centuries. One gallery is devoted to Admiral Lord Nelson, Britain's most

---

GREENWICH FOOT TUNNEL

In a brilliant piece of foresight in 1849, Greenwich Hospital bought Island Gardens, on the other side of the Thames, to guard against industrial sprawl and preserve one of the most beautiful views in London. Take the stone spiral steps down into Greenwich Foot Tunnel and head under the Thames (enjoying the magnificently creepy echo) to Island Gardens, at the southern tip of the Isle of Dogs. Then look back over the river for a magnificent vista: the Old Royal Naval College and Queen's House in all their glory, framed by the verdant green borders of the park.

Without a central support, the Tulip Stair spirals up to the Great Hall of Queen's House.

famous naval commander, and among the exhibits is the uniform he was wearing, complete with bloodstains, when he died at the Battle of Trafalgar in 1805. Temporary exhibitions here are usually fascinating; those in recent years have included the Arctic convoys of World War II and how the race to measure longitude (east–west position) at sea opened the door to global exploration on an unprecedented scale. The museum has a good café with views over Greenwich Park. The adjacent **Queen's House** is home to the museum's art collection, the largest collection of maritime art in the world, including works by William Hogarth, Canaletto, and Joshua Reynolds. Permission for its construction was granted by Queen Anne only on condition that the river vista from the house be preserved, and there are few more majestic views in London than Inigo Jones's awe-inspiring symmetry. Completed around 1638, the Tulip Stair, named for the fleur-de-lis-style pattern on the balustrade, is especially fine, spiraling up without a central support to the Great Hall. The Great Hall itself is a perfect cube, exactly 40 feet in all three dimensions, decorated with paintings of the Muses and the Virtues. ⊠ *Romney Rd., Greenwich* ☎ *020/8858–4422* ⊕ *www.rmg. co.uk/national-maritime-museum* 🖼 *Free* ☉ *Daily 10–5; last admission 4:30* Ⓜ *DLR: Greenwich.*

Fodor'sChoice ★ **Old Royal Naval College.** Begun by Christopher Wren in 1694 as a rest home for ancient mariners, the college became a school in 1873. It's still used for classes by the University of Greenwich and the Trinity College of Music, although you're more likely to recognize it as a film location—recent blockbusters to have made use of its elegant interiors include *Skyfall*, *Les Misérables*, and *The King's Speech*. Architecturally, you'll notice how the structures part to reveal the **Queen's House** across the central lawns. Behind the college are two more buildings you can visit. The **Painted Hall,** the college's dining hall, which derives its name from the baroque murals of William and Mary (reigned jointly 1689–95; William alone 1695–1702) and assorted allegorical figures. James Thornhill's frescoes, depicting scenes of naval grandeur with a suitably pro-British note, were painstakingly completed 1708–12 and 1718–26, and were good enough to earn him a knighthood. In the opposite building stands the **College Chapel,** which was rebuilt after a fire in 1779 in an altogether more restrained, neo-Grecian style. Check the website for an outstanding program of special events, including talks, tours, and concerts—many of them free. ⊠ *King William Walk, Greenwich* ☎ *020/8269–4747* ⊕ *www.ornc.org* ✉ *Free, guided tours £6* ⊙ *Painted Hall and chapel daily 10–5 (Sun. chapel from 12:30); grounds 8–6* Ⓜ *DLR: Greenwich.*

Royal Observatory.
See the highlighted listing in this chapter.

WORTH NOTING

Clock Tower Antiques Market. The weekend Clock Tower Antiques Market on Greenwich High Road has more vintage shopping, and browsing among the "small collectibles" makes for a good half-hour diversion. ⊠ *166 Greenwich High Rd., Greenwich* ☎ *020/7237–2001* ⊕ *www.clocktowermarket.co.uk* ⊙ *Weekends and holiday Mon. 10–5.* Ⓜ *Greenwich Rail.*

Up at the O2. Certainly one of the most unique ways to see London, this thrilling urban expedition takes you on a journey across the giant dome of the O2 arena. After a short briefing, you're dressed in safety gear and taken in small groups across a steep walkway, running all the way to the summit and down the other side. The high point (literally) is a viewing platform, 161 feet aboveground, with magnificent views of the city. On a clear day you can see for 15 miles. Climbs at sunset and twilight are also available. It's quite an experience, but unsurprisingly there are restrictions: you have to be at least 10 years old, more than 4 feet tall, have a waist measurement that's less than 49 inches, and weigh less than 286 pounds. Wheelchairs can be accommodated on a few tours. Advanced booking is essential. ⊠ *Peninsula Sq.* ☎ *020/463–2000* ⊕ *www.theo2.co.uk/upattheo2* ✉ *From £26 (varies according to time and date)* ⊙ *Tours daily, around 10–10 summer, 10–6 winter* Ⓜ *North Greenwich.*

THE THAMES
UPSTREAM

GETTING ORIENTED

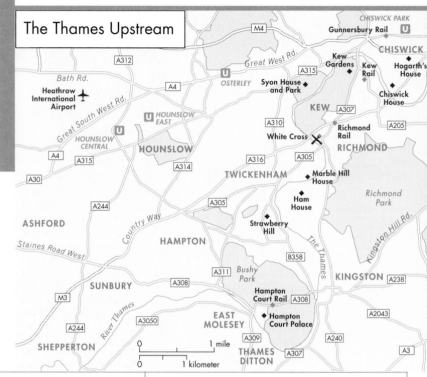

The Thames Upstream

A GOOD WALK	MAKING THE MOST OF YOUR TIME

A GOOD WALK

From Chiswick House, follow Burlington Lane and take a left onto Hogarth Lane—which, in reality, is anything but a lane—to reach Hogarth's House. Chiswick's Church Street (reached by a rather unappealing under-pass from Hogarth's House) is the nearest thing to a sleepy country village street you're likely to find in London. Follow it down to the Thames and turn left at the bottom to reach the 18th-century riverfront houses of Chiswick Mall, referred to by locals as "Millionaire's Row." There are several pretty river-side pubs near Hammersmith Bridge.

MAKING THE MOST OF YOUR TIME

Hampton Court Palace requires half a day to experience its magic, though you could make do with a few hours for the other attractions. Because of the distance between sights, it's best to focus on one sight, add in some others within the area, then a riverside walk and pint at a pub.

FEELING PECKISH?

The Original Maids of Honour. This most traditional of Old English tearooms is named for a type of jam tart invented here and still baked by hand on the premises. Legend has it that Henry VIII loved them so much he had the recipe kept under armed guard. Full afternoon tea is served daily 2:30–6, and lunch in two sittings at 12:30 and 1:45. Or opt to take out food for a picnic at Kew Gardens or on Kew Green. (While you do, keep an eye out for their 1930s-era delivery van, which still makes the rounds daily.) ⊠ *288 Kew Rd., Kew* ☎ *020/8940–2752* ⊕ *www.theoriginalmaidsofhonour. co.uk* ☉ *Daily 8:30–6.*

13

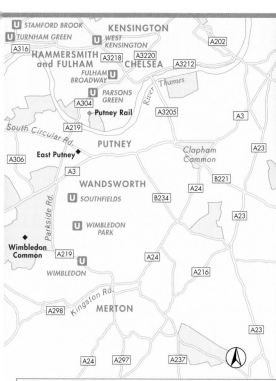

TOP REASONS TO GO

Explore Hampton Court Palace: Go ghost hunting or just admire the beautiful Tudor architecture at Henry VIII's beloved home, then lose yourself in the maze as dusk begins to fall.

Go "Goth" at Strawberry Hill: The 19th-century birthplace of connoisseur Horace Walpole's "Gothick" style, this mock-castle is a joyous riot of color and invention.

Escape to magical Kew Gardens: See the earth from above by visiting Kew's treetop walkway at the famous Royal Botanic Gardens.

Pay your respects to Father Thames: Enjoy a pint from the creaking balcony of a centuries-old riverside pub as you watch the boats row by on the loveliest stretch of England's greatest river.

NEAREST PUBLIC RESTROOMS

Richmond Park, Kew Gardens, and all the stately homes have public restrooms.

GETTING THERE

The District line is the best of the Tube options, stopping at Turnham Green (in the heart of Chiswick but a walk from the houses), Gunnersbury (for Syon Park), Kew Gardens, and Richmond. For Hampton Court, overland train is quickest: South West trains run from Waterloo twice an hour, with roughly half requiring a change at Surbiton. There are also regular, direct trains from Waterloo to Chiswick station (best for Chiswick House), Kew Bridge, Richmond (for Ham House), and St. Margaret's (best for Marble Hill House). London overground trains also stop at Gunnersbury, Kew Gardens, and Richmond.

A pleasant way to go is by river. Boats depart from Westminster Pier, by Big Ben, for Kew (1½ hours), Richmond (2 hours), and Hampton Court (3 hours). The trip is worth taking if you make it an integral part of your day, and know that it gets breezy. Round-trip costs between £18 and £23. For more details contact **Transport For London** (0843/222–1234 ⊕ www.tfl.gov.uk).

Sightseeing
★★★★
Nightlife
★★
Dining
★★★
Lodging
★★
Shopping
★★

The upper stretch of the Thames links a string of fashionable districts—Chiswick, Kew, Richmond, and Putney—with winding old streets, horticultural delights, cozy riverside pubs, and Henry VIII's Hampton Court Palace. The neighborhoods along the way are as proud of their villagey feel as of their stately history, witnessed by such handsome estates as Strawberry Hill and Syon House. After the sensory overload of the West End, it's easy to forget you're in a capital city at all.

CHISWICK

Updated By
Jack Jewers

On the banks of the Thames just west of central London, far enough out to escape the crush and crowds you've probably just started to get used to, Chiswick is a low-key, upscale district, content with its run of restaurants, stylish shops, and film-star residents. No doubt its most famous son wouldn't approve of all the conspicuous wealth, though; Chiswick was home to one of Britain's best-loved painters, William Hogarth, who tore the fabric of the 18th-century nation to shreds with his slew of satirical engravings. **Hogarth's House** has been restored to its former glory. Incongruously stranded among Chiswick's row houses are a number of fine 18th-century buildings, which are now some of the most desirable suburban houses in London. By far the grandest of all is **Chiswick House,** a unique Palladian-style mansion born from the 3rd earl of Burlington's love of classical and Renaissance architecture—a radical style at the time.

TOP ATTRACTIONS

Fodor'sChoice
★

Chiswick House. Completed in 1729 by the 3rd earl of Burlington (also known for Burlington House—home of the Royal Academy—and Burlington Arcade on Piccadilly), this extraordinary Palladian mansion

was envisaged as a kind of temple to the arts. Burlington was fascinated by the architecture he saw in Italy while on the Grand Tour as a young man. When his country home was destroyed by fire in 1725, he seized the chance to rebuild it in homage to those classical and Renaissance styles. The building is loosely modeled on the Villa Capra near Vicenza, while the colonnaded frontage is a partial replica of the Pantheon in Rome (which also inspired the domed roof).

The sumptuous interiors were the work of William Kent (1685–1748), his most extraordinary achievement being the Blue Velvet Room, with its gilded decoration and intricate painted ceiling. The design of Chiswick House sparked a great deal of interest—such ideas were radical in England at the time—and turned Kent into a hugely influential figure in British architecture. So great was his fame that wealthy patrons clamored to have him design anything, from gardens to party frocks.

The rambling grounds are one of the hidden gems of West London. Italianate in style (of course), they are filled with classical temples, statues, and obelisks. Also on the grounds are a café and a children's play area. ⊠ *Burlington La., Chiswick* ☎ *020/8995–0508* ⊕ *www.chgt.org. uk* ⊠ *£6.10; grounds free* ☉ *Grounds daily 7 am–dusk; house late Feb.– late Mar., weekends 10–4; late Mar.–early Nov., Sun.–Wed. and holiday Mon. 10–5* Ⓜ *Turnham Green, Chiswick. National Rail: Chiswick.*

Hogarth's House. Besieged by a roaring highway that somewhat spoils the atmosphere, the home of the satirist and painter William Hogarth (1697–1764) is still worth a visit by fans of his amusing, moralistic engravings (such as "The Rake's Progress" and "Marriage à la Mode"). Recently the house has had an unlucky few years; closed by a fire in 2008, restoration work was then halted by a second fire the following year. However, the house is now fully restored, with new exhibition spaces devoted to Hogarth and his work. Look out for the 300-year-old mulberry tree in the garden—the remnant of a failed attempt to get silkworms to breed in England. Hogarth's tomb can be found in the cemetery of St. Nicholas's church on nearby Chiswick Mall. ⊠ *Hogarth La., Great West Rd. (A4), Chiswick* ☎ *020/8994–6757* ⊕ *www. hounslow.info/arts/hogarthshouse* ⊠ *Free* ☉ *Tues.–Sun. and holiday Mon. noon–5* Ⓜ *Turnham Green. National Rail: Chiswick.*

HOGARTH HEAVEN

Fosters Bookshop. A great place to buy Hogarth prints is at Fosters Bookshop, based in Chiswick's oldest shop building. The shop has its original Georgian frontage, creaking floorboards, and a glorious number of original Victorian novels and essays. ⊠ *183 Chiswick High Rd., Chiswick* ☎ *020/8995-2768* ⊕ *www. fostersbookshop.co.uk* ☉ *Tues.– Sat. 10:30–5:30.*

■ QUICK
BITES

Some of the loveliest pubs in London sit beside the Thames at Chiswick, dotted along the northern bank of the river as far as Hammersmith Mall— the last remaining fragment of what was once a pretty old village, now all but replaced by urban sprawl.

Blue Anchor. This cozy 18th-century watering hole on the Thames overlooks Hammersmith Bridge—a High Victorian, wrought-iron suspension bridge designed by Sir Joseph Bazalgette in 1887. The rowing memorabilia on the walls hints at the Blue Anchor's importance on the day of the annual Oxford-versus-Cambridge university boat race, when it's an unofficial meeting point for fans and race officials. The pub also serves light meals. ✉ *13 Lower Mall, Hammersmith* ☎ *020/8748–5774* ⊕ *www.blueanchorlondon.com* ⊙ *Mon.–Sat. noon–11, Sun. noon–10:30.*

13

City Barge. One of the few pubs in this upscale quarter of Chiswick that retains a proper, old-school feel (enhanced by a recent renovation) the City Barge overlooks a tiny island in the middle of the Thames. Stop for some excellent pub food at lunchtime (it's not-too-gentrified modern British), or just enjoy a pint and watch the river flow by. ✉ *27 Strand-on-the-Green, Chiswick* ☎ *020/8994–2148* ⊕ *www.metropolitanpubcompany.com/our-pubs/the-city-barge* ⊙ *Mon.–Thurs. noon–11, Fri. noon–midnight, Sat. 10–midnight, Sun. 10–10:30* Ⓜ *Gunnersbury. National Rail: Kew Bridge.*

Dove Inn. Retaining the charm of its 300-plus-year heritage, the Dove has a tranquil little terrace that's perfect for watching the river flow by. Check out the Lilliputian room immediately on the right as you enter—it's in the *Guinness Book of World Records* for being the smallest bar in the world. ✉ *19 Upper Mall, Hammersmith* ☎ *020/8748–9474* ⊕ *www.dovehammersmith.co.uk* ⊙ *Mon.–Sat. 11–11, Sun. noon–10:30* Ⓜ *Ravenscourt Park, Hammersmith.*

KEW

A mile or so beyond Chiswick is Kew, a leafy suburb with little to see other than its two big attractions: the lovely **Kew Palace** and the **Royal Botanic Gardens**—anchored in the landscape for several miles around by a towering, mock-Chinese pagoda.

TOP ATTRACTIONS

FAMILY **Kew Gardens.**
See the highlighted listing in this chapter.

Fodor's Choice ★ **Kew Palace and Queen Charlotte's Cottage.** The elegant redbrick exterior of the smallest of Britain's royal palaces seems almost humble when compared with the grandeur of, say, Buckingham or Kensington palaces. Yet inside is a fascinating glimpse into life at the uppermost end of society from the 17th to 19th century. This is actually the third of several palaces that stood here; once known as Dutch House, it was one of the havens to which George III retired when insanity forced him to withdraw from public life. Queen Charlotte had an *orné*—a rustic-style cottage retreat—added in the late 18th century. In a marvelously regal flight of fancy, she kept kangaroos in the paddock outside. The

KEW GARDENS

✉ *Kew Rd. at Lichfield Rd., for Victoria Gate entrance, Kew* ☎ *020/8332–5655* ⊕ *www. kew.org* 🎫 *£15* ⊘ *Mid-Feb.– Mar., daily 9:30–5:30; Apr.–late Aug., weekdays 9:30–6:30, weekends and holiday Mon. 9:30–7:30; late Aug.–late Oct., daily 9:30–6; late Oct.– mid-Feb., daily 9:30–4:15. Last admission to park, greenhouses, galleries, and treetop walkway 30 mins before closing.* Ⓜ *Kew Gardens. National Rail: Kew Gardens, Kew Bridge.*

TIPS

■ Free guided tours, run by volunteers, are held daily at 11 am and 1:30 pm, plus seasonally themed tours at noon.

■ The Kew Explorer bus runs on a 40-minute, hop-on, hop-off route around the gardens every hour from 11 to 3. Tickets cost £4.50.

■ Discovery Tours are adapted and fully accessible, aimed at disabled visitors.

■ Walking tours are £5 per group, bus tours £30 per group. Book in advance.

■ Take tea at the Victoria Plaza Café or a meal at the elegant Orangery or White Peaks.

Enter the Royal Botanic Gardens, as Kew Gardens are officially known, and you are enveloped by blazes of color, extraordinary blooms, hidden trails, and lovely old follies. Beautiful though it all is, Kew's charms are secondary to its true purpose as a major center for serious research. Academics are hard at work on more than 300 scientific projects across as many acres, analyzing everything from the cacti of eastern Brazil to the yams of Madagascar. First opened to the public in 1840, Kew has been supported by royalty and nurtured by landscapers, botanists, and architects since the 1720s. Today the gardens, now a UNESCO World Heritage site, hold more than 30,000 species of plants, from every corner of the globe.

Although the plant houses make Kew worth visiting even in the depths of winter (there's also a seasonal garden), the flower beds are, of course, best enjoyed in the fullness of spring and summer.

Highlights

Architect Sir William Chambers built a series of temples and follies, of which the crazy 10-story **Pagoda**, visible for miles around, is the star. The Princess of Wales conservatory houses 10 climate zones, and the Rhizotron and Xstrata Treetop Walkway takes you 59 feet up into the air. Two great 19th-century greenhouses—the **Palm House** and the **Temperate House**—are filled with exotic blooms, and many of the plants have been there since the final glass panel was fixed into place. Unfortunately the enormous Temperate House is closed for maintenance until 2018, so until then you won't be able to gawk at the largest greenhouse plant in the world, a Chilean wine palm planted in 1846 (and so big that you have to climb the spiral staircase to the roof to get a proper view of it).

main house and gardens are maintained in the 18th- century style. Entry to the palace itself is free, but it lies within the grounds of Kew Gardens, and you must buy a ticket to that to get here. ⊠ *Kew Gardens, Kew Rd. at Lichfield Rd., Kew* ☎ *0844/482–7777 (only in U.K.), 020/3166–6000* ⊕ *www. hrp.org.uk* ⊠ *Free with entry to Kew Gardens* ⊙ *Palace Apr.–Sept., daily 10:30–5:30 (last admission 5); Queen Charlotte's Cottage late Mar.–Sept., weekends 10–4* Ⓜ *Kew Gardens.*

> ### WORD OF MOUTH
>
> "We really enjoyed Kew Gardens. Even though we went in August, we did not find it crowded. There are quite a few benches throughout the gardens so you can sit and enjoy. We threw some picnic items in our day pack and enjoyed lunch under a huge tree on the lawn." —michele_d

13

RICHMOND

Named after the (long-vanished) palace Henry VII started here in 1500, Richmond is still a welcoming suburb with a small-town feel, marred only by choking levels of traffic. Duck away from the main streets to find many handsome Georgian and Victorian houses, antiques shops, a Victorian theater, a grand stately home—and, best of all, the largest of London's royal parks.

TOP ATTRACTIONS

Ham House. To the west of Richmond Park, overlooking the Thames and nearly opposite the memorably named Eel Pie Island, Ham House was built in 1610 and remodeled 50 years later. It's one of the most complete examples in Europe of a lavish 17th-century house, together with a restored formal garden that has become an influential source for other European palaces and grand villas. The original decorations in the Great Hall, Round Gallery, and Great Staircase have been replicated, and all the furniture and fittings are on permanent loan from the Victoria & Albert Museum. A tranquil and scenic way to reach the house on foot, which takes about 30 minutes, along the eastern riverbank south from Richmond Bridge. ⊠ *Ham St., Richmond* ☎ *020/8940–1950* ⊕ *www. nationaltrust.org.uk/hamhouse* ⊠ *House, gardens, and outbuildings £10; gardens and servants' quarters only £4* ⊙ *House late Feb.–Oct., daily 10–4. Gardens Nov.–mid-Feb., daily 10–4; mid-Feb.–Oct., daily 10–5* Ⓜ *Richmond, then Bus 65 or 371.*

Fodor's Choice ★ **Hampton Court Palace.** *See the highlighted listing in this chapter.*

Marble Hill House. This handsome Palladian mansion is set in 66 acres of parkland on the northern bank of the Thames, almost opposite Ham House. It was built in the 1720s by George II for his mistress, the "exceedingly respectable and respected" Henrietta Howard. Later the house was occupied by Mrs. Fitzherbert, who was secretly married to the Prince Regent (later George IV) in 1785. The house was restored in 1901 and opened to the public two years later, looking very much like it did in Georgian times, with extravagant gilded rooms in which Mrs. Howard entertained the literary superstars of the age, including Pope, Gay, and Swift. A ferry service from Ham House operates during the summer; access on foot is a half-hour walk south along the west bank of the Thames from Richmond Bridge. Note that entry is by guided tour only, run by English Heritage and volunteers from a local history group. ✉ *Richmond Rd., Twickenham* ☎ *020/8892–5115* ⊕ *www. english-heritage.org.uk* ✆ *£5.90 (guided tour only)* ⊙ *House and park: Apr.–Oct., Sat. 10–2, Sun. and holiday Mon. 10–5; tours 10:30 and noon on weekends, with additional tours 2:15 and 3:30 on Sun. Park only: Nov.–Mar., daily 7–5.* Ⓜ *Richmond. National Rail: St Margarets.*

FAMILY   **Richmond Park.** This enormous park was enclosed in 1637 for use as a royal hunting ground—like practically all other London parks. Unlike the others, however, Richmond Park still has wild red and fallow deer roaming its 2,360 acres (that's three times the size of New York's Central Park) of grassland and heath. Its ancient oaks are among the last remnants of the vast, wild forests that once encroached on London in medieval times. The Isabella Plantation (near the Ham Gate entrance) is an enchanting and colorful woodland garden, first laid out in 1831. There's a splendid, protected view of St. Paul's Cathedral from King Henry VIII's Mound, the highest point in the park. Find it and you have a piece of magic in your sights. The park is also home to White Lodge, a 1727 hunting lodge that now houses the Royal Ballet School. ✉ *Richmond* ☎ *030/0061–2200* ⊕ *www.royalparks.org.uk* ✆ *Free* ⊙ *Apr.–Oct., daily 7–dusk; Nov.–Mar., daily 7:30–dusk.* Ⓜ *Richmond, then Bus 371 or 65.*

QUICK BITES   **White Cross.** Overlooking the Thames so closely that the waters almost lap at the door in high tide, the White Cross is a popular spot that serves traditional, hearty, and crowd-pleasing snacks and meals. ✉ *Water La., Richmond* ☎ *020/8940–6844* ⊕ *www.youngs.co.uk* ⊙ *Mon.–Sat. 11–11, Sun. 11–10:30.*

Fodor's Choice ★   **Strawberry Hill.** From the outside, this rococo mishmash of towers, crenellations, and white stucco is dazzling in its faux-medieval splendor. Its architect and owner, Sir Horace Walpole (1717–97) knew a thing or two about imaginative flights of fancy—the flamboyant son of the first British prime minister, Robert Walpole, he all but single-handedly invented the Gothic novel with *The Castle of Otranto* (1764). Once you pass through Strawberry Hill's forbidding exterior, you'll experience explosion of color and light, for Walpole boldly decided to take elements from the exteriors of Gothic cathedrals and move them inside. The detail is extraordinary, from the cavernous entrance hall with its vast Gothic trompe l'oeil, to the Great Parlour with its Renaissance stained glass, to the Gallery, where extraordinary fan vaulting is a replica of the vaults found in Henry VIII's chapel at Westminster Abbey. Neglected for years, Strawberry Hill reopened in 2011 after a stunningly successful £9-million restoration. The gardens have also been meticulously returned to their original 18th-century design, right down to a white marble loveseat sculpted into the shape of a shell. You can

Continued on page 237

Tower Bridge

A TOUR OF THE THAMES

"I have seen the Mississippi. That is muddy water.
I have seen the St. Lawrence. That is crystal water.
But the Thames is liquid history."
—John Burns

The twists and turns of the Thames River through the heart of the capital make it London's best thoroughfare and most compelling viewing point. Once famous for sludge, silt, and sewage, the Thames is now the cleanest city river in the world. Whether you take a river cruise or a leisurely stroll along its banks and bridges, traveling on or alongside the river is an unforgettable way to soak up views of the city.

MILLENNIUM BRIDGE TO THAMES FLOOD BARRIER

Tower Bridge

The **Millennium Bridge** is the newest span across the river: **St. Paul's Cathedral** and **Tate Modern** eye each other magnificently from either side of the once worryingly wobbly strip of a bridge. Farther east, the reconstructed **Shakespeare's Globe Theatre** is resplendent in whitewash and brown timber on the South Bank.

Between Southwark and London bridges, look for the southside *Golden Hinde*, an exact scale reconstruction of Sir Francis Drake's galleon that sailed around the world.

Moored outside the Victorian shopping mall **Hay's Galleria** is **HMS** *Belfast*, Europe's last existing armored warship that saw action in World War II, now a floating naval museum on nine decks.

St. Paul's Cathedral

Blackfriars Millennium Pier

Blackfriars Br.

Waterloo Br.

Golden Jubilee Br.

Millennium Br.

Southwark Br.

Cannon St. Station

London Br.

Monument

Tower of London

Tower Millennium Pier

HMS *Belfast*

St. Katharine's Docks

Tate Modern

London Bridge City Pier

Hay's Galleria

Tower Br.

St. Katharine's Pier

Shakespeare's Globe Theatre

Waterloo Station

Westminster Br.

City Hall

London Bridge Station

Butler's Wharf

Southwark Park

London Bridge is admittedly not the river's finest, but it is the birthplace of the city. Some say the river ceases to be picturesque after St. Paul's, but we disagree: look for the flaming crown of the **Monument**, Sir Christopher Wren's tribute to those who died in the 1666 Great Fire of London.

The splendid **Tower of London** sits proudly opposite the shining egg of **City Hall** (also referred to by the former London mayor Ken Livingstone as a giant "glass testicle"—a fine match for its phallic friend across the river, the **Swiss Re Building**, aka the Gherkin, both designed by a mischievous Norman Foster). They frame the 1894 **Tower Bridge**, a magnificent feat of engineering and style, which leads past the elegant confines of **St. Katharine's Docks**, the trendy restaurants of **Butler's Wharf**, and the **Design Museum**.

LONDON BRIDGE

Viking invaders destroyed London Bridge in 1014, hence the nursery rhyme "London Bridge is falling down." By 1962, London Bridge really was falling down again, its 1831 incarnation unable to take the strain of traffic. It was saved by American tycoon Robert McCulloch, who—possibly confusing the bridge with its much more splendid neighbor, Tower Bridge—bought it in 1968 for $2.46 million and had it shipped, stone by stone, to Lake Havasu in Arizona.

Thames Flood Barrier

Walking bridge at Canary Wharf

For the pièce de résistance of London's redevelopment, stay on the river until you reach the bright lights and tall reflective sides of **Canary Wharf**, the city's new business district, robotic in its modernity.

Step back in time at **Greenwich**, with the glorious **Royal Naval College** and the **National Maritime Museum**. Round the bend and you're back to the future, with the alien spaceship **02** (formerly the Millennium Dome) and the **Thames Flood Barrier** looming.

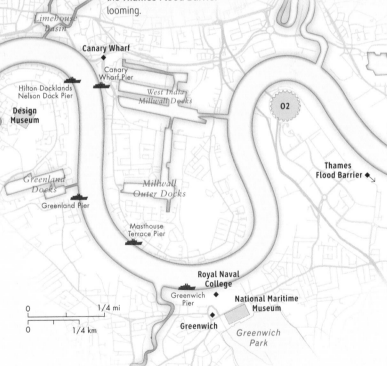

Limehouse Basin

Canary Wharf

Canary Wharf Pier

Hilton Docklands
Nelson Dock Pier

West India
Millwall Docks

Design Museum

02

Greenland Docks

Millwall
Outer Docks

Thames
Flood Barrier

Greenland Pier

Masthouse
Terrace Pier

Royal Naval
College

Greenwich
Pier

National Maritime
Museum

0   1/4 mi

0   1/4 km

Greenwich

Greenwich
Park

Blackfriars Bridge at night.

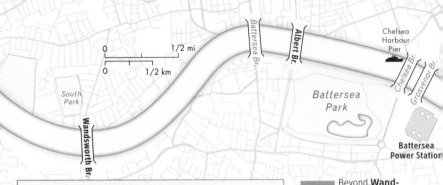

Battersea Br.

Albert Br.

Chelsea Harbour Pier

Chelsea Br.

Grosvenor Br.

South Park

Battersea Park

Wandsworth Br.

Battersea Power Station

WALKING THE THAMES

Even if you lack sea legs, you can still enjoy the river: not much beats a wander beside London's waterway. The Thames Path (www.nationaltrail.co.uk) follows the river 184 miles, from its source to the flood barriers in Greenwich. Some of the best riverside strolls:

- Hammersmith Bridge to Chiswick Mall
- Golden Jubilee Bridges to the South Bank's Queen's Walk
- Cleopatra's Needle to Parliament along Victoria Embankment
- Tate Modern to St. Paul's over Millennium Bridge

Beyond **Wandsworth Bridge**, the early part of this stretch by Battersea Bridge, rebuilt in 1890, was London's real industrial heartland, the southern side chock full of cottage housing for laborers, artisans at work, and factories.

View from London Eye (left); House's of Parliament (right)

The real treat of this stretch is the view of the **Houses of Parliament** and, beyond that, **Westminster Abbey**. Victoria Embankment, stretching all the way from Westminster to Blackfriars, was once all grim mudflats. In 1878 it became the country's first electrically illuminated street, and today its fine architecture, trees, and gardens are perfect strolling territory.

You can't miss the **London Eye**, whose parts were brought down the Thames one by one before being assembled on-location. Look out too for the London Aquarium and the Dalí museum, housed in the baroque-style County Hall.

Cleopatra's Needle, overlooking the Thames by Embankment, dates back to Heliopolis in 1450 BC. Look for World War I shrapnel holes and gouges at the base.

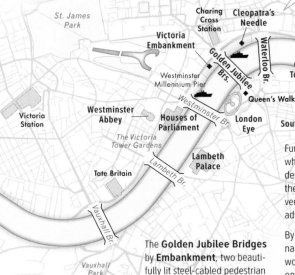

St. James Park

Charing Cross Station

Cleopatra's Needle

Victoria Embankment

Golden Jubilee Brs.

Waterloo Br.

Oxo Tower

Blackfriars Br.

Blackfriars Pier

Westminster Millennium Pier

Queen's Walk

Victoria Station

Westminster Abbey

Houses of Parliament

Westminster Br.

London Eye

South Bank

The Victoria Tower Gardens

Lambeth Palace

Tate Britain

Lambeth Br.

Vauxhall Br.

Vauxhall Park

After **Albert Bridge**—glorious at night, with lights like luminescent pearls sweeping down on strings—the Thames is a metropolitan glory of a river, charging through fashionable **Chelsea** and past the now derelict **Battersea Power Station**, under Chelsea, Vauxhall and Lambeth Bridges, with **Lambeth Palace** to the south.

The **Golden Jubilee Bridges** by **Embankment**, two beautifully lit steel-cabled pedestrian walkways, are perfect for reaching the **South Bank**.

Look out for the golden eagle, a monument to World War I RAF fighters, and **Cleopatra's Needle**. For the ultimate double-decker bus-viewing moment, look at **Waterloo Bridge**, once known as Ladies Bridge because it was built by female labor during World War II. The bridge has great views of the South Bank.

Further on is the **Oxo Tower**, whose red-glass letters were designed in 1928 to spell out the brand name while circumventing tight laws on exterior advertising.

By **Blackfriars Bridge**, named after the monks who wore black robes and lived on the north bank during the Middle Ages, the river used to run red by the riverside tanneries and slaughterhouses.

Blackfriars Bridge

HAMPTON COURT PALACE TO PUTNEY

Parliament

The Great Conservatory at Syon Park

Hampton Court Palace is a suitably lavish start or end to any trip on the Thames. The river skirts the grounds, giving magnificent views over the Tudor palace that Henry VIII and his daughter Elizabeth I made home, and continues north to **Kingston Bridge**, starting point for the river voyage of Jerome K. Jerome's *Three Men in a Boat* and home to hectic summer regattas. At **Teddington**, where the poet Alexander Pope and writer Horace Walpole entertained their female admirers in the 18th century, the river turns tidal but remains quiet and unspoiled all the way to **Kew**, passing herons and fine stately homes standing proud on the banks. From **Twickenham Bridge** you round the old deer park (to the south) and **Syon Park** (north), which has belonged to the Duke of

Waterlily House at Kew Gardens

Northumberland's family for centuries. Beyond that is an even greater treat—the UNESCO World Heritage Site of **Kew Botanical Gardens**. All manner of rowboats set up for one, two, four, or eight people pull hard under **Chiswick Bridge** and **Barnes (railway) Bridge**, past the expensive riverside frontage of Chiswick Mall and under **Hammersmith Bridge**, to **Putney** and **Fulham**—smart urban villages facing each other across the banks.

Syon Park

Kew Botanical Gardens

Twickenham Br.

Richmond Landing Stage

Richmond Br.

Marble Hill Park

Eel Pie Island

Teddington

Kingston Br.

Bushy Park

Hampton Ct. Br.

Hampton Court Palace

Hampton Court Pier

0   1 mi

0   1 km

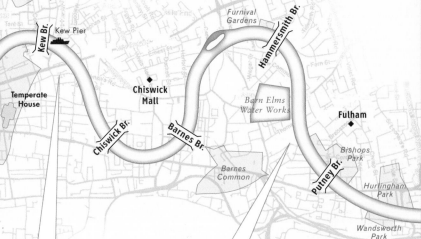

Gunnersbury Park

Kew Br.

Kew Pier

Temperate House

Chiswick Br.

♦ Chiswick Mall

Barnes Br.

Barnes Common

Furnival Gardens

Hammersmith Br.

Barn Elms Water Works

Fulham ♦

Bishops Park

Putney Br.

Hurlingham Park

Wandsworth Park

The stretch between Kew and Hammersmith is real rowing and riverside-pub territory, with a picturesque parade past Strand-on-the-Green by Kew Bridge.

ROWERS' ROW Every spring Britain's oldest universities, Oxford and Cambridge, compete not with their brains but with their brawn, in the **Boat Race**, which began in 1829. The race is 4¼ miles upstream from Putney Bridge to Chiswick Bridge: expect clashing oars, clenched teeth, and the occasional sinking (there have been six). The best views are from Hammersmith at the Surrey bend, which is also where most of the pubs are clustered. ⊕ www.theboatrace.org

A BRIEF HISTORY

An engraving by Claes Van Visscher showing Old London Bridge in 1616, with Southwark Cathedral in the foreground

The Thames has come a long way—and not just from its 344-km (214-mi) journey from a remote Gloucestershire

meadow to the sea. In the mid-19th century, the river was dying, poisoned by sewers that flushed into the river. The "Big Stink" was so awful that cholera and typhoid killed more than 10,000 in 1853, and Parliament abandoned sitting in 1858. "The odour is hardly that of frankincense," said one contemporary of the 1884 drought that forced down water levels, leaving elegant Victorian nostrils exposed to slimy ooze on the banks.

Joseph Bazalgette, star civil engineer of his time, was commissioned to design a new sewage system, and by the 1900s nearly all was forgiven. (His efforts did not go unappreciated: Bazalgette was later knighted.) Today 7.2 million people get their drinking water from the Thames River.

PLANNING A THAMES BOAT TOUR

"On the smallest pretext of holiday or fine weather the mighty population takes to the boats," wrote Henry James in 1877. You can follow in the footsteps of James, who took a boat trip from Westminster to Greenwich, or make up your own itinerary.

■ Frequent daily tourist-boat services are at their height between April and October.

■ In most cases you can turn up at a pier, and the next departure won't be far away. However, it never hurts to book ahead if you can.

■ Westminster and Tower piers are the busiest starting points, usually with boats heading east.

■TIP➜ For a rundown of all the options, along with prices and timetables, contact **London River Services** (☎ 020/7222–1234 ⊕ www.tfl.gov.uk/river), which gives details of all the operators sailing various sections of the river.

■ The trip between Westminster Pier and the Tower of London takes about 30 minutes, as does the trip between the Tower and Greenwich.

■ A full round-trip can take several hours. Ask about flexible fares and hop on/off options at the various piers.

THE BEST WAYS TO EXPERIENCE THE THAMES WHILE...

GOING OFF THE BEATEN PATH (LITERALLY)	020/7928–8933	www.londonribvoyages.com	£42
	See the river at high speed! **London RIB Voyages** use rigid inflatable boats (the kind used by coastguards) to shuttle you from Millennium Pier to Canary Wharf and back.	Varies daily according to weather, but generally hourly 10–4. Approximately 1 hr.	
SAVING TIME AND MONEY	020/7887–8888	www.tate.org.uk/tatetotate	£6.80 one-way
	The playfully polka-dotted *Tate Boat* sails across the river from the Tate Britain to the Tate Modern with a London Eye stop in between.	Departs from the pier at either museum: Daily every 40 min. Approximately 18 min. one-way.	
IMPRESSING A DATE OR CLIENT	0870/429–2451	www.bateauxlondon.com	£34–£43 (lunch), £79–£155 (dinner)
	For ultimate glamour (and expense), look into lunch and dinner cruises with **Bateaux London,** often formal affairs with surprisingly good two- to five-course meals. Variations include jazz brunch cruises on Sundays.	Departs from Embankment Pier. Departures vary but are typically noon (lunch), 3:15 (afternoon tea), and 7:15 (dinner). Check times on the day. Boarding from 30 min.	
ENJOYING ON-BOARD ENTERTAINMENT	020/7740–0400	www.citycruises.com	£79
	The *London Showboat* lives up to its name, with four-course meals, snazzy cabaret acts from West End musicals, and after-dinner dancing.	Departs from Westminster Pier, boarding point 2. Daily 7:30; boarding starts 15 min. prior to departure. Times can vary in winter; always check ahead. Approximately 3 1/2 hours.	

HAMPTON COURT PALACE

✉ *Hampton Court Rd.*
☎ *0844/482–7799 tickets, 0844/482–7777 information (24 hrs), 20/3166–6000 from outside U.K.* ⊕ *www.hrp. org.uk/hamptoncourtpalace*
🎟 *Palace, maze, and gardens £18.70; maze only £4.80; gardens only £6.40.* ☯ *Apr.– late Oct., daily 10–6; late Oct.–Mar., daily 10–4:30; last admission 1 hr before closing; last entry to maze 45 mins before closing). Formal Gardens daily: 10–6 summer, 10–4:30 winter. Informal Gardens daily: 7–8 summer, 7–6 winter.* Ⓜ *Richmond, then Bus R68. National Rail: Hampton Court Station, 35 mins from Waterloo (most trains require change at Surbiton).*

The beloved seat of Henry VIII's court, sprawled elegantly beside the languid waters of the Thames, Hampton Court is steeped in more history than virtually any other royal building in England. The Tudor mansion, begun in 1514 by Cardinal Wolsey to curry favor with the young Henry, actually conceals a larger 17th-century baroque building, which was partly designed by Christopher Wren. The earliest dwellings on this site belonged to a religious order founded in the 11th century and were expanded over the years by its many subsequent residents, until George II moved the royal household closer to London in the early 18th century.

Highlights

Wander through the **State Apartments,** decorated in the Tudor style, and on to the wood-beamed magnificence of **Henry's Great Hall,** before taking in the strikingly azure ceiling of the **Chapel Royal.** Well-handled reconstructions of Tudor life take place all year, from live appearances by "Henry VIII" to cook-historians preparing authentic Tudor feasts in the 15th-century **Henry's Kitchens.**

Watch out for the ghost of Henry VIII's doomed fifth wife, Catherine Howard, who lost her head yet is said to scream her way along the **Haunted Gallery.** Latter-day masters of the palace, the joint rulers William and Mary (reigned 1689–1702), were responsible for the beautiful **King's and Queen's Apartments** and the elaborate baroque of the **Georgian Rooms.**

Don't miss the famous **maze** (the oldest hedge maze in the world), its half mile of pathways among clipped hedgerows still fiendish to negotiate. There's a trick, but we won't give it away here: It's much more fun just to go and lose yourself.

The **Lower Orangery Exotic Garden** shows off thousands of exotic species that William and Mary, avid plant collectors, gathered from around the globe.

13

TIPS

■ Family tickets offer savings—two adults and up to three children are covered for £48, or £45 if you book online.

■ Choose which parts of the palace to explore based on a number of self-guided audio walking tours. Come Christmas time, there's ice-skating on a rink before the West Front of the palace.

■ Evening ghost tours (£28 per person) are held throughout the year. Not only are they entertainingly spooky, but they're a great opportunity to see the older parts of the palace without the crowds. Tours can sell out weeks in advance, so book ahead of time.

book a tour of the house at twilight for £20, including a glass of Prosecco. ✉ *268 Waldegrave Rd., Twickenham* ☎ *020/8744–1241* ⊕ *www. strawberryhillhouse.org.uk* 🖾 *£11* ⊙ *Timed entry, every 20 mins; see website for dates and times. Garden daily 10–6 (closed mid-Dec.–early Jan.).* Ⓜ *Richmond, then Bus 33; National Rail: Strawberry Hill Station.*

FAMILY
Fodor's Choice
★
Syon House and Park. The residence of the Duke and Duchess of Northumberland, this is one of England's most lavish stately homes. Set in a 55-acre park landscaped by "Capability" Brown, the core of the house is Tudor—it was one of the last stopping places for Henry VIII's fifth wife, Catherine Howard, and the extremely short-lived monarch, lady Jane Grey ("Queen for a day" as the saying goes—though it was actually 13), before they were sent to the Tower. It was remodeled in the Georgian style in 1761 by famed decorator Robert Adam. He had just returned from studying the sights of classical antiquity in Italy and created two rooms sumptuous enough to wow any Grand Tourist: the entryway is an amazing study in black and white, pairing neoclassical marbles with antique bronzes, and the Ante-Room contains 12 enormous verd-antique columns surmounted by statues of gold—and this was just a waiting room for the duke's servants and retainers. The Red Drawing Room is covered with crimson Spitalfields silk, and the Long Gallery is one of Adam's noblest creations. On certain Sundays and bank holidays in the summer you can take a miniature-steam-train ride in the grounds. ✉ *Syon Park, Brentford* ☎ *020/8560–0882* ⊕ *www. syonpark.co.uk* 🖾 *£11.50 for house, gardens, conservatory, and rose garden; £6.50 for gardens and conservatory* ⊙ *House mid-Mar.–Oct., Wed., Thurs., Sun., and bank holidays 11–5; gardens mid-Mar.–Oct., daily 10:30–5. Also certain dates in Dec. (call or check online). Last admission 1 hr before closing* Ⓜ *Gunnersbury, then Bus 237 or 267 to Brentlea.*

14

WHERE TO EAT

Visit Fodors.com for advice, updates, and bookings

Updated
By Alex
Wijeratna

Henry James was scathing about London's restaurants, "Whose badness is literally fabulous," he declared. But not so now, *Escoffier!* London has zoomed up the global gastro charts, and can seriously mix it now with the world's top culinary heavyweights. No other city—bar New York—has the immense range of global cuisines that London has to offer. Standards have rocketed at all price points and, dare we ask, might the London restaurant scene be in the most robust health it's ever been in?

A bottom-up local foodie revolution and a top-down cascade of *filthy* city lucre and hot global *monnay* has juiced things up fabulously. Feel like the most-tender Wagyu Shiga Omi beef steak on planet Earth? Yours for £140 at CUT at 45 Park Lane. You wanna try ultramodern old English gastronomy from the time of Henry VIII? Ashley Palmer-Watts is your man at Dinner by Heston Blumenthal. You only eat burgers and lobster? No worries, we've got just the thing: try Burger & Lobster in Soho for burgers and lobster, at £20 a pop. Can't stand any more snobby *Haw-he-haw* culinary stuff and nonsense? The low-key British wild game's so good at The Harwood in Fulham that they've bagged London's first gastropub-based Michelin star. Even the coffee shops are a marked improvement over a decade ago. While London can't compete with Rome or New York when it comes to coffee options, you'll find increasingly good quality lattes to go at Costa Coffee, Pret A Manger, Caffe Nero, and the Coffee Republic multishop chains.

Everyone's a foodie here now, and it seems everyone's blogging, Tweeting, and Instagraming their way through the latest and greatest openings. One week Portuguese chef Nuno Mendes is flavor of the month at celeb merry-go-round Chiltern Firehouse in Marylebone, the next it's the pork pie–hatted chefs brigade ripping it up at the open kitchen at spunky Israeli gastro haunt Palomar near Chinatown. Thankfully, pride in the best of British food—local, seasonal, foraged, and wild—is witnessing a genuine resurgence. And you, too, will be smitten, because you'll be spending, on average, 25% of your travel budget on eating out. Dig in. Fork up. Enjoy.

To appreciate how far London has risen in the global culinary firmament, just look back to the days of Somerset Maugham, who was once justified in warning, "To eat well in England you should have breakfast three times a day." Change was slow in coming after World War II, for then it was still understood the British ate to live, while the French lived to eat. When people thought of British cuisine, fish-and-chips—a greasy grab-and-gulp dish that tasted best wrapped in yesterday's newspaper—first came to mind. Then there was always shepherd's pie, ubiquitously found in smoky fog-filled pubs—though not made, according to *Sweeney Todd*, "With real shepherd in it."

14

These days, standards are a million times higher and poor-quality shepherd's pie has been largely replaced by the city's unofficial dish, the ubiquitous Indian curry. London's restaurant revolution is built on its extraordinary ethnic diversity, and you'll find the quality of other international cuisines has also grown immeasurably in recent years, with London becoming known for its Chinese, Japanese, Indian, Thai, Spanish, Italian, French, Peruvian, Korean, Ethiopian, and North African restaurants. With all of the choices, traditional British food, when you track it down, appears as just one more exotic cuisine in the pantheon.

PLANNING

EATING OUT STRATEGY

Where should you eat? With thousands of London eateries competing for your attention, it may seem like a daunting question. But fret not—our expert writers and editors have done most of the legwork. The selections here represent the best this city has to offer—from haute cuisine to humble dude food. *Search "Best Bets" for top recommendations by price, cuisine, and experience. Or find a review quickly in the neighborhood listings. Whichever way you look at it, you're sure to get a true taste of London.*

RESERVATIONS

Plan ahead if you're determined to snag a sought-after reservation. Some renowned restaurants like Chiltern Firehouse, Palomar, or Duck & Waffle are booked weeks or even months in advance. It's always a good idea to book as far ahead as you can and reconfirm when you arrive in London. Note that some top restaurants also now take credit card details and charge a penalty fee if you're a no-show. *In the reviews, we mention reservations only when they're essential or not accepted.*

DINING TOURS

London Food Lovers Food + Wine Tours. London is arguably the world's *top* global foodie city, and the London Food Lovers walking tour of Soho and beyond is a timely way to explore the capital's gastro delights. The half-day walk kicks off with Hawaiian blueberry pancakes at Kua'Aina burger joint off Carnaby Street and takes in offbeat stops for truffle pumpkin ravioli at Soho's Lina Stores Italian delicatessen, hot chocolate

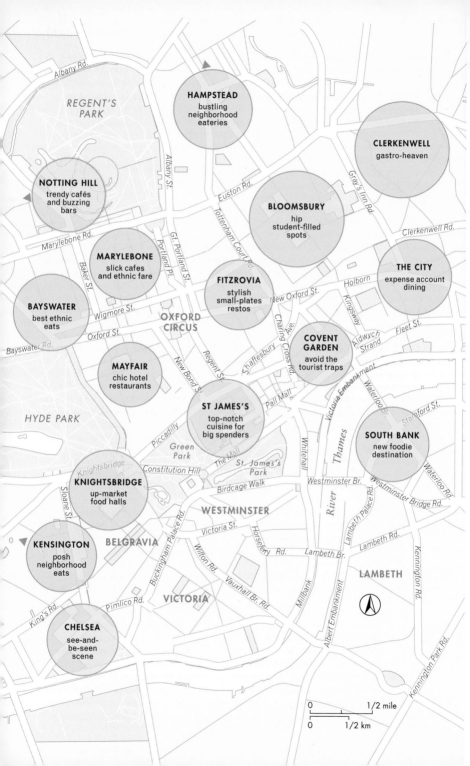

tasting at SAID artisanal Roman chocolatiers, and a sit-down lunch of battered cod and chips and pale ale in quaint Soho boozer The Dog and Duck. Participants pick up cultural and historical tidbits along the way. Well timed and synchronized throughout, you'll stop in Chinatown to sample prawn *dim sum* at Leong's Legends, and celeb spot amid the clink of fine bone china for afternoon tea at the Corinthia Hotel. The tour finishes off with a wine tasting in the Dickensian underground vaults of the 1890 Gordon's Wine Bar. ⊠ *258 Pentonville Rd., Islington* ☎ *07404–802–703* ⊕ *londonfoodlovers.com* 🖃 *£65 adults, £45 children* Ⓜ *Angel.*

WHAT TO WEAR

When in England's style capital, do as the natives do: dress up to eat out. Whatever your style, dial it up a notch. Have some fun while you're at it. Pull out the clothes you've been saving for a special occasion and get a little glamorous. As unfair as it seems, the way you look can influence how you're treated—and where you're seated. Generally speaking, jeans and a button-down shirt will suffice at most table-service restaurants in the budget to moderate range. Moving up from there, many pricier restaurants require jackets, and some like the Ritz insist on ties. Shorts, sweatpants, baseball caps, and sports jerseys are rarely appropriate. *Note that in reviews we mention dress only when men are required to wear a jacket, or a jacket and tie.*

TIPPING AND TAXES

Do not tip bar staff in pubs and bars—though you can always offer to buy them a drink. In restaurants, tip 12.5% of the check for full meals if service is not already included; tip a small token if you're just having coffee or tea. If paying by credit card, double-check that a tip has not already been included in the bill.

CHILDREN

Unless your children behave impeccably, it's best to avoid the haute-cuisine establishments, although increasingly many top places like the Wolseley and Fischer's are surprisingly child-friendly. London's many burger and rib joints, pizzerias, and Italian restaurants are popular with kids. Other family-friendly establishments include chains like Bill's, Côte, Byron, Busaba Eathai, and Wagamama.

HOURS

In London you can find breakfast all day, but it's generally served between 7 am and noon. Lunch is between noon and 3, and brunch overlaps between 11 and 4. Afternoon tea, often a meal in itself, is taken between 1 and 6, and dinner is typically eaten between 7 and 11, though it can be taken earlier. Many ethnic restaurants, especially Indian, serve food until midnight. Sunday is a proper lunch day, and some restaurants are open for lunch only. Over the Christmas period, London has a reputation for shutting down, but a growing number of hotels and other brave bastions are prepared to feed all comers.

PRICES

London is an *awfully* pricey city by global standards. A modest meal for two can easily cost £40, and the £100-a-head meal is not unknown. Damage-control strategies include making lunch your main meal—the

14

top places have bargain midday menus—going for early- or late-evening deals, or sharing an à la carte entrée and ordering a second appetizer instead. Seek out fixed-price menus, and watch for hidden extras on the check, that is, bread, vegetables, or a cover charged separately.

WHAT IT COSTS			
$	**$$**	**$$$**	**$$$$**
Restaurants	under £16	£16–£23	£24–£31	over £31

Price per person for an average main course or equivalent combination of smaller dishes at dinner. Note: If a restaurant offers only prix-fixe (set-price) meals, it has been given the price category that reflects the full prix-fixe price.

RESTAURANT REVIEWS

Listed alphabetically within neighborhoods. Use the coordinate (1:B2) at the end of each listing to locate a property on the Where to Eat and Stay in London atlas at the end of this chapter.

Prices in the reviews are the average cost of a main course at dinner or, if dinner is not served, at lunch.

WESTMINSTER, ST. JAMES'S, AND ROYAL LONDON

ST. JAMES'S

St. James's—home to Buckingham Palace and Clarence House, where Prince Charles and Camilla live—has a magnificent olde-world, royal feel. Appropriately, most of the restaurants here are fit for a future king and consort. This is where you'll find London's top-end restaurants— dining experiences that are geared toward a well-heeled, deep-pocketed clientele. Mere mortals should make reservations well in advance to dine at any of these restaurants for dinner (and reserve for the earlier or later shanks of the evening, when demand is less). Keep in mind that no-shows mean last-minute tables often crop up, and lunch here can be a great money-saving strategy.

$$$
MODERN
EUROPEAN
FAMILY

✕ **Le Caprice.** Celebville grande dame Le Caprice commands the deepest loyalty of any restaurant in London. Why? Because it gets practically everything right— *every* time. It's the 35-odd-year celebrity history—think Liz Taylor, Joan Collins, and Lady Di—the sparkling monochrome decor, the giddy David Bailey '60s black-and-white pics, charming Bolivian-born Jesus Adorno as the veteran maître'd, the pitch-perfect service, and the long-standing menu that sits somewhere between Euro peasant and trendy fashion plate. Sit at the raised counter or at a coveted corner table and enjoy calves' liver with crispy pancetta, roast pheasant with caramelized quince, yellowfin tuna with borlotti beans, and signature Scandinavian iced berries with a swirl of hot white chocolate sauce. Note the weekend live jazz sessions. $ *Average main: £24* ✉ *Arlington House, Arlington St., St. James's* ☎ *020/7629–2239* ⊕ *www.le-caprice.co.uk* ⌀ *Reservations essential* Ⓜ *Green Park* ✛ *5:A1.*

$$$$ ✕ **The Ritz Restaurant.** London's's most flamboyantly ornate dining
BRITISH room at The Ritz would moisten the eye of Marie Antoinette with its
sumptuous Belle Époque–inspired *trompe-d'oeil*, rococo garlanded gilt
chandeliers, fairy-tale silk drapery, marble statuette, and double-height
mirrored wall. A cavalcade of liveried waiters glide across the carpeted
salon, and gentlemen diners are expected to wear a jacket and tie at
all times. Sit at the late Baroness Thatcher's favorite seat overlooking
Green Park (Table 1) and enjoy unreconstructed "Palace style" British
haute cuisine. A Bresse chicken with black Périgord truffle stuffed under
its skin arrives in a pig's bladder and is carved table-side and served
with *sauce suprême.* Set and surprise menus at steep prices (£95, or
£185 with fine wine) might captivate with exquisite turbot with cep
and brown butter sauce or Anjou pigeon with *pomme Anna,* and don't
miss the famous *crêpes Suzette,* which are flambéed table-side by the
unflappable mâitre d'. $ *Average main: £38* ✉ *The Ritz London, 150
Piccadilly, St. James's* ☎ *020/7300–2370 for reservations only* ⊕ *www.
theritzlondon.com* ⚲ *Reservations essential* 🏛 *Jacket and tie* Ⓜ *Green
Park* ✦ *5:A1.*

$$$$ ✕ **Wiltons.** Aristos, Euro princes, and captains of industry blow the fam-
BRITISH ily bank at this old-fashioned bastion of English fine dining on Jermyn
Street (the place first opened on the Haymarket as a shellfish stall in
1742). Invariably fresh from a little snooze in their nearby St. James's
gentlemen's clubs, male diners are requested to wear long-sleeved shirts
and no sportswear or open-toed shoes at this linen-covered clubby time
capsule and *frightfully* snooty ode to all things English. Armigerous
signet ring–wearing posh patrons like to take half a dozen Beau Brum-
mell oysters, followed by grilled Dover sole on the bone or fabulous
native game in season, such as roast grouse, partridge, or teal. There
are antediluvian savories like soft herring roe on toast, plus desserts like
sherry trifle or bread-and-butter pudding. The use of mobile phones is
prohibited, the wine's weighed heavily toward Bordeaux claret, and
service, naturally , would put Jeeves to shame. $ *Average main: £34*
✉ *55 Jermyn St., St. James's* ☎ *020/7629–9955* ⊕ *www.wiltons.co.uk*
☾ *Closed Sun. No lunch Sat.* ⚲ *Reservations essential* 🏛 *Jacket required*
☞ *Men should wear long-sleeved shirts, with no sportswear or open-
toed shoes* Ⓜ *Green Park* ✦ *5:A1.*

$$ ✕ **The Wolseley.** A glitzy procession of stars come for the spectacle, swish
AUSTRIAN service, and soaring elegance at this bustling Viennese-style grand café
FAMILY on Piccadilly. Framed with '1920s black lacquerware in a former Wolse-
ley luxury car showroom, this all-day brasserie begins its long decadent
days with breakfasts at 7 am and serves highly adorable Dual Monarchy
delights until midnight. Don't be shy to turn up on spec (they welcome
walk-ins) to enjoy such Mitteleuropa highlights as Hungarian goulash,
Austrian pork belly, chicken soup with dumplings, or breaded *Wie-
ner schnitzel* . For dessert, go for luscious *Kaiserschmarren*—caramel-
ized pancakes with stewed fruit and raisins, or Black Forest gâteaux,
and don't forget return to savor the Viennoiserie pastries at one of
their classy £10.75 to £33.50 afternoon teas. $ *Average main: £18*
✉ *160 Piccadilly, St. James's* ☎ *020/7499–6996* ⊕ *www.thewolseley.
com* ⚲ *Reservations essential* Ⓜ *Green Park* ✦ *5:A1.*

BEST BETS FOR LONDON DINING

With 14,000 restaurants to choose from, how to decide where to eat? Fodor's writers and editors have tramped around and selected their favorite restaurants by price, cuisine, and experience in the Best Bets lists below. In the first column, Fodor's Choice properties represent the "best of the best" in every price category. You can also search by neighborhood for excellent eats—just peruse the following pages. Or find specific details about a restaurant in the full reviews, listed later in the chapter by neighborhood.

Fodor's Choice ★

Ametsa with Arzak Instruction, $$$
Berners Tavern, $$
Blanchette, $
Burger & Lobster, $$
Casse-Croûte, $$
Chiltern Firehouse, $$$
Dabbous, $$
The Delaunay, $$$
Dinner by Heston Blumenthal, $$$$
Dishoom, $
Duck & Waffle, $
Fischer's, $
Grain Store, $$
Gymkhana, $$$
The Harwood, $$$
Ivy Market Grill, $$$
The Ledbury, $$$$
Le Gavroche, $$$$
Little Social, $$

Palomar, $$
Petrus, $$$
Pollen Street Social, $$$$
Restaurant Story, $$$
The Ritz Restaurant, $$$$
Rules, $$$
Social Eating House, $$
Tommi's Burger Joint, $
Yashin, $$$
Zucca, $$

Best by Price

$

Dishoom
Duck & Waffle
Fischer's
Flat Iron
Pitt Cue Co.
Tayyabs

Tommi's Burger Joint

$$

Casse-Croûte
Palomar
Polpetto
The Riding House Café
Social Eating House

$$$

Chiltern Firehouse
Gymkhana
HKK
Restaurant Story

$$$$

Dinner by Heston Blumenthal
The Ledbury
Le Gavroche
The Ritz Restaurant

Best by Cuisine

BRITISH

Berners Tavern, $$
Duck & Waffle, $
The Harwood, $$$
Rochelle Canteen, $$
St. John, $$

CHINESE

HKK, $$$
Hunan, $$

FRENCH

Casse-Croûte, $$
Koffmann's, $$$
The Ledbury, $$$$
Le Gavroche, $$$$
The Ritz Restaurant, $$$$

ITALIAN

Bocca di Lupo, $$
Cecconi's, $$$
L'Anima, $$$
Polpetto, $
Zucca, $$

JAPANESE

Koya, $
Yashin, $$$
Zuma, $$

SEAFOOD

Bonnie Gull Seafood Shack, $$
J Sheekey, $$$
Scott's, $$$$
Sweetings, $$

STEAK

Bar Boulud, $$
Chiltern Firehouse, $$$
CUT at 45 Park Lane, $$$$
Flat Iron, $
Goodman, $$$$

Best by Experience

BRASSERIE

Balthazar, $$$
The Delaunay, $$$
Fischer's, $
The Wolseley, $$

BRUNCH

The Delaunay, $$$
Duck & Waffle, $
The Riding House Café, $
The Wolseley, $$

BUSINESS DINING

Berners Tavern, $$
The Delaunay, $$$
Fera at Claridge's, $$$$
Le Gavroche, $$$$
Scott's, $$$$

CELEB SPOTTING

34, $$$
The Delaunay, $$$
Duck & Waffle, $
J Sheekey, $$$
Scott's, $$$$

GASTROPUBS

Great Queen Street, $$
The Harwood, $$$
The Mall Tavern, $

GOOD FOR GROUPS

Bistrotheque, $$
Dean Street Townhouse, $$
Dishoom, $
Duck & Waffle, $
Pizza East, $
The Riding House Café, $

HISTORIC

Maison Bertaux, $
Rules, $$$
Simpson's Tavern, $
Sweetings, $$
Wiltons, $$$$

HOTEL DINING

Bar Boulud, $$
Berners Tavern, $$
Dinner by Heston Blumenthal, $$$$
Fera at Claridge's, $$$$
Hélène Darroze at the Connaught, $$$$

HOT SPOTS

Berners Tavern, $$
Chiltern Firehouse, $$$
Duck & Waffle, $
Gymkhana, $$$$
Palomar, $$

Restaurant Story, $$$
Social Eating House, $$

LATE-NIGHT DINING

Coya, $$
The Delaunay, $$$
Duck & Waffle, $
J Sheekey, $$$

LOCAL FAVORITES

Alounak, $
Chez Bruce, $$$
Lemonia, $
Pizza East, $

LUNCH PRIX FIXE

Galvin Bistrot de Luxe, $$$
Hereford Road, $
Le Gavroche, $$$$
The Mall Tavern, $
Merchants Tavern, $$

PRETHEATER

Côte, $
Dean Street Townhouse, $$
Opera Tavern, $
Social Eating House, $$

ROMANTIC

Berners Tavern, $$
Clos Maggiore, $$$
The Delaunay, $$$
Duck & Waffle, $
J Sheekey, $$$
Scott's, $$$$

WINE LISTS

Bocca di Lupo, $$
The Greenhouse, $$$$
Hibiscus, $$$$
The Ledbury, $$$$

14

MAYFAIR AND MARYLEBONE

If you're looking for something more wallet-friendly, head north to Marylebone, formerly dowdy but now prized for its überchic, village-like feel. Here are an array of low-key little cafés, boîtes, and tapas bars, Champagne-and-hot-dog joints, and the odd world-class sizzler, offering everything from Moroccan and Spanish to Thai and Japanese.

MAYFAIR

$$$ ✕ **34.** Megawatt celebs from Sandra Bullock to Stella McCartney head
INTERNATIONAL straight for 34 in Mayfair because . . . *all* the other stars go there, too! It must be the plush English Edwardian and art deco–inspired dining salon, the swank artwork and burnt-orange banquettes, the nightly live jazz, the interesting fish, game, steak, and seafood grill-focused menu, the copious starched white table linens, and the smooth Upper Manhattan–style service. Appetizers like salt-baked beetroot with soft burrata cheese or Dorset crab and gazpacho jelly square off against chunkier delights from the Argentinian *parrilla* charcoal grill—think 28-day Scottish Red Angus sirloin steaks, Creekstone T-bones, and Australian Wagyu flank steak. Top crowd pleasers include meatball spaghetti, cod and shallots, or Cornish lamb with pumpkin pesto, while game goes down well, too, with roast wood pigeon and damsons standing out. ⑤ *Average main: £28* ⊠ *34 Grosvenor Sq., Mayfair* ☎ *020/3350–3434* ⊕ *www.34-restaurant.co.uk* ⌦ *Reservations essential* ☞ *Entrance on South Audley St.* Ⓜ *Marble Arch* ✛ *1:G5.*

$$$ ✕ **Cecconi's.** Spot the odd glossy A-lister and wallow in glamorous all-
MODERN ITALIAN day Mayfair buzz at this upscale Italian brasserie wedged strategically between Old Bond Street, Cork Street, and Savile Row, and across from the 1768 Royal Academy of Arts. The G5 jet set and fine art world connoisseurs spill out onto pavement tables for breakfast, brunch, and *cicchetti* (Italian tapas), and return later in the day for something more substantial. À la mode English designer Ilse Crawford's luxe green-and-brown interior is a tony backdrop for well-loved classics like sea bream carpaccio, veal Milanese, and *pappardelle* pasta with Chianti ragù, and not forgetting a flavorsome pick-me-up tiramisu. It's perfect for a *what-the-hell!* pit stop during a kamikaze West End shopping spree or after old masters art buying at the nearby Mayfair auction houses, art galleries, and salons. ⑤ *Average main: £24* ⊠ *5A Burlington Gardens, Mayfair* ☎ *020/7434–1500* ⊕ *www.cecconis.co.uk* ⊗ *No dinner Sun.* ⌦ *Reservations essential* Ⓜ *Green Park, Piccadilly Circus* ✛ *3:A6.*

$$ ✕ **Coya.** London's beautiful and the damned binge on Coya's mesmer-
PERUVIAN izing array of top-end Peruvian dishes and sizzly Josper char-grilled offerings, all *boogaloo-ed* by star Indian chef Sanjay Dwivedi in a throbbing Inca-inspired, terra-cotta-floored, dimly lit basement pisco party zone. London Fashion Week buyers, bookers, and models devour no- and low-carb diced and marinated yellowfin tuna or sea bream and *aji amarillo* chili *ceviches*. They go cuckoo over the sliced raw-fish *tiraditos*—try kingfish with dashi or scallops with Peruvian *cancha* corn. Baby squid with rare Peruvian marigold or charred asparagus spears are hardly going to pile on the pounds, nor will the protein-packed *anti-cuchos* (marinated meat) grilled skewers—look for monkfish or tiger

prawns with *aji panca* red peppers—which join the party when they're ready. Afterward, the jet set slip off to the racy Pisco Bar and its riotous collection of 40 nefarious pisco sours. ⑤ *Average main: £23* ✉ *118 Piccadilly, Mayfair* ☎ *020/7042-7118* ⊕ *www.coyarestaurant.com* ⌂ *Reservations essential* Ⓜ *Green Park, Hyde Park Corner* ✛ *1:H6.*

$$$$
STEAKHOUSE

✕ **CUT at 45 Park Lane.** U.S.–based Austrian *übernuber* star chef Wolfgang Puck amps up the steak stakes at this ultraexpensive, superprime steak emporium on Park Lane. Against a mid-1990s luxe backdrop of Damien Hirst kaleidoscope paintings, globe lights, and a 1980s sound track of T'Pau and Bon Jovi, an army of hedge fund and private equity knuckleheads go gangbusters for perfectly seared prime cuts from England, Japan, and the United States. Grilled over charcoal and hardwood, and finished under a 650°C broiler, there's awesome 35-day Arkansas Creekstone filet mignon for £36, USDA Black Angus New York sirloins for £58, and a wet-aged 8-ounce rib eye of A5 100% Wagyu Omi beef from Shiga in Japan for a top whack £140. Add bone marrow, french fries, white truffles, chimichurri, or creamed spinach with a fried egg on top for the whole nine yards. ⑤ *Average main: £41* ✉ *45 Park La., Mayfair* ☎ *020/7439-4545 for reservations only* ⊕ *www.dorchestercollection.com* ⌂ *Reservations essential* Ⓜ *Marble Arch, Hyde Park Corner* ✛ *1:G5.*

$$$$
BRITISH

✕ **Fera At Claridge's.** Top toque Simon Rogan—a British local ingredient fanatic and Cumbrian field-to-fork farm owner—banishes old-school table linen at this famed restaurant inside the storied 159-year-old Mayfair institution and instead guides wowed diners on a madcap meander through his take on the best of wild, seasonal, and wickedly paired Britain. Admire the simpatico art deco walnut, nickel, and olive green hues of the Guy Olivier–designed carpeted salon—centerpieced around a spikey sandblasted Manzanita tree—before succumbing to a blizzard of edible flowers and rare herbs and shoots-strewn virtuoso dishes (from blewits to borage), served on hand-cast or carved slates, plates, and bowls of pebbles. Leap on signature Cumbrian Cartmel Valley smoked venison if it's on the menu, the duck hearts with pureed potato and Winslade cheese, or the aged lamb with pickled tongue and turnips. Desserts are occasionally batty but equally creative, ranging from a liquid nitrogen meringue of Hereford strawberries with meadsweet, to chocolate cream with rapeseed jam. ⑤ *Average main: £32* ✉ *Claridge's, 49 Brook St., Mayfair* ☎ *0207/107–8888 for reservations only* ⊕ *www. feraatclaridges.co.uk* ⌂ *Reservations essential* Ⓜ *Bond St.* ✛ *1:H4.*

$$$$
STEAKHOUSE

✕ **Goodman.** This Manhattan-themed, Russian-owned, Mayfair-based swanky steak house, named after Chicago jazz legend Benny Goodman, has everyone in agreement—these are some of the best steaks in town. USDA-certified, 150-day corn-fed and on-site dry-aged Black Angus T-bones, rib eye, Porterhouse, and New York sirloins compete for taste and tenderness with heavily marbled grass-fed prime cuts from Scotland and the Lake District. There's token Russian sweet herring, lobster bisque, beef carpaccio, and Caesar salad, but everyone at this sultry and rollicking dark-wood mecca seems to have only one big thing on their minds: the sizzling 250g–400g Josper char-grilled steaks, which come with lobster tails or panfried foie gras, truffle chips, and

14

creamed spinach, plus béarnaise pepper or Stilton sauce. $ *Average main: £34* ✉ *24–26 Maddox St., Mayfair* ☎ *020/7499–3776* ⊕ *www. goodmanrestaurants.com* ⊘ *Closed Sun.* ⌂ *Reservations essential* Ⓜ *Oxford Circus, Piccadilly Circus* ✛ *3:A5.*

$$$$
FRENCH

✕ **The Greenhouse.** Discreetly tucked away amid imposing redbrick Mayfair mansions and approached via a tranquil tree-lined, spot-lighted garden, this elegant ground-floor dining salon attracts stealth wealth new media titans and aficionados of world-class French haute cuisine at any price. Feast on complex dishes like Cornish crab on mint *gelee* with Granny Smith apple mouse or sumptuous sea bass with calamari, Sicilian prawns, black squid ink, and green "zebra" tomato sauce. A suave, well-heeled crowd comes for the attentive and smooth service, the soft lighting, the glassed-off private dining room, and the legendary 111-page wine list with more than 2,000 bottles in all, including a Domaine de la Romanée-Conti 1929 from Burgundy (a cool £14,230) and a Château Lafite Rothschild 1870 1er Grand Cru Classé at a piffling £29,500. $ *Average main: £33* ✉ *27A Hay's Mews, Mayfair* ☎ *020/7499–3331* ⊕ *www.greenhouserestaurant.co.uk* ⊘ *Closed Sun. No lunch Sat.* ⌂ *Reservations essential* Ⓜ *Green Park* ✛ *1:H5.*

$$$
MODERN INDIAN
Fodor'sChoice
★

✕ **Gymkhana.** Indian curry king Karam Sethi invokes the last days of the Raj at London's finest top-end curry emporium in Mayfair. Inspired by the Colonial-era Anglo-Indian gymkhana sporting clubs and high-society mustering points of yesteryear, you'll be charmed by the ceiling fans, rattan chairs, lacquered oak floors, and dark chocolate leather banquettes. Chuckle at the grand old Punch sketches, cricket memorabilia, and hunting trophies from the Maharajah of Jodhpur before exploring the exceptional menu. Choices include all-India delights such as a golden pancakelike *dosa* with fennel-rich Chettinad duck and coconut chutney, egg-white-soaked *kasoori* chicken tikka with *moong* beans, or wild Muntjac deer *biryani* with pomegranate and mint *raita*. There's fine *tandoori* broccoli and suckling pig vindaloo and oodles of well-spiced game—like *achari* wild roe deer or partridge pepper fry—while the saffron pistachio *kulfi falooda* (a sort of sundae) with wild basil seeds is equally sublime. $ *Average main: £27* ✉ *42 Albemarle St., Mayfair* ☎ *020/3011–5900* ⊕ *www.gymkhanalondon.com* ⊘ *Closed Sun.* ⌂ *Reservations essential* Ⓜ *Green Park* ✛ *1:H5.*

$$$$
FRENCH

✕ **Hélène Darroze at the Connaught.** London's *crème de la crème* flock to French virtuoso Hélène Darroze's restaurant at the Connaught for her dazzling regional French haute cuisine, served up in a sexy Edwardian dark-wood-paneled dining salon tricked out by Parisian It-designer India Mahdavi with geometric carpets and high-backed comfy chairs. Taking inspiration from Les Landes in southwestern France, Darroze sallies forth with a procession of *magnifique* dishes, like local Robert Dupérier foie gras with cardamom and sorrel or Limousin sweetbreads with girolles and Jerusalem artichokes. Spit-roasted and *flambéed* Racan pigeon is served gloriously pink and Pyrenean lamb is served *en rognonade* (with its kidneys). To finish, choose poached yellow peach from Provence with gingerbread cream. Darroze is perfect for a splurge, but beware the high prices: £38 for lunch, £55 for brunch, and £92–£155 for set dinner. $ *Average main: £37* ✉ *The Connaught,*

Carlos Pl., Mayfair ☎ *020/3147–7200 for reservations only* ⊕ *www. the-connaught.co.uk* ⊗ *Closed Sun. and Mon.* ⚖ *Reservations essential* ⬠ *Jacket required* ⌒ *No trainers or sportswear* Ⓜ *Green Park* ⊹ *1:H5.*

$$$$ ✕ **Hibiscus.** Burly two-starred French chef/patron Claude Bosi bosses
MODERN FRENCH the scene at this understated Mayfair epicurean mecca with nouvelle Modern French dishes, like carpaccio of hand-dived Isle of Skye scallops with blobs of truffle and pickled black radish, salted roast duck with winter *tardivo* (radicchio), or Cornish John Dory with Morteau sausage and *girolles* mushrooms. The desserts are as complex as his mains, with an unlikely sounding but wickedly flavorsome sweet cèp mushroom tart standing out. The brilliant bespoke wine list features a 25-odd selection of rare but top-rank orange biodynamic, organic, or heirloom grape variety fine wines. ⑤ *Average main: £35* ✉ *29 Maddox St., Mayfair* ☎ *020/7629–2999* ⊕ *www.hibiscusrestaurant.co.uk* ⊗ *Closed Sun. and Mon.* ⚖ *Reservations essential* Ⓜ *Oxford Circus, Piccadilly Circus* ⊹ *3:A5.*

$$ ✕ **Kitty Fisher's.** Named after a racy 18th-century courtesan who once ate
BRITISH a thousand-guinea note on a slice of bread and butter, Kitty Fisher's is situated in a classy, dark, and creaky Georgian town house in Mayfair's Dickensian Shepherd Market square. Come and be seduced here in the basement by some of the finest modern British grill and smokehouse fare around. The famed set-piece wood-grilled 12-year-old Galician beef sirloin is a singed and seared yet pink and oozing carved column of meat, accompanied by a heap of grilled onions, pickled walnuts, and barbecued pink fir potatoes with soft white Tunworth cheese. Look for the beef tartar with nasturtium, and roast leeks or charred lamb cutlets with mint and parsley. It's tony but tiny, with only 40 seats, and filled with vintage 18th-century prints and paintings, historic cast-iron wall ovens, and decadent antique silver candelabras. ⑤ *Average main: £21* ✉ *10 Shepherd Market, Mayfair* ☎ *020/3302–1661* ⊕ *www.kittyfishers. com* ⊗ *Closed Sun. and Mon. No lunch Sat.* ▭ *No credit cards* Ⓜ *Green Park* ⊹ *1:H6.*

$$$ ✕ **La Petite Maison.** With the legend *"Tous Célèbres Ici"* boldly etched
FRENCH on the frosted glass front doors, the light-filled and delightful La Petite
FAMILY Maison boasts an impressively well-sourced French Mediterranean, Côte d'Azur, Liguria, and Provençale menu. Try figure-friendly broad bean and Pecorino salad, soft burrata cheese with sweet Datterini-tomato-and-basil spread, or aromatic baked turbot with artichokes, chorizo, five spices, and gloppy white wine sauce. Based on the Riviera style of the original La Petite Maison in Nice in the south of France, dishes come to the table as soon as they're ready, and the chirpy, *très jolie*, and informal waitstaff make for a convivial Gucci Gucci party vibe. More rosé, *anyone?* ⑤ *Average main: £27* ✉ *53–54 Brook's Mews, Mayfair* ☎ *020/7495–4774* ⊕ *www.lpmlondon.co.uk* ⚖ *Reservations essential* Ⓜ *Bond St., Oxford Circus* ⊹ *1:H4.*

$$$$ ✕ **Le Gavroche.** Famed masterchef Michel Roux Jr. works the floor and
FRENCH glad-hands all comers in the old-fashioned proprietorial way at this
Fodor's Choice clubby Mayfair basement institution—established by his father and
★ uncle in 1967—and which many still rate to this day as the *best* formal dining in London. Resplendent with magnificent shiny silver domes

British Food Decoder

For pure Britishness, roast beef and Yorkshire pudding tops the list. If you want the best, go to a local gastropub where you're bound to be sharing space with local foodies. Here the Sunday roasts will be cooked with passion, and crucially with top-quality, British, organic, or free-range ingredients. The beef is served slightly pink with goose-fat roast potatoes, carrots, parsnips, and peas, and, of course, Yorkshire puddings, a savory batter baked until crisp. A dark meaty gravy is poured on top, and there's horseradish sauce on the side.

Other top tummy liners include shepherd's pie: made with minced lamb, topped with mashed potato, and baked until lightly brown. Cottage pie is similar, but made with minced beef instead of lamb. Traditional steak-and-kidney pie is made with chunky diced beef and ox kidneys, braised with onions and mushrooms in a thick, brown gravy, and encased with short-crust pastry.

Fish-and-chips, usually deep-fried battered cod, haddock, or plaice, comes with double- or triple-cooked hand-cut chips that are sprinkled with salt and malt vinegar. A "ploughman's lunch" is usually served in pubs and consists of bloomer crusty white bread, a strong English cheese (cheddar, Cheshire, or red Leicester), with a side-salad garnish and tangy onion marmalade pickle on the side.

For a hot dessert, seek out bread-and-butter pudding if you can, made with overlapping layers of buttered bread scattered with raisins and fruit peel, and baked in egg, cream, and nutmeg until crisp.

and unpriced ladies' menus, Roux's mastery of classical French haute cuisine hypnotizes all comers with signatures like foie gras with cinnamon-scented crispy duck pancake, soufflé Suissesse, roast venison with red wine *jus*, or saddle of rabbit with a crust of Parmesan cheese. Desserts like Roux's delectable chocolate omelet soufflé or upside-down apple tart are unswervingly accomplished. Notable three-course set lunches (£55) are the sanest way to experience such unashamed, overwrought flummery—with half a bottle of wine, water, coffee, and *petits fours* thrown in. $ *Average main: £41* ⊠ *43 Upper Brook St., Mayfair* ☎ *020/7408–0881* ⊕ *www.le-gavroche.co.uk* ☾ *Closed Sun. and bank holiday Mon.* ⌕ *Reservations essential* 𝄞 *Jacket required* Ⓜ *Marble Arch, Bond St.* ⊕ *1:G5.*

$$
MODERN FRENCH
Fodor's Choice
★

× **Little Social.** A neon sign may caution *Silence, Logique, Securité, Prudence* here at Jason Atherton's knock-'em-dead French *bistro de luxe* but there's always a healthy hubbub at this low-profile Mayfair hideaway. Ease into a Burgundy leather banquette booth and admire the hardwood chairs, elm tables, art deco lamps, and assorted Michelin road maps in this long and narrow dining salon before diving into an artfully classic-with-a-twist menu. The crab salad appetizer comes on a round of tomato with miso dressing and disks of beetroot and radish, while braised Irish ox cheeks with chunky roast bone marrow, carrots, and horseradish mash is top-rank comfort food of the highest order. There's always aged Scottish cheeseburger on the menu (£15), plus a cute side of unusual Québécois poutine—a bowl of fries piled high with cheese, gravy, chorizo, and jalapeños. Finally, the £7.50 hot chocolate moelleux with a dollop of sea salt and almond ice cream is near perfection. $ *Average main: £23* ✉ *5 Pollen St., Mayfair* ☎ *020/7870–3730* ⊕ *www.littlesocial.co.uk* ⌖ *Reservations essential* Ⓜ *Oxford Circus, Piccadilly Circus* ✚ *3:A4.*

$$$$
MODERN
EUROPEAN
Fodor'sChoice
★

✕**Pollen Street Social.** Unstoppable gastro god Jason Atherton knocks the London dining scene for a loop at his smash-hit flagship found in a cute alleyway off Regent Street. Braying fans enjoy refined small and large dishes ranging from a full "English breakfast" appetizer—a miniature of poached egg on tomato compote, with parsley-flecked bacon, morels, and croutons—to sublime Scottish ox cheek with 50-day Black Angus rib-eye beef, or Devon red mullet with pears and parsley. Diners can opt to get up from their tables to sit and perch at the dessert bar to watch staff as they chop, slice, squeeze, and fiddle away to prepare immaculate Eton Mess with wild strawberries and basil-ash meringue or sashimi-like pressed watermelon with an unlikely basil sorbet. Look out for Atherton, who's often around, and note the £28.50 set lunch. $ *Average main: £30* ✉ *8–10 Pollen St., Mayfair* ☎ *020/7290–7600* ⊕ *www.pollenstreetsocial.com* ⌖ *Reservations essential* Ⓜ *Oxford Circus, Piccadilly Circus* ✚ *3:A5.*

$
BURGER
FAMILY

✕**The Riding House Café.** Hirsute and hipster-chic London diners flock to this NYC-style small-plates and luxe-burgers all-day brasserie behind Oxford Circus in NOHO (North of Soho). Everything's appropriately salvaged, reclaimed, or bespoke here so you'll find stuffed squirrels, birds, and other taxidermy dotted around, reclaimed blue leather theater seats at the long bar, bright orange leather banquettes, or old snooker table legs holding up your dining table. Opt for bargain £6.50 small plates of spicy crayfish tails with lemongrass or superfood salads, and then head for poached egg chorizo hash browns, salt marsh lamb broth, 28-day hormone-free cheeseburger with chips—a steal at £12.50—or their famed lobster lasagna (£25). Service is private-members' club friendly, and you'll find neat all-day breakfasts, plus milk shakes, cocktails, and sundaes. $ *Average main: £14* ✉ *43–51 Great Titchfield St., Noho* ☎ *020/7927–0840* ⊕ *www.ridinghousecafe.co.uk* ⌖ *Reservations essential* Ⓜ *Oxford Circus* ✚ *3:A2.*

$$$$
SEAFOOD

✕**Scott's.** Bowler-hatted doormen greet the A-list with a discreet nod at this ever-fashionable seafood haven on fashion-central Mount Street in Mayfair. Originally founded in 1851, and a former haunt of James Bond author Ian Fleming (he liked the potted shrimps, apparently), these days you're more likely to see Bill Clinton in one corner, Kate Winslet in another, and former hell-raiser Brit-pack artists Damien Hirst or Tracey Emin joshing around on a burgundy banquette nearby. Scott's draws London's top-tier 1% movers and shakers who enjoy day-boat-fresh Lindisfarne oysters, baked crab, whole salt-baked turbot, cod cheeks, and scrummy shrimp burgers. Glorious standouts like sautéed razor clams with wild boar sausages or sole Colbert are similarly divine. Prices could make a Saudi sheikh blanch, but fear not: this really is the *hottest* joint in town. $ *Average main: £32* ✉ *20 Mount St., Mayfair*

14

☏ *020/7495–7309* ⊕ *www.scotts-restaurant.com* ⌑ *Reservations essential* Ⓜ *Bond St., Green Park* ✛ *1:H5.*

MARYLEBONE

$$$ ✕ **Chiltern Firehouse.** There may be a waiting list for the waiting list to
ECLECTIC   get into the red hot pap-central Chiltern Firehouse, but if you do snag
Fodor'sChoice   a table, you're in for a treat. Set beside a luxury bespoke 26-room hotel
★   of the same name opened by überchic hotelier André Balazs's in the
sensationally converted 1888 Grade II–listed redbrick fire station, the
Chiltern Firehouse sets the bar for glamour-chic dining. Once escorted
through a courtyard wildflower garden and past a pantheon of prettier-
than-thou front-of-house staff, sit at the raised open kitchen counter
and watch Portuguese maestro Nuno Mendes plate up, while taking in
the buzzy buttermilk-hued surrounds—part mid-1970s Parisian bras-
serie, and part industrial-heritage chic splendor (think huge firehouse
doors, riveted iron beams, tracery, carvings, and a fireman's pole). Pick
winners from a spanking menu—like slider-style crab meat "donuts,"
charred octopus with cep mushrooms, or red prawns in almond milk—
and get down to the business of major-league celeb spotting. Ⓢ *Average*
main: £24 ✉ *Chiltern Firehouse, 1 Chiltern St.* ☏ *00207/073–7676 for*
restaurant reservations only ⊕ *www.chilternfirehouse.com* ⌑ *Reserva-*
tions essential Ⓜ *Baker St.* ✛ *1:G3.*

$ ✕ **Fischer's.** It almost feels like Gustav Klimt, Sigmund Freud, or Egon
AUSTRIAN   Schiele might doff their Homburg hats, peel off a heavy overcoat, and
Fodor'sChoice   shuffle into a dark leather banquette at this handsomely evocative
★   early-century-styled Viennese all-day Mitteleuropa grand café. Savor
the high-gloss veneered inlaid marquetry tables, antique light fittings,
custom-made ocher tiles, hand-painted distressed wallpaper, and hodge-
podge of gilt-edged paintings of flinty *volkish* burghers and Tyrolean-
hatted wood choppers. Then dive into the menu, which includes
brötchen chopped chicken livers with dill on rye bread or the creamy
käsespätzle egg noodle/dumplings with Gruyère and bacon. Slice
through a hearty breaded *Wiener schnitzel* veal cutlet with a weighty
Sambonet knife, and be sure to try Emmental and bacon-wrapped *Ber-*
ner Würstel sausages that come on gold-rimmed monogrammed plates
piled high with sauerkraut and grain mustard–swooshed potatoes.
Note classy touches like the original Thonet bentwood chairs, muslin-
wrapped lemons, and silver coffee pots, and expect top-drawer service
from staff in natty *Tracht*-style Tyrolean green waistcoats and dark
green ties. Ⓢ *Average main: £14* ✉ *50 Marylebone High St., Maryle-*
bone ☏ *0207/466–5501* ⊕ *www.fischers.co.uk* ⌑ *Reservations essential*
Ⓜ *Baker St., Bond St.* ✛ *1:H3.*

$$$ ✕ **Galvin Bistrot de Luxe.** The successful Galvin brothers, Chris and Jeff,
BRASSERIE   blaze a spectacular trail for the time-tested French *bistrot de luxe* for-
mula on a fast-moving stretch of Baker Street in Marylebone. Sea-
soned fans return time and again for the impeccable food, traditional
black-and-white uniformed waitstaff, smart service, bentwood chairs,
and sparkling mahogany-paneled Parisian-style dining salon. There's
no finer Dorset crab lasagna in town, and mains consistently punch
above their weight: Cornish brill, calves' liver with Alsace bacon, classic stuffed pig's trotter, and sumptuous Cumbrian shorthorn beef with

bordelaise sauce are all devilishly tasty, each one a superbly executed gastro triumph. The Monday to Saturday £21.50 three-course set lunches or £23.50 early evening dinners (6–7) are top value, and look out for live Sunday afternoon jazz. $ *Average main: £25* ⊠ *66 Baker St., Marylebone* ☎ *020/7935–4007* ⊕ *www.galvinrestaurants.com* ⚭ *Reservations essential* Ⓜ *Baker St.* ✛ *1:G3.*

$
SEAFOOD
FAMILY

✕ **The Golden Hind.** You'll land some of the best fish-and-chips in town at this great British "chippy" in a cheery retro 1914 art deco café off Marylebone High Street. Gaggles of satisfied tourists and chirpy Marylebone village locals and workers alike hunker down for the homemade cod fishcakes, skate wings, feta cheese fritters, and breaded scampi tails at simple dark-wood tables, but it's the neatly prepared and decidedly nongreasy deep-fried or steamed battered cod, haddock, and plaice from Grimsby (£9.10), the classic hand-cut Maris Piper chips, and the traditional mushy peas that are the big draw. It's BYO (£1 corkage) and takeaway, but note there's no lunch Saturday and it's closed Sunday. $ *Average main: £9* ⊠ *73 Marylebone La., Marylebone* ☎ *020/7486–3644* ⊗ *Closed Sun. No lunch Sat.* ⚭ *Reservations not accepted* Ⓜ *Bond St.* ✛ *1:H3.*

$
BURGER
FAMILY
Fodor's Choice
★

✕ **Tommi's Burger Joint.** "Be Nice or Leave" and "Sharing is Caring" are a few choice aphorisms found on cardboard signs at Viking raider Tomas "Tommi" Tómasson's cult Icelandic-run burger boîte in Marylebone. The decor includes overhead fairy lights, chicken wire framing the flaming grill station Han Solo stickers, and a Chewbacca the Wookiee surfer poster. Everyone here seems to love the cool tunes (from Johnny Cash to Talking Heads), the edgy DIY vibe, and the £9.90 burger, fries, and soda deal at this no-res hamburger heaven. Aside from organic beef from top butcher HG Walter, you'll also find grilled cheese sandwiches and veggie burgers, plus a voguish steak burger made with fillet, rump, and rib eye. All come in awesome fist-size brioche buns with tomato, lettuce, onion, ketchup, mayo, and mustard, and help yourself from the estimable condiments bar, including mini pots of gherkin, relish, and horseradish sauce. $ *Average main: £10* ⊠ *30 Thayer St., Marylebone* ☎ *0782/355–7945* ⊕ *www.burgerjoint.co.uk* ⚭ *Reservations not accepted* Ⓜ *Bond St.* ✛ *1:H3.*

SOHO AND COVENT GARDEN

Soho and Covent Garden are the city's historic playground and pleasure zone, an all-day, all-night jostling neon wonderland of glitz, glamour, grit, and greasepaint. This area is London's cultural heart, with old and new media companies, late-night dive bars, cabaret, street performers, West End musicals, and world-class theater, ballet, and opera houses. High rents have recently forced out many of Soho's seedier red-light businesses and ushered in more edgy and top-notch restaurants. Just follow your nose in Covent Garden and Theatreland to find copious options for pretheater dining.

14

SOHO

$$
MODERN
EUROPEAN

✕ **10 Greek Street.** There may only be 28 table seats and nine counter stools overlooking the open kitchen at this stripped-back Modern European Soho humdinger, but Aussie chef Cameron Emirali and wine guy Luke Wilson have seriously got their *schtick* together. Great food? *Tick.* Cheap wine? *Tick.* Excellent service? *Tick.* Good prices? *Tick.* Buzz? *Tick.* The only negative is the evenings-only no-reservations policy, but most happily saunter off for a quick drink in the local pub two doors down and wait to be called back on their cell phones. Once seated, expect simple interchangeable starters and mains like butternut ravioli with sage, or scallops and chorizo. Gutsy meats like Brecon lamb shank with mash, Tamworth pork with apple chutney, or venison with potato galette are big and bold, and swing with the seasons. Top-value £5–£.50 desserts, like plum-and-apple crumble or rum panna cotta, provide a heartfelt finish. $ *Average main: £17* ✉ *10 Greek St., Soho* ☎ *020/7734–4677* ⊕ *www.10greekstreet.com* ⊘ *Closed Sun.* ⚲ *Reservations not accepted* Ⓜ *Tottenham Court Rd.* ✛ *3:D4.*

$$
MEDITERRANEAN

✕ **Andrew Edmunds.** Candlelit at night and with a haunting Dickensian vibe, Andrew Edmunds is a permanently packed, deeply romantic old-world Soho dining institution—though it could be larger, less creaky underfoot, and the reclaimed church-pew wooden bench seats more forgiving. Tucked away behind Carnaby Street in a dark and atmospheric 18th-century Soho town house, it's a cozy favorite with the boho-chic Soho media elite that come for the foolscap hand-scribbled, fixed-price lunch menus and the historic vibe. Keenly priced starters and mains draw on the tastes of Ireland, the Med, and Middle East. Harissa-spiced mackerel, woodcock on toast, seafood paella, and Herdwick lamb shanks with champ and broccoli are all deeply hale and hearty. Desserts like warm treacle tart or bread-and-butter pudding offer few surprises, but the wine's superb and the markups reasonable. $ *Average main: £17* ✉ *46 Lexington St., Soho* ☎ *020/7437–5708* ⊕ *www.andrewedmunds.com* ⚲ *Reservations essential* Ⓜ *Oxford Circus, Piccadilly Circus* ✛ *3:C5.*

$
CAFÉ

✕ **Bar Italia.** This legendary Italian coffee bar on Frith Street is Soho's unofficial beating heart and a 22-hours-a-day Soho institution. Established in 1949 during the postwar Italian coffee bar craze and still run by the founding Polledri family, it's now positively football and cycling crazy and a honeypot for an assortment of weird and wondrous Soho-ites—from dubstep clubbers and cabbies to down-home stars like Jude Law and Jason Statham. Most regulars grab an espresso or frothy cappuccino made from the vintage 50-year-old Gaggia coffee machine and wolf down a slice of pizza, *panettone*, bacon bap, or chocolate cake at one of the mirrored bar counters (or pavement seat out front). The walls are plastered with Italian flags and black-and-white photos of lusty Italian opera singers, movie legends, and '50s world boxing champs, and it's *the* primo spot in London to watch Italy play in the soccer World Cup. $ *Average main: £6* ✉ *22 Frith St., Soho* ☎ *020/7437–4520* ⊕ *www.baritaliasoho.co.uk* ⚲ *Reservations not accepted* Ⓜ *Leicester Sq.* ✛ *3:D5.*

$
TAPAS

✗**Barrafina.** London's top Spanish tapas bar is modeled on Cal Pep in old-town Barcelona, and similarly has only a few—23 in total—raised bar stools at the three-sided counter. It's no-reservations—so expect to stand in queue—but the tapas is well worth the wait. Their motto is "Sourcing Not Saucing," so get ready to nosh on brilliant small plates prepared in front of you: garlic prawns, ham *croquetas,* salt cod fritters, rare Galician *percebes* ("goose barnacles") crustaceans, baby squid, and octopus with capers, plus classics like Spanish *torilla,* spicy chorizo, and thin-sliced cured Montanera ham. There's a crack selection of Spanish reds, whites, sherries, and sparkling Cavas, and leave room for cute desserts like *crèma Catalana* or almond-based Santiago tart. ⑤ *Average main: £13* ✉ *54 Frith St., Soho* ☎ *020/7813–8016* ⊕ *www.barrafina. co.uk* ⌕ *Reservations not accepted* Ⓜ *Tottenham Court Rd.* ✛ *3:D4.*

14

$
FRENCH
Fodor'sChoice
★

✗**Blanchette.** French tapas may sound sacrilegious but the three brothers behind Blanchette—Maxime, Yannis, and Malik—hit the snail on the head at this rustic chic hipster HQ. A jazzy sound track—from Françoise Hardy to the Tom Tom Club— compliments the charming candlelit and modishly bare brick, oak tables, and swirly art nouveau-tiled interior. Visually feast on "BCBG" (*"Good class, Good taste"*) Porte de Clignancourt flee market bric-a-brac finds—Vanessa Paradis albums, a Serge Gainsbourg head, Gérard Depardieu cookbooks—and order about three or four various small— *tapas-y!*—plates per head to share. Tables may be a touch too cramped and cozy, but the crispy frogs' legs and sliced truffle saucisson are spot on, while the seasonal veg and zingy salads—like leek vinaigrette with wild mushrooms or Brillat-Savarin salad with poppy seeds—are off the scale. Baked scallops come in their shells with a spunky Café de Paris sauce (with thyme and anchovies), and authentic desserts like macerated fruits with white wine sabayon are a fitting Gallic finale. ⑤ *Average main: £6* ✉ *9 D'Arblay St., Soho* ☎ *020/7439–8100* ⊕ *www.blanchettesoho.co.uk* ⌕ *Reservations essential* ⌕ *Sun. open noon–9 pm* Ⓜ *Tottenham Court Rd.* ✛ *3:C4.*

$$
ITALIAN

✗**Bocca di Lupo.** The place is always packed and the tables jammed too close together, but everyone still comes for *la dolce vita* and chef Jacob Kenedy's wicked spread of rustic Italian regional fare. Located off Theatreland's Shaftesbury Avenue in Soho, this redbrick-fronted and always popular family-run destination offers a magnificent procession of small or large plates and peasant-based pastas, stews, roasts, and crudities from Lazio to Piedmont, Bologna to Trentino. Try drop-dead offerings like Roman veal *saltimbocca,* ear-shape Calabrian *orecchiette* pasta with *nduja* pork sausage, or Sicilian lobster spaghetti touched off with mussels and ginger. Limber up with an Aperol spritz before plunging into the regional Italian-focused wine list, which weaves from Super Tuscans to rare Barolos. There's also an intriguing marsala and a range of punchy aged grappas, plus desserts like milk-free espresso ice cream. ⑤ *Average main: £19* ✉ *12 Archer St., Soho* ☎ *020/7734–2223* ⊕ *www. boccadilupo.com* ⌕ *Reservations essential* Ⓜ *Piccadilly Circus* ✛ *3:C5.*

$$
BURGER
FAMILY
Fodor'sChoice
★

✗**Burger & Lobster.** Man up, tuck in, and don a shiny white plastic bib—à la Sopranos—at this always-rammed limited-choice burger-and-lobster zone in the heart of Soho. It's no reservations (apart from larger groups), no starters, and no printed menu, but a chalked-up blackboard kind of says it all: "Burger or lobster or lobster roll. All with chips & salad.

£20." Of the three surf 'n' turf choices available, the Nova Scotia lobster are way the best value. Flown in three times weekly, stored in giant Plexiglass tanks by the hundredweight, and stunned moments before they're steamed or finished off on the grill, the lush lobster roll comes in a butter-soaked brioche bun, with wasabi mayo sauce, a green pickle-rich salad, and a sturdy pot of fries. Sweet and moist halved lobsters are served with lemon butter, while the Worcestershire sauce-seasoned burgers are a hunky-dory mix of Irish grass-fed beef and corn-fed cuts from Nebraska, with added streaky bacon or Mont Jack cheese on top. The cocktails rock, but beware the madding crowds. $ Average main: £20 ⊠ 36 Dean St., Soho 🕾 0207/432–4800 ⊕ www.burgerandlobster. com ⩗ Reservations not accepted ⌲ Reservations only accepted for groups of 6 to 10 Ⓜ Piccadilly Circus, Tottenham Court Rd. ✛ 3:D5.

$

THAI

FAMILY

✕ **Busaba Eathai.** It's top Thai nosh for little *moolah* at this sleek and sultry modern canteen in the beating heart of Soho. Fitted with dark-wood bench seats and hardwood tables, this flagship restaurant has communal dining, rapid service, incense, low lighting, and fast-moving lineups out front. Pour yourself a lemongrass tea, then try ginger beef with Thai pepper, classic crunchy green papaya salad, Thai calamari, Massaman duck curry, or myriad other tasty winners. You'll escape well fed for about £18 a head, and, all in all, this makes for a top-value tummy-filler and a fail-safe pit stop during a West End shopping safari. $ Average main: £11 ⊠ 106–110 Wardour St., Soho 🕾 020/7255–8686 ⊕ busaba. com ⩗ Reservations not accepted Ⓜ Tottenham Court Rd. ✛ 3:C4.

$$

BRITISH

✕ **Dean Street Townhouse.** Everyone feels 10 times more glamorous at this candlelit Soho media mustering point, attached to the *swellegant* 39-room Georgian hotel of the same name. Simpatico lighting, dark oak floors, red leather banquettes, raised bar seats, crack service, and walls peppered with pictures by the likes of Brit-pack artists Tracey Emin and Mat Collinshaw create a hip hangout for London's media *haute monde*. No frills, no fuss, retro-British favorites include pea-and-ham soup, old-school mince and potatoes, twice-baked smoked haddock soufflé, toad-in-the-hole, or yummy sherry trifle. You'll find traditional fruit scones and buttered crumpets for afternoon tea, Welsh rarebit for high tea, and a smattering of vaguely familiar-looking celebs Tweeting around on their iPhones. $ Average main: £20 ⊠ 69–71 Dean St., Soho 🕾 020/7434–1775 ⊕ www.deanstreettownhouse.com ⩗ Reservations essential Ⓜ Oxford Circus, Tottenham Court Rd. ✛ 3:D5.

$

STEAKHOUSE

FAMILY

✕ **Flat Iron.** Premium steaks priced at £10 are the only mains on the printed menu at this bustling hipster canteen on Beak Street in Soho. The char-grilled "flat iron" shoulder cuts of beef arrive already sliced on wooden blocks with watercress and mini–meat cleavers. This three-story, no-reservations steak den and craft-beer basement bar is decked out in exposed brick walls, enamel lights, and bump-'n'-grind shared wooden tables. Sides include beef-dripping chips, creamed spinach, and roast eggplant with Parmesan, while sauces range from béarnaise to French horseradish cream. Shared seating is first-come, first-served, and at peak times you'll need to leave a number and hang downstairs sipping a heritage cocktail or rare small-batch beer while you wait. Check Twitter for daily specials like 12-hour braised Highland heifer steaks, a bone-in rib eye from Thirsk, or a Brazilian-style "Picanha" steak from mini grass-fed Dexter cows. $ *Average main: £10* ⊠ *17 Beak St., Soho* ⊕ *flatironsteak.co.uk* ⌲ *Reservations not accepted* ☞ *No phone* Ⓜ *Oxford Circus, Piccadilly Circus* ✛ *3:B5.*

$$$
BRITISH
Fodor's Choice
★

✕ **Ivy Market Grill.** Scrub up like Eliza Doolittle and perch at the pewter bar supping a dreamy My Fair Lady (with Ivy-made gin, Belle de Brillet, and orange blossom) at this Covent Garden piazza all-dayer and laid-back lil' sister to the famed Ivy restaurant. Radiant mottled-green leather banquettes, minibooths, dark timber tables, and hexagonal floor mosaics are stunningly set off by late-19-century antique brass lamps and chandeliers, distressed painted walls, and a glazed tiled dado panel in shades of orange, green, and teal. If a mini "Three Martini Lunch" ain't your thing, there's bargains galore on the lengthy, comfort-laden all-day menu—from five-spice warm crispy duck salad or poached lobster cocktail with Marie Rose sauce to brioche-crumbed chicken Milanese and classic shepherd's pie. Monogrammed cutlery and shiny copper serving pans proliferate, and be sure to try the chocolate bombe—a spherical chocolatey mush of milk foam, vanilla ice cream, and sticky hot salted caramel sauce. $ *Average main: £25* ⊠ *1 Henrietta St., Covent Garden* ☎ *207/307–5903* ⊕ *www.theivymarketgrill.com/* Ⓜ *Covent Garden* ✛ *3:F5.*

$
JAPANESE

✕ **Koya.** Is it all the hypnotic foot kneading that makes the hand-pulled Sanuki udon wheat-flour noodles here *so* springy, spongy, and maddeningly so *addictive*? Ever-present lines of polite Japanese diners and heritage-clad hip Soho-ites are a testament to the pull of the mega-tasty steaming dishes served at this tiny stripped-back cult noodle house on Frith Street in Soho. Once inside, start with cold udon on a bamboo basket with pungent miso and pickled pork, and then— *if* you're up for it—slurp hot udon dashi broth with smoked mackerel and Japanese green leaves, or fried tofu and green onions. There's pickled plums, Mylor prawn tempura, duck and rice in a bowl, slow-cooked *onsen tamago* poached eggs, and braised pork belly dishes, but it's the mighty udon noodle that ultimately prevails. Note it's no reservations. $ *Average main: £14* ⊠ *49 Frith St., Soho* ⊕ *www.koya.co.uk* ⌲ *Reservations not accepted* Ⓜ *Tottenham Court Rd.* ✛ *3:D5.*

$
CAFÉ

✕ **Maison Bertaux.** Francophiles and die-hard romantics cherish this quirky, two-story 1871 French patisserie, vintage tea parlor, and occasional pop-up art space, where happily nothing seems to have changed since the 1940s. Framed with classic blue-and-white striped awnings, and overflowing with art deco cake stands, fairy lights, antique mirrors, and pink-and-purple gauze drapes, the colorful pastries, tarts, croissants, and sweet cakes at this renowned time-warp Soho institution are well loved and baked on-site. The chocolate and fruit éclairs, Saint-Honoré and Black Forest gâteaux, marzipan figs, Mont Blancs, strawberry fancies, and flaky almond croissants never fail to delight. Run by Resistance-chic Soho legend, Michelle Wade, Maison Bertaux also hosts a cheery retro tea service, which come with tasty savories, like broccoli quiche or Dijon slice, with cheese, peppers, and mustard. $ *Average main: £7* ⊠ *28 Greek St., Soho* ☎ *020/7437–6007* ⊕ *www.maisonbertaux.com* ⊟ *No credit cards* ⌲ *Reservations not accepted* Ⓜ *Leicester Sq.* ✛ *3:D5.*

14

$$ ✕**Palomar.** It's Jerusalem meets Palestine meets Beirut meets a bonkers
MIDDLE EASTERN scenester vibe at this mad-as-a-hatter Israeli/Arab funky food party zone
Fodor's Choice off Shaftesbury Avenue. Perch up at the petite 16-bar stool non-kosher
★ open kitchen (there's 35 *slightly* calmer table seats at the back) and
down Arak shots and trade quips over the eclectic sound track with the
ultrapro but gregarious flat-capped–, black beret–, and "Porkie pie"–
hatted Middle Eastern chefs brigade cooking away. The menu offers a
mélange of feisty Levantine delights in between *Whoopin'!, Hollowin'!,*
and periodically banging their pots and pans. Tear away at oven-hot
Yemeni Jewish *cholla*-style *Kubaneh* bread before digging into a Kilnar
jar of truffled Jerusalem polenta with a smoky mushroom ragù. Chunky
paprika-laced pork belly tagine with dried apricots and Israeli couscous
is a must, as is the Persian oxtail stew and Palestinian steak tartare with
tahini. Look, too, for the witty *Shakshukit* "deconstructed" spiced beef
kebab with *lafah* bread, and the lavish fennel-infused Kurdish-style
mussels, inspired, naturally, by the head chef's beloved grandmother.
⑤ *Average main: £12* ✉ *34 Rupert St., Chinatown* ☎ *020/7439–8777*
⊕ *www.thepalomar.co.uk* ⊘ *No dinner Sun.* ⌣ *Reservations essential*
☞ *No counter seat bookings* Ⓜ *Piccadilly Circus, Leicester Sq.* ✛ *3:D6.*

$ ✕**Pitt Cue Co.** Everyone's gone bonkers for the supersmoky Midwest
BARBECUE American BBQ beef ribs and pulled-pork-in-a-bun combos at this Soho
trendsetter. A tiny, no-reservations corner-site joint, Pitt Cue has only 18
basement seats and eight counter stools in the ground-floor bourbon-
and-rye elbow-tight crush bar—little wonder line ups snake down the
street. Most order the £12–£13.50 finger-lickin' spreads, which come
with green slaw and house pickles in enamel *Shawshank Redemption*
baker-wear dishes. Charred rib-tips, pig's-head sausages, smoked jowl,
brisket burgers, and bone marrow butter mash sides are other tempta-
tions, but the devout devour the sloppy sliders and sticky ribs with their
mucky paws. The secret to Pitt Cue's famous BBQ pork and beef ribs?
A stonkin' coal-and-woodchip smoker, free-range Tamworth, Middle
White, and Mangalitsa pork prime cuts from Cornwall, and dry rubs
and marinades, which include smoked paprika, Sriracha chili sauce,
blackstrap molasses, and apricot preserves. ⑤ *Average main: £13* ✉ *1
Newburgh St., Soho* ⊕ *www.pittcue.co.uk* ⊘ *No dinner Sun.* ⌣ *Reser-
vations not accepted* Ⓜ *Oxford Circus* ✛ *3:B5.*

$ ✕**Polpetto.** Chef Florence Knight smashes the ruff-'n'-tumble Soho din-
ITALIAN ing scene with her Venetian-style small-plates *bàcaro* on Berwick Street
market. Peer in over old-granny lace-net curtains and step through the
heavy velvet door drapes into a feminine wonderland of tongue-in-cheek
white linen–covered hanging lamps, distressed Farrow & Ball duck-egg-
blue plaster walls, a tin-tile ceiling, and glowing maple-wood flooring,
table tops, and bar sides. Knight lets her impeccably sourced regional
and seasonal Italian ingredients do the talking—from a dazzling creamy
Puglian Burrata white buffalo's cheese with *agretti* (monk's beard) and
red chili, to simple Sardinan Camone winter tomatoes or *cavolo nero*
with a salty anchovy sauce. Besides unfussy faves like *baccalà* salt cod
or a wobbly custardlike maple tart, you'll swoon over heartier dishes
like bacon chop with pickled walnuts or beef shin *papparadelle* pasta
with an Elizabeth David chicken liver–rich ragù. Tip: Ask to dine at the

chef's table at the basement open kitchen, where you can admire Knight in full flow, but note Polpetto doesn't take evening bookings. $\boxed{\$}$ *Average main: £8* ✉ *11 Berkwick St., Soho* ☎ *0207/439–8627* ⊕ *www.polpetto. co.uk* ☾ *Closed Sun.* ⚱ *Reservations not accepted* ☞ *Lunch bookings accepted, but no evening bookings* Ⓜ *Tottenham Court Rd., Oxford Circus* ✛ *3:C4.*

$\$\$$ ✕ **Social Eating House.** Decidedly upmarket "boil-in-the-bag" aromatic

FRENCH   wild mushrooms on toast, which are snipped open and served steam-

Fodor's Choice   ing at the table, are just one of many excellent dishes found at this

★   lighthearted but technically brilliant neo-French "bistronomy" Soho hangout. Chef/patron Paul Hood casts aside uptight haute cuisine, and makes merry with witty, pretty, and winning dishes like smoked duck's "ham" (made with smoked and cured duck's breast), and Scotch egg and chips, and pulls everyone's leg with his no-bread CLT, consisting of white crabmeat, lettuce (castelfranco radiccio leaf), and roast heritage tomato. A buzzed-up Soho foodie crowd enjoy jars of shrimps and grits and perfect mains of Kentish salt-marsh lamb with mint yogurt in a rollicking, moodily lit bare-brick salon, tricked out with dark parquet floors, antique mirrored ceilings, and red-leather banquettes. Class-act hipster staff sport beards, braces, and Brylcreemed 'tashes, the first-floor copper-ceilinged speakeasy, the Blind Pig, is *most* bodacious, and the Monday-to-Saturday £19 two-course set lunch is seriously worth investigating. $\boxed{\$}$ *Average main: £18* ✉ *58 Poland St., Soho* ☎ *0207/993–3251* ⊕ *www.socialeatinghouse.com* ☾ *Closed Sun.* ⚱ *Reservations essential* Ⓜ *Oxford Circus, Tottenham Court Rd.* ✛ *3:B4.*

$\$$ ✕ **Spuntino.** Moody tin-tile ceilings, filament lights, bluegrass tunes, a

DINER   popcorn machine, and only 27 raised counter stools at this pewter-topped bar and Lower East Side–inspired diner makes for one of the *coolest* spots in town. Naturally, there's no phone, no reservations, and minimal signage, but that only adds to the speakeasy vibe. Once seated after a wait, strike up a conversation with the friendly car mechanic lookalike bar staff and settle in with a whisky-based Brooklyn Manhattan cocktail. Then dive into famed truffled egg toast before moving on to deep-fried grits, softshell crab, or three-bites-and-they're-gone Yankee sliders—try salt beef with dill or cornflake chicken with honey mustard slaw. Don't overlook the glorious mac 'n' cheese or steak and eggs. For dessert, try a PB&J sandwich, and chase it down with a slug of Elijah Craig bourbon or home-brew black treacle rum. $\boxed{\$}$ *Average main: £11* ✉ *61 Rupert St., Soho* ⊕ *www.spuntino.co.uk* ⚱ *Reservations not accepted* Ⓜ *Piccadilly Circus* ✛ *3:C5.*

COVENT GARDEN

$\$\$\$$ ✕ **Balthazar.** Brit restauranteur Keith McNally re-creates his famed New

BRASSERIE   York all-day faux Parisian brasserie at a winning spot right off the piazza in Covent Garden. The decor of brass-studded red leather banquettes, distressed vintage mirrors, illuminated columns, pewter bar tops, a seafood bar, and intricate mosaic floors creates a sparkly, soft patina, and enchanting backdrop in which to enjoy a classic all-day French brasserie menu of few surprises. Breakfast, brunch, lunch, afternoon tea, dinner, and pre- and post-theater meals are all well catered for at this bustling and notably well-serviced 175-seat venue. Pick out flavor-packed dishes

14

like macaroni and Gruyère cheese, duck shepherd's pie, or ox cheek *bourguignonne*, and kick back and linger over the diverting all-French wine list, which carries everything from a modest Chablis Colombier 2012 (£11.50 per glass) to a grand Margaux Château Palmer '71 from Bordeaux, at £540 a pop. $ *Average main: £24* ⊠ *4–7 Russell St., Covent Garden* ☎ *020/3301–1155* ⊕ *www.balthazarlondon.com* ⌂ *Reservations essential* Ⓜ *Covent Garden, Charing Cross* ✚ *3:F5.*

$$$

FRENCH

✕ **Clos Maggiore.** *Insist* on a seat in the low-lighted and white blossom-filled sky-lit conservatory at this warm and seriously romantic Provençal country inn–style bolthole in the heart of Covent Garden. A bouquet's throw away from the Royal Opera House, and once a favorite with amorous heir to the throne Prince Harry, service is decidedly Gallic and formal, while the warren of candlelit, oak-wood panel rooms, open fires, old masters oil paintings, and convex mirrors never fails to enchant. Meal deals and theater specials (£19.50–£29.50) are a cute way in, where you'll be wooed by unapologetically old-fashioned and refined French cuisine, such as Loire valley rabbit ballotine, poached wild turbot with herring roe *beurre blanc* sauce, or Charolais beef cheeks with fine French beans. $ *Average main: £26* ⊠ *33 King St., Covent Garden* ☎ *020/7379–9696* ⊕ *www.closmaggiore.com* ⌂ *Reservations essential* ☞ *Smart casual* Ⓜ *Covent Garden* ✚ *3:F5.*

$

BISTRO

FAMILY

✕ **Côte.** Where else can you find a cracking two-course French meal in Covent Garden for £11.70? The Côte brasserie chain—softly lit and decked out with gray-and-white striped awnings, banquettes, rattan chairs, and Parisian-style café tables—does the trick, and offers popular daily meal deals from noon until 7 pm. With four choices per course, you'll find all your French brasserie favorites: crepes with mushrooms and Gruyère cheese, boeuf *bourguignonne*, char-grilled Breton chicken, *moules marinières* (mussels with white wine), steak haché, and iced berries and white chocolate sauce. Service is brisk and friendly, and if you're lucky enough to be attending the nearby Royal Opera House, this is perfect for pretheater . . . *or* post-theater, come to think of it. $ *Average main: £12* ⊠ *17–21 Tavistock St., Covent Garden* ☎ *020/7379–9991* ⊕ *www.cote-restaurants.co.uk* ⌂ *Reservations essential* Ⓜ *Covent Garden* ✚ *3:G5.*

$

MODERN INDIAN

FAMILY

Fodor's Choice

★

✕ **Dishoom.** Whirring ceiling fans, Indian film posters, checkerboard tiles, oak panels, and vintage Indian cola bottles create an evocative Bombay backdrop for this inexpensive all-day Indian café off Covent Garden. Modeled after the Persian-run Irani cafés of Victorian Bombay, try the *naan* bread with keema minced lamb and peas, or classic chili jam spiked and handkerchief-thin spicy charred chicken tikka *roomali* roti rolls (£6.90). A succulent lamb *raan* bun comes on a wooden block with slow-cooked pulled lamb in a sourdough bun with pomegranate slaw, *sali* chips, and fried green chilies, while gorgeous creamy black dahl is simmered in spices for 24 hours. Drinks and tipples range from a Bollybellini to Limca lemonade or a mango-and-fennel-rich lassi. $ *Average main: £8* ⊠ *12 Upper St. Martin's La., Covent Garden* ☎ *020/7420–9320* ⊕ *www.dishoom.com* ⌂ *Reservations essential* Ⓜ *Leicester Sq.* ✚ *3:E5.*

$ ✕ **Food for Thought.** Covent Garden's throwback 1970s-style subterra-
VEGETARIAN   nean vegetarian café has a cult following, so be prepared to line up
FAMILY   down the steep stairs onto Neal Street. You'll find cramped communal
pine tables and a zingy daily changing menu of wholesome soups, salads, pulses, dhals, stews, quiches, stir-fries, bakes, and casseroles—from
mushroom Stroganoff to Rajistani red lentil curry. Wheat-free, gluten-
free, nut-free, GM–free, free range, Fair Trade, vegan, and organic
options are all usually available. Leave room for desserts like their
famous oat-based strawberry-and-banana "Scrunch." There's takeaway
and it's BYO, but note it's cash only and only open from noon until 8:30
pm Monday through Saturday, and from noon until 5:30 pm on Sunday.
⑤ *Average main: £9* ✉ *31 Neal St., Covent Garden* ☎ *020/7836–0239*
⊕ *foodforthought-london.co.uk* ▭ *No credit cards* ⌂ *Reservations not
accepted* Ⓜ *Covent Garden* ✛ *3:F4.*

$$ ✕ **Great Queen Street.** Expect a boisterous best-of-British foodie crowd
MODERN BRITISH   at one of Covent Garden's leading gastropubs, and proud doyenne of
hearty retro-British dishes. Not far from the Royal Opera House, the
ground-floor open kitchen eatery is done up with simple cardamom-
color walls and bare-oak floors and tables. Unadulterated wine-fueled
diners dive into nostalgic offerings like pressed tongue, pickled her-
rings, pigs' cheeks, and cockles or smoked mackerel with rhubarb.
You'll find stacks of other unpretentious vintage British fare, like brown
crab on toast, brawn, rabbit livers, or Swaledale beef mince pie, plus
hunking great roasts for the table—think seven-hour shoulder of lamb
with dauphinoise potatoes. Salads and veggies follow the same theme,
from sweet heritage carrots to forgotten Roseval potatoes. ⑤ *Average
main: £16* ✉ *32 Great Queen St., Covent Garden* ☎ *020/7242–0622*
⊗ *No dinner Sun.* ⌂ *Reservations essential* Ⓜ *Covent Garden, Holborn*
✛ *3:G4.*

$$$ ✕ **The Ivy.** The triple-A-list spurns The Ivy for its upstairs private mem-
BRITISH   bers' club (and other luxe spots like Scott's, 34, and Chiltern Firehouse)
but, nonetheless, this venerable luvvies landmark still receives a thousand calls a day! A mesmerizing mix of daytime TV stars, gawkers,
day-trippers, and out-of-towners dine on salt-beef hash, squash risotto,
Thai-baked sea bass, salmon fish cakes, eggs Benedict, and good ol' English classics like shepherd's pie or kedgeree (curried rice with smoked
haddock, boiled egg, and parsley) in a handsome mullioned stained-
glass and oak-paneled dining salon. Desserts are standards like Baked
Alaska or sticky toffee pudding, service is unfailingly professional, and
for low- to midrange West End star-spotting this is still a happy hunting
ground. If you can't snag a table by phone or online, try walking in on
spec—it's been known to work. ⑤ *Average main: £25* ✉ *1–5 West St.,
Covent Garden* ☎ *020/7836–4751* ⊕ *www.the-ivy.co.uk* ⌂ *Reservations essential* Ⓜ *Covent Garden* ✛ *3:E5.*

$$$ ✕ **J Sheekey.** The A-list sneaks into this classy 1896 side-alley seafood
SEAFOOD   haven, a discreet alternative to the more overtly celeb-central Scott's,
34, or Chiltern Firehouse. Umbilically linked with the surrounding
Theatreland district, J Sheekey is one of Londoners' all-time favorite
West End haunts. Beautifully orchestrated by longtime maître'd John
Andrews, Sheekey charms with warm wood paneling, vintage showbiz

14

black-and-white portraits, a warren of alcoves, and twinkly lava-rock bar tops. Opt for snappingly fresh Atlantic prawns, pickled Arctic herrings, scallop, shrimp, and salmon burgers, or famous Sheekey fish pie. Better still, sip Gaston Chiquet Champagne and slide down half a dozen Jersey rock oysters at the old mirrored oyster bar for the ultimate in true romance. Alternatively, enjoy the £26.50 weekend three-course set-lunch deals. ⑤ *Average main: £26* ⊠ *28–35 St. Martin's Ct., Covent Garden* ☎ *020/7240–2565* ⊕ *www.j-sheekey.co.uk* ⌂ *Reservations essential* Ⓜ *Leicester Sq.* ✛ *3:E6.*

$
TAPAS ✕ **Opera Tavern.** Ibérico pig's-head terrine or moreish foie gras and Manchego mini cheeseburgers are just a few of the outstanding hybrid Spanish and Italian tapas dishes found at the Opera Tavern, opposite historic Drury Lane Theatre in Covent Garden. Clamber in at the overcrowded ground-floor tapas bar (avoiding the acoustically challenged second-floor dining salon if possible) and, after enjoying a snack of crispy pigs' ears or Guindilla peppers, opt for a gentle flow of rich empanadas of venison, Italian Scotch eggs, braised cuttlefish, wood pigeon with scarmorza cheese, or char-grilled Venetian-style sardines. Vegs are specialties—like stuffed courgette flower with goat cheese and honey—and desserts like *dulche de leche* panna cotta hit the spot. Watch out for the £35 or £40 tapas set meals for groups of eight and up. ⑤ *Average main: £8* ⊠ *23 Catherine St., Covent Garden* ☎ *020/7836–3680* ⊕ *www.operatavern.co.uk* ⌂ *Reservations essential* ⌕ *No dinner Sun.* Ⓜ *Covent Garden, Holborn* ✛ *3:G5.*

$$$
BRITISH
Fodor's Choice
★ ✕ **Rules.** Come, escape the 21st century. Opened in 1798, London's oldest restaurant is, according to some, still London's most beautiful. The main dining salons are, indeed, an old-world wonderland, what Maxim's is to Paris. The decor begins with plush red banquettes, lacquered yellow walls, and spectacular etched-glass skylights. Then, in High Victorian fashion, every cranny is covered with vintage needlepoint, Regency oil paintings, figurines, antlers, antique clocks, stuffed pheasants, and endless framed prints and etchings. Little wonder Rules has been a stage across which everyone from Charles Dickens to Sir Laurence Olivier has pranced. Be sure to ask for a table in one of the "glass house" skylight rooms, the bar area, or the Margaret Thatcher corner, then dig into the menu's historic British puddings and pies, like jugged hare, steak-and-kidney pie, or roast beef and Yorkshire pudding. For a taste of the 18th century, you can choose game specials from the restaurant's High Pennines Lartington estate, including roast grouse, partridge, woodcock, snipe, and ptarmigan. ⑤ *Average main: £29* ⊠ *35 Maiden La., Covent Garden* ☎ *020/7836–5314* ⊕ *www.rules.co.uk* ⌂ *Reservations essential* 🎩 *Jacket required* Ⓜ *Covent Garden* ✛ *3:F6.*

$$$$
BRITISH ✕ **The Savoy Grill.** You can *feel* the history in the room at this glamorous 1889 art deco hotel-dining powerhouse, which has hosted everyone from Oscar Wilde and Frank Sinatra to Liz Taylor and Marilyn Monroe. Nowadays—buffed up with Swarovski chandeliers, velvet coverings, gold leaf–backed tortoiseshell walls, and vintage mirror and black-and-white pics—it caters to bulky business barons, top-end tourists, and nostalgia freaks who come for the Grill's famed table-side trolley, which might trundle up laden with hulking great roasts like beef

Wellington, rack of pork, or saddle of lamb. Savoy legends like omelet Arnold Bennett (with smoked haddock, Parmesan, and cream) or baked egg cocotte with smoked bacon, wild mushrooms, and red wine sauce are to the fore, plus there's timeless standbys like T-bone and Chateaubriand steaks, alongside Carlingford oysters and lobster thermidor. For dessert, you can't top the Baked Alaska. $ *Average main: £32* ⊠ *The Savoy, 100 The Strand, Covent Garden* ☎ *020/7592–1600 for reservations only* ⊕ *www.gordonramsay.com/thesavoygrill* ⚒ *Reservations essential* ☞ *Smart casual* Ⓜ *Charing Cross, Covent Garden* ✛ *3:G6.*

$$$ ✕ **Spring.** Australian chef Skye Gyngell worships the four seasons at
ITALIAN her high-ceilinged pastel-color pillared dining salon at historic Somerset House. A former Tudor royal palace and home to luminaries such as Elizabeth I and Catherine of Braganza and once HQ to the British Admiralty and latterly the Inland Revenue, Gyngell offers unfussy seasonal and produce-driven Italian dishes to a discerning top-end crowd—from a tousled heap of Fern Verrow salad leaves with candied walnuts to a hulking, charred veal chop with brown butter and anchovy courgettes. Alice Waters's disciple Gyngell delights in using foraged hedgerow finds—such as chickweed with onion squash ravioli—and all bread, butter, yogurt, ice cream, some of the cheese, cordials, bitters, vermouth, and tonics are resourcefully made on-site. While front-of-house staff wear dystopian health-spa Egg "smocks" and waitstaff are in pumps and jaunty Trager Delaney matelow outfits, ask to sit at one of the romantic bay window velvet booths, and look to lush buttermilk panna cotta with damsons and wood sorrel leaves to finish. $ *Average main: £30* ⊠ *Somerset House, Lancaster Pl., Haymarket* ✛ *Turn right on entering the courtyard at Someset House from the Strand* ☎ *020/011–0115* ⊕ *www.springrestaurant.co.uk* ⊘ *No dinner Sun.* ⚒ *Reservations essential* Ⓜ *Holborn, Charring Cross* ✛ *3:G6.*

$ ✕ **Wahaca.** Brace for crowds for the fab-value Mexican street food at
MEXICAN former MasterChef winner Thomasina Miers' brightly colored Covent
FAMILY Garden bolthole. Concrete walls, shared wooden bench seats, lively murals, and luminous green ceiling slats make for brisk and breezy basement surrounds, but it's the cheap-as-chips, ethically and sustainably sourced £3.95–£8.95 Mexican market-style tacos, enchiladas, quesadillas, taquitos, and burritos that pull in the budget-conscious student and touristy crowds. A generous £19.95 spread for two hungry head honchos to share will produce a feast of broad-bean quesadillas, pork pibil tacos, slaw, chicken tinga taquitas with green rice, black bean tostadas, and guacamole, but note that the Mexican music is often cranked up loud and the restaurant is invariably heaving by 6:30 pm. $ *Average main: £7* ⊠ *66 Chandos Pl., Covent Garden* ☎ *020/7240–1883* ⊕ *www. wahaca.co.uk* ⚒ *Reservations not accepted* Ⓜ *Covent Garden* ✛ *3:F6.*

BLOOMSBURY, HOLBORN, AND FITZROVIA

BLOOMSBURY

The literary giants of the Bloomsbury set—from Virginia Woolf to E.M. Forster and Vanessa Bell—may be long gone but this bluestocking enclave (centered around the British Library and University of London) still excels at a cultured and a pleasure-loving dining scene. Holborn, bordering Covent Garden, has some of those big, old-establishment hotel dining rooms, and a big, bright elegant shining star in The Delaunay on the Aldwych.

$$
MODERN FRENCH
FAMILY
Fodor's Choice
★

✕ **Grain Store.** Vegetables take pride of place at French chef Bruno Loubet's mega-hit 120-seat restaurant. Earthy beetroot, artichoke, corn, quinoa, butternut squash, onions, potatoes, and shiitake mushrooms take starring roles—and relegate proteins to the margins—on the menu at his quirky 1851 converted former grain warehouse, at spectacular Granary Square just behind King's Cross and St. Pancras stations. Watch Loubet in an "exploded" kitchen–cum–dining room as he concocts complex veg-centric surprises like spiced mash, pickled cucumber, snowball turnips, broad beans... and a *little* confit lamb. You'll smirk at flourishes like a flowerpot of radishes that you roll in "olive soil" (dried black olives), a chilled tomato water lobster "Bloody Mary," and desserts of goat's milk panna cotta with candied tomato. And yet, there's no denying the originality of Loubet's signature butternut squash ravioli or the sheer brilliance of a humble vegetable "Scotch egg" with a wicked tangle of fennel and aioli sauce. $ *Average main: £16* ⊠ *Granary Sq., 1–3 Stable St., King's Cross* ☎ *020/7324–4466* ⊕ *www.grainstore.com* ⊘ *No dinner Sun.* ⚠ *Reservations essential* Ⓜ *King's Cross, St. Pancras* ✛ *2:C1.*

HOLBORN

$$$
AUSTRIAN
FAMILY
Fodor's Choice
★

✕ **The Delaunay.** It's all *fin de siècle* Vienna and *The Radetsky March* at this magnificent art deco–style take on an all-day Viennese grand café and coffeehouse on the Aldwych. Dine like Emperor Franz Joseph I on a majestic 60-item menu that would do the dual-monarchy and Austro-Hungarian Empire proud. Dishes are von Trapp fabulous—think *Weiner schnitzels*, Hungarian goulash, and *würstchen* frankfurters and hot dogs, served with sauerkraut and onions. There are other goodies like *borscht* and beef Stroganoff, kedgeree, and sour lamb shank *sauerbraten.* Desserts delight, too, including *apfelstrudel* and an evocative three-peaked Salzburg soufflé, while the innocuous "Kinder" ice cream coupe is a blowout knickerbocker bursting with meringue, marshmallows, and whipped cream. Classy Viennese breakfast, brunch, Viennoiserie *konditorei* pastries, and afternoon teas are also served, and be sure to discover the hidden café within the café to reminisce about times past. $ *Average main: £24* ⊠ *55 Aldwych, Holborn* ☎ *020/7499–8558* ⊕ *www.thedelaunay.com* ⚠ *Reservations essential* Ⓜ *Covent Garden, Holborn* ✛ *3:G4.*

FITZROVIA

$$
MODERN BRITISH
FAMILY
Fodor's Choice
★

✕ **Berners Tavern.** All the cool cats swing by this *wowy!* grand brasserie at Ian Schrager's trendy London Edition hotel. It's hard not to feel like a million *dollah* as you enter the 18-foot triple-height all-day dining salon, crammed with 1835 ornate stucco plasterwork, Grand Central Station–style bronze chandeliers, church candles, and 150-odd stately home-style paintings. Bag a half-moon chestnut mohair-and-leather banquette and start the day with an impeccable £14 full English breakfast (with herb sausage and Stornaway black pudding) and return for a light lunch of crispy rock shrimp roll or ironbark pumpkin risotto. Reemerge refreshed for dinner, and swoon over a deep-fried duck egg, Cumbrian-ham-and-pea-puree appetizer, and then it's a toss-up between Creedy caver duck, Cornish cod, or Buccleuch Estate bavette. You'll find stunning dishes to share—like *sous vide* Romney Marsh lamb or whole Irish ox, tongue, and cheek—and battered cod, chips, and mushy peas on Fish Fridays. $ *Average main: £17* ✉ *The London Edition, 10 Berners St., Fitzrovia* ☎ *020/7908–7979* ⊕ *www.bernerstavern.com* ⌁ *Reservations essential* Ⓜ *Oxford Circus, Tottenham Court Rd.* ✛ *3:C3.*

$$
SEAFOOD

✕ **Bonnie Gull Seafood Shack.** It sort of feels like you're beside the British seaside at London's top seafood "shack" in deepest Fitzrovia, where the amazing day-boat-fresh seafood—from Shetland mussels to Brixham brill and Paignton crab—mysteriously transports all comers through a nostalgic seafood tour of the British Isles. Everything's bleached-out, shipshape, and weather-beaten at this tiny elbow-to-elbow 42-seater, where you'll spot an old ship's bell, a ship captain's hat, wall-mounted rope *appliqué*, and a mini–raw bar of iced Palourde clams and Carlingford, Jersey, and Portland oysters stashed inside an antique sea chest. Start with Dorset cockles or mini-beer-battered "queenie" scallops with tartar sauce, and move on to pristine Selsey cod with Wye Valley asparagus or line-caught sea bass with mussels and braised fennel. There are meaty razor clams and whole Dorset cock crabs, and the beef dripping chips are from a bygone age. Desserts are Brit-focused with a twist—like Eton Mess with basil jelly—while staff are all invariably pro and megafriendly. $ *Average main: £17* ✉ *21A Foley St., Fitzrovia* ☎ *0203/436–0921* ⊕ *www.bonniegullseafoodshack.com* ⌁ *Reservations essential* Ⓜ *Oxford Circus, Googe St.* ✛ *3:B2.*

$$
MODERN
EUROPEAN
Fodor'sChoice
★

✕ **Dabbous.** It's a triumph of taste over technology at wunderkind Ollie Dabbous's extraordinary game changer off Charlotte Street in Fitzrovia. Startlingly minimalist, pure, inventive, and seasonally based new-wave dishes elicit *Oohs! Aahhs!* and *Oh-my-Goshes!!* in a flummery-free hard-edged NYC–industrial–chic setting of exposed concrete, overhead ducting, and heavy metal screens and cages. Phenomenal flavors abound. Ingredient-led dishes like a peas-and-mint appetizer ping your taste buds with frozen mint tea, edible violets, and broad bean flowers, and a famed coddled hen's egg with smoked butter and woodland mushrooms sits handsomely in a rustic-chic bowl of hay. Palette-popping barbecued Ibèrico pork with acorn praline, halibut with coastal herbs (sea aster and oyster leaf), and brittle chocolate ganache with green basil moss are instant classics, and set Dabbous apart as one of London's most dazzling talents. Book far in advance. $ *Average main: £23* ✉ *39 Whitfield St., Fitzrovia* ☎ *020/7323–1544* ⊕ *www.dabbous. co.uk* ⊘ *Closed Sun. and Mon.* ⌁ *Reservations essential* Ⓜ *Goodge St.* ✛ *3:C2.*

14

CLERKENWELL AND THE CITY

Historic and just beyond The City limits, chef-centric Clerkenwell is one of the most cutting-edge, radical, and trendy quarters for London gastro-dining, which sets it in marked contrast to the adjacent City, which caters overwhelmingly to business-focused conservative dining.

In Clerkenwell, the starchiness of The City fades into relaxed artiness: a fertile ground for avant-garde chefs and restaurants.

$$ ✕ **Bistrot Bruno Loubet.** French chef Bruno Loubet rules the roost at this
FRENCH slick hotel dining room and upscale bistro at The Zetter in historic-yet-cutting-edge Clerkenwell. Loubet tinkers away and masters so many must-try regional French dishes it's genuinely hard to choose: deliciously pink quail comes with prune, Roquefort cheese, and sautéed wild mushrooms, while guinea fowl *boudin blanc* sausages sit perfectly with delicate leeks and chervil sauce, to name just two winners. You'll find fleshy sea bream with Pernod *beurre blanc*, yummy Mauricette snails and meatballs, and soothing *hare royale*, followed by tarragon poached pear, or classic *crêpes Suzette* (served with a touch of cardamom in a Mauviel shiny copper pan). The bustling ground-floor bistro is kitted with retro anglepoise lamps, earthenware jars, coat hooks, and wooden artifacts, and overlooks St. John's Square and the crenelated 14th-century St. John's Gate. ⑤ *Average main: £17* ✉ *The Zetter, 86–88 Clerkenwell Rd., Clerkenwell* ☎ *020/7324–4455* ⊕ *www.bistrotbrunoloubet. com* ⌂ *Reservations essential* Ⓜ *Farringdon St., Barbican* ✛ *2:F3.*

$ ✕ **Duck & Waffle.** Zoom up to the 40th floor of the Heron Tower near
MODERN BRITISH Liverpool Street, and head straight for the cult signature dish of crispy
FAMILY confit duck leg, fried duck egg, Belgium waffle, and grain mustard maple
Fodor's Choice syrup for a taste of awesomeness from supernova young Brit chef Dan
★ Doherty. Eclectic flourishes abound amid spectacular panoramas that take in the Tower of London, Tower Bridge, the Thames, and the Gherkin. A wax-sealed brown paper bag contains spiced pigs ears, and ox cheek doughnuts with apricot jam and smoked paprika sugar are as big as mini cannon balls. Handily open 24/7and often showcasing live music, you might satisfy the munchies with an all-day foie gras breakfast, with streaky bacon and homemade Nutella, a "Full Elvis" PBJ waffle with banana brûlée, or later share tender octopus with lemon and capers, bacon-wrapped dates, or flavor-packed baked Cornish pollock "meatballs" with lobster cream. A stunning vanilla ice-cream Baked Alaska with strawberry and mint oil is the ultimate finale. ⑤ *Average main: £8* ✉ *Heron Tower, 110 Bishopsgate, The City* ⊕ *www. duckandwaffle.com* ⌂ *Reservations essential* Ⓜ *Liverpool St.* ✛ *2:G2.*

$$ ✕ **HKK.** World-class Peking duck—some say *the* best in London—is one
CHINESE of the big things at this lauded Chinese pacesetter on the edge of The City. The amazingly succulent and brittle-skinned glazed Peking duck is cherrywood-roasted in a blazing Beech oven and carved ceremoniously by a specialist chef at an island in the middle of the neat, sleek, and minimalist dark-wood dining room. Set tasting menus—between 4, 5, 8, and 15 courses at lunch, and no-choice 10 and 15 courses at dinner—are a full-on *tour de force*. Diners are given a paintbrush to dab a caviar-topped dim sum trilogy with soy sauce (hope for the pan-fried Szechuan dumpling with Australian tiger prawns and *nameko* mushrooms), and delicate soups, such as truffled seafood soup with Osmanthus flower, are rich, pungent, and densely flavored. Sip rare white peony tea between courses of wok-fried Scottish lobster and braised Duke of Berkshire pork with XO sauce, but only attempt the epic 15-course tasting menu if you have the time…*and* the appetite.

$ *Average main: £22* ✉ *88 Worship St., The City* ☎ *0203/535–1888* ⊕ *www.hkklondon.com* ☽ *Closed Sun.* ⚐ *Reservations essential* Ⓜ *Liverpool St.* ✛ *2:G2.*

$$$
ITALIAN

✕ **L'Anima.** Top-notch southern Italian cuisine in a gleaming modern glass-sided shoe box of a restaurant characterizes the lively business-heavy dining scene here near Bishopsgate. Wavy-haired *magnifico* Italian chef Francesco Mazzei draws inspiration from Sicily, Puglia, Sardinia, and Calabria and prowls the modern high-ceilinged bar, floor, and clear-fronted kitchen like the proud owner he is. With its clean lines, soft music, and distinctive white leather seats, you'll find fresh, simple, and restrained Italian dishes like wild mushroom and black truffle tagliolini and Sardian fish stew, or incredible crispy *fritto misto* fish strips that have been soaked in milk and dipped in double-zero flour. The *baccalà* salt cod with crimson-color *n'duja* Calabrian sausage is awesome, too. Well-crafted desserts, like ricotta mousse with spicy figs, are *bellissimo*, and the winning wine list is mostly Italian. $ *Average main: £26* ✉ *1 Snowden St., Broadgate West, The City* ☎ *020/7422–7000* ⊕ *www. lanima.co.uk* ☽ *Closed Sun.* ⚐ *Reservations essential* Ⓜ *Liverpool St.* ✛ *2:G1.*

14

$$
MEDITERRANEAN
FAMILY

✕ **Moro.** Up from The City, near Clerkenwell and Sadler's Wells contemporary dance theater, is Exmouth Market, a cluster of cute indie shops, bookstores, vinyl stores, artisan bakeries, an Italian Catholic church, and more fine indie-spirited restaurants like Moro. Lovingly nurtured for over a decade by husband-and-wife chefs Sam and Sam Clark, the menu includes an expansive mélange of Spanish, Moroccan, and Moorish North African flavors. Flavor-packed and rustic tapas—like *baba ganoush* eggplant dip, Syrian lentils, baby squid with *harissa*, or ox heart tabouleh—compete with spiced meats, Serrano ham, salt cod, and seared char-grilled offerings. Wood-fired sea bass with hispi cabbage, grilled lamb with aubergine, or sea bream with chickpea salad are among the standout mains. Sidle up to the long zinc bar, or squeeze into a tiny table and lean in—it's noisy here, but then again that's all part of the buzz. $ *Average main: £19* ✉ *34–36 Exmouth Market, Clerkenwell* ☎ *020/7833–8336* ⊕ *www.moro.co.uk* ☽ *No dinner Sun.* ⚐ *Reservations essential* Ⓜ *Farringdon, Angel* ✛ *2:E3.*

$$
MODERN BRITISH

✕ **St. John.** Purists and gastronauts travel the globe for pioneering Brit-chef Fergus Henderson's nose-to-tail cuisine at this puritan stark-white converted former ham-and-bacon smokehouse near historic Smithfield Market. Henderson famously uses *all* scraps of a carcass, and his waste-not, want-not chutzpah chimes increasingly the age: one appetizer is pig's skin and others like ox heart, rolled pig's spleen, or calves' brain and chicory are marginally less extreme. Open since 1994, long-standing St. John signatures like bone marrow and parsley salad, chitterlings with dandelion, or pheasant and pig's- trotter pie appear stark on the plate, but arrive with aplomb. Look out for a metropolitan art world–and–designer crowd, who enjoy feasting meals for the table, like whole roast suckling pig or braised venison with red wine sauce. Finish with Eccles cakes and Lancashire cheese tapioca and crab apple jelly or half a dozen Madeleines. $ *Average main: £18* ✉ *26 St. John*

St., Clerkenwell ☎ *020/7251–0848* ⊕ *www.stjohnrestaurant.com* ⊗ *No dinner Sun.* ⌲ *Reservations essential* Ⓜ *Farringdon, Barbican* ✛ *2:F4.*

$$ ✕ **Sweetings.** Sweetings was established in 1889 and little seems to
SEAFOOD have changed at this time warp since the height of the British Empire. There are some things Sweetings *doesn't* do: dinner, reservations, coffee, or weekends. It does, mercifully, do seafood—and rather well. Not far from St. Paul's Cathedral, and kitted out with arcane Victoriana, sporting and Colonel Blimp cartoons, the restaurant is patronized by pinstriped and covert coated City gents who down pewter tankards of Black Velvet (Guinness and Champagne) and simply love to eat potted shrimps, soft roe on toast, Dover sole, and skate wings with black butter sauce, all this while perched on high stools at white linen–covered raised wooden counters. West Mersea oysters are fresh and plump, and desserts like spotted dick or baked jam roll are timeless public schoolboy favorites. The long-serving waitstaff wear funereal black and white and are naturally acquainted with all the regulars. Ⓢ *Average main: £23* ✉ *39 Queen Victoria St., The City* ☎ *020/7248–3062* ⊕ *www. sweetingsrestaurant.com* ⊗ *Closed weekends. No dinner* ⌲ *Reservations not accepted* Ⓜ *Mansion House* ✛ *2:H6.*

$ ✕ **Tayyabs.** Shamefaced City bankers and doctors and medics from the
PAKISTANI nearby Royal London Hospital swamp this neon-lit, high-turnover Pakistani curry specialist (set in the eastern part of Whitechapel part of The City). Expect queues after dark, and bear in mind it's BYO, jam-packed, noisy, and often maddeningly chaotic. Nonetheless, prices are keen and you can OD and gorge handsomely for less than £20 on a mixed chargrill extravaganza, which might include fiery Tandoori chicken and fish *tikka.* Other best bets include Karachi okra, slow-cooked "dry meat," minced-meat *seekh* kebabs, Karahi prawns, hot steaming naan breads, and Tayyab's famous spicy char-grilled Karahi lamb chops (cooked from a secret recipe). Ⓢ *Average main: £13* ✉ *83 Fieldgate St., The City* ☎ *020/7247–9543* ⊕ *www.tayyabs.co.uk* ⌲ *Reservations not accepted* Ⓜ *Aldgate East* ✛ *2:H2.*

EAST LONDON

$$ ✕ **Bistrotheque.** You'll need a GPS or a compass to find this East End
MODERN fashionista G-spot and all-round cool-hunters HQ located down a side
EUROPEAN alley in jam-hot Bethnal Green. Once you're inside, see the striking loft dining space and Manchichi bar in its postindustrial chic setting of all-white walls and floors, factory pipes, Crittal windows, and bentwood chairs. All the men seem to wear caps, spatz, 'tashes, cravats, Trilbys, or '30s-era tweed three-piece suits, while the Alexa Chung lookalike ladies are in faux fur leggings, *Emmanuelle 2* organza getups, shearling capes, and Scooby-Doo specs. Accomplished French and English dishes range from steak tartar, Croque Madame, and towering cheeseburgers, to cod and clams or Longhorn beef with red-wine sauce. Fashion-forward desserts like Melba toast or brioche and butter pudding stand out, and be sure to catch Xavior, the resident pianist, at weekend brunch, camping up everything from Katy Perry to Girls Aloud on the baby grand. Ⓢ *Average main: £18* ✉ *23–27 Wadeson St., Bethnal Green*

LOCAL CHAINS WORTH A TASTE

If you're zipping round town or don't have time for a fancy meal, try a top-notch local chain restaurant.

Bill's: Enjoy porridge, mezze, afternoon tea (£9.95), or cod finger sandwiches (£8.95) in a cozy setting. ⊕ www.bills-website.co.uk.

Busaba Eathai: It's always packed at these rapid Thai canteen supremos where you'll find Thai noodles, rice dishes stir-frys, currys, and spicy soups in a bowl in sultry dark-wood surrounds. ⊕ www.busaba.com.

Byron: This line of child-friendly hamburger joints mops up the mid-range burger market with its 6-ounce Scotch beef hamburgers, red onion rings, dry-cured bacon, and french fries. ⊕ www.byronhamburgers.com.

Café Rouge: An atmospheric French bistro chain that churns out great £7.95–£14.95 plats rapides and prix fixe deals—so uncool that it's now vaguely fashionable. ⊕ www.caferouge.co.uk.

Côte: High-quality £9.95–£11.90 classic French brasserie meal deals are the order of the day at this lower–upper-middle-market 23-strong chain. ⊕ www.cote-restaurants.co.uk.

Ed's Easy Diner: OD on colorful milk shakes, chili dogs, pulled pork, chicken dippers, and made-to-order British hamburgers at this six-strong chain of shiny, retro-'50s-theme, American-style diners. ⊕ www.edseasydiner.com.

Gail's Artisan Bakery: ⊕ Artisanal sourdough, spelt and German rye sandwiches, corn-bread breakfasts, and healthy lunches like chorizo, butternut squash, and quinoa salad are found at this chain of gourmet bakeries. ⊕ www.gailsbread.co.uk.

Masala Zone: The Covent Garden hub is the most popular of this chain of ocher-hued Indian restaurants, where you can feast on £13 Thali spreads of rice and curry, dhal, vegetables, papadums, chapattis, and yogurty raita. ⊕ www.masalazone.com.

Pho: Enjoy serene surrounds at this bargain-priced Vietnamese gaggle of pho rice and vermicelli noodle soup stops. ⊕ www.phocafe.co.uk.

Pret a Manger: This fast-paced take-out sandwich shop has store-made sandwiches, baguettes, sushi, salads, soups, wraps, flat breads, fruit, porridge, and tea cakes galore. ⊕ www.pret.com.

Wagamama: Londoners drain gazillions of bowls of Asian ramen and noodle soups at this high-tech, kid-friendly chain of Japanese and Asian bench-seat canteens. ⊕ www.wagamama.com.

14

☎ 020/8983–7900 ⊕ www.bistrotheque.com ⬥ Reservations essential Ⓜ Bethnal Green ✢ 2:H1.

$ ✕ **Dishoom.** The humble curry is England's surrogate national dish and

INDIAN in London you'll find some of the best around. Dark-wood and memorabilia-adorned Dishoom is modeled on the all-day Irani cafés of Victorian-era Bombay and it expertly churns out mesmerizing street food, from naan breads and handkerchief-thin roomali roti wraps, to masala prawns, black dhal, lamb biryani, and yogurt-and-milk-based sweet lassi drinks. Average price of dinner for two: £40. Ⓢ Average main: £12

⊠ *7 Boundary St., Shoreditch* ☎ *020/7420–9324* ⊕ *www.dishoom.com* ⌲ *Reservations essential* Ⓜ *Shoreditch High St., Liverpool St.* ✛ *2:G1.*

$ ✕ **E Pellicci.** It's nonstop Cockney banter and all-day full English break-
CAFÉ fasts at this tiny 1900 Grade II–listed family-run greasy spoon near
FAMILY the East End's great Brick Lane and Columbia Road street markets.
With atmospheric stained glass, chrome-lined Vitrolite panels, Formica
tables, art deco marquetry, and signed pics of *East Enders* TV soap
stars, it's a rowdy hole-in-the-wall for the greasy "fry-ups" that the
British still adore: eggs, bacon, sausages, baked beans, toast, tomatoes, mushrooms, black pudding, tea, and bubble-and-squeak (cabbage and mash). Matriarch "Mama" Maria also rustles up Toscana
spaghetti and lasagna, plus steamed sponge- and bread pudding. Your
arteries may clog up, but at least the wallet survives. Everything's less
than £8.70, but remember this is the East End, and hence it's *"Cash
only, Maaate!!"* Ⓢ *Average main: £8* ⊠ *332 Bethnal Green Rd., Bethnal
Green* ☎ *020/7739–4873* ▭ *No credit cards* ☉ *Closed Sun.* ⌲ *Reservations not accepted* Ⓜ *Bethnal Green* ✛ *2:H1.*

$$ ✕ **Merchants Tavern.** The legend on the stylish dark green frontage at
FRENCH FUSION this stealthy Hoxton sleeper reads "Merchants of Good Fortune" and
that just about sums up the exceptional smart-casual dining experience
you'll encounter within. Wonderfully self-assured seasonal and veg-
focused left-field hits from France, Italy, and Britain emerge from chef/
patron Neil Borthwick's open kitchen at this spacious dining salon and
craft-beer bar, housed in a former Victorian warehouse and onetime
apothecary. Hoxton hipsters, city folk, and social-media types all dig
the understated but *soigné* dark parquet floors, exposed walls, convex
mirrors, curved card room green leather banquettes, and a scattering
of sturdy '50s- and '60s-style bucket chairs. Plainly presented rare-pink
venison with braised red cabbage, Alsace bacon, and baked celeriac is
unbelievably good, as are other peachy dishes like roast lamb with "for-
gotten" carrots, quail with foie gras, or wild partridge with sage polenta
and scorched onions. Enjoy lemon posset or vanilla panna cotta with
unstoned damsons, and clock the cut-price £16 two-course set lunch.
Ⓢ *Average main: £19* ⊠ *38 Charlotte St., Hoxton* ☎ *0207/060–5335*
⊕ *www.merchantstavern.co.uk* ⌲ *Reservations essential* ☞ *Sun. open
until 9 pm* Ⓜ *Old St.* ✛ *2:G1.*

$ ✕ **Pizza East.** Hoxton locals seem to have taken up residence at this
PIZZA knockabout gourmet pizza parlor, which serves up chewy, 10-inch,
FAMILY wood-fired, thin-crust, crispy pizzas in Hoxton's converted Tea Build-
ing—a boisterous and achingly au courant 170-seat setting of exposed
concrete walls, raw brickwork, pipes, pillars, and ducting. Amid a
soundscape of Bow Wow Wow and X-Ray Spex, mix things up at long
refectory-style shared tables with a starter of sea bass carpaccio with
fennel and chili, or broad beans with Italian pecorino, before tearing
into one of the 11 semolina-crust pizzas, which might be topped with
veal meatballs or San Daniele ham, ricotta, and pesto. There's wine by
the tap, cocktails by the jug, plus karaoke, slam poetry, hip-hop, or old-
school vinyl sessions in the Concrete basement bar. Ⓢ *Average main:
£12* ⊠ *56 Shoreditch High St., Shoreditch* ☎ *020/7729–1888* ⊕ *www.*

pizzaeast.com ⟨ᴀ⟩ *Reservations essential* Ⓜ *Overground: Shoreditch High St.* ✛ *2:G1.*

$$ ✕ **Rochelle Canteen.** You feel quite the foodie insider once you finally track down the quirky Rochelle Canteen—it's set in an old former bike shed at the restored Victorian-era Rochelle School (off Arnold Circus in Shoreditch, not far from Liverpool Street and the trendy boutiques of Redchurch Street). Ring a buzzer next to a pale blue door, go in through the "Boys" entrance (passing a former playground), and enter chef Margot Henderson's long white, austere canteen, which has an open kitchen and two long Formica tables, Ercol chairs, and Shaker coat pegs on the wall. Gloriously understated British fare arrives at a leisurely pace, from simple deviled kidneys on toast to a retro plate of Yorkshire ham and parsley sauce. Bump along with the Frieze London art and design crowd, and enjoy seasonal guinea fowl with bacon, or skate and capers, and finish with lemon posset or quince jelly. Note it's BYO (£5 corkage), and only open 9 am to 4:30 pm weekdays for breakfast, elevenses, lunch, and tea. Ⓢ *Average main: £16* ✉ *Rochelle School, Arnold Circus, Shoreditch* ☎ *020/7729–5677 for reservations only* ⊕ *www.arnoldandhenderson.com* ☉ *Closed weekends. No dinner* ⟨ᴀ⟩ *Reservations essential* Ⓜ *Liverpool St.* ✛ *2:G1.*
BRITISH
FAMILY

14

SOUTH OF THE THAMES

First mentioned in 1276 and believed to have existed in Roman times, Borough Market in Southwark on the South Bank is a firm favorite with tourists, chefs, and foodies alike. Open Monday to Thursday (10–5), Friday (10–6), and Saturday (8–5), this Dickensian location under moody Victorian wrought-iron railway arches at London Bridge is packed with google-eyed food lovers eager to pick up the finest and freshest fruit, vegetables, and grub in town. There are more than 135 stalls, plus a bunch of nearby pubs, bars, restaurants, and specialty shops, like Neal's Yard Diary (*6 Park St.*), where you'll be bowled over by the great mountains of stinky blue Stilton cheese stacked floor to ceiling. Ever more groovy new eateries are springing up in nearby Bermondsey Street, just south of The Shard.

$$ ✕ **Casse-Croûte.** French radio plays in the background and a chubby Michelin Man perches benignly over the *'Allo 'Allo!* bar at this jaunty Parisian-style local mini-French bistro on Bermondsey Street near The Shard. Run by three friendly French guys—Alex, Hervé, and Sylvain—and miniscule with 19 tightly packed seats and six counter stools, the daily changing blackboard offers a highly restricted three-option/course menu of exceptional Gallic bistro riffs and classics. Sip Ricard pastis or an electro-green *crème de menthe* before lopping off two *ouefs à la coque* (boiled eggs with asparagus soldiers) or untangling your way through a blue cheese salad or perfectly constructed *gratinée à l'oignon* (French onion soup). With mains reasonable at £15–£18, it's elbows in as you slice into a generous *bonette* steak with pepper sauce or sublime turbot with Noilly Prat sauce. The £6 desserts like Paris-Brest choux pastry and cream will instantly transport you back to Montmartre or the Left Bank. Ⓢ *Average main: £16* ✉ *109 Bermondsey St.,*
BISTRO
Fodor's Choice
★

Bermondsey ☎ *020/7407–2140* ⊕ *www.cassecroute.co.uk* ⊘ *No dinner Sun.* ⌂ *Reservations essential* Ⓜ *London Bridge* ✛ *5:H2.*

$$$
MODERN FRENCH
FAMILY

✕**Chez Bruce.** Top-notch French and Mediterranean cuisine, faultless service, a winning wine list, copious white linen, and a straight-off-the-pistes glossy south-of-the-river Wandsworth neighborhood vibe make for one of London's all-star favorite restaurants. Take a cab or Overland train to lauded chef Bruce Poole's cozy, gimmick-free haunt overlooking Wandsworth Common and prepare for grown-up gadget-free gastro wonders, ranging from delicious homemade charcuterie or offal to lighter, simply grilled fish dishes. Pot roast pig's cheek with polenta, roast cod with truffle mash, and monkfish with scallops, ham hock, and Jerusalem artichokes are all immaculately conceived and carefully plated. Desserts like poached pear and clementine sorbet are packed with flavor and the sommelier's a hoot. Set three-course lunches are £29.50 weekdays and £35 weekends; three-course dinners are £47.50 all week. Ⓢ *Average main: £27* ✉ *2 Bellevue Rd., Wandsworth Common, Battersea* ☎ *020/8672–0114* ⊕ *www.chezbruce.co.uk* ⌂ *Reservations essential* Ⓜ *Overland: Wandsworth Common* ✛ *4:E6.*

$
TAPAS

✕**José.** Revered Spanish chef José Pizarro packs 'em in like so many slices of *jamón jamón* at this tiny tapas-and-sherry treasure trove on hot gastro-trail Bermondsey Street, just south of the Shard. With only 30 seats and no reservations, you'll be hard-pressed to find a spot at the open-kitchen tapas bar or a perch at an upturned sherry barrel after 6 pm, but stick with it *hombre*—the Spanish tapas dishes are superb. Quaff a glass of Amontillado sherry and keep those delicately handcrafted small plates a comin': *patatas bravas . . . croquetas . . .* meatballs . . . pisto and crispy duck eggs . . . hake and aioli . . . razor clams with chorizo . . . *pluma* Ibérico pork loin fillets. Everything's impeccably sourced—from the peppery Marques de Valdueza olive oil to the rare Manuel Maldonado chorizo. Service is decidedly *Excellente!*, but you'll either love or hate the *in-yer-face* crowds. Ⓢ *Average main: £9* ✉ *104 Bermondsey St., Southwark* ☎ *020/7403–4902* ⊕ *www.josetapasbar.com* ⌂ *Reservations not accepted* Ⓜ *Borough, London Bridge* ✛ *5:H2.*

$$
MODERN BRITISH
FAMILY

✕**Magdalen.** Not far from the Shard and south of the Thames between Tower and London bridges, and only a hop from the London Assembly HQ, Magdalen is a self-assured beacon of class in a remarkably rising gastrocentric part of town. Magdalen specializes in bold, inventive, but unpretentious modern British cuisine at fairly keen prices. Punchy surprises like crispy fried calves' brains with gribiche (£9.50), baked Somerset kid with butter beans and fennel (£19.50), or blackberry-and-apple trifle (£7) are hardly going to break the bank. The dark bentwood chairs, elegant chandeliers, tea candles, and enveloping ox-blood-color surrounds invite you to sit back with the short-but-sweet wine list and further ponder whether to indulge in a feast of slow-baked rabbit with white beans and roast garlic or whole stuffed suckling pig instead. The £15.50 two-course set lunch is definitely worth a gander. Ⓢ *Average main: £18* ✉ *152 Tooley St., Bermondsey* ☎ *020/7403–1342* ⊕ *www.magdalenrestaurant.co.uk* ⊘ *Closed Sun. No lunch Sat.* ⌂ *Reservations essential* Ⓜ *London Bridge* ✛ *5:H2.*

$$$ ✕ **Restaurant Story.** Ambitious young Brit hotshot Tom Sellers storms
MODERN BRITISH the ramparts at this sell-out gastro-mecca, with his conceptual take on
Fodor's Choice intensively flavored ingredient-led New British and New Nordic cui-
★ sine. Housed in a modishly Scandinavian-inspired dining space, expect
touches like edible nasturtium flowers, "trash cooking"–inspired roast
cod skin, or eel mousse Oreos to kick things off. The real fun, however,
begins with a surprise tallow beef dripping candle that melts into an
Ebenezer Scrooge–like silver candle holder, which you mop up with
own-baked bread throughout the meal. Genius dishes like pureed Dési-
rée heritage potatoes with dandelion *beurre blanc*, coal oil, and barley
grass, or meadowsweet-pickled scallops with dill ash and horseradish
cream pop up throughout the no-choice 3-, 6-, or 10-course set menus.
Standout desserts include Earl Grey–soaked prunes with lovage ice
cream, edible twig, and a smudge of milk skin. Reservations are taken
a month in advance. $ *Average main: £28* ✉ *199 Tooley St., Bermond-*
sey ☎ *020/7183–2117* ⊕ *www.restaurantstory.co.uk* ☉ *Closed Sun. and*
Mon. ⌖ *Reservations essential* Ⓜ *London Bridge* ✛ *2:H6.*

$$ ✕ **Zucca.** River Café alumni Sam Harris nails the elusive winning for-
ITALIAN mula for this ultimate modern Italian bistro, doors down from the
Fodor's Choice fab White Cube contemporary art gallery on Bermondsey Street. Any
★ restaurant that notes on its menu that "The use of mobile phones is
both unsociable and unnecessary" has its head screwed on, and this
sure touch is in evidence throughout from the open kitchen and white
melamine tables, to the passionately prepared, all-homemade Italian
breads, pasta, and ice cream. Start off sharing a punchy £7.50 anti-
pasto-like salt cod with chickpeas, then swoon maybe over the Piet-
montese egg-yoke-color *pappardelle* pasta with veal ragù, or indulgent
Le Marche white truffle and wild mushroom *vincisgrassi* pasta bake.
You'll only find three fish or meat mains to choose from at dinner, but
anything like the ink-black squid with white polenta or a blush-pink
veal chop with spinach and lemon will be *molto bellissimo!* $ *Aver-*
age main: £17 ✉ *184 Bermondsey St., Bermondsey* ☎ *020/7378–6809*
⊕ *www.zuccalondon.com* ☉ *Closed Mon. No dinner Sun.* ⌖ *Reserva-*
tions essential Ⓜ *London Bridge* ✛ *5:H2.*

14

KENSINGTON, CHELSEA, KNIGHTSBRIDGE, AND BELGRAVIA

If you're fab, famous, wealthy, or preferably all three, chances are you'll
be living—and dining—in one of these neighborhoods among London's
world-class museums, royal parks, shops, hotels, monuments, fashion
boutiques, and top restaurants (does the name of superchef Heston
Blumenthal ring a bell?). Chelsea, made famous in the swinging '60s,
is where today's Stella McCartney–velour–clad yummy mummies bomb
around in their Porsche Cayennes and Persol sunglasses. The area's
restaurants range from bijou boîtes to exclusive little froufrou places
ideal for girly gossip, an Aperol, and a no-carb bite on the go. Over in
upscale Knightsbridge, you'll find Harrods and the high-end fashion
boutiques of Sloane Street, plus a heap of platinum-class hotel-based
restaurants. Come here for an amazing celebration dining experience,
but don't expect bargains (except at lunch). Nearby, Kensington is a

Victorian residential neighborhood with a wider range of restaurants, from French bistros to funky Vietnamese hideaways.

KENSINGTON

$$$

JAPANESE

Fodor'sChoice

★

×**Yashin.** *"Without Soy Sauce...but if you want to"* proclaims the neon sign on the wall behind the sushi counter at this top London sushi bar off Kensington High Street. Take their advice, bag a ringside seat, and watch Japanese head chef and cofounder Yasuhiro Mineno tease, slice, tweak, and blowtorch his way to the most awesome, fresh, funky, spunky, colorful, and exquisite sushi, sashimi, salads, and carpaccios that you're likely to find this side of the East China Sea. Tofu-topped miso cappuccino comes in a Victorian cup and saucer, and softshell blue crab salad is a tangle of *mizuna* (Japanese greens). Delectable 5-, 11-, or 15-piece sushi spreads (£15–£60) might mesmerize with ponzu-spiked salmon, Japanese sea bream with rice cracker dust, salted Wagyu beef, or Japanese prawns. The bargain £12.50 five-piece salmon *nigiri* set lunch, with hot miso and bracing raw salad, is a smashing way to sample Yashin's below-the-radar brilliance. ⑤ *Average main: £25* ⊠ *1A Argyll Rd., Kensington* ☎ *020/7938–1536* ⊕ *yashinsushi.com* ⌕ *Reservations essential* Ⓜ *High Street Kensington* ✛ *4:B1.*

CHELSEA

$$$

MODERN BRITISH

FAMILY

Fodor'sChoice

★

×**The Harwood.** British game doesn't get much better than at this forest-floor and game-lover's paradise and London's only Michelin-starred gastropub off Fulham Broadway. Co-owned by game-shooting enthusiast and two-starred Aussie chef Brett Graham, you'll find a catalog of awesome game-based dishes like haunch of Berkshire roe deer with pickled mushrooms or Muggleswick grouse with potato and malt to keep you tickled. Tuck into game pie with Somerset cider jelly, Irish Sika deer with smoked bone marrow, or Herdwick lamb with rosemary curd in a relaxed 1840s comfy-sofas-and-Sunday-newspapers home-away-from-home Sloaney pub setting. You'll find thoughtful openers like treacle-cured smoked salmon with spelt are served on a gnarled slab of wood, and there are popular carve-your-own whole-roast lamb, pork, or beef joints for the table—and yes, you *can* ask for doggy bags on the way out! ⑤ *Average main: £24* ⊠ *27 Walham Grove, Fulham* ☎ *020/7386–1847* ⊕ *www.harwoodarms.com* ⌕ *Reservations essential* Ⓜ *Fulham Broadway* ✛ *4:A5.*

$$

HUNAN

×**Hunan.** There's no menu at this quirky, top-rated family-run Taiwanese stalwart (est. 1982), situated a few blocks south of Sloane Square in Pimlico. Instead, diners simply state how spicy they like it to owner-chef Peng, or his son Michael, and sit back, relax, and chop-stix their way through a well-paced succession of highly tasty, tapas-size Hunanese, Hakka, Cantonese, and Japanese-inspired dishes to share. Using a blizzard of garlic, ginger, fiery Szechuan chilies, and red peppercorns, a loyal, tanned, and gleaming SW1 crowd might enjoy 12 to 14 unfailingly delicious dishes like Hunan water-fried dumplings, sliced duck, signature minced pork broth with Chinese mushrooms, crispy frogs' legs, pig's ears, or pungent crab noodle soup. Chef Peng is highly thoughtful about what you might receive, the portions are generous, the wines intrigue, and the ongoing surprise is all part of the fun. ⑤ *Average main: £23* ⊠ *51 Pimlico Rd., Pimlico, Chelsea* ☎ *020/7730–5712*

⊕ *www.hunanlondon.com* ⊙ *Closed Sun.* ⚘*Reservations essential*
Ⓜ *Sloane Sq.* ✛ *4:G3.*

$$ ✕**Indian Zing.** Indian Zing's chef-patron Manoj Vasaikar woos the
INDIAN picky West London curry mafia with updated eclectic regional Indian
cuisine on King's Street's emergent "Curry Mile." Start with tamarind-
spiced Rasam mussels and move onto Khyber Pass shank of lamb
or Barbary duck with Chettinad spices. Average price of dinner
for two: £75. Ⓢ *Average main: £18* ✉ *236 King St., Hammersmith*
☏ *020/8748–5959* ⊕ *www.indianzing.co.uk* ⚘ *Reservations essential*
Ⓜ *Ravenscourt Park* ✛ *1:A2.*

$$$$ ✕**Rasoi.** Wizard Indian chef Vineet Bhatia dazzles with some of Lon-
INDIAN don's finest contemporary Indian cuisine at this tony Victorian Chelsea
town house. Ring the doorbell on arrival at this romantic celebration
venue, which is kitted out with Indian prints, masks, bells, ornaments,
and carved wooden deities. Bhatia exhibits gastro godlike qualities
of his own with ingenious surprises like popcorn prawns, crab lol-
lies with coconut soup, wild mushroom rice with tomato ice cream,
plus Bordeaux-infused lamb rogan josh and Darjeeling tea–soaked
chicken. Grilled sea bass comes crusted in South Indian lentil-based
"gunpowder" and a beetroot *molee* sauce (with coconut milk, curry
leaves, onion, turmeric, and mustard seeds), while Punjabi chicken *tikka*
is revealed from under a plume of smoke. Be sure to try the signature
warm chocolate samosas, dubbed "Choca-mosas." Ⓢ *Average main:*
£32 ✉ *10 Lincoln St., Chelsea* ☏ *020/7225–1881* ⊕ *www.rasoi-uk.com*
⊙ *No lunch Sat.* ⚘ *Reservations essential* Ⓜ *Sloane Sq.* ✛ *4:F3.*

KNIGHTSBRIDGE

$$$ ✕**Ametsa with Arzak Instruction.** Cool hunters and Hispanophiles bask in
SPANISH a fantasia of New Basque cuisine at this modernist romp at the Halkin
Fodor's Choice off Belgrave Square. The father-and-daughter team of Juan Mari and
★ Elena Arzak behind the eponymous three-Michelin-star restaurant in
San Sebastián break out triumphantly at their first European venue
outside Spain. You'll love or loath the sparkling ceiling feature which
undulates in a wave of 7,000 test tubes filled with golden-hue spices,
and look beyond the austere stark white-gray, boxy setting. Instead,
enjoy the ultrapro and passionate service, and marvel at high-spec riffs
on traditional Basque dishes, such as slow-cooked hens eggs flecked
with paprika-rich Chistorra cured sausage with dabs of wild cep mushrooms, pancetta, and chorizo. Lobster is updated with a white cas-
sava powder, and seared venison appears on a black plate with pickled
red chilies and an electric green mint and sea hawthorn mojo. Flaw-
less desserts range from clove custard to an extraordinary science
experiment—like hydromel mead "Fractal" surprise. Ⓢ *Average main:*
£27 ✉ *Halkin Hotel, 5 Halkin St., Knightsbridge* ☏ *0207/333–1234*
⊕ *www.comohotels.com/thehalkin/dining/ametsa* ⊙ *No lunch Mon.,*
no dinner Sun. ⚘ *Reservations essential* Ⓜ *Hyde Park Corner, Knights-*
bridge ✛ *4:G1.*

$$ ✕**Bar Boulud.** U.S.–based French superchef Daniel Boulud combines the
BRASSERIE best of French high-end brasserie fare with a winning dash of superior
FAMILY Yankee gourmet burgers and fries at this popular street-level, all-day
hangout at the Mandarin Oriental in Knightsbridge. Lilliputian-size

platters of the most delicate Gilles Verot charcuterie, heartier *coq au vin*, or white pork sausages with truffle mash compete with palm-size Yankee, Frenchie, Piggie, or signature "BB" foie gras–beef burgers and fries in black onion or sesame-seed buns. The knockout grazing menu has something for everyone, and professional but informal waitstaff make for a convivial vibe in this handy spot opposite Harvey Nichols department store. Note the £19 three-course noon–7 pm *prix-fixe* deals. $ *Average main: £21* ✉ *Mandarin Oriental Hyde Park, 66 Knightsbridge, Knightsbridge* ☎ *020/7201–3899 for reservations only* ⊕ *www.barboulud.com/london* ♨ *Reservations essential* Ⓜ *Knightsbridge* ✛ *4:F1.*

$$$$
BRITISH
Fodor'sChoice
★

✕ **Dinner by Heston Blumenthal.** Splendidly revived old English dishes executed with ultramodern precision in an open kitchen is the big *schtick* at Ashley Palmer-Watts' award winner at the Mandarin Oriental (Palmer-Watts is a protégée of TV chef Heston Blumenthal, who's closely involved). As you take in views of Hyde Park, you simply must slice into a chilled Meat Fruit appetizer (circa 1500), deceptively shaped like a mandarin, but encasing the smoothest foie gras and chicken liver parfait on the planet. A plate of Rice and Flesh (circa 1390) is a picture of yellow saffron rice with calf's tails and red wine, and grilled octopus Frumenty (circa 1390) is a lively dish of cracked wheat cooked with lovage in a smoked sea broth from the court of Richard II. Marvel at beef royale (circa 1720) cooked *sous vide* for 72 hours at 56°C, plus cod in cider (circa 1940), or Spiced Pigeon (circa 1780) with ale and artichokes. Head off with resplendent spit-roast pineapple Tipsy cake (circa 1810)—an homage to English spit-roasting from centuries past. $ *Average main: £34* ✉ *Mandarin Oriental Hyde Park, 66 Knightsbridge, Knightsbridge* ☎ *020/7201–3833* ⊕ *www.dinnerbyheston.com* ♨ *Reservations essential* Ⓜ *Knightsbridge* ✛ *4:F1.*

$$$
FRENCH
FAMILY

✕ **Koffmann's.** Set in the swish Berkeley in Knightsbridge, this is the last hurrah of noted veteran French superchef Pierre Koffmann. Never paying heed to trends, fads, or fashion, the ducal clientele here enjoy such signatures as gelatinous stuffed pig's trotters "Tante Claire" with sweetbreads and morels, or delicately seared scallops with a smudge of black squid ink. Unshowbizzy but culinary godfather to many of London's top chefs—from Gordon Ramsay to Tom Aikens—Gascon-born Koffmann showcases 35-odd years of experience and the best of regional Gascony cuisine in a cute, carpeted, and well-appointed basement setting. Alongside a steady stream of minor British royalty and princes in exile, be sure to experience other gastro goodies like snails with garlic and parsley, wild duck à l'orange, Gascon apple tart, or signature pistachio soufflé with pistachio ice cream. $ *Average main: £26* ✉ *The Berkeley, Wilton Pl., Knightsbridge* ☎ *020/7107–8844* ⊕ *www. the-berkeley.co.uk* ♨ *Reservations essential* Ⓜ *Knightsbridge* ✛ *4:G1.*

$$$
RUSSIAN

✕ **Mari Vanna.** All of London's Russian molls, dolls, and porcelain-skinned *babushkas* squeeze into this kitsch White Russian fantasy dining salon in Knightsbridge, which overflows with a maximalist decor of vintage chandeliers, books, pics, knickknacks, Tiffany lamps, *tchotchkes*, gilt mirrors, Cheburashkas, and a Russian *pechka* stove. Note the crochet- and linen-covered tables tended by chirpy staff (some in dirndls) and dishes proffered with what feels like great aunt Vanna's old family silver and jumbled crockery. Then snap into character with a horseradish vodka shot or two, and carb-up on *pierogi* sea bass savories, clear Siberian Pelmeni dumpling soup, or feather-light smoked salmon blinis. There's good borscht and creamy beef Stroganoff with mash and wild mushrooms, and lest we forget the sweet crepes with condensed milk. But it's the nostalgic dacha-like antebellum home-away-from-home setting that makes you feel like you're participating in some kind of *Anna Karenina*–esque historical reenactment. $ *Average main: £28* ⊠ *The Wellington Court, 116 Knightsbridge, Knightsbridge* ☎ *020/7225–3122* ⊕ *www.marivanna.ru/london* ⟷ *Reservations essential* Ⓜ *Knightsbridge* ✛ *4:F1.*

$$ ✕ **Zuma.** Hip, hip, hurray for this ever-fashionable informal Tokyo-style
JAPANESE modern sushi joint and slim-hipsters' hangout near Harrods and Harvey
FAMILY Nichols in Knightsbridge. Well lit and designed with polished granite, blond cedar wood, exposed pipes, and open timberwork, Zuma takes in a sake bar, robata grill, and famed open sushi counter—and attracts *all* the Isabel Marant and J Crew beautiful people from SW7 on a rolling basis. You can't go wrong with the fresh California maki rolls, tuna sushi, sea bass sashimi, pork with yuzo, or robata-grilled Wagyu beef that comes on a hoba leaf. Sip a rare sake, relax, enjoy the super-polite service, marvel at the engrossing petro dollar, Ruski, and spray-tanned "Made In Chelsea" *Mwah! Mwah!* set, and be sure to collar the sake sommelier to guide you through the 40-odd varieties of exquisite sake rice wines. $ *Average main: £22* ⊠ *5 Raphael St., Knightsbridge* ☎ *020/7584–1010* ⊕ *www.zumarestaurant.com* ⟷ *Reservations essential* Ⓜ *Knightsbridge* ✛ *4:F1.*

14

BELGRAVIA

$$$ ✕ **Pétrus.** A talented Gordon Ramsay stable team conducts a flawless
MODERN FRENCH dining experience at this Belgravia French haute cuisine honeypot. The
Fodor's Choice soft-carpeted ground-floor dining salon may be a bit beige and dated,
★ and a central circular glass wine cellar a tad passé , but add in the warm welcome, bonhomie, impeccable nibbles, *bonne bouches*, assured sommelier, stonking cheese board, *petits fours*, and charming fleet-footed service, and you've got an unrivaled full-court gastro press. The cuisine here is all *Technique! Technique! Technique!* and it's impossible not to gasp at starters like exemplary Les Landes duck foie gras with figs and bee pollen, or lobster ravioli swimming in creamed leaks and Champagne velouté. Bliss out on 25-day Casterbridge beef fillet with sticky Barolo sauce, and watch for surprises toward the end, like a dark chocolate bomb that theatrically melts before your eyes, or mini white choc ices on sticks that emerge from a bowl of dry ice. $ *Average main: £29* ⊠ *1 Kinnerton St., Belgravia* ☎ *020/7592–1609* ⊕ *www.gordonramsay.com/petrus* ⟷ *Reservations essential* Ⓜ *Knightsbridge, Hyde Park Corner* ✛ *4:G1.*

NOTTING HILL AND BAYSWATER

Ever since Hugh Grant and Julia Roberts starred in *Notting Hill* and put the area on the global map, Notting Hill's had a rep as London's most glammy neighborhood, with its myriad boutiques, chic cafés, pâtisseries, restaurants, buzzy bars, and the famous Portobello Road Market's collection of antiques shops, bric-a-brac, vintage-clothing stands, and food stalls. Portobello is one of London's most popular street markets, so get there early on Saturday morning (the market is open 8–6) to beat the crowds. Peruse the antiques and vintage clothes stalls, and when you want to eat, head to the north end where you'll find fresh fruit-and-veg stalls, artisan bakeries, rare Spanish olive and French cheese purveyors, plus numerous hot-food stalls peddling savory crepes, gourmet hamburgers, spicy German chicken rolls, paella, Moroccan kebabs, and Malaysian noodles.

NOTTING HILL

$

MODERN ASIAN

✕ **E&O.** *Slummin'*-it celebs and the perma-tanned Notting Hill brigade give a well-manicured thumbs up to this long-standing Asian tapas supremo off Portobello Road street market. E&O's size-8 figure-friendly medley of blue-chip Japanese, Vietnamese, Chinese, and Thai all-star favorite dishes includes dim sum, sushi, sashimi, and tempura, with a slew of low-carb/no-carb options. Don't skip lychee martinis in the singles-heavy see-and-be-seen bar, before mooching over to the moody monochrome and well-mirrored dining room for miso black cod, snow-crab maki, papaya salad, Thai rare beef, or lamb rendang; the sea bass sashimi is achingly fresh. There are pavement tables and comfy curbside bench seats to people-watch on Blenheim Crescent. ⑤ *Average main: £13* ⊠ *14 Blenheim Cres., Notting Hill* ☎ *020/7229–5454* ⊕ *www.rickerrestaurants.com/e-and-o* ⊜ *Reservations essential* Ⓜ *Ladbroke Grove, Westbourne Grove* ✛ *1:B1.*

$$$$

MODERN FRENCH

Fodor's Choice

★

✕ **The Ledbury.** Acclaimed Aussie chef Brett Graham wins hearts, minds—and *serious* global accolades—at this no-diary, no-carbs high-ceilinged modern French (with Pacific and British hints) dining landmark in deepest Notting Hill. In a handsome four-square salon full of drapes, mirrored walls, and plush cream leather seats, you won't find a more inventive vegetable dish than Graham's ash-baked celeriac with hazelnut and wood sorrel, and it's impossible to best his pretty and complex mains like roast quail with walnut cream, roe deer with bone marrow, or Cornish turbot with Riesling, cockles, and sea lettuce. Besides his obsessive interest in all things British game, Graham's also famed for wicked desserts, so why not finish with thinly sliced figs with honey, olives, and sourdough ice cream? The assured service and sommelier round out this peerless proposition. ⑤ *Average main: £34* ⊠ *127 Ledbury Rd., Notting Hill* ☎ *0207/7792–9090* ⊕ *www. theledbury.com* ☾ *No lunch Mon. or Tues.* ⊜ *Reservations essential* Ⓜ *Westbourne Park, Ladbroke Grove* ✛ *1:A4.*

$

MODERN BRITISH

FAMILY

✕ **The Mall Tavern.** It's all things British at this charming 1856 Notting Hill gastropub, which overflows with relaxed *rus en urbe* Sloane Rangers and discerning Notting Hillers. Check out the Coronation mugs, Royal wedding trinkets, Diamond Jubilee and Prince Charles and Lady

Diana memorabilia before sampling some great British bar snacks like pork scratchings or lop-eared sausage rolls. Move through to the simple dark-oak-floored dining room to feast on hearty beefy pie with bone marrow poking through the crust, or wallow in '70s nostalgia with mac 'n' cheese or high-quality smoked-salmon fish cakes with spinach and a coddled egg. There's salted caramel chocolate Rolos or blood-orange cheesecake for dessert, plus some stonking British farmhouse cheeses, like Shorrock's Bombor Leagram blue. Note the bargain £10 two-course weekday lunches. ⑤ *Average main: £15* ⌧ *71–73 Palace Gardens Terr., Notting Hill* ☎ *020/7229–3374* ⊕ *www.themalltavern.com* ⌲ *Reservations essential* Ⓜ *Notting Hill Gate* ✛ *1:B5.*

BAYSWATER

$ ✕**Alounak.** Wonderous Persian dips, unleavened *taftoon* breads, small

MIDDLE EASTERN tasty plates, steaming lamb bakes, and flame-grilled kebabs are found at this lantern-filled Aladdin's Cave, a warm Iranian canteen beloved by hoards of local Middle Easterners. Lines form onto Westbourne Grove for the hot pita and taftoon breads straight from the curved clay oven by the door, and you may have to wait to get in. Once inside, try grilled eggplant puree with walnuts, feta, mint, and tarragon, the Alounak kebabs, skewered marinated lamb with rice and grilled tomatoes, or the *Zereshk polo*—pungent saffron chicken with sweet-and-sour Iranian forest berries. Enjoy the Persian black cardamom teas and sweets, and lime juice–and–pistachio *faloodeh* Persian sorbet, but know that the sour yogurt drinks are not to everyone's taste. ⑤ *Average main: £12* ⌧ *44 Westbourne Grove, Bayswater* ☎ *020/7229–4158* ⌲ *Reservations essential* Ⓜ *Queensway, Bayswater* ✛ *1:B4.*

$$$ ✕**Angelus.** Owner, sommelier, and former pro-rugby union player Thi-

BRASSERIE erry Tomasin scores a brilliant individual try at this upmarket French brasserie near Lancaster Gate and Hyde Park. Styled with swirly art nouveau mirrors and button-back banquettes in a 200-year-old converted former pub, Angelus has a rep for unrivaled Parisian-style *brasserie de luxe* dishes; the ducks liver crème brûlée, egg cocotte, frogs' legs, saddle of lamb, or Grand Marnier soufflé are as good as they get. Classy £14 breakfasts, all-day brunch (10–10), and light bites like three-egg omelet and truffled brioche steak sandwiches are well conceived, and service is notoriously— *how* should we say this?— *Gallic!* Ex-Le Gavroche sommelier Tomasin is sure to Umm and Ahh!, shrug, sniff, gently smile, and then select an absolutely cracking bottle from the extensive and mainly French-focused wine list and Tomasin's opus and all-round master work. ⑤ *Average main: £26* ⌧ *4 Bathurst St., Hyde Park* ☎ *020/7402–0083* ⊕ *www.angelusrestaurant.co.uk* ⌲ *Reservations essential* Ⓜ *Lancaster Gate* ✛ *1:D4.*

$ ✕**Hereford Road.** Bespeckled chef and co-owner Tom Pemberton

MODERN BRITISH mans the busy front-of-house grill station at this Bayswater favorite, renowned for its pared-down, pomp-free, and ingredient-driven seasonal British fare. With an accent on well-sourced honest-to-goodness seasonal and regional British produce, many dishes are as unfussy as you'll find. Slide into side booths, and work your way though pure and uncluttered combos like steamed mussels with cider and thyme, lemon sole with sea dulse, duck breast with old-fashioned pickled walnuts, or

14

warm and soothing English rice pudding with strawberry jam. Expect to brush past the entire Tory party leadership and the rest of the well-heeled Notting Hill set on the way out. Note the £9.50 to £15.50 set lunches are arguably the *best* high-quality weekday set lunch deals, bar none. $ *Average main: £14* ⊠ *3 Hereford Rd., Bayswater* ☎ *020/7727–1144* ⊕ *www.herefordroad.org* ⊜ *Reservations essential* Ⓜ *Bayswater, Queensway* ✛ *1:B4.*

REGENT'S PARK, HAMPSTEAD, AND ISLINGTON

Stucco-fronted Regent's Park and Primrose Hill attract a boho-chic media and artsy crowd who love the slightly rough-and-rowdy neighborhood home-away-from-home restaurants like vine-decked Lemonia. Meanwhile, farther north in leafy Hampstead, it's all Dick Turpin 17th-century wood-beamed coaching houses and inns with roaring fires, house ales, and trouser-busting Sunday lunches that predominate.

REGENT'S PARK

$

GREEK

FAMILY

✕ **Lemonia.** Primrose Hill's favorite Greek Cypriot, vine-decked, and '80s-taverna-style Lemonia is large and light, and always packed with hoards of hungry families and hobo-chic locals. Besides an endless supply of Hellenic small-dish meze dips, hot breads, and starters, there are un-jazzed-up rustic mains like slow-baked *kleftiko* lamb in lemon, classic eggplant, Greek yogurt–and–potato *moussaka*, herb-stuffed tomatoes, grilled prawns, calamari, souvlaki, and pleasing beef on the bone stewed in red wine. Expect friendly Greek service and hospitality, plus an airy glass-domed atrium out the back, and the odd fly-by from the Jude Law Primrose Hill megastar set. Generous spreads are £21.50 and weekday set lunches are £12.50. $ *Average main: £14* ⊠ *89 Regent's Park Rd., Regent's Park* ☎ *020/7586–7454* ⊘ *No lunch Sat. No dinner Sun.* ⊜ *Reservations essential* Ⓜ *Chalk Farm* ✛ *1:F1.*

ISLINGTON

$

CAFÉ

FAMILY

✕ **Ottolenghi.** Captivating meringue-filled foodie window displays and a funky modern all-white interior characterize this flagship North African, Middle Eastern, and Mediterranean deli/bakery/café set in Islington's main Upper Street drag. Sit at white melamine tables and dig into exceptionally inventive, tasty, and healthy dishes like roasted sweet potatoes with burnt eggplant and pomegranate, lamb cutlets with okra, Tunisian harissa-spiced chicken, or golden beetroot, red cabbage, and sour cream, along with cult Ottolenghi fresh salads, savories, soups, flaky pastries, and artisanal cakes. Go home with a knockout take-out chocolate meringue or plum-and-quince tart, and pick up Ottolenghi's outstanding Israeli- *and* Palestinian-inspired cookbook, *Jerusalem,* on the way out, too. $ *Average main: £13* ⊠ *287 Upper St., Islington* ☎ *020/7288–1454* ⊕ *www.ottolenghi.co.uk* Ⓜ *Angel* ✛ *2:F1.*

THE THAMES UPSTREAM

These wealthy, westerly, leafy suburbs may be under the Heathrow flight path and follow the meandering course of the River Thames, but there's nothing sleepy about the neighborhood dining scene here, which

BEST BREAKFASTS

Dean Street Townhouse. Plump for the traditional Full English breakfast (£12) at this deeply English Georgian town-house boutique hotel and swank restaurant in Soho, where you'll bliss out on boiled eggs with buttered soldiers, streaky bacon, Lorne sausages, grilled mushrooms and tomatoes, and a slab of earthy black pudding. ✉ *Dean Street Townhouse, 69–71 Dean St., Soho* ☎ *020/7434–1775* ⊕ *www. deanstreettownhouse.com* Ⓜ *Tottenham Court Rd., Oxford Circus.*

The Delaunay. Luxuriate in exemplary Mitteleuropa breakfasts and enjoy a high staff-to-customer ratio at this elegant dark-wood-and-leather banquettes grand café. There's porridge, oatmeal soufflé, or gorgeous mixed baskets of Viennoiserie pastries, plus a full English (£16.50) or a classic Viennese breakfast (£11.50), with smoked ham, salami, artisan Gouda, boiled egg, and pretzel. ✉ *55 Aldwych, Haymarket* ☎ *020/7499–8558* ⊕ *www. thedelaunay.com* ⬟ *Reservations essential* Ⓜ *Holborn, Covent Garden, Charring Cross.*

Dishoom. Indian curry addicts dart into this all-day Bombay-style street-food canteen off Covent Garden for a "Big Bombay" breakfast (£11.50) of Parsi *Akuri* scrambled eggs, Shropshire pork sausages, masala baked beans, and buttered *pau* buns. There's green chili–spiced omelet, "fire toast," milky hot *chai* tea, plus tomato chili jam–spiked smoked bacon *naan* rolls. ✉ *12 Upper St. Martin's La., Covent Garden* ☎ *020/7420–9320* ⊕ *www.dishoom. com* Ⓜ *Leicester Sq.*

Duck & Waffle. Clubbers and night-shift medics are bowled over by the stupendous 40th-floor panoramas and Dan Doherty's cult munchies-style breakfast combos at this 24-hour (and London's highest) restaurant at the Heron Tower. Try Belgium waffles with fried egg, confit duck, and mustard maple syrup, or head for an ox cheek Benedict or full English breakfast with duroc bacon, black pudding, sourdough toast, and hash browns. ✉ *Heron Tower, 110 Bishopsgate, The City* ☎ *020/7222–2555* ⊕ *duckandwaffle.com* Ⓜ *Liverpool St.*

Fischer's. Marylebone's enjoy impeccable service and hearty Austrian of paprika-fried potatoes and onions, bacon, and fried hen's egg at this turn-of-the-20th-century Viennese-style high-gloss neighborhood café. There's also prunes, and ginger, and potatoes with black pudding and Asbach sauce. ✉ *50 Marylebone High St., Marylebone* ☎ *020/7466–5501* ⊕ *www.fischers. co.uk* Ⓜ *Bond St.*

The Wolseley. Mayfair's head honchos dive into kedgeree, haggis with fried duck eggs, and deviled lambs kidneys with bacon at this Austro-Hungarian grand café on Piccadilly. Full English breakfasts are complemented by Cumberland sausage sandwiches, smoked salmon bagels, French toast, and Croque Madame. ✉ *160 Piccadilly, St. James's* ☎ *020/7499–6996* ⊕ *www. thewolseley* Ⓜ *Green Park.*

14

is becoming more and more West End in style and substance by the day. One fanatical locavore maverick stands out: the bearded Mikael Jonsson, a self-taught Swedish obsessive genius, who knows his wild scallops from his foraged blueberries, and produces six- and seven-course seasonal tasting menus of staggering class and brilliance.

CHISWICK

$$$

MODERN
EUROPEAN

✕**Hedone.** Only a loony or genius would serve an appetizer of half a Cévennes onion with a few pear shavings and *beurre blanc*, but luckily maverick Swedish chef Mikael Jonsson falls triumphantly in the latter camp at his wild foodie haven in outlying Chiswick. A former lawyer and food blogger, Jonsson's *obsessive* approach to the provenance of his largely British-sourced ingredients—often rare, wild, or foraged— means that his dishes are some of the most intense and vivid around. Sit up on stools and watch Jonsson in an open kitchen prepare ingredient-driven marvels like wild Dorset sea bass with pickled black radishes and hyssop oil, hand-caught Devon scallops with a strikingly stuffed zucchini flower, or gloriously marbled 55-day-aged Darragh O'Shea Black Angus beef on the bone with juniper-smoked potatoes. Jonsson's spelt sourdough is extraordinary, and, for afters, a Cox-and-cobnut tart or English blueberries with rosemary sorbet are as pure and vital as the mains. Book far in advance. ⑤ *Average main: £27* ✉ *301–303 Chiswick High Rd., Chiswick* ☎ *020/8747–0377* ⊕ *www.hedonerestaurant.com* ☾ *Closed Sun. and Mon. No lunch Mon.–Wed.* ⬥ *Reservations essential* Ⓜ *Chiswick Park* ✛ *1:A2.*

LONDON DINING AND LODGING ATLAS

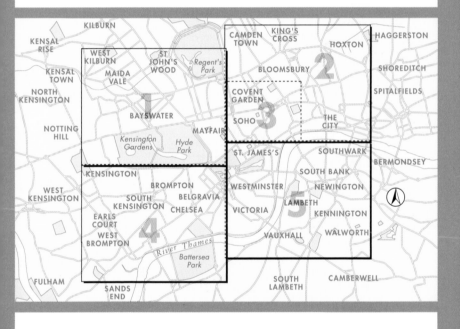

KEY

☐ Hotels
■ Restaurants
◪ Restaurant in Hotel
Ⓤ **WESTMINSTER**
⎿ Station
London Underground

⇄ National Rail Connection

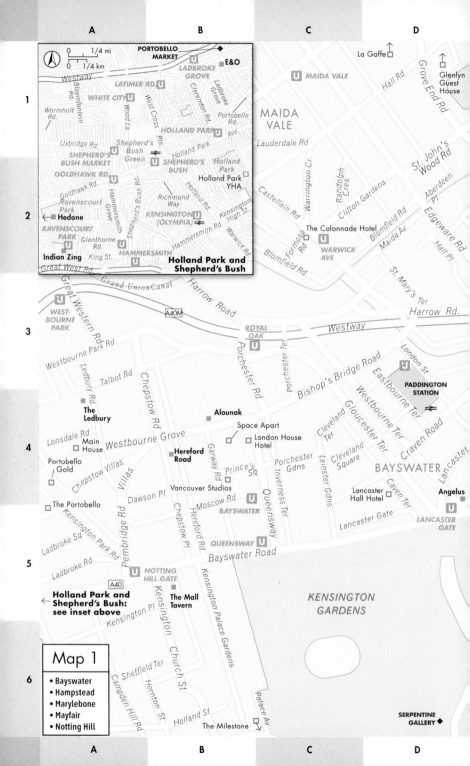

PORTOBELLO MARKET ◆ E&O

LADBROKE GROVE

LATIMER RD. Ⓤ

WHITE CITY Ⓤ

Wormholt Rd.

Westway

Bloemfontein Rd.

West Cross Rte.

Wood La.

Clarendon Rd.

Ladbroke Grove

Portobello Rd. Ave.

HOLLAND PARK Ⓤ

Uxbridge Rd.

SHEPHERD'S BUSH MARKET Ⓤ

GOLDHAWK RD. Ⓤ

Goldhawk Rd.

Ravenscourt Park

Hammersmith Grove

Shepherd's Bush Green Ⓤ

SHEPHERD'S BUSH

Holland Park

Richmond Way

Holland Park YHA

Holland Rd.

Kensington High St.

RAVENSCOURT PARK

Hedone ←🚊

Glenthorne Rd.

Indian Zing ■

Shepherd's Bush Rd.

HAMMERSMITH Ⓤ

King St.

Hammersmith Rd.

KENSINGTON (OLYMPIA) Ⓤ🚊

Warwick Rd.

Great West Rd.

Holland Park and Shepherd's Bush

0 ___ 1/4 mi
0 ___ 1/4 km

La Gaffe 🏠

Glenlyn Guest House

Grove End Rd.

Hall Rd.

MAIDA VALE Ⓤ

MAIDA VALE

St. John's Wood Rd.

Lauderdale Rd

Aberdeen Pl.

Edgware Rd.

Hall Pl.

Castellain Rd

Warrington Cr.

Randolph Cres.

Clifton Gardens

Blomfield Rd

Maida Av

The Colonnade Hotel 🏠

WARWICK AVE Ⓤ

Formosa Rd.

Blomfield Rd.

St. Mary's Ter.

Great Western Rd

Grand Union Canal

Harrow Road

Harrow Rd.

Westway

WEST-BOURNE PARK Ⓤ

Westbourne Park Rd.

Porchester Rd.

ROYAL OAK Ⓤ

A40M

Porchester Ter.

Bishop's Bridge Road

London St.

PADDINGTON STATION 🚂

Westbourne Park Rd.

Talbot Rd.

Ledbury Rd.

Chepstow Rd.

The Ledbury ■

Alounak ■

Space Apart

London House Hotel

Cleveland Ter.

Gloucester Ter.

Eastbourne Ter.

Westbourne Ter.

Craven Road

Lonsdale Rd

Main House 🏠

Westbourne Grove

Hereford Road ■

Garway Rd.

Prince's Sq.

Porchester Gdns

Leinster Gdns

Cleveland Square

BAYSWATER

Lancaster

Portobello Gold 🏠

Chepstow Villas

Dawson Pl.

Vancouver Studios

Moscow Rd.

Inverness Ter.

Lancaster Hall Hotel 🏠

Caven Ter.

Angelus ■

The Portobello 🏠

Pembridge Rd.

Chepstow Pl.

Hereford Rd.

BAYSWATER Ⓤ

Queensway

Lancaster Gate

LANCASTER GATE

Kensington Park Rd.

Ladbroke Sq.

QUEENSWAY Ⓤ

Ladbroke Rd.

Holland Park and Shepherd's Bush: see inset above ←

A40

NOTTING HILL GATE Ⓤ

Bayswater Road

Kensington Palace Gardens

Kensington Pl.

The Mall Tavern ■

Church St.

KENSINGTON GARDENS

Sheffield Ter.

Hornton St.

Campden Hill Rd.

Holland St.

Palace Av

The Milestone 🏠

SERPENTINE GALLERY ◆

Map 1

• Bayswater
• Hampstead
• Marylebone
• Mayfair
• Notting Hill

A   B   C   D

1   2   3   4   5   6

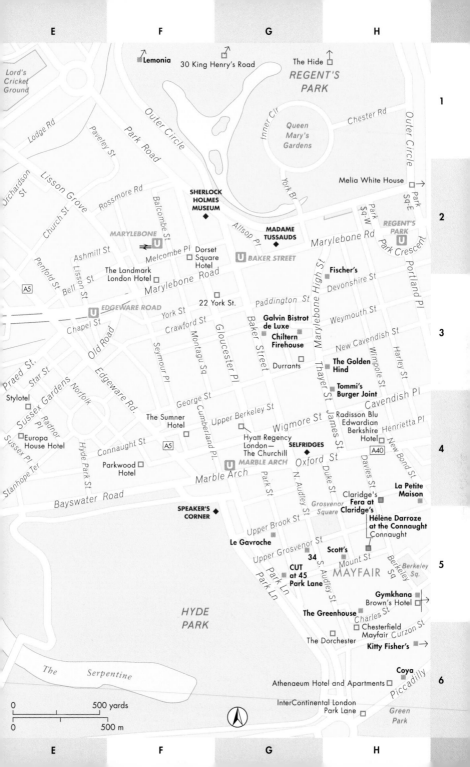

E   **F**   **G**   **H**

Lord's
Cricket
Ground

1

Lemonia

30 King Henry's Road

The Hide

REGENT'S
PARK

Outer Circle

Park Road

Paveley St

Lodge Rd

Lisson Grove

Chester Rd

Inner Cir

Queen
Mary's
Gardens

Outer Circle

York Br

Richardson St

Church St

Rossmore Rd

Batcombe St

Melia White House

Park Sq-E

2

REGENT'S
PARK

SHERLOCK
HOLMES
MUSEUM

Park Sq-W

Park Crescent

MARYLEBONE

Allsop Pl

MADAME
TUSSAUDS

Marylebone Rd

REGENT'S
PARK

Pentold St

Lisson St

Bell St

Ashmill St

Dorset
Square
Hotel

Melcombe Pl

BAKER STREET

Marylebone Rd

Fischer's

Portland Pl

The Landmark
London Hotel

Marylebone Road

Devonshire St

Marylebone High St

A5

22 York St.

Paddington St

Weymouth St

3

EDGEWARE ROAD

Chapel St

Old Road

York St

Crawford St

Seymour Pl

Montagu Sq

Gloucester Pl

Baker Street

Galvin Bistrot
de Luxe

Chiltern
Firehouse

Durrants

New Cavendish St

The Golden
Hind

Thayer St

Wimpole St

Harley St

Tommi's
Burger Joint

Cavendish Pl

Praed St.

Star St

Sussex Gardens

Norfolk

Edgeware Rd.

George St.

Cumberland Pl

Upper Berkeley St

Wigmore St

James St

Radisson Blu
Edwardian
Berkshire
Hotel

Henrietta Pl

New Bond St

4

Stylotel

Radnor
Pl

Sussex Pl

Europa
House Hotel

Hyde Park St

Connaught St

A5

The Sumner
Hotel

Hyatt Regency
London—
The Churchill

MARBLE ARCH

SELFRIDGES

Oxford St

Duke St

Davies St

A40

Stanhope Ter

Parkwood
Hotel

Marble Arch

Park St

N. Audley St

La Petite
Maison

Bayswater Road

SPEAKER'S
CORNER

Claridge's
Fera at
Claridge's

Grosvenor
Square

Hélène Darroze
at the Connaught
Connaught

5

Upper Brook St

Le Gavroche

Upper Grosvenor St

34

Scott's

S. Audley St

Mount St

MAYFAIR

Berkeley
Sq.

HYDE
PARK

CUT
at 45
Park Lane

Park Ln

Park Ln

Gymkhana

Brown's Hotel

The Greenhouse

Charles St

Chesterfield
Mayfair

Curzon St

Kitty Fisher's

The Dorchester

The
Serpentine

Coya

Athenaeum Hotel and Apartments

Piccadilly

6

InterContinental London
Park Lane

Green
Park

0   500 yards

0   500 m

E   **F**   **G**   **H**

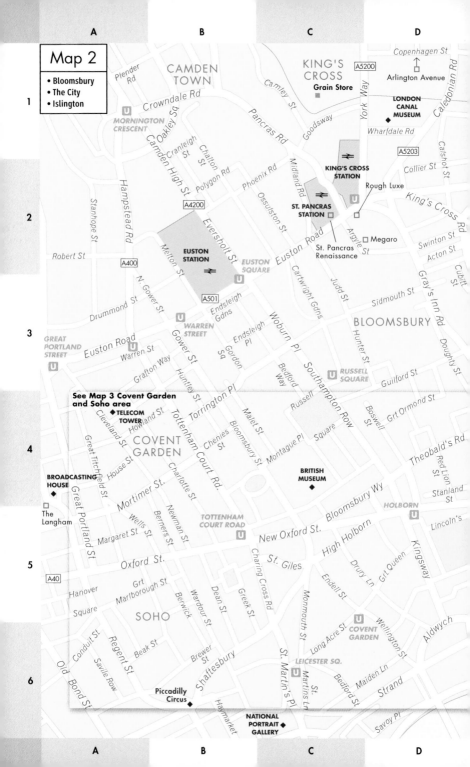

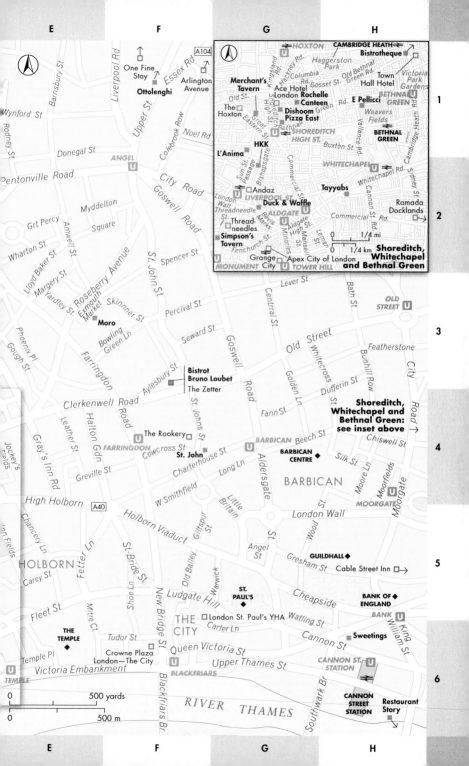

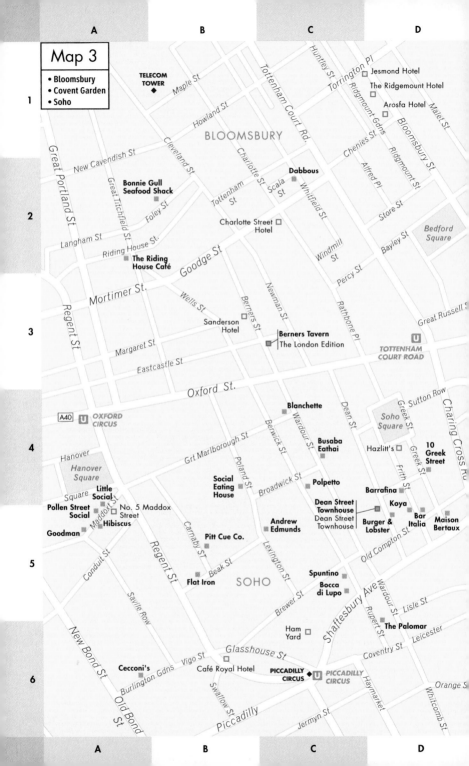

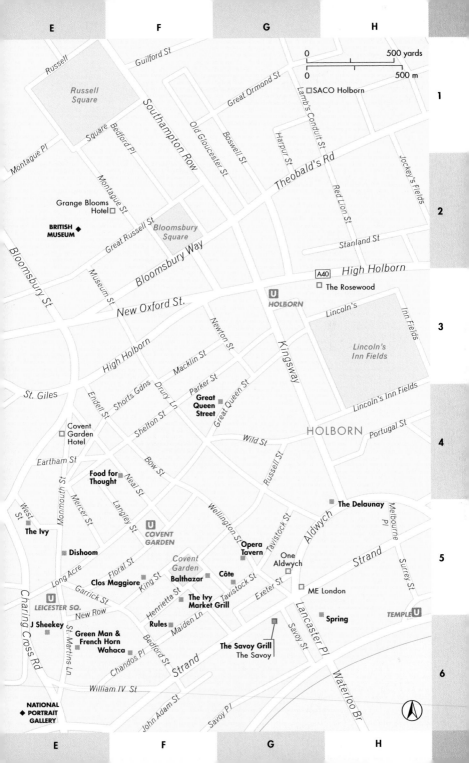

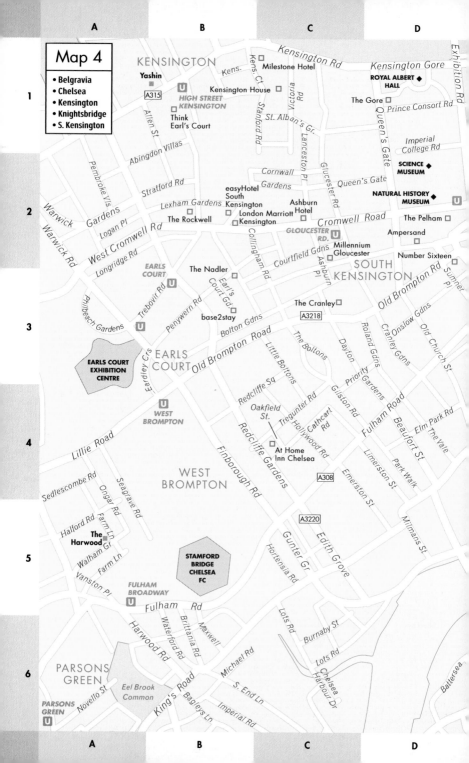

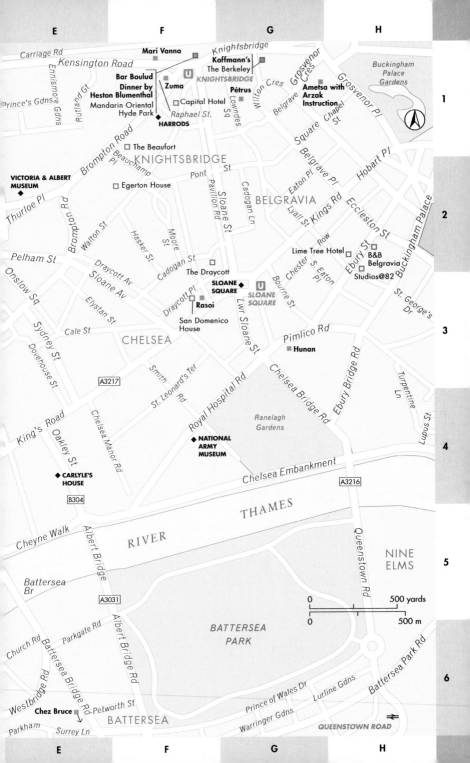

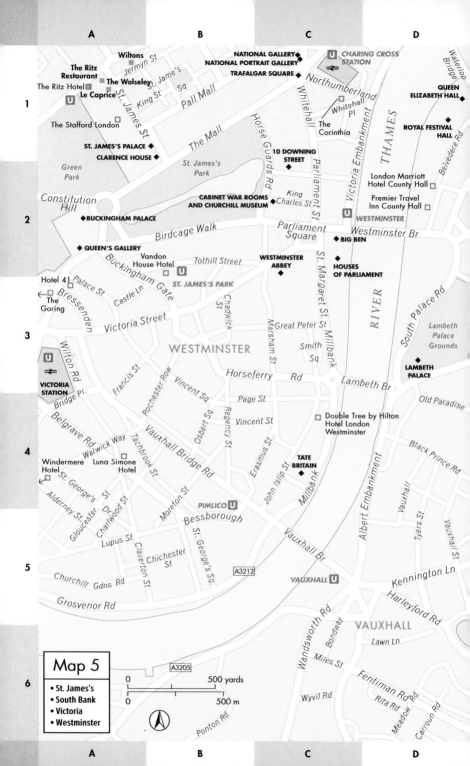

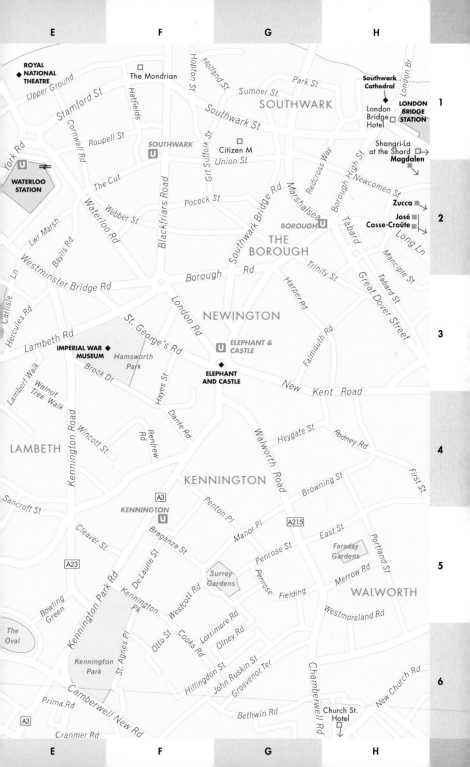

Dining
10 Greek Street, 3:D4
34, 1:G5
Alounak, 1:B4
Ametsa with Arzak Instruction, 4:G1
Andrew Edmunds, 3:C5
Angelus, 1:D4
Balthazar, 3:F5
Bar Boulud, 4:F1
Bar Italia, 3:D5
Barrafina, 3:D4
Berners Tavern, 3:C3
Bistrot Bruno Loubet, 2:F3
Bistrotheque, 2:H1
Blanchette, 3:C4
Bocca di Lupo, 3:C5
Bonnie Gull Seafood Shack, 3:B2
Burger & Lobster, 3:D5
Busaba Eathai, 3:C4
Casse-Croûte, 5:H2
Cecconi's, 3:A6
Chez Bruce, 4:E6
Chilten Firehouse, 1:G3
Clos Maggiore, 3:F5
Côte, 3:G5
Coya, 1:H6
CUT at 45 Park Lane, 1:G5
Dabbous, 3:C2
Dean Street Townhouse, 3:D5
The Delaunay, 3:G4
Dinner by Heston Blumenthal, 4:F1
Dishoom, 2:G1, 3:E5
Duck & Waffle, 2:G2
E Pellicci, 2:H1
E&O, 1:B1
Fera at Claridge's, 1:H4
Fischer's, 1:H3
Flat Iron, 3:B5
Food for Thought, 3:F4
Galvin Bistrot de Luxe, 1:G3
The Golden Hind, 1:H3
Goodman, 3:A5
Grain Store, 2:C1
Great Queen Street, 3:G4
The Greenhouse, 1:H5
Gymkhana, 1:H5
The Harwood, 4:A5
Hedone, 1:A2
Hélène Darroze at the Connaught, 1:H5
Hereford Road, 1:B4
Hibiscus, 3:A5

HKK, 2:G2
Hunan, 4:G3
Indian Zing, 1:A2
The Ivy, 3:E5
Ivy Market Grill, 3:F5
J Sheekey, 3:E6
José, 5:H2
Kitty Fisher's, 1:H6
Koffmann's, 4:G1
Koya, 3:D5
L'Anima, 2:G1
La Petite Maison, 1:H4
Le Caprice, 5:A1
Le Gavroche, 1:G5
The Ledbury, 1:A4
Lemonia, 1:F1
Little Social, 3:A4
Magdalen, 5:H2
Maison Bertaux, 3:D5
The Mall Tavern, 1:B5
Mari Vanna, 4:F1
Merchants Tavern, 2:G1
Moro, 2:E3
Opera Tavern, 3:G5
Ottolenghi, 2:F1
Palomar, 3:D6
Petrus, 4:G1
Pitt Cue Co, 3:B5
Pizza East, 2:G1
Pollen Street Social, 3:A5
Polpetto, 3:C4
Rasoi, 4:F3
Restaurant Story, 2:H6
The Riding House Café, 3:A2
The Ritz Restaurant, 5:A1
Rochelle Canteen, 2:G1
Rules, 3:F6
St. John, 2:F4
The Savoy Grill, 3:G6
Scott's, 1:H5
Social Eating House, 3:B4
Spring, 3:G6
Spuntino, 3:C5
Sweetings, 2:H6
Tayyabs, 2:H2
Tommi's Burger Joint, 1:H3
Wahaca, 3:F6
Wiltons, 5:A1
The Wolseley, 5:A1
Yashin, 4:B1
Zucca, 5:H2
Zuma, 4:F1

Lodging
22 York Street, 1:G3
30 King Henry's Road, 1:G1
Ace Hotel London, 2:G1
Ampersand, 4:D2
Andaz, 2:G2
Apex City of London, 2:G2
Arlington Avenue, 2:D1
Arosfa, 3:D1
Ashburn Hotel, 4:C2
Athenaeum Hotel and Apartments, 1:H6
B&B Belgravia, 4:H2
The Beaufort, 4:F1
The Berkeley, 4:G1
Brown's Hotel, 1:H5
Cable Street Inn, 2:H5
The Capital Hotel, 4:F1
Charlotte Street Hotel, 3:C2
Chesterfield Mayfair Hotel, 1:H6
Church Street Hotel, 5:H6
CitizenM London Bankside, 5:G1
Claridge's, 1:H4
Colonnade, 1:C2
The Connaught, 1:H5
The Corinthia, 5:C1
Covent Garden Hotel, 3:E4
The Cranley Hotel, 4:C2
Crowne Plaza London—The City, 2:F6
Dean Street Townhouse, 3:D5
The Dorchester, 1:H6
Dorset Square Hotel, 1:F2
DoubleTree by Hilton Hotel London Westminster, 5:C4
The Draycott, 4:F2
easyHotel South Kensington, 4:B2
Egerton House, 4:F2
Glenlyn Guest House, 1:D1
The Gore Hotel, 4:D1
The Goring, 5:A3
Grange Blooms Hotel, 3:F2
Grange City Hotel, 2:G2
Ham Yard Hotel, 3:C6
Hazlitt's, 3:D4
The Hide, 1:H1
Hotel 41, 5:A3
The Hoxton Hotel, 2:G1

Hyatt Regency London—The Churchill, 1:G4
InterContinental London Park Lane, 1:H6
Jesmond Hotel, 3:C1
La Gaffe, 1:D1
Lancaster Hall Hotel, 1:D4
The Langham, 2:A4
Lime Tree Hotel, 4:H2
London Bridge Hotel, 5:H1
The London Edition, 3:C3
London House Hotel, 1:B4
London Marriott Hotel County Hall, 5:D2
London Marriott Kensington, 4:B2
The Luna Simone Hotel, 5:A4
The Main House, 1:A4
Mandarin Oriental Hyde Park, 4:F1
Meliá White House, 1:H2
ME London, 3:G5
The Megaro, 2:C2
Millennium Gloucester, 4:C2
The Millstone Hotel, 4:C1
The Mondrian, 5:F1
The Nadler, 4:B3
No. 5 Maddox Street, 3:A5
Number Sixteen, 4:D2
One Aldwych, 3:G5
Parkwood Hotel, 1:F4
The Pelham Hotel, 4:D2
Portobello Gold, 1:A4
The Portobello Hotel, 1:A5
Premier Travel Inn County Hall, 5:D2
Radisson Blu Edwardian Berkshire Hotel, 1:H4
The Ridgemount Hotel, 3:D1
The Ritz, 5:A1
The Rockwell, 4:B2
The Rookery, 2:F4
Rough Luxe, 2:C2
SACO Holborn, 3:G1
St. Pancras Renaissance, 2:C2
Sanderson Hotel, 3:B3
San Domenico House, 4:F3
The Savoy, 3:G5
The Shangri-La Hotel, at The Shard, 5:H1
Space Apart Hotel, 1:B4

The Stafford London, 5:A1
Studios@82, 4:H2
The Sumner, 1:F4
Threadneedles Hotel, 2:G2
Town Hall Hotel and Apartments, 2:H1
Vancouver Studios, 1:B4
Windermere Hotel, 5:A4
The Zetter, 2:F3

WHERE TO STAY

Updated By
Jack Jewers

Queen Elizabeth hasn't invited you this time? No matter. Staying at one of London's grande-dame hotels is the next-best thing to being a guest at the palace—and some say it's even better. Happily, however, there is no dearth of options where friendliness outdistances luxe—London, thank goodness, has plenty of atmospheric places that won't cost a king's ransom.

That noted, until fairly recently it was extremely difficult to find a decent hotel in the center for less than £150 per night. Things have improved somewhat in recent years, but this is still one of the world's most expensive cities to visit. Still, thanks in part to the global recession, London is slowly amassing new mid-price hotels. You'll still have to look pretty hard to find the real bargains—and the "old London" tourist traps of horrible, badly maintained, and overpriced places to stay are still out there—but things are definitely improving. There are some beautiful historic and unique places to stay here without breaking the bank. Just . . . not all that many.

It's all so different if money is no object. At the top end, London has some of the very best and most luxurious hotels in the world. Freshly minted billionaires favor the rash of new hot spots, like the Corinthia or ME London, while fashion plates always book Kit Kemp's superstylish hotels (such as the Covent Garden and the Charlotte Street). But even these places have sales, and you can sometimes snag a bargain within the reach of ordinary mortals—particularly in the off-season—or just be a spectator to all the glamour by visiting for that most traditional of high-society treats, afternoon tea.

Meanwhile, several mid-range hotels have dropped their average prices in response to the choppy waters of the global economy, which has pulled some fantastic places, such as Hazlitt's, the Rookery, and Town Hall, back into the affordable category. And there's a clutch of new, stylish, and supercheap hotels that are a real step forward for the city. The downside is that these places tend to be a little out of the way, but that's often a price worth paying. Another attractive alternative includes hotels in the Premier and Millennium chains, which offer fairly basic but modern rooms, lots of up-to-date conveniences, and sales that frequently bring room prices well below £100 a night.

At the budget level, London has also come a long way in the last couple of years, albeit with a catch: to find a good, reasonably priced B&B, you must be prepared to look outside the very center of London. This means that you have to subtract the city's notoriously high transport costs from any savings—but on the plus side, the Tube can shuttle you out to even some far-flung suburbs in less than 20 minutes. Prepare to be just a little adventurous with your London base and you will be rewarded by a scattering of unique and interesting bed-and-breakfasts, in the kinds of neighborhoods real Londoners live in—places like 30 King Henry's Road, the Cable Street Inn, and the Church Street Hotel. And if you're willing to fend for yourself, the city has some great rental options, too.

But if you are interested in luxury, London is just the place. Although the image we love to harbor about Olde London Towne may be fast fading in the light of today's glittering city, when it comes time to rest your head, the old-fashioned clichés remain enticing. Choose one of London's heritage-rich hotels—Claridge's perfect parlors; the Savoy's ultimate river view—and these fantasies can, and always will, be fulfilled.

15

PLANNING

LODGING STRATEGY

Where should you stay? With hundreds of London hotels, it may seem like a daunting question. But it doesn't have to be. *The 130-plus selections here represent the best this city has to offer—from the most-for-your-money budget B&Bs to the sleekest designer hotels. Scan "Best Bets" on the following pages for top recommendations by price and experience. Or look through the reviews. To find one quickly, search by neighborhood, then alphabetically. Happy hunting!*

NEED A RESERVATION?

Yes, hotel reservations are an absolute necessity when planning your trip to London, so book your room as far in advance as possible. The further in advance you can book, the better the deal you're likely to get. Just watch out if you change your mind—cancellation fees can be hefty. On the other hand, it is possible to find some amazing last-minute deals at mid- to high-range places, but this is a real gamble, as you could just as easily end up paying full rate. Fierce competition means properties undergo frequent improvements, so when booking inquire about any ongoing renovations that may interrupt your stay.

CHECKING IN

Typical check-in and checkout times are 2 pm and 11 am, respectively. Many flights from North America arrive early in the morning, but having to wait six hours for a room after arriving jet-lagged at 8 am isn't the ideal way to start a vacation. Alert the hotel of your early arrival; large hotels can often make special early check-in arrangements, but almost all will look after your luggage in the meantime. Be prepared to drop your bags and strike out for a few hours. On the plus side, this can effectively give you a whole extra day for sightseeing.

HOTEL QUALITY

Note that rooms can vary considerably in a single hotel. If you don't like the room you're given, ask to see another. Hotels often renovate room by room—you might find yourself allocated a dark, unrenovated room, whereas a bright, newly decorated room awaits just down the hall. Be prepared for the fact that, while smoking is now banned in public areas, this doesn't apply to hotel rooms—so be firm and ask to change if you're given a smoking room and didn't request one.

BREAKFAST

Some hotels include breakfast in the price of the room. It ranges from a gourmet spread to what is known as the "full English" (one fried egg, two "bangers"—that's English-style sausage links—two thick slices of bacon, a grilled tomato, sautéed mushrooms or baked beans, and toast). In many budget hotels and B&Bs, this is the only hot breakfast available. Most expensive hotels (and the most imaginative small ones) may also offer pancakes, French toast, waffles, and omelets. Luckily, virtually all accommodations also offer packaged cereals, muffins, yogurt, and fresh fruit, so when the sausage-and-bacon brigade begins to get you down, go continental.

FACILITIES

Keep in mind that some facilities come with the room rate while others cost extra. So, when pricing accommodations, always ask what's included. Modern hotels usually have air-conditioning, but B&Bs and hotels in older buildings often do not, and it is generally not the norm in London. Wi-Fi is common, but don't assume it's free (large hotels in particular can charge outrageous fees). If you want a double room, specify whether you want a double bed or a twin (two single beds next to each other). *All hotels listed here have private bathrooms unless otherwise noted.*

PRICES

If you're planning to visit in the fall, winter, or early spring, start monitoring bargain online prices a few months before your trip and book whenever you see a good rate. Chains such as Hilton, Premier, and Millennium are known for their low-season sales in which prices can be as little as half the normal rate. Business-oriented hotels frequently have lower rates on weekends.

The exchange rate between the pound and the dollar is also unpredictable, so if it's looking good when you book, an advance-payment deal could end up saving you a decent amount of money. ■ TIP→ **The Visit London Accommodation Booking Service (020/7932–2020, www.visitlondon.com) offers a best-price guarantee. Also try the clearinghouse websites Late Rooms (www.laterooms.com), Booking (www.booking.com), and Last Minute (www.lastminute.com).**

WHAT IT COSTS IN POUNDS				
	$	$$	$$$	$$$$
Hotels	under £116	£116–£200	£201–£300	over £300

Prices are for two people in a standard double room in high season.

HOTEL REVIEWS

Listed alphabetically by neighborhood. Use the coordinate (1:B2) at the end of each listing to locate a site on the corresponding map. To locate the property on a map, turn to the London Dining and Lodging Atlas at the end of the Where to Eat chapter. The first number after the symbol indicates the map number. Following that is the property's coordinate on the map grid.

Hotel reviews have been shortened. For full information, visit Fodors. com.

15

WESTMINSTER, ST. JAMES'S, AND ROYAL LONDON

WESTMINSTER

$$$$
HOTEL
Fodor's Choice
★
The Corinthia. The London outpost of the exclusive Corinthia chain is design heaven-on-earth, with levels of service that make anyone feel like a VIP. **Pros:** so much luxury and elegance you'll feel like royalty. **Cons:** prices jump to the stratosphere once the cheapest rooms sell out. $ *Rooms from: £426* ⊠ *Whitehall Pl., Westminster* ☎ *020/7930–8181* ⊕ *www.corinthia.com* ➴ *294 rooms* ⊙| *Breakfast* Ⓜ *Embankment* ✚ *5:C1.*

$$$
HOTEL
FAMILY
DoubleTree by Hilton Hotel London Westminster. Spectacular views of the river, Big Ben, and the London Eye fill the floor-to-ceiling windows in this rather stark, steel-and-glass building steps from the Tate Britain, and a plethora of techy perks await inside. **Pros:** amazing views; flat screens and other high-tech gadgetry. **Cons:** small bedrooms; tiny bathrooms; TV has to be operated through a computer (confusing if you're not used to it). $ *Rooms from:* ⊠ *30 John Islip St., Westminster* ☎ *020/7630–1000* ⊕ *www.doubletreewestminsterhotel.com* ➴ *444 rooms, 16 suites* ⊙| *Some meals* Ⓜ *Westminster, Pimlico* ✚ *5:C4.*

$$$$
HOTEL
The Goring. With Buckingham Palace just around the corner, this hotel, built in 1910 and now run by third-generation Gorings, has always been a favorite among discreet VIPs—including Kate Middleton's family on the night before her marriage to Prince William in 2011. **Pros:** elegant, spacious rooms; overlooks Buckingham Palace; great attention to detail. **Cons:** price is still too high for what you get; interiors a bit fussy. $ *Rooms from: £315* ⊠ *15 Beeston Pl., Grosvenor Gardens, Victoria* ☎ *020/7396–9000* ⊕ *www.thegoring.com* ➴ *69 rooms, 6 suites* ⊙| *Some meals* Ⓜ *Victoria* ✚ *5:A3.*

$$$$
HOTEL
Fodor's Choice
★
Hotel 41. Faultless service; sumptuous designer furnishings and a sense of fun to boot—this impeccable hotel breathes new life into the cliche "thinks of everything." Yet the epithet is really quite apt. **Pros:** impeccable service; beautiful and stylish; Buckingham Palace is on

WHERE SHOULD I STAY?

	Neighborhood Vibe	Pros	Cons
Westminster, St. James's, and Royal London	This historic section is home to major tourist attractions like Buckingham Palace.	Central area near tourist sites; easy Tube access; considered a safe area to stay.	Mostly expensive lodging options; few good restaurants and entertainment venues nearby.
Mayfair and Marylebone	Traditional, old money; a mixture of the business and financial set with fashionable shops.	In the heart of the action; some of London's best hotels are found here.	Pricey part of town; the city-that-never-sleeps buzz makes peace and quiet hard to come by.
Soho and Covent Garden	A tourist hub with endless entertainment—this is party central for young adults.	Buzzing area with plenty to see and do; late-night entertainment abounds; wonderful shopping district.	Perhaps London's busiest (and noisiest) district after dark; few budget hotels.
Bloomsbury and Holborn	Diverse area that is part bustling business center and part tranquil respite with tree-lined streets and parks.	Easy access to Tube, and 15 minutes to city center; major sights, like British Museum in Bloomsbury.	Holborn has busy and noisy streets; the area around King's Cross can be sketchy—particularly at night.
The City	London's financial district, where most of the city's banks and businesses are headquartered.	Extremely central with easy transportation access and great hotel deals.	The City can be as quiet as a tomb at weekends—even the pubs close.
East London	Increasingly trendy area east of the city center, with a great arts scene.	Great for art lovers, shoppers, and business execs with meetings in Canary Wharf.	Still a transitional area; parts of Hoxton can be a bit dodgy at night; 20-minute Tube ride from central London.
South of the Thames	South of the river is a vibrant cultural hub, centered on the South Bank, the Globe, and the Royal National Theatre.	South of the river is London's unofficial cultural quarter, and walking distance from the West End theaters.	You don't have to go very far from the South Bank before you hit some of London's dodgiest neighborhoods.
Kensington, Chelsea, Knightsbridge, and Belgravia	These are some of London's most upscale neighborhoods and a hub of London's tourist universe.	Diverse hotel selection; great area for meandering urban walks; London's capital of high-end shopping.	Depending on where you are, the nearest Tube might be a hike; residential area might be too quiet for some.
Notting Hill and Bayswater	This is an upscale, trendy area favored by locals, with plenty of good hotels.	Hotel deals abound if you know where to look; gorgeous greenery in Hyde Park.	Choose the wrong place and you may end up in a flea pit; residential area may be quiet.
Regent's Park and Hampstead	A mix of arty, fashionable districts with a villagelike feel in other places.	Some of London's most fashionable neighborhoods; easy to fall in love with.	Some distance from center; lack of hotel options.

BEST BETS FOR LONDON LODGING

Fodor's offers a selective listing of high-quality lodging experiences at every price range, from the city's best budget motel to its most sophisticated luxury hotel. Here, we've compiled our top recommendations by price and experience. The very best properties—in other words, those that provide a particularly remarkable experience in their price range—are designated in the listings with the Fodor's Choice logo.

Fodor's Choice ★

30 King Henry's Road, $$
Cable Street Inn, $
Charlotte Street Hotel, $$$$
Church Street Hotel, $
Claridge's, $$$$
The Connaught, $$$$
The Corinthia, $$$$
Covent Garden Hotel, $$$$
Dean Street Townhouse, $$$
Dorset Square Hotel, $$$
The Draycott, $$
Ham Yard Hotel, $$$$
The Hide, $
Hotel 41, $$$$
The Hoxton Hotel, $
The Langham, $$$$
The London Edition, $$$$
The Main House, $
Mandarin Oriental Hyde Park, $$$$

ME London, $$$$
The Milestone Hotel, $$$$
The Mondrian, $$$
The Rookery, $$
San Domenico House, $$$
The Savoy, $$$$
The Shangri-La Hotel of the Shards, $$$$
The Stafford London, $$$$
St. Pancras Renaissance, $$$
The Zetter, $$$

Best by Price

$

Arlington Avenue
At Home Inn Chelsea
Cable Street Inn
Church Street Hotel
CitizenM London Bankside
The Hide
The Hoxton Hotel

London House Hotel
The Rockwell
The Sanctuary House Hotel

$$

Ashburn Hotel
King Henry's Road
The Luna Simone Hotel
The Rookery

$$$

Athenaeum Hotel and Apartments
The Cadogan
Egerton House
Number Sixteen
St. Pancras Renaissance

$$$$

The Berkeley
Claridge's
The Connaught
The Corinthia
Covent Garden Hotel
The Dorchester

Ham Yard Hotel
The Langham
The Savoy

Best by Experience

BUSINESS TRAVELERS

Crowne Plaza London–The City, $$
Grange City Hotel, $
Threadneedles Hotel, $$
The Zetter, $$$

HISTORIC HOTELS

Claridge's, $$$$
The Dorchester, $$$$
The Langham, $$$$
The Rookery, $$
The Savoy, $$$$
St. Pancras Renaissance, $$$$

MOST KID-FRIENDLY

DoubleTree by Hilton Hotel London Westminster, $$$
No. 5 Maddox Street, $$$
Premier Travel Inn County Hall, $

15

your doorstep. **Cons:** unusual design is not for everyone. ⑤ *Rooms from:* ✉ *41 Buckingham Palace Rd., Victoria* ☎ *020/7300–0041* ⊕ *www.41hotel.com* ⟿ *26 rooms, 4 suites, 2 apartments* ◯| *Breakfast* Ⓜ *Victoria* ✛ *5:A3.*

$$
HOTEL
⌂ **Lime Tree Hotel.** In a central neighborhood where hotels veer from wildly overpriced at one extreme to grimy boltholes at the other, the Lime Tree gets the boutique style just about right—and at a surprisingly reasonable cost for the neighborhood. **Pros:** lovely and helpful hosts; great location; rooms are decent size. **Cons:** cheaper rooms are small; some are up several flights of stairs and there's no elevator; two-night minimum on weekends. ⑤ *Rooms from: £165* ✉ *135–137 Ebury St., Victoria* ☎ *020/7730–8191* ⊕ *www.limetreehotel.co.uk* ⟿ *25 rooms* ◯| *Breakfast* Ⓜ *Victoria, Sloane Sq.* ✛ *4:H2.*

$$$
HOTEL
Fodors Choice
★
⌂ **San Domenico House.** Discreet, beautiful, and exceptionally well run, this converted Chelsea town house makes for a restful hideaway. **Pros:** unique and beautiful design; great neighborhood, with the King's Road and Saatchi Gallery a short walk away; exceptional service. **Cons:** no bar or restaurant; not even including a basic breakfast for the (pretty expensive) cheapest rates is cheeky. ⑤ *Rooms from: £264* ✉ *29-31 Draycott Pl.* ☎ *020/7581–5757* ⊕ *www.sandomenicohouse.com* ⟿ *12 rooms, 5 suites* ◯| *Breakfast* Ⓜ *Sloane Sq.* ✛ *4:F3.*

$$
HOTEL
⌂ **Windermere Hotel.** This sweet and rather elegant old hotel, on the premises of London's first B&B (in 1881), is a decent, well-located option. **Pros:** good location close to Victoria Station; free Wi-Fi; good amenities for an old hotel of this size, including air-conditioning and an elevator. **Cons:** rooms and bathrooms are tiny. ⑤ *Rooms from: £148* ✉ *142–144 Warwick Way, Victoria* ☎ *020/7834–5163* ⊕ *www.windermere-hotel.co.uk* ⟿ *19 rooms* ◯| *Breakfast* Ⓜ *Victoria* ✛ *5:A4.*

ST. JAMES'S

$$$$
HOTEL
⌂ **The Ritz.** Want to know if the *Downton Abbey*–style world of the old British upper class still exists? Then look no further than here—the Ritz is as synonymous with London's high society and superrich decadence today as it was in 1906. **Pros:** historic luxury hotel; service at every turn. **Cons:** snooty service; some rooms have views of a nearby wall; tediously old-fashioned dress code. ⑤ *Rooms from:* ✉ *150 Piccadilly, St. James's* ☎ *020/7493–8181* ⊕ *www.theritzlondon.com* ⟿ *136 rooms* ◯| *Some meals* Ⓜ *Piccadilly Circus* ✛ *5:A1.*

$$$$
HOTEL
Fodors Choice
★
⌂ **The Stafford London.** This is a rare find: a posh hotel that's equal parts elegance and friendliness, and located in one of the few peaceful spots in the area, down a small lane behind Piccadilly. **Pros:** great staff; big, luxurious rooms; quiet location. **Cons:** traditional style is not to all tastes; perks in the more expensive rooms could be more generous (free airport transfer, but only one-way, free clothes pressing, only one item per day). ⑤ *Rooms from: £365* ✉ *St. James's Pl., St. James's* ☎ *020/7493–0111* ⊕ *www.thestaffordlondon.com* ⟿ *81 rooms* ◯| *Breakfast* Ⓜ *Green Park* ✛ *5:A1.*

MAYFAIR AND MARYLEBONE

MAYFAIR

$$
B&B/INN
22 York Street. This Georgian town house has a cozy, family feel, with polished pine floors and fetching antiques decorating the homey, individually furnished guest rooms. **Pros:** good location for shoppers; friendly hosts; nicely flexible check-in times; entirely no-smoking. **Cons:** if you take away the great location, you're paying a lot for a B&B; not everyone enjoys socializing with strangers over breakfast. $ *Rooms from: £150 ⊠ 22 York St., Mayfair ☎ 020/7224–2990 ⊕ www.22yorkstreet. co.uk ➘ 10 rooms* ⦿ *Breakfast* Ⓜ *Baker St.* ✛ *1:G3.*

$$$
B&B/INN
Athenaeum Hotel and Apartments. This grand hotel overlooking Green Park offers plenty for the money: rooms are both comfortable and lavishly decorated, with deeply comfortable Hypnos beds, plasma-screen TVs, luxurious fabrics, and original contemporary artworks. **Pros:** peaceful park views; handy for Buckingham Palace and Piccadilly; great value for elegant setting. **Cons:** bathrooms are almost all small. $ *Rooms from: £287 ⊠ 116 Piccadilly, Mayfair ☎ 020/7499–3464 ⊕ www.athenaeumhotel.com ➘ 111 rooms, 46 suites and apartments* ⦿ *Breakfast* Ⓜ *Green Park* ✛ *1:H6.*

$$$$
HOTEL
Brown's Hotel. Founded in 1837 by James Brown, Lord Byron's "gentleman's gentleman," this hotel occupying 11 Georgian town houses holds a treasured place in London society. **Pros:** elegant spaces; attentive service; good afternoon tea. **Cons:** even the most basic room is very pricey. $ *Rooms from: £392 ⊠ 34 Albemarle St., Mayfair ☎ 020/7493–6020, 888/667–9477 in U.S. ⊕ www.roccofortehotels.com ➘ 88 rooms, 29 suites* ⦿ *Breakfast* Ⓜ *Green Park* ✛ *1:H5.*

$$$
HOTEL
Chesterfield Mayfair Hotel. Deep in the heart of Mayfair, the former town house of the Earl of Chesterfield welcomes guests in wood-and-leather public rooms that match the dark-wood furnishings in the bedrooms—small, but like fashion magazine spreads, with bold designer wallpaper or tones of fawn and gray. **Pros:** laid-back atmosphere; attentive service; great afternoon tea. **Cons:** prices rise sharply if you don't get the cheapest rooms; some rooms are tiny; restaurant is old-fashioned and very expensive. $ *Rooms from: £245 ⊠ 35 Charles St., Mayfair ☎ 020/7491–2622, 877/955–1515 in U.S. ⊕ www.chesterfieldmayfair. com ➘ 94 rooms, 13 suites* ⦿ *Breakfast* Ⓜ *Green Park* ✛ *1:A6.*

$$$$
HOTEL
FAMILY
Fodor's Choice
★
Claridge's. The well-heeled have been meeting—and eating—at Claridge's for generations, and the tradition continues in the original art deco public spaces of this super-glamorous London institution. **Pros:** see-and-be-seen dining and drinking; serious luxury everywhere—this is an old-money hotel; comics, books, and DVDs to help keep kids amused. **Cons:** better pack your designer wardrobe if you want to fit in with the locals. $ *Rooms from: £480 ⊠ Brook St., Mayfair ☎ 020/7629–8860, 866/599–6991 in U.S. ⊕ www.claridges.co.uk ➘ 136 rooms, 678 suites* ⦿ *Breakfast* Ⓜ *Bond St.* ✛ *1:H4.*

$$$$
HOTEL
FAMILY
Fodor's Choice
★
The Connaught. A huge favorite of the "we wouldn't dream of staying anywhere else" monied set since its opening in 1917, the Connaught has many dazzlingly modern compliments to its famously historic delights. **Pros:** legendary hotel; great for star-spotting. **Cons:** history comes at a price; bathrooms are small. $ *Rooms from: £540 ⊠ Carlos Pl., Mayfair*

15

☎ 020/7499–7070, 866/599–6991 *in U.S.* ⊕ *www.the-connaught.co.uk* 🛏 *87 rooms, 34 suites* ⎮◎⎮ *Breakfast* Ⓜ *Bond St.* ✢ *1:H5.*

$$$$ 🏨 **The Dorchester.** Few hotels this opulent manage to be as personable
HOTEL as the Dorchester, which opened in 1939 and boasts a prime Park Lane location with unparalleled glamour—gold leaf and marble adorn the public spaces, and guest quarters are awash in English country house–meets–art deco style. **Pros:** historic luxury in 1930s building; lovely views of Hyde Park; top-notch star-spotting; excellent spa; Michelin-starred dining from Alain Ducasse. **Cons:** traditional look is not to all tastes; prices are high; some rooms are rather small. 🛈 *Rooms from: £505* ✉ *Park La., Mayfair* ☎ *020/7629–8888* ⊕ *www.thedorchester. com* 🛏 *195 rooms, 55 suites* ⎮◎⎮ *Breakfast* Ⓜ *Marble Arch, Hyde Park Corner* ✢ *1:H6.*

$$$ 🏨 **InterContinental London Park Lane.** Overlooking busy Hyde Park Corner
HOTEL and the grounds of Buckingham Palace (much to the Queen's chagrin, allegedly), this hotel's luxurious rooms are aimed at high-end business travelers. **Pros:** central location; business facilities. **Cons:** no park views with standard rooms; prices can shoot up in mid-summer; £15 a day charge for Internet access is a bit rich given the room rates. 🛈 *Rooms from: £275* ✉ *1 Hamilton Pl., Park La., Mayfair* ☎ *020/7409–3131* ⊕ *www.intercontinental.com* 🛏 *447 rooms, 60 suites* ⎮◎⎮ *Some meals* Ⓜ *Hyde Park Corner* ✢ *1:H6.*

$$$$ 🏨 **The Langham.** Hotel pedigrees don't come much greater than this
HOTEL one—built in 1865, the Langham was *the* original luxury hotel in the
Fodor's Choice city, all but inventing the very image of what a great London hotel
★ looked like. **Pros:** beautiful building; impeccably good service; comfortable bedrooms; great restaurant and bar. **Cons:** price rises considerably once cheapest rooms sell out; bathrooms in basic rooms are somewhat utilitarian. 🛈 *Rooms from: £370* ✉ *1C Portland Pl., Mayfair* ☎ *020/7636–1000* ⊕ *www.langhamhotels.co.uk* 🛏 *331 rooms, 47 suites* ⎮◎⎮ *Some meals* Ⓜ *Oxford Circus* ✢ *2:A4.*

$$$ 🏨 **No. 5 Maddox Street.** Just five minutes' walk from Oxford Street, this
RENTAL is a great option for those who tire of traditional hotels: 12 luxury
FAMILY suites—some with balconies and working fireplaces—filled with everything you could ever need, including a handy kitchen. **Pros:** cozy and private; room service will deliver meals from local restaurants; guests have access to nearby health club. **Cons:** no elevator; no communal lobby can make you feel isolated; suites get booked far in advance. 🛈 *Rooms from: £266* ✉ *5 Maddox St., Mayfair* ☎ *020/7647–0200* ⊕ *www.living-rooms.co.uk/hotel/no5maddoxstreet* 🛏 *12 suites* ⎮◎⎮ *No meals* Ⓜ *Oxford Circus* ✢ *3:A5.*

$$$ 🏨 **Radisson Blu Edwardian Berkshire Hotel.** In a dangerously good loca-
HOTEL tion for shopaholics, with Oxford Street on the doorstep, the pleasant and well-run Radisson Berkshire offers a similar level of service to some of the more established hotels in the neighborhood, at a lower rate. **Pros:** great location; good restaurant; free Wi-Fi; worthwhile deals and promotions. **Cons:** walk-in rate is still quite expensive; small bedrooms. 🛈 *Rooms from: £210* ✉ *350 Oxford St., Mayfair* ☎ *020/7629–7474, 0800/374–411 toll-free in U.K., 1800/333–3333 toll-free in U.S.*

⊕ *www.radissonblu-edwardian.com* ↩ *145 rooms, 2 suites* |○| *Some meals* Ⓜ *Bond St., Oxford Circus* ✛ *1:H4.*

MARYLEBONE

$$$ ⊡ **Dorset Square Hotel.** Reopened in June 2012 after extensive updates
HOTEL and refurbishment, this boutique hotel, in one of London's most fash-
Fodor'sChoice ionable neighborhoods, occupies a charming town house. **Pros:** ideal
★ location; lovely design; welcoming vibe. **Cons:** some rooms are small;
no bathtub in some rooms; fee for Wi-Fi. Ⓢ *Rooms from: £300* ⊠ *39
Dorset Sq., Marylebone* ☎ *020/7723–7874* ⊕ *www.firmdalehotels.com*
↩ *35 rooms, 3 suites* |○| *Breakfast* Ⓜ *Baker St.* ✛ *1:F2.*

$$$ ⊡ **Hyatt Regency London—The Churchill.** Even though it's one of London's
HOTEL largest hotels, the Churchill is always abuzz with guests smiling at the
purring perfection they find here, including warmly personalized service
and calmly alluring guest rooms. **Pros:** comfortable and stylish; efficient
service; up to three can stay in one room. **Cons:** feels more geared to
business than leisure travelers. Ⓢ *Rooms from: £232* ⊠ *30 Portman
Sq., Marylebone* ☎ *020/7486–5800* ⊕ *www.london.churchill.hyatt.com*
↩ *389 rooms, 45 suites* |○| *Breakfast* Ⓜ *Marble Arch* ✛ *1:G4.*

$$$ ⊡ **The Sumner.** You can feel yourself relaxing the minute you enter this
HOTEL elegant Georgian town house. **Pros:** excellent location for shopping;
small enough that the staff knows your name; attractive conservatory
and garden. **Cons:** services are limited but prices high. Ⓢ *Rooms from:
£201* ⊠ *54 Upper Berkley St., Marble Arch, Marylebone* ☎ *020/7723–
2244* ⊕ *www.thesumner.com* ↩ *20 rooms* |○| *Breakfast* Ⓜ *Marble Arch*
✛ *1:F4.*

SOHO AND COVENT GARDEN

SOHO

$$$ ⊡ **Dean Street Townhouse.** Discreet and unpretentious, but oh-so-stylish—
HOTEL and right in the heart of Soho—this place has a bohemian vibe and an
Fodor'sChoice excellent modern British restaurant, hung with pieces by renowned
★ artists like Peter Blake and Tracy Emin. **Pros:** übercool; resembles
an upper-class pied-à-terre. **Cons:** some rooms are extremely small;
rooms at the front of the building can be noisy, especially on weekends. Ⓢ *Rooms from: £260* ⊠ *69–71 Dean St., Soho* ☎ *020/7434–1775*
⊕ *www.deanstreettownhouse.com* ↩ *39 rooms* |○| *Breakfast* Ⓜ *Leices-
ter Sq., Tottenham Court Rd.* ✛ *3:D5.*

$$$ ⊡ **Hazlitt's.** This disarmingly friendly place, full of personality, robust
HOTEL antiques, and claw-foot tubs, occupies three connected early-18th-
century houses, one of which was the last home of essayist William
Hazlitt (1778–1830). **Pros:** great for lovers of art and antiques; historic
atmosphere with lots of small sitting rooms and wooden staircases;
truly beautiful and relaxed. **Cons:** no in-house restaurant; breakfast
is £12 extra; no elevators. Ⓢ *Rooms from: £225* ⊠ *6 Frith St., Soho*
☎ *020/7434–1771* ⊕ *www.hazlittshotel.com* ↩ *20 rooms, 3 suites*
|○| *No meals* Ⓜ *Tottenham Court Rd.* ✛ *3:D4.*

15

BED-AND-BREAKFASTS

You can stay in small, homey B&Bs for an up-close-and-personal brush with city life (Parkwood Hotel; Arlington Avenue), or find yourself in what is really a modern guest-house, where you never meet the owners (B&B Belgravia; The Main House). The main benefit of staying in a B&B is that the price is usually cheaper than a hotel room of comparable quality, and you receive more personal service. However, the limitations may be off-putting for some: although you can sometimes arrange for daily maid service, there's usually no restaurant, bar, or room service. Prices start at around £60 a night, and in that bracket the grimmer places are legion, so make your choice carefully. Prices usually (though not always) go up for more central neighborhoods and larger and more luxurious homes. It's a nice option, both for seasoned travelers who want a more authentic taste of London, and for those trying to travel well without busting their budgets.

AirBnB. This popular global network of private lets and small bed-and-breakfasts has several hundred London-based properties listed on its website. ⊠ ⊕ *www.airbnb.co.uk* .

COVENT GARDEN

$$$$
HOTEL
Fodor's Choice
★
⚘ **Covent Garden Hotel.** It's little wonder this is now the London home-away-from-home for off-duty celebrities, actors, and style mavens, with its Covent Garden location and guest rooms that are design-magazine stylish. **Pros:** great for star-spotting; supertrendy. **Cons:** you can feel you don't matter if you're not famous; location in Covent Garden can be a bit boisterous. $ *Rooms from: £384* ⊠ *10 Monmouth St., Covent Garden* ☎ *020/7806–1000, 800/553–6674 in U.S.* ⊕ *www.firmdale. com* ⮢ *55 rooms, 3 suites* ❏ *Some meals* Ⓜ *Covent Garden* ✛ *3:E4.*

$$$$
HOTEL
FAMILY
Fodor's Choice
★
⚘ **Ham Yard Hotel.** Luxurious, playful, and riotously good fun, the Ham Yard Hotel is the latest addition to the burgeoning hit parade of London hotel designer extraordinaire, Kit Kemp. **Pros:** great design; excellent service; great facilities. **Cons:** eye-wateringly pricey. $ *Rooms from: £462* ⊠ *1 Ham Yard, Soho* ☎ *020/3642–2000* ⊕ *www.firmdalehotels. com/hotels/london/ham-yard-hotel* ⮢ *81 rooms, 10 suites* ❏ *Some meals* Ⓜ *Piccadilly Circus* ✛ *3:C6.*

$$$$
HOTEL
Fodor's Choice
★
⚘ **ME London.** One can only imagine the endless concept meetings that went into this shiny fortress of luxury that brought a splash of modern cool to a rather stuffy patch of the Strand when it opened in 2013—and the result is almost achingly on-trend. **Pros:** sleek and fashionable; full of high-tech comforts; excellent service; stunning views from rooftop bar. **Cons:** design can sometimes verge on form over function; very small closets and in-room storage areas; ludicrously high average price tag. $ *Rooms from: £510* ⊠ *336 The Strand, Covent Garden* ☎ *0808/234–1953* ⊕ *www.melia.com* ⮢ *141 rooms, 16 suites* ❏ *Breakfast* Ⓜ *Covent Garden* ✛ *3:G5.*

$$$
HOTEL
⚘ **One Aldwych.** An Edwardian building, with an artsy lobby and under-stated blend of contemporary and classic, provides pure, modern luxury in a great location for theaters and shopping. **Pros:** understated luxury; ultracool atmosphere; good deals and special offers, including big

advance booking discounts. **Cons:** all this luxury doesn't come cheap; fashionable ambience is not always relaxing; design sometimes verges on form over function. $ *Rooms from: £284* ✉ *1 Aldwych, Covent Garden* ☎ *020/7300–1000* ⊕ *www.onealdwych.co.uk* ⤳ *93 rooms, 12 suites* ⑩ *Breakfast* Ⓜ *Charing Cross, Covent Garden* ✛ *3:G5.*

$$$$ 🏨 **The Savoy.** One of London's most iconic hotels maintains its status at
HOTEL the top with winning attributes of impeccable service, stunning decor,
Fodor'sChoice and a desirable Covent Garden location. **Pros:** one of the top hotels in
★ Europe; iconic pedigree; Thames-side location. **Cons:** everything comes with a price tag; busy rooms can be noisy, particularly on lower floors; right off the superbusy Strand. $ *Rooms from: £354* ✉ *The Strand, Covent Garden* ☎ *020/7836–4343, 800/257–7544 in U.S.* ⊕ *www. fairmont.com/savoy-london* ⤳ *206 rooms, 62 suites* ⑩ *Breakfast* Ⓜ *Covent Garden, Charing Cross* ✛ *3:G6.*

BLOOMSBURY, HOLBORN, AND FITZROVIA

15

BLOOMSBURY

$$ 🏨 **Arosfa.** Simple, friendly, and pleasantly quirky, this little B&B, once
B&B/INN the home of pre-Raphaelite painter Sir John Everett Millais, is on an elegant Georgian street within walking distance of the West End and the British Museum. **Pros:** friendly staff; check-in from 7 am; good location for museums and theaters; free Wi-Fi. **Cons:** some rooms are very small; bathrooms have showers only; few services. $ *Rooms from: £138* ✉ *83 Gower St., Bloomsbury* ☎ *020/7636–2115* ⊕ *www.arosfalondon.com* ⤳ *16 rooms* ⑩ *Breakfast* Ⓜ *Goodge St., Euston Sq.* ✛ *3:D1.*

$$$$ 🏨 **Charlotte Street Hotel.** Tradition and modern flair are fused together in
HOTEL this superstylish Soho retreat, a short walk from Oxford Street. **Pros:**
Fodor'sChoice elegant, luxurious; great attention to detail. **Cons:** the popular bar can
★ be noisy; reservations are necessary for the restaurant. $ *Rooms from: £342* ✉ *15 Charlotte St., Bloomsbury* ☎ *020/7806–2000, 800/553– 6674 in U.S.* ⊕ *www.firmdalehotels.com* ⤳ *46 rooms, 6 suites* ⑩ *Breakfast* Ⓜ *Goodge St.* ✛ *3:C2.*

$ 🏨 **Grange Blooms Hotel.** In this white Georgian town-house hotel, just
HOTEL around the corner from the British Museum, rooms are not too tiny by London standards, and those in the back look out onto a leafy green garden. **Pros:** great location; overall good value; good prices if you book early through the website. **Cons:** bathrooms could use an upgrade; guests can be bumped to sister hotel if fully booked; no air-conditioning; street noise in some rooms; price rises steeply on weekdays. $ *Rooms from: £122* ✉ *7 Montague St., Bloomsbury* ☎ *020/7323– 1717, 800/2247–2643* ⊕ *www.grangehotels.com* ⤳ *26 rooms, 1 suite* ⑩ *Some meals* Ⓜ *Russell Sq.* ✛ *3:F2.*

$ 🏨 **Jesmond Hotel.** This friendly little hotel is great value given the loca-
B&B/INN tion: a short walk from the British Museum in one direction, and Soho and Covent Garden in the other. **Pros:** great location; friendly staff; free Wi-Fi; 15% discount on stays of one week. **Cons:** some rooms are very small; nearly half have shared bathrooms. $ *Rooms from: £85* ✉ *63 Gower St., Bloomsbury* ☎ *020/7636–3199* ⊕ *www.jesmondhotel.org. uk* ⤳ *15 rooms* ⑩ *Breakfast* Ⓜ *Goodge St., Euston Sq., Warren St., Russell Sq.* ✛ *3:C1.*

$$ ⬚ **Megaro.** Directly across the street from St Pancras International sta-
HOTEL tion (for the Eurostar), the snazzy, well-designed, modern bedrooms
here surround guests with startlingly contemporary style and ameni-
ties that include powerful showers and espresso machines. **Pros:** com-
fortable beds; great location for Eurostar; short hop on Tube to city
center. **Cons:** neighborhood isn't great; standard rooms are small; inte-
riors may be a bit stark for some. Ⓢ *Rooms from: £170* ⊠ *Belgrove
St., King's Cross* ☎ *020/7843–2222* ⊕ *www.hotelmegaro.co.uk* ⤶ *49
rooms* ❡⦵ *Breakfast* Ⓜ *Kings Cross, St. Pancras* ✛ *2:C2.*

$ ⬚ **The Ridgemount Hotel.** Mere blocks away from the British Museum and
B&B/INN London's West End theaters, this handsomely fronted guesthouse has
clean, neat, and plainly decorated rooms at a bargain. **Pros:** good loca-
tion for theaters and museum; helpful staff; family rooms (accommodat-
ing up to five) are excellent value. **Cons:** decoration is basic; no elevator;
cheapest rooms have shared bathrooms. Ⓢ *Rooms from: £82* ⊠ *65–67
Gower St., Bloomsbury* ☎ *020/7636–1141* ⊕ *www.ridgemounthotel.
co.uk* ⤶ *32 rooms, 15 with bath* ❡⦵ *Breakfast* Ⓜ *Goodge St.* ✛ *3:D1.*

$$ ⬚ **Rough Luxe.** Bloomsbury's most avant-garde hotel won't be for every-
B&B/INN one, but this 19th-century building has been renovated with an appeal-
ing mix of shabby chic and modern comfort. **Pros:** art and design lovers
will be dazzled; free Wi-Fi. **Cons:** no restaurant or bar; cheapest rooms
book up fast; in a neighborhood locals would describe as somewhat
"dodgy"; some rooms share bathrooms. Ⓢ *Rooms from: £159* ⊠ *1
Birkenhead St., Bloomsbury* ☎ *020/7837–5338* ⊕ *www.roughluxe.
co.uk* ⤶ *10 rooms* ❡⦵ *Breakfast* Ⓜ *Kings Cross* ✛ *2:C2.*

$$$ ⬚ **St. Pancras Renaissance.** Reopened in 2011 after nearly a century of
HOTEL dereliction, this stunningly restored Victorian landmark—replete with
Fodor$Choice gingerbread turrets and castlelike ornaments—started as a love letter
★ to the golden age of railways; now it's one of London's most sophisti-
cated places to stay. **Pros:** unique and beautiful; faultless service; just
an elevator ride to the Eurostar. **Cons:** very popular bar and restaurant;
streets outside are busy 24 hours. Ⓢ *Rooms from: £219* ⊠ *Euston Rd.,
King's Cross* ☎ *020/7841–3540* ⊕ *www.marriott.com* ⤶ *207 rooms,
38 suites* ❡⦵ *Breakfast* Ⓜ *Kings Cross St. Pancras. National Rail: Kings
Cross St. Pancras* ✛ *2:C2.*

HOLBORN

$$$ ⬚ **SACO Holborn.** Down a quiet backstreet, a 10-minute walk from
RENTAL the British Museum, these serviced apartments are spacious, modern,
and extremely well equipped, including a kitchen with dishwasher
and washing machine. **Pros:** more independence than hotels; pleasant and spacious accommodations; on-site parking. **Cons:** exterior is
dated; you must provide own bedding for baby cots. Ⓢ *Rooms from:
£246* ⊠ *82 Lamb's Conduit St., Holborn* ☎ *0845/122–0405* ⊕ *www.
sacoapartments.co.uk* ⤶ *30 apartments (mixture of studios, 1-, 2-, and
3-bed)* ❡⦵ *No meals* Ⓜ *Russell Sq.* ✛ *3:G1.*

FITZROVIA

$$$$ ⬚ **The London Edition.** A solidly bohemian air permeates this handsome
HOTEL new hotel in the heart of Fitzrovia, which opened to much fanfare in
Fodor$Choice the fall of 2013. **Pros:** very fashionable; great bars; beautifully designed
★ bedrooms. **Cons:** rooms may feel small to some; lobby can get crowded

LONDON CHAIN HOTEL PRIMER

Here's a quick rundown of some hotel chains worth considering:

easyHotel: One of the first chains to bring "pod hotels" to London, the easyHotel chain specializes in very cheap (less than £50 a night for a double) rooms that are clean, secure, and offer all the basics, but are teeny-tiny and have no free extras at all. ⊕ *www.easyhotel.com.*

Grange Hotels: This chain includes a mix of moderately priced hotels with neutral interior design, good service, and gadgets for business travelers. ⊕ *www.grangehotels.com.*

Malmaison: With lavish, elegant small hotels around the country, this upscale chain offers luxurious designer style, good restaurants, and trendy bars. ⊕ *www.malmaison.com.*

Millennium: Similar in style to Premier Inns, Millennium (and its other brand, Copthorne) hotels are targeted at both business and leisure travelers. They offer well-designed rooms with plenty of gadgets and have frequent sales. ⊕ *www.millenniumhotels.co.uk.*

myhotel: A chain of pricey hotels with designer style and trendy bars. myhotels offer reliable comfort and service, if you don't mind the price tag. ⊕ *www.myhotels.com.*

Premier Inns: This chain features medium-size, moderately priced hotels. They're known for their attractive look, and for frequent sales, which keep prices low. ⊕ *www.premierinn.com.*

15

with trendsetters descending upon the bars and nightclub. Ⓢ *Rooms from: £345* ✉ *10 Berners St., Fitzrovia* ☎ *020/7781–0000* ⊕ *edition-hotels.marriott.com/london* ⤴ *173 rooms* ⏐⊙⏐ *Breakfast* Ⓜ *Oxford Circus* ✛ *3:C3.*

$$ ⊞ **Sanderson Hotel.** At this fashionable and surreal "urban spa" in a
HOTEL converted 1950s textile factory, the lobby looks like a design museum: bedrooms have sleigh beds and a mix of over-the-top Louis XV and postmodern furnishings. **Pros:** popular with design mavens; your every whim gratified. **Cons:** "designer cool" can be self-consciously hip; bar and restaurant are so exclusive it's hard to get in. Ⓢ *Rooms from: £186* ✉ *50 Berners St., Fitzrovia* ☎ *020/7300–1400* ⊕ *www.sandersonlondon.com* ⤴ *150 rooms* ⏐⊙⏐ *Breakfast* Ⓜ *Oxford Circus, Tottenham Court Rd.* ✛ *3:B3.*

THE CITY

$$ ⊞ **Apex City of London.** At this sleek, modern branch of the small Apex
HOTEL chain near the Tower of London, bedrooms are reasonably spacious, with contemporary color schemes, 40-inch flat screen TVs, and little sofas. **Pros:** great location; helpful staff; good advance booking discounts; free Wi-Fi. **Cons:** geared more to business than leisure travelers; price can rise sharply during busy times. Ⓢ *Rooms from: £159* ✉ *1 Seething La., The City* ☎ *020/7702–2020* ⊕ *www.apexhotels.co.uk* ⤴ *130 rooms, 49 suites* ⏐⊙⏐ *Breakfast* Ⓜ *Tower Hill* ✛ *2:G2.*

$$
HOTEL
⬚ **Crowne Plaza London—The City.** Don't let the hotel's all-business appearance put you off—it's a polished operation, with stylish minimalist rooms, and just steps from the gleaming new Blackfriars Tube and train station in one direction, and bustling Fleet Street in the other. **Pros:** good prices available with advance booking; great location near the river and transport. **Cons:** neighborhood is super busy during the day and empty at night. ⑤ *Rooms from: £157* ⊠ *19 New Bridge St., The City* ☎ *0871/942–9190* ⊕ *www.cplondoncityhotel.co.uk* ⤶ *203 rooms, 3 suites* ❡◎❡ *Breakfast* Ⓜ *Blackfriars* ✛ *2:F6.*

$
HOTEL
⬚ **Grange City Hotel.** With an eye on business, this sleek City hotel has everything the workaholic needs to feel right at home—chic bedrooms subtly decorated, modern furnishings, plenty of space (by London standards), and more. **Pros:** good-size rooms; prices can drop considerably on weekends; female-friendly rooms are great for lone female travelers. **Cons:** a bit off the tourist track; some rooms overlook train platform; prices can soar midweek; online discounts tend to not allow changes or cancellation. ⑤ *Rooms from: £112* ⊠ *8–14 Cooper's Row, The City* ☎ *020/7863–3700* ⊕ *www.grangehotels.com* ⤶ *307 rooms, 11 suites* ❡◎❡ *Some meals* Ⓜ *Tower Hill, Aldgate, Monument* ✛ *2:G2.*

$$
HOTEL
Fodor's Choice
★
⬚ **The Rookery.** An absolutely unique and beautiful 1725 town house, the Rookery is the kind of place where you want to allow quality time to enjoy and soak up the atmosphere. **Pros:** helpful staff; free Wi-Fi; good deals in the off-season. **Cons:** breakfast costs extra; Tube ride to tourist sites. ⑤ *Rooms from: £165* ⊠ *12 Peter's La., at Cowcross St., The City* ☎ *020/7336–0931* ⊕ *www.rookeryhotel.com* ⤶ *30 rooms, 3 suites* ❡◎❡ *No meals* Ⓜ *Farringdon* ✛ *2:F4.*

$$
HOTEL
⬚ **Threadneedles Hotel.** The elaborate building housing this grand hotel in the financial district is a former bank, and the vast old banking hall—beautifully adapted as the lobby, with luxurious marble and mahogany panels—really sets the scene. **Pros:** lap of luxury; excellent service. **Cons:** a bit stuffy for some tastes; can be at least three times more expensive weekdays; neighborhood is quiet at night. ⑤ *Rooms from: £152* ⊠ *5 Threadneedle St., The City* ☎ *020/7657–8080* ⊕ *www.hotelthreadneedles.co.uk* ⤶ *63 rooms, 6 suites* ❡◎❡ *Breakfast* Ⓜ *Bank* ✛ *2:G2.*

$$$
HOTEL
Fodor's Choice
★
⬚ **The Zetter.** The five-story atrium, art deco staircase, and slick European restaurant hint at the delights to come in this converted warehouse—a breath of fresh air with its playful color schemes, elegant wallpapers, and wonderful views of The City from the higher floors. **Pros:** huge amounts of character; big rooms; free Wi-Fi; award-winning restaurant. **Cons:** rooms with good views cost more. ⑤ *Rooms from: £205* ⊠ *86–88 Clerkenwell Rd., Clerkenwell* ☎ *020/7324–4444* ⊕ *www.thezetter.com* ⤶ *59 rooms* ❡◎❡ *Breakfast* Ⓜ *Farringdon* ✛ *2:F3.*

EAST LONDON

$$
HOTEL
⬚ **Ace Hotel London.** The first European outlet of the superhip Ace hotel chain fits right into the scenery in achingly cool Shoreditch, surrounded by galleries and on-trend boutiques every bit as style conscious as its own creatively minimalist interiors. **Pros:** extremely fashionable; large and comfortable bedrooms; great bar. **Cons:** not everyone will enjoy

being surrounded by hipsters; price rises sharply midweek; street noise can be a problem. $ *Rooms from: £159* ✉ *100 Shoreditch High St., Shoreditch* ☎ *020/7613–9800* ⊕ *www.acehotel.com* ➲ *258 rooms* ❍| *Breakfast* Ⓜ *Shoreditch High St.* ✛ *2:G1.*

$$ 🛏 **Andaz.** Swanky and upscale, this hotel sports a modern, masculine
HOTEL design, and novel check-in procedure—instead of standing at a desk, guests sit in a lounge while a staff member with a handheld computer takes their information. **Pros:** nice attention to detail; guests can borrow an iPod from the front desk; no standing in line to check in; "healthy minibars" are stocked with nuts, fruit, and yogurt. **Cons:** sparse interior design is not for all; rates rise significantly for midweek stays. $ *Rooms from: £155* ✉ *40 Liverpool St., East End* ☎ *020/7961–1234, 800/492–8804 in U.S.* ⊕ *www.andaz.hyatt.com* ➲ *267 rooms* ❍| *Breakfast* Ⓜ *Liverpool St.* ✛ *2:G2.*

$ 🛏 **Cable Street Inn.** Wonderful modern art lines the walls of this for-
B&B/INN mer Victorian pub a mile east of the Tower of London, which has
Fodor's Choice been beautifully restored and converted into a modern B&B. **Pros:** true
★ one-of-a-kind place; beautiful art; wonderful host; free Wi-Fi. **Cons:** 20-minute journey by DLR then Tube to the center; historic nature of the building makes it unsuitable for those with mobility problems. $ *Rooms from: £110* ✉ *232 Cable St., East End* ☎ *020/7790–4019* ⊕ *www.cablestreetinn.co.uk* ➲ *3 rooms* ❍| *Breakfast* Ⓜ *DLR: Shadwell* ✛ *2:H5.*

$ 🛏 **The Hoxton Hotel.** The design throughout this trendy East London
HOTEL lodging is contemporary—but not so modern as to be absurd—and
Fodor's Choice in keeping with a claim to combine a country-lodge lifestyle with true
★ urban living, a fire crackles in the lobby. **Pros:** cool vibe; neighborhood known for funky galleries and boutiques; huge weekend discounts; way-cool restaurant; one hour of free international calls. **Cons:** price rockets during the week; away from tourist sights. $ *Rooms from: £69* ✉ *81 Great Eastern St., East End* ☎ *020/7550–1000* ⊕ *www.hoxtonhotels. com* ➲ *205 rooms* ❍| *Breakfast* Ⓜ *Shoreditch High St.* ✛ *2:G1.*

$$ 🛏 **Town Hall Hotel and Apartments.** An art deco town hall, abandoned in
HOTEL the early 1980s and turned into a chic hotel in 2010, is now a lively and stylish place, with the best of the building's elegant original features intact. **Pros:** beautifully designed; lovely staff; big discounts on weekends. **Cons:** though touted as "cool" and "cutting edge," this is not a great part of town; a 15-minute Tube ride from Central London. $ *Rooms from: £148* ✉ *Patriot Sq., Bethnal Green, East End* ☎ *020/7657–8080* ⊕ *www.townhallhotel.com* ➲ *98 rooms, 86 suites* ❍| *Breakfast* Ⓜ *Bethnal Green* ✛ *2:H1.*

SOUTH OF THE THAMES

$ 🛏 **Church Street Hotel.** Like rays of sunshine in gritty South London, these
HOTEL rooms above a popular tapas restaurant are individually decorated in
Fodor's Choice rich, bold tones and authentic Central American touches—elaborately
★ painted crucifixes; tiles handmade in Guadalajara; homemade iron bed frames. **Pros:** unique and arty; great breakfasts; lovely staff; closer to central London than it might appear. **Cons:** a trendy but not great part of town (stay out of neighboring Elephant and Castle); would suit

15

adventurous young things more than families; a mile from a Tube station (though bus connections are handier); some rooms have shared bathrooms. $ *Rooms from: £90* ⊠ *29–33 Camberwell Church St., Camberwell, South East* ☎ *020/7703–5984* ⊕ *www.churchstreethotel.com* ⇱ *31 rooms* |◯| *Breakfast* Ⓜ *Oval St.* ✛ *5:H6.*

$ ⬚ **CitizenM London Bankside.** High concept, high tech and supertrendy,
HOTEL   the CitizenM chain has a unique selling point—as much as possible is self-service. **Pros:** great budget concept; stylish and modern; no waiting in line for checkout. **Cons:** only really qualifies as "budget" on certain nights (price is higher midweek); true technophobes will be turned off by too much tech. $ *Rooms from: £93* ⊠ *20 Lavington St., Bankside* ☎ *020/3519–1680* ⊕ *www.citizenm.com/destinations/london/london-bankside-hotel* ⇱ *192 rooms* |◯| *No meals* Ⓜ *Southwark* ✛ *5:G1.*

$$ ⬚ **London Bridge Hotel.** Steps away from the London Bridge rail and
HOTEL   Tube stations, and handy for the South Bank, this thoroughly modern, stylish hotel is popular with business travelers, but leisure travelers find it just as handy and appealing. **Pros:** good location for visiting South Bank attractions; free Wi-Fi; good deals available online in the off-season. **Cons:** small bedrooms; prices rise by £100 or more midweek. $ *Rooms from: £156* ⊠ *8–18 London Bridge St., Southwark* ☎ *020/7855–2200* ⊕ *www.london-bridge-hotel.co.uk* ⇱ *138 rooms, 3 apartments* |◯| *Breakfast* Ⓜ *London Bridge* ✛ *5:H1.*

$$$ ⬚ **London Marriott Hotel County Hall.** This grand hotel on the Thames
HOTEL   enjoys perhaps the most iconic view in the city—right next door is the London Eye, and directly across the River Thames are the Houses of Parliament and Big Ben. **Pros:** handy for South Bank arts scene, London Eye, and Westminster; great gym; good weekend discounts. **Cons:** interior design can be overdone for some tastes; breakfasts are pricey; rooms facing the river cost extra. $ *Rooms from: £255* ⊠ *County Hall, Westminster Bridge Rd., South Bank* ☎ *020/7928–5200, 888/236–2427 in U.S.* ⊕ *www.marriott.com* ⇱ *186 rooms, 14 suites* |◯| *Breakfast* Ⓜ *Westminster, Waterloo. National Rail: Waterloo* ✛ *5:D2.*

$$$ ⬚ **The Mondrian.** Opened at the tail end of 2014 to much fanfare, the
HOTEL   Mondrian is a quirky yet sophisticated addition to the burgeoning South
Fodor's Choice   Bank. **Pros:** quirky and refreshing; great service; excellent bars and
★   restaurants; beautiful river views; short riverside walk to Tate Modern and Shakespeare's Globe. **Cons:** river-view rooms are pricey (of course); public areas, outside the lobby and bars, are a little bland; ever wondered what a paint can sneezing would look like? No? Then you may not like the art in the bedrooms; standard rooms are small. $ *Rooms from: £200* ⊠ *Sea Containers House, 20 Upper Ground* ☎ *020/3747–1000* ⊕ *www.morganshotelgroup.com/mondrian/mondrian-london* ⇱ *339 rooms, 20 suites* |◯| *Breakfast* Ⓜ *Blackfriars, Southwark* ✛ *5:F1.*

$ ⬚ **Premier Travel Inn County Hall.** The small but nicely decorated rooms
HOTEL   at this budget choice share the same County Hall complex as the fan-
FAMILY   cier London Marriott Hotel County Hall, and though it has none of the spectacular river views, and the facilities are more basic, the selling point is the same convenient location at a fraction of the price. **Pros:** fantastic location for the South Bank; bargains to be had if you book in advance; kids (sharing with adults) stay free. **Cons:** no river views;

limited services; cookie-cutter chain hotel atmosphere; on a busy road. ⑤ *Rooms from: £90* ✉ *Belvedere Rd., South Bank* ☎ *0871/527–8648* ⊕ *www.premierinn.com* ⤵ *313 rooms* ⑩ *Breakfast* Ⓜ *Westminster, Waterloo. National Rail: Waterloo* ✛ *5:D2.*

$$$$ 🛏 **The Shangri-La Hotel, at The Shard.** The Shangri-La Hotel, at the Shard, **HOTEL** which opened in summer 2014 , boasts floor-to-ceiling windows, the **Fodor'sChoice** city's highest cocktail bar and infinity pool, and unrivaled views of the ★ London skyline from 1,016 feet above the South Bank of the Thames. **Pros:** matchless views; excellent service; superb restaurants and cocktail bar; high-tech bells and whistles in guest rooms. **Cons:** a "currently being worked on" design flaw caused by glass wings that protrude from the corners of the building allows guests to see into their neighbor's room at night; decor may feel cold to some; restaurant, bar, and elevator often overcrowded due to popularity of the view. ⑤ *Rooms from: £520* ✉ *The Shangri-La at the Shard, 32 London Bridge St., South Bank* ☎ *0207/234–8000* ⊕ *www.the-shard.com/shangri-la/* ⤵ *185 rooms, 17 suites* ⑩ *No meals* Ⓜ *London Bridge Station* ✛ *5:H1.*

KENSINGTON, CHELSEA, KNIGHTSBRIDGE, AND BELGRAVIA

KENSINGTON

$$ 🛏 **Ampersand.** A sense of style emanates from every surface of this sump- **HOTEL** tuous hotel in the heart of Kensington—but the playful, vintage vibe lends the property a refreshingly down-to-earth feel in a neighborhood that often feels cooler-than-thou. **Pros:** flawless design; great service; good restaurant. **Cons:** ground floor rooms can be noisy. ⑤ *Rooms from: £216* ✉ *10 Harrington Rd., Kensington* ⊕ *www.ampersandhotel. com* ⤵ *106 rooms, 5 suites* ⑩ *Breakfast* Ⓜ *Gloucester Rd.* ✛ *4:D2.*

$$ 🛏 **Ashburn Hotel.** A short walk from Gloucester Road Tube station and **HOTEL** within walking distance of Harrods and the Kensington museums, the Ashburn is one of the better "boutique" hotels in this part of town. **Pros:** friendly atmosphere; free Wi-Fi; turndown gift (different every night). **Cons:** summer prices sometimes hike the cost. ⑤ *Rooms from: £179* ✉ *111 Cromwell Rd., Kensington* ☎ *020/7938–5930 reservations, 020/7244–1999* ⊕ *www.ashburn-hotel.co.uk* ⤵ *55 rooms, 3 suites* ⑩ *Breakfast* Ⓜ *Gloucester Rd.* ✛ *4:C2.*

$$ 🛏 **The Cranley Hotel.** Old-fashioned British propriety is the overall feel- **HOTEL** ing at this small, Victorian town-house hotel, where high ceilings, huge windows, and a pale, creamy color scheme flood the bedrooms with light. **Pros:** good-size rooms; attractively decorated; friendly staff; free evening nibbles are a nice touch. **Cons:** steep stairs into lobby; no restaurant; prices rise in mid-summer. ⑤ *Rooms from: £168* ✉ *10–12 Bina Gardens, South Kensington* ☎ *020/7373–0123* ⊕ *www.thecranley.com* ⤵ *29 rooms, 5 suites, 4 apartments* ⑩ *Breakfast* Ⓜ *Gloucester Rd.* ✛ *4:C3.*

$ 🛏 **easyHotel South Kensington.** London's original "pod hotel" has tiny **HOTEL** rooms with a double bed, private shower room, and little else—each brightly decorated in the easyGroup's trademark orange and white (to match their budget airline easyJet). **Pros:** amazing price; safe and decent enough space. **Cons:** not for the claustrophobic—rooms are truly tiny and most have no windows; six floors and no elevator; basic as basic

15

can be; inquiries are via the website only—they don't even have a phone. $ *Rooms from: £47* ✉ *14 Lexham Gardens, Kensington* ⊕ *www. easyhotel.com* ⟿ *34 rooms* ⦿*No meals* Ⓜ *Gloucester Rd.* ✛ *4:B2.*

$$ ⟐ **The Gore Hotel.** Just down the road from the Albert Hall, this gor-
HOTEL   geous, friendly hotel has a luxurious mixture of the comfortable and the extraordinary. **Pros:** gorgeously designed spacious rooms; outstanding, attentive service; air-conditioning in all rooms. **Cons:** Wi-Fi is not free; bar can be noisy. $ *Rooms from: £162* ✉ *190 Queen's Gate, Kensington* ☎ *020/7584–6601, 888/757–5587 in U.S* ⊕ *www.gorehotel.com* ⟿ *50 rooms* ⦿*Breakfast* Ⓜ *Gloucester Rd.* ✛ *4:D1.*

$$ ⟐ **London Marriott Kensington.** A big favorite for the business crowd,
HOTEL   this pleasant, modern outpost of the Marriott megachain is just one of several big-name hotels on the busy Cromwell Road. **Pros:** friendly, effi-cient service; good neighborhood; one-minute Tube ride to Kensington museums. **Cons:** "could be anywhere in the world" business ambience feels impersonal; bedrooms are on the small side. $ *Rooms from: £175* ✉ *147 Cromwell Rd., Kensington* ☎ *020/7973–1000* ⊕ *www.marriott. com* ⟿ *216 rooms* ⦿*Some meals* Ⓜ *Earl's Ct., Gloucester Rd.* ✛ *4:B2.*

$$$$ ⟐ **The Milestone Hotel.** This pair of intricately decorated Victorian
HOTEL   town houses overlooking Kensington Palace and Gardens is an inti-
Fodor's Choice   mate, luxurious alternative to the city's more famous high-end hotels,
★   offering thoughtful hospitality and sumptuous, distinctive rooms full of antiques. **Pros:** beautiful and elegant; big rooms, many with park views; excellent location; good package deal includes tickets to Kens-ington Palace and £50 of shopping vouchers. **Cons:** actual room rate discounts are rare. $ *Rooms from: £342* ✉ *1 Kensington Ct., Kensing-ton* ☎ *020/7917–1000* ⊕ *www.milestonehotel.com* ⟿ *44 rooms, 12 suites, 6 apartments* ⦿*Breakfast* Ⓜ *High Street Kensington* ✛ *4:C1.*

$ ⟐ **Millennium Gloucester.** With a Tube station opposite and Kensington's
HOTEL   many attractions nearby, this hotel is both convenient and alluring, its sleek and opulent lobby, with polished wood columns, a warming fireplace, and glittering chandeliers giving way to guest rooms with a traditionally masculine look. **Pros:** good deals available if you book in advance. **Cons:** lighting in some bedrooms is a bit too subtle; bathrooms are relatively small. $ *Rooms from: £91* ✉ *4–18 Harrington Gardens, Kensington* ☎ *020/7373–6030* ⊕ *www.millenniumhotels.co.uk* ⟿ *610 rooms* ⦿*Breakfast* Ⓜ *Gloucester Rd.* ✛ *4:C2.*

$$ ⟐ **The Nadler.** This newly refurbished "aparthotel" in a creamy white
HOTEL   Georgian town house offers a useful compromise between full-service hotel and the freedom of self-catering in the form of comfortable rooms with a stylish, modern look and tiny kitchenettes. **Pros:** great alterna-tive to hotel; handy mini-kitchens; free Wi-Fi; 24-hour reception. **Cons:** basic rooms are small; movies in entertainment system are pay-per-view; 15-minute Tube ride to central London. $ *Rooms from: £142* ✉ *25 Courtfield Gardens, South Kensington* ☎ *020/7244–2255* ⊕ *www. thenadler.com* ⟿ *65 rooms* ⦿*No meals* Ⓜ *Earls Ct.* ✛ *4:B3.*

$$$ ⟐ **Number Sixteen.** Guest rooms at this lovely luxury guesthouse, just
HOTEL   around the corner from the Victoria & Albert Museum, look like they come from the pages of *Architectural Digest,* and the delightful garden is an added bonus. **Pros:** just the right level of helpful service; interiors

are gorgeous. **Cons:** no restaurant; small elevator. $ *Rooms from: £294* ⊠ *16 Sumner Pl., South Kensington* ☎ *020/7589–5232, 888/559–5508 in U.S.* ⊕ *www.firmdale.com* ⮎ *42 rooms* ⟲| *Breakfast* Ⓜ *South Kensington* ✛ *4:D2.*

$$
HOTEL
🛏 **The Pelham Hotel.** One of the first and most stylish of London's famed "boutique" hotels, this still-chic choice is but a short stroll away from the Natural History, Science, and V&A museums. **Pros:** great location for museum-hopping; gorgeous marble bathrooms; soigné interior design; lovely staff; good package deals for online booking. **Cons:** taller guests will find themselves cursing the top-floor rooms with sloping ceilings. $ *Rooms from: £187* ⊠ *15 Cromwell Pl., South Kensington* ☎ *020/7589–8288, 888/757–5587 in U.S.* ⊕ *www.pelhamhotel.co.uk* ⮎ *47 rooms, 4 suites* ⟲| *Breakfast* Ⓜ *South Kensington* ✛ *4:D2.*

$$
HOTEL
🛏 **The Rockwell.** Despite being on the notoriously traffic-clogged Cromwell Road, this excellent little place is one of the best boutique hotels in this part of London—and windows have good soundproofing. **Pros:** large bedrooms; stylish surroundings; helpful staff; advance booking can drop the price below £100. **Cons:** on a busy road; 20-minute Tube ride to central London. $ *Rooms from: £127* ⊠ *181 Cromwell Rd., South Kensington* ☎ *020/7244–2000* ⊕ *www.therockwell.com* ⮎ *38 rooms, 2 suites* ⟲| *Breakfast* Ⓜ *Earls Court* ✛ *4:B2.*

CHELSEA

$$
HOTEL
FAMILY
Fodor'sChoice
★
🛏 **The Draycott.** This elegant yet homey boutique hotel near Sloane Square is the stuff London dreams are made on—if your dream is to live like a pleasantly old-fashioned, impeccably mannered, effortlessly stylish Chelsea lady or gentleman. **Pros:** lovely traditional town house; great service; discreet and peaceful; free afternoon tea, Champagne, and evening cocoa. **Cons:** no restaurant or bar; single rooms are very small; elevator is tiny. $ *Rooms from: £186* ⊠ *26 Cadogan Gardens, Chelsea* ☎ *020/7730–0236* ⊕ *www.draycotthotel.com* ⮎ *35 rooms* ⟲| *Breakfast* Ⓜ *Sloane Sq.* ✛ *4:F3.*

KNIGHTSBRIDGE

$$$$
HOTEL
🛏 **The Beaufort.** This gracious boutique hotel is a favorite entry in the little black books of many a visiting high-society *fashionista*—Harrods is the merest toss of a diamond from the front door. **Pros:** gorgeous interiors; friendly and professional staff; air-conditioning; free Wi-Fi. **Cons:** standard doubles are much smaller than the price might indicate. $ *Rooms from: £312* ⊠ *33 Beaufort Gardens, Knightsbridge* ☎ *020/7584–5252* ⊕ *www.thebeaufort.co.uk* ⮎ *22 rooms, 7 suites* ⟲| *Breakfast* Ⓜ *Knightsbridge* ✛ *4:F1.*

$$$$
HOTEL
🛏 **The Berkeley.** Convenient for Knightsbridge shopping, the very elegant Berkeley is known for its renowned restaurants and luxuries that culminate—literally—in a splendid penthouse swimming pool. **Pros:** lavish and elegant; attentive service; prices aren't quite as stratospheric as some high-end places. **Cons:** you'll need your best designer clothes to fit in. $ *Rooms from: £480* ⊠ *Wilton Pl., Knightsbridge* ☎ *020/7235–6000, 800/637–2869 in U.S.* ⊕ *www.the-berkeley.co.uk* ⮎ *103 rooms, 55 suites* ⟲| *Breakfast* Ⓜ *Knightsbridge* ✛ *4:G1.*

$$$$
HOTEL
🛏 **The Capital Hotel.** Nothing is ever too much at this elegant hotel that was formerly a private house—mattresses are handmade, sheets are

RENTALS AND HOME EXCHANGES

APARTMENT RENTALS

For a home base that's roomy enough for a family and that comes with cooking facilities, consider renting furnished "flats" (the British word for apartments).

INTERNATIONAL AGENTS

Hideaways International. This company offers boutique hotels, tours, and cruises. ⊠ *767 Islington St.* ☎ *603/430–4433, 800/843–4433* ⊕ *www.hideaways.com* .

LOCAL AGENTS

The Apartment Service. This agency specializes in executive apartments for business travelers, so prices are high, but so is the quality. ⊠ *5 Francis Grove, Wimbledon* ☎ *020/8944–1444* ⊕ *www.apartmentservice.com* .

At Home in London. Rooms in private homes in Knightsbridge, Kensington, Mayfair, Chelsea, and West London are handled by this agency. ⊠ *70 Black Lion La., Hammersmith* ☎ *020/8748–2701* ⊕ *www.athomeinlondon.co.uk* .

The Bed and Breakfast Club. Contact this company for delightful little London apartments, in Kensington, Chelsea, and Knightsbridge, costing from around £50–£140 per night with full English breakfasts. ⊠ *405 Kings Rd., Suite 192, Chelsea* ☎ *01243/370–692* ⊕ *www.thebedandbreakfastclub.co.uk* ☞ *There's a 2.5% fee for using a credit card; debit cards incur no fees; the full price of room must be paid in advance. Check cancellation policies carefully* .

Landmark Trust. Specializing in unusual and historic buildings, this agency has London apartments starting at around £650 for a four-night-minimum stay. ⊠ *Shottesbrooke* ☎ *01628/825–925* ⊕ *www.landmarktrust.org.uk* .

HOME EXCHANGES

If you would like to exchange your home for someone else's, join a home-exchange organization, which will send you its updated listings of available exchanges for a year.

Intervac U.S. It costs from $99 per year for a listing and online access with this company. ☎ *866/884–7567* ⊕ *us.intervac-homeexchange.com* .

450-thread count, bathrooms are marble, and everything is done in impeccable taste. **Pros:** beautiful space; handy for shopping at Harrods. **Cons:** breakfast is expensive. ⑤ *Rooms from: £340* ⊠ *22–24 Basil St., Knightsbridge* ☎ *020/7589–5171, 800/926–3199 in U.S.* ⊕ *www.capitalhotel.co.uk* ⌷ *40 rooms, 9 suites* ❑ *Breakfast* Ⓜ *Knightsbridge* ✛ *4:F1.*

$$$$
HOTEL

❑ **Egerton House.** Sensationally soigné, chicly decorated, and feeling like your own private London home, this hotel has some truly luxuriant design touches, including guest rooms lavishly decorated with rich fabrics and a knockout white-on-gold dining room. **Pros:** lovely staff; magnificent interiors; striking art; seniors discounts available. **Cons:** some style touches a little too froufrou—even if Toulouse-Lautrec would have approved. ⑤ *Rooms from: £315* ⊠ *17–19 Egerton Terr., Knightsbridge* ☎ *020/7589–2412, 877/955–1515 in U.S.* ⊕ *www.redcarnationhotels.*

com ↙ *23 rooms, 6 suites* ⏐◎⏐ *Breakfast* Ⓜ *Knightsbridge, South Kensington* ✛ *4:F2.*

$$$$ 🖼 **Mandarin Oriental Hyde Park.** Built in 1880, the Mandarin Oriental
HOTEL welcomes you with one of the most exuberantly Victorian facades in
Fodor'sChoice town, then fast-forwards you to high-trend modern London, thanks to
★ striking and luxurious guest rooms filled with high-tech gadgets. **Pros:**
great shopping at your doorstep; amazing views of Hyde Park; excellent service. **Cons:** nothing comes cheap; you must dress for dinner
(and lunch and breakfast). Ⓢ *Rooms from: £462* ✉ *66 Knightsbridge,
Knightsbridge* ☎ *020/7235–2000* ⊕ *www.mandarinoriental.com/
london* ↙ *177 rooms, 23 suites* ⏐◎⏐ *Breakfast* Ⓜ *Knightsbridge* ✛ *4:F1.*

BELGRAVIA

$$ 🖼 **B&B Belgravia.** At this modern guesthouse near Victoria Station, a
B&B/INN clean, chic white color scheme, simple modern furniture, and a lounge
where a fire crackles away in the winter are all geared to homey com-
forts. **Pros:** nice extras like free use of a laptop in the hotel lounge; cof-
fee and tea always available. **Cons:** rooms and bathrooms are small;
unimaginative breakfasts; can be noisy, especially on lower floors; decor
a bit tired around the edges. Ⓢ *Rooms from: £120* ✉ *64–66 Ebury
St., Victoria* ☎ *020/7259–8570* ⊕ *www.bb-belgravia.com* ↙ *17 rooms*
⏐◎⏐ *Breakfast* Ⓜ *Sloane Sq., Victoria* ✛ *4:H2.*

$$ 🖼 **The Luna Simone Hotel.** This delightful and friendly little family-run
HOTEL hotel, a short stroll from Buckingham Palace, is a real find for the price
in central London. **Pros:** friendly and well run; family rooms are outstanding value; superb location. **Cons:** tiny bathrooms; thin walls; no
elevator or air-conditioning. Ⓢ *Rooms from: £134* ✉ *47–49 Belgrave
Rd., Pimlico* ☎ *020/7834–5897* ⊕ *www.lunasimonehotel.com* ↙ *36
rooms* ⏐◎⏐ *Breakfast* Ⓜ *Pimlico, Victoria* ✛ *5:A4.*

$$ 🖼 **Studios@82.** A great little side operation from **B&B Belgravia,** these
RENTAL self-catering apartments represent fantastic value for money. **Pros:** great
price; lovely location; all the independence of self-catering. **Cons:** lots of
stairs and no elevator; check-in is at B&B Belgravia, six doors down the
street. Ⓢ *Rooms from: £125* ✉ *82 Ebury St., Victoria* ☎ *020/7259–8570*
⊕ *www.bb-belgravia.com* ↙ *9 apartments* ⏐◎⏐ *Breakfast* Ⓜ *Knights-
bridge* ✛ *4:H2.*

NOTTING HILL AND BAYSWATER

NOTTING HILL

$ 🖼 **The Main House.** A stay in this delightfully welcoming B&B feels more
B&B/INN like sleeping over at a friend's house than in a hotel—albeit a par-
Fodor'sChoice ticularly wealthy and well-connected friend. **Pros:** unique and unusual
★ place; charming and helpful owners. **Cons:** three-night-minimum stay
is restrictive; few in-house services. Ⓢ *Rooms from: £110* ✉ *6 Colvile
Rd., Notting Hill* ☎ *020/7221–9691* ⊕ *www.themainhouse.com* ↙ *4
rooms* ⏐◎⏐ *Breakfast* Ⓜ *Notting Hill Gate* ✛ *1:A4.*

$ 🖼 **Portobello Gold.** This no-frills B&B, in the heart of the Portobello
B&B/INN Road antiques area above the pub and restaurant of the same name,
offers comfortable guest rooms where double beds take up almost all
the space. **Pros:** great Notting Hill location; pleasant staff; free Wi-Fi.

15

Cons: tiny bedrooms; "wet rooms" replace proper bathrooms (be prepared to shower by the sink); can be noisy; no elevator; if you want more than a continental breakfast, you have to pay £8 extra. ⑤ *Rooms from: £75 ⊠ 95–97 Portobello Rd., Notting Hill ☎ 020/7460–4910 ⊕ www.portobellogold.com ⌇ 6 rooms, 1 apartment* |⦶| *Breakfast* Ⓜ *Notting Hill Gate ✣ 1:A4.*

$$ ⛫ **The Portobello Hotel.** One of London's quirkiest hotels, the little Por-
HOTEL   tobello (formed from two adjoining Victorian houses) has attracted scores of celebrities to its small but stylish rooms over the years, and the decor reflects these hip credentials with joyous abandon. **Pros:** stylish and unique; celebrity vibe; guests have use of nearby gym and pool. **Cons:** all but the priciest rooms are quite small; may be too eccentric for some. ⑤ *Rooms from: £195 ⊠ 22 Stanley Gardens, Notting Hill ☎ 020/7727–2777 ⊕ www.portobello-hotel.co.uk ⊘ Closed 10 days at Christmas ⌇ 21 rooms* |⦶| *Breakfast* Ⓜ *Notting Hill Gate ✣ 1:A5.*

BAYSWATER

$$ ⛫ **Colonnade.** Near a canal filled with colorful "narrowboats" in the
HOTEL   Little Venice neighborhood, this lovely town house offers individually styled rooms—some are split-level; others have balconies—filled with rich brocades, velvets, and antiques. **Pros:** beautifully decorated; unique and little-known part of London, five minutes from Paddington Station; free Wi-Fi. **Cons:** you have to go through shoddier parts of town to get here; rooms are small. ⑤ *Rooms from: £125 ⊠ 2 Warrington Crescent, Bayswater ☎ 020/7286–1052 ⊕ www.colonnadehotel.co.uk/ ⌇ 15 rooms, 28 suites* |⦶| *Breakfast* Ⓜ *Warwick Ave. ✣ 1:C2.*

$ ⛫ **Lancaster Hall Hotel.** This cheap and cheerful choice just north of Hyde
HOTEL   Park offers clean, simple rooms at a decent price, along with a good buffet breakfast. **Pros:** decent, inexpensive, no-frills accommodations; excellent central location five-minute walk to Hyde Park; short Tube or bus ride away from many sights. **Cons:** just the basics; only the Youth Wing has nonsmoking rooms; street noise; cheap beds; all double rooms are actually "twins" (two separate single beds). ⑤ *Rooms from: £95 ⊠ 35 Craven Terr., Bayswater ☎ 020/7723–9276 ⊕ www.lancaster-hall-hotel.co.uk ⌇ 180 rooms* |⦶| *Breakfast* Ⓜ *Lancaster Gate, Paddington. National Rail: Paddington ✣ 1:D4.*

$ ⛫ **London House Hotel.** Set in a row of white Georgian town houses, this
HOTEL   excellent budget option in hit-or-miss Bayswater is friendly, well run, and spotlessly clean. **Pros:** friendly and efficient; emphasis on value for money; good location. **Cons:** some public areas feel a bit too clinical; smallest rooms are tiny. ⑤ *Rooms from: £100 ⊠ 81 Kensington Garden Sq., Bayswater ☎ 020/7243–1810 ⊕ www.londonhousehotels.com ⌇ 100 rooms* |⦶| *Breakfast* Ⓜ *Queensway, Bayswater ✣ 1:B4.*

$ ⛫ **Parkwood Hotel.** Just seconds from Hyde Park in one of London's
B&B/INN   swankiest enclaves (the Blairs live a few doors away), this sweet little guesthouse is an oasis of value for money, with warm and helpful hosts and bright guest rooms that are simply furnished with pastel color schemes and reproduction antique beds. **Pros:** lovely hosts; free Wi-Fi; hotel guarantees to match or beat price of any other hotel of its class in the area. **Cons:** often booked up in advance; no elevator; front-facing rooms can be noisy. ⑤ *Rooms from: £89 ⊠ 4 Stanhope Pl., Bayswater*

LODGING ALTERNATIVES

London School of Economics Vacations. London School of Economics Vacations costs around £88 for a double with shared bathroom, or £92 for a double with private bathroom. ⊠ *Passfield Hall, 1–7 Endsleigh Pl., Bloomsbury* ☎ *020/7955-7676* ⊕ *www.lsevacations.co.uk* ▭ *No credit cards* ⦿ *No meals .*

University College London. University College London opens up its accommodations from mid-June to mid-September (for two-night minimum stays). ⊠ *Residence Manager, Campbell House, 5–10 Taviton St.* ☎ *020/7837-6704* ⊕ *www.ucl.ac.uk/residences* ⦿ *No meals .*

15

☎ *020/7402–2241* ⊕ *www.parkwoodhotel.com* ⇆ *18 rooms* ⦿ *Breakfast* Ⓜ *Marble Arch* ✛ *1:F4.*

$$ 🛏 **Space Apart Hotel.** These studio apartments near Hyde Park are done
RENTAL in soothing tones of white and gray, with polished wood floors and attractive modern kitchenettes equipped with all you need to make small meals. **Pros:** especially good value for the money; the larger suites have space for four people; handy location. **Cons:** no in-house restaurant or bar; minimum two-night stay required. Ⓢ *Rooms from: £140* ⊠ *32–37 Kensington Gardens Sq., Bayswater* ☎ *020/7908–1340* ⊕ *www.aparthotel-london.co.uk* ⇆ *30 rooms* ⦿ *No meals* Ⓜ *Bayswater* ✛ *1:B4.*

$$ 🛏 **Vancouver Studios.** This pleasant aparthotel, in a converted Victorian
RENTAL town house, is full of quirky design flourishes, from flock wallpaper in the sitting room to a suit of armor at the top of the stairs. **Pros:** more space than most traditional hotel rooms; unique and pleasantly designed little apartments. **Cons:** a bit out of the way. Ⓢ *Rooms from: £154* ⊠ *30 Prince's Sq., Bayswater* ☎ *020/7243–1270* ⊕ *vancouverstudios.co.uk* ⇆ *45 studios* ⦿ *No meals* Ⓜ *Bayswater, Queensway* ✛ *1:B4.*

REGENT'S PARK AND HAMPSTEAD

REGENT'S PARK

$$ 🛏 **Meliá White House.** Converted from a beautiful modernist 1930s
HOTEL apartment block, this stylish hotel is filled with nods to its prewar ori-
FAMILY gins. **Pros:** great location near Regent's Park and Oxford Street; good restaurant; families are well treated—kids get a gift on arrival. **Cons:** classic rooms are small. Ⓢ *Rooms from: £180* ⊠ *Albany St., Regent's Park* ☎ *020/393–000* ⊕ *www.melia.com* ⇆ *581 rooms, 112 apartments* ⦿ *Some meals* Ⓜ *Great Portland St.* ✛ *1:H2.*

HAMPSTEAD

$ 🛏 **Glenlyn Guest House.** An excellent option for travelers who don't mind
B&B/INN being a long Tube ride away from the action, this converted Victorian town house offers a high standard of accommodation a few miles north of Hampstead. **Pros:** comfortable and friendly; you get more for your money than you would in central London; adjoining rooms can

be converted to family suites; five-minute walk to Tube station. **Cons:** you have to factor in the cost and inconvenience of a ½-hour Tube ride to central London; no restaurant. $ *Rooms from: £90* ⊠ *6 Woodside Park Rd., North Finchley* ☎ *020/8445–0440* ⊕ *www.glenlynhotel.com* ⇥ *27 rooms, 2 apartments* ⦾ *Breakfast* Ⓜ *Woodside Park* ✛ *1:D1.*

$ ▦ **The Hide.** This cozy, chic little hideaway is exceptional value for

HOTEL money and exceeds virtually anything you could hope to find in cen-

Fodor's Choice tral London for the price; the great downside is that the half-hour

★ Tube ride into town can start to feel like penance at the end of a long day of sightseeing. **Pros:** excellent value for money; great service; free Wi-Fi; close to Tube station. **Cons:** far from the center; dull neighborhood. $ *Rooms from: £100* ⊠ *230 Hendon Way, Hendon, Hampstead* ☎ *020/8203–1670* ⊕ *www.thehidelondon.com* ⇥ *22 rooms* ⦾ *Breakfast* Ⓜ *Hendon Central* ✛ *1:H1.*

$ ▦ **La Gaffe.** The name of this simple B&B (located above an Italian

B&B/INN restaurant) means "the mistake" in Italian, and is also the punchline to the unlikely tale of how the original husband-and-wife proprietors met in the 1950s—but it also rather neatly chimes with the cockney term "gaff," meaning a simple, cozy residence. **Pros:** unusual place with a cheerful atmosphere; no shared bathrooms. **Cons:** few services; no elevator; outside city center. $ *Rooms from: £99* ⊠ *107–111 Heath St., Hampstead* ☎ *020/7435–8965* ⊕ *www.lagaffe.co.uk* ⇥ *18 rooms, 3 suites* ⦾ *Breakfast* Ⓜ *Hampstead* ✛ *1:D1.*

ISLINGTON

$ ▦ **Arlington Avenue.** A find like this in London is as rare as hen's teeth:

B&B/INN an immaculate, friendly, Georgian town-house B&B, full of character, not too far from the city center, *and* at a rock-bottom price. **Pros:** genuinely stylish and comfortable; friendly hosts; quiet street; cheap as you'll ever hope to find for a place this nice in London. **Cons:** really more a private house with guest rooms than a B&B—not to all tastes; shared guest bathroom; neighborhood is trendy but verging on not-so-nice. $ *Rooms from: £65* ⊠ *Arlington Ave., Islington* ☎ *07711/265–183* ⊕ *www.arlingtonavenue.co.uk* ⇥ *2 rooms* ⦾ *Breakfast* Ⓜ *Angel, Essex Rd.* ✛ *2:D1.*

PRIMROSE HILL

$$ ▦ **30 King Henry's Road.** Floor-to-ceiling books and a wealth of art dec-

B&B/INN orate this lovely little B&B in Primrose Hill, the perennially trendy

Fodor's Choice "village" neighborhood north of Regent's Park. **Pros:** unique, homey

★ atmosphere; lovely hosts; great neighborhood. **Cons:** no extras; not very central; smaller rooms share a bathroom. $ *Rooms from: £130* ⊠ *30 King Henry's Rd., Primrose Hill* ☎ *020/7483–2871* ⇥ *5 rooms* ⦾ *Breakfast* Ⓜ *Chalk Farm* ✛ *1:G1.*

PUBS AND
NIGHTLIFE

Updated By
Jo Caird

There isn't a London nightlife scene—there is a multitude of them. As long as there are crowds for obscure teenage rock bands, Dickensian-style pubs, comedy cabarets, and "bodysonic" dance nights, someone will create clubs and venues for them in London. The result? London has become a veritable utopia for excitement junkies, culture fiends, and those who—simply put—like to party.

Nearly everyone who visits London these days is mesmerized by the city's energy, which reveals itself in layers. Whether you prefer rhythm and blues with fine French food, the gritty guitar-riff music of Camden Town, the boutique beers of East London, a pint and gourmet pizza at a local gastropub, or swanky cocktails and sushi at London's sexiest lair, London is sure to feed your fancy.

PLANNING

GETTING AROUND
Tube lines serving central London (check ⊕ *www.tfl.gov.uk* for details) now run all night on Friday and Saturday, making getting home after a late night cheaper and easier than ever before. The rest of the network stops running around 12:30 am Monday–Saturday and midnight on Sunday. Night buses are largely safe and reliable, but far slower than taxis, as you'd expect. The best place to hail a black taxi is at the front door of one of the major hotels; or find a licensed local minicab firm on the Transport for London website. Avoid unlicensed taxis that tout for business around closing time.

LIQUOR AND SMOKING LAWS
Laws now allow London drinking establishments to extend their opening hours beyond the traditional 11 pm closing, and smoking is banned. Most pubs and bars still close by midnight or a few short hours later.

CAN I TAKE MY KIDS TO THE PUB?

As pubs increasingly emphasize what's coming out of the kitchen alongside what's flowing from the tap, bringing the kids is more of an option. The law dictates that children 14 to 17 may enter a pub but are not permitted to purchase or drink alcohol, and children under 14 are not permitted in the bar area of a pub unless the pub has a "Children's Certificate" and the kids are accompanied by an adult. Some pubs have a section set aside for families, especially during the day, but many don't allow children in the evening.

WHAT TO WEAR

As a general rule, you won't see too many people in the upscale London nightspots wearing jeans and sneakers. People are more likely to dress down for an evening in the pub.

FIND OUT WHAT'S PLAYING WHERE

Because today's cool spot is often tomorrow's forgotten or closed venue, check out the weekly listings in the *Evening Standard* (⊕ *www.standard. co.uk*) and, especially, *Time Out* (⊕ *www.timeout.com/london*). Other websites to consult are ⊕ *www.londontown.com*, ⊕ *www.allinlondon. co.uk*, and ⊕ *www.viewlondon.co.uk*. Although most clubs are frequented by those under 30, there are plenty of others that are popular with patrons of all ages and types. A particularly useful website for clubs and club nights is ⊕ *www.residentadvisor.net*.

Door and bar staff are hawkish about underage drinking, so be sure that you take photo ID with you on a night out.

PUBS

Pubs are where Londoners go to hang out, see and be seen, act out the drama of life, and, for some, drink themselves into varying degrees of oblivion. The pub is still a vital part of London life, though many of the traditions of the pub experience are evolving. There are few better places to meet Londoners in their local habitat. There are somewhere around 4,000 pubs in London—some are dark and woody, others plain and functional, a few still have original Victorian etched glass, Edwardian panels, and art nouveau carvings.

Not long ago, before the smoking ban, pubs tended to be smoky, male-dominated places with a couple of ubiquitous beers on tap and the only available food a packet of salt-and-vinegar-flavor crisps (potato chips). All that has changed. Gastropub fever swept through London around the turn of the 21st century and at many places, char-grills are installed in the kitchen and inventive pub grub is on the menu. A new wave of enthusiasm for craft beers is now having a similar effect on the liquid offerings.

The big decision is what to drink. The beer of choice among Britons is **"bitter,"** lightly fermented, with an amber color, and getting its bitterness from hops. It's usually served at cellar temperature (that is, cooler than room temperature but neither chilled, nor, as common misconception would have it, warm). **Real ales,** served from wooden kegs and made without chilling, filtering, or pasteurization, are flatter than other bitters and are enjoying a renaissance. Many small London breweries have sprung up in recent years, and bottled designer and American beers can be found in most bars across London. **Stouts,** like Guinness, are a meal in themselves and something of an acquired taste—they have a dark, caramel-infused flavor and look like thickened flat Coke with a frothy top. Chilled **lagers,** most familiar to American drinkers, are light in color and carbonated. ■TIP→ **The most commonly served lagers in Britain are from continental Europe.**

Many English pubs are owned by chains such as Mitchells and Butlers, Punch Taverns, or Samuel Smith, and are tenanted, meaning that they are run on a sort of franchise basis. Most are not obviously branded and retain at least some independence. Independently owned pubs, sometimes called "free houses," tend to offer a more extensive selection of beer. Other potations available include apple-based **ciders,** ranging from sweet to dry and from alcoholic to very alcoholic (Irish cider, served over ice, is now also ubiquitous), and **shandies,** a mix of beer and lemonade or a citrus-flavored soda. Friendly pubs will usually be happy to give you a taste of the brew of your choice before you order.

The list below offers a few pubs selected for interesting beer, historical interest, a pleasant garden, music, or good food, but you might just as happily adopt your own temporary "local."

MAYFAIR

The pubs in this central London neighborhood tend to be as upscale as the people that frequent them, but you'll also find plenty of informal establishments with a lot of character.

Audley. Big, smart, old-school, and a little brash, the Audley makes up in friendly atmosphere what it lacks in charm. There's a good selection of beer on tap, and it's far enough away from the tourist hot spots that, on the right day, it can feel like a village pub. ⊠ *41–43 Mount St., Mayfair* ☎ *020/7499–1843* ⊕ *www.taylor-walker.co.uk* Ⓜ *Bond St., Green Park.*

Punch Bowl. In a quiet corner of Mayfair, the cozy little Punch Bowl has a worn wood floor and well-spoken staff. The pub dates from 1750 and the interior remains steadfastly old-fashioned, with a painting of Churchill, candles, polished dark wood, and engraved windows. Try the place's own ale, made specially in Scotland by Caledonian. A dining area at the rear buzzes at lunchtime with locals who come for the upscale English pub food, and there's a fancier restaurant upstairs. ⊠ *41 Farm St., Mayfair* ☎ *020/7493–6841* ⊕ *www.punchbowllondon.com* Ⓜ *Green Park, Bond St.*

16

SOHO AND COVENT GARDEN

Traditional British "boozers" stand side-by-side with informal continental-style drinking dens in this buzzing central neighborhood. Drop by for a late drink and you may find yourself rubbing shoulders with musicians and actors from the West End's many theaters.

SOHO

Dog and Duck. A beautiful example of a late 19th-century London pub, the Dog and Duck has a well-preserved interior furnished with tiles, mirrors, and polished wood, though it's often so packed that it's hard to get a good look. There's a good selection of real ales at the bar, and a restaurant serving standard pub dishes upstairs. ⊠ *18 Bateman St., Soho* ☎ *020/7494–0697* ⊕ *www.nicholsonspubs.co.uk* Ⓜ *Tottenham Court Road.*

French House. In the pub where the French Resistance convened during World War II, Soho hipsters and eccentrics now rub shoulders with theater people and the literati—more than shoulders, actually, because this tiny, tricolor-waving, photo-lined pub is almost always packed. In the French style, beer is served in half-pints only. If you're around on July 14, come and join in the rapturous Bastille Day celebrations. ⊠ *49 Dean St., Soho* ☎ *020/7437–2477* ⊕ *www.frenchhousesoho.com* Ⓜ *Tottenham Court Rd.*

COVENT GARDEN

Harp. This is the sort of friendly little local you might find on some out-of-the-way backstreet, except that it's right in the middle of town, between Trafalgar Square and Covent Garden. As a result, the Harp can get crowded, especially because it was named British pub of the year by the Campaign for Real Ale, but the squeeze is worth it for the excellent beer (there are usually 10 carefully chosen ales, often including a London microbrew) and a no-frills menu of high-quality British sausages, cooked behind the bar. ⊠ *47 Chandos Pl., Covent Garden* ☎ *020/7836–0291* ⊕ *www.harpcoventgarden.com* Ⓜ *Charing Cross.*

Lamb & Flag. This refreshingly ungentrified 17th-century pub was once known as the Bucket of Blood because the upstairs room was used as a ring for bare-knuckle boxing. Now it's a friendly—and bloodless—place, serving food and real ale. It's on the edge of Covent Garden, up a hidden alley off Garrick Street. ⊠ *33 Rose St., Covent Garden* ☎ *020/7497–9504* ⊕ *www.lambandflagcoventgarden.co.uk* Ⓜ *Covent Garden.*

BLOOMSBURY, HOLBORN, AND FITZROVIA

The gorgeous pubs in this literary neighborhood attract tourists in the daytime and huge crowds of after-work drinkers in the early evening. They tend to quiet down as the night advances, making this area a great spot for a relaxing evening out.

BLOOMSBURY

The Lamb. Charles Dickens and his contemporaries drank here, but today's enthusiastic clientele make sure this intimate and eternally popular pub avoids the pitfalls of feeling too old-timey. For private chats at the bar, you can close a delicate etched-glass "snob screen" to the bar staff, opening it only when you fancy another pint. ☒ *94 Lamb's Conduit St., Bloomsbury* ☎ *020/7405–0713* ⊕ *www.youngs. co.uk* Ⓜ *Russell Sq.*

Museum Tavern. Across the street from the British Museum, this friendly and classy Victorian pub makes an ideal resting place after the rigors of the culture trail. Karl Marx unwound here after a hard day in the Library. He could have spent his *Kapital* on any of 15 well-kept beers available on tap. ☒ *49 Great Russell St., Bloomsbury* ☎ *020/7242–8987* ⊕ *www.taylor-walker. co.uk* Ⓜ *Tottenham Court Rd., Holborn.*

The Queen's Larder. The royal associated with this tiny pub is Queen Charlotte, who is said to have stored food here for her "mad" husband, George III, when he was being treated nearby. The interior preserves its antique feel, with dark wood and old posters, and in the evenings fills up quickly with office workers and students. In good weather, you might prefer to grab one of the seats outdoors. ☒ *1 Queen's Sq., Bloomsbury* ☎ *020/7837–5627* ⊕ *www.queenslarder.co.uk* Ⓜ *Russell Sq.*

HOLBORN

Holborn Whippet. An impressive number of craft beers are served from unmarked taps set into a brick column behind the bar in this new-breed London pub. Names of the brews are all chalked onto boards, while empty barrels outside testify to the popularity of the best; lunch and supper are served daily. It's popular, especially when nearby offices empty out in early evening, with punters spilling out onto ornate, pedestrian-only Sicilian Avenue. Inside, it's a deliberately plain affair, with little to detract from the liquid experience. ☒ *Sicilian Ave., Holborn* ☎ *020/3137–9937* ⊕ *holbornwhippet.com* Ⓜ *Holborn.*

Fodor's Choice
★

Princess Louise. This fine, popular pub is an exquisite museum piece of a Victorian interior, with glazed tiles and intricately engraved glass screens that divide the bar area into cozy little annexes. It's not all show, either. There's a good selection of excellent-value Yorkshire real ales from the Samuel Smith's brewery. ☒ *208 High Holborn, Holborn* ☎ *020/7405–8816* Ⓜ *Holborn.*

FITZROVIA

The Green Man. This bright and friendly pub is a great refueling stop for Oxford Street shoppers. Cider is the specialty, with nine varieties on tap, plus bottled beers from around the world. Board games, tasty pub food, and Sunday roasts make it the sort of place you'll find hard to leave. ☒ *36 Riding House St., Fitzrovia* ☎ *020/7580–9087* ⊕ *www. thegreenmanw1.co.uk* Ⓜ *Goodge St., Oxford Circus.*

16

WHAT'S IN A NAME?

Pictorial signs traditionally helped illiterate customers identify establishments. The practice goes back to Roman times, with tavernas hanging vines outside to advertise the fact that they sold wine. The naming of pub and inns was widespread by the 12th century, and in 1393 King Richard II made it law for all pubs to display a sign, the idea being to make it easier for the official ale-taster to find the establishments he needed to visit.

The most common pub names offer an illustrated guide to Britain's past, with various monarchs, legends and eras referenced in the colorful signs swinging above the doors of drinking dens all over the country. The Red Lion, for example, one of the most common pub names in use today, dates from when King James VI of Scotland became James I of the united kingdoms of England and Scotland and ordered that the heraldric lion of Scotland be displayed on all important buildings. Other pub names highlight the importance of specific events (the Trafalgar), mythical figures (Robin Hood), and technological advances (the Railway).

In "pub cricket," a game traditionally played on long car journeys in the United Kingdom, player take turns at "bat." For each pub passed, the batter gets a score corresponding to the number of legs possessed by any beings that are part of the pub's name. For instance, passing the Swan gets you two points, because swans have two legs. The batter continues to accrue points until he or she is "batted out" by passing a pub with "head" or "arms" in its name (the Queen's Head, for example). The next player then takes over and the game continues until the end of the journey, when whoever has the highest score is declared the winner.

CLERKENWELL AND THE CITY

Workers from The City's many finance firms pour into the neighborhood's pubs at the end of the day, but by 8 pm the party is pretty much over and you'll have no trouble finding a place to sit. It's always worth ducking down a side street, as this is where some of the area's most interesting establishments can be found.

Fodor's Choice ★ **The Blackfriar.** A step from Blackfriars Tube station, this spectacular pub has an Arts and Crafts interior that is entertainingly, satirically ecclesiastical, with inlaid mother-of-pearl, wood carvings, stained glass, and marble pillars all over the place. Under finely lettered temperance tracts on view just below the reliefs of monks, fairies, and friars, there is a nice group of ales on tap from independent brewers. The 20th-century poet Sir John Betjeman once led a successful campaign to save the pub from demolition. ⊠ *174 Queen Victoria St., The City* ☏ *020/7236–5474* ⊕ *www.nicholsonspubs.co.uk/theblackfriarblackfriarslondon* Ⓜ *Blackfriars.*

Craft Beer Company. With 37 beers on tap and 300 more in bottles (some brewed exclusively for the Craft Beer Company), the main problem here is knowing where to start. Luckily, friendly and knowledgeable staff are happy to advise or give tasters—or why not sign up for a guided tasting session? A huge chandelier and a mirrored ceiling lend antique charm to the interior, and a smattering of tourists and beer pilgrims break up the crowds of Leather Lane workers and locals. ⊠ *82 Leather La., Clerkenwell* ⊕ *www.thecraftbeerco.com* Ⓜ *Chancery La.*

Fodor's Choice **Jerusalem Tavern.** Owned by the well-respected St. Peter's Brewery from
★ Suffolk, the Jerusalem Tavern is one-of-a-kind: small, and endearingly eccentric. Ancient Delft-style tiles meld with wood and concrete in a converted watchmaker and jeweler's shop dating back to the 18th century. The beer, both bottled and on tap, is some of the best available anywhere in London. It's loved by Londoners and is often busy, especially after work. ⊠ *55 Britton St., Clerkenwell* ☎ *020/7490–4281* ⊕ *www. stpetersbrewery.co.uk/london-pub* Ⓜ *Farringdon.*

Viaduct Tavern. Queen Victoria opened the nearby Holborn Viaduct in 1869, and this eponymous pub honored the road bridge by serving its first pint the same year. Much of the Victorian decoration is still extant, with gorgeous paintings (depicting the statues on the viaduct), carved wood, and engraved glass. The tavern has a haunted reputation, which stems from its proximity to the former Newgate Prison and its gallows. Prison cells in the basement, once used for debtors, can be seen with a free tour when staff aren't busy with customers. There are usually three or four ales on tap; lunch is also served. ⊠ *126 Newgate St., The City* ☎ *020/7600–1863* ⊕ *viaducttavern.co.uk* ⊗ *Closed weekends* Ⓜ *St. Paul's.*

Ye Olde Cheshire Cheese. Yes, this extremely historic pub (it dates from 1667, the year after the Great Fire of London) is full of tourists, but it deserves a visit for its sawdust-covered floors, low wood-beam ceilings, and the 14th-century crypt of Whitefriars' monastery under the cellar bar. This was the most regular of Dr. Johnson's and Dickens's many locals. Food is served. ⊠ *145 Fleet St., The City* ☎ *020/7353–6170* ⊗ *Closed Sun.* Ⓜ *Blackfriars.*

Ye Olde Mitre. Hidden off the side of 8 Hatton Gardens, this cozy pub's roots go back to 1546, though it was rebuilt around 1782. Originally built for the staff of the Bishop of Ely, whose London residence was next door, it remained officially part of Cambridgeshire until the 20th century. It's a friendly little labyrinthine place, with a fireplace, well-kept ales, wooden beams, and traditional bar snacks. ⊠ *1 Ely Ct., The City* ☎ *020/7405–4751* ⊕ *yeoldemitreholborn.co.uk* ⊗ *Closed weekends* Ⓜ *Chancery La.*

EAST LONDON

East London is better known these days for its bars and clubs than for its pubs, but in historic neighborhoods such as Spitalfields and Wapping there's a cozy old drinking den around practically every corner.

Prospect of Whitby. Named after a ship, this is one of London's oldest riverside pubs, dating from around 1520. Once upon a time it was called the Devil's Tavern because of the lowlives—thieves and smugglers—who congregated here. Ornamented with pewter ware and nautical objects,

16

this much-loved "boozer" has a terrace with views of the Thames, from where boat trips often point it out. ⊠ *57 Wapping Wall, East End* ☎ *020/7481–1095* ⊕ *www.taylor-walker.co.uk* Ⓜ *Wapping; DLR: Shadwell.*

Sebright Arms. This surprisingly enormous pub is on a small alley that's off that hipsters' favorite, Hackney Road. During the day it's a chilled-out place to grab a craft beer, but at night a party atmosphere reigns, with fuel provided by tasty burgers and fries. Always informal, the pub attracts a young, alternative crowd. ⊠ *31–35 Coate St., Bethnal Green* ☎ *020/7729–0937* ⊕ *www.sebrightarms.co.uk* Ⓜ *Bethnal Green, Cambridge Heath.*

SOUTH OF THE THAMES

Head to the area around Borough Market—one of London's oldest neighborhoods—for lively historic pubs where locals and tourists jostle for craft ales and gourmet snacks.

Anchor & Hope. One of London's most popular gastropubs, the Anchor & Hope doesn't take reservations (except for the three-course prix-fixe Sunday lunch that begins at 12:30 pm). Would-be diners snake around the red-walled, wooden-floored pub, kept happy by some good real ales and a fine wine list as they wait for at least 45 minutes for a table. The excellent, meaty food is old-fashioned English—for instance, salt cod, tripe, and chips (fries)—with a few modern twists. ⊠ *36 The Cut, South Bank* ☎ *020/7928–9898* ⊕ *www.charleswells.co.uk* Ⓜ *Southwark.*

FAMILY **Cutty Sark.** Take a break from Greenwich's cultural and historical attractions at this spacious riverside pub, which dates back to the late 1700s. Mismatched furniture give the large rooms a homey feel, while the wood-burning stove keeps things cozy. There's outdoor seating, too, with fantastic views of the Thames. A classic pub menu includes several tasty sharing platters, and the beer list includes tipples from local London breweries. ⊠ *4–6 Ballast Quay, Greenwich* ☎ *020/8858–3146* ⊕ *www.cuttysarkse10.co.uk* Ⓜ *Cutty Sark, Maze Hill.*

Market Porter. Opposite the foodie treasures of Borough Market, this atmospheric pub opens at 6 am (weekdays) for the stallholders, and always seems busy. Remarkably, the place manages to remain relaxed, with helpful staff and happy customers spilling out onto the road right through the year. The wide selection of real ales is lovingly tended. The pub was used as a set for one of the Harry Potter movies. ⊠ *9 Stoney St., Borough* ☎ *020/7407–2495* ⊕ *www.markettaverns.co.uk* Ⓜ *London Bridge.*

The Mayflower. This atmospheric 17th-century riverside inn (rebuilt in the following century) has exposed beams and a terrace near the one-time berth of the famous ship on which the Pilgrims sailed to what became the American colonies. The pub has a heated jetty where customers can sit outside; alternatively, opt to enjoy the wood-beamed interiors, although this can get quite packed with sightseers. ⊠ *117 Rotherhithe St., South Bank* ☎ *020/7237–4088* ⊕ *themayflowerrotherhithe.com* Ⓜ *Rotherhithe.*

CHELSEA AND BELGRAVIA

Pubs in this upmarket central west neighborhood range from classy modern affairs with impressive wine lists and sharing platters to tiny local institutions guaranteed to make you feel like you've stepped back in time.

CHELSEA

The Antelope. Just around the corner from chic Sloane Square is the perfect spot to grab an unpretentious pint. Wood paneling and comfy seating create a snug environment, and there's a more genteel dining room upstairs. ⊠ *22 Eaton Terr., Chelsea* ☎ *020/7824–8512* ⊕ *www. antelope-eaton-terrace.co.uk* Ⓜ *Sloane Sq.*

BELGRAVIA

Fodor'sChoice ★

The Nag's Head. The landlord of this idiosyncratic little mews pub in Belgravia runs a tight ship, and no mobile phones are allowed. The lovingly collected artifacts (including antique penny arcade games) that decorate every inch of the place, high-quality beer, and old-fashioned pub grub should provide more than enough distraction. ⊠ *53 Kinnerton St., Belgravia* ☎ *020/7235–1135* Ⓜ *Knightsbridge, Hyde Park Corner.*

16

NOTTING HILL

The line between pub and bar is frequently blurred in this trendy area on the west side of the capital, with the emphasis on good—often haute—food, sleek style, and extensive wine lists.

The Cow. Crowds head to this chic mix of fun, haute food, and friendly, retro style for Guinness and oysters, either enjoying them in the unpretentious downstairs bar or the upstairs, more formal restaurant. The pub food is all excellent, though pricey, with lots of seafood and steaks (and sometimes a mix, as in the smoked eel with mash and bacon). The atmosphere's always warm, welcoming, and buzzing. ⊠ *89 Westbourne Park Rd., Notting Hill* ☎ *020/7221–0021* ⊕ *www.thecowlondon.co.uk* Ⓜ *Royal Oak, Westbourne Park.*

REGENT'S PARK AND HAMPSTEAD

London's village-like northern neighborhoods—Hampstead, Highgate, and Primrose Hill, to name a few—all boast fantastic local boozers where you can easily while away an afternoon. Camden Town has more of a buzz to it and attracts a younger crowd.

HAMPSTEAD

The Holly Bush. A short walk up the hill from Hampstead Tube station, the friendly Holly Bush was a country pub before London spread this far north. It retains something of a rural feel, with stripped wooden floors and an open fire, and is an intimate place to enjoy great ales and organic and free-range pub food. Try the homemade pork scratchings (rinds) and pickled eggs. ⊠ *22 Holly Mount, Hampstead* ☎ *020/7435–2892* ⊕ *www.hollybushhampstead.co.uk* Ⓜ *Hampstead.*

Spaniards Inn. Ideal as a refueling point when you're on a hike in Hampstead Heath, this historic, country-style, oak-beam pub has a gorgeous garden—the scene of the tea party in Dickens's *Pickwick Papers*. Dick Turpin, the highwayman, frequented the inn before Dickens's time, and Shelley, Keats, and Byron hung out here as well. The place is extremely popular, especially on Sunday, when Londoners roll in. It's canine friendly, too—there's even a dog wash in the garden. ⊠ *Spaniards Rd., Hampstead* ☎ *020/8731–8406* ⊕ *www.thespaniardshampstead.co.uk* Ⓜ *Hampstead.*

HIGHGATE

FAMILY **The Bull and Last.** A luxurious menu featuring the likes of roast venison and handmade ricotta and black cabbage ravioli makes this large corner pub a must-visit for visitors to Parliament Hill (aka Kite Hill), the area of Hampstead Heath that's just across the road. It's a good idea to make a reservation, particularly on Sunday, when the roasts attract punters from far and wide. Or in the summertime (April–September) order a hamper and have a picnic with London spreading out beneath you and kites flying overhead. ⊠ *168 Highgate Rd., Highgate* ☎ *020/7267–3641* ⊕ *www.thebullandlast.co.uk* Ⓜ *Kentish Town.*

THE THAMES UPSTREAM

A pint in a riverside pub is a London must, and the capital's western reaches offer some truly picturesque drinking opportunities. Pick a traditional establishment and you'll feel like you've ventured far from the Big Smoke.

RICHMOND

Roebuck. Perched on top of Richmond Hill, the Roebuck has perhaps the best view of any pub in London. The most sought-after seats are the benches found directly across the road, which look out over the Thames as it winds its way into the countryside below. Friendly and surprisingly unpretentious, given its lofty surrounds, it is well worth the long climb up the hill from the center of Richmond. ⊠ *130 Richmond Hill, Richmond* ☎ *020/8948–2329* ⊕ *www.taylor-walker.co.uk* Ⓜ *Richmond. National Rail: Richmond.*

HAMMERSMITH

Blue Anchor. This unaltered Georgian pub has been seen in the movie *Sliding Doors* and was the site where *The Planets* composer Gustav Holst wrote his *Hammersmith Suite*. Sit out by the river, or shelter inside with a good ale. ⊠ *13 Lower Mall, Hammersmith* ☎ *020/8748–5774* ⊕ *www.blueanchorlondon.com* Ⓜ *Hammersmith.*

Dove Inn. Read the list of famous ex-regulars, from Charles II and Nell Gwyn to Ernest Hemingway, as you wait for a beer at this smart, comely, and popular 16th-century riverside pub. An Irish folk band play on Monday nights, squeezing into the miniature front bar. If (as is often the case) the Dove is too full, stroll upstream along the bank to the Old Ship or the Blue Anchor. ⊠ *19 Upper Mall, Hammersmith* ☎ *020/8748–9474* ⊕ *www.dovehammersmith.co.uk* Ⓜ *Hammersmith.*

NIGHTLIFE

The pace with which London bars and clubs go in and out of fashion is mind-boggling. New trends, likewise, emerge all time. In one somewhat recent development, the dreaded velvet rope has been usurped by the doorbell-ringing mystique of members-only drinking clubs. Some of the city's most talked-about nightlife spots these days are those attached to some of the best restaurants and hotels—no wonder, when you consider the increased popularity of London cuisine in international circles. Moreover, the gay scene in London continues to flourish. One constant on the nightlife scene is variety. The understated glamour of north London's Primrose Hill, which makes movie stars feel so at ease, might be considered dull by the übertrendy club goers of London's East End. Likewise, the price of a pint in Chelsea would be considered blasphemous by the musicians and poets of multicultural Peckham.

Whatever your pleasure, however your whim turns come evening, chances are you'll find what you're looking for in London's ever-changing arena of activity and invention.

JAZZ AND BLUES

Jazz in London may include anything from danceable, smooth tunes played at a supper club to groovy New Orleans–style blues to exotic world-beat rhythms, which can be heard at some of the less central venues. London hosts the **London Jazz Festival** (⊕ www.efglondonjazzfestival.org.uk) in November, which showcases top and emerging artists in experimental jazz. The **Ealing Jazz Festival** (⊕ www.ealing.gov.uk), at the end of July, claims to be the biggest free jazz event in Europe.

16

WESTMINSTER, ST. JAMES'S, AND ROYAL LONDON

Elegant drinking holes catering to London's political and social elites abound in these central neighborhoods. Streets that are thronged with tourists and workers by day quiet down by the evening, leaving the area to its few residents and a handful of sophisticated drinkers and diners.

WESTMINSTER

BARS

Cinnamon Club. In the basement of what was once the Old Westminster Library, the Club Bar of this contemporary Indian restaurant (the curries are superb) has Bollywood scenes projected onto the glass back wall, Asian-theme cocktails (mango mojitos, "Delhi mules"), delicious bar snacks, and a clientele that includes fashionable young politicos. Upstairs, the Library Bar also serves cocktails through the day. ⊠ *The Old Westminster Library, Great Smith St., Westminster* ☎ *020/7222–2555* ⊕ *www.cinnamonclub.com* ⊗ *Daily noon–midnight* Ⓜ *Westminster.*

Fodor's Choice **Gordon's Wine Bar.** Nab a rickety table in the atmospheric, vaulted interior of what claims to be the oldest wine bar in London, or fight for standing room in the long pedestrian-only alley that runs alongside it.

THE GAY SCENE

Gay nightlife is as busy as it is in New York or Los Angeles. Soho's the traditional hub, and "Voho," the previously unfashionable Vauxhall, south of the river, is one upstart area for gay London.

Clubs in London cater to almost every desire, whether that be the suited-up Tommy Hilfiger–look-alike scene, dingy dives for cruising, flamboyant drag shows, lesbian tea dances, or themed fetish nights.

There's also a cornucopia of queer theater and performance art that runs throughout the year. Whatever your tastes, you'll be able to satisfy them with a night on the town in London.

Choices are admittedly much better for men than women; although many of the gay clubs are female-friendly, those catering strictly to lesbians are rare.

The British Film Institute puts on BFI Flare: London LGBT Film Festival (⊕ www.bfi.org.uk/flare) in late March and early April every year.

Pride London in June (an annual event that encompasses a parade, sports, art, comedy, theater, music, cabaret, and dance) welcomes anyone and everyone, and claimed around 800,000 participants in 2014. This extravagant 30,000-strong pageant spirals its way through London's streets, with major events taking place in Trafalgar Square and Leicester Square, then culminates in Victoria Embankment with ticketed parties continuing on afterward. See ⊕ prideinlondon.org for details.

For up-to-date listings, consult *Time Out* (⊕ www.timeout.com/london/lgbt), *Boyz* (⊕ www.boyz.co.uk), *Gay Times* (⊕ www.gaytimes.co.uk), *Attitude* (⊕ www.attitude.co.uk), or the lesbian monthly *Diva* (⊕ www.divamag.co.uk).

BARS, CAFÉS, AND PUBS

Most bars in London are gay-friendly, though there are a number of cafés and pubs that are particularly known as gay hangouts after-hours. The latest serve drinks until 3 am (11 pm on Sunday).

CLUBS

Many of London's best gay dance clubs are on particular nights in mixed clubs like Fabric.

Either way, the mood is always cheery as a diverse crowd sips on more than 60 different wines, ports, and sherries. Tempting cheese and meat plates are great for sharing. ⊠ *47 Villiers St., Westminster* ☎ *020/7930–1408* ⊕ *www.gordonswinebar.com* ⊗ *Mon.–Sat. 11–11, Sun. noon–10* Ⓜ *Charing Cross, Embankment.*

The Mint Leaf Bar. The renowned long bar is stocked with more than 500 spirits and serves more than 1,000 well-prepared cocktails. Nibbles and light snacks with an Indian twist are available, and if you're up for some more substantial spicy food, there's also a full restaurant. DJs play nightly from Wednesday to Saturday. A sister bar and restaurant is in Angel Court in The City. ⊠ *Suffolk Pl., Haymarket* ☎ *020/7930–9020* ⊕ *www.mintleafrestaurant.com* ⊗ *Mon.–Wed. and Sun. noon–3 pm, and 5 pm–midnight, Thurs.–Sat. 5 pm–1 am* Ⓜ *Piccadilly Circus.*

ST. JAMES'S

BARS

Fodor'sChoice **American Bar.** Festooned with a chin-dropping array of club ties, signed
★ celebrity photographs, sporting mementos, and baseball caps, this sensational hotel cocktail bar has superb martinis. The name dates from the
1930s, when hotel bars in London started to cater to growing numbers
of Americans crossing the Atlantic in ocean liners, but it wasn't until
the 1970s, when a customer left a small carved wooden eagle, that
the collection of paraphernalia was started. ✉ *Stafford Hotel, 16–18
St. James's Pl., st. James's* ☎ *020/7493–0111* ⊕ *www.thestaffordhotel.
co.uk* ☉ *Daily 11:30 am–11 pm* Ⓜ *Green Park.*

MAYFAIR

Bars in this upmarket central neighborhood—many of which can be
found within luxury hotels—attract a polished crowd. Cocktails, fine
wines, and rare aged spirits are the tipples of choice.

BARS

Oscar Wilde Bar at Hotel Café Royal. Sit where Oscar Wilde once sat in this
beautifully restored bar and tearoom at the luxurious Hotel Café Royal.
Established in 1865, the Grill Room (as it was known until recently)
was the place where Wilde met Lord Alfred Douglas, and over the years
it has hosted everyone from Mick Jagger and Elizabeth Taylor to Kanye
West and Kate Moss. The bar has a very fine Champagne list—including some delicious Champagne cocktails—but for the really Wilde, it's
got to be absinthe. On Friday and Saturday night, the gold leaf ceiling
and mirrored walls ring with the sultry sounds of Black Cat Cabaret's
Salon des Artistes; DJs take over at the end of the show. An indulgent
afternoon tea is served daily at noon, 2, and 4. ✉ *Hotel Café Royal, 68
Regent St., Piccadilly Circus* ☎ *020/7406–3333* ⊕ *www.hotelcaferoyal.
com* ✉ *Free; cabaret £30* ☉ *Afternoon tea daily noon–6; bar Tues.–
Thurs. 6:30 pm–1 am, Fri. and Sat. 6:30 pm–3 am* Ⓜ *Piccadilly Circus.*

16

Fodor'sChoice **Sketch.** One seat never looks like the next at this downright extraordi-
★ nary collection of esoteric living-room bars. The exclusive Parlour, a
patisserie during the day, exudes plenty of rarefied charm; the intimate
East Bar at the back is reminiscent of a sci-fi film set; and in the Glade
it's permanently sunset in a forest. The restrooms are surely London's
quirkiest. ✉ *9 Conduit St., Mayfair* ☎ *020/7659–4500* ⊕ *www.sketch.
london* ☉ *Parlour weekdays 8 am–2 am, Sat. 10 am–2 am, Sun. 10 am–
midnight; the Glade Mon.–Thurs. 1 pm–2 am, Fri. and Sat. noon–2 am,
Sun. noon–midnight; East Bar daily 6:30 pm–2 am* Ⓜ *Oxford Circus.*

SOHO AND COVENT GARDEN

The center of town is famous for its vibrant gay scene, atmospheric
music, cabaret venues, and acclaimed comedy clubs. In Covent Garden,
recent bar openings have also brought in some new buzz.

SOHO

BARS

The Blind Pig. Chances are you won't have heard of half the ingredients on the cocktail menu at this dark and sultry bar above Jason Atherton's casual restaurant, Social Dining House, but the sense of mystery only adds to the experience. So, too, do the antique mirrored ceilings, the delectable small plates (for instance, macaroni and cheese with shaved mushroom, and black pepper prawn crackers), and the knowledge that you've nabbed a seat at one of the coolest spots in Soho. ⊠ *58 Poland St., Soho* ☎ *020/7993–3251* ⊕ *www.socialeatinghouse.com* ⊗ *Mon.– Sat. noon–midnight* Ⓜ *Oxford Circus, Tottenham Court Rd.*

Le Beaujolais. Around 60 lovingly selected French wines are available here, and you can snack on olives, charcuterie, and homemade croque monsieurs (grilled ham-and-cheese sandwiches) while staying snug and warm under a bottle-laden ceiling as a funky blues sound track plays. The romantic, shabby-around-the-edges feel and authentic French insouciance may come as a surprise in the heart of tourist-centric London. ⊠ *25 Litchfield St., Soho* ☎ *020/7836–2955* ⊗ *Weekdays noon–11 am, Sat. 5 pm–11 pm* Ⓜ *Leicester Sq.*

DANCE CLUBS

Disco. At the end of an unlikely looking alley in the Newburgh Quarter is the entrance to Disco, a fun club playing, yep, you've guessed it, disco (from classic '70s to Daft Punk and beyond). The dance floor is the focus at this unpretentious basement joint, where staff dressed as airline stewards invite you to "check-in" your coat and give you a "boarding pass" in exchange for your entry fee. Technically it's members only, so email ahead to get your name on the list. You must be over 21 to enter. ⊠ *13 Kingly Ct., Soho* ⚓ *Beak St. entrance* ☎ *020/7036–0609* ⊕ *www. disco-london.com* 🎟 *£20* ⊗ *Thurs.–Sat. 10 pm–3 am* Ⓜ *Piccadilly Circus, Oxford Circus.*

COMEDY AND CABARET

100 Club. Since this small club opened in 1942, many of the greats have played here, from Glenn Miller and Louis Armstrong to the Who and the Sex Pistols. Saved from closure in 2010 by a campaign led by Sir Paul McCartney, the space now reverberates to jazz, '60s R&B, and northern soul. ⊠ *100 Oxford St., Soho* ☎ *020/7636–0933* ⊕ *www. the100club.co.uk* 🎟 *£5–£17* ⊗ *Fri.–Sun. 7:30 pm–late; weekdays vary, depending on gigs* Ⓜ *Oxford Circus, Tottenham Court Rd.*

Comedy Store. Before heading off to prime time, some of the United Kingdom's funniest stand-ups cut their teeth here, at what's considered the birthplace of alternative comedy. Comedy Store Players, a team with six comedians doing improvisation with audience suggestions, entertain on Wednesday and Sunday; the Cutting Edge steps in every Tuesday. Thursday, Friday, and Saturday have the best stand-up acts. There's also a bar with food. You must be over 18 to go here. ⊠ *1A Oxendon St., Soho* ☎ *0844/871–7699 ticket and booking line* ⊕ *www. thecomedystore.co.uk* 🎟 *£14–£26* ⊗ *Shows daily 7:30 or 8 pm, with extra shows Fri. and Sat. at 11 pm* Ⓜ *Piccadilly Circus, Leicester Sq.*

JAZZ AND BLUES

Ain't Nothin' but . . . The Blues Bar. This sweaty, fun place does exactly what its name suggests. Local musicians, as well as some notable names, squeeze onto the tiny stage and there's good bar food of the chili-and-gumbo variety. Most weekday nights there's no cover. ✉ *20 Kingly St., Soho* ☎ *020/7287–0514* ⊕ *www.aintnothinbut.co.uk* 💷 *£5 Fri. and Sat. after 8:30 pm, otherwise free* ⊙ *Mon.–Thurs. 5 pm–1 am, Fri. 5 pm–2:30 am, Sat. 3 pm–2:30 am, Sun. 3 pm–midnight* Ⓜ *Oxford Circus.*

Fodor'sChoice
★
Pizza Express Jazz Club Soho. One of the United Kingdom's most ubiquitous pizza chains also runs a leading Soho jazz venue. The dimly lighted restaurant hosts top-quality international jazz acts every night. The Italian-style thin-crust pizzas are about what you'd expect from a major chain. ✉ *10 Dean St., Soho* ☎ *0845/602–7017 club, 020/7437–9595 restaurant* ⊕ *www.pizzaexpresslive.com* 💷 *£10–£30* ⊙ *Mon.–Sat. 11:30 am–midnight, Sun. 11:30 am–11:30 pm for food; music after 7:30 pm (times vary)* Ⓜ *Tottenham Court Rd.*

Ronnie Scott's. This legendary jazz club has attracted big names since the 1960s. It's usually crowded and hot, but the food and service are much better than they used to be. The mood can't be beat, even since the sad departure of the eponymous founder and saxophonist. Reservations are recommended. ✉ *47 Frith St., Soho* ☎ *020/7439–0747* ⊕ *www.ronniescotts.co.uk* 💷 *£25–£42.50* ⊙ *Mon.–Sat. 6 pm–3 am, Sun. noon–4 pm and 6:30 pm–midnight* Ⓜ *Leicester Sq.*

THE GAY SCENE

Fodor'sChoice
★
Friendly Society. An unremarkable-looking door in a Soho alleyway leads down some dingy steps into one of the most fun joints in the neighborhood. Hopping with activity almost any night of the week, the place is known for being gay but also with a friendly place for women. The decor alone—including garden gnome stools and a ceiling covered in Barbie dolls and disco balls—is enough to lift the spirits. ✉ *79 Wardour St., Soho* ⊙ *Mon.–Thurs. 4 pm–11:30 pm, Fri. and Sat. 4 pm–midnight, Sun. 4 pm–10:30 pm* Ⓜ *Leicester Sq.*

Ku Bar. A deliciously camp vibe, toned bar staff, and a friendly atmosphere make this one of Soho's most popular gay bars. The crowd is mostly male, but women are very welcome. Head to the quieter upstairs lounge bar for a more laid-back mood, or dance the night away at Ku Klub in the basement. There's a second branch around the corner on Frith Street. ✉ *30 Lisle St., Soho* ☎ *020/7437–4303* ⊕ *www.ku-bar. co.uk* ⊙ *Mon.–Sat. noon–3 am, Sun. noon–midnight* Ⓜ *Leicester Sq.*

The Shadow Lounge. This fabulous little lounge and dance club glitters with twinkling fiber-optics after an extensive makeover. It has a serious A-list celebrity factor, with the glamorous London glitterati camping out in the snug booths around the dance floor. Members are given priority to enter when the place gets full, especially on weekends, so show up early, book onto the guest list online, or prepare to wait in line. ✉ *5–7 Brewer St., Soho* ☎ *020/7317–9270* ⊕ *www.theshadowlounge.co.uk* 💷 *Mon. and Tues. free, Wed.–Sat. £5–£10* ⊙ *Mon.–Sat. 9 pm–3 am (Fri. and Sat. 9 pm–4:30 am in Dec.)* Ⓜ *Leicester Sq.*

16

The Yard. A corridor of kitsch leads to a surprisingly laid-back bar and spacious terrace at The Yard. This oasis of calm in the middle of Soho attracts a mixed, friendly crowd. ✉ *57 Rupert St., Soho* ☎ *020/7437–2652* ⊕ *www.yardbar.co.uk* ☉ *Mon.–Wed. 4 pm–11:30 pm, Thurs. 3 pm–11:30 pm, Fri. and Sat. 2 pm–midnight, Sun. 2 pm–10:30 pm* Ⓜ *Piccadilly Circus.*

COVENT GARDEN

BARS

Bedford and Strand. The wine bar enjoyed something of a renaissance in the first decade of the 21st century in London, and this is one of the best of a new generation. You'll find it down below the streets of Covent Garden, with dark wood and hanging shades; the wine list is short but well chosen, the service is faultless, and the bistro food is created with plenty of care. ✉ *1A Bedford St., Charing Cross* ☎ *020/7836–3033* ⊕ *www.bedford-strand.com* ☉ *Weekdays noon–midnight, Sat. 5 pm–midnight* Ⓜ *Charing Cross.*

Earlham Street Clubhouse. Reasonably priced cocktails and super-thin-crust pizzas are the order of the day at this vaulted basement bar in Covent Garden. A fun atmosphere reigns in the main bar area, where the decor is "college kids do speakeasy," according to the manager. Nooks and crannies abound for those more in the mood for a quiet drink. ✉ *35 Earlham St., Covent Garden* ☎ *020/7240–5142* ⊕ *www.esclubhouse.com* ☉ *Mon.–Sat. 5–midnight* Ⓜ *Covent Garden.*

Terroirs. Specializing in "natural wines" (organic and sustainably produced with minimal added ingredients), Terroirs has an unusually careful selection of 200 wines from small French and Italian winemakers. These are served, along with delicious, relatively simple dishes: charcuterie, tapas, and more substantial French-inspired dishes, at a bar and tables surrounded by whitewashed walls and wooden floors. ✉ *5 William St., Covent Garden* ☎ *020/7036–0660* ⊕ *www.terroirswinebar. com* ☉ *Mon.–Sat. noon–11 pm (bar menu only 3–5:30)* Ⓜ *Charing Cross.*

THE GAY SCENE

Fodor's Choice ★   **Heaven.** With the best light show on any London dance floor, Heaven is unpretentious, loud, and huge, with a labyrinth of rooms, bars, and live-music parlors. Friday and Saturday nights there's a gay comedy night (£13–£15, 7–10 pm). Check in advance about live performances—they can take place any night of the week. If you go to just one gay club in London, Heaven should be it. ✉ *The Arches, Villiers St., Covent Garden* ☎ *020/7930–2020* ⊕ *www.heavennightclub-london.com* 💷 *£4–£12* ☉ *Mon. 11 pm–5:30 am, Tues.–Fri. 11 pm–4 am, Sat. 10:30 pm–5 am* Ⓜ *Charing Cross, Embankment.*

BLOOMSBURY, FITZROVIA, AND ISLINGTON

The ongoing redevelopment of the area around King's Cross St. Pancras station has invigorated Bloomsbury's nightlife scene. Fitzrovia, meanwhile, manages to blend sophistication, informality, and a certain edginess that's not found elsewhere in the center of town.

BLOOMSBURY

BARS

Booking Office. Taking full advantage of the soaring Victorian red-brick vaults and arches of the restored St. Pancras Renaissance Hotel, Booking Office is closer in feel to a cathedral than a traditional station bar. Seasonal cocktails using traditional English ingredients are high on flavor and low on mixers, and there's also a restaurant and live music Thursday through Saturday evenings. ✉ *St. Pancras Renaissance Hotel, Euston Rd., King's Cross* ☎ *020/7841–3566* ⊕ *www.bookingofficerestaurant.com* ☾ *Mon.–Wed. 6:30 am–2 am, Thurs.–Sat. 6:30 am–3 am, Sun. 6:30 am–1 am* Ⓜ *Kings Cross St Pancras.*

Big Chill House. King's Cross has changed almost beyond recognition in recent years, thanks to the wonders of culture-focused neighborhood regeneration. What used to be an area you avoided or hurried through has become a major destination, particularly on the food front. That said, this fun bar, which occupies a big old Victorian pub, has been a draw since long before the area started smartening up its act. It's at its best on Friday and Saturday night (over 21s only), when DJs keep the party going until late, and when the spacious outdoor terrace buzzes with life. ✉ *257–59 Pentonville Rd., King's Cross* ☎ *020/7427–2540* 🎟 *Free* ☾ *Mon.–Wed. 9 am–midnight, Thurs. 9 am–1 am, Fri. 9 am–3 am, Sat. 11 am–3 am, Sun. 11 am–midnight* Ⓜ *King's Cross St. Pancras.*

FITZROVIA

BARS

The London Edition bars. Visitors to the London Edition hotel are spoiled for choice when it comes to bars. High ceilings, eclectic artwork, and innovative cocktails can be found at the all-day Berners Tavern and Lobby Bar, which opens in the evening. You'll need a reservation to get into the cozy Punch Room, but the bar's reinventions of traditional (and communal) punches and the exemplary service are worth the extra effort. At the weekend there's dancing until late in the more informal Basement (guest list only; visit *www.basementldn.com* for the current lineup). ✉ *10 Berners St., Fitzrovia* ☎ *020/7908–7979* ⊕ *www.edition-hotels.marriott.com/london* ☾ *Berners Tavern daily 7 am–midnight; Lobby Bar daily 9 am–1 am; Punch Room daily 5 pm–1 am* Ⓜ *Tottenham Court Rd., Oxford Circus.*

ISLINGTON

Exmouth Market and Upper Street are the main nightlife hot spots in this neighborhood just north and east of central London. The fun and informal bars in Islington make it a reliable choice for going out.

BARS

69 Colebrooke Row. This elegant faux speakeasy must be London's tiniest cocktail lounge. Book one of the handful of tables or a seat at the diminutive bar to sample perfectly made twists on classic cocktails, like the panettone bellini, which uses a puree of the sweet Italian bread instead of peach. Staff are immaculate but approachable. ✉ *69 Colebrooke Row, Islington* ☎ *07540/528–593* ⊕ *www.69colebrookerow.com* ☾ *Sun.–Wed. 5 pm–midnight, Thurs. 5 pm–1 am, Fri. and Sat. 5 pm–2 am* Ⓜ *Angel.*

16

ECLECTIC

Union Chapel. The beauty of this sublime old chapel and its impressive multicultural programming make this spot one of London's best musical venues, especially for acoustic shows. Performers have included Björk, Beck, and Goldfrapp, though now you're more likely to hear lower-key alternative country, world music, and jazz, alongside poetry and literary events, film screenings, and stand-up gigs. ⊠ *Compton Terr., Islington* ☎ *020/7226–1686 Venue (no box office; ticket sales numbers vary with each event)* ⊕ *www.unionchapel.org.uk* ✉ *Free–£25* ⊗ *Hrs vary* Ⓜ *Highbury & Islington.*

CLERKENWELL AND THE CITY

BARS

Café Kick. This homey continental-style café-bar is open all day for meals, snacks, coffee, and cocktails. It's famous for its foosball tables, which give the place a fun, informal environment. Deals are available on "cocktails of the month" and house beers during happy hour (4–7). You can reserve foosball tables in advance. There's another branch in Shoreditch. ⊠ *43 Exmouth Market, Clerkenwell* ☎ *020/7837–8077* ⊕ *www.cafekick.co.uk* ⊗ *Mon.–Thurs. 11–11, Fri. and Sat. 11 am–midnight, Sun. noon–10:30 pm* Ⓜ *Angel.*

DANCE CLUBS

Fabric. This sprawling subterranean club opposite Smithfield Meat Market is a firm fixture on the London scene and is regularly voted as one of the top clubs in the world. "FabricLive" hosts drum 'n' bass, dubstep, and hip-hop crews and live acts on Friday; international big-name DJs play slow, sexy bass lines, and cutting-edge music on Saturday. The devastating sound system ensures that bass riffs vibrate through your entire body. Get there early to avoid a lengthy line-up and don't wear a suit. Expect a mainly young crowd. ⊠ *77A Charterhouse St., The City* ☎ *020/7336–8898* ⊕ *www.fabriclondon.com* ✉ *£7–£26; discounts after 3 or 4 am* ⊗ *Fri. 11 pm–7 am, Sat. 11 pm–8 am, Sun. 11 pm–5:30 am* Ⓜ *Farringdon.*

EAST LONDON

East London's bar scene is ever evolving, with the trendy crowd constantly pushing farther east in search of the next big thing. Shoreditch has bars and clubs to suit nearly all tastes these days, while Dalston, the neighborhood to its north, attracts a younger clientele.

BARS

Birthdays. Dalston is probably London's hippest neighborhood for nightlife right now. This stark, industrial bar near the top of the main drag is as hot as it gets. Join the youngish crowd for craft beers and high-end burgers. There's a club in the basement that hosts DJs and live gigs. ⊠ *33–35 Stoke Newington Rd., Dalston* ☎ *020/7923–1680* ⊕ *www. birthdaysdalston.com* ✉ *Free–£12.50* ⊗ *Mon.–Thurs. 4 pm–midnight, Fri. 4 pm–3 am, Sat. noon–3 am, Sun. 11 am–midnight* Ⓜ *Dalston Junction.*

Book Club. Light and friendly, the Book Club tops off a dose of Shoreditch's fashionable industrial chic with a dollop of culture. White tiles, bare brick walls, and big black-and-white photos set the tone, and there's a separate room for table tennis. Breakfast is served weekday mornings, a full lunch menu is offered through the week, and a modern menu of cocktails accompanies music, book launches, and workshops in the evenings. It's best avoided on weekend evenings, when it heaves with a raucous crowd. ⊠ *100 Leonard St., Shoreditch* ☏ *020/7684–8618* ⊕ *www.wearetbc.com* ☉ *Mon.–Wed. 8 am–midnight, Thurs. and Fri. 8 am–2 am, Sat. 10 am–2 am, Sun. 10 am–midnight* Ⓜ *Shoreditch High St., Old St.*

Crate Bar and Pizzeria. Canal-side craft beer and pizza at the busiest of a handful of grown-up bars in this übertrendy area of East London. Rub shoulders with the locals—the community still has its share of artists who made their way east following rent hikes in Shoreditch—as well as visitors who come for late-night raves in the area's many warehouses. There's a warm atmosphere inside, with quirky upcycled decor and DJs playing on weekend evenings. The beer comes from the on-site brewery, while thin-rust pizzas emerge from the open kitchen. ⊠ *Unit 7, Queens Yard, Hackney* ☏ *07834/275–687* ⊕ *www.cratebrewery.com* ☉ *Sun.–Thurs. noon–11, Fri. and Sat. noon–midnight (pizzeria closes 1 hr before)* Ⓜ *Hackney Wick.*

Fodor's Choice ★ **White Lyan.** Cocktail making has been turned into an exact science at this stark Hoxton bar, with everything made in-house and all ice, perishables, and visible liquor brands outlawed to ensure that drinks turn out perfectly every time (they're chilled ahead of time). It's fascinating to watch the bartenders at work over their digital scales (they're more exact than spirit measures), using eye-droppers and spritzing bottles to add precise quantities of unusual ingredients like blueberry vinegar or lager syrup. It sounds pretentious but it manages not to be, and the results are delicious. Over 21s only. ⊠ *153–155 Hoxton St., Hoxton* ☏ *020/3011–1153* ⊕ *www.whitelyan.com* ☉ *Sun.–Thurs. 6 pm–midnight, Fri. and Sat. 6 pm–1 am* Ⓜ *Hoxton, Old St.*

COMEDY AND CABARET

Comedy Cafe Theatre. Upstairs from the Bedroom Bar, the Comedy Cafe Theatre hosts at least three mixed-bill nights a week, including the free New Act Night every Wednesday. Up-and-coming comics appear alongside big international names such as Tony Law and Andrew Maxwell on Friday and Saturday, and when the show's over, DJs take the stage, transforming the bare brick space into a dance club. The buzzing downstairs bar hosts five live bands a week, as well as a tasty Korean canteen. ⊠ *68 Rivington St., Shoreditch* ☏ *020/7739–5706* ⊕ *www.comedycafetheatre.co.uk* ☎ *Free–£20* ☉ *Tues.–Thurs. noon–1 am, Fri. and Sat. noon–3 am* Ⓜ *Old St., Shoreditch High St.*

DANCE CLUBS

Cargo. Housed under a series of old railroad arches, this spacious brick-wall bar, restaurant, dance floor, and live-music venue pulls a young, international crowd with its hip vibe and diverse selection of music. Long tables bring people together, as does the food, which draws on

16

global influences and is served tapas-style. Drinks are expensive. ⊠ *83 Rivington St., Shoreditch* ☎ *020/7739–3440* ⊕ *www.cargo-london.com* 🖘 *Free–£20* ⊗ *Mon.–Thurs. noon–1 am, Fri. and Sat. noon–3 am, Sun. noon–midnight* Ⓜ *Old St.*

Fodor'sChoice
★
Cafe Oto. A relaxed café by day, and London's leading venue for experimental music by night, Cafe Oto is a Dalston institution. Its programming of free jazz, avant-garde electronica, and much more is enough of a draw that it regularly sells out, with music fans steaming up the windows and spilling out onto the pavement and road outside to smoke in the breaks. Healthy Japanese food is served in the daytime, before customers are kicked out at 5:30 pm to make way for sound checks. It's open as a bar (with no admission charge) on nights when no concerts are taking place. ⊠ *18–22 Ashwin St., Dalston* 🖘 *Café free; concerts £8–£18* ⊗ *Café weekdays 8:30 am–5:30 pm, Sat. 9:30 am–5:30 pm, Sun. 10:30 am–5:30 pm; concerts daily 8 pm–12:30 am* Ⓜ *Dalston Junction.*

XOYO. Big international DJs regularly play this cool Shoreditch spot that's on a small side street off the main drag. The decor is industrial chic, with some banquet seating in the relaxed upstairs room and a downstairs that's a bit more hard core. A youngish crowd dances the night away on the weekend, while weeknight live gigs attract a more diverse bunch. ⊠ *32–37 Cowper St., Shoreditch* ☎ *020/7354–9993* ⊕ *www.xoyo.co.uk* 🖘 *Club nights £12.50–£20; gig ticket prices vary* ⊗ *Fri. and Sat. 9 pm–4 am, Sun.–Thurs. hrs vary* Ⓜ *Old St.*

SOUTH OF THE THAMES

Recent years have seen an explosion in South London nightlife, including the gentrification of Brixton, the artistic colonization of Peckham, and the continuing popularity of Vauxhall's gay clubs.

BARS

Aqua Shard. This classy bar on level 31 of the Shard, London's new skyscraper and the tallest building in Western Europe, is worth a visit for the phenomenal views alone. The cocktail list is pretty special, too, with ranges inspired by teas and botanicals, as well as all the usual classics. No reservations are taken in the bar, so be prepared to wait during busy periods. ⊠ *Level 31, The Shard, 31 St. Thomas St., London Bridge* ☎ *020/3011–1256* ⊕ *www.aquashard.co.uk* ⊗ *Daily noon–1 am* Ⓜ *London Bridge.*

Fodor'sChoice
★
Bussey Building. This multilevel warehouse (officially called the CLF Art Cafe) is the epicenter of nightlife and culture in Peckham, attracting an edgy and young crowd. Have a chilled-out drink at Rye Wax, the record store–café bar in the basement; catch a theater performance, indie movie, or comedy gig on levels two through four, or dance the night away as big DJs and live acts work their magic. Expect an eclectic mix of soul, hip-hop, dubstep, house, and electronica, plus an anything-goes vibe that keeps this one of the best places to party in South London. ⊠ *133 Rye La., South East* ☎ *020/7732–5275* 🖘 *Free–£15* ⊗ *Daily from noon; closing times vary* Ⓜ *Overground: Peckham Rye.*

The Dogstar. This popular South London hangout was here years before Brixton's hipster renaissance and is still going strong today. The vibe is unpretentious, with top-name DJs playing cutting-edge sounds every night in the main bar, comedy and cabaret upstairs, and pizza available until late. ✉ *389 Coldharbour La., Brixton* ☎ *020/7733–7515* ⊕ *dogstarbrixton.com* 🖃 *Free; Fri. and Sat. £5 after 10 pm* ☉ *Tues. and Wed. 4 pm–11 pm, Thurs. 4 pm–2 am, Fri. 4 pm–4 am, Sat. noon–4 am, Sun. noon–10:30 pm* Ⓜ *Brixton.*

Fodor's Choice ★ **Three Eight Four.** Epitomizing a new breed of Brixton bar, Three Eight Four mixes up inventive cocktails. Don't miss whatever's being cooked up at the flambé station at the end of the bar—perhaps the peach-theme Mr. Flambastic, for instance. Bare light bulbs and brick walls seem to be the decor of choice for lots of cool London bars these days, but this place manages it with particular panache. A delectable selection of small dishes is also available. ✉ *384 Coldharbour La., Brixton* ☎ *02/3417–7309* ⊕ *www.threeeightfour.com* ☉ *Mon.–Wed. 5 pm–midnight, Thurs. and Fri. 5 pm–2 am, Sat. 11 am–2 am, Sun. 11 am–midnight* Ⓜ *Brixton.*

DANCE CLUBS

Ministry of Sound. This is more of an industry than a club, with its own record label, online radio station, and international DJs. Though it's too much a part of the establishment these days to be at the forefront of cool, the stripped-down warehouse-style club has a super sound system and still pulls in the world's most legendary names in dance. There are chill-out rooms, four bars, four dance floors, and a spacious smoking area with its own snack bar. ✉ *103 Gaunt St., Borough* ☎ *0870/060–0010* ⊕ *www.ministryofsound.com* 🖃 *£15–£25* ☉ *Fri. 10:30 pm–6 am (last entry 4 am), Sat. 11 pm–7 am (last entry 5 am)* Ⓜ *Elephant & Castle.*

ECLECTIC MUSIC

Fodor's Choice ★ **O2 Academy Brixton.** This legendary Brixton venue has seen it all—mods and rockers, hippies and punks—and it remains one of the city's top indie and rock venues. Despite a capacity for almost 5,000, this refurbished Victorian hall with original art deco fixtures retains a clublike charm; it has plenty of bars and upstairs seating. ✉ *211 Stockwell Rd., Brixton* ☎ *0844/477–2000 box office* ⊕ *www.o2academybrixton.co.uk* 🖃 *£15–£50* ☉ *Hrs vary* Ⓜ *Brixton.*

CHELSEA AND KNIGHTSBRIDGE

The pages of society magazines are full of photographs of gorgeous young people dancing the night away at clubs—many of which are members only—in these famously swanky neighborhoods. Dress up and be prepared to splurge.

CHELSEA

JAZZ AND BLUES

606 Club. This Chelsea jazz club has been doing things speakeasy-style since long before it became a nightlife trend in London. Buzz the door and you'll find a basement venue showcasing mainstream and contemporary jazz by well-known British-based musicians. You must eat a meal in order to consume alcohol, so allow for an extra

£30. Reservations are advisable. Sunday lunchtime jazz takes place on selected Sundays; call ahead. ⊠ *90 Lots Rd., Chelsea* ☎ *020/7352–5953* ⊕ *www.606club.co.uk* ◲ *£10–£12 music charge added to bill* ⊙ *Mon.– Thurs. 7 pm–11:15 pm, Fri. and Sat. 8 pm–12:45 am, Sun. 12:30 pm–3:30 pm and 7 pm–11:15 pm* Ⓜ *Earl's Ct., Fulham Broadway.*

KNIGHTSBRIDGE

BARS

The Blue Bar at the Berkeley Hotel. With low-slung dusty-blue walls, this hotel bar is ever so slightly sexy. Immaculate service, an excellent seasonal cocktail list and a trendy David Collins design make this an ideal spot for a romantic tête-à-tête, complete with jazzy music in the background. ⊠ *Wilton Pl., Knightsbridge* ☎ *020/7235–6000* ⊕ *the-berkeley. co.uk* ⊙ *Mon.–Sat. 9 am–1 am, Sun. 9 am–11 pm* Ⓜ *Knightsbridge.*

NOTTING HILL

The focus is more on bars than clubs in this West London neighborhood, though late-night fun is on offer at a few notable exceptions. In general, you can expect a young, moneyed crowd making this their first stop on a wild night out elsewhere.

BARS

Beach Blanket Babylon. In a Georgian house close to Portobello Market, this always-packed bar is distinguishable by its eclectic indoor-outdoor spaces with Gaudí-esque curves and snug corner spaces—like a fairytale grotto or a medieval dungeon. A sister restaurant-bar-gallery offers a slightly more modern take on similar themes in an ex-warehouse in Shoreditch (19–23 Bethnal Green Rd.; 020/7749–3540). ⊠ *45 Ledbury Rd., Notting Hill* ☎ *020/7229–2907* ⊕ *www.beachblanket.co.uk* ⊙ *Mon. 6–midnight, Tues.–Fri. noon–midnight, weekends 10 am–midnight* Ⓜ *Notting Hill Gate.*

Electric Diner. A huge selection of bottled beers and quirky twists on classic cocktails (Courvoisier, mint, and Champagne anyone?) are the attractions at this bar and diner next to Notting Hill's famed Electric Cinema. Run by the people behind the member's-only Soho House, the place exudes the same mixture of posh and cool, but is open to anyone and everyone. Sit in the window and watch the world go by along Portobello Road, or opt for one of the luxury takes on classic diner fare at a table in the moody, vaulted interior. ⊠ *191 Portobello Rd., Notting Hill* ☎ *020/7908–9696* ⊕ *www.electricdiner.com* ⊙ *Mon.–Wed. 8 am–midnight, Thurs.–Sat. 8 am–1 am, Sun. 8 am–11 pm* Ⓜ *Ladbroke Grove.*

DANCE CLUBS

Notting Hill Arts Club. Rock stars like Liam Gallagher and Courtney Love have been seen at this small basement club-bar. What the place lacks in looks it makes up for in mood, and an alternative crowd swills beer to eclectic music that spans Asian underground, hip-hop, Latin-inspired funk, deep house, and jazzy grooves. ⊠ *21 Notting Hill Gate, Notting Hill* ☎ *020/7460–4459* ⊕ *www.nottinghillartsclub.com* ◲ *Free–£8* ⊙ *Tues.–Sat. 7 pm–2 am, alternate Sun. 6 pm–1 am* Ⓜ *Notting Hill Gate.*

REGENT'S PARK AND HAMPSTEAD

Camden Town boasts a handful of dance clubs, but it's this north London neighborhood's music venues that are the big draw for most. Every genre is covered, from folk and pop, to jazz and world music, with interesting gigs taking place every night of the week.

REGENT'S PARK

COMEDY AND CABARET

Canal Café Theatre. Famous comics and cabaret stars perform every night of the week in this intimate, canal-side venue. The long-running News-Revue is a topical song-and-sketch show performed Thursday–Sunday evenings. ✉ *Bridge House, Delamere Terr., Little Venice* ☎ *020/7289–6054* ⊕ *www.canalcafetheatre.com* 🎫 *Free–£15; NewsRevue £12.50* ⊘ *Pub Mon.–Thurs. noon–11 pm, Fri. and Sat. noon–11:30 pm, Sun. noon–10:30 pm* Ⓜ *Warwick Ave., Royal Oak, Paddington.*

DANCE CLUBS

KOKO. This Victorian theater has seen acts from Charlie Chaplin to Madonna, and genres from punk to rave. Furnished with lush reds that make it not unlike a cockney Moulin Rouge, this is still one of London's most stunning venues. Sounds of live indie rock, cabaret, funky house, and club classics keep the big dance floor moving, even when it's not heaving. ✉ *1A Camden High St., Camden Town* ☎ *0870/432–5527* ⊕ *www.koko.uk.com* 🎫 *£5–£30* ⊘ *Hrs vary, depending on shows and club nights* Ⓜ *Mornington Crescent.*

ECLECTIC

Roundhouse. This former steam-engine repair shed hosts some of the most atmospheric medium-scale rock and pop gigs in the capital, plus a varied program of circus, theater, dance, and the occasional art installation. There's a good restaurant on the first floor, and in the summer the terrace bar is transformed into an "urban beach," complete with sand. ✉ *Chalk Farm Rd., Camden* ☎ *0844/482–8008 box office, 020/7424–9991 enquiries* ⊕ *www.roundhouse.org.uk* 🎫 *Free–£40* ⊘ *Daily 9:30–5 (later when performances are taking place; times vary)* Ⓜ *Chalk Farm.*

JAZZ AND BLUES

Jazz Café. A palace of cool in bohemian Camden, this remains an essential hangout for fans of both the mainstream end of the jazz repertoire and hip-hop, funk, world music, and Latin fusion. It's also the unlikely venue for "I Love the 80s Vs I Love the 90s," on Saturday nights. Book ahead if you want a prime table in the balcony restaurant overlooking the stage. ✉ *5 Parkway, Camden Town* ☎ *020/7485–6834 venue info, 0844/847–2514 tickets (Ticketmaster)* ⊕ *mamacolive.com/thejazzcafe* 🎫 *£6–£35* ⊘ *Sun.–Thurs. 7 pm–10:30 pm, Fri. and Sat. 7 pm–3 am* Ⓜ *Camden Town.*

ROCK

Barfly Club. At one of the finest small clubs in the capital, punk, indie guitar, and new metal rock attract a nonmainstream crowd. Weekend club nights upstairs host DJs (and live bands) who rock the decks. ✉ *49 Chalk Farm Rd., Camden Town* ☎ *020/7424–0800 venue, 0844/847–2424 tickets* ⊕ *mamacolive.com/thebarfly* 🎫 *Free–£11* ⊘ *Mon. and*

16

Thurs. 3 pm–2 am, Tues. and Wed. 3 pm–1 am, Fri. and Sat. 3 pm–3 am, Sun. 3 pm–midnight Ⓜ *Camden Town, Chalk Farm.*

Dublin Castle. Run by the same family for nearly three decades, the Dublin Castle has hosted almost every British rock group you care to name, from Madness to Coldplay. With four bands on the bill almost every night, and DJs taking over afterward on Friday and weekends, there's something for most tastes at this legendary venue. ✉ *94 Parkway, Camden Town* ☎ *020/7485-1773* ⊕ *www.thedublincastle.com* 🎫 *£4-£8* ⊙ *Mon.–Wed. 1–1, Thurs.–Sun. noon–2 am* Ⓜ *Camden Town.*

PERFORMING
ARTS

Updated By
Jo Caird

"All the world's a stage," said Shakespeare, immortal words heard for the first time right here in London. And whether you prefer your theater, music, and art classical or modern, or as contemporary twists on time-honored classics, you'll find that London's vibrant cultural scene more than holds its own on the world stage.

Divas sing original-language librettos at the Royal Opera House, Shakespeare's plays are brought to life at the reconstructed Globe Theatre, and challenging new writing is produced at the Royal Court. Whether you feel like basking in the lighthearted extravagance of a West End musical or taking in the next shark-in-formaldehyde at the White Cube gallery, the choice is yours.

PLANNING

TOP THEATER TIPS
Behind the pillars. Many theaters and concert halls sell discounted seats with restricted views.

Matinees. Afternoon performances are almost always a better value than evening ones.

Previews. Tickets to shows are usually less expensive in the first few weeks of their run, before the critics have had their say.

Monday. Most cinemas and some theaters, including the Royal Court, have a reduced-price ticketing policy on Monday.

Standing. Shakespeare's Globe Theatre and the BBC Proms are the two most prominent places where remaining upright saves you money.

FIND OUT WHAT'S PLAYING WHERE
To find out what's showing now, the free weekly magazine *Time Out* (issued every Tuesday outside major stations and around the city; also online at ⊕ *www.timeout.com*) is invaluable.

The free *Evening Standard* carries listings, many of which are also available online at ⊕ *www.standard.co.uk. Metro*, London's other widely available free newspaper, is also worth checking out, as are many Sunday papers, and the Saturday *Independent, Guardian,* and *Times.*

The website ⊕ *www.whatsonstage.com* is an invaluable resource for theater listings.

There are hundreds of small private galleries all over London with interesting work by famous and not-yet-famous artists. The bimonthly free pamphlet "new exhibitions of contemporary art" (⊕ *www. newexhibitions.com*), available at most galleries, lists and maps nearly 200 art spaces in London.

PERFORMING ARTS REVIEWS

ST. JAMES'S AND WESTMINSTER

Wander the streets of this chic central London neighborhood—home to aristocrats in the 17th century—and you'll discover small commercial galleries, fine-art auction houses, and antiques dealers mixed in among the high-end tailors and gentlemen's clubs.

ART GALLERIES

Institute of Contemporary Arts. Housed in an elegant John Nash–designed Regency terrace, the ICA's two galleries have changing exhibitions of contemporary visual art. The ICA also programs performances, underground and vintage movies, talks, and photography, and there's an excellent arts bookstore, cafeteria, and a funky bar. ⊠ *Nash House, The Mall, St. James's* ☎ *020/7930–3647* ⊕ *www.ica.org.uk* ☐ *Free* ☉ *Tues.–Sun. 11–11; galleries Tues., Wed., and Fri.–Sun. 11–6, Thurs. 11–9* Ⓜ *Charing Cross, Piccadilly Circus.*

White Cube. The English role in the exploding contemporary art scene has been major, thanks in good portion to Jay Joplin's influential gallery, which has regularly moved around London since 1993. This striking modern concrete structure was the first freestanding building to be built in the area for 30 years when it opened in 2006. It is home base for an array of British artists who have won the Turner Prize, including Damien Hirst, Tracey Emin, and Gary Hume. ⊠ *25–26 Mason's Yard, St. James's* ☎ *020/7930–5373* ⊕ *whitecube.com* ☐ *Free* ☉ *Tues.–Sat. 10–6* Ⓜ *Green Park, Piccadilly Circus.*

CLASSICAL MUSIC

St. James's Church. The organ was brought here in 1691 after fire destroyed its former home, the Palace of Whitehall. St. James's holds regular classical-music concerts and free lunchtime recitals Monday, Wednesday, and Friday at 1:10 pm (free but donation of £3.50 suggested). ⊠ *197 Piccadilly, St. James's* ☎ *020/7381–0441 concert program and tickets* ⊕ *www.sjp.org.uk* Ⓜ *Piccadilly Circus, Green Park.*

St. John's Smith Square. This baroque church behind Westminster Abbey offers chamber music and organ recitals as well as orchestral concerts. There are two or three lunchtime recitals a month for £10. ⊠ *Smith Sq., Westminster* ☎ *020/7222–1061* ⊕ *www.sjss.org.uk* Ⓜ *Westminster.*

17

Random Dance Company performs at Sadler's Wells.

St. Martin-in-the-Fields Concerts. Popular lunchtime concerts (£3.50 donation suggested) are held in this lovely 1726 church, as are regular evening concerts. Stop for a snack at the Café in the Crypt. ⊠ *Trafalgar Sq., Westminster* ☎ *020/7766–1100* ⊕ *www.stmartin-in-the-fields.org* Ⓜ *Charing Cross.*

MAYFAIR AND MARYLEBONE

The historic center of the London art world, Mayfair has a thriving gallery scene that has undergone a renaissance in recent years. With East End gallerists relocating to central London and a number of top international galleries opening new premises here, there's a real buzz about the place. Directly north of Mayfair, Marylebone has more of a village atmosphere, with a few choice galleries and arts institutions dotted around.

MARYLEBONE

ART GALLERY

Lisson. Owner Nicholas Logsdail represents about 50 blue-chip artists, including the minimalists Sol LeWitt and Dan Graham, at one of the most respected galleries in London. The gallery is most associated with New Object sculptors like Anish Kapoor and Richard Deacon, many of whom have won the Turner Prize. A branch down the road at 27 Bell Street features work by up-and-coming artists. ⊠ *52–54 Bell St., Marylebone* ☎ *020/7724–2739* ⊕ *www.lissongallery.com* ⌧ *Free* ⊙ *Weekdays 10–6, Sat. 11–5* Ⓜ *Edgware Rd., Marylebone.*

DANCE: LONDON TODAY

Dance fans in London can enjoy the classicism of the world-renowned Royal Ballet, as well as innovative works by several contemporary dance companies—including Rambert Dance Company and Matthew Bourne's New Adventures—and scores of independent choreographers. The English National Ballet and visiting international companies perform at the Coliseum and at Sadler's Wells, which also hosts various other ballet companies and dance troupes. Encompassing the refurbished Royal Festival Hall, the Southbank Centre has a seriously good contemporary dance program that hosts top international companies and important U.K.

choreographers, as well as multicultural offerings, such as Japanese *butoh*, and Indian classical, and hip-hop. The Place and the Lilian Baylis Theatre at Sadler's Wells are where you'll find the most daring, cutting-edge performances.

Check ⊕ *londondance.com* for current performances and fringe venues.

Dance Umbrella. The biggest annual event is Dance Umbrella, a 15-day festival in October that hosts international and British-based artists at venues across the city. ✉ ☎ *020/7407-1200* ⊕ *www.danceumbrella.co.uk.*

CLASSICAL MUSIC

Fodor's Choice ★ **Wigmore Hall.** Hear chamber music and song recitals in this charming hall with near-perfect acoustics. Don't miss the Sunday morning concerts (11:30 am). ✉ *36 Wigmore St., Marylebone* ☎ *020/7935-2141* ⊕ *www.wigmore-hall.org.uk* Ⓜ *Bond St.*

SOHO AND COVENT GARDEN

London's hip center has it all, from multiplexes playing the biggest blockbuster movies to niche contemporary art galleries tucked away in backstreets, and from world-famous opera houses to sultry cabaret joints.

SOHO

ART GALLERIES

Fodor's Choice ★ **Photographer's Gallery.** Britain's first and foremost photography gallery programs cutting-edge and provocative photography exhibitions. The prestigious Deutsche Börse Photography Prize is exhibited and awarded here annually. The gallery also has a print sales room, a bookstore, and a café-bar—a great spot to escape the bustle of nearby Oxford Street. ✉ *16–18 Ramillies St., off Oxford St., Soho* ☎ *020/7087–9300* ⊕ *www.thephotographersgallery.org.uk* ✉ *Free; prices for exhibitions vary, but free admission available weekdays 10–noon* ☉ *Mon.–Wed. 9:30–6, Thurs. 9:30–8, Fri. and Sat. 10–6, Sun. 11:30–6* Ⓜ *Oxford Circus.*

Sadie Coles HQ. This light-filled art space overlooking busy Regent Street marked a major expansion for respected British gallerist Sadie Coles when it opened in fall 2013. You'll find the work of important British and international artists such as Sarah Lucas and Wilhelm Sasnal. ✉ *62*

17

The Royal Opera House, one of the world's greatest opera houses and home to the Royal Ballet, offers regular tours of the auditorium and backstage.

Kingly St., Soho ☎ *020/7493–8611* ⊕ *www.sadiecoles.com* ⊗ *Tues.– Sat. 11–6.*

FILM

Curzon Soho. This popular, comfortable movie theater runs a vibrant and artsy program of mixed repertoire and mainstream films, with a good calendar of director talks and other events, too. The bar is great for a quiet drink, even when Soho is crawling with people. There are branches in Mayfair, Bloomsbury, Victoria, Chelsea, and Richmond. ⊠ *99 Shaftesbury Ave., Soho* ☎ *0330/500–1331* ⊕ *www.curzoncinemas. com* Ⓜ *Piccadilly Circus, Leicester Sq.*

FAMILY **Prince Charles Cinema.** This repertory cinema right off Leicester Square offers a chance to catch up with independent features, documentaries, and even blockbusters you may have missed. Tickets start at £8, or £4 if you purchase a £10 annual membership. A second screen upstairs shows newer movies at more usual West End prices. This is where the "sing-along" screening took off—come in character and warble along to *The Sound of Music, Grease,* or *The Rocky Horror Picture Show.* ⊠ *7 Leicester Pl., Soho* ☎ *020/7494–3654* ⊕ *www.princecharlescinema. com* Ⓜ *Leicester Sq., Piccadilly Circus.*

THEATER

Fodor's Choice **Soho Theatre.** This sleek theater in the heart of Soho is devoted to foster-
★ ing new work and is a prolific presenter of plays by emerging writers, comedy performances, cabaret shows, and other entertainment. The bar is always buzzing. ⊠ *21 Dean St., Soho* ☎ *020/7478–0100* ⊕ *www. sohotheatre.com* Ⓜ *Tottenham Court Rd.*

TOP FIVE FOR THE ARTS

Stand with the "plebs" in Shakespeare's Globe Theatre. There are seats, but to really experience theater Shakespearean-style you should stand in the yard, with the stage at eye level (plus, it's a bargain at £5).

Visit the latest grand art installation in the Turbine Hall at Tate Modern. The enormity of the Tate's central space regularly inspires striking work.

Catch a world-class performance at the BBC Proms. There's a surprisingly down-to-earth atmosphere among the elated company at these great concerts.

Enjoy a night at the BFI Southbank. Mingle with the real aficionados at screenings of foreign, classic, and experimental films.

Watch a Hollywood star in a West End production. Film stars often come to London to boost their artistic credibility in small-scale theaters.

COVENT GARDEN

DANCE

The London Coliseum. Ballet troupes are booked into the spectacular Coliseum during the summer and at Christmas, and any time when the resident English National Opera is not in town. The Edwardian baroque theater is known for its magnificent auditorium and a glass dome. The top dance company to perform here is the English National Ballet (*www.ballet.org.uk*). ⊠ *St. Martin's La., Covent Garden* ☎ *020/7845–9300* ⊕ *www.eno.org* Ⓜ *Leicester Sq.*

Fodor's Choice ★ **Royal Opera House.** As well as the Royal Opera, the renowned Royal Ballet performs classical and contemporary repertoire in this spectacular theater, where the interior may be Victorian but the stagecraft behind the red velvet curtain is state-of-the-art. Backstage tours are £12. They don't take place when rehearsals or performances are taking place, so check the schedule in advance of your visit. ⊠ *Bow St., Covent Garden* ☎ *020/7304–4000* ⊕ *www.roh.org.uk* ☉ *Backstage tours (75 mins) weekdays 10:30, 12:30, and 2:30; Sat. 10:30, 11:30, 12:30, 1:30, and 2:30* Ⓜ *Covent Garden.*

OPERA

The London Coliseum. A veritable architectural extravaganza of Edwardian exoticism, the baroque-style theater has a magnificent auditorium and a rooftop glass dome with a bar and great views. As one of the city's most venerable theaters, the Coliseum functions mainly as the home of the English National Opera which continues to produce innovative opera, sung in English, for lower prices than the Royal Opera House. During opera's off-season, the house hosts the English National Ballet (*www.ballet.org.uk*). Guided tours (every other Saturday at 11:30 am, when productions are scheduled) cost £10. ⊠ *St. Martin's La., Covent Garden* ☎ *020/7845–9300 box office, 020/7836–0111 inquiries* ⊕ *www.eno.org* Ⓜ *Leicester Sq.*

Fodor's Choice ★ **Royal Opera House.** Along with Milan's La Scala, New York's Metropolitan, and the Palais Garnier in Paris, this is one of the world's greatest

THEATER: LONDON TODAY

In London the play really *is* the thing, ranging from a long-running popular musical like *Mamma Mia!*, a groundbreaking reworking of Pinter, imaginative physical theater from an experimental company like Complicite, a lavish Disney spectacle, or a small fringe production above a pub. West End glitz and glamour continue to pull in the audiences, and so do the more innovative productions.

In London the words "radical" and "quality," or "classical" and "experimental," are not mutually exclusive. The Royal Shakespeare Company (⊕ www.rsc.org.uk) and the National Theatre (⊕ www.nationaltheatre.org.uk) often stage contemporary versions of the classics. The Almeida, Donmar Warehouse, Royal Court Theatre, Soho Theatre, and Old Vic attract famous actors and have excellent reputations for new writing and innovative theatrical approaches. These are the venues where you'll see an original production before it becomes a hit in the West End or on Broadway (and for a fraction of the cost).

The London theater scene remains vibrant throughout the summer months. Open-air productions of Shakespeare are particularly well served, whether in the faithful reconstruction of the Elizabethan Globe Theatre or under the stars in Regent's Park's Open Air Theatre. Theater festivals such as **LIFT** (the London International Festival of Theatre; ⊕ www.liftfestival.com) and the **London International Mime Festival** (⊕ www.mimelondon.com) provide the chance to see international and cutting-edge companies throughout the year.

Theatergoing isn't cheap. Tickets less than £15 are a rarity, although designated productions at the National Theatre have seats at this price. At the commercial theaters you should expect to pay from £20 for a seat in the upper balcony to at least £40 for a good one in the stalls (orchestra) or dress circle (mezzanine). However, last-minute returns available on the night may provide some good deals. Tickets may be booked through ticket agents, at individual theater box offices in person or online, or over the phone by credit card. Be sure to inquire about any extra fees—prices can vary enormously, but agents are legally obliged to reveal the face value of the ticket if you ask. All the larger hotels offer theater bookings, but they tack on a hefty service charge.

Ticketmaster (⊕ www.ticketmaster.co.uk) sells tickets to a number of different theaters, although they charge a booking fee. For discount tickets, **Society of London Theatre** (⊕ www.tkts.co.uk) operates "tkts," a half-price ticket booth on the southwest corner of Leicester Square, and sells the best available seats to performances at about 30 theaters. It's open Monday–Saturday 10–7, Sunday 11–4:30; there's a £3 service charge (included in the price). Major credit cards are accepted.

■TIP➔ Be very wary of ticket touts (scalpers) and unscrupulous ticket agents outside theaters and working the line at "tkts."

opera houses. The resident troupe has mounted spectacular productions in the past, though recent productions have tended toward more contemporary operas. Whatever the style of the performance, the extravagant theater—also home to the famed Royal Ballet—delivers a full dose of opulence. Tickets range in price from £3 to £235. The box office opens at 10 am, but lines for popular productions start as early as 7 am; unsold tickets are offered at half price four hours before a performance. If you wish to see the hall but are not able to procure a ticket, you can join a backstage tour (£12) or one of the infrequent tours of the auditorium (£9.50). ⊠ *Bow St., Covent Garden* ☎ *020/7304–4000* ⊕ *www.roh.org.uk* ☉ *Public areas generally 10–3:30; backstage tours weekdays 10:30, 12:30, and 2:30, Sat. 10:30, 11:30, 12:30, and 1:30 (check in advance)* Ⓜ *Covent Garden.*

THEATER

Donmar Warehouse. Hollywood stars often perform in this not-for-profit theater in diverse and daring new works, bold interpretations of the classics, and small-scale musicals. Nicole Kidman, Gwyneth Paltrow, and Ewan McGregor have all been featured. ⊠ *41 Earlham St., Seven Dials, Covent Garden* ☎ *0844/871–7624* ⊕ *www.donmarwarehouse. com* Ⓜ *Covent Garden.*

BLOOMSBURY AND HOLBORN

Once the heart of fashionable literary London, there's still an air of refinement about this neighborhood. A handful of small theaters with links to the colleges with campuses in the area create a vibrant small-scale performance scene with theater, dance, and stand-up comedy.

Kings Place. This airy concert venue opened in 2008. The cultural jewel in the huge new developments near the Eurostar terminal in King's Cross, it is the permanent home of the London Sinfonietta and the Orchestra of the Age of Enlightenment. It offers weeklong programs by musicians in a range of genres and a hugely varied cultural calendar of jazz, comedy, folk, and political and literary lectures, plus two gallery spaces. ⊠ *90 York Way, King's Cross* ☎ *020/7520–1490 box office, 020/7520–1440 inquiries* ⊕ *www.kingsplace.co.uk* Ⓜ *King's Cross.*

Peacock Theatre. Sadler's Wells's West End annex, this modernist theater near the London School of Economics (which uses it as a lecture hall during the day) focuses on younger companies and shows in popular dance genres like flamenco, tango, and hip-hop. ⊠ *Portugal St., Holborn* ☎ *0844/412–4322 box office* ⊕ *www.sadlerswells.com* Ⓜ *Holborn.*

The Place. The Robin Howard Dance Theatre at The Place is London's only theater dedicated to contemporary dance, and with tickets often under £15 (tickets to performances by student dancers cost just £5) it's good value, too. "Resolution!" is the United Kingdom's biggest platform event for new choreographers. ⊠ *17 Duke's Rd., Bloomsbury* ☎ *020/7121–1100* ⊕ *www.theplace.org.uk* Ⓜ *Euston.*

17

The giants of modern art are on display at South Bank's Tate Modern, one of the largest modern art galleries in the world and housed in a former power station.

ISLINGTON

Close to central London, yet with its own unique atmosphere, this neighborhood is home to a handful of renowned theaters and music venues that make the short journey northeast well worth the effort.

ART GALLERY

Victoria Miro Gallery. This large, important commercial gallery, in a former furniture factory, has exhibited some of the biggest names on the British contemporary art scene—Grayson Perry, the Chapman Brothers, and Peter Doig, to name a few. Some exhibitions spill out into the gallery's own garden. It also brings in exciting talent from abroad. ⊠ *16 Wharf Rd., Islington* ☎ *020/7336–8109* ⊕ *www.victoria-miro. com* ⊠ *Free* ☉ *Tues.–Sat. 10–6* Ⓜ *Old St., Angel.*

DANCE

FAMILY
Fodor's Choice
★

Sadler's Wells. This gleaming building opened in 1998, the seventh on the site in its 300-year history. Head here to see performances by leading classical and contemporary dance companies. The Random Dance Company is in residence, and the little Lilian Baylis Theatre hosts avant-garde work. ⊠ *Rosebery Ave., Islington* ☎ *0844/412–4300 tickets* ⊕ *www.sadlerswells.com* Ⓜ *Angel.*

THEATER

Almeida Theatre. This Off–West End venue, helmed by director Rupert Goold, premiers excellent new plays and exciting twists on the classics, often featuring high-profile actors. There's a good café and a licensed bar that serves "sharing dishes" as well as tasty main courses.

CONTEMPORARY ART: LONDON TODAY

In the 21st century, the focus of the city's art scene has shifted from the past to the future. Helped by the prominence of Tate Modern, London's contemporary art scene has never been so high profile. In publicly funded exhibition spaces like the Barbican Gallery, the Hayward Gallery, the Institute of Contemporary Arts, and the Serpentine Galleries, London now has a modern-art environment on par with that of Bilbao and New York. The so-called Young British Artists (YBAs, though no longer that young) Damien Hirst, Tracey Emin, and others are firmly planted in the public imagination. The celebrity status of British artists is in part thanks to the annual Turner Prize, which always stirs up controversy in the media during the display of the work, usually at Tate Britain.

Depending on whom you talk to, the Saatchi Gallery is considered to be either the savior of contemporary art or the wardrobe of the emperor's new clothes. After a couple of moves it is now ensconced in the former Duke of York's barracks off Chelsea's King's Road.

The South Bank's Tate Modern may house the giants of modern art, but East London is where the innovative action is. There are dozens of galleries in the fashionable spaces around Old Street, and the truly hip have already moved even farther afield, to areas such as Bethnal Green, to the east, and Peckham, to the south. The Whitechapel Art Gallery and Jay Jopling's influential White Cube, with branches in Bermondsey and St. James's, remain essential parts of the new art establishment and continue to show exciting work by emerging British artists.

On the first Thursday of every month, more than 130 museums and galleries of East London stay open until late and host talks, workshops, and other events (more information at ⊕ www.firstthursdays.co.uk).

⊠ *Almeida St., Islington* ☎ *020/7359–4404* ⊕ *www.almeida.co.uk* Ⓜ *Angel, Highbury & Islington.*

FAMILY **Little Angel Theatre.** Innovative puppetry performances for children and adults have been taking place in this adorable former temperance hall since 1961. The theater runs a number of festivals a year, including the biennial Suspense festival, with puppetry for adults. ⊠ *14 Dagmar Passage, Islington* ☎ *020/7226–1787 box office* ⊕ *www.littleangeltheatre. com* Ⓜ *Angel, Highbury & Islington.*

THE CITY

It may seem at first glance like the denizens of London's financial center are far too busy to take time out for culture, but if you look a little closer you'll see that arts events are taking place all over, courtesy of a number of acclaimed annual festivals. Art exhibits in empty offices and chamber performances in historic churches are regular occurrences.

PERFORMANCE CENTER

FAMILY **Barbican Centre.** Opened in 1982, The Barbican is an enormous Brutalist concrete maze that Londoners either love or hate—but its importance to the cultural life of the capital is beyond dispute. At the largest performing arts center in Europe, you could listen to Elgar, see 1960s photography, and catch German animation with live accompaniment. The main theater, known for its acoustics, is most famous as the home of the London Symphony Orchestra. The Barbican is also a frequent host of the BBC Symphony Orchestra. ⊠ *Silk St., The City* ☎ *020/7638–8891 box office* ⊕ *www.barbican.org.uk* ☉ *Mon.–Sat. 9 am–11 pm, Sun. 10 am–11 pm* Ⓜ *Barbican.*

EAST LONDON

Artists and other creative types, no longer able to afford central London rents, have been making their way eastward for years. It began in Shoreditch, but as rents increased there, too, neighborhoods farther and farther out have taken on these new residents. Go gallery hopping in Vyner Street in Bethnal Green or catch a hip band in action at one of Shoreditch's myriad music venues.

Fodor'sChoice **Wilton's.** Arguably London's most atmospheric cultural space, Wilton's
★ has been entertaining the crowds since 1743, first as an alehouse, then as a music hall. It now hosts gigs, talks, theater performances, movie screenings (often with live scores), and swing-dance evenings. The cozy Mahogany Bar, the oldest part of the building, serves a good range of quality local ales, along with typical pub food. ⊠ *1 Graces Alley, East End* ☎ *020/3468–5670* ⊕ *www.wiltons.org.uk* Ⓜ *Aldgate East, Tower Hill.*

SOUTH OF THE THAMES

The South Bank and its easterly near neighbor Bankside together make up one of the richest areas in London when it comes to arts and entertainment. Whether you want to watch a play, hear a concert, or see an art exhibit, you won't have to wander far to find something top class. Venture a little farther into South London, and you'll be rewarded with a sprinkling of fringe theaters that act as incubators for the capital's mainstream theater scene.

ART GALLERY

Fodor'sChoice **Tate Modern.** This converted power station is one of the largest modern-
★ art galleries in the world, so give yourself time to take it all in. The temporary installations in the gallery's Turbine Hall are always a must-see. The permanent collection includes work by all the major 20th-century artists, though only a fraction is shown at any one time. There are also touring shows and solo exhibitions of international artists. The oil tanks of the old power station were opened up in 2012 for a season of performance art. These new spaces are the first stage in a new extension of the gallery that is scheduled for completion in 2016. ⊠ *Bankside, South Bank* ☎ *020/7887–8888* ⊕ *www.tate.org.uk* 🖾 *Free; exhibitions from £12.50* ☉ *Sun.–Thurs. 10–6, Fri. and Sat. 10–10* Ⓜ *Southwark, St. Paul's, London Bridge.*

FILM: LONDON TODAY

There are many wonderful movie theaters in London and several that are committed to nonmainstream and repertory cinema, in particular the excellent Curzon cinemas and the British Film Institute. The **BFI London Film Festival** (⊕ *www.bfi. org.uk/lff*) brings hundreds of films made by masters of world cinema to London each October, accompanied by often sold-out talks and other events. The smaller, avant-garde **Raindance Film Festival** (⊕ *www. raindance.co.uk*) highlights independent filmmaking, September into October.

Open-air screenings of new releases and classic movies take place throughout the summer months at atmospheric locations including Somerset House, and the 19th-century Brompton Cemetery (⊕ *www.whereisthenomad.com*).

West End movie theaters continue to do good business. Most of the major houses, such as the Odeon Leicester Square and the Empire, are in the Leicester Square–Piccadilly Circus area, where tickets average £15. Monday and matinees are often cheaper, at around £8–£12, and there are also smaller crowds.

Check out *Time Out*, one of the London papers, or *www.viewlondon. co.uk* for listings.

FILM

FAMILY **BFI London IMAX Cinema.** The British Film Institute's glazed drum-shaped IMAX theater (now, confusingly, operated by Odeon) has the largest screen in the United Kingdom (approximately 75 feet wide and the height of five double-decker buses). It shows state-of-the-art 2-D and 3-D films. ⊠ *1 Charlie Chaplin Walk, South Bank* ☎ *0330/333–7878* ⊕ *www.bfi.org.uk/imax* Ⓜ *Waterloo.*

FAMILY **BFI Southbank.** With the best repertory programming in London, the three movie theaters and studio here are effectively a national film center run by the British Film Institute. More than 1,000 titles are screened each year, with art-house, foreign, silent, overlooked, classic, noir, and short films favored over recent Hollywood blockbusters. The center also has a gallery, bookshop, and "mediatheque" where visitors can watch film and television from the National Archive for free (closed Monday). This is one of the venues for the BFI London Film Festival; throughout the year there are minifestivals, seminars, and guest speakers. ⊠ *Belvedere Rd., South Bank* ☎ *020/7928–3232 box office* ⊕ *www. bfi.org.uk* Ⓜ *Waterloo.*

PERFORMANCE CENTER

Southbank Centre. The Royal Festival Hall is one of London's best spaces for large-scale choral and orchestral works and is home to the Philharmonia and London Philharmonic orchestras. The Queen Elizabeth Hall is a popular venue for top-tier soloists, and the Purcell Room is known for chamber music recitals. Free events take place in foyer spaces around the complex. Southbank hosts everything from the London International Mime festival to large-scale dance performances, plus highly regarded pop, rock and jazz acts. Also part of the complex is the **Hayward Gallery** (Mon. noon–6; Tues., Wed., and weekends 11–7; Thurs.

London's Royal Opera House is also home to the Royal Ballet and an in-house orchestra.

and Fri. 11–8), a landmark 1960s building and one of London's best contemporary art venues. ⊠ *Belvedere Rd., South Bank* ☏ *020/7960-4200,* ⊕ *www.southbankcentre.co.uk* Ⓜ *Waterloo, Embankment.*

THEATER

BAC. Battersea Arts Centre has a reputation for producing innovative new work, as well as hosting top alternative stand-up comics. Performances take place in quirky spaces all over this atmospheric former town hall. Check out Scratch events, low-tech theater where the audience provides feedback on works-in-progress. Entry for Scratch events is on a pay-what-you-can basis (minimum £1). There's also a fun bar that serves good food. ⊠ *176 Lavender Hill, Battersea* ☏ *020/7223–2223* ⊕ *www.bac.org.uk* Ⓜ *National Rail: Clapham Junction.*

FAMILY
Fodor's Choice
★

National Theatre. When this theater designed by Sir Denys Lasdun opened in 1976, Londoners weren't all so keen on the low-slung Brutalist block. Prince Charles described it as "a clever way of building a nuclear power station in the middle of London without anyone objecting." But whatever its merits or demerits, the National Theatre's interior spaces are worth a visit. Interspersed with the three theaters—the 1,150-seat Olivier, the 890-seat Lyttelton, and the 450-seat Dorfman—is a multilayered foyer with exhibitions, bars, restaurants, and free entertainment. Musicals, classics, and plays are performed by top-flight professionals. The Clore Learning Centre offers courses and events on all aspects of theater making, and you can watch staff at work in the backstage workshops from the Sherling High-Level Walkway. ⊠ *Belvedere Rd., South Bank* ☏ *020/7452–3000* ⊕ *www.nationaltheatre.org.uk* ✉ *Tour £8.50* ☉ *Foyer Mon.–Sat. 9:30 am–11 pm; selected Sun. noon–6 pm; 75-min tour backstage, times vary* Ⓜ *Waterloo.*

CLASSICAL MUSIC: LONDON TODAY

Whether it's a concert by pianist Lang Lang or a Mozart requiem by candlelight, it's possible to hear first-rate musicians in world-class venues almost every day of the year. The London Symphony Orchestra is in residence at the Barbican Centre, although other top orchestras—including the Philharmonia and the Royal Philharmonic—also perform here. The Barbican also hosts chamber-music concerts, with celebrated orchestras such as the City of London Sinfonia. Kings Place has a varied calendar of musical events. The Southbank Centre also has a varied and impressive international music season. Full houses are rare, so even at the biggest concert halls you should be able to get a ticket for £12. If you can't book in advance, arrive at the hall an hour before the performance for a chance at returns.

■TIP→ Lunchtime concerts take place all over the city in smaller concert halls, arts-center foyers, and churches; they usually cost less than £5 or are free. St. John's Smith Square and St. Martin-in-the-Fields are popular locations. Performances usually begin about 1 pm and last one hour.

Classical-music festivals include the stimulating avant-garde **Meltdown** (⊕ meltdown.southbankcentre. co.uk), curated each year by a prominent musician—James Lavelle in 2014—at the Southbank Centre in June, the **Spitalfields Festival** (⊕ www.spitalfieldsfestival.org.uk), a program of recitals held in beautiful, historic East End churches in June and December, and the **City of London Festival** (⊕ www.colf. org), held in the Square Mile for a month in summer. A great British tradition since 1895, the **Henry Wood Promenade Concerts,** better known as the "Proms" (⊕ www. bbc.co.uk/proms), run eight weeks, from July to September, at the Royal Albert Hall and Cadogan Hall. Despite its numerous high-quality concerts, it's renowned for its (atypical) last night: a very patriotic display of singing "Land of Hope and Glory," Union Jack–waving, and general madness. For regular Proms, tickets run £5–£95, with hundreds of standing tickets for £5 available at the hall on the night of the concert.

■TIP→ The last night is broadcast in Hyde Park on a jumbo screen, but even here a seat on the grass requires a paid ticket that costs around £40.

17

The Old Vic. In 2015 Matthew Warchus, the director behind *Matilda the Musical*, took over as artistic director at this grand old theater, the former haunting grounds of such stage legends as John Gielgud, Vivien Leigh, Peter O'Toole, Richard Burton, and Judi Dench. The venue had suffered decades of financial duress before being brought under the ownership of a dedicated trust headed by its previous artistic director, the actor Kevin Spacey. It's now in great shape, secure for the future and producing some of the best theater in London. ✉ *The Cut, Southwark* ☎ *0844/871–7628 box office* ⊕ *www.oldvictheatre.com* Ⓜ *Waterloo, Southwark.*

FAMILY
Fodor's Choice
★

Shakespeare's Globe Theatre. This faithful reconstruction of the open-air playhouse where Shakespeare wrote many of his greatest plays marvelously re-creates the 16th-century theater experience. Standing room in the "yard" in front of the stage costs £5. The season runs April through October, but an exhibition and theater tours run year-round. The Sam Wanamaker Playhouse, a replica Jacobean (early-17th-century) indoor theater named after the Globe's founder, opened in early 2014. It hosts plays, concerts, and operas by candlelight in winter, when the open-air theater is closed. Tours of the playhouse are available on selected dates. ⌧ *21 New Globe Walk, Bankside, South Bank* ☎ *020/7401–9919 box office, 020/7902–1400 inquiries* ⊕ *www.shakespearesglobe. com* ⬚ *Exhibition and Globe Theatre Tour £13.50* ☽ *Exhibition daily 9–5:30; Globe Theatre Tour daily 9:30–5* Ⓜ *London Bridge, Mansion House (then cross Southwark Bridge), Blackfriars (then cross Blackfriars Bridge), St. Paul's (then cross Millenium Bridge).*

Southwark Playhouse. This impressive little theater, in what was once a car showroom, produces award-winning new musicals and gritty drama for a fraction of the cost of the West End. The bar/café is good, too, which is fortunate—the surrounding area is something of a no-man's-land. ⌧ *77-85 Newington Causeway, Borough* ☎ *020/7407–0234* ⊕ *www.southwarkplayhouse.co.uk* Ⓜ *Borough, Elephant & Castle.*

FAMILY
Fodor's Choice
★

Unicorn Theatre. Dedicated to innovative work for young audiences, this modern theater programs plays, musicals, and interactive theater for everyone from babies on up. Inclusivity is a major focus, with performances for those with visual and hearing and other impairments taking place regularly. ⌧ *147 Tooley St., Borough* ☎ *020/7645–0560 box office, 020/7645–0500 inquiries* ⊕ *www.unicorntheatre.com* Ⓜ *London Bridge.*

Fodor's Choice
★

Young Vic. In a home near Waterloo, big names perform alongside young talent, often in daring, innovative productions of classic plays that appeal to a more diverse audience than is traditionally found in London theaters. Good food is served at the bustling bar. ⌧ *66 The Cut, Waterloo, South Bank* ☎ *020/7922–2922 box office* ⊕ *www.youngvic. org* Ⓜ *Southwark, Waterloo.*

KENSINGTON AND CHELSEA

These refined neighborhoods just west of central London have a wide variety of galleries and performance spaces, with several located within the area's large public green spaces.

KENSINGTON

ART GALLERY

Serpentine Galleries. Built in 1934 as a tea pavilion in Kensington Gardens, the Serpentine has an international reputation for exhibitions of modern and contemporary art. Henry Moore, Andy Warhol, Bridget Riley, Damien Hirst, and Rachel Whiteread are a few of the artists who have exhibited here. It's a seven-minute walk across the park from the main gallery. The annual summer Pavilion, a striking temporary structure designed by a different leading architect every year, is always worth catching. ⌧ *Kensington Gardens, Kensington* ☎ *020/7402–6075* ⊕ *www.serpentinegalleries.org* ⬚ *Free* ☽ *Tues.–Sun. 10–6* Ⓜ *Lancaster Gate, Knightsbridge, South Kensington.*

OPERA: LONDON TODAY

The two key players in London's opera scene are the internationally renowned Royal Opera House and the more innovative English National Opera (ENO), which presents English-language productions at the London Coliseum. Only the Theatre Royal, Drury Lane, has a longer theatrical history than the Royal Opera House—the third theater to be built on the site since 1858.

Despite occasional performances by the likes of Björk, the Royal Opera House struggles to shrug off its reputation for stuffiness. Ticket prices can rise to £800, though some are less than £10.

In summer, the increasingly adventurous Opera Holland Park presents the usual warhorses alongside some obscure works under a canopy in leafy Holland Park.

International touring companies often perform at Sadler's Wells, the Barbican, the Southbank Centre, and Wigmore Hall, so check the weekly listings for details.

CLASSICAL MUSIC

Cadogan Hall. Once a church, this spacious venue is home to the Royal Philharmonic Orchestra, and the English Chamber Orchestra performs here regularly. ✉ *5 Sloane Terr., Kensington* ☎ *020/7730–4500* ⊕ *www.cadoganhall.com* Ⓜ *Sloane Sq.*

Fodor's Choice ★ **Royal Albert Hall.** Opened in 1871, this splendid iron-and-glass–dome auditorium hosts everything from pop and classical headliners to Cirque du Soleil, awards ceremonies, and sumo wrestling championships, but is best known for the annual July–September BBC Promenade Concerts. Bargain-price standing (or promenading, or sitting-on-the-floor) tickets for "the Proms" are sold on the night of the concert. The domed, circular 5,272-seat auditorium has a terra-cotta exterior surmounted by a mosaic frieze depicting figures engaged in cultural pursuits. The hall is open daily for daytime guided tours (£12.25) and, Wednesday–Sunday, afternoon tea (£10.50–£33). ✉ *Kensington Gore, Kensington* ☎ *0845/401–5034* box office ⊕ *www.royalalberthall.com* Ⓜ *South Kensington.*

OPERA

FAMILY **Opera Holland Park.** In summer, well-loved operas and imaginative productions of lesser-known works are presented under a spectacular canopy against the remains of Holland House, one of the first great houses built in Kensington. The company has successfully branched out into opera for families in recent years, too. Ticket prices range from £10 to £75, with around 1,000 tickets offered free to young people ages 9–18 every season. Tickets go on sale in March. ✉ *Holland Park, Kensington High St., Kensington* ☎ *0300/999–1000 box office (opens Mar.), 020/7361–3570 inquiries* ⊕ *www.operahollandpark.com* Ⓜ *High Street Kensington, Holland Park.*

CHELSEA

ART GALLERY

Saatchi Gallery. In the late 1980s and 1990s, Charles Saatchi lit the fuse to the contemporary art explosion in Britain, and although he and his art investments may not be quite as ubiquitous as they once were, he

17

remains a key figure. After migrating to several museums and being shown around the world, Saatchi's collection now resides in this modern gallery that sprawls through 70,000 square feet of the Duke of York's HQ building in Chelsea, complete with a bookshop and café-bar. ⊠ *Duke of York's HQ, King's Rd., Chelsea* ☎ *020/7811–3070* ⊕ *www. saatchi-gallery.co.uk* ⌑ *Free* ⊙ *Daily 10–6* Ⓜ *Sloane Sq.*

THEATER

Royal Court Theatre. Britain's undisputed epicenter of new theatrical works, the Court continues to produce gritty British and international drama. Don't miss the best deal in town—four 10-pence standing tickets go on sale one hour before each performance, and £10 tickets are available on Monday. ⊠ *Sloane Sq., Chelsea* ☎ *020/7565–5000* ⊕ *www. royalcourttheatre.com* Ⓜ *Sloane Sq.*

NOTTING HILL

This cosmopolitan West London neighborhood, shown to advantage in the 1999 film that bears its name, is best known for the Notting Hill Carnival, a lively music-focused street festival that takes over the wider area on the final weekend of August each year. There's a year-round culture scene, too, catering mainly to the neighborhood's trendy young professionals.

FILM

FAMILY **The Electric Cinema.** This refurbished Portobello Road art house screens mainstream and international movies. The emphasis is on comfort, with leather sofas for two, armchairs, and coffee tables for your wine and appetizers. Edible Cinema combines experimental food and cocktails with a movie. The Electric also has another movie theater in east London, on Redchurch Street, with sofas and wine coolers. ⊠ *191 Portobello Rd., Notting Hill* ☎ *020/7908–9696* ⊕ *www.electriccinema.co.uk* ⌑ *£15.50–£22.50* Ⓜ *Ladbroke Grove, Notting Hill Gate.*

REGENT'S PARK AND HAMPSTEAD

Leafy north London has long been a stomping ground for the capital's cultural elite—stroll through Primrose Hill and you're practically guaranteed to spot a film star or musician—but there's diversity here, too. Camden Town is justifiably famous for its indie music scene, while respected fringe theaters in Swiss Cottage and Kilburn don't shy away from major topics.

REGENT'S PARK

THEATER

FAMILY **Open Air Theatre.** On a warm summer evening, open-air theater in the
Fodor's Choice pastoral Regent's Park is hard to beat. Enjoy a supper before the performance, a bite during the intermission on the lawn, or drinks in the bar. The only downside is that warm summer nights in London are not always reliable—a raincoat is advisable. ⊠ *Inner Circle, Regent's Park* ☎ *0844/826–4242* ⊕ *openairtheatre.com* Ⓜ *Baker St., Regent's Park.*

SHOPPING

Updated By
Ellin Stein

The keyword of London shopping has always been "individuality," whether expressed in the superb custom tailoring of Savile Row, the nonconformist punk roots of quintessential British designer Vivienne Westwood, or the unique small stores that purvey the owner's private passion, whether paper theaters, toy soldiers, or buttons. This tradition is under threat from the influx of chains—global luxury, domestic mid-market, and international youth—but the distinctively British mix of quality and originality, tradition and character, remains.

You can try on underwear fit for a queen at Her Majesty's lingerie supplier, track down a leather-bound Brontë classic at an antiquarian bookseller, or find a bargain antique on Portobello Road. Whether you're just browsing—there's nothing like the size, variety, and sheer theater of London's street markets to stimulate the acquisition instinct—or on a fashion-seeking mission, London shopping offers something for all tastes and budgets.

Although it's impossible to pin down one particular look that defines the city, London style tends to fall into two camps: one is the quirky, individualistic, somewhat romantic look exemplified by homegrown designers like Matthew Williamson, Vivienne Westwood, and Lulu Guinness. The other reflects Britain's celebrated tradition of classic knitwear and suiting, with labels like Jaeger, Pringle, and Brora, while Oswald Boateng, Paul Smith, and Richard James take tradition and give it a very modern twist. Traditional bespoke men's tailoring can be found in the menswear stores of Jermyn Street and Savile Row—there's no better place in the city to buy custom-made shirts and suits, while the handbags at Mulberry, Asprey, and Anya Hindmarch are pure classic quality. If your budget can't stretch this far, no problem; the city's chain stores like Topshop, Zara, and H&M, aimed at the younger end of the market, are excellent places to pick up designs copied straight from the catwalk at a fraction of the price, while mid-market chains like Reiss, Jigsaw, and L.K. Bennett offer smart design and better quality for the more sophisticated shopper.

If there's anything that unites London's designers, it's a commitment to creativity and originality, underpinned by a strong sense of heritage. This combination of posh and rock-n-roll sensibilities turns up in everyone from Terence Conran, who revolutionized product and houseware design in the '60s (and is still going strong), to Alexander McQueen, who combined the Punk aesthetic with the rigor of couture. You'll see it in fanciful millinery creations by Philip Treacy and Stephen Jones, and in the work of imaginative shoemakers Nicholas Kirkwood, United Nude, and Terry de Havilland; and it keeps going, right through to current hot designers Erdem, Christopher Kane, and Christopher Bailey, the latter responsible for making traditional label Burberry relevant again.

One reason for London's design supremacy is the strength of local fashion college Central St. Martin's, whose graduates include Conran, Kane, McQueen, his successor at his eponymous label—and designer of the Duchess of Cambridge's wedding dress—Sarah Burton, and Stella McCartney's equally acclaimed successor at Céline, Phoebe Philo.

To find the McQueens, McCartneys, and Baileys of tomorrow, head for the independent boutiques of the East End and Bermondsey. If anything, London is even better known for its vibrant street fashion than for its high-end designers. Stock up from the stalls at Portobello, Camden, and Spitalfields markets.

Aside from bankrupting yourself, the only problem you may encounter is exhaustion. London's shopping districts are spread out all over the city, so do as savvy locals do: plan your excursion with military precision, taking in only one or two areas in a day, and stop for a lunch with a glass of wine or a pint at a pub.

18

PLANNING

OPENING HOURS

Most shops are open from about 9:30 or 10 am to 6 or 6:30 pm. Some may open at 11 and stay open until 7. Because shop hours, particularly for the smaller shops, are varied, it's a good idea to phone or check websites ahead. Stores that have late shopping—and not all do—are usually open until 7 or 8 pm on Wednesday or Thursday only. Most department stores stay open late one day a week. On Sunday, many shops open between 11 am and noon and close at 5 or 6 pm. Most stores are open on Sunday in December for the Christmas season.

WATCH YOUR LANGUAGE

Locals like to say that Brits and Americans are separated by a common language. Here are a few confusing terms to watch for when out and about in the shops:

Pants means underwear. Every other type of long-legged bottoms (except jeans) are called **trousers**. Also in the underwear category is the **vest**

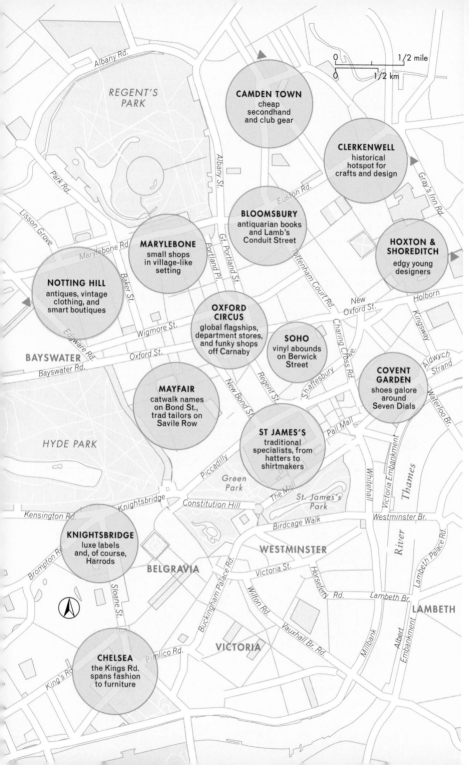

REGENT'S PARK

Albany Rd.

Park Rd.

Lisson Grove

Marylebone Rd.

Baker St.

Edgware Rd.

BAYSWATER

Wigmore St.

Oxford St.

Bayswater Rd.

HYDE PARK

Kensington Rd.

Knightsbridge

Brompton Rd.

Sloane St.

King's Rd.

Pimlico Rd.

Albany St.

Gt. Portland St.

Portland Pl.

Euston Rd.

Tottenham Court Rd.

New Oxford St.

Charing Cross Rd.

Shaftesbury

Regent St.

New Bond St.

Piccadilly

Pall Mall

The Mall

Green Park

Constitution Hill

St. James's Park

Birdcage Walk

WESTMINSTER

Victoria St.

Buckingham Palace Rd.

Willow Rd.

VICTORIA

BELGRAVIA

Vauxhall Br. Rd.

Horseferry Rd.

Millbank

Westminster Br.

River Thames

Victoria Embankment

Whitehall

Gray's Inn Rd.

Kingsway

Holborn

Aldwych

Strand

Waterloo Br.

Albert Embankment

Lambeth Palace Rd.

Lambeth Br.

LAMBETH

0 — 1/2 mile
0 — 1/2 km

CAMDEN TOWN
cheap secondhand and club gear

CLERKENWELL
historical hotspot for crafts and design

BLOOMSBURY
antiquarian books and Lamb's Conduit Street

HOXTON & SHOREDITCH
edgy young designers

MARYLEBONE
small shops in village-like setting

NOTTING HILL
antiques, vintage clothing, and smart boutiques

OXFORD CIRCUS
global flagships, department stores, and funky shops off Carnaby

SOHO
vinyl abounds on Berwick Street

COVENT GARDEN
shoes galore around Seven Dials

MAYFAIR
catwalk names on Bond St., trad tailors on Savile Row

ST JAMES'S
traditional specialists, from hatters to shirtmakers

KNIGHTSBRIDGE
luxe labels and, of course, Harrods

CHELSEA
the Kings Rd. spans fashion to furniture

(undershirt in the United States); if you are looking for a vest, ask for a waistcoat.

Knickers are ladies' underwear. If you want pantyhose, ask for **tights.**

Jumper means sweater—unless it's a cardigan, in which case it may be shortened to **cardie.** If you ask for a **sweater,** you may be offered a sweatshirt.

Men use **braces** to hold up their trousers; in England **suspenders** is another word for garters.

If you want some Adidas- or Nike-type athletic shoes, ask for **trainers,** not sneakers.

Don't ask for a **pocketbook** or a **purse** if you mean a handbag—the former will be incomprehensible, and the latter will produce a coin purse. Ask for a **fanny pack** and it will produce a laugh—"fanny" means something altogether different in the United Kingdom, so ask for a "bum-bag."

Nightgowns are usually abbreviated to **nighties** and bathrobes may be **dressing gowns.**

A WORD ABOUT SERVICE

American standards of customer service are rare in London—you may find attentive customer service at old-school, traditional names and some independent stores, but salespeople elsewhere can seem abrupt or indifferent.

SHOPPING REVIEWS

18

ST. JAMES'S

ACCESSORIES: HATS

Fodor's Choice ★ **James Lock & Co. Hatters.** Need a silk top hat, a flat-weave Panama, or a traditional tweed flat cap? Or, for ladies, an occasion hat? James Lock of St. James's has been providing hats from this cozy shop since 1676 for customers ranging from Admiral Lord Nelson, Oscar Wilde, and Frank Sinatra to, more recently, Robert Downey Jr. and Guy Ritchie, as well as trendsetting musicians and models. ⊠ *6 St. James's St., St. James's* ☏ *020/7930–8884* ⊕ *www.lockhatters.co.uk* ☉ *Closed Sun.* Ⓜ *Green Park.*

Fodor's Choice ★ **Swaine Adeney Brigg.** Providing practical supplies for country pursuits since 1750, Swaine Adeney Brigg carries beautifully crafted umbrellas, walking sticks, and hip flasks, or ingenious combinations, such as the umbrella with a slim tipple-holding flask secreted inside the stem. The same level of quality and craftsmanship applies to the store's leather goods, which include attaché cases (you can buy the "Q Branch" model that James Bond carried in *From Russia With Love*) and wallets. You'll find scarves, caps, and the Herbert Johnson "Poet Hat," the iconic headgear (stocked since 1890) worn by Harrison Ford in every Indiana Jones film. ⊠ *7 Piccadilly Arcade, St. James's* ☏ *020/7409–7277* ⊕ *www.swaineadeney.co.uk* ☉ *Closed Sun.* Ⓜ *Green Park.*

CLOSE UP

Know Your Shopping Personality

"Where is the best place to shop in London?" There are thousands of shops in the city, and dozens of neighborhoods worth shopping in. Start by identifying your shopping personality to narrow your choices for a successful outing.

Easygoing. If you want to pop in and out of a variety of shops, as well as avoid the crowds around Oxford Street, head to King's Road in Chelsea. You'll find department store Peter Jones, plus Marks & Spencer and plenty of chains and trendy boutiques. Another safe bet is High Street Kensington for the usual big chains, in addition to some smaller ones less oriented toward disposable fashion, such as Cos, Karen Millen, and Oliver Bonas.

Eclectic. If you are looking for well-crafted, original items, start at Liberty on Regent Street, then head to Marylebone to the north, or the warren of cobblestone streets lined with independent shops off Carnaby Street, immediately to the south.

Fashionista. When only the top designers will do, start at the designer boutiques along Sloane Street in Knightsbridge before hopping on bus No. 19 to Green Park. From there you can cover Bond Street (both Old and New) finishing at Fenwick, or veer off onto Conduit Street, designer-heavy Bruton Street, or, at the northwest end of Berkeley Square, ultrachic Mount Street. If you still have time and energy, check out South Molton Street opposite Bond Street Tube or St. Christopher's Place across Oxford Street.

Funky and Avant-Garde. For cutting-edge fashion and housewares, head to the East End neighborhoods. Start at Columbia Road in Hoxton, with its charming specialty shops (and the Sunday flower market), then wander through Shoreditch, Spitalfields, and Bethnal Green, where you'll find stores filled with one-of-a-kind designs. There's also lots here to appeal to vintage hunters.

Whirlwind. If you're after a one-stop-shopping experience, head to one of the big department stores. Selfridges and Fenwick are near the Bond Street Tube station, Liberty is near Oxford Circus Tube station, while Harvey Nichols and Harrods share the Knightsbridge Tube station.

BEAUTY

Floris. What do Queen Victoria and Marilyn Monroe have in common? They both used fragrances from Floris, one of the most beautiful shops in London, with gleaming glass-and-Spanish-mahogany showcases salvaged from the Great Exhibition of 1851. In addition to scents for both men and women, Floris makes its own shaving products, reflecting its origins as a barbershop. Other gift possibilities include goose-down powder puffs, a famous rose-scented mouthwash, and beautifully packaged soaps and bath essences. There's another branch in Belgravia. ⊠ *89 Jermyn St., St. James's* ☎ *0845/702–3239* ⊕ *www.florislondon. com* ☉ *Closed Sun.* Ⓜ *Piccadilly Circus, Green Park.*

BOOKS

Fodor'sChoice
★

Hatchards. This is the United Kingdom's oldest bookshop, open since 1797 and beloved by writers themselves (customers have included Oscar Wilde, Rudyard Kipling, and Lord Byron). Despite its wood-paneled, "gentleman's library" atmosphere, and eclectic selection of books, Hatchards is owned by the large Waterstone's chain. Nevertheless, the shop still retains its period charm, aided by the staff's old-fashioned helpfulness and expertise. Look for the substantial number of books signed by notable contemporary authors on the well-stocked shelves. ✉ *187 Piccadilly, St. James's* ☎ *020/7439–9921* ⊕ *www.hatchards.co.uk* Ⓜ *Piccadilly Circus.*

> ### ROYAL WARRANT
>
> Many stores carry items with the Royal Warrant seal (even some sugar brands). Though this doesn't mean that the products have been personally endorsed by the royals, it does mean that the palace has used such items for five consecutive years—and it could enliven a gift for royal-watchers.

CLOTHING: MEN

Turnbull & Asser. The Jermyn Street store sells luxurious jackets, cashmere sweaters, suits, ties, pajamas, ready-to-wear shirts, and accessories perfect for the billionaire who has everything. The brand is best known for its superb custom-made shirts—worn by Prince Charles, Woody Allen, and every filmic James Bond to name a few. These can be ordered at the nearby Bury Street branch. At least 15 separate measurements are taken, and the cloth, woven to the company's specifications, comes in 1,000 different patterns—the cottons feel as good as silk. The first order must be for a minimum of six shirts, which start from £195 each. There's another branch in The City. ✉ *71–72 Jermyn St., St. James's* ☎ *020/7808–3000* ⊕ *www.turnbullandasser.com* ☾ *Closed Sun.* Ⓜ *Green Park.*

FOOD

Fodor'sChoice
★

Berry Bros. & Rudd. Nothing matches Berry Bros. & Rudd for rare offerings and a unique shopping experience. A family-run wine business since 1698, BBR stores its vintage bottles and casks in vaulted cellars that are more than 300 years old. The in-house wine school offers educational tasting sessions, while the dedicated whisky room also has an excellent selection. The shop has a quirky charm and the staff is extremely knowledgeable—and not snooty if you're on a budget. ✉ *3 St. James's St., St. James's* ☎ *800/280–2440* ⊕ *www.bbr.com* ☾ *Closed Sun.* Ⓜ *Green Park.*

Fodor'sChoice
★

Fortnum & Mason. Although F&M is jokingly known as "the Queen's grocer," and the impeccably mannered staff still wear traditional tailcoats, its celebrated food hall stocks gifts for all budgets, including irresistibly packaged luxury foods stamped with the gold "By Appointment" crest for under £5. Try the teas, preserves (including the unusual rose-petal jelly), condiments, or Gentleman's Relish (anchovy paste). The store's famous hampers are always a welcome gift. The gleaming food hall spans two floors and incorporates a sleek wine bar, with the rest of the store devoted to upscale housewares, men and women's accessories and toiletries, a dedicated candle room, a jewelry department featuring

18

LONDON SHOPPING STEALS AND DEALS

Even at the best of times London has never been known as a budget-shopping destination, and when the pound is strong prices can seem stratospheric. However, whatever the exchange rate, there are still bargains to be had as long as you know where, and when, to look. To get the maximum mileage out of your cash, visit during the widespread biannual sales, which kick off in late June and just after Christmas, and last about a month.

Fashion insiders attend the many sales held throughout the year, from big warehouse clearances, such as the Designer Warehouse Sales (⊕ www.designerwarehousesales. com) and Designer Sales UK (⊕ designersales.co.uk), to individual designers' sample sales—check out

⊕ www.fashionconfidential.co.uk or *Time Out* (⊕ www.timeout.com) for information, and to register for updates. London outlets, such as Browns Labels for Less, Paul Smith Sale Shop, and the Joseph Sale Shop on King's Road offer year-round designer bargains. If time permits, travel outside London to Bicester Village (⊕ www.bicestervillage.com), a luxury outlet mall in Oxfordshire. It's completely worth the nearly one-hour train journey, if only for the opportunity to score an item from such highly coveted British brands as Alexander McQueen, Temperley, Mulberry, Burberry, and Aquascutum, as well as other top labels.

If you're not fussy about labels, there are even more choices, including Primark *(see Soho listings)*.

exclusive designs by breakthrough talent, and clothing and toys for children. If you start to flag, break for afternoon tea at the juice bar or one of the four other restaurants (one's an indulgent ice-cream parlor)—or a treatment in the Beauty Rooms. There's another branch at St. Pancras International. ⊠ *181 Piccadilly, St. James's* ☎ *020/7734–8040* ⊕ *www. fortnumandmason.com* Ⓜ *Green Park*.

Paxton & Whitfield. In business for more than 200 years, this venerable and aromatic London shop stocks hundreds of the world's greatest artisinal cheeses, particularly British and French varieties (a homesick General de Gaulle shopped here during World War II). The cheeses are laid on straw on refrigerated shelves, with tasting samples set out on a marble-top counter. You can pick up some ham, pâté, condiments, preserves, wine, or port, as well as cheese-related accessories like boards or knives. ⊠ *93 Jermyn St., St. James's* ☎ *020/7930–0259* ⊕ *www.paxtonandwhitfield.co.uk* ⊘ *Closed Sun.* Ⓜ *Piccadilly Circus, Green Park*.

SHOES

Loake Shoemakers. Long established in England's Midlands and a provider of boots to the British armed forces in both world wars, this family-run firm specializes in classic handcrafted men's shoes. Whether you're after brogues, loafers, or deck shoes, the staff will take the time to ensure you have the right fit. In terms of quality and service, Loakes represents real value for money, though they definitely aren't inexpensive. There's another branch on Bow Street in The City. ⊠ *8–10 Princes*

Arcade, off Jermyn St., St. James's ☎ *020/7734–8643* ⊕ *www.loake. co.uk* ☉ *Closed Sun.* Ⓜ *Piccadilly.*

SPECIALTY STORES

Geo F. Trumper. If you don't have the time for an old-fashioned hot-towel shave, pick up some accessories to take home for yourself or as a gift. The Extract of West Indian Lime is a popular, zingy aftershave, and the Coconut Oil Hard Shaving Soap, which comes in a hand-turned wooden bowl, is a classic. There is also a store at 9 Curzon Street in Mayfair. ✉ *1 Duke of York St., St. James's* ☎ *020/7734–6553* ⊕ *www. trumpers.com* ☉ *Closed Sun.* Ⓜ *Piccadilly Circus.*

TOYS

The Armoury of St. James's. The fine toy soldiers and military models in stock here are collectors' items. Painted and mounted knights only 6 inches high can cost up to £1,200 (though figures start at a mere £7.50 for a toy soldier). Besides lead and tin soldiers, the shop has regimental brooches, historic orders and medals, and military antiques. ✉ *17 Piccadilly Arcade, St. James's* ☎ *020/7493–5082* ⊕ *www.armoury.co.uk* ☉ *Closed Sun.* Ⓜ *Piccadilly Circus.*

MAYFAIR AND MARYLEBONE

MAYFAIR

ACCESSORIES

Mulberry. Staying true to its roots in rural Somerset, this luxury goods company epitomizes *le style Anglais*, a sophisticated take on the earth tones and practicality of English country style. Best known for highly desirable luxury handbags, such as those in the Cara Delevigne line and the Bayswater, the company also produces gorgeous leather accessories, from wallets to luggage, as well as shoes and clothing for men and women. Aside from the New Bond Street flagship, there are branches in Knightsbridge and Covent Garden, and Mulberry concessions in most of the major department stores. The small store on St. Christopher's Place in Marylebone stocks accessories only. ✉ *50 New Bond St., Mayfair* ☎ *020/7491–3900* ⊕ *www.mulberry.com* Ⓜ *Bond St.*

William & Son. William Asprey, scion of a jewelry dynasty, sells his carefully chosen, British-made luxury goods using a friendlier and less-formal approach. Here's where you'll find all sorts of items you didn't know you needed, like silver-tipped retractable pencils, lizard-skin passport holders, crocodile backgammon sets, or a silver piggy bank. The jewelry is tasteful and subtle rather than knock-your-eyes-out, and the store will also do custom work. ✉ *10 Mount St., Mayfair* ☎ *020/7493–8385* ⊕ *www.williamandson.com* ☉ *Closed weekends* Ⓜ *Bond St.*

ANTIQUES

Grays Antique Market. Open weekdays from 10 to 6 and from 11 to 5 on Saturday (when not all stalls are open), Grays has approximately 200 dealers specializing in everything from Bakelite items to Mughal art. The majority focus on jewelry, ranging from contemporary to antique. Bargains are not out of the question, and proper pedigrees are guaranteed. Also try Grays in the Mews around the corner—stalls there sell

18

less expensive merchandise, including antique dolls at Glenda's and excellent vintage clothing at Vintage Modes. ⊠ *58 Davies St. & 1–7 Davies Mews, Mayfair* ☎ *020/7629–7034* ⊕ *www.graysantiques.com* ☉ *Closed Sun.* Ⓜ *Bond St.*

BOOKS AND STATIONERY

Fodor's Choice
★

Heywood Hill. Open since 1936, Heywood Hill is considered by some to be the best small bookstore in the English-speaking world—John Le Carré, who set a scene in *Tinker Tailor Soldier Spy* here, is a long-standing customer. Here's where you can pick up a leather-bound volume on architecture, gardening, natural history, and topography—just some of the topics in which the antiquarian collection specializes. The contemporary selection emphasizes literature, history, biography, travel, architecture, and children's books. During World War I, author Nancy Mitford helped keep the bookstore going. Today, the 12th Duke of Devonshire, a descendant of her brother-in-law, the 11th Duke, is the owner. ⊠ *10 Curzon St., Mayfair* ☎ *020/7629–0647* ⊕ *www.heywoodhill.com* ☉ *Closed Sun.* Ⓜ *Green Park.*

Maggs Bros. Ltd. How could any book lover resist a shop with such a Dickensian name? Located in a Georgian town house in one of Mayfair's toniest squares, Maggs, established in 1853, is one of the world's oldest and largest rare-book dealers. The staff is expert enough to advise important collectors, but they're friendly and helpful to all interested visitors. Far from being fussy, the store includes a "counterculture" section with works on subversion, extremism, punk, the occult, and more. ⊠ *50 Berkeley Sq., Mayfair* ☎ *020/7493–7160* ⊕ *www.maggs. com* ☉ *Closed weekends* Ⓜ *Green Park.*

Smythson of Bond Street. No hostess of any standing would consider having a leather-bound guest book made by anyone other than this elegant stationer, and the shop's social stationery and distinctive diaries, with pale-blue pages, are the epitome of British good taste. Diaries, stationery, and small leather goods can be personalized. Smythson also produces a small line of leather handbags and purses. You'll find other branches in Chelsea, Notting Hill, and The City. ⊠ *40 New Bond St., Mayfair* ☎ *020/7629–8558* ⊕ *www.smythson.com* Ⓜ *Bond St., Oxford Circus.*

Waterstone's. At this mega-bookshop (Europe's largest) located in a former art deco department store near Piccadilly Circus, browse through your latest purchase or admire the view with a glass of wine or a snack at the 5th View Bar and Grill, which is open until 9. Waterstone's is the country's leading book chain, and they've pulled out all the stops to make their flagship as comfortable and welcoming as a bookstore can be. There are several smaller branches throughout the city. ⊠ *203–206*

BESPOKE LONDON

Having anything superbly cut and supremely fashionable used to be restricted to the upper class, who had such items made to order. One had one's tailor, one's milliner, one's dressmaker, and so forth. Things are more egalitarian these days, but whether you want a bespoke Savile Row suit or custom-made leather shoes, the prices remain steep.

Those who want the best and have the budget to afford it head for Mayfair and St. James's.

Piccadilly, Mayfair ☎ *0207/851–2400* ⊕ *www.waterstones.com* Ⓜ *Piccadilly Circus.*

CLOTHING

Belstaff. For years purveyors of Britain's coolest motorcycle leathers, Belstaff has expanded into dresses, skirts, and handbags, as well as knitwear, boots, tops, and trousers for both men and women, all reflecting the brand's functional but unconventional heritage (previous customers include Lawrence of Arabia, Amelia Earhart, and Che Guevara). Outerwear in general and leather jackets in particular remain a strength. ⊠ *135–137 New Bond St., Mayfair* ☎ *020/7495–5897* ⊕ *www.belstaff. co.uk* Ⓜ *Bond St.*

Burberry. Known for its trademark tartan, this company has cultivated an edgy, high-fashion image in recent years, with designs like fetish-y boots and sexy leather jackets perfect for any catwalk. The raincoats are still a classic buy, along with plaid scarves in every color imaginable and handbags. If you're up for a trek, there's a huge factory outlet in Hackney on Chatham Place that has clothes and accessories for men, women, and children at half price or less. There are also branches in Mayfair, Knightsbridge, and Covent Garden, in addition to this spectacular flagship store. ⊠ *121 Regent St., Mayfair* ☎ *020/7806–8904* ⊕ *uk.burberry.com* Ⓜ *Piccadilly Circus.*

Fodor's Choice
★

Dover Street Market. With its creative displays and eclectic, well-chosen mix of merchandise, this six-floor emporium is as much art installation as store. The merchandise and its configuration change every six months, so you never know what you will find, which is half the fun. The creation of Comme des Garçons' Rei Kawakubo, Dover Street

Market showcases all of the label's collections for men and women alongside a changing roster of other designers, including Erdem, Alexander Wang, and Givenchy—all of whom have their own customized mini-boutiques—plus avant-garde art books, vintage couture, and curiosities, such as antique plaster anatomy models. An outpost of the Rose Bakery on the top floor makes for a good break. ⊠ *17–18 Dover St., Mayfair* ☎ *020/7518–0680* ⊕ *www.doverstreetmarket.com* Ⓜ *Green Park.*

Isabel Marant London. The first London store from the designer, who is a favorite of French fashion editors, this airy skylit space is full of her signature skinny jeans, slouchy knits, wedge sneakers, and rock-chick miniskirts, all exuding Left Bank boho cool. ⊠ *29 Bruton St., Mayfair* ☎ *020/7499–7887* ⊕ *www.isabelmarant.com* ☾ *Closed Sun.* Ⓜ *Bond St.*

CLOTHING: MENSWEAR

Alfred Dunhill. For more than 100 years, Dunhill has been synonymous with the most luxurious and sophisticated men's goods, including accessories, briefcases, and superbly tailored clothes. This Georgian mansion, the flagship, also offers a barbershop, men's spa, humidor, cellar bar, courtyard restaurant, and bespoke services, where you can order custom-fitted menswear or unique versions of the brand's celebrated leather goods. The smaller, original St. James's shop has been on Jermyn Street since 1906. ⊠ *2 Davies St., Mayfair* ☎ *020/7853-4440* ⊕ *www. dunhill.com* ☾ *Closed Sun.* Ⓜ *Bond St.*

Gieves and Hawkes. One of the grand men's tailoring houses of Savile Row, this company made its name outfitting British royals who served as officers in the armed forces. The company still supplies custom-made military uniforms, as well as beautifully tailored civilian wear. Prices for a bespoke suit start around £3,800, but you can find ready-made designs starting at around £600. There's also a branch in The City. ⊠ *1 Savile Row, Mayfair* ☎ *020/7432–6403* ⊕ *www.gievesandhawkes.com* Ⓜ *Piccadilly Circus.*

Ozwald Boateng. The dapper menswear by Ozwald Boateng (pronounced Bwa-teng) combines contemporary funky style with traditional Savile Row quality. His made-to-measure suits have been worn by trendsetters such as Jamie Foxx, Mick Jagger, and Laurence Fishburne, who appreciate the sharp cuts, luxurious fabrics, and occasionally vibrant colors (even the more conservative choices sport jacket linings in bright silk). ⊠ *30 Savile Row, Mayfair* ☎ *020/7437-2030* ⊕ *www.ozwaldboateng. co.uk* ☾ *Closed Sun.* Ⓜ *Piccadilly Circus.*

CLOTHING: WOMEN'S WEAR

Alexander McQueen. Since McQueen's untimely death in 2010, his right-hand woman Sarah Burton has been at the helm, receiving raves for continuing his tradition of theatrical, darkly romantic, and beautifully cut clothes incorporating corsetry, lace, embroidery, and hourglass silhouettes, all of which were exemplified in Burton's celebrated wedding dress for Kate Middleton. Can't afford a gala gown? Go home with a skull-printed scarf. ⊠ *4–5 Old Bond St., Mayfair* ☎ *020/7355–0088* ⊕ *www.alexandermcqueen.com* Ⓜ *Bond St.*

Browns. This shop—actually a collection of small shops—was a pioneer designer boutique in the 1970s and continues to talent-spot the newest and best around. You may find the windows showcasing the work of top graduates from this year's student shows or displaying well-established designers such as Christopher Kane, Valentino, or Balenciaga. The men's store at No. 23 has a similar designer selection, while Browns Focus at No. 24 showcases youthful, hip designs and denim. There is a smaller boutique on Sloane Street, too. If you're about to go down the aisle, check out the two bridal boutiques, one at 12 Hinde Street, which stocks various designers, and another at 59 Brook Street, devoted to Vera Wang gowns exclusive to Browns in the United Kingdom. ✉ *24–27 S. Molton St., Mayfair* ☎ *020/7514–0016* ⊕ *www.brownsfashion.com* ✆ *Closed Sun.* Ⓜ *Bond St.*

Fodor'sChoice
★
Fenwick. A manageably sized department store, Fenwick is a welcome haven of affordability in a shopping area where stratospheric prices are the norm. The store is particularly strong on accessories (notably lingerie, wraps, and hats), cosmetics, perfumes, and chic, wearable fashion by both established and emerging designers such as Issa, Goat, and Theory. There are also three small spas (Chantecaille, Clarins, and Pure Massage), various beauty services, and two restaurants, plus a men's department in the basement. ✉ *163 New Bond St., Mayfair* ☎ *020/7629–9161* ⊕ *www.fenwick.co.uk* Ⓜ *Bond St.*

Matthew Williamson. Sinuous, feminine, and floaty, and often incorporating bright prints and embellishment, Williamson's designs are the epitome of rich-hippie chic. They are favorites with such well-heeled free spirits as Kate Moss and Sienna Miller. Even if you can't manage to get to a beach party on Ibiza, a Williamson dress will put you in the spirit. ✉ *28 Bruton St., Mayfair* ☎ *020/7629–6200* ⊕ *www.matthewwilliamson.com* ✆ *Closed Sun.* Ⓜ *Bond St.*

Stella McCartney. It's not easy emerging from the shadow of a Beatle father, but Stella McCartney has become a major force in fashion in her own right. Her signature jumpsuits and tuxedo pantsuits embody her design philosophy, combining minimalist tailoring with femininity and sophistication with ease of wear. Her love of functionality and clean lines has led to her branching off into sportswear, designing a line for Adidas and dressing Team GB for the London Olympics. A vegetarian like her parents, she refuses to use fur or leather, making her a favorite with similarly minded fashionistas. There's another boutique in South Kensington. ✉ *30 Bruton St., Mayfair* ☎ *020/7518–3100* ⊕ *www.stellamccartney.com* Ⓜ *Bond St.*

Vivienne Westwood. From beginnings as the most shocking and outré designer around, Westwood (now Dame Vivienne) has become a standard bearer for high-style British couture. From the boutique in Chelsea she first sold the lavish corseted ball gowns, the dandyfied nipped-waist jackets, and the tartan with a punk edge that formed the core of her signature look. Here you can still buy ready-to-wear, mainly the more casual Anglomania diffusion line and the exclusive Worlds End label, based on the archives. The small Davies Street boutique sells only the more expensive Gold Label and Couture collections (plus bridal), while

18

the flagship Conduit Street store carries all of the above. ✉ *44 Conduit St., Mayfair* ☎ *020/7439–1109* ⊕ *www.viviennewestwood.co.uk* ⊗ *Closed Sun.* Ⓜ *Oxford Circus.*

DEPARTMENT STORES

Thomas Goode. This spacious luxury housewares shop has been at the same smart Mayfair address since 1845. The china, silver, crystal, and linen, whether from the store's own line or from luxury brands like Christofle and Puiforcat, are simply the best that money can buy, a legacy of its original customer base of international royals and heads of state. The store still holds two royal warrants, but anyone who can afford it can commission their own bespoke set of china. If such luxury is beyond you, visit anyway for the shop's small museum of plates, either antique or designed for royalty, including some created for Princess Diana's wedding. ✉ *19 South Audley St., Mayfair* ☎ *020/7499–2823* ⊕ *www.thomasgoode.co.uk* Ⓜ *Green Park.*

FOOD

Charbonnel et Walker. Established in 1875, this master chocolatier's Mayfair shop specializes in traditional handmade chocolates (violet and rose-petal creams, for example) and has been creating these beautifully packaged, high-quality sweets from long before most of today's fashionable brands appeared. Their drinking chocolate—coarsely grated fine chocolate in a tin—is worth carrying home in a suitcase. ✉ *The Royal Arcade, 28 Old Bond St., Mayfair* ☎ *020/7491–0939* ⊕ *www. charbonnel.co.uk* Ⓜ *Green Park.*

JEWELRY

Asprey. Refurbished a decade ago by architect Norman Foster and interior designer David Mlinaric (some 155 years after Asprey first moved in), this "global flagship" store displays exquisite jewelry—as well as silver and leather goods, watches, china, and crystal—in a discreet, very British setting that oozes quality, expensive good taste, and hushed comfort. If you're in the market for an immaculate 1930s cigarette case, a silver cocktail shaker, a pair of pavé diamond and sapphire earrings, or a ladylike handbag, you won't be disappointed. And, for the really well-heeled, there's a custom-made jewelry service available as well. ✉ *167 New Bond St., Mayfair* ☎ *020/7493–6767* ⊕ *www.asprey.com* ⊗ *Closed Sun.* Ⓜ *Green Park.*

Garrard. The oldest jewelry house in the world, Garrard has been in business since 1735. Between 1843 and 2007, the company was responsible for the upkeep of the Crown Jewels in the Tower of London and for creating several royal crowns (you can see some on display in the Tower.) Today the focus is on precious gems in simple, classic settings, along with silver accessories. Although some collections are definitely contemporary (for instance, minimalist hoop earrings), many of the designs are traditional and impressive, which will be handy should you be in the market for an old-school diamond tiara. ✉ *24 Albemarle St., Mayfair* ☎ *207/518–1070* ⊕ *garrard.com/* ⊗ *Closed Sun.* Ⓜ *Green Park.*

SHOES

Nicholas Kirkwood. Kirkwood is one of Britain's most fashionable shoe designers, and this is his first retail boutique. You won't be able to hike in his imaginative, elegant, sky-high stilettos (be warned: prices are similarly high), but you will be able to make quite an entrance. There are also more wearable shoes that are equally flattering and distinctive. ⊠ *5 Mount St., Mayfair* ☎ *020/7499–5781* ⊕ *www.nicholaskirkwood. com* ⊙ *Closed Sun.* Ⓜ *Green Park.*

Rupert Sanderson. Designed in London and made in Italy, Sanderson's elegant shoes have been a huge hit in fashion circles. Red-carpet-ready high heels as worn by Claire Danes and Sandra Bullock, bright colors, tough motorcycle boots, and a penchant for peep toes are signature elements. The high prices reflect the impeccable craftsmanship. ⊠ *19 Bruton Pl., Mayfair* ☎ *0207/491–2260* ⊕ *www.rupertsanderson.com* ⊙ *Closed Sun.* Ⓜ *Bond St., Green Park.*

MARYLEBONE

ANTIQUES

Alfie's Antique Market. This four-story, bohemian-chic labyrinth is London's largest indoor antiques market, housing over 75 dealers specializing in art, lighting, glassware, textiles, jewelry, furniture, and collectibles, with a particular strength in vintage clothing and 20th-century design. Come here to pick up vintage (1900–70) clothing, accessories, and luggage from Tin Tin Collectables, art deco items (lamps, small furnishings, and mirrors) at Andrew Martin, or a spectacular mid-20th-century Italian lighting fixture at Vincenzo Caffarrella. There's also a rooftop restaurant if you need a coffee break. In addition to the market, this end of Church Street is lined with excellent antiques shops. ⊠ *13–25 Church St., Marylebone* ☎ *020/7723–6066* ⊕ *www.alfiesantiques.com* ⊙ *Closed Sun. and Mon.* Ⓜ *Marylebone.*

BOOKS

Daunt Books. An independent bookstore chain (there are additional branches in Belsize Park, Chelsea, Hampstead, Holland Park, and Cheapside), Daunt favors a thoughtful selection of contemporary and classic fiction and nonfiction. The striking Marylebone branch is an original Edwardian bookstore where a dramatic room lined with oak galleries under lofty skylights houses the noted travel section, which includes not only guidebooks but also related literature and poetry. The Hampstead branch is strong on children's books. ⊠ *83 Marylebone High St., Marylebone* ☎ *020/7224–2295* ⊕ *www.dauntbooks. co.uk* Ⓜ *Baker St.*

CLOTHING

Matches. The rising British designers featured in this carefully curated boutique include Christopher Kane, Erdem, and JW Anderson, as well as more-established figures like McCartney and McQueen and international labels such as Isabel Marant, Peter Piloto, Bottega Veneta, Valentino, Saint Laurent, Marni, and Chloe. There's also an equally stylish menswear department, plus jewelry, lingerie, and accessories. Other branches are in Notting Hill and southwest London. ⊠ *87 Marylebone*

18

High St., Marylebone ☎ *020/7487–5400* ⊕ *www.matchesfashion.com* Ⓜ *Regent's Park, Baker St.*

Reiss. With an in-house design team whose experience includes stints at Gucci and Calvin Klein and customers like Beyoncé and the Duchess of Cambridge, who wore a Reiss dress for her official engagement picture, this hot chain brings luxury standards of tailoring and details to mass-market women and menswear. The sleek and contemporary style doesn't come cheap, but does offer value for money. There are branches in Knightsbridge, The City, Covent Garden, Chelsea, Hampstead, Islington, Soho, Kensington, and basically all over London. ⊠ *10 Barrett St., Marylebone* ☎ *020/7486–6557* ⊕ *www.reiss.com* Ⓜ *Oxford St.*

DEPARTMENT STORES

Marks & Spencer. You'd be hard-pressed to find a Brit who doesn't have something in the closet from Marks & Spencer (or "M&S," as it's popularly known). This major chain is famed for its classic, dependable clothing for men, women, and children—affordable cashmere and lambswool sweaters are particularly good buys—and occasionally scores a fashion hit. The food department at M&S is consistently good, especially for frozen food, and a great place to pick up a sandwich or premade salad on the go (look for M&S Simply Food stores all over town). The flagship branch at Marble Arch and the Pantheon location at 173 Oxford Street have extensive fashion departments. ⊠ *458 Oxford St., Marylebone* ☎ *020/7935–7954* ⊕ *www.marksandspencer. com* Ⓜ *Marble Arch.*

Fodor's Choice ★ **Selfridges.** This giant, bustling store (the second largest in the United Kingdom after Harrods) gives Harvey Nichols a run for its money as London's most fashionable department store. Packed to the rafters with clothes ranging from mid-price lines to the latest catwalk names, the store continues to break ground with its innovative retail schemes, especially the ground-floor Wonder Room (for extravagant jewelry and luxury gifts), the self-contained Louis Vuitton "town house," a dedicated Denim Studio, an array of pop-up shops, and the Concept Store, used for a rotating series of themed displays There are so many zones that merge into one another—from youth-oriented Miss Selfridge to audio equipment to the large, comprehensive cosmetics department—that you practically need a map. Don't miss the Shoe Galleries, the world's largest shoe department, which is filled with more than 5,000 pairs from 120 brands, displayed like works of art under spotlights. Take a break with a glass of wine at the rooftop restaurant or pick up some tea in the Food Hall as a gift. At the Everyman movie theater in the basement, you can watch first-run art-house movies. ⊠ *400 Oxford St., Marylebone* ☎ *0800/123400* ⊕ *www.selfridges.com* Ⓜ *Bond St.*

JEWELRY

Fodor's Choice ★ **The Button Queen.** Extremely specialized shops like this one once helped make London so distinctive, but now they are in danger of disappearing. The Button Queen began life as a market stall in the 1950s, and now has amassed a vast selection of buttons, from antique to modern, encompassing an array of styles and prices. You can also have a set made using fabric you supply. ⊠ *76 Marylebone La., Marylebone*

☎ *020/7935–1505* ⊕ *www.thebuttonqueen.co.uk* ☽ *Closed Sun.* Ⓜ *Oxford Circus.*

Kabiri. A carefully curated array of exciting contemporary jewelry by emerging and established designers from around the world is packed into this small shop. There is something to suit most budgets and tastes, from flamboyant statement pieces to subtle, delicate adornment. Look out for British talent Johanne Mills, among many others. There's another branch in Chelsea. ✉ *37 Marylebone High St., Marylebone* ☎ *020/7317–2150* ⊕ *www.kabiri.co.uk* Ⓜ *Baker St.*

SOHO AND COVENT GARDEN

SOHO
ACCESSORIES

Fodor's Choice
★

Peckham Rye. On the small cobblestone streets leading off Carnaby Street you'll find small specialty shops like the family-run Peckham Rye, which sells heritage-style men's accessories—handmade silk and twill ties, bow ties, and scarves, all using traditional patterns drawn from the archives going back to 1799. More Ralph Lauren than Ralph Lauren, the socks, striped shirts, and handkerchiefs attract modern-day dandies such as Mark Ronson and David Beckham. ✉ *11 Newburgh St., Soho* ☎ *0207/734–5181* ⊕ *www.peckhamrye.com* Ⓜ *Oxford St.*

BOOKS

Fodor's Choice
★

Foyles. Founded in 1903 by the Foyle brothers after they failed the Civil Service exam, this family-owned bookstore is in a 1930s art deco building, once the home of the legendary art college Central Saint Martins. Foyles carries almost every title imaginable on its 4 miles of bookshelves. One of London's best sources for textbooks and the United Kingdom's largest retailer of foreign language titles, Foyles also stocks everything from popular fiction to military history, sheet music, medical tomes, graphic novels, and handsome illustrated fine arts books. It also offers the store-within-a-store Ray's Jazz (one of London's better outlets for music) and a cool café. Foyles has branches in the Southbank Centre, St. Pancras International train station (the Eurostar's U.K. terminus), Waterloo station, and the Westfield shopping centers in Shepherd's Bush and Stratford. ✉ *107 Charing Cross Rd., Soho* ☎ *020/7437–5660* ⊕ *www.foyles.co.uk* Ⓜ *Tottenham Court Rd.*

CLOTHING

Other. Aimed at men and women in search of stylish cool, this independent boutique stocks its own brand of entirely made-in-England clothing, as well as accessories, housewares, books, and clothing from other carefully selected brands such as Opening Ceremony, Christopher Lemaire, and Peter Jensen. The look is understated, slightly geeky, and totally contemporary. ✉ *21 Kingly St., Soho* ☎ *020/7734–6846* ⊕ *www.other-shop.com* Ⓜ *Oxford Circus.*

Primark. Primark's huge, two-story flagship is fantastic for low-cost, trendy clothing (there are other branches in Hammersmith and Kilburn). But keep in mind, you get what you pay for: some of the fabrics and finishes reflect the store's budget prices, and its labor practices have

18

attracted criticism. This is the home of fast, youthful, disposable fashion, so don't expect attentive service or classic styling and you won't be disappointed. ⊠ *499–517 Oxford St., Soho* ☎ *020/7495–0420* ⊕ *www.primark.co.uk* Ⓜ *Marble Arch.*

CLOTHING: WOMEN'S WEAR

Wolsey. Specializing in men's knitwear since 1755, Wolsey now sells rugged but stylish outerwear, sweaters, shirts, hats, scarves, socks, T-shirts, sweatshirts, and underwear (as worn by both Roald Amundsen and Captain Robert Scott on their race to the South Pole). There's another branch in Covent Garden. ⊠ *83A Brewer St., Soho* ☎ *020/7434–4257* ⊕ *www.wolsey.com* Ⓜ *Piccadilly Circus.*

DEPARTMENT STORE

Fodor'sChoice ★ **Liberty.** The wonderful black-and-white mock-Tudor facade, created from the timbers of two Royal Navy ships, reflects this store's origins in the late-19th-century Arts and Crafts movement. Leading designers were recruited to create the classic art nouveau Liberty prints that are still a centerpiece of the brand, gracing everything from cushions and silk kimonos to embossed leather bags and photo albums. Inside, Liberty is a labyrinth of nooks and crannies stuffed with thoughtfully chosen merchandise. Clothes for both men and women focus on high quality and high fashion with labels like Helmut Lang and Roland Mouret. The store regularly commissions new prints from contemporary designers, and sells both these and its classic patterns by the yard. If you're not so handy with a needle, an interior design service will create soft furnishings for you. ⊠ *Regent St., Soho* ☎ *020/7734–1234* ⊕ *www.liberty.co.uk* Ⓜ *Oxford Circus.*

FOOD

Fodor'sChoice ★ **The Vintage House.** If whiskey is more to your taste than wine, visit the Vintage House, which has the country's largest selection of single malts (more than 1,350), many notable for their age. You'll also find more than 100 tequilas as well as Cuban cigars. The shop is until 11 pm except Sunday. ⊠ *42 Old Compton St., Soho* ☎ *020/7437–2592* ⊕ *freespace.virgin.net/vintagehouse.co* Ⓜ *Leicester Sq.*

SHOES

Irregular Choice. If you want to blend in with the crowd, these shoes are not for you. But if you like footwear that is fun and flattering (not to mention reasonably priced), head for Irregular Choice. Styles tend toward Louis XIV–like court shoes ornamented with ribbon ties or silk flowers; pumps in interesting patterns ranging from polka dots to houndstooth; as well as bejeweled flats, leopard-print boots, and red patent leather stilettos. Best of all, many have round toes and supportive heels, proving that comfortable doesn't have to be dull. There's another branch near Camden Market. ⊠ *35 Carnaby St., Soho* ☎ *020/7494–4811* ⊕ *www.irregularchoice.com* Ⓜ *Oxford Circus.*

TOYS

FAMILY **Hamleys.** When British children visit London, Hamleys is at the top of their agenda. This institution (the oldest toy store in the world) has six floors of the latest dolls, soft toys, video games, and technological devices (plus such old-fashioned pleasures as train sets, drum kits, and magic tricks), with every must-have on the preteen shopping list—although some parents may find the offerings to be overly commercialized (it's heavy on movie and TV tie-ins). Hamleys is a madhouse at Christmastime, but the Santa's grotto is one of the best in town. There's a smaller branch in St. Pancras International train station. ✉ *188–196 Regent St., Soho* ☎ *0871/704–1977* ⊕ *www.hamleys.com* Ⓜ *Oxford Circus, Piccadilly Circus.*

COVENT GARDEN

BOOKS AND PRINTS

Grosvenor Prints. London's largest collection of 17th- to-early 20th-century prints emphasizes views of the city and architecture as well as sporting and decorative motifs. The selection is eclectic, with prices ranging from £5 into the thousands. ✉ *19 Shelton St., Covent Garden* ☎ *020/7836–1979* ⊕ *www.grosvenorprints.com* ⊘ *Closed Sun.* Ⓜ *Covent Garden, Leicester Sq.*

Fodor's Choice ★ **Stanfords.** When it comes to encyclopedic coverage, there is simply no better travel shop on the planet. Stanfords is packed with a comprehensive selection of maps, travel books, travel gadgets, globes, notebooks, replicas of antique maps, and more. Even the floor is decorated with giant maps. Whether you're planning a day trip to Surrey or an adventure to the South Pole, this should be your first stop. ✉ *12–14 Long Acre, Covent Garden* ☎ *020/7836–1321* ⊕ *www.stanfords.co.uk* Ⓜ *Covent Garden.*

CLOTHING

Paul Smith. British classics with an irreverent twist define Paul Smith's collections for women, men, and children. Beautifully tailored suits for men and women take hallmarks of traditional British style and turn them on their heads with humor and color, combining exceptional fabrics with flamboyant linings or unusual detailing. Gift ideas abound—wallets, scarves, diaries, spectacles, even a soccer ball—all in Smith's signature rainbow stripes. There are several branches throughout London, in Notting Hill, Soho, Canary Wharf, and Borough Market, plus a Mayfair shop that includes vintage furniture and a shoes-and-accessories shop on Marylebone High Street. ✉ *40–44 Floral St., Covent Garden* ☎ *020/7379–7133* ⊕ *www.paulsmith.co.uk* Ⓜ *Covent Garden.*

Fodor's Choice ★ **Tabio.** For everything hosiery—knee socks, ankle socks, leggings, leg warmers, pantyhose, tights—this is the place. Patterns range from simple and elegant to lively and attention-getting and come in a wide assortment of weights, but all are functional without being boring. There's another branch on King's Road in Chelsea. ✉ *66 Neal St., Covent Garden* ☎ *020/7836–3713* ⊕ *www.tabio.com* Ⓜ *Covent Garden.*

United Nude. Cocreated by the famed architect Rem Koolhaas (who also designed this Covent Garden flagship store) and Galahad Clark (of the Clarks shoes dynasty), this brand sells distinctive, futuristic designs use up-to-the-minute techniques such as carbon fiber heels and injection-molded soles. The shoes are also flattering and surprisingly comfortable. ✉ *13 Floral St., Covent Garden* ☎ *0207/240–7106* ⊕ *www.unitednude.com* Ⓜ *Covent Garden.*

18

BRING A BIT OF ENGLAND HOME

To avoid panic-buying a bulk pack of Cadbury chocolate at Heathrow, it's wise to plan your gift purchasing with care.

For a well-chosen, eclectic selection, unique department store Liberty is hard to beat—here you'll find everything from exquisite Miller Harris fragrances by British perfumer Lyn Harris to small leather goods embossed with the famous Liberty prints.

Fortnum & Mason has equally carefully curated, though perhaps more sedate, offerings, such as leather-covered hip flasks and model boats with Union Jack sails. The big

attraction here is the world-famous food hall, which carries cookies, teas, and unusual condiments. A. Gold is another source of British-made treats.

Looking for a gift for the hard-to-shop-for man in your life? Consider some traditional shaving cream from Geo. F. Trumper.

The museum shops are also bursting with original gift ideas, from art books and posters at Tate Modern or the Fashion Museum to double-decker bus models and Tube-map mouse pads at the London Transport Museum, in Covent Garden.

HOUSEHOLD
Cath Kidston. If you love chintz and colorful patterns, you'll love Cath Kidston's bright feminine signature look. Textiles bearing ginghams, polka dots, and lots of big, blooming roses appear on everything in sight, from ceramics and bed linens to fine china, stationery, and doggie beds. There are clothing and nightwear lines for women and children, along with handbags, totes, and cosmetic bags. Branches can be found throughout the city, including ones in Marylebone and a new flagship store on Piccadilly. ✉ *28–32 Shelton St., Covent Garden* ☎ *020/7836–4803* ⊕ *www.cathkidston.co.uk* Ⓜ *Covent Garden.*

MARKET
Covent Garden. Covent Garden is actually three markets. Forty stalls selling handcrafted jewelry, clothes, ceramics, and other unique items are in the covered area, which was originally designed by Inigo Jones and is known as the Apple Market. The Jubilee Market, in Jubilee Hall toward Southampton Street, tends toward the more pedestrian (kitschy T-shirts, unremarkable household goods, and the like) on Tuesday through Friday, but has vintage collectibles on Monday and worthwhile hand-made goods on weekends. A "Real Food" market on Thursday offers artisanal street food, while the East Colonnade market has stalls with specialty items that include handmade soaps and magic tricks. Covent Garden is something of a tourist magnet, and the prices can be high, but don't miss the magicians, musicians, and escape artists who perform in the open-air piazza. Covent Garden has recently started aiming for a more sophisticated image with the opening of upscale restaurants and chains in the surrounding arcades (including the world's largest Apple Store) and boutiques for brands like Dior, Aesop, Mulberry, Kate Spade, and Jo Malone. Even the noted celebrity haunt The Ivy has a branch

there now. ⊠ *The Piazza, off Wellington St., Covent Garden* ⊕ *www. coventgardenlondonuk.com* Ⓜ *Covent Garden.*

TOYS

FAMILY
Fodor'sChoice
★

Benjamin Pollock's Toyshop. This landmark shop still carries on the tradition of its founder, who sold miniature theater stages made from richly detailed paper from the late 19th century until his death in 1937. Among his admirers was Robert Louis Stevenson, who wrote, "If you love art, folly, or the bright eyes of children, speed to Pollock's." Today the antique model theaters are expensive, but there are plenty of magical reproductions for less than 10 pounds. There's also an extensive selection of new but nostalgic puppets, marionettes, teddy bears, spinning tops, jack-in-the-boxes, and similar traditional children's toys from the days before batteries were required (or even possible). ⊠ *44 The Market Building, Covent Garden* ☎ *020/7379–7866* ⊕ *www.pollocks-coventgarden.co.uk* Ⓜ *Covent Garden.*

BLOOMSBURY, HOLBORN, ISLINGTON, AND FITZROVIA

BLOOMSBURY

ACCESSORIES

Fodor'sChoice
★

James Smith & Sons Ltd. This has to be the world's ultimate umbrella shop, and a must for anyone interested in real Victorian London. The family-owned shop has been in this location on a corner of New Oxford Street since 1857, and sells every kind of umbrella, cane, and walking stick imaginable. The interior is unchanged since the 19th century; you will feel as if you have stepped back in time. Umbrellas range from about £60 for a folding umbrella to more than £250 for a classic man's umbrella with a carved handle. If the umbrellas seem too high, James Smith also sells smaller accessories and handmade wooden bowls. ⊠ *Hazelwood House, 53 New Oxford St., Bloomsbury* ☎ *020/7836–4731* ⊕ *www.james-smith.co.uk* ☉ *Closed Sun.* Ⓜ *Tottenham Court Rd., Holborn.*

18

BOOKS

Gay's the Word. Open since 1979, this is London's leading gay and lesbian bookshop. Thousands of titles, from literature and thoughtful nonfiction to erotica and prodiversity children's books, fill the shelves. The shop is a well-loved fixture on the scene (it features prominently in the 2014 movie *Pride*) and often hosts discussion groups, readings, and other events. ⊠ *66 Marchmont St., Bloomsbury* ☎ *020/7278–7654* ⊕ *www.gaystheword.co.uk* Ⓜ *Russell Sq.*

Persephone Books. A must for all lovers of women's fiction and nonfiction, Persephone is a gem of a bookshop specializing in their own reprints of mostly neglected 20th-century works from predominately female writers. Exquisitely decorated endpapers make these books perfect gifts for your bibliophile friends. ⊠ *59 Lamb's Conduit St., Bloomsbury* ☎ *020/7242–9292* ⊕ *www.persephonebooks.co.uk* ☉ *Closed Sun.* Ⓜ *Russell Sq., Holborn.*

SPECIALTY STORES

Blade Rubber. This unique shop near the British Museum specializes in rubber stamps, with everything from businesslike "Paid" stamps to Alice in Wonderland characters, Egyptian gods, VW Beetles, flying saucers, and more. Get a custom-made personal stamp—a great gift for a young person—or bring back an iconic double-decker bus stamp as a souvenir. It also carries scrapbooking materials. ✉ *12 Bury Pl., Bloomsbury* ☎ *020/7831–4123* ⊕ *www.bladerubber.co.uk* Ⓜ *Holborn.*

HOLBORN

ANTIQUES

London Silver Vaults. Housed in a basement vault, this extraordinary space holds stalls from more than 30 silver dealers. Products range from the spectacularly over-the-top costing thousands to smaller items—like teaspoons, candlesticks, or a set of Victorian cake forks—starting at £25. Most of the silver merchants actually trade out of room-size, underground vaults, which were originally rented out to London's upper crust to store their valuables. ✉ *53–64 Chancery La., Holborn* ☎ *020/7242–3844* ⊕ *www.thesilvervaults.com* ⊙ *Closed Sat. after 1 and Sun.* Ⓜ *Chancery La.*

ISLINGTON

HOUSEHOLD

Fodor's Choice ★ **TwentyTwentyOne.** A must for lovers of modernist design. Among the huge selection of 20th-century classics here are a chaise lounge from Le Corbusier as well as pieces from Noguchi, Aalto, Prouvé, Saarinen, and the husband-and-wife team Robin and Lucienne Day, in the form of both originals and licensed reissues, along with contemporary pieces from modern masters like Tom Dixon, Thomas Heatherwick, and Marc Newson. The kids' line is particularly cool, with items like a classic elephant sculpture/toy from another married design team, Charles and Ray Eames. Small accessories like tote bags and cushions will easily fit into your luggage. There's another branch in Clerkenwell. ✉ *274–275 Upper St., Islington* ☎ *020/7288–1996* ⊕ *www.twentytwentyone.com* Ⓜ *Highbury & Islington.*

FITZROVIA

CLOTHING

Topshop. A hot spot for straight-from-the-runway affordable fashion, Topshop is destination shopping for teenagers and fashion editors alike. Clothes and accessories are geared to the youthful end of the market, although women who are young at heart and girlish of figure can find plenty of wearable items here. However, you will need a high tolerance for loud music and busy dressing rooms. The store also features collections designed by a rotating roster of high-end designers as well as offering its own premium designer line called Topshop Unique. Topman brings the same fast-fashion approach to clothing for men. If the crowds become too much, head to one of the smaller Topshops in Kensington High Street, Knightsbridge, Victoria, Marble Arch, The City, or Holborn. ✉ *214 Oxford St., Fitzrovia* ☎ *0844/848–7487* ⊕ *www.topshop. com* Ⓜ *Oxford Circus.*

CAMDEN

MARKETS

The Camden Markets. Grouped around two locks on the Regent's Canal, Camden Lock Market proper began in the early 1970s, when weekend stalls sold the output of nearby craft workshops. It later expanded to four markets—Camden, Camden Lock, The Stables, and Camden Lock Village. For many years, the markets have hosted more than 1,000 stalls offering a spectacular array of merchandise: vintage and new clothes, antiques and junk, rare vinyl, ceramics, Indian bedspreads, fetishwear, obscure band memorabilia, and toys.

The outdoor Camden Market on Camden High Street mainly sells cheap jeans, secondhand clothes, and tacky pop-culture paraphernalia; it's best to head to Camden Lock Market for crafts and the Stables Market for furniture. The Stables Market recently expanded into the so-called Catacombs, which are Victorian brick arches, and now has more than 700 shops and stalls. Camden Lock Village (formerly the Canal Market) has more than 500 shop units, many specializing in vintage clothes, plus street-food stalls. Though much of the merchandise is targeted for the young, aging hippies, street-fashion aficionados, and anyone with a taste for alternative culture (Goths are particularly well catered for) will also find plenty that appeals. This shopping experience is best suited to those who don't mind large crowds and a boisterous atmosphere, especially on weekends. Camden Market, Camden Lock Market, Camden Lock Village, and Stables Market are open daily (9:30 or 10 until 6). In 2014 all four markets came under the same ownership and were earmarked for redevelopment, so their focus is likely to change. ✉ *Camden High St.–Chalk Farm Rd., Camden Town* ⊕ *www.camdenlockmarket.com* Ⓜ *Camden Town, Chalk Farm.*

18

EAST LONDON

ACCESSORIES: HATS

Fodor's Choice
★

Bernstock Speirs. Here since 1982, Paul Bernstock and Thelma Speirs put a quirky spin on traditional hats for men and women, with streetsmart trilbies, whimsical rabbit-ear baseball caps, and knitted beanies that feature unusual colors and detailing (like veils, for instance). ✉ *234 Brick La., Spitalfields* ☎ *020/7739–7385* ⊕ *www.bernstockspeirs.com* Ⓜ *London Overground: Shoreditch High St.*

CLOTHING

Absolute Vintage. This is a warehouse of handpicked items from the 1930s through the 1980s, but the specialty here is shoes and bags. The shop has the largest collection of vintage shoes in the United Kingdom—more than 1,000 pairs—and, best of all, prices are reasonable. There's another branch on Berwick Street in Soho. ✉ *15 Hanbury St., Spitalfields* ☎ *020/7274–3883* ⊕ *www.absolutevintage.co.uk* Ⓜ *London Overground: Shoreditch High St.*

Beyond Retro. The more than 10,000 vintage items for men and women here—from cowboy boots to bowling shirts to prom dresses—include the largest collection of American retro in the United Kingdom. There's another outpost in Dalston and one in Soho. ✉ *110–112 Cheshire St.,*

Spitalfields ☎ *020/7613–3636* ⊕ *www.beyondretro.com* Ⓜ *Whitechapel. London Overground: Shoreditch High St.*

Fodor'sChoice ★ **Hostem.** Drawing style-conscious customers from nearby tech start-ups, Hostem is for the man who wants to be well dressed without looking like he's trying too hard, with a mixture of casual luxury, street wear, and fashion-forward edge. You'll find established names like Thom Browne and Ann Demeulemeester as well as beautiful cashmere sweaters from newcomers like The Elder Statesmen. The womenswear area offers pieces by designers like Commes des Garçons and Rick Owens. It's achingly hip, so expect lots of black. ⊠ *41–43 Redchurch St., Shoreditch* ☎ *020/7739–9733* ⊕ *www.hostem.co.uk* Ⓜ *London Overground: Shoreditch High St.*

The Laden Showroom. Sienna Miller and Victoria Beckham are among the celebs who regularly check out emerging talent at this East End showroom for young designers. The store retails the work of more than 50 new designers, some selling one-off items—so the look you find is likely to be original. ⊠ *The Rib Man, 103 Brick La., Spitalfields* ☎ *020/7247-2431* ⊕ *www.laden.co.uk* Ⓜ *London Overground: Shoreditch High St.*

Rokit. Magazine and music stylists love this place. It consists of two shops along Brick Lane that carry everything from handbags and ball gowns to jeans, military garb, and Western wear. The ever-changing stock spans the 1920s to the 1990s. There are also branches in Camden and Covent Garden. ⊠ *101 and 107 Brick La., Spitalfields* ☎ *020/7375-3864* ⊕ *www.rokit.co.uk* Ⓜ *London Overground: Shoreditch High St.*

Fodor'sChoice ★ **Start London.** An ever-changing roster of cutting-edge designers like Acne, Helmut Lang, and Alexander Wang is on offer here, and, for men (down the street at No. 59), designers like Comme des Garçons to Nudie Jeans. Despite all the chic fashion on offer, the co-owner and American expat Brix Smith-Start is more mother hen than formidable fashionista and is happy to gently guide customers into trying something new. ⊠ *42–44 Rivington St., Shoreditch* ☎ *020/7729–3334* ⊕ *www.start-london.com* Ⓜ *Old St. London Overground: Shoreditch High St.*

Fodor'sChoice ★ **Sunspel.** This British firm has been making fine men's underwear since the mid-19th century and it's still their specialty, along with luxury basics. Prince Charles is a real-life customer and James Bond a cinematic one (he wore their shorts in *Thunderball* and polo shirt in *Quantum of Solace*). They also carry elegant, minimalist T-shirts, sweaters, and sweats for women. There are other branches in Marylebone, St. James's, and Soho. ⊠ *7 Redchurch St., Shoreditch* ☎ *020/7739–9729* ⊕ *www.sunspel.com* Ⓜ *London Overground: Shoreditch High St.*

FOOD

Fodor'sChoice ★ **A. Gold.** All of the traditional or retro foodstuffs—such as jars of locally produced honey, relish, or even gin—are British-made and make excellent and portable presents. Also available in this re-creation of a village shop are stylish gift baskets and old-fashioned picnic hampers, as well as freshly made take-out sandwiches (like roast chicken with herb and onion stuffing), salads, and hot daily specials. ⊠ *42 Brushfield St., Spitalfields* ☎ *020/7247-2487* ⊕ *www.agoldshop.com* Ⓜ *London Overground: Shoreditch High St.*

HOUSEHOLD

Fodor's Choice
★
Labour & Wait. Although mundane items like colanders and clothes-pins may not sound like ideal souvenirs, this shop (selling both new and vintage) will make you reconsider. The owners are on a mission to revive retro, functional British household goods, such as enamel kitchenware, genuine feather dusters, bread bins, and traditional Welsh blankets. ⊠ *85 Redchurch St., Shoreditch* ☎ *020/7729–6253* ⊕ *www.labourandwait.co.uk* ⊗ *Closed Mon.* Ⓜ *London Overground: Shoreditch High St.*

MARKETS

Brick Lane. The noisy center of the Bengali community is a hubbub of buying and selling. Sunday stalls have food, hardware, household and electrical goods, books, bikes, shoes, clothes, spices, and traditional saris. At least some of the CDs and DVDs are pirated, and the bargain iron may not have a plug, so be careful. Shoppers nevertheless flock to the market to enjoy the ethnic buzz, sample curries and Bengali sweets, or indulge in salt beef on a bagel at Beigel Bake—London's 24-hour bagel bakery, a survivor of the neighborhood's Jewish past. Brick Lane's activity spills over into nearby Petticoat Lane Market, where there are similar goods but less atmosphere. ⊠ *Brick. La., Shoreditch* ⊕ *www.visitbricklane.org* ⊗ *Sun. 9–5* Ⓜ *Aldgate East. London Overground: Shoreditch High St.*

Fodor's Choice
★
Columbia Road Flower Market. London's premier flower market is about as pretty and photogenic as they come, with more than 50 stalls selling flowers, shrubs, bulbs, and trees—everything from bedding plants to 10-foot banana trees—as well as garden tools, pots, and accessories at competitive prices. The stallholders' patter is part of the fun. Columbia Road itself is lined with interesting independent shops selling art, fashion, furnishings, and jewelry, and the local cafés are superb. ⊠ *Columbia Rd., Hoxton* ⊕ *www.columbiaroad.info* ⊗ *Sun. 8–2* Ⓜ *Old St. London Overground: Hoxton.*

Old Spitalfields Market. Once the East End's wholesale fruit and vegetable market and now restored to its original splendor, this fine example of a Victorian market hall is at the center of the area's gentrified revival. The original building is largely occupied by shops, with traders' stalls in the courtyard. A modern shopping precinct under a Norman Foster–designed glass canopy adjoins the old building and holds many more traders' stalls. You may have to wade through a certain number of stalls selling cheap imports to find the good stuff, which includes crafts, vintage and new clothing, handmade rugs, jewelry, hand-carved toy trains, unique baby clothes, rare vinyl, and cakes. Thursday is particularly good for antiques; Friday for fashion, art, and a biweekly record fair; and Saturday for produce and handmade crafts. The food outlets (mostly small, upscale chains but some indies as well) sell Spanish tapas, Thai satays, and many other dishes from all over. ⊠ *16 Horner Sq., Brushfield St., Spitalfields* ☎ *020/7375–2963* ⊕ *www.oldspitalfieldsmarket.com* ⊗ *Stalls Mon.–Wed. 10–5, Thurs. and Sun. 9–5, Fri. 10–4, Sat. 11–5; restaurants weekdays 11–11, Sun. 9–11 am; retail shops daily 10–7* Ⓜ *Liverpool St. London Overground: Shoreditch High St.*

18

MUSIC

Rough Trade East. Although many London record stores are struggling, this veteran indie-music specialist in the Old Truman Brewery seems to have gotten the formula right. The spacious surroundings are as much a hangout as a shop, complete with a stage for live gigs, a café, and Internet access. There's another branch on Portobello Road in Notting Hill. ⊠ *Dray Walk, Old Truman Brewery, 91 Brick La., Spitalfields* ☎ *020/7392–7788* Ⓜ *Liverpool St. London Overground: Shoreditch High St.*

SOUTH OF THE THAMES

ART

Oxo Tower Wharf. The artisans creating fashion, jewelry, home accessories, textiles, prints and photographs, furniture, and other design items have to pass rigorous selection procedures to set up in these prime riverside studios, where they make, display, and sell their work. The Oxo Tower Restaurant & Brasserie on the top floor is expensive, but with its fantastic view of London, it's worth popping up for a drink. There's also a public terrace where you can take in the view. ⊠ *Oxo Tower Wharf, Bargehouse St., South Bank* ☎ *020/7021–1686 24-hour information line* ⊕ *www.coinstreet.org* ⊘ *Closed Mon.* Ⓜ *Waterloo.*

MARKETS

Fodor's Choice
★

Borough Market. There's been a market in Borough since Roman times. This latest incarnation, spread under the arches and railroad tracks leading to London Bridge station, is where some of the city's best food sellers set up stalls. Fresh coffees, gorgeous cheeses, olives, and baked goods complement the organically farmed meats, fresh fish, fruits, and vegetables.

Don't make any other lunch plans for the day; this is where celebrity chef Jamie Oliver's scallop man cooks them up fresh at Shell Seekers, and The Ginger Pig's rare-breed sausages sizzle on grills, while for the sweet lover there are chocolates, preserves, and Whirld's artisanal confectionery, as well as 18 restaurants and cafés, most above average. The Market Hall hosts workshops, tastings, and demonstrations and also acts as a greenhouse (even hops are being grown here).

Seven of the original Borough Market traders, including the celebrated Kappacasein Swiss raclette stand that serves heaping plates of melted Ogleshield cheese, have established a separate market on nearby Maltby Street. This opens on Saturday morning from 9 am. ⊠ *8 Southwark St., Borough* ☎ *020/7402–1002* ⊕ *www.boroughmarket.org.uk* ⊘ *Mon. and Tues. 10–5 (lunch stalls only), Wed. and Thurs. 10–5, Fri. 10–6, Sat. 8–5* Ⓜ *London Bridge.*

KENSINGTON, CHELSEA, KNIGHTSBRIDGE, AND BELGRAVIA

KENSINGTON

CLOTHING

FAMILY **Marie-Chantal.** If you love beautiful, tasteful clothing for babies and children, head to this boutique created by Princess Marie-Chantal of Greece. As you'd imagine, the look is elegant and the prices are high. Materials used include silk, linen, and Liberty prints. There's another branch in Notting Hill. ✉ *148 Walton St., South Kensington* ☎ *020/7838–1111* ⊕ *www.mariechantal.co.uk* ⊘ *Closed Sun.* Ⓜ *South Kensington.*

Orsini. High-end vintage fashion from the 1930s to 1980s is the trademark at this tiny but desirable boutique, which sells big designer names like Pucci, Hermès, Chanel, and Alaïa at bargain prices. There's also an in-house line of made-to-measure dresses based on Vogue patterns from the same period. ✉ *76 Earl's Court Rd., Kensington* ☎ *020/7937–2903* ⊕ *www.orsinivintage.co.uk* Ⓜ *Earl's Court.*

HOUSEHOLD

The Conran Shop. This is the brainchild of Sir Terence Conran, who has been a major influence on British taste since he opened Habitat in the 1960s. Although he is no longer associated with Habitat, his Conran Shops remain bastions of similarly clean, unfussy modernist design. Housewares from furniture to stemware and textiles—both handmade and mass-produced, by famous names and emerging designers—are housed in a building that is a modernist design landmark in its own right. Both the flagship store and the branch on Marylebone High Street are bursting with great gift ideas. ✉ *Michelin House, 81 Fulham Rd., South Kensington* ☎ *020/7589–7401* ⊕ *www.conranshop.co.uk* Ⓜ *South Kensington.*

Mint. Owner Lina Kanafani has scoured the globe to curate an eclectic mix of conceptual statement furniture, art, ceramics, and home accessories. Mint also showcases works by an international selection of up-and-coming designers and sells plenty of limited edition and one-off pieces. If you don't want to ship a couch home, consider a miniature flower vase or a handmade ceramic pitcher. ✉ *2 North Terr., Alexander Sq., South Kensington* ☎ *020/7225–2228* ⊕ *www.mintshop.co.uk* ⊘ *Closed Sun.* Ⓜ *South Kensington.*

Skandium. Largely thanks to its thrillers and chefs, Scandinavia is having a moment in Britain. Skandium brings together many of the region's top designers of furniture, lighting, rugs, and housewares under one roof. Designers include Artek, Aalto, Saarinen, and Georg Jensen, as well as non-Scandinavian modernists, such as Ron Arad. Clean lines and stripped-back, unfussy elegance abounds (although the Moomins make an appearance on ceramics). There's another branch in Marylebone. ✉ *245–249 Brompton Rd., South Kensington* ☎ *020/7584–2066* ⊕ *www.skandium.com* Ⓜ *South Kensington.*

18

JEWELRY

Butler & Wilson. Specialists in bold costume jewelry and affordable glamor, Butler & Wilson have added semiprecious stones to their foundation diamanté, colored rhinestone, and crystal collections. Flamboyant skull brooches or dainty floral earrings make perfect gifts. ✉ *189 Fulham Rd., South Kensington* ☎ *020/7352–3045* ⊕ *www.butlerandwilson.co.uk* Ⓜ *South Kensington.*

CHELSEA

ACCESSORIES

The Shop at Bluebird. The brainchild of the couple behind popular womenswear brand Jigsaw, this 10,000-square-foot space in the old Bluebird garage brings together men's and women's fashion from of-the-moment designers like Raf Simons and Christopher Kane. There's also furniture, collectibles, designer tech accessories, and music—all chosen for style and originality. It's worth visiting for the displays alone, which change regularly, although the funky ceiling-light installation of more than 1,000 bulbs seems to be a constant feature. After browsing, unwind with a treatment at the on-site spa or join the ladies who lunch at the restaurant in the same complex. It's a good 20-minute walk from the nearest Tube station at Sloane Square, so catch a No. 11 or No. 22 bus along King's Road. ✉ *350 King's Rd., Chelsea* ☎ *020/7351–3873* ⊕ *www.theshopatbluebird.com* Ⓜ *Sloane Sq.*

ANTIQUES

Rupert Cavendish. Having cornered the Biedermeier market, this most high-end of Chelsea dealers has now expanded into art deco, with pieces that are often museum quality. Look out for Frank Lloyd Wright–designed carpets and other 20th-century classics. ✉ *1 Penywern Rd., Kensington* ☎ *020/7731–7041* ⊕ *www.rupertcavendish.co.uk* Ⓜ *Earls Court.*

BOOKS

Fodor'sChoice
★ **Green & Stone Art Materials.** This fabulous cave of artists' materials, papers, art books, easels, and mannequins is one of the longest-established shops on King's Road. It began life in 1927 as part of the Chenil Gallery, run by a distinguished group that included the artist Augustus John and the playwright George Bernard Shaw. At the current location since 1934, the shop also has a framing service, antique paint boxes, and craft supplies. Francis Bacon and David Hockney have been among their clients. ✉ *259 King's Rd., Chelsea* ☎ *020/7352–0837* ⊕ *www.greenandstone.com* Ⓜ *Sloane Sq.*

John Sandoe [Books] Ltd. This atmospheric warren that crams some 25,000 titles into an 18th-century building off King's Road is the antithesis of a soulless chain bookstore—no surprise it has attracted equally idiosyncratic customers like Tom Stoppard and Keith Richards. Staff members are wonderfully knowledgeable (don't try to figure out how the stock is organized without their help) and there are a lot of them per customer. If a book isn't in stock, they will try to find it for you, even if it is out of print. ✉ *10 Blacklands Terr., Chelsea* ☎ *020/7589–9473* ⊕ *www.johnsandoe.com* Ⓜ *Sloane Sq.*

CLOTHING

FAMILY

Fodor's Choice

★

Brora. The knitwear is cozy, but the style is cool in this contemporary Scottish cashmere emporium for men, women, and kids. There are dressed-up camisoles, sweaters, and cardigans, and adorable baby ensembles, as well as noncashmere items such as picnic blankets and scarves. Other branches are in Notting Hill, Marylebone, Islington, Covent Garden, and Sloane Square. ✉ *344 King's Rd., Chelsea* ☎ *020/7352–3697* ⊕ *www.brora.co.uk* Ⓜ *Sloane Sq.*

Hackett. If J. Crew isn't preppy enough for you, try Hackett, with branches in Covent Garden, Spitalfields, St. James's, Soho, Mayfair, and The City. Originally a posh thrift shop recycling cricket flannels, hunting pinks, Oxford brogues, and other staples of a British gentleman's wardrobe, Hackett now creates its own line and has become a genuine—and very good—men's outfitter. The look is traditional and classic, with best buys including polo shirts, corduroys, and striped scarves. There's also a boys' line for the junior man-about-town. ✉ *137–138 Sloane St., Chelsea* ☎ *020/7730–3331* ⊕ *www.hackett. com* Ⓜ *Sloane Sq.*

Jack Wills. Jack Wills specializes in heritage and country sports-inspired styles, giving them a fresh, sexy edge. This means crowds of lithe young things who don't mind the pumping music while browsing for slim-line Fair Isle sweaters, fitted plaid shirts, and short floral sundresses for the girls, plus sweatshirts, blazers, skinny cords, and rugby shirts for the boys. The store also carries Union Jack carry-on bags, bobble hats galore, knitted jackets for hot-water bottles, and other traditional-with-irony items. Other branches are in Notting Hill, Covent Garden, Islington, Soho, and Shoreditch. ✉ *72 Kings Rd., Chelsea* ☎ *020/7581–0347* ⊕ *www.jackwills.com* Ⓜ *Sloane Sq.*

Jigsaw. Jigsaw specializes in clothes that are classic yet trendy, ladylike without being dull. The style is epitomized by the former Kate Middleton, who was a buyer for the company before her marriage. The quality of fabrics and detailing belie the reasonable prices, and the cuts are kind to the womanly figure. Although there are numerous branches across London, no two stores are the same. Preteens have their own line, Jigsaw Junior. ✉ *The Chapel, 6 Duke of York Sq., Chelsea* ☎ *020/730–4404* ⊕ *www.jigsawonline.com* Ⓜ *Sloane Sq.*

FOOD

L'Artisan du Chocolat. Praised by top chefs Gordon Ramsay and Heston Blumenthal , L'Artisan raises chocolate to an art form. "Couture" chocolates are infused with fruits, nuts, and spices (including such exotic flavorings as Szechuan pepper and tobacco). This is one of the few chocolate shops in the world that makes liquid salted caramels. There are also branches in Notting Hill and Borough Market. ✉ *89 Lower Sloane St., Chelsea* ☎ *0845/270–6996* ⊕ *www.artisanduchocolat.co.uk* Ⓜ *Sloane Sq.*

SHOES

Fodor's Choice

★

Manolo Blahnik. Blink and you'll miss the discreet sign that marks fashionista footwear central. Blahnik, the man who single-handedly managed to revive the sexy stiletto, has been trading out of this small shop

18

on a Chelsea side street since 1973. It's a must for shoe lovers with generous budgets. If you decide to wear your new Manolos, hop on the No. 11 or No. 22 bus or grab a cab—the nearest Tube station is about a 20-minute totter away. ✉ *49–51 Old Church St., Chelsea* ☎ *020/7352–8622* ⊕ *www.manoloblahnik.com* ☼ *Closed Sun.* Ⓜ *Sloane Sq., South Kensington.*

KNIGHTSBRIDGE

ACCESSORIES

Fodor's Choice
★

Anya Hindmarch. Exquisite leather bags and personalized, printed canvas totes are what made Hindmarch famous. Here you'll find her complete collection of bags and shoes. You can also order a custom piece, such as the "Be A Bag," a tote bag imprinted with your chosen photo. There are also branches around the corner on Pont Street, in Mayfair, in Hackney, and in Notting Hill. ✉ *157–158 Sloane St., Knightsbridge* ☎ *020/7730–0961* ⊕ *www.anyahindmarch.com* Ⓜ *Sloane Sq., Knightsbridge.*

CLOTHING

Egg. Tucked away in a residential mews, this spartan shop in a former Victorian dairy is the brainchild of Maureen Doherty, once Issey Miyake's assistant. More than half the minimalist, unstructured styles for men and women in natural fabrics such as silk, cashmere, and antique cotton are handmade. Garments may be casually hung on hooks or folded on wooden tables, but the price tags are anything but unassuming. The clientele includes the likes of Donna Karan and photographer Bruce Weber. Unusual ceramics and jewelry are also on display. ✉ *36 Kinnerton St., Knightsbridge* ☎ *020/7235–9315* ☼ *Closed Sun.* Ⓜ *Knightsbridge.*

FAMILY **Rachel Riley.** Specializing in traditional English style for boys and girls, Riley's luxurious, vintage-inspired collection includes classics like duffle coats and hand-smocked floral dresses. Mothers who love the Riley look (including the Duchess of Cambridge, who has put Prince George in Riley clothes) can pick up coordinating outfits for themselves here or at the Marylebone High Street location. ✉ *14 Pont St., Knightsbridge* ☎ *020/7259–5969* ⊕ *www.rachelriley.co.uk* ☼ *Closed Sun.* Ⓜ *Knightsbridge.*

Rigby & Peller. Lovers of luxury lingerie shop here for brands like Prima Donna and Aubade, as well as R&P's own line. If the right fit eludes you, the made-to-measure service starts at around £300. Many of London's most affluent women shop here, not only because this is the Queen's favored underwear supplier but also because the quality is excellent and the service impeccably knowledgeable while being much friendlier than you might expect. There are also branches in Mayfair, Chelsea, and The City. ✉ *2 Hans Rd., Knightsbridge* ☎ *020/7225–4760* ⊕ *www.rigbyandpeller.com* Ⓜ *Knightsbridge.*

DEPARTMENT STORES

Harrods. With an encyclopedic assortment of luxury brands, this Knightsbridge institution, now owned by the State of Qatar, has more than 300 departments and 20 restaurants, all spread over 1 million square feet on a 5-acre site. If you approach Harrods as a blingtastic tourist attraction rather than as a center of elegant sophistication, you won't be disappointed. Focus on the spectacular food halls, the huge ground-floor perfumery, the revamped toy and technology departments, the excellent Urban Retreat spa, and the Vegas-like Egyptian Room. Nevertheless, standards of taste are enforced with a customer dress code (no shorts, ripped jeans, or flip-flops). Be prepared to brave the crowds, especially on weekends. ⊠ *87–135 Brompton Rd., Knightsbridge* ☎ *020/7730–1234* ⊕ *www.harrods.com* Ⓜ *Knightsbridge.*

Fodor's Choice
★ **Harvey Nichols.** While visiting tourists flock to Harrods, fashionistas shop at Harvey Nichols, aka "Harvey Nicks." The womenswear and accessories departments are outstanding, featuring top designers like McQueen, Alexander Wang, Lanvin, Louboutin, and just about every trendy name you can think of. The furniture and housewares are equally gorgeous (and pricey), though they become somewhat more affordable during the twice-annual sales in January and July. The Fifth Floor restaurant is the place to see and be seen, but if you're just after a quick bite, there's also a more informal café on the same floor or sushi-to-go from Yo! Sushi. To keep you looking as fresh as the fashion, there's also a MediSpa, an Elemis spa, and a hair salon, plus nail and brow bars. ⊠ *109–125 Knightsbridge, Knightsbridge* ☎ *020/7235–5000* ⊕ *www. harveynichols.com* Ⓜ *Knightsbridge.*

BELGRAVIA
ACCESSORIES

Fodor's Choice
★ **Lulu Guinness.** Famous for her flamboyantly themed bags (think the satin "bucket" topped with roses or the elaborately beaded red "lips" clutch), Guinness also showcases vintage-inspired luggage and beauty accessories in this frilly little shop, which is just as whimsical as her designs. There are other branches in Mayfair, and The City. ⊠ *3 Ellis St., Belgravia* ☎ *020/7823–4828* ⊕ *www.luluguinness.com* ☯ *Closed Sun.* Ⓜ *Sloane Sq.*

Fodor's Choice
★ **Philip Treacy.** Magnificent hats by Treacy are annual showstoppers on Ladies Day at the Royal Ascot races and regularly grace the glossy magazines' society pages. Part Mad Hatter, part Cecil Beaton, Treacy's creations always guarantee a grand entrance (remember Princess Beatrice's eye-catching headdress at the Royal Wedding?). In addition to the extravagant, haute couture hats handmade in the atelier, ready-to-wear hats are also for sale, as are some bags. ⊠ *69 Elizabeth St., Belgravia* ☎ *020/7730–3992* ⊕ *www.philiptreacy.co.uk* ☯ *Closed Sun.* Ⓜ *Sloane Sq.*

SPECIALTY STORES

Mungo & Maud. If you don't want to leave London without buying something for your pet, pick up a well-designed coat, collar, leash, blanket, bowl, toy, or comfortable bed that will make your dog the snazziest pooch in town. Cats are also catered for with baskets, suede collars, and catnip toys. Even owners get a nod with luxurious merino throws (soon to be covered in pet hair) and a leather poop pouch. There's also a branch in Notting Hill. ⊠ *79 Elizabeth St., Belgravia* ☎ *020/022–1207* ⊕ *www.mungoandmaud.com* Ⓜ *Sloane Sq.*

18

NOTTING HILL

BOOKS

Books for Cooks. It may seem odd to describe a bookshop as delicious-smelling, but the aromas wafting out of the tiny test kitchen—which serves daily-changing lunch dishes drawn from recipes in the 8,000 cookbooks on the shelves, as well as cakes and culinary experiments—will whet your appetite even before you've opened one of the books. Just about every world cuisine is represented, along with a complete lineup of works by celebrity chefs. Before you come to London, visit the shop's website to sign up for a cooking class. ⊠ *4 Blenheim Cres., Notting Hill* ☎ *020/7221–1992* ⊕ *www.booksforcooks.com* ⊗ *Closed Sun. and Mon.* Ⓜ *Notting Hill Gate, Ladbroke Grove.*

CLOTHING

Aimé. French-Cambodian sisters Val and Vanda Heng-Vong launched this shop to showcase the best of French clothing and designer housewares. Expect to find cult French labels like Isabel Marantand A.P.C. as well as a couple of Italian brands like Forte Forte along with housewares and a well-chosen collection of ceramics. Petit Aimé, next door, sells children's clothing. There's also a Shoreditch branch. ⊠ *32 Ledbury Rd., Notting Hill* ☎ *020/7221–7070* ⊕ *www.aimelondon.com* ⊗ *Closed Sun.* Ⓜ *Notting Hill Gate.*

FAMILY **Caramel Baby & Child.** Here you'll find adorable yet unfussy clothes for children six months and up: handcrafted Peruvian alpaca cardigans in sherbet colors, floral cotton dresses for girls; check shirts and earth-tone tees for boys; comfortable pants in twill, corduroy, and cotton for both; and merino cashmere sweaters for extremely fashionable babies. Caramel also sells a small selection of decorative-functional items like mobiles and child-friendly chairs and stools. There are also branches in South Kensington and Soho. ⊠ *77 Ledbury Rd., Notting Hill* ☎ *020/7727–0906* ⊕ *www.caramel-shop.co.uk* Ⓜ *Westbourne Park, Notting Hill Gate.*

The Cross. One of the first "lifestyle boutiques" and still one of the best, this West London favorite carries fashion by in-the-know favorites like Vanessa Bruno, Bella Freud, Frame Denim, Dosa, and more, plus accessories, housewares, and kids clothes. The emphasis is on the feminine and quirky. ⊠ *141 Portland Rd., Notting Hill* ☎ *020/7727–6760* ⊕ *www.thecrossshop.co.uk* ⊗ *Closed Sun.* Ⓜ *Holland Park.*

Rellik. Now in the modernist landmark known as the Trellick Tower and favored by the likes of Kate Moss, Rellik began as a stall in the Portobello Market. Vintage hunters looking to splurge can find a selection of YLS, Dior, Pierre Cardin, and Ossie Clark as well as items from lesser-known designers. ⊠ *Trellick Tower, 8 Golborne Rd., Notting Hill* ☎ *020/8962–0089* ⊕ *www.relliklondon.co.uk* ⊗ *Closed Sun.* Ⓜ *Westbourne Park.*

MARKET

Portobello Market. Still considered the best all-round market in town by many fans, and certainly the most famous, Portobello Market stretches almost 2 miles, from fashionable Notting Hill to the lively cultural melting pot of North Kensington, changing character as it goes.

The southern end, starting at Chepstow Villas and going to Elgin Crescent, is lined with shops, stalls, and arcades selling antiques, silver, and bric-a-brac on Saturday. The middle, from Elgin Crescent to Talbot, is devoted to fruit and vegetables, interspersed with excellent hot food stalls. On Friday and Saturday, the area between Talbot Road and the elevated highway (called the Westway) becomes more of a flea market specializing in new household and mass-produced goods sold at a discount. North of the Westway up to Goldborne Road are more stalls selling even cheaper secondhand household goods and bric-a-brac. Scattered throughout but mostly concentrated under the Westway are clothing stalls selling vintage pieces and items from emerging designers, custom T-shirts, and supercool baby clothes, plus jewelry. New and established designers are also found in the boutiques of the Portobello Green Arcade.

Some say Portobello Road has become a tourist trap, but if you acknowledge that it's a circus and get into the spirit, it's a lot of fun. Perhaps you won't find many bargains, but this is such a fascinating part of town that just hanging out is a good enough excuse to come. There are some food and flower stalls throughout the week (try the Hummingbird Bakery for delicious cupcakes) but Saturday is when the market in full swing. Serious shoppers avoid the crowds and go on Friday morning. Bring cash (several vendors don't take credit cards), but also be sure to keep an eye on it. ⊠ *Portobello Rd., Notting Hill* ⊕ *www.portobelloroad.co.uk* ☽ *Mon.–Wed. 9–6, Thurs. 9–1, Fri. and Sat. 9–7* Ⓜ *Notting Hill Gate.*

MUSIC

Music & Video Exchange. This store is a music collector's treasure trove, with a constantly changing stock refreshed by customers selling and exchanging as well as buying. The main store focuses on rock pop, soul, and dance, both mainstream and obscure, in a variety of formats ranging from vinyl to CD, cassette, and even mini-disk. Don't miss the discounts in the basement and the rarities upstairs. Classical music is at No. 40, comics and books on nearby Pembridge Road, and there are branches in Soho and Greenwich. ⊠ *38 Notting Hill Gate, Notting Hill* ☎ *020/7243–8573* ⊕ *www.mgeshops.com* Ⓜ *Notting Hill Gate.*

SHOES

Emma Hope. The signature look of the footwear here is elegant and ladylike, with pointed toes and kitten heels, often ornamented with bows, lace, crystals, or exquisite embroidery (such craftsmanship doesn't come cheap, unfortunately). Ballet flats and sneakers in velvet or animal prints provide glamor without sacrificing comfort. Small, but perfectly formed, handbags, as well as shoes and accessories for men, are stocked both here and in the Sloane Square branch. ⊠ *207 Westbourne Grove, Notting Hill* ☎ *020/7313–7490* ⊕ *www.emmahope.com* Ⓜ *Notting Hill Gate.*

18

REGENT'S PARK AND HAMPSTEAD

HOUSEHOLD

Graham & Green. Combining style with practicality and an added whimsical twist, this delightful interiors shop carries faux fur and mohair throws, elegant lamps and lampshades, embroidered cushions, felt animal rugs for children, Venetian glass doorknobs, folding deckchairs (as found in the Royal Parks), shabby chic sofas, and even a pedal-powered kiddie car that's a replica of a classic Bugatti. There's another branch in Notting Hill. ⊠ *164 Regent's Park Rd., Primrose Hill* ☎ *020/7586–2960* ⊕ *www.grahamandgreen.co.uk* Ⓜ *Chalk Farm.*

SHOES

Spice. Touring London requires a lot of walking, so if your feet are crying out for mercy, stop in at this long-established boutique that specializes in spiffy but comfortable shoes and boots for men and women from brands like Unisa, Aubrey, and their own Spice line. There's another branch in Islington. ⊠ *162 Regents' Park Rd., Primrose Hill* ☎ *020/7722–2478* ⊕ *www.spiceshu.co.uk* Ⓜ *Chalk Farm.*

SIDE TRIPS FROM LONDON

Updated By
Kate Hughes
and Jack
Jewers

Londoners are undeniably lucky. Few urban populations enjoy such glorious—and easily accessible—options for day-tripping. Even if you have only one day to spare, head out of the city. A train ride past hills dotted with sheep, a stroll through a medieval town, or a visit to one of England's great castles could make you feel as though you've added another week to your vacation.

Not only is England extremely compact, the train and bus networks, although somewhat inefficient and expensive compared with their European counterparts, are extensive and easily booked (though pricing structures can be confusing), making "a brilliant day out" an easy thing to accomplish.

Although you can do the Warner Bros. Harry Potter Studio Tour in a day, visiting many of the towns near London would be a frenzied day trip. Heavy summer crowds make it difficult to cover the sights in a relaxed manner, so consider staying for a day or two. You'd then have time to explore a different England—one with quiet country pubs, tree-lined lanes, and neat fields. No matter where you go, lodging reservations are a good idea from June through September, when foreign visitors saturate the English countryside.

PLANNING

GETTING AROUND

Normally the towns near London are best reached by train. Bus travel costs less, but can take twice as long. Wherever you're going, plan ahead: check the latest timetables before you set off, and try to get an early start. ⇨ *Also see Travel Smart London.*

STATION TIPS

You can reach any of London's main-line train stations by Tube. London's bus stations can be confusing for the uninitiated, so here's a quick breakdown:

Green Line Coach Station is on Bulleid Way (in front of the Colonnades Shopping Centre on Buckingham Palace Road) and is the departure point for most Green Line and Megabus services.

Victoria Bus Station is where many of the local London bus services arrive and depart, and is directly outside the main exits of the train and Tube stations.

Victoria Coach Station is on Buckingham Palace Road: it's a five-minute walk from Victoria Tube station. This is where to go for coach departures; arrivals are at a different location, a short walk from here.

TO GET TO...		
	Take the Train From...	Take the Bus From...
Cambridge	King's Cross (45–90 minutes; every 10 or 20 minutes); Liverpool St. (80 minutes; every 30 minutes)	Victoria Coach (about 3 hours; every hour–90 minutes)
Oxford	Paddington (55–110 minutes; every 3–20 minutes)	Victoria Coach (100 minutes; every half hour; Oxford Tube, Buckingham Palace Rd. (100 minutes; every 12–20 minutes)
Stratford-upon-Avon	Marylebone (2 hours to 2½ hours; every 2 hours); or Euston (1½ hours; every 20 or 40 minutes or hourly)	Victoria Coach (3 hours, 25 minutes; about 3 times daily)
Warner Bros. Harry Potter Studio Tour	Euston Station (20 minutes) to Watford; then shuttle bus to attraction	Watford (15 minutes; every 20 minutes; after taking London train from Euston).
Windsor	Paddington (25–50 minutes; every 5–30 minutes) or Waterloo (1 hour, 5 minutes; every half hour)	Green Line Bus Station, Victoria (1 hour, 5 minutes; hourly)

19

CAMBRIDGE

60 miles northeast of London.

With the spires of its university buildings framed by towering trees and expansive meadows, its medieval streets and passages enhanced by gardens and riverbanks, the city of Cambridge is among the loveliest in England. The city predates the Roman occupation of Britain, but there's confusion over exactly how the university was founded. The most widely accepted story is that it was established in 1209 by a pair of scholars from Oxford, who left their university in protest over the wrongful execution of a colleague for murder.

This university town may be beautiful, but it's no museum. Even when the students are on vacation, there's a cultural and intellectual buzz here. Well-preserved medieval buildings sit cheek-by-jowl next to the latest in modern architecture (for example the William Gates building, which houses Cambridge University's computer laboratory) in this growing city dominated culturally and architecturally by its famous university (whose students make up around one-fifth of the city's 109,000 inhabitants), and beautified by parks, gardens, and the quietly flowing River Cam. A quintessential Cambridge pursuit is punting on the Cam (one occupant propels the narrow, square-end, flat-bottom boat with a long pole), followed by a stroll along the Backs, the left bank of the river fringed by St. John's, Trinity, Clare, King's, and Queens' colleges, and by Trinity Hall.

VISITING THE COLLEGES

College visits are certainly a highlight of a Cambridge tour, but remember that the colleges are private residences and workplaces, even when school isn't in session. Each is an independent entity within the university; some are closed to the public, but at others you can see the chapels, dining rooms (called halls), and sometimes the libraries, too. Some colleges charge a fee for the privilege of nosing around. All are closed during exams, usually from mid-April to late June, and the opening hours often vary. Additionally, all are subject to closures at short notice, especially King's; check the websites in advance. For details about visiting specific colleges not listed here, contact Cambridge University.

TOURS

City Sightseeing. This company operates open-top bus tours of Cambridge, including the Backs, colleges, and Botanic Gardens. Tours can be joined at marked bus stops in the city. Ask the tourist office about additional tours. ⊠ *Cambridge Train Station, Station Rd., Cambridge* ☎ *01223/433250* ⊕ *www.city-sightseeing.com* 🎫 *From £14.*

Visit Cambridge. Visit Cambridge. Walking tours, as well as other tours, are led by an official Blue Badge guide. The two-hour tours leave from the tourist information center at Peas Hill. Hours vary according to the tour, with the earliest leaving at 11 am and the latest at 1 or 2 pm. ⊠ *Peas Hill, Cambridge* ☎ *0871/226–8006* ⊕ *www.visitcambridge.org/ official-tours* 🎫 *From £18.50.*

ESSENTIALS

Visitor Information Cambridge University. ☎ *01223/337733* ⊕ *www.cam. ac.uk.*

EXPLORING

TOP ATTRACTIONS

Fodor'sChoice ★ **Fitzwilliam Museum.** In a Classical Revival building renowned for its grand Corinthian portico, this museum, founded by the seventh viscount Fitzwilliam of Merrion in 1816, has one of Britain's most outstanding collections of art and antiquities. Highlights include two large Titians, an extensive collection of French Impressionist paintings, and many works by Matisse and Picasso. The opulent interior displays its treasures to marvelous effect, from Egyptian pieces such as inch-high figurines and painted coffins, to sculptures from the Chinese Han dynasty of the 3rd century BC. Other collections of note here are a fine assortment of medieval illuminated manuscripts and a fascinating room full of armor

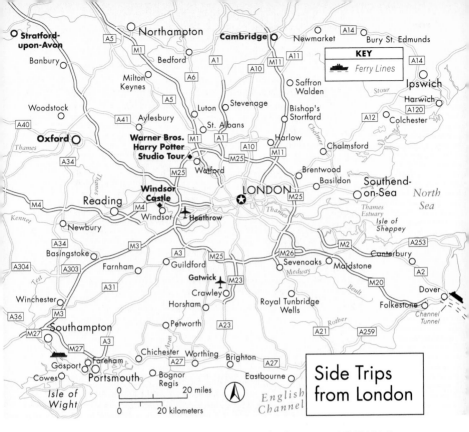

Side Trips from London

---

and muskets. ✉ *Trumpington St., Cambridge* ☎ *01223/332900* ⊕ *www. fitzmuseum.cam.ac.uk* 🎟 *Free* ⏱ *Tues.–Sat. 10–5, Sun. noon–5.*

King's College. Founded in 1441 by Henry VI, King's College has a magnificent late-15th-century chapel that is its most famous landmark. Other notable architecture is the neo-Gothic Porters' Lodge, facing King's Parade, which was a comparatively recent addition in the 1830s, and the classical Gibbs building. ■TIP→ **Head down to the river, from where the panorama of college and chapel is one of the university's most photographed views.** Past students of King's College include the novelist E.M. Forster, the economist John Maynard Keynes, and the World War I poet Rupert Brooke. ✉ *King's Parade, Cambridge* ☎ *01223/331212* ⊕ *www.kings.cam.ac.uk* 🎟 *£8, includes chapel* ⏱ *Term time: Mon. 9:45–3:30, Tues.–Fri. 9:30–3:30, Sat. 9:30–3:15, Sun. 1:15–2:30. Out of term: Mon. 9:45–4:30, Tues.–Sun. 9:30–4:30.*

Fodor's Choice
★

King's College Chapel. Based on Sainte-Chapelle, the 13th-century royal chapel in Paris, this house of worship is perhaps the most glorious flowering of Perpendicular Gothic in Britain. Henry VI, the king after whom the college is named, oversaw the work. From the outside, the most prominent features are the massive flying buttresses and the fingerlike spires that line the length of the building. Inside, the most obvious impression is of great space—the chapel was once described as "the noblest barn in Europe"—and of light flooding in from its huge windows. The brilliantly colored bosses (carved panels at the intersections of the roof ribs) are particularly intense, although hard to see without binoculars. An exhibition in the chantries, or side chapels, explains more about the chapel's construction. Behind the altar is *The Adoration of the Magi*, an enormous painting by Peter Paul Rubens. ■ TIP➜ **The chapel, unlike the rest of King's College, stays open during exam periods.** Every Christmas Eve, a festival of carols is sung by the chapel's famous choir. It's broadcast on national television and considered a quintessential part of the traditional English Christmas. To compete for the small number of tickets available, join the line at the college's main entrance early—doors open at 7 am. ⊠ *King's Parade, Cambridge* ☎ *01223/331212* ⊕ *www.kings.cam.ac.uk* ⊒ *£8, includes college and grounds* ☉ *Term time: Mon. 9:45–3:30, Tues.–Fri. 9:30–3:30, Sat. 9:30–3:15, Sun. 9:45–4:30. Out of term: Mon. 9:45–5:30, Tues.–Sun. 9:30–4:30. Sometimes closed for events; call ahead to confirm.*

WORD OF MOUTH

"It's perfectly possible to get a HUGE amount out of a 6-hour Oxford stay—especially by following the self-guided tours on the Oxfordshire official tourist site or booking a Blue Badge walking tour at the city's Tourist Information Centre. Or opt to spend a month there. Neither strategy (or anything in between) is self-evidently wrong." —flanneruk

Fodor'sChoice ★ **Polar Museum.** Beautifully designed, this museum at Cambridge University's Scott Polar Research Institute chronicles the history of polar exploration. There's a particular emphasis on the British expeditions of the 20th century, including the ill-fated attempt by Robert Falcon Scott to be the first to reach the South Pole in 1912. Norwegian explorer Roald Amundsen reached the pole first; Scott and his men perished on the return journey, but their story became legendary. There are also collections devoted to the science of modern polar exploration; the indigenous people of northern Canada, Greenland, and Alaska; and frequently changing art installations. ⊠ *Scott Polar Research Institute, Lensfield Rd., Cambridge* ☎ *01223/336540* ⊕ *www.spri.cam.ac.uk/museum* ⊒ *Free* ☉ *Tues.–Sat. 10–4. Closed Sat. of holiday weekends.*

WORTH NOTING

Emmanuel College. The master hand of architect Christopher Wren (1632–1723) is evident throughout much of Cambridge, particularly at Emmanuel, built on the site of a Dominican friary, where he designed the chapel and colonnade. A stained-glass window in the chapel has a likeness of John Harvard, founder of Harvard University, who studied here. The college, founded in 1584, was an early center of Puritan learning; a number of the Pilgrims were Emmanuel alumni, and they remembered their alma mater in naming Cambridge, Massachusetts. ⊠ *St. Andrew's St., Cambridge* ☎ *01223/334200* ⊕ *www.emma.cam. ac.uk* ⊒ *Free* ☉ *Daily 9–6, except exam period.*

Queens' College. One of the most eye-catching colleges, Queens' is named after Margaret, wife of Henry VI, and Elizabeth, wife of Edward IV. Founded in 1448, the college is tucked away on Queens' Lane, next to the wide lawns that lead down from King's College to the Backs. The secluded "cloister court" looks untouched since its completion in the 1540s. Queens' masterpiece is the **Mathematical Bridge,** the original version of which is said to have been built without any fastenings. The current bridge (1902) is securely bolted. The college is closed to visitors late May to late June. ⊠ *Queens' La., Cambridge* ☎ *01223/335511* ⊕ *www.quns.cam.ac.uk* 🖾 *£3* ⊙ *Daily 10–4:30; closed during exam study periods certain wks Apr.–July. Call to confirm.*

Trinity College. Founded in 1546 by Henry VIII, Trinity replaced a 14th-century educational foundation and is the largest college in either Cambridge or Oxford, with nearly 700 undergraduates. In the 17th-century great court, with its massive gatehouse, is **Great Tom,** a giant clock that strikes each hour with high and low notes. The college's greatest masterpiece is Christopher Wren's **library,** colonnaded and seemingly constructed with as much light as stone. Among the things you can see here is A. A. Milne's handwritten manuscript of *The House at Pooh Corner.* Trinity alumni include Isaac Newton, William Thackeray, Lord Byron, Alfred Tennyson, and 31 Nobel Prize winners. ⊠ *St. John's St., Cambridge* ☎ *01223/338400* ⊕ *www.trin.cam.ac.uk* 🖾 *£2* ⊙ *College and chapel daily 10–4, except exam period and event days; Wren Library weekdays noon–2, Sat. in term time 10:30–12:30; Great Court daily 10–4:30.*

WHERE TO EAT

$$
SEAFOOD

✕ **Loch Fyne.** Part of a Scottish chain that harvests its own oysters, this airy, casual place across from the Fitzwilliam Museum is deservedly popular. The seafood is fresh and well prepared, served in a traditional setting with a modern ambience. Try the Bradan Rost smoked salmon if it's on the menu; it's flavored with Scotch whisky. The restaurant is also open for breakfast. $ *Average main: £17* ⊠ *37 Trumpington St., Cambridge* ☎ *01223/362433* ⊕ *www.lochfyne-restaurants.com.*

$$
MODERN BRITISH

✕ **River Bar Steakhouse & Grill.** Across the river from Magdalene College, this popular waterfront bar and grill serves delicious steak and burgers, plus specialties such as lobster mac and cheese, and roast chicken with a bourbon barbecue glaze. Light lunches are served in the afternoon, and the evening cocktail list is small but elegant. Try the French 75, which is gin with lemon juice, sugar, and sparkling wine. $ *Average main: £20* ⊠ *Quayside, Thompsons Ln., off Bridge St., Cambridge* ☎ *01223/307030* ⊕ *www.riverbarsteakhouse.com* ⌕ *Reservations essential.*

19

OXFORD

55 miles northwest of London.

With arguably the most famous university in the world, Oxford has been a center of learning since 1167, with only the Sorbonne preceding it. It doesn't take more than a day or two to explore its winding medieval streets, photograph its ivy-covered stone buildings and ancient churches and libraries, and even take a punt down one of its placid waterways. The town center is compact and walkable, and at its heart is Oxford University. Alumni of this prestigious institution include 48

Nobel Prize winners, 26 British prime ministers (including David Cameron), and 28 foreign presidents (including Bill Clinton), along with poets, authors, and artists such as Percy Bysshe Shelley, Oscar Wilde, and W. H. Auden.

Oxford is northwest of London, at the junction of the rivers Thames and Cherwell. The city is more interesting and more cosmopolitan than Cambridge, and although it's also bigger, its suburbs aren't remotely interesting to visitors. The interest is all at the center, where the old town curls around the grand stone buildings, great restaurants, and historic pubs. Victorian writer Matthew Arnold described Oxford's "dreaming spires," a phrase that has become famous. Students rush past on the way to exams, clad with antiquarian style in their requisite mortar caps, flowing dark gowns, stiff collars, and crisp white bow ties. ■TIP➜ Watch your back when crossing roads, as bikes are everywhere.

VISITING THE COLLEGES

You can explore major sights in town in a day, but it takes more than a day to spend an hour in each of the key museums and absorb the college scene. Some colleges are open only in the afternoons during university terms. When undergraduates are in residence, access is often restricted to the chapels, dining rooms, and libraries, and you're requested to refrain from picnicking in the quadrangles. All are closed certain days during exams, usually from mid-April to late June.

TOURS

City Sightseeing. This company offers hop-on, hop-off bus tours with 19 stops around Oxford; your ticket, purchased from the driver, is good for 24 hours. ☎ *01865/790522* ⊕ *www.citysightseeingoxford. com* ✉ *From £14.*

Oxford Tourist Information Centre. You can find information here on the many guided walks of the city. The best way of gaining access to the collegiate buildings is to take the two-hour university and city tour, which leaves the Tourist Information Centre at 10:45 and 1 daily, 1 and 2 on Saturdays. You can book in advance. ✉ *15/16 Broad St., Oxford* ☎ *01865/252200* ⊕ *www.visitoxfordandoxfordshire.com.*

EXPLORING

TOP ATTRACTIONS

Fodor's Choice ★ **Ashmolean Museum.** Britain's oldest public museum displays its rich and varied collections from the Neolithic to the present day over five floors. Innovative and spacious galleries on the theme of "Crossing Cultures, Crossing Time" explore connections between the priceless Greek, Roman, and Indian artifacts, as well as the Egyptian and Chinese objects, all of which are among the best in the country. In regards to the superb art collection, not to be missed are drawings by Raphael, the shell-encrusted mantle of Powhatan (father of Pocahontas), the lantern belonging to Guy Fawkes, and the Alfred Jewel, set in gold, which dates from the reign of King Alfred the Great (ruled 871–899). There's too much to see in one visit, but the free admission makes return trips easy. The Ashmolean Dining Room, the rooftop restaurant, is a good spot

Radcliffe Camera, an unmissable circular library at Oxford University

for refreshments. ✉ *Beaumont St., Oxford* ☎ *01865/278002* ⊕ *www.ashmolean.org* ✉ *Free* ☉ *Tues.–Sun. and bank holiday Mon. 10–5.*

Fodor's Choice ★ **Magdalen College.** Founded in 1458, with a handsome main quadrangle and a supremely monastic air, Magdalen (pronounced *maud*-lin) is one of the most impressive of Oxford's colleges and attracts its most artistic students. Alumni include such diverse people as P.G. Wodehouse, Oscar Wilde, and John Betjeman. The school's large, square tower is a famous local landmark. ■TIP➜ **To enhance your visit, take a stroll around the Deer Park and along Addison's Walk; then have tea in the Old Kitchen, which overlooks the river.** ✉ *High St., Oxford* ☎ *01865/276000* ⊕ *www.magd.ox.ac.uk* ✉ *£5* ☉ *July–Sept., daily noon–7 or dusk; Oct.–June, daily 1–6 or dusk.*

19

FAMILY **Fodor's** Choice ★ **Pitt Rivers Museum.** More than half a million intriguing archaeological and anthropological items from around the globe, based on the collection bequeathed by Lieutenant-General Augustus Henry Lane Fox Pitt Rivers in 1884, are crammed into a multitude of glass cases and drawers. Items are organized thematically rather than geographically, an eccentric approach that's surprisingly thought-provoking. Labels are handwritten, and children are given flashlights to explore the farthest corners and spot the world's smallest dolly. Give yourself plenty of time to wander through the displays of shrunken heads, Hawaiian feather cloaks, and fearsome masks. Children will have a field day. ✉ *S. Parks Rd., Oxford* ☎ *01865/270927* ⊕ *www.prm.ox.ac.uk* ✉ *Free, suggested donation £3* ☉ *Mon. noon–4:30, Tues.–Sun. and bank holiday Mon. 10–4:30.*

WORTH NOTING

Christ Church. Built in 1546, the college of Christ Church is referred to by its members as "The House." This is the site of Oxford's largest quadrangle, Tom Quad, named after the huge bell (6¼ tons) that hangs in the Christopher Wren–designed gate tower and rings 101 times at five past nine every evening in honor of the original number of Christ Church scholars. The vaulted, 800-year-old chapel in one corner has been Oxford's cathedral since the time of Henry VIII. The college's medieval dining hall contains portraits of many famous alumni, including 13 of Britain's prime ministers, but you'll recognize it from its recurring role in the Harry Potter movies (although they didn't actually film here, the room was painstakingly recreated in a film studio). ■ TIP→ **Plan carefully, as the dining hall is only open weekdays 10:30–11:40 and 2:30–4:30, and weekends 2:30–4:30.** Lewis Carroll, author of *Alice in Wonderland*, was a teacher of mathematics here for many years; a shop opposite the meadows on St. Aldate's sells Alice paraphernalia. ⊠ *St. Aldate's, Oxford* ☎ *01865/276492* ⊕ *www.chch.ox.ac.uk* ✉ *£8; £9 in July and Aug.* ☉ *Mon.–Sat. 10–5, Sun. 2–5; last admission 45 mins before closing. Sometimes closed for events; call to confirm.*

Radcliffe Camera and Bodleian Library. A vast library, the domed Radcliffe Camera is Oxford's most spectacular building, built in 1737–49 by James Gibbs in Italian baroque style. It's usually surrounded by tourists with cameras trained at its golden-stone walls. The Camera contains part of the Bodleian Library's enormous collection, begun in 1602 and one of six "copyright libraries" in the U.K. Like the Library of Congress in the United States, this means it must by law contain a copy of every book printed in Great Britain. This means very crowded shelves—the collection grows by about 5,000 items a week. It also contains valuable treasures such as a Gutenberg Bible and a Shakespeare First Folio. Tours reveal the magnificent Duke Humfrey's Library, which was the original chained library and completed in 1488. (The ancient tomes are dusted once a decade.) Guides will show you the spots used for Hogwarts School in the Harry Potter films. ■ TIP→ **Arrive early to secure tickets for the two to six daily tours. 10:30 am tours can be pre-booked, as can the extended tours on Wednesday and Saturday. Otherwise tours are first-come, first-served.** Audio tours, the only tours open to kids under 11, don't require reservations. Call ahead to confirm times, as tours don't run on days when private events are booked at the library. ⊠ *Broad St., Oxford* ☎ *01865/287400* ⊕ *www.bodleian.ox.ac. uk* ✉ *Audio tour £2.50, minitour £5, standard tour £7, extended tours £13* ☉ *Bodleian and Divinity School weekdays 9–5, Sat. 9–4:30, Sun. 11–5. Sometimes closed for events; call to confirm.*

St. John's College. One of Oxford's most attractive campuses, St. John's has seven quiet quadrangles surrounded by elaborately carved buildings. You enter the first through a low wooden door. This college dates to 1555, when Sir Thomas White, a merchant, founded it. His heart is buried in the chapel (by tradition, students curse as they walk over it). The Canterbury Quad represented the first example of Italian Renaissance architecture in Oxford, and the Front Quad includes the buildings of the old St. Bernard's Monastery. ⌂ *St. Giles, Oxford* ☎ *01865/277300* ⊕ *www.sjc.ox.ac.uk* ✉ *Free* ☼ *Daily 1–5 or dusk.*

University Church of St. Mary the Virgin. Seven hundred years' worth of funeral monuments crowd this galleried and spacious church, including the tombstone, on the altar steps, of Amy Robsart, the wife of Robert Dudley, Elizabeth I's favorite. One pillar marks the site where Thomas Cranmer, author of the *Anglican Book of Common Prayer*, was brought to trial and executed for heresy by Queen Mary I (Mary restored Catholicism to England after her father, Henry VIII, broke with the Catholic Church; Cranmer had been a key player in the Protestant reforms). The top of the 14th-century tower has a panoramic view of the city's skyline. It's worth the 127 steps. The Vaults and Garden Café, a part of the church accessible from Radcliffe Square, serves breakfasts and cream teas as well as good lunches. ⌂ *High St., Oxford* ☎ *01865/279111* ⊕ *www.university-church.ox.ac.uk* ✉ *Church free, tower £4* ☼ *Sept.–Jun., daily 9–5; Jul.–Aug., daily 9–6; last admission 30 mins before closing.*

WHERE TO EAT

$$ ✕ **Brasserie Blanc.** Raymond Blanc's sophisticated brasserie in the Jericho
FRENCH neighborhood isthe more affordable,chain restaurant cousin of Le Manoir aux Quat' Saisons in Great Milton. Wood floors, pale walls, and large windows keep the restaurant open and airy. The changing menu always lists innovative adaptations of bourgeois French fare, sometimes with Mediterranean or Asian influences. Try thecod filet marinated in lemon, or the chicken served with mousseline potato. There's a good selection of steaks as well. The £12 fixed-price lunch is a good value, and kids have their own menu. ⒮ *Average main: £16* ⌂ *71–72 Walton St., Oxford* ☎ *01865/510999* ⊕ *www.brasserieblanc.com.*

$$ ✕ **Jamie's Italian.** One of chef Jamie Oliver's missions is to re-create the
ITALIAN best rustic Italian fare all over the country, and it's no different at this big and buzzing eatery. There's a diverting range of starters, pastas, and mains such as truffle tagliatelle with Parmesan and nutmeg or British lamb lollipops with toasted nuts and lemon yogurt. Desserts are light and refreshing—tutti frutti lemon meringue pie and granola crumble, for example—and the lively crowd appreciates it all. ⒮ *Average main: £14* ⌂ *24–26 George St., Oxford* ☎ *01865/838383* ⊕ *www.jamieoliver.com.*

19

STRATFORD-UPON-AVON

104 miles north of London.

Stratford-upon-Avon has become adept at accommodating the hordes of people who stream in for a glimpse of William Shakespeare's world. Filled with distinctive, Tudor half-timber buildings, this is certainly a handsome town, and the Royal Shakespeare Theatre is a don't-miss for those who want to see Shakespeare performed in England. But the town can feel, at times, like a literary amusement park, so if you're not a fan of the Bard, you may want to explore elsewhere.

Stratford-upon-Avon honors Shakespeare's birthday with an annual procession.

TOURS AND TICKETS

City Sightseeing. Hop-on hop-off guided tours of Stratford are run by City Sightseeing, and you can combine the tour (about an hour with no stops) with entry to either three or five Shakespeare houses. ☎ *01789/412680* ⊕ *www.city-sightseeing.com* ✉ *From £12.50.*

Shakespeare Birthplace Trust. The main places of Shakespearean interest (Anne Hathaway's Cottage, Hall's Croft, Mary Arden's House, New Place and Nash's House, Shakespeare's Birthplace, and Shakespeare's Grave) are run by the Shakespeare Birthplace Trust. Buy a money-saving combination ticket to five properties for £23.90, or pay separate entry fees if you're visiting only one or two. Family tickets are an option, too. Advance booking online gives you a 10% discount, and tickets are valid for a year. Tickets for Hall's Croft and New Place andNash's House are available only as a rather pricey (£15.90) joint ticket, which includes the birthplace and grave. ☎ *01789/204016* ⊕ *www.shakespeare.org.uk.*

Stratford Town Walk. This walking tour runs year-round and also offers ghost-themed walks and cruises. ☎ *0785/576–0377, 01789/292478* ⊕ *www.stratfordtownwalk.co.uk* ✉ *From £5* ☉ *Weekdays at 11, week-ends at 11 and 2.*

ESSENTIALS

Visitor Information Stratford-upon-Avon Tourist Information Centre. ☎ *01789/264293* ⊕ *www.discover-stratford.com.*

EXPLORING

Hall's Croft. One of the finest surviving Jacobean (early 17th-century) town houses, this impressive residence has a delightful walled garden. Hall's Croft was the home of Shakespeare's elder daughter, Susanna, and her husband, Dr. John Hall, a wealthy physician who, by prescribing an herbal cure for scurvy, was well ahead of his time. One room is furnished as a medical dispensary of the period, and throughout the building are fine examples of heavy oak Jacobean furniture, including a child's high chairand some 17th-century portraits. The café serves light lunches and afternoon teas. ✉ *Old Town, Stratford-upon-Avon* ☎ *01789/292107* ⊕ *www.shakespeare.org.uk* 💷 *£15.90, includes admission to Shakespeare's Birthplace, New Place and Nash's House, and Shakespeare's Grave* ⊙ *Mid-Mar.–Oct., daily 10–5; Nov.–mid-Mar., daily 11–4.*

Holy Trinity Church. The burial place of William Shakespeare, this 13th-century church sits on the banks of the Avon, with a graceful avenue of lime trees framing its entrance. Shakespeare's final resting place is in the chancel, rebuilt in 1465–91 in the late Perpendicular style. He was buried here not because he was a famed poet but because he was a lay rector of Stratford, owning a portion of the township tithes. On the north wall of the sanctuary, over the altar steps, is the famous marble bust created by Gerard Jansen in 1623 and thought to be a true likeness of Shakespeare. The bust offers a more human, even humorous, perspective when viewed from the side. Also in the chancel are the graves of Shakespeare's wife, Anne; his daughter Susanna; his son-in-law John Hall; and his granddaughter's husband, Thomas Nash. Nearby, the Parish Register is displayed, containing Shakespeare's baptismal entry (1564) and his burial notice (1616). ✉ *Trinity St., Stratford-upon-Avon* ☎ *01789/266316* ⊕ *www.stratford-upon-avon.org* 💷 *£2 for chancel* ⊙ *Mar. and Oct., Mon.–Sat. 9–5, Sun. 12:30–5; Apr.–Sept., Mon.–Sat. 8:30–6, Sun. 12:30–5; Nov.–Feb., Mon.–Sat. 9–4, Sun. 12:30–5; last admission 20 mins before closing.*

19

New Place and Nash's House. Originally built in 1483 "of brike and tymber" for a lord mayor of London, **New Place** was Stratford's grandest piece of real estate when Shakespeare bought it in 1597 for £60. Along with a celebrated mulberry tree, revered as planted by Shakespeare himself, the house was torn down in 1759 by the Reverend Francis Gastrell, who was angry at the hordes of Shakespeare-related sightseers. This in turn provoked the wrath of the local inhabitants, who drove him out of town. Now imaginatively reinterpreted to mark the 400th anniversary of Shakespeare's death in 1616, it shows the footprint of the original house and focuses on a deep, illuminated pool. Next door is **Nash's House,** the residence of Thomas Nash, who married Shakespeare's last direct descendant, his granddaughter Elizabeth Hall; it holds finds from recent excavations of the area. The gardens contain a restored Elizabethan knot garden and a fine display of cloud topiary. Currently closed for renovations, the site reopens in April 2016. ✉ *Chapel St., Stratford-upon-Avon* ☎ *01789/292325* ⊕ *www.shakespeare. org.uk* 💷 *£15.90, includes admission to Shakespeare's Birthplace,*

Hall's Croft, and Shakespeare's Grave ⊙ Mid-Mar.–Oct., daily 10–5; Nov.–mid-Mar., daily 11–4.

Fodor's Choice
★
Royal Shakespeare Company. One of the finest repertory troupes in the world and long the backbone of the country's theatrical life, the company performs plays year-round in Stratford and at venues around Britain. The stunning Royal Shakespeare Theatre, home of the RSC, has a thrust stage based on the original Globe Theater in London. The Swan Theatre, part of the theater complex and also built in the style of Shakespeare's Globe, stages plays by Shakespeare and contemporaries such as Christopher Marlowe and Ben Jonson, as well as works by contemporary playwrights. Prices range from £5 to £50. ■TIP→ **Seats book up fast, but day-of-performance and returned tickets are sometimes available.** ⊠ *Waterside, Stratford-upon-Avon* ☎ *0844/800–1110 ticket hotline* ⊕ *www.rsc.org.uk.*

Fodor's Choice
★
Shakespeare's Birthplace. A half-timber house typical of its time, the playwright's birthplace is a much-visited shrine that has been altered and restored since he lived here. Passing through the modern visitor center, you are immersed in the world of Shakespeare through an exhibition that displays the First Folio, deeds to his properties, what is thought to be his signet ring, busts and other memorabilia. The house itself is across the garden from the visitor center. Colorful wall decorations and the furnishings reflect comfortable, middle-class Elizabethan domestic life. Shakespeare's father, John, a glove maker and wool dealer, purchased the house; a reconstructed workshop shows the tools of the glover's trade. Mark Twain and Charles Dickens were both pilgrims here, and you can see the signatures of Thomas Carlyle and Walter Scott scratched into Shakespeare's windowpanes. In the garden, actors present excerpts from the plays. There's also a café and bookshop on the grounds. ⊠ *Henley St., Stratford-upon-Avon* ☎ *01789/201822* ⊕ *www. shakespeare.org.uk* ⊠ *£15.90, includes entry to Hall's Croft, Nash's House and New Place, and Shakespeare's Grave* ⊙ *Mid-Mar.–June, Sept., and Oct., daily 9–5; July and Aug., daily 9–6; Nov.–mid-Mar., daily 10–4.*

STRATFORD ENVIRONS

Two additional stops on the Shakespeare trail are just outside Stratford; also nearby is spectacular Warwick Castle.

Fodor's Choice
★
Anne Hathaway's Cottage and Gardens. The most picturesque of the Shakespeare Trust properties, on the western outskirts of Stratford, was the family home of the woman Shakespeare married in 1582. The "cottage," actually a substantial Tudor farmhouse, has latticed windows and a grand thatch roof. Inside is period furniture, including the settle where Shakespeare reputedly conducted his courtship, and a rare carved Elizabethan bed; outside is a garden planted in lush Edwardian style with herbs and flowers. A stroll through the adjacent orchard takes you to willow cabins where you can listen to sonnets and view sculptures with Shakespearean themes, while the nearby arboretum has trees, shrubs, and roses mentioned in Shakespeare's works. ■TIP→ **The best way to get here is on foot, especially in late spring when the apple trees**

are in blossom. The signed path runs from Evesham Place (an extension of Grove Road) opposite Chestnut Walk. Pick up a leaflet with a map from the tourist office; the walk takes a good half hour. ⊠ *Cottage La., Shottery* ☎ 01789/295517 ⊕ *www.shakespeare.org.uk* ⊠ *£9.50; £23.90 with the Five House Pass which includes Hall's Croft, Mary Arden's Farm, New Place and Nash's House, Shakespeare's Birthplace, and Shakespeare's Grave* ⊙ *Mid-Mar.–Oct., daily 9–5; Nov.–mid-Mar., daily 10–4.*

FAMILY **Mary Arden's Farm.** A working farm, where food is grown using methods common in the 16th century, is the main attraction at Mary Arden's House (the childhood home of Shakespeare's mother) and Palmer's Farm. This bucolic stop is great for kids, who can try their hand at basket weaving and gardening, listen as the farmers explain their work in the fields, and watch the cooks prepare food in the Tudor farmhouse kitchen. It all brings the past to life. There are crafts exhibits, a café, and a garden. The site is 3 miles northwest of Stratford; you need to walk or drive here, or else go with a tour. ⊠ *Off A3400, Wilmcote* ☎ 01789/293455 ⊕ *www.shakespeare.org.uk* ⊠ *£12.50; £23.90 with the Five House Pass which includes Anne Hathaway's Cottage and Gardens, Hall's Croft, Mary Arden's Farm, Nash's House and New Place, Shakespeare's Birthplace, and Shakespeare's Grave* ⊙ *Mid-Mar.–Oct., daily 10–5.*

FAMILY
Fodor's Choice
★
Warwick Castle. The vast bulk of this medieval castle rests on a cliff overlooking the Avon—"the fairest monument of ancient and chivalrous splendor which yet remains uninjured by time," to use the words of Sir Walter Scott. Today the company that runs the Madame Tussauds wax museums owns the castle, and the exhibits and diversions can occupy a full day. Warwick is a great castle experience for kids, though it's pricey (there are family rates). Warwick's two soaring towers, bristling with battlements, can be seen for miles: the 147-foot-high Caesar's Tower, built in 1356, and the 128-foot-high Guy's Tower, built in 1380. The castle's most powerful commander was Richard Neville, earl of Warwick, known during the 15th-century Wars of the Roses as the Kingmaker. Warwick Castle's monumental walls enclose an impressive armory of medieval weapons, as well as state rooms with historic furnishings and paintings by Peter Paul Rubens, Anthony Van Dyck, and other old masters. Twelve rooms are devoted to an imaginative wax exhibition, "A Royal Weekend Party—1898." Other exhibits display the sights and sounds of a great medieval household as it prepares for an important battle, and of a princess's fairy-tale wedding. At the Mill and Engine House, you can see the turning water mill and the engines used to generate electricity early in the 20th century. In the spooky dungeon exhibit, you can wander by wax re-creations of decaying bodies, chanting monks, witches, executions, and "the labyrinth of lost souls"—a modern mirror maze. Elsewhere, a working trebuchet (a kind of catapult), falconry displays, and rat-throwing (stuffed, not live) games add to the atmosphere. Below the castle strutting peacocks patrol the 60 acres of grounds elegantly landscaped by Capability Brown in the 18th century. ■ TIP→ Arrive early to beat the crowds. If you book online, you save 20% on ticket prices. Lavish medieval banquets (extra charge) and

19

special events, including festivals, jousting tournaments, and a Christmas market, take place throughout the year, and plenty of food stalls serve lunches. For the ultimate castle experience, you can glamp (glamorously camp) in a medieval tent or stay in your own luxury suite in Ceasar's Tower, ⊠ *Castle La., off Mill St., Warwick* ☎ *01926/495421, 0871/265–2000 24-hr information line, 01926/406–660 for accommodation* ⊕ *www.warwick-castle.com* ⊠ *Castle, Dragon Tower, and Dungeon £30.60; Castle and Dungeon £28.20; Castle £22.80; parking £6* ☉ *Late July and Aug., daily 10–6; mid-Sept.–mid-July, daily 10–5; last admission 30 mins before closing.*

WHERE TO EAT

$ ╳ **The Black Swan/The Dirty Duck.** The only pub in Britain to be licensed under two names (the more informal one came courtesy of American GIs who were stationed here during World War II), this is one of Stratford's most celebrated pubs—it's attracted actors since the 18th-century thespian David Garrick's days. A little veranda overlooks the theaters and the river here. Along with your pint of bitter, you can choose from the extensive menu ofbaked potatoes, steaks, burgers, and grills; there are also good-value set menus. Few people come here for the food, though you will need to book ahead for dinner: the real attraction is the ambience and your fellow customers. ⑤ *Average main: £8* ⊠ *Waterside, Stratford-upon-Avon* ☎ *01789/297312* ⊕ *www.oldenglishinns.co.uk.*

BRITISH
Fodor'sChoice
★

$ ╳ **Opposition.** Hearty, warming meals are offered at this informal, family-style restaurant in a 16th-century building on the main dining street near the theaters. The English and international dishes—chicken roasted with banana and served with curry sauce and basmati rice, for instance—win praise from the locals. There's a good range of lighter and vegetarian options and fixed-price menus as well. Make reservations a month ahead in summer. ⑤ *Average main: £14* ⊠ *13 Sheep St., Stratford-upon-Avon* ☎ *01789/269980* ⊕ *www.theoppo.co.uk* ☉ *Closed Sun.*

MODERN BRITISH

WARNER BROS. HARRY POTTER STUDIO TOUR

20 miles northwest of London.

Popular and family friendly, the Warner Bros. Harry Potter Studio Tour has sets and props from the successful films, and plenty of engaging interactive diversions for all ages. The train and a special shuttle bus from Watford get you here.

FAMILY
Fodor'sChoice
★

Warner Bros. Harry Potter Studio Tour. Muggles, take note: this spectacular attraction just outside Watford will give you a good three hours of experiencing the magical world of Harry Potter. From the Great Hall of Hogwarts–faithfully restored–to magical props beautifully displayed in a vast studio space, each section of this attraction showcases the real sets, props, and special effects used in the eight movies. Visitors enter the Great Hall, a fitting stage for costumes from each Hogwarts house. You can admire the intricacies of the huge Hogwarts Castle model , ride a broomstick, try butterbeer, explore Platform 9¾, or just

take refuge in the comforting confines of Dumbledore's office. The
new Hogwarts Express section–
in a faithfully reproduced King's
Cross Station–allows you to walk
through the actual steam train and
see what it's like to ride with Harry
and the gang. Tickets, pegged to a
30-minute arrival time slot, must
be prebooked online. The studio
tour is a 20-minute drive from St.
Albans. You can also get here by
taking a 20-minute train ride from

London's Euston Station to Watford Junction (then a 15-minute shuttle
bus ride). Via car from London, use M1 and M25—parking is free.
⊠ *Studio Tour Dr., Leavesden* ☎ *0845/084–0900* ⊕ *www.wbstudiotour.
co.uk* 🎫 *£35* ☉ *Daily times vary; generally 10–8 in summer months
(last tour slot 2½–3½ hrs before closing). Call or check website to
confirm daily times.*

WINDSOR CASTLE

21 miles west of London.

The tall turrets of Windsor Castle, one of the homes of the Royal Family, can be seen for miles around. The grand stone building is the star
attraction in this quiet town with some remaining medieval elements—
though Eton College, England's most famous public school, is also just
a lovely walk away across the Thames.

ESSENTIALS

Visitor Information Royal Windsor Information Centre. ☎ *01753/743900,
01753/743907 for accommodations* ⊕ *www.windsor.gov.uk.*

19

EXPLORING

Fodor's Choice
★

Windsor Castle. From William the Conqueror to Queen Victoria, the
kings and queens of England added towers and wings to this brooding,
imposing castle, visible for miles and now the largest inhabited castle
in the world. Despite the multiplicity of hands involved in its design,
the palace manages to have a unity of style and character. The most
impressive view of Windsor Castle is from the A332 road, coming into
town from the south. Admission includes an audio guide and, if you
wish, a guided tour of the castle precincts. Entrance lines can be long in
season, and you're likely to spend at least half a day here, so come early.

William the Conqueror began work on the castle in the 11th century,
and Edward III modified and extended it in the mid-1300s. One of
Edward's largest contributions was the enormous and distinctive **Round
Tower.** Later, between 1824 and 1837, George IV transformed the still
essentially medieval castle into the fortified royal palace you see today.
Most of England's kings and queens have demonstrated their undying

attachment to the castle, the only royal residence in continuous use by the Royal Family since the Middle Ages.

As you enter the castle, **Henry VIII's gateway** leads uphill into the wide castle precincts, where you're free to wander. Across from the entrance is the exquisite **St. George's Chapel** (closed Sunday). Here lie 10 of the kings of England, including Henry VI, Charles I, and Henry VIII (Jane Seymour is the only one of his six wives buried here). One of the noblest buildings in England, the chapel was built in the Perpendicular style popular in the 15th and 16th centuries, with elegant stained-glass windows; a high, vaulted ceiling; and intricately carved choir stalls. The colorful heraldic banners of the Knights of the Garter—the oldest British Order of Chivalry, founded by Edward III in 1348—hang in the choir. The ceremony in which the knights are installed as members of the order has been held here with much pageantry for more than five centuries. The elaborate **Albert Memorial Chapel** was created by Queen Victoria in memory of her husband.

The **North Terrace** provides especially good views across the Thames to Eton College, perhaps the most famous of Britain's exclusive public-schools (confusingly, "public schools" in Britain are highly traditional, top-tier private schools). From the terrace, you enter the **State Apartments,** which are open to the public most days. On display to the left of the entrance to the State Apartments in Windsor Castle, **Queen Mary's Dolls' House** is a perfect miniature Georgian palace-within-a-palace, created in 1923. Electric lights glow, the doors all have tiny keys, and a miniature library holds Lilliputian-size books written especially for the young queen by famous authors of the 1920s. Five cars, including a Daimler and Rolls-Royce, stand at the ready. In the adjacent corridor are exquisite French couturier–designed costumes made for the two Jumeau dolls presented to the Princesses Elizabeth and Margaret by France in 1938.

Although a fire in 1992 gutted some of the State Apartments, hardly any works of art were lost. Phenomenal repair work brought to new life the **Grand Reception Room,** the **Green and Crimson Drawing Rooms,** and the **State and Octagonal Dining Rooms.** A green oak hammer-beam (a short horizontal beam that projects from the tops of walls for support) roof looms magnificently over the 600-year-old **St. George's Hall,** where the Queen gives state banquets. The State Apartments contain priceless furniture, including a magnificent Louis XVI bed and Gobelin tapestries; carvings by Grinling Gibbons; and paintings by Canaletto, Rubens, Van Dyck, Holbein, Dürer, and Bruegel. The tour's high points are the **Throne Room** and the **Waterloo Chamber,** where Sir Thomas Lawrence's portraits of Napoléon's victorious foes line the walls. You can also see arms and armor—look out for Henry VIII's ample suit. A visit between October and March also includes the Semi-State rooms, the private apartments of George IV, resplendent with gilded ceilings.

To see the castle come magnificently alive, check out the Changing of the Guard, which takes place daily at 11 am from April through July and on alternate days at the same time from August through March. Confirm the exact schedule before traveling to Windsor. ⊠ *Castle Hill,*

Windsor ☎ *020/7766–7304 tickets, 01753/831118 recorded information* ⊕ *www.royalcollection.org.uk* ☒ *£19.50 for Precincts, State
Apartments, Gallery, St. George's Chapel, and Queen Mary's Dolls'
House; £10.50 when State Apartments are closed* ⊙ *Mar.–Oct., daily
9:45–5:15; Nov.–Feb., daily 9:45–4:15; last admission 1 hr 15 min
before closing.*

Fodor's Choice
★

Eton College. Signs warn drivers of "Boys Crossing" as you approach the
splendid Tudor-style buildings of Eton College, the distinguished boarding school for boys ages 13 through 18 founded in 1440 by King Henry
VI. It's all terrifically photogenic, because during the college semester
students still dress in pin-striped trousers, swallow-tailed coats, and stiff
collars. Rivaling St. George's at Windsor in terms of size, the Gothic
Chapel contains superb 15th-century grisaille wall paintings juxtaposed
against modern stained glass by John Piper. Beyond the cloisters are the
school's playing fields where, according to the Duke of Wellington, the
Battle of Waterloo was really won, since so many of his officers had
learned discipline and strategy during their school days. Among the
country's prime ministers to be educated here is David Cameron. The
Museum of Eton Life has displays on the school's history and vignettes of
school life. The school gives public tours, although as of this writing
they were suspended due to construction. They are set to resume again
by early 2016, but call ahead for more information. ☒ *Brewhouse Yard,
Eton* ☎ *01753/370100* ⊕ *www.etoncollege.com.*

WHERE TO EAT

$$
BRITISH

✕ **Two Brewers.** Locals congregate in a pair of low-ceiling rooms at this
tiny 17th-century establishment by the gates of Windsor Great Park.
Those under 18 aren't allowed inside the pub (though they can be
served at a few outdoor tables), but adults find a suitable collection of
wine, espresso, and local beer, plus an excellent menu with such dishes
as sausages with mash and pea gravy, fish cakes, and a good selection
of hot and cold sandwiches. On Sunday the pub serves a traditional,
hearty lunchtime roast. ⑤ *Average main: £15* ☒ *34 Park St., Windsor*
☎ *01753/855426* ⊕ *www.twobrewerswindsor.co.uk* ⊙ *No dinner Fri.–
Sun.* ⌁ *Reservations essential.*

19

UNDERSTANDING LONDON

London At-a-Glance

English Vocabulary

Books and Movies

LONDON AT-A-GLANCE

FAST FACTS

Type of government: Representative democracy. In 1999 the Greater London Authority Act reestablished a single local governing body for the Greater London area, consisting of an elected mayor and the 25-member London Assembly. Elections, first held in 2000, take place every four years.

Population: Inner city 3 million, Greater London 7.7 million

Population density: 12,331 people per square mile

Median age: 38.4

Infant mortality rate: 5 per 1,000 births

Language: English. More than 300 languages are spoken in London. All city government documents are translated into Arabic, Bengali, Chinese, Greek, Gujurati, Hindi, Punjabi, Turkish, Urdu, and Vietnamese.

Ethnic and racial groups: White British 70%, White Irish 3%, Other White 9%, Indian 6%, Bangladeshi 2%, Pakistani 2%, other Asian 2%, Black African 6%, Black Caribbean 5%, Chinese 1%, Other 3%.

Religion: Christian 58%, nonaffiliated 15%, Muslim 8%, Hindu 4%, Jewish 2%, Sikh 1%, other religion 1%, Buddhist 0.8%.

When a man is tired of London, he is tired of life; for there is in London all that life can afford.

—Samuel Johnson

GEOGRAPHY AND ENVIRONMENT

Latitude: 51° N (same as Calgary, Canada; Kiev, Ukraine; Prague, Czech Republic)

Longitude: 0° (same as Accra, Ghana). A brass line in the ground in Greenwich marks the prime meridian (0° longitude).

Elevation: 49 feet

Land area: City, 67 square miles; metro area, 625 square miles

Terrain: River plain, rolling hills, and parkland

Natural hazards: Drought in warmer summers, minor localized flooding of the Thames caused by surge tides from the North Atlantic

Environmental issues: The city has been improving its air quality, but up to 1,600 people die each year from health problems related to London's polluted air. Only half of London's rivers and canals received passing grades for water quality from 1999 through 2001. More than £12 million ($22 million) is spent annually to ensure the city's food safety.

I'm leaving because the weather is too good. I hate London when it's not raining.

—Groucho Marx

ECONOMY

Workforce: 3.8 million; financial/real estate 28%, health care 10%, manufacturing 4%, education 7%, construction 5%, public administration 5%

Unemployment: 7.2%

Major industries: The arts, banking, government, insurance, tourism

London: a nation, not a city.

—Benjamin Disraeli, Lothair

ENGLISH VOCABULARY

You and a Londoner may speak the same language, but some phrases definitely get lost in translation once they cross the Atlantic.

BRITISH ENGLISH	ENGLISH

BASIC TERMS AND EVERYDAY ITEMS

bill	check
flat	apartment
holiday	vacation
lift	elevator
nappy	diaper
note	bill (currency)
plaster	Band-Aid
queue	line
row	argument
rubbish	trash
tin	can
toilet/loo/WC	bathroom

CLOTHING

braces	suspenders
bum bag	fanny pack
dressing gown	robe
jumper	sweater
pants/knickers	underpants/briefs
rucksack	backpack
suspender	garter
tights	pantyhose
trainers	sneakers
trousers	pants
vest	undershirt
waistcoat	vest

TRANSPORTATION

bonnet	hood
boot	trunk

BRITISH ENGLISH	ENGLISH
coach	long-distance bus
pavement	sidewalk
petrol	gas
pram	baby carriage
puncture	flat
windscreen	windshield

FOOD

aubergine	eggplant
banger	sausage
biscuit	cookie
chips	fries
courgette	zucchini
crisps	potato chips
jam	jelly
main course (or main)	entrée
pudding	dessert
rocket	arugula
starter	appetizer
sweet	candy
tea	early dinner

SLANG

all right	hi there
Cheers	thank you
chuffed	pleased
fit	attractive
geezer	dude
guv'nor, gaffer	boss
hard	tough
mate	buddy
sound	good
Ta	thank you

BOOKS AND MOVIES

London in Books

London has been the focus of countless books and essays. For sonorous eloquence, you still must reach back more than half a century to Henry James's *English Hours* and Virginia Woolf's *The London Scene*. Today most suggested reading lists begin with V. S. Pritchett's *London Perceived* and H. V. Morton's *In Search of London*, both decades old. Four more-up-to-date books with a general compass are Peter Ackroyd's *Thames* and anecdotal *London: The Biography*, which traces the city's growth from the Druids to the 21st century; John Russell's *London*, a sumptuously illustrated art book; and Christopher Hibbert's *In London: The Biography of a City*. Stephen Inwood's *A History of London* explores the city from its Roman roots to its swinging '60s heyday. Piet Schreuders's *The Beatles' London* follows the footsteps of the Fab Four.

That noted, there are books galore on the various facets of the city. *The Art and Architecture of London*, by Ann Saunders, is fairly comprehensive. *Inside London: Discovering the Classic Interiors of London*, by Joe Friedman and Peter Aprahamian, has magnificent color photographs of hidden and overlooked shops, clubs, and town houses. For a wonderful take on the golden age of the city's regal mansions, see Christopher Simon Sykes's *Private Palaces: Life in the Great London Houses*. For various other aspects of the city, consult Mervyn Blatch's helpful *A Guide to London's Churches*, Andrew Crowe's *The Parks and Woodlands of London*, Sheila Fairfield's *The Streets of London*, Ann Saunders's *Regent's Park*, Ian Norrie's *Hampstead, Highgate Village, and Kenwood*, and Suzanne Ebel's *A Guide to London's Riverside: Hampton Court to Greenwich*. For keen walkers, there are two books by Andrew Duncan: *Secret London* and *Walking Village London*. *City Secrets: London*, edited by Robert Kahn, is a handsome book of anecdotes from London writers, artists, and historians about their favorite places in the city. For the last word on just about every subject, see *The London Encyclopaedia*, edited by Ben Weinreb and Christopher Hibbert. HarperCollins's *London Photographic Atlas* has a plethora of bird's-eye images of the capital. For an alternative view of the city, it would be hard to better Iain Sinclair's witty and intelligent *London Orbital: A Walk Around the M25* in which he scrutinizes the history, mythology, and politics of London from the viewpoint of its ugly ring road. Sinclair is also the editor of *London: City of Disappearances*, an anthology exploring what has vanished.

Of course, the history and spirit of the city are also to be found in celebrations of great authors, British heroes, and architects. Peter Ackroyd's massive *Dickens* elucidates how the great author shaped today's view of the city; Martin Gilbert's magisterial, multivolume *Churchill* traces the city through some of its greatest trials; J. Mansbridge's *John Nash* details the London buildings of this great architect. Liza Picard evokes mid-18th-century London in *Dr. Johnson's London*. For musical theater buffs, Mike Leigh's *Gilbert and Sullivan's London* takes a romantic look at the two artists' lives and times in the capital's grand theaters and wild nightspots. *Rodinsky's Room*, by Rachel Lichtenstein and Iain Sinclair, is a fascinating exploration of East End Jewish London and the mysterious disappearance of one of its occupants.

Maureen Waller's *1700: Scenes from London Life* is a fascinating look at the daily life of Londoners in the 18th century. Nineteenth-century London—the city of Queen Victoria, Tennyson, and Dickens—comes alive through *Mayhew's London*, a massive study of the London poor by Henry Mayhew, and Gustave Doré's *London*, an unforgettable series of engravings of the city (often reprinted in modern editions) that detail its horrifying slums and grand avenues. When it comes to fiction, of course, Dickens's immortal works top the list. Stay-at-home detectives have long walked the streets of London, thanks to great mysteries by Dorothy L. Sayers, Agatha Christie, Ngaio Marsh, and Antonia Fraser. Cops and bad guys wind their way around 1960s London in Jake Arnott's pulp fiction books, *The Long Firm* and *He Kills Coppers*. Martin Amis's *London Fields* tracks a murder mystery through West London. For so-called "tart noir," pick up any Stella Duffy book. Marie Belloc-Lowndes's *The Lodger* is a fictional account of London's most deadly villain, Jack the Ripper. Victorian London was never so salacious as in Sarah Waters's story of a young girl who travels the theaters as a singer, the Soho squares as a male prostitute, and the East End as a communist in *Tipping the Velvet*. Late-20th-century London, with its diverse ethnic makeup, is the star of Zadie Smith's famed novel *White Teeth*. The vibrancy and cultural diversity of London's East End come to life in Monica Ali's *Brick Lane*.

London in Film

Many films—from *Waterloo Bridge* and *Georgy Girl* to *Secrets and Lies* and *Notting Hill*—have used London as their setting. The great musicals Walt Disney's *Mary Poppins*, George Cukor's *My Fair Lady,* and Sir Carol Reed's *Oliver!* evoke the Hollywood soundstage version of London.

Children of all ages enjoy Stephen Herek's *101 Dalmatians*, with Glenn Close as fashion-savvy Cruella de Vil. King's Cross Station in London was shot to cinematic fame by the movie version of J.K. Rowling's *Harry Potter and the Philosopher's Stone*. Look for cameos by the city in all other *Harry Potter* films.

The swinging '60s are loosely portrayed in M. Jay Roach's *Austin Powers: International Man of Mystery*, full of references to British slang and some great opening scenes in London. For a truer picture of the '60s in London, Michelangelo Antonioni weaves a mystery plot

around the world of a London fashion photographer in *Blow-Up*. British gangster films came into their own with Guy Ritchie's amusing tales of London thieves in *Lock, Stock, and Two Smoking Barrels,* filmed almost entirely in London, and the follow-up *Snatch*. More sobering portraits of London criminal life include Neil Jordan's *Mona Lisa*, Paul McGuigan's *Gangster No. 1*, and John Mackenzie's *The Long Good Friday*. Of course, the original tough guy is 007, and his best exploits in London are featured in the introductory chase scene in *The World Is Not Enough*.

Sir Arthur Conan Doyle knew the potential of London as a chilling setting, and John Landis's *An American Werewolf in London* and Hitchcock's *39 Steps* and *The Man Who Knew Too Much* exploit the Gothic and sinister qualities of the city. For a fascinating look at Renaissance London, watch John Madden's *Shakespeare in Love*. Dickens's London is indelibly depicted in David Lean's *Oliver Twist*.

Some modern-day romantic comedies that use London as a backdrop are Peter Howitt's *Sliding Doors* with Gwyneth Paltrow and the screen adaptations of Helen Fielding's *Bridget Jones's Diary* (and its sequel), starring Renée Zellweger, Hugh Grant, and Colin Firth. Glossy London is depicted in Woody Allen's *Match Point,* bohemian London in David Kane's *This Year's Love,* gritty London in Shane Meadow's *Somers Town,* and post-zombie London in Danny Boyle's *28 Days Later,* while Patrick Kellior's *London* offers a uniquely informed, idiosyncratic view of the city.

TRAVEL SMART
LONDON

GETTING HERE AND AROUND

Central London and its surrounding districts are divided into 32 boroughs—33, counting the City of London. More useful for finding your way around, however, are the subdivisions of London into postal districts. Throughout the guide we've given the full postal code for most listings. The first one or two letters give the location: N means north, NW means northwest, and so on. Don't expect the numbering to be logical, however. You won't, for example, find W2 next to W3. The general rule is that the lower numbers, such as W1 or SW1, are closest to Buckingham Palace, but it is not consistent—SE17 is closer to the city center than E4, for example.

■ AIR TRAVEL

Flying time to London is about 6½ hours from New York, 7½ hours from Chicago, 11 hours from San Francisco, and 21½ hours from Sydney.

For flights out of London, the general rule is that you should be at the airport at least one hour before your scheduled departure time for domestic flights and two hours before international flights for off-peak travel.

Airline Security Issues Transportation Security Administration. ☎ 866/289-9673 ⊕ www.tsa.gov.

AIRPORTS

Most international flights to London arrive at either Heathrow Airport (LHR), 15 miles west of London, or at Gatwick Airport (LGW), 27 miles south of the capital. Most flights from the United States go to Heathrow, which is divided into five terminals, with Terminals 3, 4, and 5 handling transatlantic flights. Gatwick is London's second gateway. It has grown from a European airport into an airport that also serves dozens of U.S. destinations. A third airport, Stansted (STN), is 35 miles northeast of the city; it handles European and domestic traffic. Three

smaller airports, Luton (LTN), 30 miles north of town, Southend (SEN), 40 miles to the east, and business-oriented London City (in East London E16) mainly handle flights to Europe.

Airport Information Gatwick Airport. ☎ 0844/892-0322 ⊕ www.gatwickairport.com. **Heathrow Airport.** ☎ 0844/335-1801 ⊕ www.heathrowairport.com. **London City Airport.** ☎ 020/7646-0088 ⊕ www.londoncityairport.com. **Luton Airport.** ☎ 01582/405-100 ⊕ www.london-luton.co.uk. **Southend Airport.** ☎ 01702/538-500 ⊕ www.southendairport.com. **Stansted Airport.** ☎ 0844/355-1803 ⊕ www.stanstedairport.com.

GROUND TRANSPORTATION

London has excellent if pricey bus and train connections between its airports and central London. If you're arriving at Heathrow, you can pick up a map and fare schedule at the Transport for London (TfL) Information Centre, located in the Underground station serving Terminals 1, 2, and 3. Train service can be quick, but the downside (for trains from all airports) is that you must get yourself and your luggage to the train via a series of escalators and connecting trams. Airport link buses (generally National Express Airport buses) may ease the luggage factor and drop you closer to central hotels, but they're subject to London traffic, which can be horrendous and make the trip drag on for hours. Taxis can be more convenient than buses, but beware that prices can go through the roof. Airport Travel Line has additional transfer information and takes advance booking for transfers between airports and into London.

FROM HEATHROW TO CENTRAL LONDON		
TRAVEL MODE	TIME	COST
Taxi	1 hour+	£45–£70 (depending on traffic)+
Heathrow Express Train	15 minutes	£21 (£34 round-trip) and £29 for first class
Underground	50 minutes	£5.70 one-way (less with Oyster card)
National Express Bus	1 hour	From £5.50 one-way
Hotel by Bus	1 hour+	£22.50 one-way

Heathrow by Bus: National Express buses take one hour to reach the city center (Victoria) and cost from £5.50 one-way and £11 round-trip (book online for best prices). The National Express Hotel Hoppa service runs from all airports to around 20 hotels near the airport (from £4.50). Alternatively, nearly every hotel in London itself is served by the Hotel By Bus service. Fares to central London average around £22.50. SkyShuttle also offers a shared minibus service between Heathrow and any London hotel. The N9 night bus runs to Aldwych every 20 minutes from midnight to 5 am; it takes an hour and costs £2.40.

Heathrow by Train: The cheap, direct route into London is via the Piccadilly line of the Underground (London's extensive subway system, or "Tube"). Trains normally run every four to eight minutes from all terminals from early morning until just before midnight. The 50-minute trip into central London costs £5.70 one-way and connects with other central Tube lines. The Heathrow Express train is comfortable and convenient, if costly, speeding into London's Paddington station in 15 minutes. Standard one-way tickets cost £21 (£34 round-trip) and £29

NAVIGATING LONDON

London is a confusing city to navigate, even for people who've visited it a few times. Its streets are arranged in medieval patterns that no longer make much sense, meaning that you can't always use logic to find your way around. A good map is essential, and public transportation can be a lifesaver: buses will take you magically from point A to point B, and the Tube is often the quickest way to reach your destination. Here are some basic tips to help you find your way around.

■ Although free tourist maps can be handy, they're usually quite basic and include only major streets. If you're going to be doing lots of wandering around, buy the pocket-size map book *London A–Z*, which is sold in bookstores and Tube and train stations throughout the city. Its detailed maps are invaluable.

■ To find your way, look for tall landmarks near where you are headed: the London Eye, for example, or the cross atop St. Paul's Cathedral—or the most obvious of all, Big Ben.

■ If you get properly lost, the best people to ask are the Londoners hustling by you, who know the area like nobody else. The worst people to ask are the people working in souvenir kiosks, and street vendors handing out the local *Evening Standard* newspaper; they're famously rude and unhelpful to lost tourists.

■ The tourist hubs of Soho, Covent Garden, Leicester Square, and Trafalgar Square are separated from one another by only a few blocks. Taking the Tube from one to another actually takes longer than walking.

■ On the other hand, when you're lost, the Tube is often the shortest distance between two points. Don't hesitate to use it.

for first class. Book ahead (online is the cheapest option; at a counter/kiosk less so), as tickets are more expensive to buy on board. There's daily service from 5:10 am (6:25 am on Sunday) to 11:25 pm, with departures every 15 minutes. The Heathrow Connect service leaves from Paddington station and makes five local stops before arriving at Terminals 1, 3, and 5. It takes 25 minutes, only a little more time than the Express, though trains are less frequent (two an hour in peak times). One-way tickets are £9.90.

Gatwick by Bus: An hourly bus service runs from Gatwick's north and south terminals to London's Victoria station, with stops at Hooley, Coulsdon, Mitcham, Streatham, Stockwell, and Pimlico. The journey takes upward of 90 minutes (depending on time of day) and costs from £10 one-way. The easyBus service runs to West London (Earl's Court) or Waterloo from as little as £2; the later the ticket is booked online, the higher the price (up to £10 on board).

Gatwick by Train: The fast, nonstop Gatwick Express leaves for Victoria station every 15 minutes 4:35 am–1:35 am. The 30-minute trip costs £19.90 one-way, and £34.90 round-trip, though cheaper tickets are available online. The Thameslink Great Northern rail company runs nonexpress services that are cheaper; Thameslink train runs regularly throughout the day to St. Pancras International, London Bridge, and Blackfriars stations; departures are every 15 minutes (hourly during the night), and the journey takes 45–55 minutes. Tickets are from £10 one-way to St. Pancras International. FlyBy service to Victoria (£15 single) is not express, taking almost an hour, and the fare applies only on trains operated by Southern Trains.

Stansted by Bus: Hourly service on National Express Airport bus A6 (24 hours a day) to Victoria Coach station costs from £12 one-way, £19 round-trip, and takes about 1 hour and 40 minutes. Stops include Golders Green, Finchley Road, St. John's Wood, Baker Street, Marble Arch, and Hyde Park Corner. The easyBus service to Victoria via Baker Street costs from £2 one-way, but book early and online for best prices.

Stansted by Train: The Stansted Express to Liverpool Street station (with a stop at Tottenham Hale) runs daily every 15 minutes, from 5:30 am to 12:30 am. The 50-minute trip costs £23.40 one-way, £33.20 round-trip if booked online. Tickets cost more when purchased on board.

Luton by Bus and Train: An airport shuttle runs from Luton Airport to the nearby Luton Airport Parkway station, from which you can take a train or bus into London (this shuttle is free if you have bought a rail ticket in advance; otherwise it's £1.60 one-way). From there, the Thameslink Great Northern train service runs to St. Pancras, Farringdon, Blackfriars, and London Bridge. The journey takes about 35 minutes. Trains leave every 10 minutes or so during the day, and hourly during the night. Single tickets cost from £9 one-way, if booked in advance. The Green Line 757 bus service from Luton to Victoria station runs three times an hour, takes about 90 minutes, and costs from £8 one-way, if booked in advance.

Heathrow, Gatwick, Stansted, and Luton by Taxi: This is an expensive and time-consuming option. The city's congestion charge (£10) may be added to the bill if your hotel is in the charging zone, you run the risk of getting stuck in traffic, and if you take a taxi from the stand, the price will be even more expensive (whereas a minicab booked ahead is a set price). The trip from Heathrow, for example, can take more than an hour and can cost more than £55.

TRANSFERS BETWEEN AIRPORTS

Allow at least two to three hours for an inter-airport transfer. The cheapest option—but most complicated—is public transportation: from Gatwick to Stansted, for instance, you can catch the nonexpress commuter train from Gatwick to Victoria station, take the Tube to Liverpool Street station, then catch the train to Stansted from there. To get from Heathrow to Gatwick by public transport, take the Tube to King's Cross, then change to the Victoria line, get to Victoria station, and then take the commuter train to Gatwick.

The National Express Airport bus is the most direct option between Gatwick and Heathrow. Buses pick up passengers every 15 to 20 minutes from 5:35 am to midnight from both airports. The trip takes around 70 minutes, and the fare is from £25 one-way, but it's advisable to book tickets in advance. National Express buses between Stansted and Gatwick depart every 30 to 45 minutes and can take around 3 hours and 45 minutes. The adult one-way fare is from £22. Some airlines may offer shuttle services as well—check with your travel agent in advance of your journey.

Contacts easyBus. ⊕ www.easybus.co.uk. **Gatwick Express.** ☎ 0345/850–1530 ⊕ www.gatwickexpress.com. **Heathrow Express.** ☎ 0345/600–1515 ⊕ www.heathrowexpress.com. **National Express.** ☎ 08717/818–178 ⊕ www.nationalexpress.com. **SkyShuttle.** ☎ 0845/481–0960 ⊕ www.skyshuttle.co.uk. **Stansted Express.** ☎ 0345/600–7245 ⊕ www.stanstedexpress.com. **Thameslink Great Northern.** ☎ 0345/026–4700 ⊕ www.thameslinkrailway.com.

Transfer Information Airport Travel Line. ☎ 0871/200–2233 ⊕ www.travelline.co.uk.

FLIGHTS

British Airways is the national flagship carrier and offers mostly nonstop flights from 16 U.S. cities to Heathrow and Gatwick airports, along with flights to Manchester, Birmingham, and Glasgow. It also offers flights to New York from London City Airport near Docklands.

Airline Contacts American Airlines. ☎ 207/660–2300, 0844/369–9899 in London ⊕ www.aa.com. **British Airways.** ☎ 0344/493–0787, 0844/493–0787 in London ⊕ www.britishairways.com. **Delta Airlines.** ☎ 800/241–4141 for international reservations, 207/660–0767 in London ⊕ www.delta.

com. **United Airlines.** ☎ 800/864–8331 for international reservations, 0845/607–6760 in London ⊕ www.united.com. **US Airways.** ☎ 800/428–4322 for international reservations, 0845/600–3300 in London ⊕ www.usairways.com. **Virgin Atlantic.** ☎ 800/862–8621, 0344/209–7777 in London ⊕ www.virgin-atlantic.com.

▌ BIKE TRAVEL

London's mayor, Boris Johnson, is a real cycling enthusiast and keen to make the capital more bike-friendly. A 24-hour bike-rental program, currently called Barclays Cycle Hire but with a new sponsor set to be announced in 2015, enables Londoners to pick up a "Boris bike" at one of more than 700 docking stations and return it at another. The first 30 minutes are free. After that, charges rise incrementally from £1 for one hour up to £50 for the entire 24 hours. There is also a £2-per-day access charge. Fees are payable online, by phone, or at docking stations, by credit or debit cards only—cash is not accepted. To sign up, a user goes to the TfL (Transport for London) website and then receives a bike key in the mail, so this very popular system is really only practical for locals, not most tourists.

▌ BUS TRAVEL

ARRIVING AND DEPARTING

National Express is the biggest British long-distance bus operator and the nearest equivalent to Greyhound. It's not as fast as traveling by train, but it's comfortable (with bathrooms on board). Services depart mainly from Victoria Coach station, a well-signposted short walk behind the Victoria mainline train station. The departures point is on the corner of Buckingham Palace Road; this is also the main information point. The arrivals point is opposite, at Elizabeth Bridge. National Express buses travel to all large and midsize cities in southern England and the midlands. Scotland and the north are not as well served. The station is extremely busy around holidays and weekends. Arrive at least 30 minutes before departure so you can find the correct exit gate. Smoking is not permitted on board.

Another bus company, Megabus, offers cross-country fares for as little as £1 per person. The company's single- and double-decker buses serve an extensive array of cities across Great Britain with a cheerful budget attitude. In London, buses for all destinations depart from the Green Line bus stand at Victoria station. Megabus does not accommodate wheelchairs, and the company strictly limits luggage to one piece per person checked, and one piece of hand luggage.

Green Line serves the counties surrounding London, as well as airports. Bus stops (there's no central bus station) are on Buckingham Palace Road, between the Victoria train station and Victoria Coach station.

Tickets on many long-distance routes are cheaper if purchased in advance, and traveling midweek costs less than over weekends and at holiday periods.

GETTING AROUND LONDON

Private, as opposed to municipal, buses are known as coaches. Although London is famous for its double-decker buses, the old beloved rattletrap Routemasters, with the jump-on/off back platforms, now only serves a single "heritage" route: the No. 15 travels from Trafalgar Square down Fleet Street and on to St. Paul's Cathedral. That said, a modernized Routemaster has taken to the streets in recent times.

Bus stops are clearly indicated; signs at bus stops feature a red TfL symbol on a plain white background. You must flag the bus down at some stops. Each numbered route is listed on the main stop, and buses have a large number on the front with their end destination. Not all buses run the full route at all times; check with the driver to be sure. You can pick up a free bus guide at a TfL Travel Information Centre (at Euston, Liverpool Street,

Piccadilly Circus, King's Cross, and Victoria Tube stations; and at Heathrow Airport).

Buses are a good way of seeing the town, particularly if you plan to hop on and off to cover many sights, but don't take a bus if you're in a hurry, as traffic can really slow them down. To get off, press the red "Stop" buttons mounted on poles near the doors. You will usually see a "Bus Stopping" sign light up. Expect to get sardined during rush hour, from 8 am to 9:30 am and 4:30 pm to 6:30 pm.

Night buses, denoted by an "N" before their route numbers, run from midnight to 5 am on a more restricted route than day buses. However, some night-bus routes should be approached with caution, and the top deck avoided (the danger is that muggings are most likely to occur there, since it's farthest from both the exit doors and the drivers). All night buses run by request stop, so flag them down if you're waiting or push the button if you want to alight.

All London buses are now cash-free, which means you must buy your ticket *before* you board the bus. Ticket machines are located at most bus stops, but they can be the most expensive option: tickets bought here cost £2.40 for all journeys, as opposed to £1.45 if you pay by prepaid Oyster card or a "contactless" payment card. Visitor Oyster cards cost £3, but must be purchased either before you arrive or at London's Standsted airport. Normal Oyster cards, which cost £5, are available from ticket desks at all major airports or at any Tube station and are transferable if you have money left over. Contactless cards are meant to be the future of London travel: you place a compatible debit or credit card near a bus or Tube-station's reader reader, and the fare is automatically debited from your bank account.

An alternative is to buy a one- or seven-day Travelcard, which is good for both Tube and bus travel. Travelcards can be bought at Tube stations, travel information centers, and some newsagents, However, note that seven-day Travelcards bought in London *must be loaded onto an Oyster card*. Although using a Travelcard may save you some money, it might be easier to just add additional money to your Oyster card as needed, since there are machines at all Tube stations and at lots of London newsagents. A seven-day paper Travelcard can only be purchased in advance, online. However you buy your ticket, just make sure you have one: traveling without a valid ticket makes you liable for a significant fine (£80). Buses are supposed to swing by most stops every five or six minutes, but in reality, you can often expect to wait a bit longer, although those in the city center are quite reliable.

Bus Information easyBus. ⊕ www.easybus. co.uk. **Green Line.** ☎ 0844/801–7261 ⊕ www. greenline.co.uk. **Megabus.** ☎ 0900/160–0900 ⊕ www.megabus.com. **National Express.** ☎ 08717/818–178 ⊕ www.nationalexpress. com. **Transport for London.** ☎ 0343/222–1234 ⊕ www.tfl.gov.uk. **Victoria Coach Station.** ☎ 0343/222–1234.

▌ CAR TRAVEL

The best advice on driving in London is this: don't. London's streets are a winding mass of chaos, made worse by one-way roads. Parking is also restrictive and expensive, and traffic is tediously slow at most times of the day; during rush hours—from 8 am to 9:30 am and 4:30 pm to 6:30 pm—it often grinds to a standstill, particularly on Friday, when everyone wants to leave town. Avoid city-center shopping areas, including the roads feeding Oxford Street, Kensington, and Knightsbridge. Other main roads into the city center are also busy, such as King's Cross and Euston in the north. Watch out also for cyclists and motorcycle couriers, who weave between cars and pedestrians that seem to come out of nowhere, and you may get a heavy fine for straying into

a bus lane during its operating hours—check the signs.

If you are staying in London for the duration of your trip, there's virtually no reason to rent a car, because the city and its suburbs are widely covered by public transportation. However, you might want a car for day trips to castles or stately homes out in the countryside. Consider renting your car in a medium-size town in the area where you'll be traveling, and then journeying there by train and picking up the car once you arrive. Rental rates are generally reasonable, and insurance costs are lower than in comparable U.S. cities. Rates generally begin at £25 a day for a small economy car (such as a subcompact General Motors Vauxhall Corsa, or Renault Clio), usually with manual transmission. Air-conditioning and unlimited mileage generally come with the larger-size automatic cars.

In London your U.S. driver's license is acceptable (as long as you are over 23 years old, with no driving convictions). If you have a driver's license in a country other than the United States, it may not be recognized in the United Kingdom. An International Driver's Permit is a good idea no matter what; it's available from the American (AAA) or Canadian (CAA) Automobile Association and, in the United Kingdom, from the Automobile Association (AA) or Royal Automobile Club (RAC). International permits are universally recognized, and having one may save you a problem with the local authorities.

Remember that Britain drives on the left, and the rest of Europe on the right. Therefore, you may want to leave your rented car in Britain and pick up a left-side drive if you cross the Channel.

CONGESTION CHARGE

Designed to reduce traffic through central London, a congestion charge has been instituted. Vehicles (with some exemptions) entering central London on weekdays from 7 am to 6 pm (excluding public holidays) have to pay a £11.50 daily fee; it can be paid up to 90 days in advance, or on the day of travel, or on the following "charging day," when the fee goes up to £14. Day-, month-, and yearlong passes are available on the Congestion Charging page of the Transport for London website, at gas stations, parking lots (car parks), by mail, by phone, and by SMS text message. One day's payment is good for all access into the charging zone on that day. Traffic signs designate the entrance to congestion areas, and cameras read car license plates and send the information to a database. Drivers who don't pay the congestion charge by midnight of the next charging day following the day of driving are penalized £130, which is reduced to £65 if paid within 14 days.

Information Congestion Charge Customer Service. ☎ 0343/222–2222 in UK, 0044 207/649–9122 outside UK ⊕ www.cclondon. com. **Transport for London.** ☎ 0343/222–1234 ⊕ www.tfl.gov.uk.

GASOLINE

Gasoline (petrol) is sold in liters and is expensive (at this writing about £1.27 per liter—around $7.50 per gallon). Unleaded petrol, denoted by green pump lines, is predominant. Premium and Super Premium are the two varieties, and most cars run on regular Premium. Supermarket pumps usually offer the best value. You won't find many service stations in the center of town; these are generally on main, multilane trunk roads out of the center. Service is self-serve, except in small villages, where gas stations are likely to be closed on Sunday and late evening. Most stations accept major credit cards.

PARKING

During the day—and probably at all times—it's safest to believe that you can park nowhere except at a meter, in a pay-and-display bay, or in a garage; otherwise, you run the risk of an expensive ticket, plus possibly even more expensive clamping and towing fees (some boroughs are clamp-free). Restrictions are indicated by the "No Waiting" parking signpost on the sidewalk (these restrictions vary from street to street), and restricted areas include single yellow lines or double yellow lines, and Residents' Parking bays. Parking at a bus stop is prohibited; parking in bus lanes, restricted. On Red Routes, indicated by red lines, you are not allowed to park or even stop. It's illegal to park on the sidewalk, across entrances, or on white zigzag lines approaching a pedestrian crossing.

Meters have an insatiable hunger in the inner city—a 20p coin may buy just three minutes—and some will permit only a maximum two-hour stay. Meters take 20p and £1 coins, pay-and-display machines 10p, 20p, 50p, £1, and £2 coins. Some take payment by credit card. In some parts of central London, meters have been almost entirely replaced by pay-and-display machines that require payment by cell phone. You will need to set up an account to do this (⊕ www.westminster. gov.uk). Meter parking is free after 6:30 or 8:30 in the evening, on Sunday, and on holidays. Always check the sign. In the evening, after restrictions end, meter bays are free. After meters are free, you can also park on single yellow lines—but not double yellow lines. In the daytime, take advantage of the many NCP parking lots in the center of town (from about £8 per hour, up to six hours).

Information NCP. ☎ 0345/050–7080 ⊕ www. ncp.co.uk.

ROADSIDE EMERGENCIES

If your car is stolen, you're in a car accident, or your car breaks down and there's nobody around to help you, contact the police by dialing 999.

The general procedure for a breakdown is the following: position the red hazard triangle (which should be in the trunk of the car) a few paces away from the rear of the car. Leave the hazard warning lights on. Along highways (motorways), emergency roadside telephone booths are positioned at intervals within walking distance. Contact the car-rental company or an auto club. The main auto clubs in the United Kingdom are the Automobile Association (AA) and the RAC. If you're a member of the American Automobile Association (AAA), check your membership details before you depart for Britain, as, under a reciprocal agreement, roadside assistance in the United Kingdom should cost you nothing. You can join and receive roadside assistance from the AA on the spot, but the charge is higher—around £95—than a simple membership fee.

Emergency Services American Automobile Association. ☎ *800/564–6222* ⊕ *www.aaa. com.* **Automobile Association.** ☎ *0800/085– 2721, 161/333–0004 from outside the U.K., 0800/887–766 for emergency roadside assistance from cell phones* ⊕ *www.theaa. com.* **RAC.** ☎ *0800/828–282 for emergency roadside assistance, 0333/200–0999 for emergency roadside assistance* ⊕ *www.rac. co.uk.*

RULES OF THE ROAD

London is a mass of narrow, one-way roads, and narrow, two-way streets that are no bigger than the one-way roads. If you must risk life and limb and drive in London, note that the speed limit is either 20 or 30 mph—unless you see the large 40 mph signs found only in the suburbs. Speed bumps are sprinkled about with abandon in case you forget. Speed is strictly controlled and cameras, mounted on occasional lampposts, photograph speeders for ticketing.

Medium-size circular intersections are often designed as "roundabouts" (marked by signs in which three curved arrows form a circle). On these, cars travel left in a circle and incoming cars must yield to those already on their way around from the right. Signal when about to leave the roundabout.

Jaywalking is not illegal in London and everybody does it, despite the fact that striped crossings with blinking yellow lights mounted on poles at either end—called "zebra crossings"—give pedestrians the right-of-way to cross. Cars should treat zebra crossings like stop signs if a pedestrian is waiting to cross or already starting to cross. It's illegal to pass another vehicle at a zebra crossing. At other crossings (including intersections) pedestrians must yield to traffic, but they do have the right-of-way over traffic turning left at controlled crossings—if they have the nerve.

Traffic lights sometimes have arrows directing left or right turns; try to catch a glimpse of the road markings in time, and don't get into the turn lane if you mean to go straight ahead. Turning on a red light is not permitted. Signs at the beginning and end of designated bus lanes give the time restrictions for use (usually during peak hours); if you're caught driving on bus lanes during restricted hours, you will be fined. By law, seat belts must be worn in the front and back seats. Drunk-driving laws are strictly enforced, and it's safest to avoid alcohol altogether if you'll be driving. The legal limit is 80 milligrams of alcohol per 100 milliliters of blood, which roughly translated means two units of alcohol—two small glasses of wine, one pint of beer, or one glass of whiskey.

▌ DLR: DOCKLANDS LIGHT RAILWAY

For reaching destinations in East London, the quiet, driverless Docklands Light Railway (DLR) is a good alternative, with interesting views of the area.

The DLR connects with the Tube network at Bank and Tower Hill stations as well as at Canary Wharf. It goes to London City Airport, the Docklands financial district, and Greenwich, running 5:30 am–12:30 am Monday–Saturday, 7 am–11:30 pm Sunday. The DLR takes Oyster cards and Travelcards, and fares are the same as those on the Tube. A £17 River Rover ticket (£15.30 if booked online) combines one-day DLR travel with hop-on, hop-off travel on City Cruises riverboats between Westminster, Waterloo, Tower, and Greenwich piers.

Information Transport for London.
☎ *0343/222–1234* ⊕ *www.tfl.gov.uk.*

■ RIVER BUS

One legacy of the 2012 Olympics was a new push to develop river travel as part of London's overall public transportation system. The service now stops at 10 piers between London Eye/Waterloo and Greenwich, with peak-time extensions to Putney in the west and Woolwich Arsenal in the east. The Waterloo-Woolwich commuter service runs 6:30 am–11 pm on weekdays, 9:30 am–midnight on weekends (peak-time frequency: every 20 minutes). Tickets are £6.80, with a one-third discount for Travelcard holders and a 10% discount for Oyster card holders. When there are events at the O2 (North Greenwich Arena), a half-hourly express service runs to and from Waterloo starting three hours before the event. There is also the special Tate to Tate express, a 15-minute trip between Tate Modern and Tate Britain that costs £6.80. Boats run every 40 minutes from 10 am to 5 pm. A £16.50 per day River Roamer ticket offers unlimited river travel after 9 am.

Contacts Thames Clippers. ☎ ⊕ *www. thamesclippers.com.*

■ TAXI

Universally known as "black cabs" (even though many of them now come in other colors), the traditional big black London taxicabs are as much a part of the city's streetscape as red double-decker buses, and for good reason: the unique, spacious taxis easily hold five people, plus luggage. To earn a taxi license, drivers must undergo intensive training on the history and geography of London. The course, and all that the drivers have learned in it, is known simply as "the Knowledge." There's almost nothing your taxi driver won't know about the city. Partly because of lobbying efforts by the black car industry, Uber and similar companies have yet to make significant inroads into the London market.

Hotels and main tourist areas have cabstands (just take the first in line), but you can also flag one down from the roadside. If the orange "For Hire" sign on the top is lighted, the taxi is available. Cabdrivers sometimes cruise at night with their signs unlighted so that they can choose their passengers and avoid those they think might cause trouble. If you see an unlighted, passengerless cab, hail it: you might be lucky.

Fares start at £2.40 and charge by the minute—a journey of a mile (which might take between 6 and 13 minutes) will cost anything from £5.60 to £8.80 (the fare goes up between 10 pm and 6 am—a system designed to persuade more taxi drivers to work at night). A surcharge of £2 is applied to a telephone booking. At Christmas and New Year, there is an additional surcharge of £4. You can, but do not have to, tip taxi drivers 10% of the tab. Usually passengers round up to the nearest pound.

Minicabs, which operate out of small, curbside offices throughout the city, are generally cheaper than black cabs, but are less reliable and less trustworthy. These are usually unmarked passenger cars, and their drivers are often not native Londoners, and do not have to take or pass "the Knowledge" test. Still, Londoners use them in droves because they are plentiful and cheap. If you choose to use them, do not ever take an unlicensed cab: anyone who curb-crawls looking for customers is likely to be unlicensed. Unlicensed cabs have been associated with many crimes and can be dangerous. All cab companies with proper dispatch offices are likely to be licensed. Look for a small purple version of the Underground logo on the front or rear window with "private hire" written across it.

There are plenty of trustworthy and licensed minicab firms. For London-wide service try Lady's and Gent's Mini Cabs, or Addison Lee, which uses comfortable minivans but requires that you know the full postal code for both your pickup location and your destination. When using a minicab, always ask the price in advance when you phone for the car, then verify with the driver before the journey begins.

Black Cabs Dial-a-Cab. ☎ *020/7253–5000 cash bookings, 020/7426–3420 credit/debit card bookings* ⊕ *www.dialacab.co.uk.* **Radio Taxis.** ☎ *020/7272–0272* ⊕ *www.radiotaxis. co.uk.*

Minicabs Addison Lee. ☎ *020/7407–9000* ⊕ *www.addisonlee.com.* **Lady's and Gent's MiniCabs.** ☎ *020/7272–3300* ⊕ *www. ladysandgentsminicabs.com.*

❚ TRAIN TRAVEL

The National Rail Enquiries website is the clearinghouse for information on train times and fares as well as the main place for booking rail journeys around Britain—and the earlier the better. Tickets bought two to three weeks in advance can cost a quarter of the price of tickets bought on the day of travel. However, journeys within commuting distance of city centers are sold at unvarying set prices, and those can be purchased on the day you expect to make your journey without any financial penalty. You may also be able to purchase a PlusBus ticket, which adds unlimited bus travel at your destination. Note that, in busy city centers such as London, all travel costs more during morning rush hour. You can purchase tickets online, by phone, or at any train station in the United Kingdom. Check the website or call the National Rail Enquiries line to get details of the train company responsible for your journey and have them give you a breakdown of available ticket prices. Regardless of which train company is involved, many discount passes are available, such as the 16–25 Railcard (for which you must be under 26 and provide a passport-size photo), the Senior Railcard, and the Family &

Friends Travelcard, which can be bought from most mainline stations. But if you intend to make several long-distance rail journeys, it can be a good idea to invest in a BritRail Pass (which you must buy in the United States).

You can get a BritRail Pass valid for London and the surrounding counties, for England, for Scotland, or for all of Britain. Discounts (usually 20%–25%) are offered if you're between 16 and 25, over 60, traveling as a family or a group, or accompanied by a British citizen. The pass includes discounts on the Heathrow Express and Eurostar. BritRail Passes come in two basic varieties. The Classic pass allows travel on consecutive days, and the FlexiPass allows a number of travel days within a set period of time. The cost (in U.S. dollars) of a BritRail Consecutive Pass adult ticket for 8 days is $409 standard and $615 first class; for 15 days, $615 and $919; and for 22 days, $775 and $1,165. The cost of a BritRail FlexiPass adult ticket for 4 days' travel in two months is $365 standard and $539 first class; for 8 days' travel in two months, $525 and $785; and for 15 days' travel in two months, $795 and $1,179. Prices drop by about 25% for off-peak travel passes between November and February.

Most long-distance trains have refreshment carriages, called buffet cars. Most trains these days also have "quiet cars" where the use of mobile phones and music devices is banned. Smoking is forbidden in all railcars.

Generally speaking, rail travel in the United Kingdom is expensive and the ticketing system unnecessarily convoluted: for instance, a round-trip ticket to Bath from London can cost more than £150 per person at peak times, although for an off-peak ticket purchased far enough in advance, that fee can drop to £20 or even less. It's best to avoid the frantic business commuter rush (before 9:30 am and 4:30 pm–7 pm). Credit cards are accepted for train fares paid in person, by phone, and online.

Delays are not uncommon, but they're rarely long. You almost always have to go to the station to find out if there's going to be one (because delays tend to happen at the last minute). Luckily, most stations have coffee shops, restaurants, and pubs where you can cool your heels while you wait for the train to get rolling. National Rail Enquiries provides an up-to-date state-of-the-railroads schedule.

Most of the time, first-class train travel in England isn't particularly first class. Some train companies don't offer at-seat service, so you still have to get up and go to the buffet car for food or drinks. First class is generally booked by business travelers on expense accounts because crying babies and noisy families are quite rare in first class and quite common in standard class.

Short of flying, taking the Eurostar train through the Channel Tunnel is the fastest way to reach the continent: it's 2 hours and 15 minutes from London's St. Pancras International station to Paris's Gare du Nord. You can also go from St. Pancras to Midi station in Brussels in around two hours. If purchased in advance, round-trip tickets from London to Belgium or France cost from as little as £69, especially if you travel in the very early or very late hours of the day. If you want to bring your car over to France (if it's a rental, ask the rental company if this is permitted), you can use the Eurotunnel Shuttle, which takes 35 minutes from Folkestone to Calais, plus at least 30 minutes to check in. The Belgian border is just a short drive northeast of Calais.

Information BritRail Travel. ☎ *866/938–7245 in U.S. and Canada* ⊕ *www.britrail.com.* **Eurostar.** ☎ *03432/186–186, 1233/617–575 outside U.K.* ⊕ *www.eurostar.com.* **National Rail Enquiries.** ☎ *0845/748–4950* ⊕ *www. nationalrail.co.uk.*

Channel Tunnel Car Transport
Eurotunnel. ☎ *0844/335–3535 in U.K.,*

+33/3-21-00-20-61 from outside Europe ⊕ *www.eurotunnel.com.*

▮ UNDERGROUND TRAVEL: THE TUBE

London's extensive Underground train (Tube) system has color-coded routes, clear signage, and many connections. Trains run out into the suburbs, and all stations are marked with the London Underground circular symbol. (Do not be confused by similar-looking signs reading "subway" this is British for "pedestrian underpass.") Trains are all one class; smoking isn't allowed on board or in the stations. There is also an Overground network serving the farther reaches of Inner London. These now accept Oyster cards.

Some lines have multiple branches (Central, District, Northern, Metropolitan, and Piccadilly), so be sure to note which branch is needed for your particular destination. Do this by noting the end destination on the lighted sign on the platform, which also tells you how long you'll have to wait until the train arrives. Compare that with the end destination of the branch you want. When the two match, that's your train.

London is divided into six concentric zones (ask at Underground ticket booths for a map and booklet, which give details of the ticket options), so be sure to buy a ticket for the correct zone or you may be liable for an on-the-spot fine of £80. Don't panic if you do forget to buy a ticket for the right zone: just tell a station attendant that you need to buy an "extension" to your ticket. Although you're meant to do that in advance, if you're an out-of-towner, they generally don't give you a hard time.

For one-way fares paid in cash, a flat £4.70 price per journey now applies across all central zones (1–2), whether you're traveling 1 stop or 12 stops. If you're planning several trips in one day, it's much cheaper to buy a visitor Oyster card or even a Travelcard, which is good for unrestricted travel on the Tube, buses, and some Overground railroads for the day. The off-peak Oyster-card fare for Zones 1–2, for example, is £2.20. An Off-Peak one-day Travelcard for Zones 1–2 costs £8.90. The more zones included in your travel, the more the Travelcard will cost. For example, Kew is Zone 4, and Heathrow is Zone 6. If you're going to be in town for several days, buy a seven-day Travelcard (£31.40 for Zones 1–2, £57.20 for Zones 1–6). Children 11–15 can travel at discounted rates on the Tube and free on buses and trams with an Oyster photocard (order at least four weeks before date of travel), while children under 11 travel free on the Tube if accompanied by an adult or with an Oyster photocard and on buses at all times. Young people 16–18 and students over 18 get discounted Tube fares with an Oyster photocard.

Oyster cards are "smart cards" that can be charged with a cash value and then used for discounted travel throughout the city. A Visitor Oyster card, which you must buy before arriving in the United Kingdom, costs £3. Normal Oyster cards cost £5. Each time you take the Tube or bus, you place the blue card on the yellow readers at the entrance and the amount of your fare is deducted. Passengers using Oyster cards pay lower rates. Oyster-card Tube fares start at £1.60 and go up depending on the number of zones you're covering, time of day, and whether you're traveling into Zone 1. You can open an Oyster account online or pick up an Oyster card at any London Underground station, and then prepay any amount you wish for your expected travel while in the city. Using an Oyster card, bus fares are £1.45 instead of £2.40. If you make numerous journeys in a single day, your Oyster card deductions will always be capped: at £6.40 for travel in Zones 1–2 and £7.50 for Zones 1–3.

However, although Oyster cards sound like the way of the future, they will soon be a thing of the past. Starting in 2015, Oyster cards will begin to be gradually phased out and passengers encouraged to move to a system of direct payments using their bank debit or credit cards. In practice, this will mean swiping a "contactless" bank card instead of your Oyster card at ticket barriers.

Starting in late 2015, Tube trains will run for 24 hours a day on weekends on five major lines: Piccadilly, Victoria, Northern, Central, and Jubilee. If successful, this initiative will be expanded to other lines. Until then, the usual timetable will apply on all lines, with trains running from just after 5 am Monday–Saturday, and with the last services leaving central London between midnight and 12:30 am. On Sunday, trains start two hours later and finish about an hour earlier. The frequency of trains depends on the route and the time of day, but normally you should not have to wait more than 10 minutes in central areas.

There are TfL Travel Information Centres at the following Tube stations: Euston and Liverpool Street (open 7:15 am–7 pm), Piccadilly Circus (8 am–7 pm), King's Cross and Victoria open 7:15 am–8 pm); and at Heathrow Airport (in Terminals 1, 2, and 3), open 7:30 am–10 pm. New Visitor Information Centres are due to open at Paddington Station and Gatwick airport (North Terminal) in December 2015.

Important note: As with the Metro system in Paris—and unlike the subway system in New York City—you need to have your ticket (Oyster-card, Travelcard, or regular ticket) handy in order to exit the turnstiles of the Tube system, not just to enter them.

Information Transport for London.
☎ *0343/222–1234* ⊕ *www.tfl.gov.uk.*

ESSENTIALS

▌ BUSINESS SERVICES AND FACILITIES

There are several Color Company outlets (formerly known as FedEx Kinko's) and Mail Boxes Etc. locations in London to handle your photocopying, next-day mail, and packaging needs. Check their websites for more locations.

Contacts The Color Company (*FedEx Kinko's*). ☎ *0800/939–493* ⊕ *www.color.co.uk.* **Mail Boxes Etc.** ☎ *020/7224–2666* ⊕ *www. mailboxes-etc.co.uk.*

▌ COMMUNICATIONS

INTERNET

If you're traveling with a laptop, carry a spare battery and adapter: new batteries and replacement adapters are expensive. If you do need to replace them, head to Tottenham Court Road (W1), which is lined with computer specialists. For Macintosh computers, Micro Anvika is a good chain for parts and batteries, and the Apple Stores on Regent Street off Oxford Street and in the Covent Garden Piazza do repairs. John Lewis department store and Selfridges, on Oxford Street (W1), also carry a limited range of computer supplies.

In London, free Wi-Fi is increasingly available in hotels, pubs, coffee shops—even certain branches of McDonald's—and broadband coverage is widespread; generally speaking, the pricier the hotel, the more likely you are to find Wi-Fi there, though it is not usually included in rates.

Contacts Cybercafes. ⊕ *www.cybercafes. com.* **My Hot Spots.** ⊕ *www.myhotspots.co.uk.*

PHONES

The good news is that you can now make a direct-dial telephone call from virtually any point on Earth. The bad news? You can't always do so cheaply. Calling from a hotel is almost always the most expensive option; hotels usually add huge surcharges to all calls, particularly international ones. Calling cards usually keep costs to a minimum, but only if you purchase them locally. And then there are cell phones, which are also likely to be cheaper than calling from your hotel.

The minimum charge from a public phone is 60p for a 120-second call. To make cheap calls it's a good idea to pick up an international phone card, available from newsstands, which can be used from residential, hotel, and public pay phones. With these, you can call the United States for as little as 5p per minute.

To dial from the United States or Canada, first dial 011, then Great Britain's country code, 44. Continue with the local area code, dropping the initial "0." The code for London is 020 (so from abroad you'd dial 20), followed by a 7 for numbers in central London, or an 8 for numbers in the Greater London area. Freephone (toll-free) numbers start with 0800, 0500, or 0808; low-cost national information numbers start with 0845, 0343, or 0844.

A word of warning: 0900 numbers are *not* toll-free numbers; in fact, numbers beginning with this prefix are "premium rate" numbers, and it costs extra to call them. The amount varies and is usually relatively small when dialed from within the country but can be excessive when dialed from outside the United Kingdom.

CALLING WITHIN BRITAIN

There are three types of phones: those that accept (1) only coins, (2) only British Telecom (BT) phone cards, or (3) BT phone cards and credit cards, although with the advent of cells, it's increasingly difficult to find any type of public phone, especially in London.

The coin-operated phones are of the push-button variety; the workings of coin-operated telephones vary, but there are usually instructions on each unit. Most take 10p, 20p, 50p, £1, and £2 coins. Insert the coins *before* dialing (the minimum charge is 60p). If you hear a repeated single tone after dialing, the line is busy; a continual tone means the number is unobtainable (or that you have dialed the wrong—or no—prefix). The indicator panel shows you how much money is left; add more whenever you like. If there is no answer, replace the receiver and your money will be returned.

There are several different directory-assistance providers. For information anywhere in Britain, try dialing 118–888 (59p per call, then £1.29 per minute); you'll need to know the town and the street (or at least the neighborhood) of the person or organization for which you're requesting information. For the operator, dial 100.

You don't have to dial London's central area code (020) if you are calling inside London itself—just the eight-digit telephone number. However, you do need to use it if you're dialing a 0207 (Inner London) number from a 0208 (Outer London) number, and vice versa.

For long-distance calls within Britain, dial the area code (which begins with 01), followed by the number. The area-code prefix is used only when you are dialing from outside the destination. In provincial areas, the dialing codes for nearby towns are often posted in the booth.

CALLING OUTSIDE BRITAIN
For assistance with international calls, dial 155.

To make an international call from London, dial 00, followed by the country code and the local number.

When calling from overseas to access a London telephone number, drop the first 0 from the prefix and dial only 20 (or any other British area code) and then the eight-digit phone number.

The United States country code is 1.

Access Codes AT&T Direct. ☎ *0800/890–011 in U.K., 0500/890–011 in U.K.* **MCI.** ☎ *0800/279–5088 in U.K., 800/888–8000 for*

U.S. and other areas. **Sprint International Access.** ☎ *0808/234–6616 in U.K.*

CALLING CARDS
Public card phones operate either with cash or with special cards that you can buy from post offices or newsstands. Ideal for longer calls, they are composed of units of 10p, and come in values of £5, £10, and more. To use a card phone, lift the receiver, insert your card, and dial the number. An indicator panel shows the number of units used. At the end of your call, the card will be returned. Where credit cards are taken, slide the card through, as indicated.

CELL PHONES
If you have a multiband phone (Britain uses different frequencies from those used in the United States) and your service provider uses the world-standard GSM network (as do T-Mobile, AT&T, and Verizon), you can probably use your phone abroad. Roaming fees can be steep, however: 99¢ a minute is considered reasonable. And overseas you normally pay the toll charges for incoming calls. It's almost always cheaper to send a text message than to make a call, since text messages have a very low set fee (often less than 5¢).

If you just want to make local calls, consider buying a new SIM card (note that your provider may have to unlock your phone for you to use a different SIM card) and a prepaid service plan in London. You'll then have a local number and can make local calls at local rates. If your trip is extensive, you could also simply buy a new cell phone in your destination, as the initial cost will be offset over time.

■TIP→ **If you travel internationally frequently, save one of your old cell phones or buy a cheap one online; ask your cell phone company to unlock it for you, and take it with you as a travel phone, buying a new SIM card with pay-as-you-go service in each destination.**

Any cell phone can be used in Britain if it's tri-band/GSM. Travelers should ask their cell phone company if their phone is tri-band and what network it uses, and make sure it is activated for international calling before leaving their home country.

You can rent a cell phone from most car-rental agencies in London. Some upscale hotels now provide loaner cell phones to their guests. Beware, however, of the per-minute rates charged, as these can be shockingly high.

Contacts **Cellular Abroad.** ☎ *800/287–5072 in U.S., 310/862–7100 International, 800/3623–3333 in U.K.* ⊕ *www.cellularabroad. com.* **Mobal.** ☎ *888/888–9162 in U.S., 01543/426–999 in U.K.* ⊕ *www.mobal.com.* **Planet Fone.** ☎ *888/988–4777* ⊕ *www. planetfone.com.*

∎ CUSTOMS AND DUTIES

You're always allowed to bring goods of a certain value back home without having to pay any duty or import tax. But there's a limit on the amount of tobacco and liquor you can bring back duty-free, and some countries have separate limits for perfumes; for exact figures, check with your customs department. The values of so-called "duty-free" goods are included in these amounts. When you shop abroad, save all your receipts, as customs inspectors may ask to see them as well as the items you purchased. If the total value of your goods is more than the duty-free limit, you'll have to pay a tax (most often a flat percentage) on the value of everything beyond that limit.

There are two levels of duty-free allowance for entering Britain: one for goods bought outside the European Union (EU) and the other for goods bought within the EU.

Of goods bought outside the EU you may import the following duty-free: 200 cigarettes or 100 cigarillos or 50 cigars or 250 grams of tobacco; 4 liters of still wine and 16 liters of beer and, in addition, either 1 liter of alcohol over 22% by volume (most spirits), or 2 liters of alcohol under 22% by volume (fortified or sparkling wine or liqueurs).

Of goods bought within the EU, you should not exceed the following (unless you can prove they are for personal use): 800 cigarettes, 400 cigarillos, 200 cigars, or 3 kilos of tobacco, plus 10 liters of spirits, 20 liters of fortified wine such as port or sherry, 90 liters of wine, or 110 liters of beer.

Pets (dogs and cats) can be brought into the United Kingdom from the United States without six months' quarantine, provided that the animal meets all the PETS (Pet Travel Scheme) requirements, including microchipping and vaccination. Other pets have to undergo a lengthy quarantine, and penalties for breaking this law are severe and strictly enforced.

Fresh meats, vegetables, plants, and dairy products may be imported from within the EU. Controlled drugs, switchblades (aka flick knives), obscene material, counterfeit or pirated goods, and self-defense sprays may not be brought into the United Kingdom; firearms (both real and imitation) and ammunition, as well as souvenirs made from endangered plants or animals, are barred except with relevant permits.

Information **HM Revenue and Customs.** ☎ *0300/200–3700* ⊕ *www.hmrc.gov.uk.* **U.S. Customs and Border Protection.** ⊕ *www. cbp.gov.*

∎ ELECTRICITY

The electrical current in London is 220–240 volts (coming into line with the rest of Europe at 230 volts), 50 cycles alternating current (AC); wall outlets take three-pin plugs, and shaver sockets take two round, oversize prongs. For converters, adapters, and advice, stop in one of the many STA Travel shops around London or at Nomad Travel.

Consider making a small investment in a universal adapter, which has several types of plugs in one lightweight, compact unit. Most laptops and cell phone chargers are dual voltage (i.e., they operate equally well on 110 and 220 volts), and thus require only an adapter. These days the same is true of small appliances such as hair dryers. Always check labels and manufacturer instructions to be sure. Don't use 110-volt outlets marked "For Shavers Only" for high-wattage appliances such as hair dryers.

Contacts Nomad Travel. ☎ *0134/155–5061* ⊕ *www.nomadtravel.co.uk.* **Walkabout Travel Gear.** ⊕ *www.walkabouttravelgear.com.*

▌ EMERGENCIES

London is a relatively safe city, though crime does happen (more so than in New York City), especially in areas of built-up public project housing or in tourist meccas. If you need to report a theft or an attack, head to the nearest police station (listed in the Yellow Pages or the local directory) or dial 999 for police, fire, or ambulance (be prepared to give the telephone number you're calling from). National Health Service hospitals give free round-the-clock treatment in Accident and Emergency sections, where waits can be up to four hours, depending on the severity of your ailment or injury. As a non-EU foreign visitor, you will be expected to pay for any treatment you receive before you leave the country. Prescriptions are valid only if made out by doctors registered in the United Kingdom. All branches of Boots are dispensing pharmacies.

Doctors and Dentists Dental Emergency Care Service. ☎ *020/8748–9365* ⊕ *www.24hour-emergencydentist.co.uk.* **Medical Express Clinic.** ☎ *020/7499–1991, 0800/980–0700* ⊕ *www.medicalexpressclinic. co.uk.* **UCL Eastman Dental Hospital.** ☎ *020/3456–7899* ⊕ *www.uclh.nhs.uk.*

Foreign Embassies U.S. Embassy. ☎ *020/7499–9000* ⊕ *www.usembassy.org.uk.*

General Emergency Contacts Ambulance, fire, police. ☎ *999 U.K. only, 112 pan-European.*

Hospitals and Clinics Charing Cross Hospital. ☎ *020/3311–1234* ⊕ *www.imperial. nhs.uk/charingcross.* **Royal Free Hospital.** ☎ *020/7794–0500* ⊕ *www.royalfree.nhs.uk.* **St. Thomas's Hospital.** ☎ *020/7188–7188* ⊕ *www.guysandstthomas.nhs.uk.* **University College Hospital.** ☎ *0845/155–5000, 020/3456–7890* ⊕ *www.uclh.nhs.uk.*

Hotlines Samaritans. ☎ *020/7734–2800* ⊕ *www.cls.org.uk.*

Pharmacies Boots. ☎ *0345/070–8090* ⊕ *www.boots.com.*

▌ HOLIDAYS

Standard holidays are New Year's Day, Good Friday, Easter Monday, May Day (first Monday in May), spring and summer bank holidays (last Monday in May and August, respectively), Christmas, and Boxing Day (December 26). On Christmas Eve and New Year's Eve, some shops, restaurants, and businesses close early. Some museums and tourist attractions may close for at least a week around Christmas, or operate on restricted hours—call to verify.

▌ MAIL

Stamps can be bought from post offices (generally open weekdays 9–5:30, Saturday 9–noon), from stamp machines outside post offices, and from some newsagents and newsstands. Mailboxes are known as post or letter boxes and are painted bright red; large tubular ones are set on the edge of sidewalks, whereas smaller boxes are set into post-office walls. Allow seven days for a letter to reach the United States. Check the Yellow Pages for a complete list of branches, though you cannot reach individual offices by phone.

Airmail letters up to 10 grams (0.35 ounce) to North America, Australia, and New Zealand cost 97p. Letters under 9.4 inches by 6.4 inches within Britain are from 62p for first class, 53p for second class. Large letters (over 9.4 inches by 6.4 inches, under 13.8 inches by 9.8 inches) cost from 93p first class, 73p second class within the United Kingdom, depending on weight. Airmail is assessed by weight alone.

If you're uncertain where you'll be staying, you can have mail sent to you at the London Main Post Office, c/o poste restante. The post office will hold international mail for one month.

Contact Post Office. ☏ *0345/611–2970* ⊕ *www.postoffice.co.uk.*

Main Branches London Main Post Office. ⊕ *www.postoffice.co.uk.* **London Main Post Office. London Main Post Office. London Main Post Office. London Main Post Office.**

SHIPPING PACKAGES

Most department stores and retail outlets can ship your goods home. You should check your insurance for coverage of possible damage. Private delivery companies such as DHL, FedEx, and Parcelforce offer two-day delivery service to the United States, but you'll pay a considerable amount for the privilege.

Express Services DHL. ☏ *0844/248–0844* ⊕ *www.dhl.com.* **FedEx.** ☏ *0845/600–0068* ⊕ *www.fedex.com.* **Parcelforce.** ☏ *0344/800– 4466* ⊕ *www.parcelforce.com.*

▌ MONEY

London is one of the most expensive cities in the world: getting around is expensive, eating can be pricey, travel costs are steep, and hotels aren't cheap. However, for every yin there's a yang, and travelers do get a break in other places: most museums are free, for example, and Oyster cards help cut the price of travel.

ATMS AND BANKS

Your own bank will probably charge a fee for using ATMs abroad; the foreign bank you use may also charge a fee. Nevertheless, you'll usually get a better rate of exchange at an ATM than you will at a currency-exchange office or even when changing money in a bank. And extracting funds as you need them is a safer option than carrying around a large amount of cash.

▌TIP➔ **PIN numbers with more than four digits are not recognized at ATMs in many countries. If yours has five or more, remember to change it before you leave.**

Credit cards or debit cards (also known as check cards) will get you cash advances at ATMs, which are widely available in London. To make sure that your Cirrus or Plus card (to cite just two of the leading names) works in European ATMs, have your bank reset it to use a four-digit PIN number before your departure.

CREDIT CARDS

▌TIP➔ **Remember to inform your credit-card company before you travel, especially if you're going abroad and don't travel internationally very often.** Otherwise, the credit-card company might put a hold on your card owing to unusual activity—not a good thing halfway through your trip. Record all your credit-card numbers—as well as the phone numbers to call if your cards are lost or stolen—in a safe place, so you're prepared should something go wrong. MasterCard and Visa have general numbers you can call (collect if you're abroad) if your card is lost, but you're better off calling the number of your issuing bank, because MasterCard and Visa usually just transfer you to your bank; your bank's number is usually printed on your card.

If you plan to use your credit card for cash advances, you'll need to apply for a PIN at least two weeks before your trip. Although it's usually cheaper (and safer) to use a credit card abroad for large purchases (so you can cancel payments or be reimbursed if there's a problem), note that some credit-card companies *and* the banks that issue them add substantial percentages to all foreign transactions, whether they're in a foreign currency or not. Check on these fees before leaving home, so there won't be any surprises when you get the bill.

■TIP➔ Before you charge something, ask the merchant whether he or she plans to do a dynamic currency conversion (DCC). In such a transaction the credit-card processor

Dynamic currency conversion programs are becoming increasingly widespread. Merchants who participate in them are supposed to ask whether you want to be charged in dollars or the local currency, but they don't always do so. And even if they do offer you a choice, they may well avoid mentioning the additional surcharges. The good news is that you *do* have a choice. And if this practice really gets your goat, you can avoid it entirely thanks to American Express; with its cards, DCC simply isn't an option.

Credit cards are accepted virtually everywhere in London.

Reporting Lost Cards American Express. ☏ 800/528–4800 in U.S., 01273/696–933 in U.K. ⊕ *www.americanexpress.com.* **Diners Club.** ☏ 800/234–6377 in U.S., 514/877–1577 collect from abroad ⊕ www.dinersclub.com. **MasterCard.** ☏ 800/627–8372 in U.S., 0800/964–767 in U.K. ⊕ www.mastercard.com. **Visa.** ☏ 800/847–2911 in U.S., 020/7795–5777 in U.K. ⊕ www.visa.com.

CURRENCY AND EXCHANGE

The units of currency in Great Britain are the pound sterling (£) and pence (p): £50, £20, £10, and £5 bills (called notes); £2, £1 (100p), 50p, 20p, 10p, 5p, 2p, and 1p coins. At this writing, the exchange rate was about Australian $1.79, Canadian $1.76, New Zealand $1.97, U.S. $1.56, and €1.25 to the pound (also known as quid).

Even if a currency-exchange booth has a sign promising no commission, rest assured that there's some kind of huge, hidden fee. (Oh…that's right. The sign didn't say no *fee*.) And as for rates, you're almost always better off getting foreign currency at an ATM or exchanging money at a bank or post office.

■TIP➔ Banks never have every foreign currency on hand, and it may take as long as a week to order. If you're planning to exchange funds before leaving home, don't wait until the last minute.

▌ PACKING

London's weather is unpredictable. It can be cool, damp, and overcast, even in summer, but the odd summer day can be uncomfortably hot, as not many public venues, theaters, or the Tube are air-conditioned. In general, you'll need a heavy coat for winter and light clothes for summer, along with a lightweight coat or jacket. Always pack a small umbrella that you can easily carry around with you. Pack as you would for any American city: jackets and ties for expensive restaurants and nightspots, casual clothes elsewhere. Jeans are popular in London and are perfectly acceptable for sightseeing and informal dining. Sports jackets are popular with men. In five-star hotels men can expect to be asked to wear a jacket and tie in the restaurant and bar, and women might feel out of place unless they're in smart clothes. Otherwise, for women, ordinary dress is acceptable just about everywhere.

▌ PASSPORTS AND VISAS

U.S. citizens need only a valid passport to enter Great Britain for stays of up to six months. If you're within six months of your passport's expiration date, renew it before you leave—nearly extinct passports are not strictly banned, but they make immigration officials anxious, and may cause you problems.

PASSPORTS

It's always surprising how few Americans have passports—only 35% at this writing. This number is expected to grow now that it is impossible to reenter the United States from trips to neighboring Canada or Mexico without one. Remember this:

A passport verifies both your identity and nationality—a great reason to have one.

U.S. passports are valid for 10 years. You must apply in person if you're getting a passport for the first time; if your previous passport was lost, stolen, or damaged; or if your previous passport has expired and was issued more than 15 years ago or when you were under 16. All children under 18 must appear in person to apply for or renew a passport. Both parents must accompany any child under 14 (or send a notarized statement with their permission) and provide proof of their relationship to the child.

There are 24 regional passport offices, as well as 7,000 passport acceptance facilities in post offices, public libraries, and other governmental offices. If you're renewing a passport, you can do so by mail. Forms are available at passport acceptance facilities and online.

The cost to apply for a new passport is $140 for adults, $95 for children under 16; renewals are $140. There is an additional "execution fee" of $25. Allow six weeks for processing, both for first-time passports and renewals. For an expediting fee of $60 you can reduce this time to about two weeks. If your trip is less than two weeks away, you can get a passport even more rapidly by going to a passport office with the necessary documentation. Private expediters can get things done in as little as 48 hours, but charge hefty fees for their services.

■TIP→ Before your trip, make two copies of your passport's data page (one for someone at home and another for you to carry separately). Or scan the page and email it to someone at home and/or yourself.

VISAS

A visa is essentially formal permission to enter a country. Visas allow countries to keep track of you and other visitors—and generate revenue (from application fees). You *always* need a visa to enter a foreign country; however, many countries routinely issue tourist visas on arrival, particularly to U.S. citizens. When your passport is stamped or scanned in the immigration line, you're actually being issued a visa. Sometimes you have to stand in a separate line and pay a small fee to get your stamp before going through immigration, but you can still do this at the airport on arrival. Getting a visa isn't always that easy. Some countries require that you arrange for one in advance of your trip. There's usually—but not always—a fee involved, and said fee may be nominal ($10 or less) or substantial ($100 or more).

If you must apply for a visa in advance, you can usually do it in person or by mail. When you apply by mail, you send your passport to a designated consulate, where your passport will be examined and the visa issued. Expediters—usually the same ones who handle expedited passport applications—can do all the work of obtaining your visa for you; however, there's always an additional cost (often more than $50 per visa).

Most visas limit you to a single trip—basically during the actual dates of your planned vacation. Other visas allow you to visit as many times as you wish for a specific period of time. Remember that requirements change, sometimes at the drop of a hat, and the burden is on you to make sure that you have the appropriate visas. Otherwise, you'll be turned away at the airport or, worse, deported after you arrive in the country. No company or travel insurer gives refunds if your travel plans are disrupted because you didn't have the correct visa.

U.S. Passport Information U.S. Department of State. ☎ 877/487–2778 ⊕ travel.state.gov/passport.

U.S. Passport and Visa Expediters A. Briggs Passport & Visa Expeditors. ☎ 800/806–0581, 202/388–0111 ⊕ www.abriggs.com. **American Passport Express.** ☎ 800/455–5166 ⊕ www.americanpassport.com. **Travel Document Systems.** ☎ 800/874–5100,

202/638–3800 ⊕ www.traveldocs.com. **Travel the World Visas.** *☎ 866/886–8472 ⊕ www. world-visa.com.*

Advisories U.S. Department of State. *⊕ travel.state.gov.*

▮ SAFETY

The rules for safety in London are the same as in New York City or any big metropolis. If you're carrying a considerable amount of cash and do not have a safe in your hotel room, it's a good idea to keep it in something like a money belt, but don't get cash out of it in public. Keep a small amount of cash for immediate purchases in your pocket or handbag.

Beyond that, use common sense. In central London, nobody will raise an eyebrow at tourists studying maps on street corners, and don't hesitate to ask for directions. However, outside of the center, exercise general caution about the neighborhoods you walk in: if they don't look safe, take a cab. After midnight, outside of the center, take cabs rather than wait for a night bus. Although London has plenty of so-called minicabs—normal cars driven by self-employed drivers in a cab service—don't ever get into an unmarked car that pulls up offering you "cab service." Take a licensed minicab only from a cab office, or, preferably, a normal London "black cab," which you flag down on the street. Unlicensed minicab drivers have been associated with a slate of violent crimes in recent years.

If you carry a purse, keep a firm grip on it (or even disguise it in a local shopping bag). Store only enough money in the purse to cover casual spending. Distribute the rest of your cash and any valuables among deep front pockets, inside jacket or vest pockets, and a concealed money pouch. Some pubs and bars have "Chelsea clips" under the tables where you can hang your handbag at your knee. Never leave your bag beside your chair or hanging from the back of your chair. Be careful with backpacks, as pickpockets can unzip them on the Tube, or even as you're traveling up an escalator.

▮ TAXES

Departure taxes are divided into four bands, depending on destination. The Band A tax on a per-person Economy fare is £13, Band B is £69, Band C is £85, and Band D is £97. The fee is subject to government tax increases.

The British sales tax (V.A.T., value-added tax) is 20%. The tax is almost always included in quoted prices in shops, hotels, and restaurants.

Most travelers can get a V.A.T. refund by either the Retail Export or the more cumbersome Direct Export method. Many, but not all, large stores provide these services, but only if you request them; they will handle the paperwork. For the Retail Export method, you must ask the store for Form VAT 407 when making a purchase (you must have identification—passports are best). Some retailers will refund the amount on the spot, but others will use a refund company or the refund booth at the point when you leave the country. For the latter, have the form stamped like any customs form by U.K. customs officials when you leave the country, or, if you're visiting several European Union countries, when you leave the EU. After you're through passport control, take the form to a refund-service counter for an on-the-spot refund (which is usually the quickest and easiest option), or mail it to the address on the form (or the envelope with it) after you arrive home. You receive the total refund stated on the form (the retailer or refund company may deduct a handling fee), but the processing time can be long, especially if you request a credit-card adjustment. This may be preferable to a check, however, as U.S. banks will charge a fee for depositing a check in a foreign currency.

With the Direct Export method, the goods are shipped directly to your home. You must have a Form VAT 407 certified by customs, the police, or a notary public when you get home and then send it back to the store, which will refund your money. For inquiries, contact Her Majesty's Revenue & Customs office.

Global Blue (formerly, Global Refund) is a worldwide service with 270,000 affiliated stores and more than 200 Refund Offices. Its refund form, called a Tax Free Check, is the most common across the European continent. The service issues refunds in the form of cash, check, or credit-card adjustment. Again, the cost of cashing a foreign currency check may exceed the amount of the refund.

V.A.T. Refunds Global Blue. ☏ 866/706–6090 in U.S., 800/32–111–111 in U.K. ⊕ www.globalblue.com. **Her Majesty's Revenue & Customs.** ☏ 0300/200–3700 within U.K., 292/050–1261 from outside U.K. ⊕ www.hmrc.gov.uk/vat.

▌TIME

London is five hours ahead of New York City at most times of the year. In other words, when it's 3 pm in New York (or noon in Los Angeles), it's 8 pm in London. Note that Great Britain and most European countries also move their clocks ahead for the one-hour differential when daylight saving time goes into effect (although they make the changeover several weeks after the United States).

Time Zones Timeanddate.com. ⊕ www.timeanddate.com/worldclock.

▌TIPPING

Tipping is done in Britain just as in the United States, but at a lower level. Tipping less than you would back home in restaurants—and not tipping at all in pubs—is not only accepted, but standard. Tipping more can look like you're showing off. Do not tip movie or theater ushers, elevator operators, or bar staff in pubs—although you can always offer to buy the latter a drink.

TIPPING GUIDELINES FOR LONDON

Bartender	In cocktail bars, if you see a tip plate, it's fine to leave £1 or £2. For table service, tip 10% of the cost of the bill. However, the gratuity is often included in the check at more expensive bars.
Bellhop	£1 per bag, depending on the level of the hotel.
Hotel Concierge	£5 or more, if a service is performed for you.
Hotel Doorman	£1 for hailing taxis or for carrying bags to check-in desk.
Hotel Maid	It's extremely rare for hotel maids to be tipped; £1 or £2 would be generous.
Porter at Airport or Train Station	£1 per bag
Skycap at Airport	£1–£3 per bag
Taxi Driver	Optional 10%–12%, perhaps a little more for a short ride.
Tour Guide	Tipping optional; £1 or £2 would be generous.
Waiter	10%–15%, with 15% being the norm at high-end restaurants; nothing additional if a service charge is added to the bill.
Other	Restroom attendants in expensive restaurants expect some small change (50p or so). Tip coat-check personnel £1 unless there is a fee (then nothing). Hairdresser and barbers get 10%–15%.

▌TOURS

BIKE TOURS

Whether you join the Barclays Cycle Hire scheme or just, per usual, get one from a rental shop, remember that London is still a busy metropolis: unless you're familiar with riding in London traffic, the best way to see it on two wheels is probably to contact one of the excellent cycle-tour companies.

Tour Operators Barclays Cycle Hire. ☏ *0343/222–6666 within U.K., 208/216–6666 from outside U.K.* ⊕ *https://web. barclayscyclehire.tfl.gov.uk/maps.* **Cycle Tours of London.** ☏ *07788/994–430* ⊕ *www. biketoursoflondon.com.* **Fat Tire Bike Tours.** ☏ *07882/338–779* ⊕ *www.fattirebiketours. com.* **London Bicycle Tour Company.** ☏ *020/7928–6838* ⊕ *www.londonbicycle.com.*

BOAT TOURS

Year-round, but more frequently from April to October, boats cruise the Thames, offering a different view of the London skyline. Most leave from Westminster Pier, Charing Cross Pier, and Tower Pier. Downstream routes go to the Tower of London, Greenwich, and the Thames Barrier via Canary Wharf. Upstream destinations include Kew, Richmond, and Hampton Court (mainly in summer). Most of the launches seat between 100 and 250 passengers, have a public-address system, and provide a running commentary on passing points of interest. Some include musical entertainment. Depending on the destination, river trips may last from one to four hours.

Details on all other operators are available as a PDF from Transport for London's River Services page ⊕ *www.tfl.gov.uk.*

River Cruise Operators Bateaux London. ☏ *020/7695–1800* ⊕ *www.bateauxlondon. com.* **London Duck Tours.** ☏ *020/7928–3132* ⊕ *www.londonducktours.co.uk.* **Thames Cruises.** ☏ *020/7928–9009* ⊕ *www. thamescruises.com.* **Thames River Boats.** ☏ *020/7930–2062* ⊕ *www.wpsa.co.uk.* **Thames River Services.** ☏ *020/7930–4097* ⊕ *www.thamesriverservices.co.uk.*

BUS, COACH, AND TAXI TOURS

Guided sightseeing tours from the top of double-decker buses, which are open-top in summer, are a good introduction to the city, as they cover all the main central sights. A number of companies run daily bus tours that depart (usually between 8:30 and 9 am) from central points. In hop-on, hop-off fashion, you may board or alight at any of the numerous stops to view the sights, and reboard on the next bus. Most companies offer this hop-on, hop-off feature but others, such as Best Value, remain guided tours in traditional coach buses. Tickets can be bought from the driver and are good all day. Prices vary according to the type of tour, although £25 is the benchmark. For that more personal touch, try out a tour in a guided taxi. Other guided bus tours, like those offered by Golden, are not open-top or hop-on, hop-off, but enclosed (and more expensive) coach bus versions.

Bus Tour Operators Best Value Tours. ☏ *0870/803–1316* ⊕ *www.bestvaluetours. co.uk.* **Big Bus Tours.** ☏ *020/7808–6753* ⊕ *www.bigbustours.com.* **Black Taxi Tour of London.** ☏ *020/7935–9363* ⊕ *www. blacktaxitours.co.uk.* **Golden Tours.** ☏ *020/7630–2028 in U.K., 800/509–2507 in U.S.* ⊕ *www.goldentours.co.uk.* **Original London Sightseeing Tour.** ☏ *020/8877–1722* ⊕ *www.theoriginaltour.com.* **Premium Tours.** ☏ *020/7713–1311, 800/815–4003 from the US* ⊕ *www.premiumtours.co.uk.*

CANAL TOURS

The tranquil side of London can be found on narrow boats that cruise the city's two canals, the Grand Union and Regent's Canal; most vessels operate on the latter, which runs between Little Venice in the west (nearest Tube: Warwick Avenue on the Bakerloo line) and Camden Lock (about 200 yards north of Camden Town Tube station). Fares start at about £9 for 1½-hour round-trip cruises.

Canal Tour Operators Canal Cruises. ☏ *020/8440–8962* ⊕ *www.londoncanalcruises. com.* **Jason's Trip.** ⊕ *www.jasons.co.uk.* **London Waterbus Company.** ☏ *020/7482–2660* ⊕ *www.londonwaterbus.co.uk.*

EXCURSIONS

Evan Evans, Green Line, and National Express all offer day excursions by bus to places within easy reach of London, such as Hampton Court, Oxford, Stratford-upon-Avon, and Bath.

Tour Operators Evan Evans. ☎ *020/7950–1777, 866/382–6868 in U.S.* ⊕ *www.evanevanstours.co.uk.* **Green Line.** ☎ *0844/801–7261* ⊕ *www.greenline.co.uk.* **National Express.** ☎ *0871/781–8178* ⊕ *www.nationalexpress.com.*

WALKING TOURS

One of the best ways to get to know London is on foot, and there are many guided and themed walking tours available. Richard Jones's London Walking Tours includes the Jack the Ripper Walk, following in his footsteps, as does the Blood and Tears Walk. Other tours include Secret London, the West End with Dickens, and Hampstead—A Country Village. Context London's expert docents lead small groups on walks with art, architecture, and similar themes. The London Walks Company hosts more than 100 walks every week on a variety of themes, including a Thames pub walk, Literary Bloomsbury, and Spies and Spycatchers. For more options, pick up a copy of *Time Out* magazine and check the weekly listings for upcoming one-off tours.

Walking Tour Operators Blood and Tears Walk. ☎ *07905/746–733* ⊕ *www.shockinglondon.com.* **Blue Badge.** ☎ *020/7403–1115* ⊕ *www.britainsbestguides.org.* **Context London.** ☎ *020/3514–1780, 800/691–6036 in U.S.* ⊕ *www.contexttravel.com/london.* **London Walks.** ☎ *020/7624–3978* ⊕ *www.walks.com.* **Richard Jones's London Walking Tours.** ☎ *020/8530–8443* ⊕ *www.londondiscoverytours.co.uk.* **Shakespeare City Walk.** ☎ *07905/746–733* ⊕ *www.shakespeareguide.com.*

▍ VISITOR INFORMATION

You can get good information at the Travel Information Centre near the Eurostar arrivals area at St. Pancras International train station and at Victoria and Liverpool Street stations. These are helpful if you're looking for brochures for London sights, or if something's gone horribly wrong with your hotel reservation—if, for example, you don't have one—as they have a useful reservations service. The Victoria station center, opposite Platform 8, is open Monday–Saturday 7:15 am–8:15 pm, Sunday 8:15 am–7 pm; the St. Pancras center Monday–Saturday 7:15 am–8:15 pm, Sunday 8:15 am–7 pm; while Liverpool Street and Euston station centers are open Monday–Thursday 7:15 am–7 pm, Friday and Saturday 7:15 am–8 pm and Sunday 8:15 am–7 pm. The one at Piccadilly Circus Tube station is open weekdays 8 am–7 pm, Saturday 9:15 am–7 pm, Sunday 9:15 am–6 pm. The Travel Information Centre at Heathrow is open daily 7:30 am– 7:30 pm. There are also London Tourist Information Centres in Greenwich and some other Outer London locations with new centers set to open in Paddington station and Gatwick airport (North Terminal).

Official Websites ⊕ *www.visitbritain.com,* ⊕ *www.visitlondon.com*

Other Websites ⊕ *www.londontown.com, the Evening Standard online,* ⊕ *www.standard.co.uk, and the BBC* ⊕ *www.bbc.co.uk.*

Entertainment Information ⊕ *www.timeout.com/london,* ⊕ *www.officiallondontheatre.co.uk.*

INDEX

PHOTO CREDITS

Upstream: 219, Mark6138 | Dreamstime.com. 221 and 222, Danilo Donadoni/Marka/age fotostock. 223, Terry Harris / Alamy. 226, britainonview.com. 229, Rich B-S/Flickr. 230, Rafael Campillo/age fotostock. 231 (left), British Tourist Authority. 231 (right), Danilo Donadoni/Marka/age fotostock. 232, photogl/Shutterstock. 233 (top left), Roger Hutchings/Alamy. 233 (top right), Corbis. 233 (bottom), Lyndon Giffard/Alamy. 234 (top), Mike Booth/Alamy. 234 (bottom), Danilo Donadoni/Marka/age fotostock. 235, wikipedia.org. 237, britainonview.com. Chapter 14: Where to Eat: 239, Presselect / Alamy. 240, Atlantide S.N.C./age fotostock. Chapter 15: Where to Stay: 297, Danita Delimont/Alamy. 298, Araraadt | Dreamstime.com. Chapter16: Pubs & Nightlife: 323, Peter Phipp/Travelshots.com / Alamy. 324, Everynight Images/Alamy. Chapter 17: Arts & Entertainment: 349, James McCormick/ BritishTourist Authority. 350, David Jensen 2013. 352, Hugo Glendinning. 354, Bettina Strenske / age fotostock. 358, Claudiodivizia | Dreamstime.com. 362, Lebrecht Music and Arts Photo Library/Alamy. Chapter 18: Shopping: 367, Anizza | Dreamstime.com. 368, Edonalds | Dreamstime.com. 377, Jim Batty/Alamy. Chapter 19: Side Trips from London: 401, Andrew Holt/Alamy. 402, Mark Sunderland/ Alamy. 409, British Tourist Authority/Tourism South East. 412, John Martin/Alamy. Back cover (from left to right), WH Chow/Shutterstock; James D. Hay/Shutterstock; Paul B. Moore/Shutterstock. Spine: Ron Ellis / Shutterstock.

About Our Writers: All photos are courtesy of the writers except for the following: Kate Hughes, courtesy of Ellen Hughes; Ellin Stein, courtesy of Paul Rider; Alex Wijeratna, courtesy of Heathcliff O'Malley.

NOTES

NOTES

NOTES

ABOUT OUR WRITERS

 Jo Caird is a travel and arts journalist who writes on theater, visual arts, film, literature, and food and drink, as well as cycling and scuba diving. Her travel stories, city guides, and arts features appear regularly in *The Guardian, The Independent, The Sunday Telegraph, The Economist, Condé Nast Traveller,* and *World of Interiors.* Born and raised in London, Caird has an endless fascination for the city, and is delighted to write about it whenever the opportunity arises. For this edition, she updated the Pubs and Nightlife, Performing Arts, and Soho and Covent Garden chapters. Follow her on Twitter at ⊕ *www.twitter.com/jocaird* or visit her website at ⊕ *www.jocaird.com.*

 Writer and editor **Kate Hughes** studied classical literature in Liverpool and also has a master's degree in garden history, so she feels qualified to pass judgment on matters both urban and rural. She is responsible for Stratford-upon-Avon and various Thames Valley side trips in *Fodor's London,* and also updates parts of *Fodor's England.*

 Jack Jewers updated the Where to Stay chapter, along with the neighborhood chapters on Greenwich, Thames Upstream, Westminster, St. James and Royal London, and The City. A resident of London and its penumbra since public transport was cheap, Jack knows slightly more than is healthy about the city's secret underground world of abandoned train lines, mysterious tunnels, and other things hidden below the streets. When he isn't writing guidebooks, he makes independent films.

 James O'Neill loves London and—as his work updating our chapters on Mayfair and Marylebone, Bloomsbury and Holborn, and Travel Smart for this edition proves—loves rediscovering it, too. Although originally from Ireland, he's lived in London for almost 20 years—and still loves it just as much now as he did back then. He has written extensively for TV (BBC and Channel 4), the stage, and the page. He is currently finishing his debut novel, which is set in—where else? —London.

 Ellin Stein has written for publications on both sides of the Atlantic, including the *New York Times,* the *Times [London],* the *Guardian,* the *Telegraph,* and *InStyle,* for whom she was European correspondent. Her book *That's Not Funny, That's Sick: The National Lampoon and the Comedy Insurgents Who Captured the Mainstream,* was published by W. W. Norton & Co. in 2013. Originally from Manhattan, she has lived in London for two decades. For this edition, she updated our chapters on Kensington, Chelsea, Knightsbridge, and Belgravia; East London; South of the Thames; Notting Hill and Bayswater; Regent's Park and Hampstead; and Shopping.

 London restaurant maven **Alex Wijeratna** is permanently blown away by the capital's rocket-fueled restaurant scene. From locavore heroes and street food gourmet-democrats, to global gastro-panjandrums, Alex tickles out the best joints that restaurant-mad London has to offer. With his first full Fodor's guidebook out last year (*Around London with Kids*), Alex has written for *The Times, Guardian, Independent, Daily Mail, Daily Express,* and *The Face.* For this edition, he updated the Where to Eat and Experience London chapters.

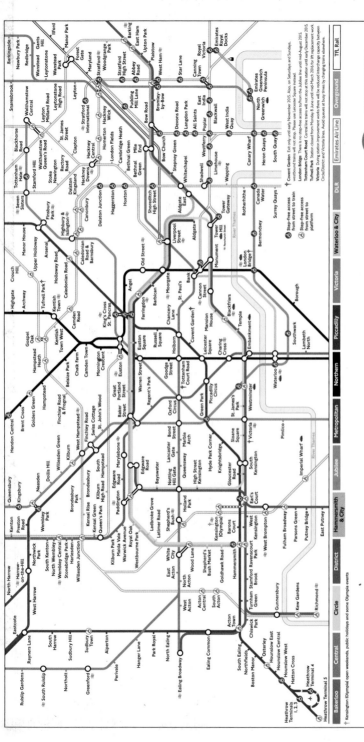